A History of Chinese Buddhist Faith and Life

# Studies on East Asian Religions

*Edited by*

James A. Benn (*McMaster University*)
Jinhua Chen (*University of British Columbia*)

VOLUME 3

The titles published in this series are listed at *brill.com/sear*

# A History of Chinese Buddhist Faith and Life

*By*

Kai Sheng

*Translated by*

Jeffrey Kotyk
Matt Orsborn
Gina Yang

*Edited by*

Jinhua Chen

BRILL

LEIDEN | BOSTON

This publication has been made possible with the support of the Chinese Fund for the Humanities and Social Sciences.

Abridged and updated English edition of *Zhongguo Fojiao xinyang yu shenghuo shi* 中國佛教信仰與生活史, Jiangsu Renmin Press 江苏人民出版社 2016.

Cover illustration: Bhikṣu Sponsor in the Gong county 鞏縣 Grotto Complex dated to the Northern Wei (386-534).

Library of Congress Cataloging-in-Publication Data

Names: Sheng, Kai, 1972- author. | Chen, Jinhua, 1966- editor.
Title: A history of Chinese Buddhist faith and life / by Kai Sheng; translated by Jeffrey Kotyk, Matt Osborn, Gina Yang ; edited by Jinhua Chen.
Other titles: Zhongguo fo jiao xin yang yu sheng huo shi. English
Description: Leiden ; Boston : Brill, [2020] | Series: Studies on East Asian religions, 2452-0098 ; volume 3 | Includes bibliographical references and index.
Identifiers: LCCN 2020015832 (print) | LCCN 2020015833 (ebook) | ISBN 9789004431522 (hardback) | ISBN 9789004431775 (ebook)
Subjects: LCSH: Buddhism--China--History. | Buddhism--Social aspects--China.
Classification: LCC BQ626 .S54213 2020 (print) | LCC BQ626 (ebook) | DDC 294.30951--dc23
LC record available at https://lccn.loc.gov/2020015832
LC ebook record available at https://lccn.loc.gov/2020015833

Typeface for the Latin, Greek, and Cyrillic scripts: "Brill". See and download: brill.com/brill-typeface.

ISSN 2452-0098
ISBN 978-90-04-43152-2 (hardback)
ISBN 978-90-04-43177-5 (e-book)

# Contents

# Figures

All photos were taken by the author.

INTRODUCTION

# Expression and Transformation of Chinese Buddhist Faith: Perspectives of Institutional History, Social History, Cultural History, and Scholarship History

## 1 "Holistic Buddhism" and the Sinicization of Buddhism

What is Buddhism? This seems like a very simple question. However, as a religious tradition that has been passed along for 2600 years, Buddhism is rich in thought, scripture, history, and customs. In his *Fojiao changshi dawen* 佛教常識答問 (Buddhist General Knowledge Questions and Answers), Zhao Puchu 趙樸初 (1907-2000) explains "Buddhism" as:

> Buddhism, in the broad sense, is a kind of religion, which includes its scriptures, rituals, customs, religious organizations, and more. In the narrow sense, it is the teachings given by the Buddha. If we use Buddhism's own technical term, it should be called "Buddha Dharma."[1]

The core of Buddhism is the Three Jewels, Buddha, Dharma and *Saṃgha*. That is, the three major essential elements of faith, thought and institution. Therefore, Buddhism relies on the Buddha, Dharma and *Saṃgha* as its core and as a root to establish itself as a religion. This includes the doctrinal teaching and soteriological path of religious cultivation from the time of Śākyamuni onwards, its common ideas of religious faith and lifestyle, as well as the religious culture that gradually formed in various countries and regions throughout the world. The "Buddha" is the element of "faith" in Buddhism and refers to the founder of Buddhism, Śākyamuni Buddha. Gradually, concepts of the Buddha and the Buddha's bodies, as well as faith in Bodhisattvas and Pure Lands, extended out from the stories of the Buddha's past lives. Furthermore, these also brought about institutions of worship and art depicting elements of Buddhist faith. The "Dharma" is the element of "thought" in Buddhism, namely the theoretical thought that issued forth from the central teaching of the four noble truths. The "*Saṃgha*" is the element of "institution" in Buddhism, it refers to the monastic community which has faith in, propagates and actualizes

1 Zhao, *Wenji* (I), 571.

 | DOI:10.1163/9789004431775_002

Buddhist thought. Is also includes the community of lay followers who have faith in Buddhism. Based on the "*Saṃgha*", there are regulatory systems of monastic precepts and the pure rules, as well as later Chinese Buddhist cult of the *arhat*s, and cult of the patriarchs. Apart from these, from the perspectives of history and actualization, Buddhism as a religious social entity also includes society and culture, two major categories that function as Buddhism's external extensions. So-called "holistic Buddhism" refers to Buddhism's entire connected existence, including the three essential elements and the three major levels—Buddhism, society and culture.

The modern anthropologist Melford E. Spiro,[2] utilizing a study of the changes of Theravada Buddhism in Burmese society, analyzes Buddhism as an ideological system, ritual system and monastic system, with a final section on "Buddhism and the world". Within Buddhism's ideological system there are two main types: one, the soteriological system, which has "Nibbanic Buddhism" and "Kammatic Buddhism". "Nibbanic Buddhism" is normative Buddhism, concerned with liberation from cyclic existence; "Kammatic Buddhism" is not normative liberating Buddhism, focusing on the accumulation of merit and elimination of karma, raising people's position within cyclic existence. Two, a non-liberating system, namely including a third kind—"Apotropaic Buddhism"—which deals with benefits for secular humanity, such as the treatment of illness, protection from *yakṣa* demons, and the avoidance of disaster and calamity.[3] From the anthropological perspective, Spiro explores the mutually interactive relationship between the doctrines of the scriptures and the concepts of the lay community—that is, the relationship between religious concepts, ordinary social order, and cultural lifestyle. It is well worth our serious consideration and reflection.

Therefore, Buddhist studies must be conducted from the three major levels of Buddhism, Buddhism and society, and Buddhism and culture to carry out a comprehensive, three dimensional, and integrated exploration. One, from the point of view of Buddhism itself: its scripture, faith, thought, and institution compose four main areas of research. Two, from Buddhism and society: politics, economics, charitable and philanthropic works, and social life make up four large areas of research. Three, speaking from Buddhism and culture: Buddhist literature, art and architecture are important research subjects.

2 Melford Spiro defines religion as "an institution consisting of culturally patterned interaction with culturally postulated superhuman beings". See Spiro, "religion", 96. Cf. Bowie, *Anthropology of Religion*, 25.

3 Spiro, *Buddhism and Society*, 50.

FIGURE 1 The remains on Mount Gṛdhrakūṭa ("Vulture Peak"), India.

When Buddhism was transmitted from India to China, not only did it bring a completely new spiritual world to the Chinese people, it also transplanted a completely new lifestyle into the living world of the Chinese, enriching the life of the Chinese. At the same time, it also provided a completely new momentum and influence upon Chinese society, influencing the politics, economics, charitable and philanthropic works, and social life of the Chinese. Lastly, Confucianism and Daoism as the social "background" of Chinese people's social life, were also the "background" for the development of Buddhism, with the three of them forming an intimate mutually interactive relationship. Clashing, communicating, accepting and merging, they each appreciated the others' good qualities, and with such good qualities being of benefit for all, together they all provided resources for Chinese people for contemplation and action.

When studying Chinese Buddhism, it is necessary to take China's previously existent faith, thought, institutions, social life, cultural psychology and so on as "background", to then explore the intellectual questions such as Buddhism's "transformation" in China, Buddhism and Chinese society, Buddhism and Chinese culture. That is, the question of "Sinicization". Many scholars divide "Buddhism in China" and "Chinese Buddhism", each emphasizing their own subjectivity. For example, Lü Cheng 呂澂 (1896-1989) rejected the idea that Chinese Buddhism was a "transplanting" of Indian Buddhism, but advocated a "theory of grafting". He said, "Chinese Buddhism is a 'graft' of Indian Buddhism, and therefore the root of Chinese Buddhism is in China, not in India."[4] Mou Zongsan 牟宗三 (1909-1995) emphasized in his book *Foxing yu bore* 佛性與般若 (Buddha-Nature and *Prajñā*):

> Buddhism never changed its character in Sinicization. Rather, the Chinese discoursed on pure Buddhism, directly discussing the doctrinal principles of the *sūtras* and commentaries, and developing them to a state of complete fulfillment. If one claims that Chinese Buddhism has something that Indian Buddhism original did not have, that is because that original content of Indian Buddhism, such as the two schools of emptiness and existence, are not the final stage of doctrinal principles from Buddhist *sūtras* and commentaries. This difference is a difference of continual development, not a difference of opposition.[5]

Mou Zongsan's standpoint can be said to be completely different from that of Lü Cheng. Emphasizing Chinese Buddhology as a "continual development" of

4 Lü, *lüejiang*, 4.

5 Mou, *Foxing*, 7.

Indian Buddhology is the point of view of the "theory of transplanting". We must take note that the object of concern for both scholars is just Buddhist thought, i.e. the "Dharma", disconnected from Buddhist faith and institution.

In the middle of the 20th century, Western Sinologists came up with the theories of "assimilation" and "transformation" in their research of Chinese Buddhism, for example, the famed work by Sinologist Erik Zürcher from the Netherlands, *The Buddhist Conquest of China: The Spread and Adaptation of Buddhism in Early Medieval China*, which was translated into Chinese in 1998. Because the title of the translated book lost its subtitle, there was a debate about whether it was "The Buddhist Conquest of China" or "The Chinese Conquest of Buddhism".[6] However, we have discovered that the original sense of Zürcher's "conquest" was stated in reference to Buddhism's "overcoming" various difficulties in its development, during its process of transmission and adjustment in China. It did not have the sense of the Chinese characters *zhengfu* 征服 (conquest), i.e. a kind of subjective transformation. In his book, Zürcher states:

> Buddhism is not and has never pretended to be a "theory", an explanation of the universe; it is a way to salvation, a way of life. Its introduction into China means not only the propagation of certain religious notions, but also the introduction of a new form of social organization: the monastic community, the *saṃgha*. To the Chinese Buddhism has always remained a doctrine of monks. The forces and counter-forces which were evoked by the existence of the Buddhist Church in China, the attitudes of the intelligentsia and of the government, the social background and status of the clergy and the gradual integration of the monastic community into medieval Chinese society are social phenomena of fundamental importance which have played a decisive role in the formation of early Chinese Buddhism.[7]

This book summarizes the history of Buddhism's transmission into China before the 5th century CE, as well as the process of its mutual adaptation with Chinese culture. From the perspective of cultural history, it analyzes the conflicts and merging between Buddhism and the learned classes of China, and the history of its eventual acceptance into Chinese culture. Buddhism clashed with Confucians over their politics, patriarchal ethics, and notions of the relations between Chinese and foreigners. In the end, patriarchal society was able

6 The subtitle is added in the reprint in 2003. See Zürcher, *Buddhist Conquest of China*.

7 Zürcher, *Buddhist Conquest of China*, 1.

to accept the existence of the monastic community of renunciants, which was not only an assimilation on the level of thought, but also a mutual "overcoming" and "integration" between the institutional systems of society.

In 1973, Kenneth Ch'en published a work named *The Chinese Transformation of Buddhism*, which analyzes the process of adaptation and transformation after Buddhism entered into China from the five aspects of ethical life, political life, economic life, literary life and educational social life.[8] Ge Zhaoguang 葛兆光 cites the expression of this book, and raises a question on Zürcher's conclusions. In his *Qi shiji qian Zhongguo de zhishi, sixiang, yu xinyang shijie* 七世紀前中國的知識、思想與信仰世界 (An Intellectual History of China: Knowledge, Thought, and Belief Before the Seventh Century CE), Ge states:

> The course of Chinese intellectual history from the fifth to the seventh centuries does not seem to have confirmed the Buddhist conquest of China, but rather to have witnessed a transformation of Buddhist thought under the influence of Chinese culture. Buddhism underwent a quiet shift in the three aspects of the relations between (1) the Buddhist community and secular political power, (2) Buddhist precepts and social ethics, and (3) the essential spirit of Buddhism and ethnic Han Chinese nationalism. As noted above, to survive in the area of Chinese culture with its long historical tradition of civilization, Buddhism could not help but adjust to Chinese ways. Under the rule of authoritarian Chinese political power, they could only accept the divine laws unconditionally, and acknowledge that religion should exist under imperial power.[9]

Given that China's collective consciousness at the time was predominantly ethnically Han, Buddhism avoided any forceful resistance against ethnic sentiment. While continuing and extending Buddhism's subjectivity, it vigorously adjusted and transformed Buddhism's thought, faith, ethics, organization, and institution.

Therefore, "the Chinese transformation of Buddhism" is precisely Buddhism's "Sinicization". However, most of the research on Chinese Buddhism in the last 100 years has focused on the area of Buddhist thought in its exploration of "Sinicization", and in examining this question, very little has come from the perspective of "Holistic Buddhism". Furthermore, research on the "Sinicization of Buddhism" fails to consider China's "holistic" background. Finally, researchers each come from the backgrounds of their own disciplines, and will

8 Ch'en, *The Chinese Transformation of Buddhism*.

9 Ge, *Xinyang shijie*, 594.

favor the relevant fields within Buddhism that relate to their own backgrounds (such as thought and philosophy, society and economics, faith and culture, history and archeology, and texts and manuscripts), but they lack the illumination of "Holist Buddhism". Concerning the development of Buddhist studies, further attention must be paid to the "Sinicization" of Buddhist faith and Buddhist regulations.

## 2 The Perspective of Institutional History in Chinese Buddhist Faith

In addition to its own unique qualities, Buddhist faith has commonalities with religious faith in general. Renowned anthropologist Émile Durkheim (1858-1917) emphasizes that "religion is a whole composed of parts—a more or less complex system of myths, dogmas, rites, and ceremonies."[10] He divides all religious phenomena into two fundamental categories: beliefs and rites. Beliefs are states of public opinion, and are formed through all manner of expressions. Rites are rather some specific modes of behavior. He states that: "Between these two categories of phenomena lies all that separates thinking from doing."[11] He makes a bipartite division of things of the world, i.e. the sacred and profane, and in his view:

> Beliefs, myths, dogmas, and legends are either representations or systems of representations that express the nature of sacred things, the virtues and powers attributed to them, their history, and their relationships with one another as well as with profane things. Rites are rules of conduct that prescribe how man must conduct himself with sacred things.[12]

Durkheim also points out that religion has another necessary feature that distinguishes itself from magic: the church. This is because a proper religious faith has some kind of common faith within their specific group, and this group not only professes loyalty to that faith, but it also has to perform the various rites corresponding to that faith. The members of the group not only think in the same way about the world of the sacred and related issues in the profane world, but they also turn these common views into common practices, thus forming their society, which is referred to as the "church". However, magic lacks this kind of commonality. Lastly, he defines religion as follows: "A religion is a

10 Durkheim, *The Elementary Forms of Religious Life*, 36.

11 Ibid.

12 Ibid., 37 & 41.

unified system of beliefs and practices relative to sacred things, that is to say, things set apart and forbidden beliefs and practices which unite into one single moral community called a Church, all those who adhere to them."[13] This fully explains how the concept of religion and the concept of church cannot be separated, and that religion is a matter of the collective group. Therefore, Durkheim emphasizes the three essential elements of religions as faith, rite and church. The core feature of faith is its sacredness—the qualities, character and power of sacred things, and the relationship between the sacred and the profane. Rites are a mode of symbolic action, expressing ideals of faith, as well as the intention to influence the sacred or produce profane results such as the treatment of illness. They are an important way to express notions of faith through symbolic actions, and are also an important pathway to produce religious experiences.[14] The church uses shared expressions of faith to collectively demonstrate some form of regulation.

The three essential elements of Buddhism, Buddha, Dharma and *Saṃgha*, are all sacred, and are the core elements of Buddhist faith. Within the history of Chinese Buddhist faith, the objects of faith such as Śākyamuni Buddha, Maitreya Buddha, Amitābha Buddha, Avalokiteśvāra, Mañjuśrī, Samantabhadra and Kṣitigarbha are constantly in a state of transformation. For example, in Hou Xudong's study of Buddhist faith in the northern populace during the 5th and 6th centuries, he indicates that Śākyamuni, Maitreya and Avalokiteśvāra were the figures with the broadest influence at that time. Apart from the cult of Avalokiteśvāra which was more stable, worship of Śākyamuni during the later Northern dynasties gradually changed to worship of Maitreya. Contemplation of Maitreya and Prabhūtaratana Buddha was popular for a period, and the influence of Amitābha and Vairocana slowly ascended during the end of the Northern dynasties. During the Northern dynasties, the "Three Sages of the West" were not very influential.[15] Faith in the Buddhas and bodhisattvas not only used the construction of statues to manifest the goal of votive prayers, but also combined with repentance rites, such as the worship repentance rites of the Western Pure Land, the Medicine Buddha repentances, Maitreya repentances, and Avalokiteśvāra repentances, which have continued to be transmitted up to the present day, and have remained popular without decline.

*Śarīra* are the relics of the Buddha, which Buddhists have worshipped and made offerings to throughout history. The Buddha's *śarīra* were transmitted to China during the Northern and Southern dynasties. Due to the promotion by

13 Ibid., 47.

14 Argyle, *Psychology* and *Religion*, 184-85.

15 Hou, *Fojiao xinyang*, 290.

FIGURE 2 Pagoda dedicated to Kumārajīva's (344-413) Reputed Tongue.

Emperor Wen of Sui (Sui Wendi 隋文帝 [r. 581-604]; i.e. Yang Jian 楊堅 [541-604]), common people participated enthusiastically, and offerings to *śarīra* became a shared religious activity for all society. The *śarīra* cult formed an important component of politics and society during medieval China. When Emperor Wen of Chen (r. 559-566) in the Southern dynasty founded the state, he used the Buddha's tooth *śarīra* to embellish his own political legitimacy. Sui Wendi made an intimate union of his Buddhist faith and ideals of state governance. Within the four years of the Renshou period (601-604), he mobilized the entire state's force of human and material, and issued three decrees to construct *śarīra* pagodas in every province throughout the land. The imperial house of the Tang continuously developed *śarīra* offering activities around Famen Monastery in Shaanxi. In his *Zhongguo gudai sheli yimai zhidu yanjiu* 中國古代舍利瘞埋制度研究 (Research on *Śarīra* Entombment Regulations in Medieval China), Ran Wanli 冉萬里 studies the system for the burial of *śarīra* during medieval China, including content on the types of *śarīra*, and their incoming transmission and external dissemination. In addition, based on archeological data, he undertakes an in-depth exploration of the issues with the appearance of vaults under pagodas, their evolution, and the relationship between vaults and tombs. He also makes a detailed analysis of the arrangement of *śarīra* containment vessels and their special features during each of the historical periods.[16] With the ongoing discovery of *śarīra* and underground vaults in many locations, *śarīra* scholarship will deepen further under the comprehensive viewpoints of religious sociological, historical, and archeological methodologies.

Faith in the "Dharma" is mainly shown through worship of *sūtra* texts and rituals for lecturing the *sūtra*s. In particular, there has historically been an emphasis on the merit of transcribing, making offerings to, reciting, explaining and contemplating Mahayana *sūtra*s such as the *Fahua jing* 法華經 (Lotus *Sūtra*), *Huayan jing* 華嚴經 (Flower Adornment *Sūtra*), *Da boniepan jing* 大般涅槃經 (*Mahāparinirvāṇa-sūtra*) and others. This has brought about the notion of Chinese Buddhists worshipping scripture. The thought and faith of the *Fahua jing* has had immense influence on Chinese Buddhism, and it ultimately became the central text for the Tiantai tradition. Japanese scholarship on the textual history of the *Da boniepan jing* and the history of its religious community has already achieved important results.[17] However, in the course of history of Chinese Buddhist faith, a "*Nirvāṇa* repentance (*Niepan chan* 涅槃懺)" centered on the *Niepan jing* appeared, and it was quite popular during the Southern

16 Ran, *Yimai zhidu*.

17 Mochizuki, *Daijō Nehangyō*; Shimoda, *Nehangyō no kenkyū*.

dynasties period. In Buddhist monasteries during the Tang and Five dynasties periods, it was popular to hold "*Nirvāṇa* services (*Niepan hui* 涅槃會)" to commemorate the Buddha's *parinirvāṇa*. The Northern Song Tiantai scholar monk Jingjue Renyue 淨覺仁嶽 (992-1064) specifically composed the *Shijia rulai niepan lizan wen* 釋迦如來涅槃禮讚文 (Śākyamuni Tathāgata *Nirvāṇa* Worship and Praise Text, *T* 1947) for holding Nirvana service. Concerning research on the *Huayan jing*, Korean scholar Lee Do-op has explored the thought of the Dharma-body Buddha, Bodhisattvas, consciousness only, dependent origination and the Pure Land, as well as the key content for each assembly in the *Huayan jing*.[18] "*Huayan* vegetarian feasts" (*Huayan zhai* 華嚴齋) and "Samantabhadra vegetarian feasts" (*Puxian zhai* 普賢齋) appeared from the Northern and Southern dynasties to the Sui and Tang periods. As the practice of forming Buddhist societies became popular, societies with the *Huayan jing* as their center of faith appeared during the Song dynasty. The Huayan school system of repentance practices includes Guifeng Zongmi's 圭峰宗密 (780-841) *Yuanjue jing daochang xiuzheng yi* 圓覺經道場修證儀 (Ritual for the Realisation in the Altar of the *Sūtra of Perfect Awakening*, *XZJ* 1454) in 18 fascicles and Huijue's 慧覺 (d.u) *Huayan jing haiyin daochang chanyi* 華嚴經海印道場懺儀 (Repentance Ritual in the Ocean Seal Altar of the *Huayan Jing*, *XZJ* 1452) in 40 fascicles as its most representative works. These are two of the largest of all presently extant repentance services in terms of their textual length. Zongmi based his ritual on the methods of cultivation in the *Yuanjue jing* and the systems of actual practice from Daoan 道安 (314-385) in the Eastern Jin to Zhiyi 智顗 (538-597). He used Zhiyi's *Tiantai xiao zhiguan* 天台小止觀 (Tiantai Lesser Teaching of Calm and Insight, *T* 1915) and *Fahua sanmei chanyi* 法華三昧懺儀 (*Lotus Samādhi* Repentance Ritual, *T* 1941) to explain the methods of sitting meditation and contemplation and repentance of transgressions that Buddhist practitioners should engage, in terms of actual cultivation and religious activity. He also made rules for the practices of praise, recitation and worship, and composed the *Practice and Realization Rite* in 18 fascicles. Later, Jingyuan of the Song dynasty simplified the *Practice and Realization Rite* into the *Yuanjue jing daochang lüeben xiuzheng yi* 圓覺經道場略本修證儀 (Abbreviated Ritual for the Realisation in the Altar of the *Sūtra* of Perfect Awakening, *XZJ* 1455), in one fascicle.

The union of faith in the "Buddha" and "Dharma" ultimately manifests in the popularity of repentance practices. We can see the influence and status of repentance practices in Chinese Buddhism from the wealth of writings on

18 Lee, *Kegonkyō shisō*.

repentance practices preserved in the *Taishō* and *Manji Zokuzōkyō* canons.[19] There are two categories of repentance practices that have been in common use through history. The first category is collations of the teachings in the *sūtra*s, which are routines for the repentance of transgressional faults. The second category is based on the Dharma method of the five regrets (prostrations, repentance, beseeching, rejoicing and dedication), and is practiced to cultivate the practices of calm and insight.[20] However, the reason why repentance practices have particular characteristics of Chinese Buddhism is because of the influence of local Chinese culture, especially the influence of Confucian and Daoist thought. The Chinese Buddhist repentance practices, which are based on various elaborations about repentance practices in the *sūtra*s, formed different rituals for repentance in different schools and sects. In particular, Tiantai's *Fahua sanmei chanyi* had an important influence on the composition of later repentance methods. In terms of their thought, when each school interprets their thought on repentance, they all express different ideas. However, some more universal ideas of Chinese Buddhist repentance practices can still be seen. From the Ming and Qing dynasties on, the development of repentance practices slowly diverged from their original concepts and led to some abuse, which became a predicament for their further development.

In the last twenty years of research on Buddhism, repentance practice has gradually become a hot topic. Scholars across the Taiwan strait, in Japan, Europe, America and elsewhere, such as Shioiri Ryōdō 鹽入良道, Kuo Li-ying (Guo Liying) 郭麗英, Wang Juan 汪娟, Shi Darui 釋大睿 have achieved many results in their studies of Buddhist repentance practices.[21] Research on Buddhist repentance practices includes ideas on repentance, transgressive karma and meditative contemplation. It also touches upon the origins and transmission of repentance ritual texts, the history of transmission of repentance practices, and also the interactive relationship between repentance, society and politics. In particular, research on the Yoga Flaming Mouth Service,[22] the Water and Land Rite,[23] and Water and Land Paintings[24] continues to find new information and breakthroughs.

---

19 In vol. 45 and vol. 46 of the *Taishō* canon, there are 13 repentance texts, while there are 36 repentance texts in the "repentance section" of the vols. 128-130 of the *Manji Zokuzōkyō* canon.

20 Sheng, *Hanchuan fojiao liyi*, 3.

21 Wang, *Dunhuang lichanwen yanjiu*; Idem, *Tang Song guyi fojiao chanyi yanjiu*; Shi, *Tiantai chanfa zhi yanjiu*; Sheng, *Zhongguo fojiao chanfa yanjiu*; Bai, *Tangdai Chanzong chanhui sixiang yanjiu*.

22 Yuan, *Yankou shishi yishi*.

23 Hong, *Shuilu fahui yigui*.

24 Dai, *Fojiao shuilu hua yanjiu*.

The "*Saṃgha*" represents the aspect of Buddhist institutional systems. It includes the disciplinary precepts and religious lifestyle of the monastic community. Common society does not share the disciplinary precepts, though it does share some elements with the monastic community's lifestyle. Faith in the "*Saṃgha*" primarily refers to the institutional expression of faith or, we could say, an expression of the sacredness of the monastic lifestyle. For example: although the arhats are the *śrāvaka* disciples at the time of the Buddha, however, the *Fazhu ji* 法住記 (Record of the Perpetuity of the Dharma, *T* 2030) states that sixteen *arhat*s vowed to remain in the world for a long time and not enter *parinirvāṇa* in order to act as fields of merit for living beings during the Dharma ending age and to safeguard the Dharma-body ideals of Mahayana. From this, the "cult of arhats" in Chinese Buddhism was formed.[25] Another example is the formation of the tradition of vegetarianism for monks and nuns in Chinese Han tradition Buddhism. This has its textual basis in Mahayana scriptures, but also includes Emperor Wu of the Liang's (Liang Wudi 梁武帝 [r. 502-549]) promotion of a policy of uniting politics and religion, in addition to his advocating Mahayana Bodhisattva precepts. This dual tiered application of "royal law" and "Buddhist law" pushed the development of the "prohibition of alcohol and meat" movement.

Within the Buddha, Dharma and *Saṃgha* faith, faith in the Buddhas and bodhisattvas has the power of being a call to inspiration for religious faith, and the lifestyle of the *Saṃgha* of religious faith has the power of practical influence. Therefore, Buddhist faith gradually permeated into society, and became an element of shared spiritual life for Chinese civilization.

## 3 The Perspective of Social History in Chinese Buddhist Faith

When many scholars discuss the types of Buddhism, they are influenced by Western Sinology, and often divide Buddhism into "elite Buddhism" and "popular Buddhism". The term "popular religion" is often used in Western Sinology, which is translated in Chinese as "folk religion" (*minjian zongjiao* 民間宗教)[26] or "Buddhism for the masses" (*dazhong zongjiao* 大眾佛教)[27]. The popularity of this concept indicates that scholars have paid attention to the social history dimension of religion besides its doctrinal system. When discussing the function of "popular religion", Victor Turner emphasizes that:

25 Chen, *Luohan tuxiang yanjiu*.
26 Feuchtwang, *Popular Religion in China*.
27 Averill, *Zhongguo dazhong zongjiao*, 1-11.

> Society (societas) seems to be a process rather than a thing—a dialectical process with successive phases of structure and communitas. There would seem to be—if one can use such a controversial term—a human "need" to participate in both modalities. Persons starved of one in their functional day-to-day activities seek it in ritual liminality. The structurally inferior aspire to symbolic structural superiority in ritual; the structurally superior aspire to symbolic communitas and undergo penance to achieve it.[28]

Through participation in Buddhist ritual activities, individual members use rituals to establish a relationship of equality, which displays the integration of a communally shared lifestyle.[29] This instigates a loosening of rigid notions of social structure, and thus fulfills Buddhism's social function.

The relationship between Buddhism and society is shown mainly in the interaction and influence between Buddhism and politics, economics, charitable and philanthropic works, and social activities. The relationship between the history of the monastic community of Buddhist monastics codes and social activities has been given a great deal of attention by academia.[30] For example, Japanese scholar Moroto Tatsuo 諸戶立雄 has discussed specific issues in Buddhist monastic codes such as moral standards for the *Saṃgha*, regulations for monastic tonsure, and so on. He has also examined the relationships between the Buddhist monastic community and regulations for tax exemption, and between the monastic community and the start of the Tang dynasty.[31] Hasebe Yūkei 長谷部幽蹊 has mainly explored questions in sectarian consciousness during the Ming and Qing. He has also worked on Ming and Qing dynasty royal law and Buddhist Dharma, monastics' internal politics and external assistance, monastic institutional organization, and social ethics and so forth.[32] However, the relationship between Buddhism and medieval society was made extremely complicated by the conflict between Buddhism and political power, and also mutual exchange and exploitation between officials and Buddhism. The influence of Buddhism upon Chinese traditional local society includes the appearance of prohibitions against slaughter, vegetarian fasting precepts, and other such folk customs, as well as local public engineering works and construction for other charitable works. Furthermore, there is the influence of the uniquely

28 Turner, *The Ritual Process Structure and Anti-structure*, 203.

29 Georg Simmel emphasizes that "totalitarian integration" is religion's social function. See Simmel, *Sociology of Religion*, 37-46.

30 Yan, *Fojiao jielü yu Zhongguo shehui*.

31 Moroto, *Chūgoku bukkyō seidoshi*.

32 Hasebe, *Min Shin bukkyō kyōdanshi*.

Buddhist customs of funerals and mourning upon Chinese folk society, which brought about forest burial, rock cave burial and pagoda burial practices.[33] We have mainly discussed Liang Emperor Wu's promotion of the vegetarian tradition, inner altars in the Sui and Tang periods, and Emperor Taizu of Ming's rectification of *sūtra* recitation and repentance services, which all show the interactive relationship between Buddhism and politics.

The cult of the patriarchs is originally a system of faith from within the Chinese Buddhist monastic community. However, the cult of the patriarchs slowly joined with folk faith practices such as Fu Xi's 傅翕 (497-569) revolving Buddhist canon, Wanhui's 萬回 (632-712) transformation into a god of harmony, Hongren 弘忍 (602-675) and other patriarchs becoming gods of industries, the popularization of the Venerable Budai 布袋和尙 (?-916) within Chinese folk beliefs, faith in Yizhong 義忠 (781-872), Yinsu 印肅 (1115-1169), Daoji 道濟 (1149-1209), Dingguang 定光 and so forth,[34] which demonstrate the simplified and practical attitude of Chinese people toward Buddhist faith.[35] The particular features of openness and sociality of Buddhist faith encouraged its own merging into society, slowly entering into the daily life of the common people. For example, the custom of life release not only had scriptural support and advocacy from eminent monastics, it also had the promotion of emperors and participation of the populace. From the Northern and Southern dynasties up until the present, it has always flourished without decline.

Buddhism advocates concepts such as "loving kindness and compassion", cause and effect, and merit, which have always instigated the Buddhist world to engage in works of charity, relief and so on. Through Buddhist folk organizations such as "groups" (*yi* 邑), "associations" (*yi* 義) and "societies" (*she* 社), Buddhism in the Northern and Southern dynasties were dedicated to disaster relief, care for the sick and hospital works, drilling wells, building bridges and construction of roads. From this, there was the development of charitable works such as public wells, bridges and grave sites. Through the cooperation of Buddhism and government during the Tang dynasty, institutions for compassion field infirmaries, hospitals and so on were first set up. Many types of charitable institutions appeared in Song dynasty Buddhism, such as nursing homes and rest homes for taking in sick and destitute elderly, orphanages for taking in abandoned infants and children, grain subsidies to assist indigent families for

---

33 Liu, *Zhonggu de fojiao yu shehui*; Chikusa, *chūgoku bukkyō shakaishi*.

34 Since the end of the Tang dynasty, there appeared a group of monks that were called manifestations of the Dīpaṃkara Buddha, which together constitutes the faith of Dīpaṃkara Buddha. See Yang, "Dingguangfo xinyang", 50-63.

35 Nagai, *Zenshū kyōdan*, 1-278.

raising their children, as well as professional funereal services for unidentified decedents and the remains of the poor.

The interaction between Buddhism and society includes both the mutual influence between Buddhist faith and social ideas and the constraint and support between Buddhist monasteries as public institutions and political power, economics, social life and charitable works. Timothy Brook explores donations to monasteries by the late Ming gentry, and points out that there are three constraining environments for religions as public institutions: One, the relationship between religious groups and the leadership of state power creates a kind of political constraint on the organization of religious activities. Two, economic resources and labor relations determine the feasibility of funding religious works. Three, social structures shape the supporters of religious works and their internal relationships.[36] Based on these points of view, the constraining environment of Buddhist monasteries as public institutions indirectly influences the content of Buddhist doctrines and faith. To put it more precisely, the Buddhist social ecosystem indeed constrains the social expression of Buddhist faith, and influences the interaction in daily life between Buddhism and the common populace.

Ge Zhaoguang promotes the research of intellectual history on "worlds of general knowledge, thought and belief".[37] He opposes turning intellectual history into the intellectual history of elites and scripture, and rejects arranging elites at the center. His reasons are as follows.[38] First, thought which is formed by intellectual elites and scriptural texts does not necessarily have a definite thread with a very clear continuity. Rather, knowledge and thought of the kind which actually exists within universal life does instead continue and evolve in some slow manner, allowing us to clearly see its conceptual lines. Second, thought from elites and scripture does not necessarily play the most important role in the world of daily life. Therefore, Ge states that apart from elites and scriptures, "there is another form of general knowledge, thought and belief that served as the background and the cornerstone. This general knowledge, thought and belief genuinely function in people's decisions, interpretations and dealings with the world around them."[39] For example, Stephen Teiser has two works which aid in understanding the influence of Buddhism upon society: One, *The Ghost Festival in Medieval China*.[40] It explains how the Buddhist Ullambana festival evolved into the Daoist ghost festival, as well as the

36 Brook, *Praying for Power*, 1.

37 Ge, *Xinyang shijie*, 9.

38 Ibid., 9-24.

39 Ibid., 13.

40 Teiser, *The Ghost Festival in Medieval China*.

influence that this kind of evolution produced on the social life of the populace. The emphasis is on analyzing the story of "Maudgalyāyana saves his mother". Two, *Scripture of the Ten Kings and the Making of Purgatory in Medieval Chinese Buddhism*.[41] This is a study of the religious cultural background to the *Scripture of the Ten Kings*, the manuscript of which was found in Dunhuang. It discusses the historical and cultural context of this text and how the medieval cult of the "Ten Kings" entered into the Chinese funeral rites for the deceased. We may ask: what is the common foundation for the interaction between Buddhism and society? In other words, apart from the constraining environments of politics, economics, social life, charitable works and so forth, which concepts of Buddhist faith were accepted by the people of China, and ultimately became "general knowledge, thought and belief"? This requires us to turn from a perspective of social history of Chinese Buddhist faith, to a perspective of cultural history.

## 4 The Perspective of Cultural History in Chinese Buddhist Faith

For Buddhism in China to take root and develop, in terms of thought, it needed to incorporate the original Chinese cultures of Confucianism and Daoism; in terms of faith, it needed to integrate with the culture of "ritual" (*li* 禮); in terms of institution, it had to receive acceptance from imperial power; in terms of propagation, it had to gain the tolerance and support of society; in terms of economics, it needed the sustenance of flourishing economic development. From the Han, Wei, Jin, Northern and Southern dynasties, up until the Tang and Song, Buddhism successfully completed the process of Sinicization. Since Confucianism and Daoism were parts of China's original culture, Buddhism's entry inevitably brought about confrontation and conflict with Confucianism and Daoism. The "cultural dialogue" between Confucianism, Buddhism and Daoism became an important element of Chinese culture.

However, when discussing Chinese Buddhist faith and lifestyle from the perspective of cultural history, the influence of intellectual elites and scriptures of the three religions (Confucianism, Buddhism and Daoism) upon the lives of the common people was very limited. Also, between the three religions there are some fundamental conceptual ideas that through "cultural dialogue" entered into each other's conceptual systems, and have together influenced the material and spiritual lives of Chinese society. Feng Youlan 馮友蘭 (1895–1990) examined the background of Chinese philosophy, and emphasized the

41 Teiser, *Scripture of the Ten Kings*.

FIGURE 3 The grotto remains of the Nālandā University, India.

geographic and economic background of the Chinese people, the systems of families and clans, the socially engaged and the transcendent.[42] Because of its special family and clan institution, Chinese civilization places heavy emphasis on "filial piety" and ancestor worship. Among debates between the three religions from the Northern and Southern dynasties to the Sui and Tang, the ethics of "filial piety" was the biggest problem that Buddhism faced. It was because of this that the *Sanpo lun* 三破論 (Treatise on the Three Ruinations), the conflict between foreigners and the Chinese and other issues all come about. Therefore, Buddhism continuously "transformed" and "adjusted" its own theories and standpoint, emphasizing that many Buddhist scriptures also gave favorable attention to the way of filial piety. It created many "apocryphal scriptures", and even emphasized that Buddhist "filial piety" was loftier than that of Confucianism.[43] For example, the *Lianghuang chan* 梁皇懺 (Emperor Liang Repentance; i.e. *Cibei daochang chanfa* 慈悲道場懺法 [Repentance Rituals of Compassion Altar], *T* 1909) strongly proclaims the grace of one's mother and father, and hopes that those who perform the repentance will generate gratitude toward that grace, and states that one should worship the Buddha on behalf of one's past mothers and fathers:

> Today, in the great assembly of common practice at the altar, there are some people who lost their parents when they were young. They wish to meet their parents with no avail. Since they have not attained transcendental powers, they are unable to know which realms their parents have been reborn to. The only thing they can do now is to do good deeds and transfer the merits to their parents. If they do not cease performing good deeds, they will certainly achieve success. The *sūtra* says: Accumulating the merits for the deceased is like giving gifts to someone who lives far away. If the deceased were reborn in the realms of human and heaven, the merits would increase their virtues. If the deceased were reborn in the three evil destinies or under the eight difficult conditions, they would be liberated from all sufferings forever. They would live in a period when the Buddha is still alive, receive the proper Dharma, and thus attain enlightenment. The worries and fears of their parents of the past seven lives

42 Feng, *Zhongguo zhexue jianshi*, 14-20.

43 Jan Yün-hua points out that though filial piety was noticed in Indian Buddhism, its status was not as important and lofty as that in Chinese Buddhism. It is manifested from three aspects: the Chinese politics, society and culture emphasized filial piety much more than the Indian tradition; the pressure of filial piety that Chinese Buddhists faced was much heavier that the Indian; the combination of filial piety and bureaucracy in China never happened in Indian history. See Jan, *Cong Yindu fojiao dao Zhongguo fojiao*, 44.

> and of their relatives of past eons would be eliminated. Therefore the wise ones know that the best way to repay the gratitude is to be compassionate and kind to their parents.[44]

For one's parents of this life, one should care for them and be filial. For one's parents of past lives, one should let them grow in merit and become liberated by performing repentance and worship of buddhas. This idea is founded on the assumption that one can communicate with the spiritual world through one's mind. As long as one is sincere and devout, one thought of sincerity is able to directly communicate with the activity of the spirits (souls) of one's deceased family and friends. This concept not only successfully resolved the gulf which was present early on between Buddhist ethics and Chinese indigenous filial ethics, it also fully satisfied the thought of filial piety of the Chinese people. Repentance rites have been popular right up to the present without decline, and can be said to have an intimate connection with the continuity of China's filial ethics.[45]

From the expression of faith in Chinese Buddhism, the greatest element of constraint is "ritual" (*li*). "Ritual" (*li*) is the value goal of ancient Chinese society, where seeking rank and order within human interaction is a common social ideal. "Ritual" (*li*) not only manifests as many diffuse forms of ritual institution and ethical norms, it is also a universal social institution. With centralized concentration of power institutions and institutions for ritual as background, Chinese Buddhism took Buddhist ethical precepts as the source of their thought, and in the middle of the Tang period established Chan-school pure rules which have particular Chinese characteristics. This provided an essential institutional safeguard for the survival and development of the Chan school.

From the latter half of the Six dynasties up until the Sui and Tang, the Daoist and Confucian rejection of Buddhism was mainly from the standpoints of the ethics of the three mainstays and five constants, politics of the royal way, and the dispute between foreigners and the Chinese. These three aspects are the special feature of the Chinese sociopolitical system, cultural tradition, and

---

44 *Cibei daochang chanfa*, *T* no. 1909, 45: 8.956b15-23:
今日道場, 同業大眾, 其中若有父母, 少便孤背, 難復再遇. 萬劫悠然, 既未得天眼, 死生智明, 不知父母舍報, 神識更生何道. 唯當競設福力功德, 追而報恩. 爲善不止, 功成必致. 經言：爲亡人作福, 如餉遠人. 若生人天, 增益功德；若處三途, 或在八難, 速令解脫. 生若値佛, 受正法教, 永離眾苦憂畏, 悉除七世久遠歷劫親緣, 十方眾生同得解脫. 是爲智者至慈至孝, 最上報恩.

45 You, "Fojiao chanhui lunli", 125.

ethnical psychology.[46] The setting up of Buddhist repentance practices was influenced by Chinese Confucian culture's emphasis on "ritual" (*li*). This is just as indicated by Max Weber: the obvious contrast between Confucianism and Buddhism is that Confucianism wanted an adaptation to secular life and its social order and customs, which would be no more than a large canon of laws for the educated to establish political standards and social rites and protocol.[47] Within the conflict between the ideas of the three religions, China's indigenous thinking criticized Buddhism because it is a "religion of the Western barbarians", and only appropriate for the needs of undeveloped foreign people. Confronted with China, a nation of ritual and protocol, Buddhism had to adapt to the demands of Chinese "ritual" culture, and thus formulated repentance practices. For example, during the Liu Song period, Huitong 慧通 (415-477) refuted the Daoist master Gu Huan's 顧歡 (420-483) *Yixia lun* 夷夏論 (Treatise on Foreigners and Chinese), stating:

> If one burns incense at the altar in the evening, intones a Buddhist scripture at the temple in the morning, worships, repents and entreats unceasingly, [the merit] will reach his relatives in successive eons, and below [will reach] all people of the world. The immensity of filial piety and benevolence like this cannot be surmised by the ignorant.[48]

Under the influence of Chinese culture, and in the unconscious process of countering Chinese "ritual" (*li*), Buddhism was gradually melted down, and thus Buddhist rituals such as repentance practices were born. Therefore, Jacques Gernet has pointed out that procedures for prayer rituals pose an issue which is both fundamental and significant, namely, that Buddhism had been assimilated by religious lifestyle in Chinese society.[49]

Comparing Buddhism and Daoism, in terms of doctrine, Buddhism far surpasses Daoism, but in terms of the arrangement of rituals, Daoism is richer than Buddhism. Therefore, in its process of development, it was inevitable that Chinese Buddhism absorbed the ritual of Daoism. Xiao Dengfu 蕭登福 has thus directly stated that Buddhist repentance texts, considering their concepts of repentance before the buddhas of the past, present and future, prayers to eliminate calamity and extinguish transgression, and liberating the deceased

46 Lai, *Zhongguo fojiao wenhua lun*, 82.

47 Weber, *Confucianism and Taoism*, 152.

48 *Hongming ji*, *T* no. 2102, 52: 7.46a24-27:
若乃煙香夕臺，韻法晨宮，禮拜懺悔，祈請無輟，上逮歷劫親屬，下至一切蒼生，若斯孝慈之弘大，非愚瞽之測也.

49 Gernet, *A History of Chinese Civilization*, 215.

to higher rebirth, have the same motivation as Daoist memorial presentations. As early as in the Eastern Han, Daoism already had the practice of memorial presentations to the three officials of the heaven, earth and water, during which one writes all of one's transgressions on a sheet of paper and repents before the three officials, seeking amnesty. Daoist *Yulu* 玉錄 (Jade Records), *Tutan* 塗炭 (Mud and Soot) and *Bajie* 八節 (Eight Seasons) vegetarian offerings take repentance as their focus, and thus the practice of Daoist memorial presentations (*shangzhang shouguo* 上章首過) appear to have inspired Buddhist repentance practices.[50] An additional example is the ritual of reciting the benediction text during services in Han tradition Buddhism, which also an absorption from Daoism: a reshaping of the blue paper prayer ritual (*qingci biaowen* 青詞表文) used during vegetarian offerings.[51]

The most popular and representative elements of ancient Chinese religion are with respect to heaven, service to spirits, and worship of ancestors. Within these three, religious studies scholarship can include worship of ancestors within the scope of worship of spirits, and the worship of spirits is founded on the idea of the imperishability of the soul.[52] Ancient Chinese usually considered that after a person is dead, the independent existence of the soul which has left the physical body was called a "spirit". The "Jifa" 祭法 ("Law of Sacrifices") in the *Liji* 禮記 (Book of Rites) states: "All that lives within heaven and earth is called a 'life' (*ming* 命). The death of the myriad things is called 'departing' (*zhe* 折); a human who dies is called a 'spirit' (*gui* 鬼)."[53] The concept that people die and become spirits is a common notion in ancient China. Later Daoism and Chinese Buddhism all took this as a fundamental doctrine of their own.

That serving the dead just as one serves the living, and serving gods just as one serves humans, is a religious tradition, and is also a basic principle of Confucianism in their treatment of spirits. Therefore, toward this kind of spirit which comes from the "immortal soul", one should choose an attitude of respect, yet from a distance. However, toward the spirits of ancestors, one should instead reverently respect and worship them. Therefore, the Chapter of "Xueer" 學而 (Learning) in the *Analects* records: "One takes care to the end of life, and

50 Xiao, *Daojiao yu fojiao*, 43.

51 Buddhist repentance rituals certainly influenced Daoist repentance and sacrifice rituals as well. For example, the famous Daoist *Jiuyou chan* 九幽懺 (*Jiuyou Repentance*) in the Tang dynasty is composed by imitating the Buddhist *Lianghuang chan* 梁皇懺 (Emperor Liang Repentance). These two show great similarity in procedures and content of the words. See Sheng, *Hanchuan fojiao liyi*, 3-4.

52 Lai & Wang, *Zongjiao yu daode quanshan*, 15.

53 *Liji*, 606: 大凡生於天地之間者皆曰命, 其萬物死皆曰折, 人死曰鬼.

commemorates after they are long passed, the people's virtue will return to its depth."[54] This was explained by Zhu Xi 朱熹 (1130-1200), as follows:

> "Takes care to the end of life", is their ritual of bereavement. "Commemorates after they are long passed", is their sincerity of sacrifice. "The people's virtue will become deep", means the common people are educated by it, and their virtue will return to a deep state.
>
> So, "the end of life", is easily overlooked by people, yet it is to be taken seriously; "long passed", is easily forgotten by people, yet it is to be commemorated; "depth", is the way (*dao*).
>
> Thus, one so acts, and one's virtue is deep; the common people are educated, and their virtue also returns to a deep state.[55]

It was precisely under the influence of these kinds of ideas like "deceased people become spirits" and "one takes care to the end of life, and commemorates after they are long passed", that there was recitation of *sūtras* and performance of repentance for the deceased in order to save the departed. Only under these circumstances did the commemoration and memorialization of the deceased by the living come about.

In ancient China, the idea that "beneath the broad heavens, all land belongs to the monarch" was already a natural truth ordained by heaven and earth. This kind of divinely mandated power extended to all aspects of the state. Once Indian Buddhism, which originally transcended and kept itself removed from politics, was transmitted into the great land of China, it brought about a conflict between religious and secular power. Thus, there were the matters of the debate "on why monks do not bow down before kings" in the Southern dynasties, and the event that "the emperors are Tathāgatas" in the Northern dynasties. Therefore, Buddhism could not help but adapt to China: Under the governance of autocratic Chinese political power, Chinese Buddhism could only unconditionally accept the political power that was ordained by heaven and earth, and accept that religion could only survive beneath imperial power.[56] For example, in the *Lianghuang chan*, there is worship of the Buddhas on

54 Cheng, *Lunyu jishi*, 47: 愼終追遠, 民德歸厚矣.

55 Zhu Xi, *Sishu zhangju jizhu*, 5:
愼終者, 喪盡其禮. 追遠者, 祭盡其誠. 民德歸厚, 謂下民化之, 其德亦歸於厚. 蓋終者, 人之所易忽也, 而能謹之; 遠者, 人之所易忘也, 而能追之; 厚之道也. 故以此自爲, 則己之德厚; 下民化之, 則其德亦歸於厚也.

56 Ge, *Xinyang shijie*, 594. Kamata Shigeo names this phenomenon of Chinese Buddhism as "State Buddhism"; see Kamata, *Chūgoku bukkyō shi*, 3-8.

behalf of the king and princes,[57] and the *Guoqing bailu* 國淸百錄 (Hundred Records of Guoqing Monastery, *T* 1934), "Practices of Respect and Worship", teaches the respect and worship of the Buddhas for the emperor, empress and princes:

> For the sake of Emperor Wuyuan, Empress Dowager Yuanming, and the holy spirits of the seven shrines, wish that [they] spiritually travel to the pure land and enter the status of the Dharma Cloud; respect and worship the eternally abiding Buddhas.
>
> For the sake of the Holy Lord Emperor, wish that the precious age will last for prosperity, that the heavenly blessings will continue forever, that they kindly come to the many states and save the four classes of living beings; respect and worship the eternally abiding Buddhas.
>
> For the sake of the Revered Empress, wish [her] adorned with a hundred merits and protected by the thousand sages; respect and worship the eternally abiding Buddhas.
>
> For the sake of the Prince and those of his court, wish that [they] guard the nation and bring peace to the people, that blessings be extended for ten thousand lives; respect and worship the eternally abiding Buddhas.
>
> For the sake of the many ministers of the court, the hundred officials, and five grades, wish that [they] support and praise the imperial household, fulfilling all responsibilities; respect and worship the eternally abiding Buddhas.[58]

There are blessings and dedications of merit for the state and emperor like this everywhere in the repentance texts. We can thus see that repentance practices display the special feature of Chinese Buddhism as a "State Buddhism". In addition, it also shows the special feature that Chinese Buddhist repentances emphasize practical benefits.

To summarize, looking from the perspective of cultural history, the concepts of filial piety, ritual institutions, spirits of the deceased and the state are constraining elements on the expression and transformation of Chinese Buddhist faith. During the process of the formation of Chinese Buddhist faith, it has also continuously responded to the constraints of these concepts. For example, the

57 *Cibei daochang chanfa*, *T* no. 1909, 45: 8.955b11-956a11.

58 *Guoqing bailu*, *T* no. 1934, 46: 1.794c4-13:
爲武元皇帝、元明皇太后、七廟聖靈, 願神遊淨國, 位入法雲, 敬禮常住諸佛. 爲至尊聖御, 願寶曆遐長, 天祚永久, 慈臨萬國, 拯濟四生, 敬禮常住諸佛. 爲皇后尊體, 願百福莊嚴, 千聖擁護, 敬禮常住諸佛. 爲皇太子殿下, 願保國安民, 福延萬世, 敬禮常住諸佛. 爲在朝群臣百司五等, 願翼贊皇家, 務盡成節, 敬禮常住諸佛.

Kṣitigarbha cult states that Kṣitigarbha Bodhisattva takes care of the nether world, which has very vigorously merged into the culture of filial piety.[59] Yü Chün-fang mentions another example: the cult of Avalokiteśvara is a response produced by the positivistic faith and practical system of "neo-Confucianism" (Lixue 理學).[60] The most representative result of the Sinicization of Buddhist faith is the formation of the "Four Great Mountains". The general layout of the cult of the "Four Great Mountains" began in the period of Wanli (1572-1620). During the reign of Kangxi (1662-1722), it had already become a consensus within Chinese Buddhism, and became a "central dream" within the Chinese sense of cultural superiority.[61]

59 Zhang, *Dizang xinyang yanjiu*; Yin, *Zhongguo Dizang xinyang yanjiu*.

60 Yü, *Kuan-yin*, 491. Cf. Li, *Guanyin xinyang de yuanyuan yu chuanbo*.

61 Sheng, "On the Veneration", 121-143.

CHAPTER 1

# The Faith and Lifestyles of Buddhists During the Northern and Southern Dynasties

The faith and lifestyle of Buddhism during the Northern and Southern Dynasties (Wei-Jin) between 220 and 589 gradually took on forms that were suited to Chinese people, which built upon a foundation that absorbed forms from India and the Western Regions (i.e., Central Asia), in addition to exercising reforms to the ways that original Indian Buddhism was expressed, before finally becoming a distinct Chinese form of Buddhism.

## 1 The Formation of Buddhist Repentance

Repentance is an important form of practice in Buddhism. Repentance ceremonies were gradually incorporated into the religious lifestyle of Chinese Buddhists following the transmission and translation of ideas concerning repentance in Buddhist *sūtra*s. The reason that repentance came to be characteristic of Chinese Buddhism was a result of influences from native Chinese culture, in particular via intellectual influences from Confucianism and Daoism. Eminent Chinese monks devised Buddhist repentance within the context of debates regarding the three teachings (Buddhism, Daoism and Confucianism) during the Northern and Southern dynasties atop a foundation of repentance ceremonies that originally existed in India and the Western Regions. This kind of repentance, moreover, gradually adopted an expressed form that was suited to the culture of 'ritual' (*li* 禮) in China.

### 1.1 *Daoan's Regulations for Monks and Nuns and Confession of Transgressions*

The sinicization of the institutional systems of Buddhism commenced with Daoan 道安 (314-385). His biography in the *Gaoseng zhuan* 高僧傳 (Biographies of Eminent Monks) states the following:

> Since An's virtue functioned as a standard for the people, and his learning encompassed the Three Repositories (i.e. Tripiṭaka), the rules and regulations for the monks and nuns, [as well as] the canons and constitutions of the Buddhist Dharma formulated by him were classified under three

 | DOI:10.1163/9789004431775_003

FIGURE 4
Buddha's stucco statues from Gandhāra (private collection of HE Ping 何平).

> headings: 1) rules for circulating incense, setting the seats, going up for [reciting] the *sūtras* and attending to the exposition [of them]; 2) rules for daily observation of the processions during the six parts [of each day and night] (*pradakṣiṇa*), for the partaking of drink and food, and for the hours of chanting; 3) rules for *upavasatha*, for carrying out errands, for repenting transgressions; and so forth. The *vihāras* throughout the empire consequently took these as the standard and followed them.[1]

As far back as the period of Cao Wei 曹魏 (220-266) during the Three Kingdoms Period, Dharmakāla (Tanmojia 曇摩迦; fl.222-250) and Tandi 曇諦 (fl.254) had carried out but not yet perfected the transmission of precepts.

1 *Gaoseng zhuan*, *T* no.2059, 50: 5.353b23-27: 安既德爲物宗, 學兼三藏, 所製僧尼軌範、佛法憲章, 條爲三例：一曰行香定座, 上經上講之法;二曰常日六時行道,飲食唱時法;三曰布薩差使,悔過等法.天下寺捨,遂則而從之 (Translation after Link, "Biography of Shih Tao-an", 35-36, with slight modifications).

While in Yedu 鄴都, Daoan intended to devote himself to monastic precepts, but as a result of war could not realize his aspirations. After returning to Chang'an 長安 from Xiangyang 襄陽, he requested Zhu Fonian 竺佛念 (fl.365-416) to translate the *Shisong lü biqiu jieben* 十誦律比丘戒本 (*Bhikṣu* Precepts of the Sarvāstivāda), whereby the institutional system of Buddhism was made complete.

Daoan's establishment of monastic regulations was based on actual needs. The *Jianbei jing* 漸備經 (An Alternative translation of the *Sūtra on the Ten Stages*, *T* 285), translated in 297, includes a list of the names of the 'Ten Stages of the *Jianbei jing* Given in a Foreign Language as Well as an Exegesis' ('Jianbei jing shizhu huming bing shu xu' 漸備經十住胡名並書敘), which states the following:

> On the twenty-fourth day of the fifth month of the first year of the Taiyuan 泰元 era, a year of *bingzi* 丙子 in the Chinese calendar of the sexagenary cycle (i.e., June 27, 376), this scripture was brought to Xiangyang. In the year of [*kui*]*you* 癸酉, Shi Huichang 釋慧常 consigned this scripture to a chapman of the boundary-crossing marketplace, a certain Kang'er 康兒 (i.e. a native of Samarkand), and thus it was taken from place to place before arriving at Chang'an. An Fahua 安法華, [a monk] in Chang'an, had someone deliver it to the boundary-crossing marketplace [in Chang'an], and a peddler there carried it to Xiangyang, handing it to the monk Shi Daoan 釋道安. At that time in Xiangyang, there were three hundred monks, natives of Qi, who had the text hand-copied by the monk Shi Sengxian 釋僧顯 and delivered to a devotee of the Way, Zhu Fatai 竺法汰 (320-387), in Yangzhou 揚州.[2]

It became increasingly necessary to establish an institutional system for the *saṃgha* as the number of monks grew. The translation of monastic precepts at the time, however, was incomplete. As the preface above states:

> It is said that there are five hundred articles of Buddhist precepts and for unknown reasons they have not yet been transmitted here. This matter is most imperative. With the precepts for the Four Groups of Buddhist disciples incomplete, it would make the great cause of spiritual

2 *Chu sanzang ji ji*, *T* no. 2145, 55: 9.62c4-9:
泰元元年, 歲在丙子, 五月二十四日, 此經達襄陽. 釋慧常以酉年因此經寄互市人康兒, 展轉至長安；長安安法華遣人送至互市, 互市人送達襄陽, 付沙門釋道安. 襄陽時, 齊僧有三百人, 使釋僧顯寫送與楊州道人竺法汰.

> transformation defective. The *Bore jing* 般若經 (*Prajñāpāramitā-sūtra*) holds lay Buddhists as the primary concern of its teaching, and the precepts present the fundamentals of behavior, and were the origin of hundreds of conducts—as a tree must have its roots. I am always striken by deep regret [at such a situation].[3]

Daoan was delighted to meet Tanmoshi 曇摩侍 (fl.379).[4] It was a result of this that he established the monastic regulations based on the monastic precepts or *vinaya*, as well as on the monastic system of the Western Regions about which he had heard.

However, in later times there were differing interpretations of the concrete meaning of Daoan's monastic regulations. Fascicle 13 of the *Chu sanzang ji ji* 出三藏記集 (Document Collection from the Translation of *Tripiṭaka*) records a "*An fashi faji jiuzhi sanke*" 安法師法集舊制三科 (Three Subjects on the Old System of Practice Collections of Dharma Master [Dao]an) under the *Fayuan zayuan yuanshi ji mulu* 法苑雜緣原始集目錄 (Catalogue of the Original Collections of Miscellaneous Accounts from the Dharma Garden). The chapter on recitation (*baizan pian* 唄贊篇) of the *Fayuan zhulin* 法苑珠林 (Pearl Forest of the Dharma Garden) states, "In the past, there was a master named Daoan, who collected and amended the rules of three subjects, namely the rites for mounting scriptural sermons and for *poṣadha*, etc. The wise men of the past established these injunctions, and they have not been ignored nor have they fallen to the earth. All under Heaven holds them as laws and rules, and people have been always practicing and applying them."[5] The *Da Song sengshi lüe* 大宋僧史略 (Great Song Topical Compendium of Monks) by Zanning 贊寧 (920-1001) has the following record:

> Dharma Master Daoan of the Jin dynasty bemoaned that the Buddhist rules and regulations were unavailable [in China] and that from time to time, there were demands for the ritual gravitas and decorum. Therefore, he plugged the gap and moulded the channel for the stream [of the

3 Ibid., 9.62c17-20:
云有五百戒,不知何以不至,此乃最急.四部不具,於大化有所闕,《般若經》乃以善男子、善女人爲教首,而戒立行之本,百行之始,猶樹之有根,常以爲深恨.

4 Translator note: Tanmoshi was well-versed in *vinaya*. Daoan thus invited him to recite the bhikṣu precepts out and had it translated by others. *Chu sanzang ji ji, T* no. 2145, 55: 11.80b3-5.

5 *Fayuan zhulin, T* no. 2122, 53: 36.575c29-576a2:
昔晉時有道安法師, 集制三科, 上經上講布薩等. 先賢立制, 不墜於地, 天下法則, 人皆習行.

> practice]. [He] established three paradigms to define the chapters and inspired Buddhist faith for the entire age. These were manners in 1). Offering incense, taking and ranking seats, and mounting sermons; 2). The practice of repentance throughout the six periods of the day; and 3). Holding the precepts governing *poṣadha*. As for those beyond the above, [he] established disciplines as well.[6]

Zanning believed that the three subjects of Daoan's monastic regulations included: 1. carrying of incense for the lecture, 2. repentance ceremonies for six periods of time, and 3. procedures such as *poṣadha* (formal monastic meeting). The *Fayuan zhulin*, however, lacks the "practice for six periods of time".

Tang Yongtong 湯用彤 (1893-1964), however, argued that the three subjects of Daoan concerned *sūtra*s, lectures, and *poṣadha*, among others.[7] The section on ceremonies (*yishi bu* 儀式部) in the lecture chapter (*shuoting pian* 說聽篇) of the *Fayuan zhulin* cites the *Sanqian weiyi jing* 三千威儀經 (*Sūtra* of the Three Thousand Regulations; *T* 1470) and refers to "ascending the high seat and reading *sūtra*s", which ought to include these regulations: (a). one should first prostrate to the Buddha; (b). one should prostrate to the head monk presiding over the teachings of the *sūtras*; (c). one should first set one foot on the *āsandī* (i.e. a lower chair) and mount onto the squared seat; (d). one should go back to the Seat of Honour; and (e). one holds onto the seat with a hand and gets off it. The regulations for those seated: (a). one should sit properly in proper robes; (b). one should first chant the verses once the *ghaṇṭā* (bell) is rung; (c). one should read according to cause and condition (i.e., the immediate situation); (d). If there is someone disagreeable, anger is not to be voiced while seated; and (e). if there is someone bearing items to give, they are to be placed down in front.[8] Tang Yongtong believes that "ascending the high seat and reading *sūtra*s" refers to a practice of reading out loud while atop the high seat, since one must first read out loud scriptures before lecturing on them.[9] Daoxuan 道宣 (596-667) in the chapter on Repenting Transgressions ("Huizui pian" 悔罪篇) in the *Guang Hongming ji* 廣弘明集 (An Expansion of the Collection for Glorifying and Elucidating [Buddhism]; *T* 2103) states:

---

6 *Da Song sengshi lüe*, *T* no. 2126, 54: 2.241a28-b3:
晉道安法師傷戒律之未全,痛威儀之多缺,故彌縫其闕,埭堰其流.立三例以命章,使一時而生信.一、行香定座上講,二、六時禮懺,三、布薩等法.過逾此法者,則別立遮防.

7 Tang, "Fojiao shi", 153.

8 *Fayuan zhulin*, *T* no. 2122, 53: 23. 460a27-b4.

9 Tang, "Fojiao shi", 153.

> Daoan, Huiyuan, and their peers employed this ritual ordering without delay. Princes and ministers all held the principle and specifications in great deference, and gentlemen and ladies of pure faith never broke their pledge to the moral precepts. In days of yore, Prince Jingling 竟陵, Minister of Education of the Southern Qi, produced the *Busafa jingxingyi* 布薩法浄行儀 (Ritual Procedure of the Pure Performance of Poṣadha). The categories it covered were exhaustive, as is explained elsewhere. Since words and pages tend to grow excessive, here for brevity, I list four categories so as to illuminate fundamental principle and scope of the practice of repentance.[10]

If Daoan's monastic regulations were a search for essentialness in a foundation period of Chinese Buddhism, then Huiyuan 慧遠 (334-416) built up the monastic system even more deeply atop a foundation that began with Daoan. The *Chu sanzang ji ji* preserves the names related to the system established by Huiyuan, such as *Fashe jiedu* 法社節度 ("System of the Dharma Society"), *Waisi seng jiedu* 外寺僧節度 ("System for Monks from External Temples"), *Jiedu* 節度 ("System") and *Biqiuni jiedu* 比丘尼節度 ("System for Nuns"). The *Chu sanzang ji ji* records the *Falun mulu* 法論目錄 (Catalogues of the Dharma Treatises) by Lu Cheng 陸澄 (425-494), which records their prefaces.[11] These names reveal to us that the systems related to monks, nuns, external monks and the community at Mount Lu 廬山 were completely set up by this time. Later, the *Jingzhuzi jingxing famen* 淨住子淨行法門 (Methods of Pure Practices of the Pure Abider) by Prince Wenxuan 文宣王 (460-494) of Jingling 竟陵 of the Qi 齊 (i.e, Xiao Ziliang 蕭子良 [460-494]) and the *Cibei daochang chanfa* 慈悲道場懺法 (Repentance Rituals of Compassion Altar; *T* 1909) by Emperor Wu of the Liang Dynasty—Liang Wudi 梁武帝 (464-549)—facilitated the first appearance of truly Chinese Buddhist practices of repentance. There is, however, no way of knowing the concrete details of Daoan's monastic regulations. For instance, the *Fozu lidai tongzai* 佛祖歷代通載 (Comprehensive Registry of the Successive Ages of the Buddhas and the Patriarchs; *T* 2036) by Nianchang 念常 (b. 1282-1341) during the Yuan dynasty (1271-1368) records that Daoan "composed the *Monastic Regulations* as well as twenty-four articles related to pure ceremonies for Dharma practice. These were followed by successive

10 *Guang Hongming ji*, *T* no. 2103, 52: 28.330b24-28:
道安、慧遠之儔, 命駕而行茲術. 至於侯王宰伯咸仰宗科, 清信士女無虧誡約. 昔南齊司徒竟陵王製布薩法淨行儀, 其類備詳, 如別所顯. 今以紙墨易繁, 略列數四, 開明悔過之宗轄焉.

11 *Chu sanzang ji ji*, *T* no. 2145, 55:12.84a3-6.

generations."[12] We can, therefore, get a glimpse of the influence of said monastic regulations in later times.

With respect to the third item of the monastic regulations concerning "*busa chaishi huiguo deng fa*" 布薩差使悔過等法 (Procedures for Sending Envoys and Confession of Transgressions etc at *Poṣadha*), Daoxuan in his *Sifen lü shanfan buqüe xingshi chao* 四分律刪繁補闕行事鈔 (Transcript Regarding the Revised [Regulation] of the Practice of the Four-part *Vinaya*) mentions that "the Renunciate *Poṣadha Procedures* compiled by the *śramaṇa* Daoan the enlightening hero have been consulted throughout time."[13] This refers to the ceremonies for reciting the precepts at *poṣadha* as established on the basis of the *vinaya* canon. The extant canonical *vinaya*-related texts translated before Daoan include the following:

> *Foshuo fanjie zuibao qingzhong jing* 佛說犯戒罪報輕重經 (The *Sūtra* of the Buddha's Teaching on the Severity of Retribution for Violating Precepts; *T* 1467) translated by An Shigao 安世高 of the Latter Han dynasty (25-220) in one fascicle;
> *Da biqiu sanqian weiyi jing* 大比丘三千威儀經 (The *Sūtra* of the Great Three-Thousand Regulations of Monks; *T* 1470) in two fascicles, also by An Shigao;
> *Foshuo jie xiaozai jing* 佛說戒消災經 (The *Sūtra* of the Buddha's Teaching on Precepts and the Elimination of Disasters; *T* 1477) in one fascicle translated by Zhi Qian 支謙 (fl. 223-253) in Wu 吳;
> *Tanwude lübu za jiemo* 曇無德律部雜羯磨 (The Various Karma Proceedings of the *Dharmaguptaka Vinaya*) in one fascicle translated by Saṃghavarman 康僧鎧 (active 250s) in the Cao Wei period;
> *Jiemo* 羯磨 (The Karma Proceedings; *T* 1433), being an excerpt from the Dharmaguptaka *Vinaya*, in one fascicle translated by Tan Di in the Cao Wei period.

What was most gratifying to Daoan, however, was the *Bi'naiye* 鼻奈耶 (*Vinaya*; *T* 1464) in ten fascicles translated by Zhu Fonian. Daoan in his "*Bi'naiye* xu" 鼻奈耶序 (Preface to the *Vinaya*) states:

> The spread of Buddhist scriptures to the land of Qin (i.e. China) has a long history. The scriptures brought over by Indian monks would be

---

12 *Fozu lidai tongzai*, *T* no. 2036, 49: 6.524b19-20: 著《僧尼軌範》及法門清式二十四條，世遵行之.

13 *Sifen lü shanfan buqüe xingshi chao*, *T* no. 1804, 40:1.34b25-26: 普照沙門道安開士撰《出家布薩法》, 並行於世.

translated immediately. Among the scriptures of Twelve Divisions, the largest number comes from those belonging to *vaipulya* (i.e. Mahāyāna). This is because to people of this land, the teachings and practices of Zhuangzi and Laozi resemble "all-forgetfulness" as taught in Mahāyāna *sūtras*; that is to say, [Mahāyāna *sūtras*] easily prevailed due to indigenous conventions. Daoan often bemoaned that the three divisions of the Buddhist canon were incomplete; indeed, a flaw he believed. In the year of *renwu* 壬午 (382), Kumārabuddhi carried *Apitan chao* 阿毗曇抄 (selections from *Abhidharma*) and *Si Ahan chao* 四阿含抄 (selections from the four *Āgamas*) to Chang'an. Since monks had long yearned for [the two texts], in that very summer, [Kumārabuddhi] prepared the translation of *Apitan chao* in four *juan* and in that winter the translation of *Si Ahan chao* in four fascicles. In addition, his fellow monk Bi'nai 鼻奈 from Kāśmīra, whose dharma name was Yeshe 耶舍 (Skt. Yaśa?), adroitly recited a *vinaya* text, and [Kumārabuddhi] asked him to dictate [the text] for translation. Kumārabuddhi wrote the text down in Sanskrit, [Zhu] Fonian [竺]佛念 (active 3rd - 4th c.) conducted the translation, and Tanjing 曇景 (d.u.) acted as the scribe. The dictation was started on the twelfth day of the first month (382.2.11), and [the whole project] was completed on the twenty-fifth day of the third month (382.4.24). The translation was arranged in four *juan*, and [the content] resembled the *vinaya* text recited by Tanmochi 曇摩持 (=Tanmoshi 曇摩侍): the two texts tally with each other. All hindrances caused by those that had been uncertain of and that had been gnawing people among the two hundred and sixty monastic precepts were dissolved. Thus the Supreme Teachings (*shangwen* 上聞. i.e. the Buddha's teachings), the Singular and Essential [Path], became illuminated and could be contemplated. Within these two years, the *Tripiṭaka* became complete in the land of China.[14]

---

14 "*Bi'naiye* xu," *T* no. 1464, 24: 1.851a11-24:
經流秦地, 有自來矣. 隨天竺沙門所持來經, 遇而便出. 於十二部, 毗曰羅部最多. 以斯邦人莊老教行, 與方等經兼忘相似, 故因風易行也. 道安常恨, 三藏不具, 以爲缺然. 歲在壬午, 鳩摩羅佛提賫《阿毗曇抄》《四阿含抄》, 來至長安, 渴仰情久, 即於其夏出《阿毗曇抄》四卷, 其冬出《四阿含抄》四卷. 又其伴罽賓鼻奈, 厥名耶捨, 諷鼻奈經甚利, 即令出之, 佛提梵書, 佛念爲譯, 曇景筆受. 自正月十二日出, 至三月二十五日乃了. 凡爲四卷, 與往年曇摩寺出戒典相似, 如合符焉. 於二百六十事疑礙之滯, 都謏然焉, 上聞異要, 煥乎可觀焉. 二年之中, 於此秦邦三藏具焉.

Daoan was eager to flesh out the *Tripiṭaka* in China (including *sūtra*s, the *vinaya* and *śāstra*s). In particular, he was devoted to completely building up the precepts and monastic regulations, while exerting himself to establish the institutional systems of Buddhism.

As the number of monks from South and Central Asia increased, the Buddhist world of Chang'an had the opportunity to become familiar with the monastic systems of these regions. Moreover, as the *vinaya* was translated, Chinese monks also gradually increased their understanding of the precepts and monastic regulations. The monastic systems of *poṣadha* and other similar systems were also absorbed into temple activities. "Sending appointees" (*chaishi* 差使) refers to the system of sending appointees out of the monastic community, such as when other monasteries or nuns request teachings. "Confession of transgressions" (*huiguo fa* 悔過法) is a punitive measure employed by the *saṃgha*, such as *mānatva* (penance), after a monk has violated a precept. The "confession of transgressions" in the *vinaya* is fundamentally distinct from repentance practices of later Chinese Buddhism. The former refers to repentance carried out through the *karma* proceedings of the *saṃgha*.

## 1.2 *Preaching in the Northern and Southern Dynasties*

> According to the *Gaoseng zhuan* by Huijiao 慧皎 (497-554),
> In the past, when drafting the *Gaoseng zhuan*, I structured the biographies into eight categories. Later I realized that two categories of "Scriptural Recitation" and "Persuasive Preaching", in terms of attaining the Way, were trivial; however, considering the advantage [they have] in awakening the laity, they are commendable.[15]

Huijiao found that the "master of scriptures" (*jingshi* 經師) and "preaching" (*changdao* 唱導) functioned for the purposes of conversion, which is why they were added to comprise ten topics. On the basis of the three subjects outlined in the *Gaoseng zhuan* (recitation, the master of scriptures, and preaching), it is clear that the recitation and preaching of early-period Buddhism directly influenced the late period of the Northern and Southern dynasties and the establishment of Buddhist repentance during the Sui dynasty (581-619). Daoxuan in his *Xu Gaoseng zhuan* 續高僧傳 (Extended Biographies of Eminent Monks; *T* 2060) changes "*songjing*" 誦經 (recitation of scriptures) to "*dusong*" 讀誦 (reading and recitation), and "*jingshi*" 經師 (master of scriptures) and

15 *Gaoseng zhuan*, *T* no. 2059, 50: 13.417c28-29: 昔草創高僧本以八科成傳, 卻尋經導二技, 雖於道爲末, 而悟俗可崇.

"*changdao*" 唱導 (preaching) are combined into a category of "*zake shengde pian*" 雜科聲德篇 (Virtues of the Voice in Assorted Topics).

The topic of reciting *sūtra*s in the *Gaoseng zhuan* records that monks will, for the most part, gain spiritual experiences from asceticism, recitation, repentance, and practice of meditation. Their recitations included texts such as the *Fahua jing* 法華經 (Lotus *Sūtra*), *Weimo jing* 維摩經 (*Vimalakīrti-sūtra*), *Shidi jing* 十地經 (*Daśabhūmika-sūtra*), *Siyi fantian suowen jing* 思益梵天所問經 (*Viśeṣa-cinti-brahma-paripṛcchā*, *T* 586), *Da niepan jing* 大涅槃經 (*Mahāparinirvāṇa-sūtra*), *Jin'guangming jing* 金光明經 (*Sūtra* of Golden Light), *Shoulengyan jing* 首楞嚴經 (*Śūraṃgama-sūtra*), *Dapin bore jing* 大品般若經 (*Mahāprajñāpāramitā-sūtra*), and *Jin'gang bore jing* 金剛般若經 (Diamond *Sūtra*). Therein the first two were the primary scriptures to be recited. It is from this that we can know which scriptures were popular during the Wei-Jin Northern and Southern Dynasties period. For instance, Puming 普明 (c. 371-455 during the Jin dynasty) regarded repentance and recitation as a primary activity, prioritizing recitation of the *Fahua jing* and *Weimo jing*.[16] Fazong 法宗 (5th c.) repented and renounced because he had shot a pregnant deer. He "suffered for six periods of time to repent his earlier transgression." He also recited the *Fahua jing* and *Weimo jing*.[17] It is clear that recitation of *sūtra*s and repentance were closely linked together.

When taking meals, Buddhists during the Northern and Southern dynasties period would all first prostrate and repent, and thereafter "preach guidance" (*xuanchang huadao* 宣唱化導). The ceremony for preaching came from India and the Western Regions. The *Da Song sengshi lüe* states, "Preaching started from the Western Regions. The elder monk responds to an invitation and makes an invocation: 'May two limbs always be stable. May four limbs also be stable. May all times be auspicious to gladden the heart of the benefactor.' Śāriputra was quite eloquent and once served as an elder monk. His preaching was quite fine. The white-robed laypeople were all greatly delighted. This is the foundation for formally addressing the assembly."[18] It is clear that "preaching" means that when an elder monk receives an invitation to receive offerings, he prays for auspiciousness for the sake of the benefactor, while reciting and dedicating merit. He makes various invocations and carries out praises for the benefactor. Hence, "preaching" means to address the assembly. The *Gaoseng*

16 Ibid., 12.407b11.

17 Ibid., 12.407a8-9.

18 *Da Song sengshi lüe*, *T* no. 2126, 54: 2.242a15-18:
唱導者始則西域, 上座凡赴請, 咒願曰, 二足常安, 四足亦安, 一切時中皆吉祥等, 以悅可檀越之心也. 舍利弗多辯才, 曾作上座, 贊導頗佳, 白衣大歡喜, 此爲表白之椎輪.

*zhuan* by Huijiao states the following in the discussion on the chapter on preaching:

> Persuasive preaching is meant to explain Buddhist laws and rationale, and to inspire and guide the mind of the masses. In the former times of the early spread of the Buddha's teachings, [all Buddhists] assembled in a certain place. They [started with] chanting the Buddha's name, and paid their homage according to the prescripts. It continued until midnight, when they were extremely fatigued, and the progress of the matter needed inspiration and insights. Therefore, a venerable elder was invited to ascend the seat and deliver a sermon, who may have related various historical narratives of *Nidāna,* or eloquently cited the Avadāna scriptures. In a later period, there was Shi Huiyuan from Mount Lushan, whose spiritual attainment and practical commitment were pure and consummate, and whose demeanor and talents were brilliant and expressive. On every occasion of assembling for repentance, [Huiyuan] took the initiative to ascend the seat and present a discourse. He led the way. He would first expound the causality that spans the past, the present, and the future, and then turned to identify the fundamental significance of penance. [This procedure] was transmitted to later generations and became the established paradigm. This could be understood from that Daozhao 道照 (388-453), Tanying 曇穎 (389-471), over ten figures in total, joined the ranks of his disciple, and all of them claimed fame in the world of the day.[19]

Huijiao offered an interpretation of the origins of preaching. In gatherings during the earliest time of the Buddhadharma's transmission, people would recite the name of the Buddha and prostrate. When tired during the middle of the night, the venerable monk would be requested to preach the Dharma. Huijiao believed that Huiyan was the first one to preach from the high seat in Chinese Buddhism. During meal offering ceremonies, Huiyuan personally exercised leadership and would first speak about cause and effect through the three lifetimes while also explaining the significance of the meal offering ceremony.

19 *Gaoseng zhuan*, *T* no. 2059, 50: 13.417c7-15:
唱導者, 蓋以宣唱法理, 開導眾心也. 昔佛法初傳, 於時齊集止, 宣唱佛名, 依文致禮；至中宵疲極, 事資啓悟, 乃別請宿德升座說法, 或雜序因緣, 或傍引譬喻. 其後廬山釋慧遠, 道業貞華, 風才秀發, 每至齋集, 輒自升高座, 躬爲導首, 先明三世因果, 卻辯一齋大意. 後代傳受, 遂成永則. 故道照、曇穎等十有餘人, 並駢次相師, 各擅名當世.

This led to the formation of rules governing preaching. After Huiyuan, various teachers scrambled to learn them and they became fashionable.

In order to be a preacher, it was necessary to be widely learned and eloquently spoken. One could "point to things at the right time, not only relying on words."[20] For instance, Daozhao 道照 (388-453) preached for Emperor Wu of the Song dynasty, Song Wudi 宋武帝 (r. 420-422), explaining in brief that human life "quickly fades within a century" and that "suffering and pleasure are irregular—they necessarily stem from causes inviting results."[21] As a result of this, Daozhao moved Wudi to bestow upon him thirty-thousand coins. Huiqu 慧璩 (392-463) "read through the Buddhist scriptures and treatises and extensively went through classics and histories, and he was skilled in various arts, and was especially talented at preaching. Words flowed from his mouth as from the pen of a master, and he wielded literary expressiveness for creative writing. In every case, he improvised with various citations, and none of them would fail to be amazed."[22] Huiqu was adaptable to circumstances and eloquent in his speech. Later he received the graces of Song Wudi, becoming the "rector of the capital."[23] At the same time, preaching required "excellent guidance" (*shanyou* 善誘), such as Tanying 曇穎 (d. c. 471) who "recited *sūtras* more than a hundred-thousand times. … By nature, he was reverent and considered guidance as foremost, hence he set his mind on preaching and was naturally unmatched."[24] Tanying's individual character was humble and also committed. He was adept in guiding beings, which is why he was especially known for his preaching.

Thus, Huijiao offers a summary with respect to the four items important to preaching, i.e., voice, eloquence, ability and erudition: "Without voice, one cannot alert beings. Without eloquence, one cannot be in accord with one's circumstances. Without talent, one's words cannot be taken in. Without erudition, one's speech will be baseless."[25] These are the four conditions that a preacher must meet. The voice of a preacher should be like bells and drums, used to awaken beings. What one speaks must not be erroneous. "Eloquence" is being in accordance with the place and faculties of the audience. "Talent"

---

20 Ibid., 13.415c16-17: 指事適時, 言不孤發.

21 Ibid., 13.415c18-19: 百年迅速, 遷滅俄頃. 苦樂參差, 必由因召.

22 Ibid., 13.416a9-11:
讀覽經論, 涉獵書史, 眾技多閑, 而尤善唱導；出語成章, 動辭製作, 臨時采博, 罄無不妙.

23 Ibid., 13.416a17: 京邑都維那.

24 Ibid., 13.415c24-26: 誦經十餘萬言 ... 性恭儉, 唯以善誘爲先, 故屬意宣唱, 天然獨絕.

25 Ibid., 13.417c16-17: 非聲則無以警眾, 非辯則無以適時, 非才則言無可采, 非博則語無依據.

refers to the brilliance of the preacher, for example writing must use eloquent vocabulary and possess literary richness. “Erudition” refers to how the preacher must possess expertise, having widely read canonical texts, secular works, and history. Moreover, with respect to the matters of the audience, one must adopt different approaches to preaching. First, when addressing renunciates, one should “urgently speak of impermanence and anxiously explain repentance”[26] and thereby cause them to devote themselves to activities of the Buddhist path. Second, when addressing rulers and elders, one should “also cite worldly texts and elegantly weave one’s words together,”[27] which is to say, one should convert those in high positions by producing a sense of reverence and respect in them through erudite learning and elegant writing. Third, when addressing common people, one directly speaks of matters that come up in daily life. Fourth, when addressing bandits in the mountains, one directly and clearly speaks of the condition of sin. If a preacher “knows the time and audience”[28] in addition to also being eloquent, talented and without error, then their preaching will sincerely move people, and even convert beings, such as animals in the air and on land. This is also the foremost method of converting beings.

### 1.3 *Purification Gathering* (Zhaihui 齋會) *and Repenting Transgressions* (Huiguo 悔過)

*Poṣadha* and preaching are both related to repentance, and moreover these all came to completion through the formation of the purification gathering. The Chinese translation of *poṣadha* is *zhai* 齋, which means purity and explicit repentance. This is because the origin *poṣadha* and the day of purification are intimately related. The *saṃgha*’s primary activity on this day is recitation of precepts and pure repentance. In addition, on the six days of purification, laypeople receive the eight precepts of purification for a day and a night, during which time the core part is the precept of fasting after noon. Preaching is one of the activities that occurs during this gathering, the goal of which is actual purification of body and mind as well as repentance of karmic obstacles through preaching and recitation of scriptures. The purification gathering during the Wei-Jin Northern and Southern Dynasties period was a direct extension of the Indian system, having merged with the cultures of traditional Chinese rites and Daoist purification. As a result, a uniquely Chinese system of purification rituals gradually developed.

---

26 Ibid., 13.417c22: 切語無常, 苦陳懺悔.

27 Ibid., 13.417c23: 兼引俗典, 綺綜成辭.

28 Ibid., 13.417c26: 知時知眾.

FIGURE 5 The Buddha's footprint, dated to the second century AD (Yale University Art Gallery).

During the early period when Buddhism was being introduced into China, it was primarily comprised of miracles and purification precepts, such as Prince Ying of Chu 楚王英 (i.e. Liu Ying 劉英 [?-71]) who, during the time of Later Han dynasty Emperor Ming 明帝 (r. 57-75), "emulated the Buddha and carried out sacrificial rites with the purification precepts."[29] As a result of this, Emperor Ming decreed that "Prince of Chu recited the fine words of the Yellow Emperor and Laozi as well as carried out the beneficial rites of the Buddha during a purification period of three months, during which he made oaths with the divine."[30] Moreover, purification precepts and invocations with incense were linked together, as is recorded in Kang Sengui's 康僧會 (c. third century) biography in the *Gaoseng zhuan*, "He carried out the invocation with burning incense added to a copper vessel together with purification in a quiet room."[31] The *Da Song sengshi lüe* by Zanning states the following:

29 *Gujin tushu jicheng shijiao buhui kao*, XZJ no. 1498, 133: 1.298a1-2: 學爲浮屠, 齋戒祭禮.

30 Ibid., 298a5-6: 楚王誦黃老之微言, 尙浮屠之仁祠, 潔齋三月, 與神爲誓.

31 *Gaoseng zhuan*, *T* no. 2059, 50: 1.325b17-18: 乃共潔齋靜室, 以銅瓶加凡燒香禮請.

> Ever since the teachings of the Buddha were first spread to the East (i.e. China), in most cases, exercises were sloppy and ignorant. As is told in the *Gaoseng zhuan*, "The rite of repentance was set up, a reverse effort [echoing the Indian practice], but the procedure was identical to that of the indigenous rites of ancestor worship. During the age of Wei-Jin, monks all spread out grass when eating, and such deportment as simple as how to sit or rise from a seat, etc., and the delivering of a sermon for conversion, lacked rules of professional etiquette.[32]

In the process of transmitting purification precepts into China, it became a symbol of the Buddhism of commoners, as well as a lively expression of Mahāyāna Buddhism's active engagement in the world.

With respect to lay Buddhists, the eight purifying precepts are a system of Buddhist practice that is normally carried out. For instance, the *Guang Hongming ji* (fascicle 30) records the "Ba guangzhai shi xu" 八關齋詩序 (Preface to the Poems on the Eight Purifications), "Wuyue changzhai shi" 五月長齋詩 (Poem on the Long Purification of the Fifth Lunar Month) and "Ba guanzhai shi sanshou" 八關齋詩三首 (Three Poems on the Eight Purifications) by Zhidun 支遁 (314-355), which explains how the monks and laypeople are to cultivate the eight purifying precepts together. The first of these texts states the following:

> Lately, Cavalry General He [Chong] 何 [充] (292-346) [and I] made an appointment to hold the One-Day Observance of the Eight Precepts together. On the twenty-second day of the tenth month, [we] gathered those having the same intention at the foot of the earth burial mound in Wu County. The rite started on the early morning of the twenty-third day, and there were altogether twenty-four persons, both monastics and lay devotees. The atmosphere was pure, balmy, solemn, and harmonious, and no one did not feel quiet and fulfilled. On the morning of the twenty-fourth day, the assembly of worthy men each took their leave.[33]

There were diverse activities in the purification gatherings during the Wei-Jin Northern and Southern Dynasties period. Neither the time nor the venue were settled. The *Fayuan zhulin* records that in the ninth lunar month of 425,

---

32 *Da Song sengshi lüe*, *T* no. 2126, 54: 1.238c10-12:
自佛法東傳, 事多草昧, 故《高僧傳》曰 : " 設復齋懺, 同於祠祀. 魏晉之世, 僧皆布草而食, 起坐威儀, 唱導開化, 略無規矩."

33 *Guang Hongming ji*, *T* no. 2103, 52: 30.350a17-20:
間與何驃騎期, 當爲合八關齋. 以十月二十二日, 集同意者, 在吳縣土山墓下, 三日清晨爲齋. 始道士白衣凡二十四人, 清和肅穆, 莫不靜暢. 至四日朝, 眾賢各去.

Daojing 道璟 (fl.425-430) was in Luoyang, where more than forty-thousand monastic and lay Buddhists carried out a purification gathering connected to Samantabhadara. The practice lasted for more than one week.[34] In the following year (426) in the twelfth lunar month, the laypeople again carried out the same gathering. In 432, the household of a Zhang Xuyuan 張須元 (otherwise unknown) provided an Observance of the Eight Precepts, which was participated by several tens of people, from either the clergy or the laity.[35] Twenty-four monks and laypeople participated in cultivating the eight purifications together.

Renunciates participate in the eight purifications because laypeople rely upon the monks in order to receive the precepts. The monks then lead and preside over the activities of the purification gathering. The right purification precepts are renunciate precepts upheld by laypeople, through which they experience the pure lifestyle of renunciate monks. There must be monks present to teach the Dharma and lead things so that the rites could be properly carried out. The eight purification precepts, however, gradually became superficial. Shen Yue 沈約 (441-513) in 509 in his "Sheshen yuanshu" 捨身願疏 (Treatise on Vows to Self-Sacrifice) expresses his frustrations as follows:

> [Therefore, the Buddha] unveiled the Eight Stems [of Precepts] to guide the devotees of purity so that for a day and night, they could experience the life of renunciation exemplified by the Buddha. This was meant to promote the teachings to the laity and does not belong to the monastic practice. Sentient beings in the secular world, however, tend to mistake the idea and have gone astray in this respect. They arrogantly invite famous monks and leave them in an empty room. They host householders who would lie loftily, remaining idle in a lounge. It is called "One-Day Observance of the Eight Precepts", but in reality, it is far from that. Although there is the cause of the generosity of giving, it is not the deed that would eliminate their negative karma.[36]

Aristocrats would invite monks into their own homes, but they themselves were lazy and degenerate, which is why although there were donations and offerings, these activities were still tainted.

34 *Fayuan zhulin*, *T* no. 2122, 53: 17.408c29-409a5.

35 Ibid., 40. 601c1-2.

36 *Guang Hongming ji*, *T* no. 2103, 52: 28.323c18-22:
開以八支導彼清信, 一日一夜同佛出家. 本弘外教, 事非僧法, 而世情乖舛, 同迷斯路. 招屈名僧, 置之虛室, 主人高臥, 取逸閒堂, 呼爲八關, 去之實遠. 雖有供施之緣, 而非斷漏之業.

At the same time, other activities such as self-immolation and reading of *sūtras* also appeared during the gatherings for the eight purification precepts. As the *Gaoseng zhuan* biography of Huishao 慧紹 (424-451) records, he once sought to carry out self-immolation at Zhaoti si 招提寺 in the county of Linchuan 臨川郡. The hired hands piled up several feet of firewood in a cave in Mount Dong 東山. On the day he was to carry out his self-immolation, he administered the eight purification precepts for the great assembly at Mount Dong and addressed them. Early in the night they made a procession. After Huishao offered incense, he ignited the firewood.[37]

In purification gatherings, the recitation of *sūtras* was commonly undertaken. A "Zheng fahua jing houji" 正法華經後記 (Postscript to the *Zheng fahua jing*) in the *Chu sanzang ji ji* records that in 290, at Dongniu si 東牛寺 in Luoyang there was a reading and explanation of the *Fahua jing*. The scale of the Dharma gathering was magnificent.[38] Liang Wudi's "Duan jiurou wen" 斷酒肉文 (Proscription of Alcohol and Meat) records the following:

> On the morning of the twenty-third day, [Master] Fayun 法雲 (467-529) of the Guanzhai si 光宅寺 ascended the elevated seat that faced east before the Hualin 華林 hall and served as the dharma master, and [Master] Huiming 慧明 (d.u.) of the Waguan si 瓦官寺 ascended the elevated seat facing west and acted as the Preacher. [Huiming] recited one-fourth of the chapter of "Sixiang pin" 四相品 in *Da boniepan jing*, laying out the idea that those who eat meat would eliminate their seed of great compassion. [Master] Fayun presented explanations. His Majesty graced the event with his presence, whose position was set in the north of the elevated seats. Male and female monastics respectively took seats in order. When the preaching was concluded, [Master] Daocheng 道澄 (d.u.) of the Qishe si 耆闍寺 ascended the west-facing elevated seat and read out this text about abstention from eating meat, followed by the words transmitted [by His Majesty]. After [the words were] read out, then followed the liturgical obeisance and repentance. Then a lunch for all attendants was provided, and when the lunch finished, the assembly was dismissed.[39]

---

37 *Gaoseng zhuan, T* no. 2059, 50: 12.404c22-28.

38 *Chu sanzang ji ji, T* no. 2145, 55:8.56c26-57a2.

39 *Guang Hongming ji, T* no. 2103, 52: 26.299a1-8:
二十三日旦，光宅寺法雲於華林殿前登東向高座爲法師，瓦官寺慧明登西向高座爲都講，唱《大涅槃經・四相品》四分之一，陳食肉者斷大慈種義. 法雲解釋，輿駕親御，地鋪席位於高座之北，僧尼二衆各以次列坐. 講畢，耆闍寺道澄又登西向高座，唱此斷肉之文，次唱所傳之語，唱竟又禮拜懺悔，普設中食竟出.

Liang Wudi himself attended the purification gathering to speak on the twenty-third and twenty-ninth days. During the talks there were dharma masters and preachers. After the talks, there were also people who preached and spoke about the *sūtras*. Finally, they all prostrated, repented and ate the offerings of food. It is clear that the purification gathering was a commonly held Dharma service in which monks and laypeople gathered to lecture on and discuss the meaning of scriptures.

As the above discussion suggests, purification gatherings as well as *poṣadha*, preaching, prostrations, talks, recitations, and repentance were all related. For example, the table of contents of the *Fayuan zayuan yuanshi ji* 法苑雜緣原始集 (The Original Collections of Miscellaneous Accounts from the Dharma Garden) lists the program of practices by Xiao Ziliang, Prince Jingling, from the Qi dynasty:[40]

Purification gatherings involving the practice of *poṣadha*:

*Huayan zhaiji* 華嚴齋記 (Record of the Huayan Purification Gathering), 1 *juan*;

*Xizhou Fayun, Xiao Zhuangyan, Puhong Si jiang* 西州法雲、小莊嚴、普弘寺講 (Lectures in the Fayun, Xiao Zhuangyan, and Puhong monasteries in Xizhou) and *Shu Yang Chang Hongguang zhai* 述羊常弘廣齋, together in 1 *juan*;

"Jiang *Jingzhu* ji" 講淨住記 (Notes of the Lecture on Pure Abider), 1 *juan*;

"Bari Chanling si zhai bing song" 八日禪靈寺齋並頌 (Eight-Day Purification Ceremony at Chanling si and Verses), 1 *juan*;

"Longhua Hui bing Daolin zhai" 龍華會並道林齋 (Gathering at Longhua and Purification at Daolin), 1 *juan*;

"Jingling Wenxuan Wang Longhua hui ji" 竟陵文宣王龍華會記 (Notes on a Longhua Gathering by Prince Wenxuan of Jingling);

"Busa bing Tianbao jiang" 布薩並天保講 (*Poṣadha* and the Lecture in Tianbao Monastery), 1 *juan*;

*Jingzhu zi* 淨住子 (The Pure Abider), 20 *juan*;

*Jingzhu zi cimen* 淨住子次門 (The Liturgical Sequence of the Pure Abider), 1 *juan*;

"Wenxuan wang ji youposai busa ji" 文宣王集優婆塞布薩記 (Notes on the *Upāsaka Poṣadha* Compiled by Prince Wenxuan).

Purification gatherings involving worship rituals and repentance:

*Chao Puxian guan chanhui fa* 抄普賢觀懺悔法 (Excerpts of the Repentance of Contemplation on Samantabhadra), 1 *juan*;

*Lifo wen* 禮佛文 (Liturgy of Paying Homage to the Buddha), 2 *juan*.

40 *Chu sanzang ji ji*, *T* no. 2145, 55:12.85c10-86b18, 92b12-93a19.

Purification gatherings involving precepts and taking precepts:

*Jingling Wenxuan wang shou pusajie ji* 竟陵文宣王受菩薩戒記 (The Record of Prince Wenxuan of Jingling Taking Bodhisattva Precepts);

*Tianbao si ji youposai jiang ji* 天保寺集優婆塞講記 (Notes on the Lecture on *Upāsaka* Collected in Tianbao Monastery), *Wenxuan Wang ji youposai busa ji* 文宣王集優婆塞布薩記 (Notes on *Upāsaka Poṣadha* Collected by Prince Wenxuan), *Kai "Youposai jing" ti* 開《優婆塞經》題 (Explanation of the title of the *Sūtra* on *Upāsaka*), 1 *juan*;

*Chao "Youposai shoujie pin"* 抄優婆塞受戒品 (Excerpts from the Chapter "The Precepts for *Upāsaka*"), 1 *juan*;

*Zhu "Youposai jie"* 注優婆塞戒 (Comments on Precepts on *Upāsaka*), 3 *juan*;

*Chao youposai shoujie fa* 抄優婆塞受戒法 (Excerpts from the Procedure for *Upāsaka* to Take Precepts), 1 *juan*;

*Jie guo zhuangyan* 戒果莊嚴 (The Majestic Adorment of the Fruition of Observing Precepts), 1 *juan*;

*Shu fangsheng donggong zhai* 述放生東宮齋 (An Account of the Life-releasing Ceremony in the Eastern Quarters of the Imperial Palace) and *Shu shoujie* 述受戒 (An Acount of Taking Precepts), 1 *juan*;

*Jiao xuanyue shoujie ren* 教宣約受戒人 (Instructions to Those Who Pledge to Take Precepts), 1 *juan*;

*Shoujie bing hongfa jie* 受戒並弘法戒 (Taking Monastic Precepts and Precepts for Aggrandizing the Dharma), 1 *juan*.

Purification gatherings involving hymns (*fanbai* 梵唄) and scriptural recitation (*zhuanjing* 轉經):

"Zan fanbai ji wen" 贊梵唄偈文 (Text of Praising Hymns), 1 *juan*;

"Fanbai xu" 梵唄序 (A Preface to Hymns), 1 *juan*;

"Zhuandu fa bing shizhi" 轉讀法並釋滯 (The Method of Brief Recitation of Scriptures with Resolutions of Doubts), 1 *juan*;

"Jingling Wenxuan zhuan fanli zan" 竟陵文宣撰梵禮贊 (The Ode of Buddhist Obeisance by Prince Wenxuan of Jingling);

"Jingling Wenxuan zhi chang pusa yuan zan" 竟陵文宣製唱菩薩願贊 (The Ode of The Vows of Bodhisattvas Created by Prince Wenxuan of Jingling);

"Jingling Wenxuan wang di ji zhuanjing ji" 竟陵文宣王第集轉經記 (Records of Brief Recitation of Scriptures Compiled by Prince Wenxuan of Jingling).

The purification gathering and repentance of transgressions are related. Fascicle thirteen of the *Da zhidu lun* 大智度論 (Treatise on the Great Perfection of Wisdom; *T* 1509) mentions the Eight Purification Repentance as the "one-day precept." After receiving the "three refuges" (*san guiyi* 三皈依), the precept receivers made the following vow:

> This is the person, so-and-so. If my physical activities are non-virtuous, or my spoken activities non-virtuous, or my mental activities non-virtuous, they are all caused by greed, hatred, and ignorance. If I have committed such transgressions either during this life or past lives, today I repent them sincerely. To purify my bodily actions, my speech, and my mind, I take and observe the Eight Precepts, this being *poṣadha*.[41]

It is only through sincerely repenting past life karma of the body, speech and mind that one can attain purity of the three karmas and thereafter receive the eight precepts. This is why the *Fayuan zhulin* records that Wei Shidu 衛士度 (3rd c.) produced an "Baguan chanwen" 八關懺文 (Eight Purification Repentance Text), which "was still employed at purification ceremonies during the late Jin dynasty."[42]

## 1.4 *The Formation of Repentance Rites in the Six Dynasties Period (222-589)*

Following the popularity of practices of repentance and the translation of scriptures related to this topic, the creation of repentance rites gradually matured and became complete. Scriptures related to repentance were continually translated during the early period of Buddhist translations from the first century CE onward when Buddhism was being transmitted into China. This includes scriptures such as the *Asheshi wang jing* 阿闍世王經 (*Sūtra* of King Ajātaśatru; *T* 626), which was translated between 147 and 186, and the *Shelifo huiguo jing* 舍利弗悔過經 (*Sūtra* of Śāriputra's Repentance; *T* 1492), which was translated between 148 and 170. The *Chu sanzang ji ji* records that during the time of Emperor Wen of the Wei, Wei Wendi 魏文帝 (r. 220-226), Zhi Qian between 221 and 237 translated a *Huiguo jing* 悔過經 (Repentance *Sūtra*) in one fascicle. A comment reads, "some say it narrates a repentance text of prostrating to [the Buddhas] of the Ten Directions."[43] The transmission of repentance scriptures therefore ought to have been quite early. There are a total of sixty-one scriptures concerning repentance from the Eastern Han to the Six

41 *Da zhidu lun*, *T* no. 1509, 25: 13.159b22-25: 我某甲, 若身業不善, 若口業不善, 若意業不善, 貪欲、嗔恚、愚痴故. 若今世、若過世, 有如是罪, 今日誠心懺悔. 身清淨、口清淨、心清淨, 受行八戒, 是則布薩.

42 *Fayuan zhulin*, *T* no. 2122, 53: 42. 616b27: 晉末齋者尚用之.

43 *Chu sanzang ji ji*, *T* no. 2145, 55:2.7a12: 或云序十方禮悔過文.

Dynasties in the Chinese Buddhist canon. Such rich translation of concepts concerning repentance inevitably brought about the flourishing of related rites.

At the earliest, the production of repentance rites in Chinese Buddhism started with Xuangao 玄高 (402-444) in 439, who produced a "Purification of Golden Light" (*Jin guangming zhai* 金光明齋) for Prince Huang 晃 (428-451).[44] Sengbao 僧苞 (?-452/453) of the Liu Song produced a "Twenty-One Purifying Repentance of Samantabhadra" (*Sanqi Puxian zhai chan* 三七普賢齋懺).[45] The *Lidai sanbao ji* 歷代三寶紀 (Record of the Three Jewels throughout Successive Dynasties; *T* 2034) records that in 517, Baochang 寶唱 (d. early 5th c.) during the Liang Dynasty produced the "*Zhongjing chanhui miezui fangfa*" 眾經懺悔滅罪方法 (Methods for the Repentance and Expiation of Transgressions from Various Scriptures) in three fascicles. In addition, below the titles of the eight works by Baochang, the following explanation is given:

> Appreciating that the land of the country remains hospitable and free of various disasters and hindrances, the emperor believed that it is owed firstly to the grace of the Three Jewels and secondly to the Four Heavenly Kings [...] Therefore, during the Tianjian 天監 era, [His Majesty] issued a decree year after year, ordering that the monk Baochang 寶唱 (495?-528?) of Zhuangyan si 莊嚴寺, among others, to prepare a comprehensive compilation for future use. [The work covers the practices of] cultivating Dharmic merits to ward off disasters, worshipping and repenting to remove the Dharmic hindrances, and offering sacrifice to the *nāga*-kings—all such various practices of prayer were reviewed by the emperor in person. The practices of sacrifice and prayer were so clearly illustrated that miraculous responses were numerous. Thus, this was what the myriad people relied upon during that fifty years—it was due to the power of this [work].[46]

Liang Wudi made a great contribution to the establishment and development of Chinese Buddhist repentance practices. Therein the greatest influence was with the production of the *Cibei daochang chanfa*. This is the earliest established repentance practice in Chinese Buddhism.

The *Chu sanzang ji ji* lists the titles of some of the repentance rites:

44 *Gaoseng zhuan*, *T* no. 2059, 50: 11.397c8-9.

45 Ibid., 7.369b16.

46 *Lidai sanbao ji*, *T* no. 2034, 49: 11.99b13-21:
帝以國土調適住持, 無諸災障, 上資三寶, 中賴四天 ...... 故天監中頻年降敕, 令莊嚴寺沙門釋寶唱等總撰集錄以備要須. 或建福禳災, 或禮懺除障, 或饗鬼神, 或祭龍王, 諸所祈求, 帝必親覽. 指事祠禱, 訖多感靈, 所以五十年間兆民荷賴, 緣斯力也.

*Zhou yong yangzhi jingshui yuanji* 咒用楊枝淨水緣記, derived from *Qing Guanshiyin jing* 請觀世音經 (*Sūtra* of the Request for Avalokiteśvara), trans. Nanti 難提 (Skt. Nandi, b. 419);
*Mile liushi chanhui fa yuanqi* 彌勒六時懺悔法緣起, derived from *Mile wen benyuan jing* 彌勒問本願經 (*Maitreyaparipṛcchā-sūtra* or *Sūtra* about Maitreya Inquiring about the Original Vows), trans. Zhu Fahu 竺法護 (239-316);
*Puxian liugen chanhui fa* 普賢六根悔法, derived from *Puxian guan jing* 普賢觀經 (*Sūtra* of Meditating on Samantabhadra Bodhisattva), trans. Tanmomiduo 曇摩蜜多 (Skt. Dharmamitra, 356-442);
*Xukongzang chanhui ji* 虛空藏懺悔記, derived from *Xukongzang jing* 虛空藏經 (*Sūtra* of Meditating on Ākāśagarbha Bodhisattva), trans. Tanmomiduo;
*Fangguang tuoluoni qihui fayuan ji* 方廣陀羅尼七悔法緣記, derived from the very *sūtra* (*Mahāvaipulya Dhāraṇī sūtra*, or *Sūtra* of the *Dhāraṇī* of Universality), trans. Fazhong 法眾 (402-413);
*Jin guangming chanhui fa* 金光明懺悔法, derived from *Jinguangming jing* (*Suvarṇa prabhāsôttama sūtra*, or *Sūtra* of Golden Light), trans. Tanwuchen 曇無讖 (Skt. Dharmakṣema in 412).

It is clear that repentance rites based on Maitreya, Avalokiteśvara, Samantabhadra, Ākāśagarbha, *Mahāvaipulya*, and the *Jin'guangming jing* very much flourished during the period of the Southern dynasties, and moreover became daily rituals observed by monks.

After the Northern and Southern Dynasties period, there were a great number of repentance rites produced under royalty. The *Guang Hongmingji* (see the chapter on repentance in fascicle 28) lists the repentance texts produced by kings of the Southern Dynasties as well as Shen Yue and Jiang Zong 江總 (519-594).[47]

These repentance texts might be regarded as the opening remarks before activities such as reciting *sūtra*s, since these texts have no definite ritual form

47 *Guang Hongming ji*, *T* no. 2103, 52: 28.330c05-335a24: Emperor Jianwen of Liang's 梁簡文帝 "Xiechi wei jian *Niepan* chan qi" 謝敕爲建涅槃懺啓, "Liugen chanwen" 六根懺文, "Hui gaoman wen" 悔高慢文; Shen Yue's 沈約 (441-513) "Chanhui wen" 懺悔文; Jiang Zong's "Qunchen Chen Wudi chanwen" 群臣陳武帝懺文; Liang Gaozu's 梁高祖 "*Mohe bore* chanwen" 摩訶般若懺文; Liang Wudi's 梁武帝 "*Jingang bore* chanwen" 金剛般若懺文; Emperor Xuan of Chen's 陳宣帝 "*Shengtian bore* chanwen" 勝天王般若懺文; Emperor Wen of Chen's 陳文帝 "*Miaofa lianhua jing* chanwen" 妙法蓮華經懺文, "*Jinguangming* chanwen" 金光明懺文, "*Datong fangguang* chanwen" 大通方廣懺文, "*Xukongzang pusa* chanwen" 虛空藏菩薩懺文, "*Fangdeng tuoluoni* zhai chanwen" 方等陀羅尼齋懺文, "Yaoshi zhai chanwen" 藥師齋懺文, "Suoluo zhai chanwen" 娑羅齋懺文, "Wuai hui sheshen chanwen" 無礙會捨身懺文.

in writing. Moreover, judging from the opening lines in each text, "Now, reverentially, a repentance rite is held by a certain number of monks for a certain number of days according to the formula of *Dapin* Repentance, or *Jin'gang Bore* Repentance…," these texts must have been applied universally for various rites. Looking at the repentance texts, the aim of such practice is to gain worldly benefits, such as eliminating obstacles, remedying illnesses, praying for the protection of the realm, and increasing fortune. This emerged from the desires of Chinese people, whereby seeking peace in the present world, freedom from hardships, and the practice of repentance to eliminate past transgressive karmas were all brought together.

The *Fayuan zhulin* (the Chapter on Repentance) includes a "Shi'e chanwen" 十惡懺文 (Repentance Text for the Ten Evils) produced by Tanqian 曇遷 (543-608) as well as a "Zongchan shi'e jiwen" 總懺十惡偈文 (Verse for the Total Repentance of the Ten Evils) by Lingyu 靈裕 (518-605).[48]

The Cult of the Three Stages (Sanjie jiao 三階教) during the late Southern Dynasties and early Sui widely promoted the *Qijie mingli chanyi* 七階名禮懺儀 (Stages of Worship and Repentance), the founder of this cult being Xinxing 信行 (540-594), who produced the *Zhouye liushi fayuan fa* 晝夜六時發願法 (Practice of Aspirations for the Nocturnal and Diurnal Six Periods of Time). Included in this is a *Li Fo chanhui wen* 禮佛懺悔文 (Text on Venerating the Buddha and Repentance) in one fascicle, which is a repentance ritual that includes reciting the Fifty-Three and Thirty-Five Buddhas.[49]

Zhiyi 智顗 (538-597) brought together Buddhist theory and repentance practice on the basis of Mahāyāna scriptures related to repentance, producing a number of repentance practices. He became a synthesizer of Chinese Buddhist repentance practices. Zhiyi produced the *Fahua sanmei chanyi* 法華三昧懺儀 (Lotus *Samādhi* Repentance Practice; *T* 1941) based on the *Guan Puxian pusa xingfa jing* 觀普賢菩薩行法經 (*Sūtra* of Meditating on Samantabhadra Bodhisattva; *T* 277), the *Fangdeng chanfa* 方等懺法 (Mahāvaipulya Repentance Practice) based on the *Da fangdeng tuoluoni jing* 大方等陀羅尼經 (*Mahāvaipulya-dhāraṇī-sūtra, T* 1339), the *Jin'guangming chanfa* 金光明懺法 (*Golden Light* Repentance Practice) based on the *Jin'guangming jing*, and *Qing Guanshiyin chanfa* 請觀世音懺法 (Repentance Ritual of Petitioning Avalokiteśvara) based on the *Qing Guanshiyin jing* 請觀世音經 (*Sūtra* of Petitioning Avalokiteśvara; *T* 1043). Among his repentance practices, the *Fahua sanmei chanyi* is the most complete.

48 *Fayuan zhulin*, *T* no. 2122, 53: 86.918b09-919b17.

49 Huang (comp.), *Dunhuang baozang*, 21: 202.

The establishment and development of repentance rituals were subject to cultural influences from Chinese Confucian notions of rites (*li* 禮). In the debates concerning the "Three Teachings" (Buddhism, Daoism and Confucianism), native Chinese thought criticized Buddhism, in that it was regarded as a "Barbarian Teaching" (*hujiao* 胡教) suited to the needs of uncivilized foreigners. Relative to China, which is a country of rites, Buddhism could only meet the cultural needs of "rites" in China and subsequently established practices of repentance. For instance, Huitong 慧通 (415-477), from the period of the Liu Song, says in the *Yixia lun* 夷夏論 (Treatise on the Distinction between the Barbarian and Chinese) when refuting the Daoist priest Gu Huan 顧歡 (420-483), "Consider that every dawn and dusk in the palace rise plumes of incense smoke and rhyming sounds of the Dharma, when worship rituals are held with repentance and prayer goes on without cessation. The [blessings it begets] will extend to all families of ones' past *kalpas* as well as to all sentient beings. So great is such a practice of filial and parental affection that it is beyond the appreciation of the narrow-minded!"[50] Buddhism was gradually assimilated under the influence of Chinese culture in the process of its unconscious resistance to the Chinese culture of rites, which subsequently led to the production of Buddhist rites such as repentance.

### 1.5 *Zhenguan* 真觀 *(538-611) and the Formation of the* Lianghuang Chan 梁皇懺

The *Cibei daochang chanfa* is also called the *Lianghuang baochan* 梁皇寶懺 (Precious Repentance of the Liang Emperor) or *Lianghuang chan* 梁皇懺 (Emperor Liang Repentance). Later on, it was always called the latter. Legend has it that Liang Wudi produced this. This is the most important of all repentance practices in Chinese Buddhist history. The procedures for this repentance practice have been continually transmitted until today. It is also the most widespread among contemporary repentance practices. The "Cibei daochang chanfa zhuan" 慈悲道場懺法傳 (Account of the Repentance Rituals of Compassion Altar) ahead of the *Lianghuang chan* points out that contemporary eminent monks produced this practice at the request of Liang Wudi in order to expiate the sins of his late Empress, *née* Xi 郗. People have presented doubts concerning the authenticity of this practice as a result of the explanations of the received text and differing accounts in orthodox histories.

50 *Hongming ji*, *T* no. 2102, 52: 7.46a24-27:
若乃煙香夕台,韻法晨宮,禮拜懺悔,祈請無輟,上逮歷劫親屬,下至一切蒼生.若斯孝慈之弘大,非愚瞽之測也.

Regarding the author of the *Lianghuang chan*, there are three different opinions among modern scholarship:

a. Zhou Shujia 周叔迦 (1899-1970) in his *Fayuan tancong* 法苑談叢 (Discussions on the Dharma Garden) believed that the *Lianghuang chan* was personally compiled by Liang Wudi.[51]
b. Zhou Shujia in *Shidian conglu* 釋典叢錄 (Collected Record of Buddhist Scriptures), however, thought that the *Lianghuang chan* was compiled by Baochang.[52]
c. Yinshun 印順 (1906-2005) thought that the *Lianghuang chan* was put together during the Yuan dynasty, borrowing Liang Wudi's name in order for the text to be promulgated.[53]

Among these three views, the second view of Zhou Shujia and the viewpoint of Yinshun are quite stimulating.

Zhou Shujia thought that there were two editions of the repentance practice established by Liang Wudi. The first was the *Liugen dachan* 六根大懺 (Great Repentance of the Six Faculties). The second was the *Liudao cichan* 六道慈懺 (Compassion for the Sixth Paths Repentance). At the same time, he thought that the latter constituted the extant *Lianghuang chan*. Zhou points out that the *Da Tang neidian lu* 大唐內典錄 (Great Tang Catalog of Buddhist Scriptures) records that a "Zongjing chanhui miezui fangfa" 眾經懺悔滅罪方法 (Methods for the Repentance and Expiation of Transgressions from Various Scriptures) in three fascicles was compiled by Baochang,[54] which he thought was the *Lianghuang chan*, but the number of fascicles differs from the extant version's ten fascicles. Fascicle eleven of the *Lidai sanbao ji* 歷代三寶紀 (Record of the Three Jewels throughout Successive Dynasties) states the following:

> *Zhongjing chanhui miezui fangfa* is in three or four fascicles, both cases are seen under the "Sixteenth Year" in the [Buddhist] Catalgue of Baochang (*Baochang lu* 寶唱錄) [...] Appreciating that the land of the country remains hospitable and free of various disasters and hindrances, the emperor believed that it was owed firstly to the grace of the Three Jewels, secondly to the Four Heavenly Kings, and lastly to the protection and support of the *nāga*-kings. [Because of] these various [benevolences], sentient beings in the world could have peace and happiness. Although

51 Zhou, "Lunzhu ji," 636.

52 Ibid., 1060.

53 Yinshun, "Suotan," 136-37.

54 *Da Tang neidian lu*, *T* no. 2149, 55: 4.266c7.

> recorded in detail, [these themes are] scattered in different scriptural and exegetical texts. In case there is an urgent need to investigate, it would be difficult to have a thorough investigation. Therefore, during the Tianjian era, [His Majesty] issued a decree year after year, ordering the monk Shi Baochang of the Zhuangyan monastery, among others, to prepare a comprehensive compilation for future use. [The work covers the practices of] cultivating Dharmic merits to ward off disasters, worshipping and repenting to remove the Dharmic hindrances, and offering sacrifice to the *nāga*-kings—the emperor reviewed all such various practices of prayer in person. The practices of sacrifice and prayer were so clearly illustrated that miraculous responses were quite numerous. Thus, this was what the myriad people relied on during those fifty years—it was due to the power of this [work].[55]

Later, Daoxuan's *Da Tang neidian lu* followed the explanation of the *Lidai sanbao ji*. Fascicle four of the former reads, "Zhongjing chanhui miezui fangfa."[56] The Song, Yuan and Ming versions all read, "Otherwise four fascicles. Sixteenth year. See *Baochang lu* 寶唱錄 (Record of Baochang)."[57] Daoxuan's biography of Baochang in the *Xu Gaoseng zhuan* also records the following:

> In the fourth year of the Tianjian era, [Baochang] was back to the capital city. [The emperor] then decreed that [he] be the Abbot of Xin'an si 新安寺. The emperor appreciates that the time sees wise administration, and that it is peaceful and pleasant near and far, the wind and rain coming on time, and that there is an abundant harvest of all crops; these all owe firstly to the grace of the Three Jewels, secondly to the Four Heavenly [Kings], and lastly to the protection and support of the divine *nāga*s. Because of the concerted support of the unfathomable spirits, blessings could spread to the masses. We gratefully admire their profound virtue, but since the textual references were scattered in various divisions [of the Buddist canon], it is hard to make a thorough investigation. [The

55 *Lidai sanbao ji*, *T* no. 2034, 49: 11.99b13-21:
《眾經懺悔滅罪方法》三卷, 或四卷, 十六年, 並見《寶唱錄》. …… 帝以國土調適, 住持無諸災障, 上資三寶, 中賴四天, 天下藉龍王眾神祐助, 如是種種, 世間蒼生始獲安樂. 雖具有文, 散在經論, 急要究尋, 難得備睹. 故天監中, 頻年降敕, 令莊嚴寺沙門釋寶唱等總撰集錄, 以備要須. 或建福攘災, 或禮懺除障, 或饗神鬼, 或祭龍王, 諸所祈求, 帝必親覽. 指事祠禱, 訖多靈感, 所以五十年間, 兆民荷賴, 緣斯力也.

56 *Da Tang neidian lu*, *T* no. 2149, 55: 4.266c7:《眾經懺悔滅罪方法》三卷.

57 *Lidai sanbao ji*, *T* no. 2034, 49: 11.99b12: 或四卷, 十六年, 並見《寶唱錄》.

> emperor] issued a decree ordering Baochang to prepare a comprehensive compilation, so as to prepare occasional imperatives. [The work covers the practices of] cultivating Dharmic merits to ward off disasters, worshipping and repenting to remove the Dharmic hindrances, and offering sacrifice to the *nāga*-kings. The content is divided into nearly one hundred categories, and the names of the Deities of Eight Divisions take up three *juan*. It collects the mysterious and the abstruse and reasonably details cases from the past and present. All such various practices of prayer were reviewed by the emperor in person. The practices of sacrifice and prayer were so clearly illustrated that impressive responses were quite a few. Thus, this was why our Yangzi valley had been free of disasters for some fifty years, and the myriad people had something to fall back on because of the power of this [work].[58]

Thus, Baochang certainly compiled a *Zhongjing chanhui miezui fangfa* in three fascicles, but why is it not found in the extant canon? Zhisheng in the *Kaiyuan Shijiao lu* 開元釋教錄 (Record of Śākyamuni's Teachings Compiled during the Kaiyuan Period; *T* 2154) states that Baochang was a monk of Zhuangyan si in the Liang capital. In 516, he compiled the *Jinglü yixiang* 經律異相 (Spiritual Wonders from Scriptures and *Vinaya* Texts), in one fascicle, at imperial order, and he also compiled a *Biqiuni zhuan* 比丘尼傳 (Biographies of Nuns) in four fascicles. The catalogue compiled by Fei Zhangfang 費長房 (ca. 6th c.) includes seven titles under his name beginning with the *Mingseng zhuan* 名僧傳 (Biographies of Famed Monks); since these works were not included in the Buddhist canon, here they are left undiscussed. His other writing activities are all addressed in the *Xu Gaoseng zhuan*.[59] Zhisheng never entered the *Zhongjing chanhui miezui fangfa* in three fascicles into the canon, which is why it was not later preserved.

Zhou Shujia thought that the *Zhongjing chanhui miezui fangfa* in three fascicles was the *Lianghuang chan* in ten fascicles, and the different numbers of

---

58 *Xu Gaoseng zhuan*, *T* no. 2060, 50: 1.426b27-c7:
天監四年, 便還都下, 乃敕爲新安寺主. 帝以時會雲雷, 遠近清晏, 風雨調暢, 百穀年登, 豈非上資三寶, 中賴四天, 下藉神龍. 幽靈葉贊, 方乃福被黔黎, 歆茲厚德, 但文散群部, 難可備尋. 下敕令唱總撰集錄, 以擬時要. 或建福禳災, 或禮懺除障, 或饗接神鬼, 或祭祀龍王, 部類區分近將百卷, 八部神名以爲三卷, 包括幽奥祥略, 詳備古今. 故諸所祈求, 帝必親覽, 指事祠禱, 多感、威靈. 所以五十許年, 江表無事, 兆民荷賴, 緣斯力也.

59 *Kaiyuan Shijiao lu*, *T* no. 2154, 55: 6.538a3-9:
沙門釋寶唱, 梁都莊嚴寺僧也. ...... 十五年景申又敕撰《經律異相》一卷, 唱又別撰《尼傳》四卷, 《房錄》之中複有《名僧傳》等七部, 非入藏故缺不論, 餘並備在《續高僧傳》.

fascicles are a result of different divisions. The three and ten fascicle versions are compared as follows:

| *Zhongjing chanhui miezui fangfa* 眾經懺悔滅罪法 | *Lianghuang chan* 梁皇懺 | |
|---|---|---|
| | *juan* | Contents |
| 1 | 1 | 1. Taking refuge in the Three Jewels 歸依三寶<br>2. Breaking doubt 斷疑<br>3. Repentance 懺悔 |
| | 2 | 4. Arousing the enlightened mind 發菩提心<br>5. Making vows 發願<br>6. Enlightening the mind of merit transference 發回向心 |
| 2 | 3 | Illuminating the fruition of karma 顯果報 |
| | 4 | Illuminating the fruition of karma and breaking away from hell 顯果報、出地獄 |
| | 5 | Dissolving the bond of hatred 解怨結 |
| | 6 | Dissolving the bond of hatred, making vows 解怨結、發願 |
| 3 | 7 | Self-celebration, offering obeisance to the Buddha for sentient beings in the Six Realms (for the various transcendentals and the god Brahmā in the Realm of Heaven) 自慶、爲六道禮佛（爲天道、諸仙、梵王） |
| | 8 | Offering obeisance to the Buddha for sentient beings in the Six Realms (for *asuras*, kind deities, *nāga* kings, the Māra king, and human) 爲六道禮佛（爲阿修羅等善神、龍王、魔王、人） |
| | 9 | Offering obeisance to the Buddha for sentient beings in the Six Realms (for sentient beings in various hells, hungry ghosts, and animals), and performing merit transference 爲六道禮佛（爲各種地獄、餓鬼、畜生）、回向 |
| | 10 | Performing merit transference, making vows, and the final instruction 回向、發願、囑累 |

We know from the above discussion that Baochang compiled the *Zhongjing chanhui miezui fangfa* in three fascicles and that Liang Wudi also personally performed repentance to eliminate obstacles based on this practice.

We can get a grasp of the situation concerning repentance practices of Liang Wudi from the above catalogs and the biography of Baochang. At the same time, in fascicle twenty-nine of the *Xu Gaoseng zhuan*, we discover remarks by Daoxuan on repentance practices as follows:

> In the early period of the Liang dynasty, the repentance practice of Correctness and Broadness originated in the region around Jing 荆 and Xiang 襄. Initially, due to an outbreak of plague, people prayed sincerely and repented their misdeeds; they bewailed their karma, so anguished and depressed. When they had their heads touched by the hand of the Buddhist statues, their afflictions would immediately disappear. Since people of the same disease worsened the condition of others, this practice became widespread. [The court ordered] excerpts from various scriptures to be taken and compiled into a separate work. People clapped in celebration, and common masses gathered [to repent]. They talked about and related their sinful deeds that conditioned [the plague], to the extent that sweat poured and tears were shed; counting their blessings and happiness, they conceived admiration for those lucky from their innards. Thereupon, the various offices restored governance, and myriads of matters were transformed. By perfecting this single practice, the era was benefited and the world saved. This indeed deserved praise. What was regretful was that the work was a derivative of scriptures and not original in its own right, and therefore it was subject to evaluation. Initially, the *Liugen dachan* was practiced by Liang Wudi, and His Majesty nursed pity for beings of common consciousness. Therefore, the text says, "When the myriad regions are guilty of crimes, the responsibility is on my person." Because the root consciousness has not been adjusted, the mind is excessively defiled by sensations and objects. Each year, the work was widely practiced, and [His Majesty] forsook the Great Treasure (i.e. the sovereignty) and took the role of the servant; because of the power of the mind, the earth responded by shaking, and heaven sent an auspicious sign. Thus, it became prevalent and stood out as the universal canon. There was one Zhenguan in the Chen dynasty, who embraced and expanded the work. His writing is flowery, while the message of being intent on practice became weak.[60]

60 *Xu Gaoseng zhuan*, *T* no. 2060, 50: 29.699c15-28:

Daoxuan in this paragraph explains the form and function of repentance practices during the Southern Dynasties. These practices were produced by copying from various scriptures. Later the causes and conditions of one's own transgressions are to be explained in accordance with scriptural meaning. Inner repentance would then lead to external sweat and tears. Daoxuan also comments upon the *Liugen dachan* carried out by Liang Wudi. This work was originally only personally practiced by Liang Wudi himself and later as a result of having had a spiritual experience he broadly disseminated it into society, it thereby becoming widely carried out. Daoxuan in this paragraph also informs us of some most important information: that the original meaning of repentance in the *Liugen dachan*, which was expanded by Zhenguan 真觀 (of 6th c.) during the Chen Dynasty (557-589), became quite diluted as a result of flowery language.

Zanning's 贊寧 (919 -1001) *Song Gaoseng zhuan* 宋高僧傳 (Song Biographies of Eminent Monks; *T* 2061) mentions this matter as follows:

> In the past, the Grand Steward of the Qi dynasty composed *Jingzhu fa* 淨住法, Emperor of the Liang repented according to his *Liugen men* 六根門, Chengzhao 澄照 (i.e. Daoxuan) completed *Zhufa tu* 住法圖 in a brief manner, and Zhenguang expanded [*Liugen men*] into *Cibei chan* 慈悲懺. [...] Beyond the Huai River in the south, people show deference only to the *Liangwu chan* 梁武懺 and thereupon perform Buddhist ritual. At times, monks, several in number, would chant and sing in praise, which is regarded as the repentance rite for halting calamities.[61]

Zanning not only discusses how Zhenguan expanded the *Liugen dachan* to become the *Cibei chan*; he also mentions the widespread popularity of the *Lianghuang chan* during the Song Dynasty in the Huainan 淮南 region.

Thus, through the explanations of Daoxuan and Zanning we can confirm that the *Lianghuang chan* was produced through Zhenguan's expansion of the

---

梁初方廣, 源在荆襄. 本以厲疾所投, 祈誠悔過, 哀茲往業, 悲慟酸涼. 能使像手摩頭, 所苦郯 (欻) 然平復, 同疾相重, 遂廣其塵. 乃依約諸經, 抄撮成部. 擊聲以和, 動發恆流. 談述罪緣, 足使汗垂淚瀉；統括福慶, 能令藏府俱傾. 百司以治一朝, 萬化惟通一道, 被時濟世, 諒可嘉之. 而恨經出非本, 事須品藻, 六根大懺, 其本惟梁武帝親行, 情矜默 (= 黔) 識. 故文云：萬方有罪, 在予一人. 當由根識未調, 故使情塵濫染. 年別廣行, 捨大寶而充僮僕. 心力所被感, 地震而天降祥. 是稱風靡, 郁成恆則. 有陳真觀, 因而廣之, 但爲文涉菁華, 心行頗淡.

61 *Song Gaoseng zhuan*, *T* no. 2061, 50: 28.888b6-12:
昔者齊太宰作《淨住法》, 梁武帝懺《六根門》, 澄照略成《住法圖》, 真觀廣作《慈悲懺》. ...... 自淮以南, 民間唯禮《梁武懺》以爲佛事. 或數僧唄 嚯 歌讚相高, 謂之禳懺法也.

*Liugen dachan*, but to what does the latter refer? In fascicle thirteen of the *Chaxiangshi congchao* 茶香室叢鈔 (Collected Notes of the Tea and Fragrance Room) by Deqing Yuyue 德清俞樾 (1821-1907) we find a detailed explanation of the formative process of the *Lianghuang chan* as follows:

> The *Nanbu xinshu* 南部新書 (The New History of the South) composed by Qian Yi 錢易 (968-1026) of the Song dynasty relates, "The [promotion of] repentance started with Prince Jingling of the Qi of Southern Dynasties. This was because one night, he dreamed that he went to the place of the Buddha in the east, called the King of Universal Illumination, and that having heard the Dharma talk of that Buddha, he uttered his confession. He awoke and invited [the future] Liang Wudi, Wang Rong 王融 (466-493), Xie Tiao 謝眺 (464-499), and Shen Yue 沈約 (441-513) to discuss this matter. Thus, the Prince composed the *Jingling ji* 竟陵集, consisting of twenty chapters, one chapter being "Chanhui" 懺悔. Afterwards, when Emperor Wu took the throne, [His Majesty] was thinking of repenting for his sinful karma made through the Six Sense Organs. Before putting it into practice, he ordered Master Zhenguan Huishi 真觀慧式 to expand the content. It was not created for Empress Xi 郗.
> Here is my comment. The present version of *Jingling wang ji* 竟陵王集 contains *Jingzhu zi* in thirty-one chapters wherein the third chapter is "The Section of Purifying the Three Dharmas." The chapter reads, "The key to eliminating suffering is none other than repentance. The way of repentance should start with purifying one's mind, cleansing one's own thoughts, straightening posture, adjusting appearance, making one's behaviour reverential and visage solemn, etc. etc." May that be the very chapter of "Chanhui" mentioned above?[62]

The *Chaxiangshi congchao* is based on the explanation of the *Nanbu xinshu* by Qian Yi. It mentions that Liang Wudi ordered Zhenguan to expand the section on repentance in the *Jingzhu zi*. Zhenguan passed away in 611 at the age of seventy-four, thus he was born under Liang Wudi in 537. At the age of sixteen,

62 *Chaxiangshi congchao* 13.318-319:
錢易《南部新書》云：懺之始, 本自南齊竟陵王, 因夜夢往東方普光王如來所, 聽彼如來說法後, 因述懺悔之言. 覺後即賓席, 梁武、王融、謝眺、沈約, 共言其事, 王因茲乃述成《竟陵集》二十篇, 《懺悔》一篇. 後梁武得位, 思懺六根罪業, 即將懺悔, 召真觀法師慧式, 廣演其文, 非是爲郗后所作.
按：今《竟陵王集》, 有《凈住子》三十一篇, 內第三篇爲《滌除三業門》. 其文云："滅苦之發, 莫過懺悔. 懺悔之法, 先當潔其心、凈其意、端其形、整其貌、恭其身、肅其容"云云. 豈即所謂《懺悔篇》乎？

he renounced his home life and became a monk. At the time, Liang Wudi (464-549) had already passed away. Liang Wudi could not, therefore, have ordered Zhenguan to expand the *Liugen dachan*. The accounts of Daoxuan and Zanning clearly mention that Zhenguan expanded the *Liugen dachan* of Liang Wudi, which is why it was called *Lianghuang chan*. The second fascicle of the *Da Song sengshi lüe* records that Prince Jingling of the Qi and Zhenguan were both adept in preaching and, moreover, that Zhenguan led the collection of texts. The production of the *Lianghuang chan*, therefore, ought to have been during the Chen Dynasty and not the Liang Dynasty.

Although Daoxuan and Zanning both mention that Zhenguan expanded the *Cibei chan*, perplexingly, the biography of Zhenguan in the *Xu Gaoseng zhuan* does not record this matter. When Zhenguan became a monk, Liang Wudi granted him a set of monastic garments and a begging bowl. Zhenguan accomplished eight sorts of skills, which included doctrinal explanation, proselytizing, calligraphy, writing poems, polemics, physiognomy, singing, and planning. He composed proselytizing texts numbering over twenty fascicles, and collections of poems, rhapsodies, and stele inscriptions numbering over thirty fascicles. We can find in the *Guang Hongming ji* his three writings, "Meng fu" 夢賦 (Ode of Dream), "*Yinyuan wuxing lun* xu" 因緣無性論序 (Preface of the Treatise on the No Self-Nature of Causes and Conditions), and "Yu Xu puye lingjun shu yiseng shu" 與徐僕射領軍述役僧書 (Letter to Chief Administrator General commanding the army Xu on Corvée of Monastics). His biography also contains his "Chou fu" 愁賦 (Ode of Sorrow).[63] Zhenguan and Zhiyi's relationship was quite close. The biography of Zhenguan states the following:

> The fame and conduct of the Sage of Tiantai were peerless. Due to past karmic connections, [Zhenguang] and he were friends, so intimate that they had never misunderstood each other. Being the same age, both in the worldly and the monastic sense, they were Dharma brothers. They travelled together to Mount Qinling and visited the old chamber of cloud-reaching height. In the bright sunshine in the morning, they enjoyed lofty talks full of the illumination of wisdom; at nightfall when brightness dimmed, they entered deeply into meditative quiescence. [...] [Zhenguan] dreamed that he shared a chariot with the Sage [of Tiantai], flanking a venerable Buddhist statue and escorting it back to the mountain. [...] On that day, [the Sage of] Tiantai sent a letter and incense, butter, and sugar to Zhenguan, who read through the letter and sighed, "Our karmic association extends back into many lives, and this is our last letter." [He]

63 *Xu Gaoseng zhuan*, *T* no. 2060, 50: 30.701c12-703c8.

> ordered that of the pair of *ruyi* scepters, one was sent eastward to [the Sage of] Tiantai, and the other remained in this western region, left to *Fazhi* 法志.[64]

From the above we can see that Zhenguan and Zhiyi were very friendly with one another. Zhiyi was the true originator of Chinese Buddhist repentance practices. This is why when Zhenguan expanded the then-relatively popular *Liugen dachan*, he could only be influenced by Zhiyi. During the Chen dynasty, the court prepared to forcibly disrobe monks and draft them into the army. Zhenguan sent a letter and humbly presented himself before Xu Ling 徐陵 (507-583). He petitioned the Emperor and subsequently this issue was settled. Zhenguan in his letter to Xu Ling writes:

> [As for those who are devoted themselves to] meditation, chanting, learning, and explanation [leading lives of] vegetarianism, austerity, aloofness, and quietism, those whose public sermon is meritorious and the Dharma voice deserves note, those who dedicate themselves to repairing *stūpas* and temples and reproducing scriptures, those who concentrate their minds on salvation and apply themselves to listening to and practice Dharma teachings, and the aged, the infirm, the deprived, and the sick, [I request that] they be immune from household registration since they would be of no use [to the government] and that [they] be allowed to live in monasteries and logged in the monastic registration.[65]

At the same time, he earnestly addressed these monastic matters at the court, Zhenguan also confirmed that he would adopt some measures in the *saṃgha*. It is quite possible that the *Liugen dachan* was therefore supplemented with ideas concerning vegetarianism, filial piety and the afterlife. As a result of his literary talents, Zhenguan's *Lianghuang chan* was regarded by Daoxuan as "flowery in writing, but weak in intention on practice."[66]

---

64 Ibid., 30.702b15-18, 702c18-19, 702c24-26:
天台智者, 名行絕倫, 先世因緣, 敦猷莫逆. 年臘既齊, 爲法兄弟, 共游秦嶺, 凌雲舊房. 朝陽澄景, 則高談慧照；夕陰匿採, 則深安禪寂. …… 又夢與智者同輿, 夾侍尊像, 翼佛還山. …… 爾日天台送書, 並致香蘇石蜜, 觀覽書嘆曰：宿世因緣, 最後信矣. 命兩如意, 一東向天台, 一留西法 [志].

65 "Yu Xu puye lingjun shu yiseng shu," *Guang Hongming ji, T* no. 2103, 52: 24.277c21-24:
禪誦知解, 蔬素清虛；或宣唱有功, 梵聲可錄；或繕修塔廟, 建造經書；救濟在心, 聽習爲務；乃至羸老之屬, 貧病之流. 幸於編戶, 無所堪用, 並許停寺, 仍上僧籍.

66 *Xu Gaoseng zhuan, T* no. 2060, 50: 29.699c27-28: 文涉菁華, 心行頗淡.

Daoxuan does not only point out the history of the *Lianghuang chan*. He also analyzes the circumstances surrounding the circulation of repentance practices during the Tang Dynasty. We can understand the real situation with respect to the *Lianghuang chan* during this period, especially when considering Daoxuan's explanation. He states:

> The establishment of the practice of repentance has its pith in absorption and sincerity. It is meant to repose one's full confidence in the assembly and to inspire shame in one's own moral inferiority and wrongdoings. This ensures the end of one's sinful actions, the nascence of dharma merits, and the reliability of one's words and deeds. Taking *Jingzhu zi* created by Wenxuan (i.e. Xiao Ziliang) as an example, his accounts are veracious. He cites the scriptural teachings as if the Buddha were present, and his descriptions of the likes and dislikes conjure up facial expressions. Although the work numbers as many as twenty fascicles, readers would not find it voluminous. Despite that fact that the wording is grave and abstruse, readers would not consider it troublesome. It has been widely regarded as the literary ocean, and surely it is no adulation. There are those who run imprudently into reading the text of confession and undertaking the ritual of repentance; they leave the various sinful acts into disorder without due understanding and arranged them into ten articles. This causes confusion, for they do not understand that [all sinful acts] originate in the Three Troubles. They vainly recite the texts through the last pages while the muddled message is transmitted from one to another. It is hard to act for them as masters, as remissness and violation of precepts result from each other. Disposing of karmic burden in such a way could never be regarded as thorough. Therefore, the above discussion is made only to roughly set up the principle. The rationale of the *Liudao cichan* is the same as that given above; the event is to be arranged at the end of year—only then the ritual is performed. Sacrifices are held according to which one of the Six Paths [the recipient has been reborn], and delicacies from sea and land are set out; as per the specific one of the Six Destinies, blessings are prayed for, and the import of compassion is thus enlarged.[67]

67 Ibid., 29.699c28-700a11:
原夫懺悔之設, 務在專貞, 欲使肝膽露於眾前, 慚愧成於即日, 固得罪終福始, 言行可依. 如文宣之製《淨住》, 言詞可屬, 引經教如對佛, 述欣厭如寫面. 卷雖二十, 覽者不覺其繁；文乃重生, 讀人不嫌其妨. 世稱筆海, 固匪浮言. 又有妄讀懺文, 行於悔法, 罪事雜叢, 不解位以十條；因構煩拿, 未知本於三惱. 浪誦盡紙, 昏憒通於自他；爲師難哉, 墮負歸於彼此. 如斯遺累, 未曰清澄. 固約前論, 薄爲準

Daoxuan points out that the core point of repentance is in being "intent and ardent (*zhuanzhen* 專貞)."[68] This would enable the repenter to exercise true repentance. Also, he especially praises the *Jingzhu zi*. Although it included many fascicles, no one felt that it was complex. At the same time, Daoxuan also offered criticism on the situation of contemporary repentance, namely that repenters did not understand the true meaning of repentance, nor did they understand the causes and conditions underlying transgressive karma. They only read the repentance text.

During the Tang, the *Lianghuang chan* was carried out at the end of the year. The sacrificial offerings were made in accordance with the differences of beings on the six paths. "Sacrifices are held according to which one of the Six Paths [in which the recipient has been reborn], and delicacies from sea and land are laid out; as per the specific one of the Six Destinies, blessings are prayed for, and the import of compassion is thus enlarged."[69] From these words we can tell that this is the scene in the *Lianghuang chan* concerning worshipping the Buddha for the sake of beings in the Six Paths.

At the same time, Daoxuan expressed his own view on this method of repentance and the worship of the Buddhas connected to the Six Paths as follows:

> As for the Six Paths, the destinations of transmigration, distinctions are made roughly and delicately. Humans are so different that they can be divided into ten sub-categories, and from this fact the other Paths could be inferred. [Sentient beings in] the Path of Ruchu Hungry Ghost (*ruchu egui* 入處餓鬼), as described in the *Āgama*s, when their families offer sacrifice to them, would have the feeling of agreeable delight. Once the minds are delighted, their appetites are satiated. This is how their hunger is fed, not through the merit gained from offering sacrifices. According to the Correct Dharma, any theory must be reasonable. It would be impossible that one makes an action while the karmic effect goes to others, and this is what the story teaches us when Maudgalyāyana tried vainly to feed his hungry-ghost mother. The other five destinations are each confined in the domain conditioned by karmic recompense, and since sentient beings there are segmented according to the karmic recompense, it is impossible to make offerings to them all at the same time. Although some

---

的.《六道慈懺》源亦同前, 事在歲終, 方行此祀. 道別開奠, 海陸之味畢陳; 隨趣請祝, 慈悲之意弘矣.

68 Ibid., 699c28.

69 Ibid., 700a9-10: 道別開奠, 海陸之味畢陳; 隨趣請祝, 慈悲之意弘矣.

> people present offerings separately to each of the paths, sentient beings of the various paths would probably not show up at the site. They variously possess clairevoyence as the results of karma, as happening to the Destinations of sentient beings. There are cases that [sentient beings] are rewarded with clairvoyance into Others' Minds, and they see clearly [what are going on in the minds of their families] and wait to join the ceremony. In this way, they benefit from the sacrifice.[70]

Daoxuan cites an explanation from the *Āgama*s, that those beings of the Preta Path rejoice at their relatives making offerings. But their hunger is fed not because of the merit gained from the relatives' offerings going to the *pretas* or ghosts; they have no access to it, for, according to the law of cause and effect in Buddhadharma, you are subject to what you do yourself. Others are not subject to one's own karma. Since different paths of the Six Paths embody different karmic fruitions and are isolated from one another, and beings of different paths cannot communicate their minds, it is difficult for beings to "rejoice in mind and be physically satisfied" because the resultant karma experienced by beings on each of the Six Paths differs. Although a person might make various offerings to beings on the Six Paths, it is difficult for them to enjoy them. Among beings on the Sixth Paths, however, there are those such as *pretas*, devas and sages who are clarivoyent as a result of past karma, which is why they can read the minds of others and thereby gain benefits from the offerings.

It is through Daoxuan's explanation that we can understand the solemnness and grandeur of repentance services at the time. However, the biography of Ziyu 子瑀 (668-752) states, "He frequently offered worship to the 15,000 names of buddhas, and performed the repentance of compassion. One round lasts a day and night, or otherwise two or three days."[71]

We can see that during the Tang Dynasty there were two popular forms of the *Lianghuang chan*. First, the *Lianghuang chan* was performed as an individual practice. It was clearly simple and, moreover, relatively short in duration. Second, the *Lianghuang chan* was performed as a solemn ceremony complete with various offerings that was relatively long in duration. Modern

---

70 Ibid., 700a11-19:
六道至果, 趣別重輕, 人含十等之差, 餘則舉例可悉. 阿含所述, 入處鬼道, 有親供祭, 心生隨喜, 心喜身飽, 故曰充飢, 非由供福業令自受. 以正法義, 理有所從, 無有自作, 他人受果, 斯則目連飯母事也. 自外五趣, 報局所收, 隨報位隔, 無由通給. 今則道別陳奠, 恐非臨饗. 然又報得諸通, 事含生趣, 不妨他心, 徹視待會, 而從祭酹.

71 *Song Gaoseng zhuan*, *T* no. 2061, 50: 26. 876c19-20: 常禮一萬五千佛名, 兼禮慈悲懺. 日夜一匝, 或二日三日一匝.

Buddhism is also like this. There are some monks who practice the *Lianghuang chan* as their own individual practice, while temples on special days, such as the birthdays of buddhas and bodhisattvas, Spring Festival or when requested by a benefactor, perform it as a ceremony.

The earliest form of the *Lianghuang chan* was the "section on repentance" in the *Jingzhuzi jingxing fa* 淨住子淨行法 (Methods of Pure Practices of the Pure Abider) compiled by Prince Jingling, also called *Liugen dachan* 六根大懺. During the Chen Dynasty, Zhenguan expanded the *Liugen dachan* to become the extant *Lianghuang chan* in ten fascicles. During the Tang-Song period, it was called *Liudao cichan* 六道慈懺 (Compassion for the Sixth Paths Repentance), *Cibei chan* 慈悲懺 (Repentance of Compassion) and *Liang Wu chan* 梁武懺 (Repentance of Liang Wu). The true producer of the *Lianghuang chan*, therefore, was Zhenguan, and not Baochang.

## 2 The Formation of the Tradition of Buddhist Vegetarianism

Vegetarianism is a tradition of Han Chinese Buddhism. Vegetarianism is also advocated as a part of the monastic lifestyle in China. The formation of the tradition of vegetarianism is not only based upon Mahāyāna Buddhist scriptures, since it was influenced by intellectual trends in Buddhism at the same time during the Northern and Southern Dynasties.

### 2.1 *The Scriptural Basis of Vegetarianism*

The monastic codes from the time of early Buddhism included various explanations of the three types of clean meats, three types of unclean meats, and the ten types of unclean meats. The *saṃgha* of early and sectarian Buddhism, however, did not forbid the consumption of meat, which was clearly defined. For example, the *Sifen lü* 四分律 (*Dharmaguptaka Vinaya*; *T* 1428) states that the Buddha permitted the consumption of various types of fish and meat.[72] On the basis of valuing life, however, the Buddha promoted the three types of clean meats and opposed the three types of unclean meats. The *Sifen lü* states:

> The deliberate killings herein include those that one sees, or hears, or suspects to be for him/her; there are such unclean kinds of flesh involving those three matters which, I say, [monastics] should not consume. If one saw that it was killed for him/her, or if one hears from a trustworthy man that it was killed for him/her, or if one sees there are in his/her home a

72 *Sifen lü*, *T* no. 1428, 22: 42. 866c14-15:

> head, skin, fur, or sees there are footprints of blood, and also if the man can commit Ten Evil Activities and often act as a killer, it could be killed for him/her. The unclean flesh conditioned by these three matters may not be consumed. There are three kinds of clean flesh that could be consumed; if one does not see, or hear, or suspect that the killing is for him/her, [the flesh] may be consumed.[73]

The purity or impurity of meat is decided via three conditions related to seeing, hearing and suspicion. If one personally witnesses, hears or sees indications that that this meat was slaughtered for oneself, then this sort of meat cannot be consumed. Meat purchased at the market, therefore, is clean meat.

In addition, as a result of venerating specific lives, the *Sifen lü* forbids the consumption of the flesh of elephants, horses, people, dogs, venomous creatures, lions, tigers, leopards, bears and *nāgas* (serpents). The *Mohe sengqi lü* 摩訶僧祇律 (*Mahāsāṃghika Vinaya, T* 1425) forbids the flesh of people, serpents, elephants, horses, dogs, crows, vultures, swine, monkeys and lions. It is clear that Indian Buddhism differed with respect to its regulations on food and drink on account of regional and sectarian differences.

Scriptures forbidding the consumption of meat, however, were gradually produced following the development of Mahāyāna Buddhism and in the background of conceptions of the compassion of bodhisattvas. For instance, the *Fanwang jing* 梵網經 (Brahma Net *Sūtra*) states, "Son of the Buddha, one must not intentionally eat any meat, since it destroys the innate seed of great compassion. All beings will see you and flee. All Bodhisattvas thus must not eat the meat of any being. There are immeasurable transgressions when meat is consumed. He who intentionally eats meat commits a minor defiling transgression."[74] The proscription against meat consumption became an article of bodhisattva precepts, it being a transgression in which the seed of compassion is destroyed. The chapter on the proscription of meat eating in the *Ru Lengqie jing* 入楞伽經 (*Laṅkāvatāra-sūtra*) translated by Bodhiruci (Putiliuzhi 菩提流支; fl. 508-537) states the following:

---

73 Ibid., 872b5-12:
是中故爲殺者,若故見、故聞、故疑,有如此三事因緣不淨肉,我說不應食.若見爲我故殺,若從可信人邊聞爲我故殺,若見家中有頭有皮有毛,若見有腳血,又復此人能作十惡業常是殺者,能爲我故殺.如是三種因緣不清淨肉,不應食.有三種淨肉應食,若不故見、不故聞、不故疑,應食.

74 *Fanwang jing, T* no. 1484, 24: 2.1005b10-13:
若佛子!故食肉,一切肉不得食,斷大慈悲性種子,一切眾生見而捨去.是故一切菩薩不得食一切眾生肉,食肉得無量罪.若故食者,犯輕垢罪.

> At that time, the sage Mahāmati the Bodhisattva-Mahāsattva said this to the Buddha: "World-Honoured One, from my contemplation, the cycle of birth and death, in this world, in which the knots of hatred are tied one after another and beings tend to sink into various atrocious paths, this is caused by eating meat. And this again leads to the killing of one another and the growth of greed and hatred, so that they could never get out of [those atrocious paths]. What a great suffering! World-Honoured One, those who eat meat ruin their seed of great compassion, and those who follow the divine path should not eat meat."[75]

As the *Ru Lengqie jing* clearly suggests, the practitioner should not consume meat in order to perfect the karma of the path. The *Da boniepan jing* 大般涅槃經 (*Mahāparinirvāṇa-sūtra, T* 374) translated by Dharmakṣema (Tanwuchen 曇無讖, 385-433) during in the Northern Liang (397-439) clearly establishes the following: "Virtuous sons! From this day onward, I will not permit *śrāvaka* disciples to consume meat. When a benefactor offers it, one should view this as if you were eating the flesh of your child."[76] It also offers an interpretation of the three types of clean meat as given in the monastic codes as follows: "These three types of clean meat were gradually restricted according to circumstances."[77] It stresses that meat consumption was successively forbidden as expedient means.

### 2.2 *The Tradition of Monastic Vegetarianism before Liang Wudi*

The tradition of Chinese Buddhist vegetarianism is generally believed to have been established during the time of Liang Wudi. Prior to Liang Wudi, however, there appeared a number of eminent "vegetarian" monks in the *Gaoseng zhuan*, which furnished a historical basis for the establishment of the vegetarian tradition.

With respect to the vegetarianism of eminent monks as told in the *Gaoseng zhuan*, we have, for example, Zhiyan 智嚴 (350-427), who after becoming a monk "wore a patchwork robe in seated meditation, and was always vegetarian."[78] Guṇabhadra (Qiunabatuoluo 求那跋陀羅; 394-466) "was a vegetarian

75 *Ru Lengqie jing, T* no. 0671, 16: 8.561a21-25:
爾時, 聖者大慧菩薩摩訶薩白佛言 :" 世尊 ! 我觀世間生死流轉, 怨結相連, 墮諸惡道, 皆由食肉更相殺害, 增長貪嗔, 不得出離, 甚爲大苦. 世尊 ! 食肉之人斷大慈種, 修聖道者不應得食."

76 *Da boniepan jing, T* no. 374, 12: 4.386a12-14:
善男子, 從今日始, 不聽聲聞弟子食肉. 若受檀越信施之時, 應觀是食, 如子肉想.

77 Ibid., 386a17: 是三種淨肉, 隨事漸制.

78 *Gaoseng zhuan, T* no. 2059, 50: 3. 339b1: 納衣宴坐, 蔬食永歲.

from his youth onward."[79] The background, causes and conditions behind these were all different.

First, on one hand, there is only vegetarianism is the only option in the wilderness. On the other hand, the image of Daoist adepts seeking immortality exerted a great deal of influence upon eminent Chinese monks. Said adepts were largely required to be vegetarian, some even not eating the five cereal grains. Daoan, upon receiving ordination precepts, "resided in a mountain and ate from the trees."[80] Zhidun said of himself: "leading a life on Mt. Dongshan, having a different sense of honour from the world, and growing vegetables [by himself]."[81] He became a vegetarian for life upon seeing a chick inside a hen's egg. Bo Daoyou 帛道猷 (412-477) in a letter to Daoyi 道壹 (d.u.) states, "Wandering in the wilderness, I have the freedom to read the books of Confucius and Śākyamuni, sparking feelings for poetry. On the hills and peaks I gather medicines and take pellets to cleanse my bowels. I have abundant joy."[82] Prior to ordaination, Shan Daokai 單道開 (fl. 261-359) "abstained from cereals and took cypress seeds. When cypress seeds were hard to find, he would take pine resin. Later on, he took little stones, several in one swallow and once every few days. Occasionally, he ate a certain amount of ginger or pepper. He did so for seven years and afterwards felt no coldness or heat; to him, winter was warm and summer cool. Day or night, he would never lay down. He practiced such a dietary regime in a group of ten fellows."[83]

Daoism emphasizes internal energy practices, abstention from grains, and various techniques related to ingestion of medicinal pellets. Daoism believes that the primordial *qi* is the source of living *qi*. Where *qi* is present, the spirit accompanies life. Gaining primordial *qi* then is followed by life. Loss of primordial *qi* is followed by death. Internal energy practices or literally "subjugating the *qi*" (*fuqi* 服氣) is also called controlled breath (*tuna* 吐納) and "consumption of *qi*" (*shiqi* 食氣), which involes inhaling the living *qi* between Heaven and Earth. "Abstaining from grains" refers to not consuming the five cereal grains (*wugu* 五穀). Daoists believe that within the body there exist three demonic creatures called "Three Corpses," namely Pengju 彭倨, Pengzhi 彭質, and Pengjiao 彭矯. Respectively, they delight in treasures, five flavors, and

79 Ibid., 345a7-8: 自幼以來, 蔬食終身.

80 Ibid., 352a10: 棲山木食.

81 Ibid., 4.349b6-7: 野逸東山, 與世異榮, 菜蔬長阜.

82 Ibid., 5.357b3-5: 優遊山林之下, 縱心孔釋之書, 觸興爲詩, 陵峰采藥, 服餌蠲痾, 樂有餘也.

83 Ibid., 9.387b3-6:
絕谷餌柏實, 柏實難得, 復服松脂. 後服細石子, 一吞數枚, 數日一服, 或時多少啖姜椒. 如此七年, 後不畏寒暑, 冬溫夏涼, 晝夜不臥, 與同學十人共契服食.

sexual desire. They are the origin of desires and demons that harm the body, and they live on the *qi* of grains. Hence, if a person does not consume the five grains, and does away with the cereal *qi*, then the "Three Corpses" cannot survive within the human body. One must refrain from grains if seeking increased longevity.

One must still maintain one's body without consuming the five grains, which is why medicinal substances such as Chinese tuckahoe (*fuling* 茯苓), *jusheng* 巨勝, polygonatum (*huangjing* 黃精) and jujubes (*dazao* 大棗) were consumed. "Taking pellets" (*fuer* 服餌) refers to ingesting medicine rolled into pills.

Eminent monks carried out these Daoist arts during the early period when Buddhism was being transmitted into China. For instance, Facheng 法成 (354?-424+) "did not take the five grains—he only consumed pine sap, hiding in the caves devoted to meditation."[84] Sengcong 僧從 (389-479) "did not take the five grains, he only ate jujubes and chestnuts." Nonetheless, "He did not stop his prostrations and recitation at the age of a hundred, at which time the strength of his *qi* was firm." Faguang 法光 (447-487) after becoming a monk practiced austerities and "did away with the five grains, only eating pine needles." After making the vow to carry out self-immolation, "he ingested pine sap and drank oil."[85] Fagong 法恭 (387-466+) after becoming a monk "was peerless in austerities, wearing cloth and eating beans and wheat."[86] The same biography records that Senggong 僧恭 (fl. 399) of Wuyi si 烏衣寺 "also did not eat cereal provisions, for he only ate beans."[87]

A second cause for vegetarianism is that Confucians stress that one must refrain from meat during a period of mourning. The Chapter of "Sanfu" 喪服 (Mourning Dresses) in the *Yili* 儀禮 (Book of Etiquette and Ceremonia) says,

> Why "untrimmed"?... The principle mourner lives in a booth built of branches leant against the house. He sleeps on straw and pillows his head on a cloth. He wails day and night, with no set times. For food he sups up congee, made twice a day, morning and evening, with one handful of grain. He does not put off the head or waist fillet when he sleeps. After the sacrifice of repose, he cuts a hole in the side of the hut and the fits lintel and door-posts to it. He lays a mat over the straw, and sleeps on this. For food he eats coarse rice, and has water for his drinking. He wails once

84 Ibid., 11.399a2-3: 不餌五穀,唯食松脂,隱居岩穴,習禪爲務.
85 Ibid., 12.405c12-14: 絕五穀,唯餌松葉 ... 乃服松膏及飲油.
86 Ibid., 407c8-9: 苦行殊倫,服布衣,餌菽麥.
87 Ibid., 407c15-16: 亦不食粳糧,唯餌豆麥.

> in the morning and once at night only. When he assumes the raw-silk hat, at the end of the first year of mourning, he lodges in a structure called the "outer sleeping apartment," and eats vegetables and fruit for the first time, partaking also of his ordinary food. No definite times are then prescribed for his wailing.[88]

For example, Menicus in the "Liang Hui Wang 1" 梁惠王上 chapter states, "So is the superior man affected towards animals, that, having seen them alive, he cannot bear to see them die; having heard their dying cries, he cannot bear to eat their flesh."[89] Mourning requires vegetarianism, which becomes an expressed form of filial piety, and moreover this was implemented and supported by Chinese Buddhist monks. For instance, Zhu Fakuang 竺法曠 (327-402) "carried out full mourning rites when his mother passed. When the mourning passed, he renounced his home life."[90] Daoheng 道恒 (346-417) "after his mother also passed [he] carried out full mourning rites and thereafter renounced the home life."[91] Sengjing 僧鏡 (407?-473+) "came from a poor house and his mother passed … he carried the earth himself and planted pines and cypress trees, making a hut at the grave. He wept blood for three years and after mourning, and renounced his home life."[92] These are all rites of worship that strictly adhere to Confucian protocols. Confucian rites were deeply embedded into the level of daily life of ancient Chinese society. It was not only Buddhists—hermits were also all made to be like this. For instance, the biographies of hermits (*yinyi* 隱逸) in the *Jin shu* 晉書 (Book of Jin) record that Guo Wen 郭文 (d.u.) "after his parents had passed and the mourning was completed, did not take a wife—he left the household and wandered through famous mountains … He always wore deer hides and wrapped himself in *ko*-hemp cloth. He did not drink alcohol, nor did he eat meat. He regularized the field and planted beans and wheat and gathered bamboo leaves and tree nuts."[93] Meng Lou 孟陋 (326-388) "mourned for his mother, weakened to the point of it almost becoming fatal. He did not drink alcohol or eat meat for more than ten

---

88 *Yili zhushu*, 28.543:
斬者何？…… 居倚廬,寢苫枕塊,哭晝夜無時.歠粥,朝一溢米,夕一溢米,寢不說絰帶.既虞,翦屏柱楣,寢有席.食疏食水飲,朝一哭,夕一哭而已.既練,捨外寢,始食菜果,飯素食,哭無時. (Translated by Steele, *The I-li*, 10-11)

89 *Mengzi*, 見其生,不忍見其死！聞其聲,不忍食其肉; Legge (trans.), *Mencius*, 134.

90 *Gaoseng zhuan*, *T* no. 2059, 50: 5.356c9-10: 及母亡,行喪盡禮,服闋出家.

91 Ibid., 6. 364b28-29: 後母又亡,行喪盡禮,服畢出家.

92 Ibid., 7.373b20-22: 家貧母亡 …… 乃身自負土,種植松柏,廬於墓所,泣血三年,服畢出家.

93 *Jin shu*, 94:2440: 父母終,服畢,不娶,辭家遊名山 …… 恒著鹿裘葛巾,不飲酒食肉,區種菽麥,采竹葉木實.

years."[94] Moreover, Liang Wudi's pious Buddhist lifestyle, in which he proscribed meat consumption, actually happened after his parents passed away. As the "Jingye fu" 淨業賦 (Ode of Pure Karma) states: "We are deeply distressed at the fact that it is already impossible to serve food to my parents during summer and winter. How could we be in humour to savour such [fine] meals? Therefore, we began to dine on vegetable dishes and eat no fish or meat." It is clear that Confucian thought regarding filial piety greatly influenced the establishment of the Chinese Buddhist tradition of vegetarianism.

A third reason for vegetarianism is that it assists in maintaining precepts. It establishes the form for spiritual cultivation of austerities and moreover is symbolic of virtuous conduct. For instance, a disciple of Huiyuan, Tanshun 曇順 (347-425) "was vegetarian and virtuous in conduct."[95] The biography of Huiguan 慧觀 (366-436+) also mentions Faye 法業 (fl. 418), who "regulated himself with vegetarianism"[96] and for that reason, Princess Jinling 晉陵 built the temple called Nanlin si 南林寺 for him. Huixian 慧猷 (376?-447?) "had vegetarianism display his personal morality."[97] Fazhen 法珍 (398?-473+) "never altered his resolute practice of vegetarianism, being pure in his restraint."[98] Huiwen 慧溫 (fl. 454-456) "practiced resolute vegetarianism and was also highly self-controlled."[99] Vegetarianism controls one's desires and does away with worldly customs, with no doubt that it is a noble expression of virtuous activity.

A fourth reasons for vegetarianis is that it assists in seated meditation, recitation and the chanting of mantras. It is a necessary foundation for a lifestyle of spiritual cultivation. For instance, Daoheng 道恒 (346-417) "ate vegetables, and savoured meditation, and distanced his presence from the world."[100] Hui-an 慧安 (?-424+) "sincerely practiced vegetarianism. He thoroughly studied the meaning of scriptures and was able to skillfully explain them. He also was praised for his dedication to the precepts."[101] Puming 普明 (370-454+) "was vegetarian and recited scriptures; he was thoroughly involved in practice and self-restraint."[102] Zhu Sengxian 竺僧顯 (?-321) "sincerely cultivated virtuous precepts; he was vegetarian and recited scriptures, being dedicated to the

94 Ibid., 94.2443: 喪母, 毀瘠殆於滅性, 不飲酒食肉十有餘年.
95 *Gaoseng zhuan, T* no. 2059, 50: 6.363a23: 蔬食有德行.
96 Ibid., 7.368b29: 蔬食節己.
97 Ibid., 11.400c24: 蔬食履操.
98 Ibid., 7.374c6: 蔬苦弗改, 戒節清白.
99 Ibid., 12.408c14: 疏苦並有高節.
100 Ibid., 6.365a4-5: 蔬食味禪, 緬跡人外.
101 Ibid., 7.370a19-20: 蔬食精苦, 學通經義, 兼能善說, 又以專戒見稱.
102 Ibid., 7.372a12: 蔬食誦經, 苦節通感.

practice of meditation."[103] Zhi Tanlan 支曇蘭 (341-423) "was vegetarian and delighted in meditation; he recited scripture 300,000 times."[104] Faxu 法緒 (317?-420?) "was pure and attentive to his virtuous conduct; he was vegetarian and practiced meditation."[105] Huitong 慧通 (415-477+) "was vegetarian and recited mantras."[106] Sengfu 僧覆 (396-471) "studied thoroughly scriptures; he was vegetarian and recited mantras."[107]

A fifth reason for vegetarianism is the close relationship between vegetarianism and repentance. Prior to becoming a monk, Sengyuan 僧遠 (413-484) "was vegetarian and practiced repentance and recitation"[108] and thereupon after becoming a monk was vegetarian for more than fifty years. Senghou 僧侯 (396-485) at the age of eighteen "became vegetarian and practiced repentance", and after becoming a monk "never let fish, meat, pungent herbs and vegetables near his teeth" until his end.[109]

The number of vegetarians and their ratio in various sections of the *Gaoseng zhuan* are presented as follows:

| **Sections** | **Number of vegetarian monks** | **Monk population** | **Percentage (%)** |
|---|---|---|---|
| Translators 譯經 | 2 | 63 | 3.2 |
| Exegetes 義解 | 16 | 271 | 5.9 |
| Divine wonders 神異 | 3 | 30 | 10.3 |
| Practitioner of meditation 習禅 | 9 | 32 | 28.1 |
| *Vinaya* elucidators 明律 | 5 | 21 | 23.8 |
| Self-immolators 亡身 | 6 | 14 | 42.9 |
| Scripture chanters 誦經 | 16 | 33 | 48.5 |
| Benefactors 興福 | 5 | 16 | 31.3 |
| Proselytizers 經師 | 2 | 11 | 18.2 |
| Hymnodists 唱導 | 3 | 10 | 30.0 |
| Total | 67 | 497 | 13.4 |

103 Ibid., 11.395b24-25: 貞苦善戒節, 蔬食誦經, 業禪爲務.
104 Ibid., 11.396c10: 蔬食樂禪, 誦經三十萬言.
105 Ibid., 11.396c26: 德行清謹, 蔬食修禪.
106 Ibid., 11.398c7-8: 蔬食持咒.
107 Ibid., 12.407c18: 學通諸經, 蔬食持咒.
108 Ibid., 8.377c10: 蔬食懺誦.
109 Ibid., 12.408c4-10: 蔬食禮懺 ... 魚肉葷辛, 未嘗近齒.

From the above table it is clear that vegetarian monks in the categories of Recitation (*songjing pian* 誦經篇), Self-immolators (*wangshen pian* 亡身篇), Benefactors (*xingfu pian* 興福篇) and Preaching (*changdao pian* 唱導篇) are highest, which is because these monks regularly interacted with the populace and must have had to gain their faith and respect, and being vegetarian was undoubtedly one cause for this.

In addition, in the *Biqiuni zhuan* 比丘尼傳 (Biographies of Nuns), there are, at times, vegetarian nuns. They are presented as follows:

| Dynasty | Nuns of major biographies | Nuns of appended biographies | Total | Vegetarian nuns | Ratio |
|---|---|---|---|---|---|
| Jin | 13 | 1 | 14 | 4 | 28 |
| Song | 23 | 11 | 34 | 11 | 39 |
| Qi | 15 | 10 | 25 | 5 | 20 |
| Liang | 14 | 8 | 22 | 10 | 45 |
| In total | 65 | 30 | 95 | 30 | 32 |

It is clear that in early Chinese Buddhism, whether it be monks or nuns, there existed a large number of vegetarians. The emergence of vegetarianism among monastics was, of course, influenced by translated scriptures and monastic codes. Starting in the year 418, scriptures such as the *Da boniepan jing*, *Ru Lengqie jing*, *Fanwang jing* and *Yangjuemoluo jing* 央掘魔羅經 (*Aṅgulimālīka-sūtra*; *T* 120) greatly influenced the development of the movement prohibiting consumption of meat. This was especially so when the *Shisong lü* 十誦律 (*Sarvāstivāda Vinaya*, or Ten Recitations *Vinaya*, *T* 1435) was translated. In fascicle twenty-six, the Buddha establishes the following rule: "I permit eating the flesh of beings and consuming their blood. Eat in a sheltered place and do not allow people to see it."[110] One may eat meat when ill, but others should not be allowed to see this, which would mean that the Buddha did not permit monks who were not ill to consume flesh and blood.

A number of Southern Dynasty contemporary monks and nuns who actually consumed meat appear among the *Gaoseng zhuan* and *Biqiuni zhuan*. Liang Wudi established the foundation for vegetarianism in light of Chinese Confucian thought on filial piety, regulations for mourning, forms of Daoist practice for immortality, the regulations of scriptures and monastic codes, as well as the large number of real vegetarians.

110 *Shisong lü*, *T* no. 1435, 23: 26.185a14-15: 聽啖生肉飲血, 應屏處啖, 莫令人見.

### 2.3 *Vegetarianism of Zhou Yong* 周顒 *(?-493) and Shen Yue* 沈約 *(441-513)*

Liang Wudi's movement to prohibit alcohol and meat among monastics not only occurred within an underlying scriptural and historical background, but he also had the support of aristocratic society. In particular were those supporters like Zhou Yong and Shen Yue, who one after another advocated vegetarianism and greatly influenced Liang Wudi. Daoxuan, in the *Guang Hongming ji* (the section on salvation or "Ciji pian" 慈濟篇), records Shen Yue's "Jiujing Cibei lun" 究竟慈悲論 (Treatise on Ultimate Compassion), Zhou Yong's "Yu He Yin shu lun zhisha" 與何胤書論止殺 (Letter to He Yin Discussing Stopping the Slaughter), Liang Wudi's "Duan jiurou wen" and "Duan sha jue zongmiao yisheng zhao" 斷殺絕宗廟犧牲詔 (Edict Proscribing against Sacrifices of Animals at Ancestral Shrines), and the "Jie sha jiaxun" 誡殺家訓 (Family Precepts Admonishing Slaughter) by Yan Zhitui 顏之推 (531-602). Therein the first three sections are most important, since they advocate Buddhist vegetarian thoughts and were deeply influential.

Zhou Yong was a literati figure of the Song-Qi period. He wrote the *Sanzong lun* 三宗論 (Treatise on the Three Theses), and was also proficient with *Laozi* and *Yijing*. His biography in the *Nan Qi shu* 南齊書 (Book of the Southern Qi) states the following:

> [Zhou Yong led a life of] austerity and purging desires, and his daily dietary regime was vegetarian. Although having a wife and children, he lived alone in a lodge in a mountain. The General of Defence Wang Jian 王儉 said to Yong, "My dear friend, what substance do you eat in the mountain?" Yong said, "Red grains and white salts, green Kui and purple Liao." The crown prince Wenhui 文惠 asked Yong, "What vegetable is the tastiest?" Yong said, "The first harvest of chives in early spring, and the final harvest of cabbage in late fall." At that time, He Yin 何胤 (446-531) was also known for his sincere faith in Buddhist teachings, and he had no wife and children. The crown prince asked Yong, "My dear friend, you are so very spiritually vigorous, but what do you think of [He] Yin?" Yong replied, "The Three Evil Paths and the Eight Difficult Circumstances are what we both have not been freed of, but each of us has our own obstructions." The crown prince said, "What are your obstructions?" Yong replied, "My wife, and He [Yin]'s meat."[111]

111 *Nan Qi shu* 41.732:
清貧寡欲, 終日長蔬食, 雖有妻子, 獨處山捨. 衛將軍王儉謂顒曰：" 卿山中何所食？ "顒曰：" 赤米白鹽, 綠葵此蓼. " 文惠太子問顒：" 菜食何味最勝？ "顒曰：" 春初早韭, 秋末晚菘. "時何胤亦精信佛法, 無妻妾. 太子問顒：" 卿精進何

In his later years, Zhou Young was deeply committed to vegetarianism and actively advocated it. Monks were the primary influence on his vegetarian ideas. In 464, Zhou Yong received a promotion by the prefectural governor of Yizhou 益州, named Xiao Huikai 蕭惠開 (423-471), and proceeded to Shu 蜀 (Sichuan). At the same time, when he was to go, there was a monk Senghou 僧侯 (396-484). Senghou said, "ever since becoming a monastic novice until his death, he never let fish, meat, pungent herbs nor vegetables near his teeth."[112] In 473, he was appointed county governor of Shanxian 剡縣 and studied under Huiji 慧基 (413-496). In 479, he was appointed prefectural commander of Shanyin Prefecture 山陰縣, where he came under Fahui 法慧 (411-495), who "was vegetarian and clothed in cloth, intent on immerging himself away from people."[113] The qualities of these vegetarian monks inevitably influenced the culinary habits of Zhou Yong. Shen Yue in his letter to Huiyue 慧約 (452-535) praises Zhou Yong as follows: "[Zhou Yong], throughout his lifetime, firmly believed in the rarefied and profound, and relished humble fare. As for those seasonal tributes transported in bamboo cases and bags from across the country, he invariably asked me to recommend vegetables of various descriptions. What I always did was to decline him at first and to offer him afterwards, which was intended as a tease for fun."[114] It is clear that Zhou Yong was earnestly dedicated and faithful to practicing vegetarianism.

The three brothers He Yin, He Qiu 何求 (?-486) and He Dian 何點 (437-504) successively secluded themselves in temples in the wilderness and travelled far. At the time people called them the "three eminent ones" (*sangao* 三高). He Yin enjoyed studying. He received the *Yijing* as well as the *Li ji* 禮記 (Record of Rites) and *Mao shi* 毛詩 (Mao Commentary on Classic of Poems) from Liu Xian 劉獻 (434-489). He also listened to Buddhist scriptures recited at Dinglin si 定林寺 on Mount Zhong 鍾山. He was proficient in Buddhist scriptures and all Buddhist practices. He started his official career as the Assistant in the Palace Library and then was transferred to the provincial post of Governor of Jianan 建安. Afterwards, he was summoned to the court to serve as the Cadet of the Crown Prince, and during this period he compiled the *Xin li* 新禮 (*New Rites*).

---

如何胤？"顒曰："三途八難, 共所未免. 然各有其累."太子曰："所累伊何？"對曰："周妻、何肉."

112 *Gaoseng zhuan*, *T* no. 2059, 50: 12.408c9-10: 自息慈以來至於捨命, 魚肉葷辛未嘗近齒.

113 Ibid., 408b27: 蔬食布衣, 志耽人外.

114 *Guang Hongming ji*, *T* no. 2103, 52: 28.326b17-20:
此生篤信精深, 甘此藿食. 至於歲時苞篚, 每見請求, 凡厥菜品, 必令以薦. 弟子輒靳而後與, 用爲歡謔.

In the time of Emperor Ming 明帝 (r. 494-498), he went into isolation in the mountains where he passed away.

He Yin wrote commentaries on the *Baifa lun* 百法論 (*Śatadharma-prakāśa-mukha-śāstra*) in one fascicle, the *Shi'er men lun* 十二門論 (*Dvādaśa-mukha-śāstra*) in one fascicle, and the *Zhouyi* 周易 in one fascicle. He also wrote the *Maoshi yinyi* 毛詩隱義 (Secret Meaning of the Mao Commentary on Poetry) in ten fascicles, the *Maoshi zongji* 毛詩總集 (Collection on the Mao Commentary on Poetry) in six fascicles, the *Liji yinyi* 禮記隱義 (Secret Meaning of the Book of Rites) in twenty fascicles, and the *Li dawen* 禮答問 (Questions and Answers on the Rites) in fifty-five fascicles, all of which were circulated. The *Nan shi* 南史 (History of the South) records the following:

> Initially, [He] Yin had indulged in delicacies, and whenever he was to dine, dishes would spread over one square *zhang*. Later on, he decided to dismiss those excessive fineries, but he still consumed "white fish", dried eel, wine preserved crab, considering that this was not eating live creatures. He was thinking of eating clams and oysters and let his followers discuss the matter. Zhou Yong from the Runan 汝南 area wrote to Yin, persuading him to eat [only] vegetables.[115]

He Yin believed in Buddhism, but he made careful study of culinary matters and as a result of this he defended his meat eating. Prince Jingling also criticized him for twisting of Buddhadharma. This is why Zhou Yong wrote a letter to He Yin and encouraged him to become vegetarian. In his later years, He Yin "did away with his taste for blood."[116]

Based on the "Letter to He Yin,"[117] Zhou Yong's thought on Buddhist vegetarianism becomes clear:

> First, Confucian thought on kindness emphasizes refraining from killing and not eating meat. The "Letter to He Yin" states:

---

115 *Nan shi* 30.793:
初, 胤侈於味, 食必方丈, 後稍欲去其甚者, 猶食白魚、鱔脯、糖蟹, 以為非見生物. 疑食蚶蠣, 使門人議之. …… 汝南周顒與胤書, 勸令食菜.

116 *Guang Hongming ji*, *T* no. 2103, 52: 26.293b26: 遂絕血味.

117 Zhou Yong's "Letter to He Yin" ("Yu He Yin shu" 與何胤書) is preserved in the *Guang Hongming ji* (fascicle fifty-two), the *Nan shi* (fascicle thirty) and the *Nan Qi shu* (fascicle forty-one). The version in the *Nan Qi shu* is most complete. The *Nan Qi shu* only selects the important parts, while the *Guang Hongming ji* omits the later tail-end of the text.

> The Sage set out the dietary model and further drew different grades. This is because eating animal flesh raw and drinking their blood accompanied the appearance of human beings. If one indulged in such a practice without restraint, the situation would have degenerated without end. How could those who know how to conduct themselves in the way of a Confucian not set their heart on honesty and commiseration? Mankind should live graciously within the sphere designated (by Heaven), and should not commit cruelty to [animals]. Furthermore, one of the greatest changes is the transmigration of life, and among those valued by sentient beings, nothing surpasses life. To animals, life is of paramount importance, while to us, relish could be forgone. For a whole lifetime, we consume them at two meals each day, only to contribute to longevity; whereas they end up with grievance and slaughter with nowhere to appeal against the injustice. Our karma will last long, which is indeed dreadful. Look at those poor little eggs! They are so fragile and crisp as to naturally rouse our pity. The little fawns breathe so faintly, and the sight of the way they walk makes us feel tenderness.[118]

The Confucian sense of kindness places heavy value upon life and restraining desires, and emphasizes that we should exercise mercy toward living beings.

Second, the Buddhist theories of karmic retribution and transmigration through the three times emphasizes the karmic response to be experienced for slaughtering life: "One going, one coming, one life, one death. Transmigration is continual. Various retributions are like a household. Humanity and the gods are like guests."[119] Various levels can be advanced—from Confucian ideas of kindness, to Buddhist theories of cause and effect and karmic retribution. Zhou Yong stated, "Towards living beings, those gentlemen, though they would not personally commit killing, have to approach the butcher's shop in order to acquire the food stuff such as wild duck and carp. Once the wealth had been in the hands of thieves, it would be avoided by men of honour; [similarly,] the scene that living beings under the knife furnished with rings is unbearable to the compassionate mind. The principled beast Zouyu 騶虞, even if starved, will never eat any plants other than those having died naturally. Does it not

118 *Nan Qi shu* 41.733:
觀聖人之設膳修, 仍復爲之品節. 蓋以茹毛飲血, 與生民共始, 縱而勿裁, 將無崖畔. 善爲士者, 豈不以恕己爲懷？是以各靜封疆, 罔相陵軼. 況乃變之大者, 莫過死生；生之所重, 無踰性命. 性命之於彼極切, 滋味之在我可賒, 而終身朝餔, 資之以永歲, 彼就怨殘, 莫能自列, 我業長久, 吁哉可畏. 且區區微卵, 脆薄易矜, 歆彼弱貌, 顧步宜愍.

119 Ibid., 41.733: 則一往一來, 一生一死, 輪回是常事. 雜報如家, 人天如客.

make one feel much ashamed to hear its reputation?"[120] Vegetarianism means not only personally refraining from slaughtering animals, one must also refuse to accept the results from when another carries out a slaughter. Zhou Yong emphasized avoiding killing. Underlying vegetarianism are the virtues of love and compassion. Similarly, Zhou Yong's vegetarianism was not merely for his own pursuit of enlightenment, since faithfully acting on the compassion of Buddhism also carries out the virtues of Confucian kindness. Thus, Zhou Yong developed his ideas of Buddhist vegetarianism based upon a stance that incorporated both Confucianism and Buddhism.

Shen Yue's promotion of vegetarianism is apparent in his writings: "Jiujing cibei lun" 究竟慈悲論 (Teatise on the Ultimate Compassion), "Chanhui wen" 懺悔文 (Repentance Text), and "Sheshen yuan shu" 捨身願疏 (Treatise on Self-Sacrifice). Shen Yue kept Zhou Yong's form of vegetarianism in mind and mentions in the "Jiujing cibei lun" that not only is meat consumption to be forbidden, but it is also necessary to forbid silk clothing. Shen Yue in 485 produced the "Chanhui wen," in which repentance is carried out in the order of slaughter, theft, adultery and false speech. Therein, the text dealing with the repentance of meat consumption is the lengthiest. He states,

> Ever since my childhood, I have had a mind for penchants and desires, lacking the sense of compassion and the retribution for sins. I thought that it was right and proper that fur and fin were used as foodstuff in the kitchen, and as beings of non-communication that were with us, they were beyond the range of our commiseration. [...] The way that I have been killing is all-embracing, and until the present time, I could not break [the habit] all at once.[121]
> It is clear that vegetarianism and precept against killing were significant to Shen Yue.

Following Liang Wudi, Shen Yue's stance on the precept against killing leapt ahead. The "Jiujing cibei lun" suggests that not only must we stop the consumption of meat, but we must also forbid silk clothing: "Meat consumption and silk clothing are no different, for they harm lives and young things die. Both

---

120 *Guang Hongming ji*, *T* no. 2103, 52: 26.293b22-26:
丈人於血氣之類, 雖無身踐, 至於晨鳧夜鯉, 不能不取備屠門. 財貝之一經盜手, 猶爲廉士所棄；生性之一啓鸞刀, 寧複慈心所忍. 騶虞雖饑, 非自死之草不食, 聞其風豈不使人多愧.

121 Ibid., 28.331b19-28:
爰始成童, 有心嗜欲, 不識慈悲, 莫辨罪報. 以爲毛群魪品, 事允庖廚, 無對之緣, 非惻隱所及. ...... 爲殺之道, 事無不足, 迄至於今, 猶未頓免.

matters are identical in principle."[122] Shen Yue developed a scope of restraining desires from forbidding meat consumption to including proscription against silk clothing. He also pointed out that there are worldly people who foolishly doubt this because Buddhist scriptures do not mention a proscription against silk word for word in the text: "This perhaps is overthinking the letter and being confused about a broader meaning."[123] It is clear that during the time of Xiao Liang, Shen Yue's stance on vegetarianism rapidly progressed well ahead of what it was during the Southern Qi. His demands for an end to slaughter were even harsher than that of Liang Wudi.

Shen Yue's advocacy of vegetarianism never refers to explanations of cause and effect or karmic retribution, but rather, is rooted in Buddhist compassion. He states, "The teachings of Śākyamuni in their original meaning are from compassion; the requirement of compassion is that all beings are to be valued."[124] The primary idea of Buddhism is compassion, but the core of compassion is protecting the lives of animals. This is as the *Da zhidu lun* states: "Compassion is the root of the Buddha's path."[125] At the same time, Shen Yue also advocated precepts against killing via the idea of Confucian kindness, using the example of Mengzi who started to be vegetarian from the age of sixty-nine and only wore cotton garments since turning fifty-nine. He thoroughly preached for the stoppage of meat consumption and a proscription against silk using both orthodox and heterodox texts, basing his arguments upon the *Da boniepan jing* and the texts of Confucianism.

### 2.4 *The Thought of Liang Wudi in the "Duan Jiurou Wen"*

Liang Wudi is the core figure in the formation of the tradition of Chinese Buddhist vegetarianism. With respect to the life and achievements of Liang Wudi, he was proficient in all fields of Chinese learning (Confucianism, history, metaphysics, etc.), and he also understood both Buddhism and Daoism. He harmonized the three teachings of Confucianism, Buddhism and Daoism together. On one hand, in the secular politic, Liang Wudi collapsed the structure of the aristocracy, advocating the idea that gentlemen should have their positions based on talent and learning, while also elevating the royal position. On the other hand, on the political side, he advocated an idea of "true sons of the Buddha and bodhisattva acts," creating a new outlay of a "national Buddhist structure" via the idea of the "Bodhisattva Emperor." On the eighth day of the fourth

122 Ibid., 26.292c16: 夫肉食蠶衣, 爲方未異, 害命夭生, 事均理一.
123 Ibid., 26.293a23-24: 此蓋慮窮於文字, 思迷於弘旨.
124 Ibid., 26.292c9: 釋氏之教, 義本慈悲; 慈悲之要, 全生爲重.
125 *Da zhidu lun*, *T* no. 1509, 25: 27.256c16: 慈悲是佛道之根本.

lunar month in the year 519, Liang Wudi received the bodhisattva precepts. He reformed the Buddhist community by forbidding meat and alcohol as his central aim in order to address the contemporary disorder of the *saṃgha*, which thereby served as a definitive measure with respect to the formation of the Chinese Buddhist tradition of vegetarianism.

### 2.4.1 Qi-Liang Period Buddhist Corruption and Liang Wudi's Stance in Life

Liang Wudi's advocacy for proscribing alcohol and meat not only had its scriptural basis and historical traditions, but he also implemented it personally. This was actually needed in Qi-Liang Buddhism. Buddhism in this period quickly developed with the support of Prince Jingling of the Southern Qi and Liang Wudi. The Southern Qi (479-502) had 2015 monasteries and more than 32,500 monks and nuns. The Liang Dynasty (502-557) had 2,846 monasteries and more than 82,700 monks and nuns. The development of the power of the monasteries and *saṃgha* inevitably came into conflict with regal authority. There were persecutions of Buddhism in the Northern Dynasties (under the Northern Wei and Northern Zhou), but the Southern Dynasties emphasized intellectual thought based on reason and at the same time suffered no destructive calamities. Liang Wudi actively promoted Buddhism. On one hand, this led to the sharp increase of monasteries and monastics. On the other hand, monastic corruption also continually emerged. As a result of this, figures such as Guo Zushen 郭祖深 (fl.500-526) continually petitioned Liang Wudi on matters concerning Buddhism. In his memorials, he mentions the actual situation and corruption of Buddhism at the time:

> At the time, the emperor was widely promulgating Buddhist scriptures, which were to transform customs. Zushen, in particular, spoke critically of the matter, and his opinion was laid out as follows: Buddhist temples in the capital city number over five hundred and are as stately and splendid as possible. The population of male and female monastics are up to over one-hundred thousand, and in possession of ample assets. As for the situation of the commanderies and counties, it is beyond description. Furthermore, a monk has lay followers, and a nun keeps adopted daughters. These people are not subject to household registration, and therefore of the total population of the country, almost a half are left unregistered. Monks and nuns tended to disregard the monastic rules, and the adopted daughters are all clad in fine silk fabric. Debasing customs and violating laws has its cause in this. I request that a thorough examination be imposed and that those who show no devotion to the Way and

> are under the age of forty *sui* (thirty-nine years old) resume secular and agricultural life. Dismiss the lay followers and adopted daughters, but allow them to keep slaves. Female slaves may wear only clothing of dark cloth, and monks and nuns are ordered to eat a vegetarian diet. In this way, the Buddhist teachings would thrive and social customs will be refreshed; the state would become prosperous and the people wealthy. Otherwise, every corner of the country would become a temple, and each household would have members tonsured; every square inch of the land or every single one of the people would no longer belong to the state.[126]

Guo Zushen pointed out that after Liang Wudi became Buddhist, the involved state officials and commoners also came to widely believe in Buddhism, reaching a point in which "all households take the purification precepts and everyone practices repentance."[127] In the vicinity of Jiankang there were more than five-hundred Buddhist temples, all of which were stately and grand. There were tens of thousands of monks and nuns, who possessed rich assets. Moreover, clerics protected general commoners, and nuns looked after common girls, none of whom were entered into the government registry, leading to a loss of one-half of tax revenue and countless people absent from mandatory labor duties. In this way, the monastic economy already threatened national security and moreover the monastics were not abiding by the monastic codes, their lifestyles loose and, on the contrary, destructive to the lay world and damaging to the True Dharma. Guo Zushen presented his opinion to reform Buddhism. Therein he included a rule that "the monks and nuns shall all be forced to become vegetarian."[128] This was a standard in which vegetarianism was connected to precepts and religious vocation, becoming a critical way to reform Buddhism.

Guo Zushen presented his confidential memorial in 522. This was close to the time when the "Duan jiurou wen" was produced. Liang Wudi welcomed what he wrote as correct and elevated him in rank. Hence, faced with a corrupt

---

126 *Nan shi* 70.1721-1722:
時帝大弘釋典, 將以易俗, 故祖深尤言其事, 條以爲：都下佛寺五百餘所, 窮極宏麗. 僧尼十餘萬, 資產豊沃. 所在郡縣, 不可勝言. 道人又有白徒, 尼則皆畜養女, 皆不貫人籍, 天下戸口幾亡其半. 而僧尼多非法, 養女皆服羅紈, 其蠹俗傷法, 抑由於此. 請精加檢括, 若無道行, 四十已下, 皆使還俗附農. 罷白徒養女, 聽畜奴婢, 婢唯著青布衣, 僧尼皆令蔬食. 如此, 則法興俗盛, 國富人殷. 不然, 恐未來處處成寺, 家家剃落, 尺土一人, 非復國有.

127 Ibid.: 家家齋戒, 人人禮懺.

128 Ibid.: 僧尼皆令蔬食.

*saṃgha* and its power on the rise, Liang Wudi had to adopted proactive measures in order to deal with the problems of Buddhism.

On one hand, with respect to Liang Wudi, even though he himself was of the aristocracy, after becoming Buddhist his daily lifestyle underwent great changes. Fascicle seven of the *Nan shi* states the following:

> During his later years, [the emperor] inordinately devoted himself to the Buddhist Way. He had only one meal each day, which contained no fresh or greasy foods, but only bean paste and brown rice. At times he had many affairs to handle, and if the sun had passed the midheaven, he would merely rinse his mouth. He made doctrinal notes on various *sūtra*s such as [*Da bo*]*niepan* [*jing*], *Dapin* [*jing*], *Jingming* [*jing*] 淨名 [經] (*Vimalakīrti nirdeśa-sūtra*), and *Sanhui* [*jing*] 三慧 [經] (*Sūtra* on the Three Kinds of Wisdom, *T* 768), which number hundreds of fascicles. In his spare time, after attending lectures and reading, he gave sermons in the Chongyun Hall 重雲殿 and Tongtai si 同泰寺, where renowned monks and erudite scholars—an audience comprised of the the Four Groups of Buddhist follower—often exceeded ten thousand people. He was clad in cloth and used a black canopy made of *kapok*; he had a hat that lasted for three years and a quilt for two years. After the age of fifty *sui*, he abstained from sexual life. Officials of the harem quarters of the palace below the rank of Senior Concubine all wore dresses that did not touch the floor, except for the various gowns needed for ceremonials, and there was no ornate clothing. [The emperor] did not drink alcohol or listen to music; if it was not for the sacrifice rites held in the imperial ancestral temple, banquets for the large assemblies, or various religious events, he did not allow music to be performed.[129]

Liang Wudi had a strict and sincere attitude to life and he was able to vow to refrain from killing, alcohol, and meat (i.e., the bodhisattva precepts), which is why he advocated proscribing alcohol and meat, which no doubt had great public appeal.

129 *Nan shi* 7.223:
晚乃溺信佛道, 日止一食, 膳無鮮臾, 惟豆羹糲飯而已. 或遇事擁, 日倘移中, 便漱口以過, 製《涅槃》、《大品》、《淨名》、《三慧》諸經義記載百卷. 聽覽餘閒, 即於重雲殿及同泰寺講說, 名僧碩學, 四部聽眾, 常萬餘人. 身衣布衣, 未綿皂帳, 一冠三載, 一被二年. 自五十外, 便斷房室. 後宮職司貴妃以下, 六宮褘褕三翟之外, 皆衣不曳地, 傍無錦綺, 不飲酒, 不聽音聲, 非宗廟祭祀, 大會餐宴及諸法事, 未嘗作樂.

His practice of vegetarianism probably ought to have commenced after he took refuge in Buddhism. "Jingye fu" 淨業賦 (Ode of Pure Karma) states the following:

> Back when he was still a commoner, we knew only appropriateness and rightfulness and had no sense of the devotion [to Buddhism]. We slayed various sentient beings to receive my guests. Following others, we ate meat and had no taste for vegetables. Since we seated ourselves on the throne and our wealth encompassed the entire realm, rare dainties from far away had been sent in as tributes, and distinctive food from everywhere within the seas would be brought to us in spite of any effort. Over one *zhang* square before us was loaded with various food, and hundreds of delicacies were piled on the chopping board. Starting the meal, we would drop the chopsticks and weep to face the dining table, overwhelmed by the itch for that [such food] could be available to our parents and that we could serve [such food] to them every morning and evening. How [badly] we felt when we alone enjoyed such daily meals? It is for this reason that we started eating a vegetarian diet and ceased eating fish and meat, keeping this a secret from everyone else. As for the situation where various ministers had to be feasted, dishes were arranged as usual. Since we were not used to the vegetarian food, our bodies became emaciated. Among the multitude of officials in the court, there appeared those who knew about [our diet]. Xie Fei 謝朏 (441-506) and Kong Yanying 孔彥穎 (d.u.), among others, frequently tried to persuade us to abandon vegetarianism; although out of their utmost loyalty, their words could not match up with our heart. We thought to ourselves…is there anyone who knows that we are not greedy for the power over All-under-Heaven. Only through doing that which Buddhist practitioners are unable to do, we let people all under Heaven know our heart.[130]

Hence, after ascending the throne, Liang Wudi commenced his vegetarianism. Xie Fei passed away in 506, thus Liang Wudi was vegetarian in his daily life between 502 and 505. Soon afterwards, in 517, Liang Wudi ordered ancestral shrines to no longer use blood offerings. As a result, vegetarianism went from

130 *Guang Hongming ji, T* no. 2103, 52: 29.336a13-25:
朕布衣之時, 唯知禮義, 不知信向. 烹宰眾生, 以接賓客, 隨物肉食, 不識菜味. 及至南面, 富有天下, 遠方珍羞, 貢獻相繼；海內異食, 莫不必至；方丈滿前, 百味盈俎. 乃方食輟筯, 對案流泣, 恨不得以及溫清朝夕供養, 何心獨甘此膳？因爾蔬食, 不啖魚肉, 雖自內行, 不使外知. 至於禮宴群臣, 肴膳按常, 菜食未習, 體過黃羸, 朝中斑斑, 始有知者. 謝朏、孔彥穎等, 屢勸解素, 乃是忠至, 未達朕心. 朕又自念 …… 誰知我不貪天下,唯當行人所不能行者, 令天下有以知我心.

his religious lifestyle into gradually becoming a part of the national will, which started to be promoted during the Liang Dynasty.

When, however, did Liang Wudi promote his "Duan jiurou wen"? Fascicle Thirty-seven of the *Fozu tongji* 佛祖統紀 (Complete Chronicle of the Buddha and Patriarchs; *T* 2035) records that in 511 "the monastic regulatory texts were brought together and vows were undertaken to forever abstain from alcohol eating [meat]." Perhaps Zhipan based his remarks upon the second fascicle of the *Ji Shenzhou sanbao gantong lu* 集神州三寶感通錄 (Record of Collected Spiritual Experiences of the Triple Gem in Shenzhou) by Daoxuan, which records the following:

> On the fifth day of the fourth lunar month of the tenth year of the Tianjian era (May 17, 511), [General Hao] Qian 郝騫 (d. after 511), accompanied by others, reached the city of Yangzhou. The emperor and various officials travelled forty miles on foot [to receive them] and welcomed them back to the Taiji Hall 太極殿, where a Buddhist feast was held and monastic candidates were ordained. A universal amnesty was granted, and acts of killing were banned. Weapons such as bows, swords, and spears were controlled, and a lotus flower *stūpa* was built. From then on, the emperor began to practice vegetarianism and cut off desires.[131]

Hao Qian reached Jiankang on May 17, 511. Liang Wudi welcomed up in the Taiji palace. As a result, Liang Wudi became vegetarian was after May 17, 511. In this way, there exists a definite contradiction between Daoxuan's account and the "Jingye fu".

In the dharma service for forbidding alcohol and meat, Fachong 法寵 (451-524) was one of the monks to respond. Fachong resided at Xuanwu si 宣武寺 and died on May 4, 524. The time when the "Duan jiurou wen" was produced was June 21, 523 (the twenty-third day of the fifth lunar month of the fourth year of the Putong Era), and hence the lower limit of when Liang Wudi would have promoted the "Duan jiurou wen" was June 21, 523. What would be the upper limit of time? There are two positions from we can estimate.

First is the fourth lunar month of 517, when Liang Wudi ordered that the ancestral shrines stop using blood offerings. The second is May 22, 519 (the eighth of the fourth lunar month of the eighteenth year of the Tianjian era), when Liang Wudi received the bodhisattva precepts. This is why Suwa Gijun 諏

---

131 *Ji Shenzhou sanbao gantong lu*, *T* no. 2106, 52: 2.419b27-c1:
天監十年四月五日, 騫等達於揚都, 帝與百寮徒行四十里, 迎還太極殿. 建齋度人, 大赦斷殺, 絓是弓刀槊等, 並作蓮花塔頭. 帝由此菜蔬斷欲.

訪義純 determined that the time of the production of the "Duan jiurou wen" was between 517 and June 21-27, 523.[132] The "Duan jiurou wen" mentions the vows that Liang Wudi took to maintain the bodhisattva precepts and abstain from alcohol and meat, which is why the Taiwanese scholar Yan Shangwen 顏尚文 believes that the "Duan jiurou wen" was produced between May 21, 519 and 523.[133]

Based on this we can determine the date a bit further. The Paris National Library in France houses a fascicle from Dunhuang (P. 2196) titled *Chujiaren shou pusajie fa juan diyi* 出家人受菩薩戒法卷第一 (First Fascicle for the Service of Receiving Bodhisattva Precepts for Renunciates). An inscription at the end of the document reads as follows: "The Summer Fifth Lunar Month of the eighteenth year of the Tianjian era of the Great Liang ... Shi Huiming and Huichi from Waguan-si."[134] This was personally composed by Liang Wudi after having received the bodhisattva precepts from Huiyue in order to spread the bodhisattva precepts. The "Duan jiurou wen" also was produced in the fifth lunar month, which is why the "Duan jiurou wen" ought to have been produced on June 21, 519.

### 2.4.2 The Process of the Dharma Service of Proscribing Alcohol and Meat

Fascicle twenty-six of the *Guang Hongming ji* (the chapter of "Ciji pian") includes the "Duan jiurou wen" by Liang Wudi. It provides a detailed account of the process by which the Dharma service proscribed alcohol and meat.

In order to promote his policies on Buddhism, Liang Wudi had the monk Fayun 法雲 (467-529) as his representative. He promoted a new spirit of bodhisattva compassion and strict maintenance of the precepts which aimed at the corruption of the traditional Buddhist *saṃgha*. He corrected Buddhism by first implementing the proscription on alcohol and meat. Hence, Liang Wudi used monks well-versed in scripture, doctrine and the *vinaya* to discuss the precepts and doctrines of dharma in order to remedy corrupt practices of the *saṃgha*. The movement to proscribe alcohol and meat became an inner-awakening within Buddhism and thereby avoided military clashes between regal authority and the *saṃgha*.

The Dharma service for proscribing alcohol and meat was carried out on June 21, and June 27, 523. At the fifth watch on June 20, 523, 1,448 men who

132 Suwa, "Chūsei bukkyōshi', 80. It is incorrect that this book takes the fourth year of the Putong Era as CE 525.

133 Yan, *Liang Wudi*, 230-31.

134 Huang (comp.), *Dunhuang baozang*, 116: 561: 大梁天監十八年歲次己亥夏五月 ...... 瓦官寺釋慧明慧持.

represented the monks and nuns assembled at the Fengzhuang Gate 鳳莊門. These 1,448 people were leaders of the monks and nuns. Therein there were 368 abbots and 369 abbesses. The "three officials" included the three monastic vocations: elder, abbot and rector, who were the leaders of temples. There were 574 scholar monks and 68 scholar nuns. These were scholars adept in various types of Buddhist scriptures and treatises. There were 25 senior monks of virtue, 39 monk-teachers and 5 nun-teachers, who were the most eminent monks and nuns of the whole Buddhist world. The addresses that appear in the "Duan jiurou wen" include the following: "The Disciple reverently addresses the monks and nuns of great virtue, the scholarly monks and nuns, and the three officials of the temples."[135] Liang Wudi hoped that his own idea to stop alcohol and meat could convince these leading figures of the Buddhist to give their assent and support, and through this remedy the faults of the *saṃgha*.

On June 21, 523, 1,448 monks and nuns stood in the square in front of the Hualin Hall 華林殿 of the Hualin Garden 華林園 and formally carried out the Dharma service to "proscribe alcohol and meat." Fayun of Guangzhai si and Huiming 慧明 (d.u.) of Waguan si acted as speakers and Liang Wudi personally attended. More than a thousand monks and nuns were seated accordingly in rows. First, Huiming the speaker recited a quarter of the chapter concerning the four marks in the *Da boniepan jing*, and then explained the primary meaning of "meat eaters destroying the seed of great compassion." This is recorded in its entirety in the "Duan jiurou wen." Next, Fayun interpreted the meaning of the scripture, but Fayun's interpretation was never recorded. We may only infer that Fayun interpreted "meat eaters destroying the seed of great compassion" from the "Duanrou zhi wen" 斷肉之文 (text on proscribing meat) annouced by Daocheng 道澄 (d.u.).

> The *sūtra* says, "Meat eaters destroy their seed of great compassion." What does it mean to destroy the seed of great compassion? Great compassion means to bring peace and joy to all sentient beings. If one is a meat eater, all sentient beings will take him or her as a foe and will never share peace and joy. [...] Meat eaters will struggle with the enlightened mind and will not possess the bodhisattva teachings. [...] Because they possess no bodhisattva teachings, they do not have the Four Immeasurable Minds. Because they do not have the Four Immeasurable Minds, they do not possess the great mercy and the great compassion. Due to these causes and conditions, the spiritual descendants of the Buddha will

---

135 *Guang Hongming ji*, *T* no. 2103, 52: 26.294b17-18: 弟子蕭衍敬白諸大德僧尼、諸義學僧尼、諸寺三官

> disappear. It is for this reason that the *sūtra* says, "Meat eaters will destroy the seed of great compassion."[136]

Drinking alcohol and eating beings not only destroys the seed for one's attainment of Buddhahood—being the *bodhicitta* which is of great mercy and compassion—one also kills the other beings' means to life in which they would attain Buddhahood, causing them only further great suffering and fostering much more resentment. The causes and conditions of drinking alcohol and eating meat cause "sons of the Buddha to be inconsistent"—in other words, causing the Buddhadharma to face extinction.

After Fayun's interpretation, Daocheng of Qishe si 耆闍寺 took up the west-facing high seat and preached on the "Duan jiurou wen." He also read the words conveyed by Liang Wudi. In order to correct the Buddhadharma, Liang Wudi took on the role of a Dharma-protecting king, in which he was a king who instructed people in the Buddhadharma, in line with the aspirations of a bodhisattva of great mercy and compassion. He made the following decree to the monks and nuns while proscribing alcohol and meat:

> We, Xiao Yan 蕭衍 (i.e. Liang Wudi), your disciple, respectfully explain the following to various monks and nuns of Great Virtues, various monks and nuns of doctrinal scholars, and the Three Monastic Officials of various monasteries: It is the business of monastics clad in black to remedy the situation surrounding the Buddha's teachings, not what we, your lay disciples clad in white, should worry about. The *sūtras*, however, say, "The Buddha's teachings are entrusted to human kings"; therefore, we, your disciples, must not keep silence. Today, We hope you various monks and nuns can have an open mind to listen to and accept [our words] and will not raise doubt and confusion nor harbor indignation and dissent.[137]

Liang Wudi made every effort to implement this proscription against alcohol and meat using his status as a "Bodhisattva Emperor," the compassion of the

---

136 Ibid., 26. 295c23-26, 296a19, 296a21-23:
經言 : 食肉者斷大慈種. 何謂斷大慈種 ? 凡大慈者, 皆令一切衆生同得安樂. 若食肉者, 一切衆生皆爲怨對, 同不安樂. …… 若食肉者障菩提心, 無有菩薩法. …… 以無菩薩法故, 無四無量心. 無四無量心故, 無有大慈大悲. 以是因緣, 佛子不續. 所以經言 : 食肉者斷大慈種.

137 Ibid., 26.294b17-21:
弟子蕭衍, 敬白諸大德僧尼、諸義學僧尼、諸寺三官 : 夫匡正佛法是黑衣人事, 乃非弟子白衣所急. 但經教亦云 : 佛法寄囑人王, 是以弟子不得無言. 今日諸僧尼開意聽受, 勿生疑閉, 內懷忿異.

bodhisattva precepts, and a union of regal and religious authorities. After Daocheng finished his pronouncements, the monks and nuns prostrated to the Buddha image in the Hualin hall in a great assembly and repented their transgressive karma. They then dispersed after a lunch prepared by the court.

When Fayun was lecturing on the idea of forbidding meat as found in the *Da boniepan jing*, there was a monk superintendent Huichao and monks and nuns such as Fachong who raised questions. Fayun immediately replied to them. Liang Wudi "feared that lesser monks would grasp onto doubts, thus becoming an enormous hindrance."[138] Again, after the ceremony on the twenty-third, "Monks and nuns still said, 'There is no prohibition against meat in the *vinaya*, or a practice for repenting meat eating'."[139] Thus, on the twenty-ninth day of the fifth lunar month, a second Dharma service proscribing alcohol and meat was held.

The second Dharma service centered its discussion on the "three types of unclean meat." It was ordered that 141 scholar-monks and 57 scholar-nuns carry out the service at the Huaguang Hall 華光殿 in the Hualin Garden. The representatives of the monks and nuns in the service at this venue were Fachao 法超 (456-526) of Zhuangyan si, Sengbian 僧辯 (d.u.) of Fengcheng si 奉誠寺 and Baodu 寶度 (d.u.) of Guangzhai si, all *vinaya* masters.

Fachao had studied the *Shisong lü* under Zhicheng 智稱 (429-500), and had gained the trust of Liang Wudi and served as superintendent of monks in the capital. Sengbian "was upright in nature, solid as ice with his precepts; he relished benevolence and was faithful, and he was dedicated and brave. He frequently recited the *Shisong lü*."[140] We do not know about Baodu. It is clear that these three *vinaya* masters came from the *Shisong lü* system. The authority of *vinaya* studies at the time primarily made arguments based upon the three types of unclean meat mentioned in the *vinaya* and the proscription against meat in the *Da boniepan jing*. Following the sophisticated and intense debate between Liang Wudi and the three *vinaya* masters plus Daoen 道恩 (d.u.) and Fachong, there were no further disagreements in the assembly and the three *vinaya* masters were the first to step down from the high seats. Liang Wudi also ordered Jingxian 景猷 (d.u.) of the Shixing si 始興寺 to ascend the high seat and recite Fascicle Four of the *Lengqie abaduoluo baojing* 楞伽阿跋多羅寶經 (*Laṅkāvatāra-sūtra*, *T* 670) and Fascicle One and Two of the *Yangjuemoluo jing*, which contain scriptural text concerning proscriptions against meat. After the

138 Ibid., 26.303a7: 恐諸小僧, 執以爲疑, 方成巨蔽.
139 Ibid., 26. 299a9-10: 諸僧尼或猶云, "律中無斷肉事, 及懺悔食肉法."
140 *Xu Gaoseng zhuan*, *T* no. 2060, 52: 6.475a9-10: 性廉直, 戒品冰嚴, 好仁履信, 精進勇勵, 常講《十誦》.

recitation of the scripture, Liang Wudi emphasized three times: "From today onwards, we are no longer to drink alcohol or eat meat and moreover I hope that the monks and nuns present here will broadly promulgate this." In the end, the monks and nuns made a procession, prostrated, repented and the ceremony came to a close as they exited the Huaguang Hall.

On the night of June 27, Liang Wudi felt unsettled and concerned about the debate at the Dharma service during the daytime and his will was unsatisfied, thus he issued five decrees successively to Zhou She 周捨 (469-524) who was at the time staying in the palace on guard and in charge of confidential matters. He emphasized that all the monastics would absolutely have to carry out his order proscribing alcohol and meat, and even a single thought of consuming meat would not be permitted. It is clear that Liang Wudi exerted himself to the fullest in advocating a proscription against alcohol and meat through bringing together regal and religious authority with his ambition as a "Bodhisattva Emperor."

### 2.4.3 The Content and Thought of the "Duan Jiurou Wen"

Liang Emperor's movement to proscribe alcohol and meat not only was an expression of his own individual faith and will, as he also gained the support of some monastics. In particular, Fayun of Guangzhai si offered his assistance. His biography in the *Xu Gaoseng zhuan* records Fayun's prophecy as follows:

> A fisherman in the Yiling 夷陵 county found a scroll of Buddhist *sūtra* in his fishing net, which turned out to be the "Sifa" 四法 chapter of the [*Da bo*]*Nihuan* [*jing*] [大般] 泥洹 [經] (*Mahāparinirvāṇa-sūtra, T* 376). The colophon read, "Created with reverence by Wang Baosheng 王寶勝 in the second year of Yuanhui era of the [Liu] Song dynasty, as a tribute to Master Fayun of the Guangzhai si." Let us collate this information with historical facts. At that time, Fayun was just ten years old, and surely his name had not yet spread far; the Guanzhai monastery had not come into existence. The central themes of this chapter prove to be firstly the promulgation of the Buddha's teachings and secondly the abstinence from eating fish and meat. [The two themes] foretell the thoughts and deeds [of Fayun], a remarkable concordance.[141]

141 Ibid., 5.465a13-17:
夷陵縣漁人於網中得經一卷, 是《泥洹・四法品》, 末題云：宋元徽二年, 王寶勝敬造, 奉光宅寺法雲法師. 以事勘校, 時雲年始十歲. 名未遠布, 寺無光宅. 而此品正則, 初云弘法, 次斷魚肉, 驗今意行, 頗用相符.

Fayun was a "household monk" (*jiaseng* 家僧) of Liang Wudi. He was ordered to become abbot of Guangzhai si. Later generations took up the systems that he created for monastic management to address the problems of the *saṃgha*. During the period when Liang Wudi was on the throne, Fayun and Sengmin 僧旻 (467-527) primarily managed policies concerning Buddhism. Thus, in order to completely terminate the traditional Buddhist allowances for eating the three types of clean meat, Liang Wudi must have thoroughly planned with Fayun, in terms of timing, the venue, the liturgical procedure, and the participants. Therefore, as the prophecy goes, the fisherman netted the "Sifa" 四法 chapter of the *Da bonihuan jing* which would be gifted to Fayun to promulgate Buddhist teachings and appeal to abstain from fish and meat. Thus, this story was in response to the idea in the *Da boniepan jing* that "meat eaters destroy the seed of great compassion" and the "Duan jiurou wen." Hence, the success of the Dharma service in proscribing alcohol and meat and the compilation of the "Duan jiurou wen" were definitely carried out with Fayun's assistance.

All contents of the "Duan jiurou wen" were based upon words spoken to the monks and nuns. The whole text can be divided into three parts in addition to the "words conveyed." In this way, it is divided into four parts in total.[142]

The general purport of the first part can be divided into five aspects as follows:

a. Renunciates who eat meat are no better than the heterodox or laypeople. If monastics do not maintain the precepts and *vinaya*, even violating the precepts against killing while "eating fish and meat" or violating the precept against alcohol and "still drinking alcohol," then there would not only be no difference in these acts from the heterodox, but moreover the renunciates would be all the more unfortunate. Liang Wudi pointed out nine matters in which they would be no different from the heterodox and laypeople.
b. The causes and defects concerning multiplying obstacles from meat eating. Liang Wudi, basing himself upon the *Da boniepan jing*, explained that meat eating separated oneself from the bodhisattva Dharma, the fruit of Buddhahood and *Mahāparinirvāṇa*. He also listed the unfortunate fruits such as the causes for suffering or falling into the three lower realms.
c. Meat eaters have contempt for one another and will end up eating one another as a karmic consequence.
d. Meat eaters are always held in contempt by their parents and elders from past lives.

142 *Guang Hongming ji*, *T* no. 2103, 52: 26.294b16-303c5.

e. Meat eaters are subject to hindrances of "principle" and "phenomenal" hindrances. "Principle hindrances" refer to obstacles that arise due to karmic causes and conditions. "Phenomenal hindrances" refer to obstacles in the form of rebirth on the Six Paths.

The purport of the second part:

a. God Jiang 蔣神 of Mount Bei 北山 was vegetarian and practiced the bodhisattva path. God Jiang was originally named Jiang Ziwen 蔣子文. He was from Guangling 廣陵. During the later years of the Eastern Han, he served as an officer in Moling sub-prefecture 秣陵縣. He was wounded in battle and died beneath Mount Zhong. After Jiang Ziwen died, he gradually became sacralized as a god. After the Three Kingdoms period, the status of God Jiang was elevated. During the Qi of the Southern Dynasties, Marquess of Donghun granted Jiang Ziwen the title of "Being Offered the Emperor's Gold Battle-Axe" and "Being Allowed to Hold the Imperial Tally," and even honoured him as an emperor. Liang Wudi himself lead the court ministers to the shrine of Jiang Di 蔣帝 to "cultivate respects 修謁 ".[143] Liang Wudi called on Jiang Shen in the hopes of finding a popular basis for proscribing alcohol and meat through the cult of spirit worship.
b. Compelling the shrines to never use animal sacrifices when offering formal sacrifices.

The purport of the third part:

a. Liang Wudi bowed before the Triple Gem and the monastics. If the monastics were to drink alcohol and eat meat, it would fall on the royal law to rectify the problem. Moreover, it would be according to the management procedure in which "monks are assembled, the bell is rung, precepts are abandoned and [those violators] are returned to lay life." Thus, this was a policy in which royal law and the Buddhadharma were linked together.
b. Liang Wudi, witnessed by the Dharma protection deities such as *nāga*s and *deva*s, vowed not to drink alcohol or eat beings, aspiring to the path of the Mahāyāna bodhisattva. If he broke his vow, he would suffer in Avīci Hell.
c. Monastics and monasteries were forbidden to drink alcohol and eat meat, or else "the problem would be rectified according to law."

143 Liang, "Tansuo," 98-100.

The fourth section encourages monastics to halt meat eating through mentioning the cause and effect and karmic retribution connected to good and evil. At the same time, the nourishment of vegetarianism and its benefits on the body and mind together with aspects related to the seed of awakening are together advanced in offering encouragement to monastics.

On the evening of the twenty-ninth day (June 6, 523), the five royal proclamations issued to Zhou She can be summarized as follows: (1) Correct Fachong and respond to Sengbian's criticism. (2) The transgression of buying meat is the same as that of killing by oneself. (3) Eating meat destroys compassion and increases ill-will. It is not something that should be done by Buddhist monks. (4) Scholar-monks eating meat is the greatest transgression, because they comprehend doctrines, but cannot practice according to their explanation. Their words are contradictory and they also mislead people. They will certainly fall into hell. (5) Bodhisattvas maintain mental moral discipline. There is no reason to eat beings. It is absolutely forbidden to even have a thought to drink alcohol or eat meat.

Thus, on the basis of the statement that "meat eaters destroy the seed of great compassion" in the *Da boniepan jing* as well as the ideas of anti-slaughter in the *Lengqie abaduoluo baojing* and *Yangjuemoluo jing*, Liang Wudi fully expressed the bodhisattva spirit of great mercy and compassion in his "Duan jiurou wen." In terms of the intellectual thought, this text has several particular characteristics:

First, there is a correction of the traditional *vinaya*'s idea on the "three types of clean meats", with the proscription against alcohol and meat as a new standard for the *vinaya*. The *vinaya* is the root of Buddhist practice and it was also the precondition for maintaining and developing the monastic community.

In the *vinaya*, the five precepts are foundational, which include refraining from killing, theft, sexual misconduct, false speech and the consumption of alcohol. Stemming from the five precepts, the proscription against alcohol and meat became the most foundational regulatory standard for monks and nuns. This is why the "Duan jiurou wen" emphasizes that monks and nuns are the same as the heterodox people if they should drink alcohol and eat fish or meat. The "Duan jiurou wen" quotes scripture and states, "One who carries out the ten misdeeds undergoes unfortunate karmic retribution, while one who carries out the ten virtues undergoes favorable karmic fruits."[144] This sort of union between the *vinaya* and karmic theory no doubt held popular appeal. At the

---

144 *Guang Hongming ji*, *T* no. 2103, 52: 26.294b23-24: 行十惡者受於惡報, 行十善者受於善報.

same time, the ten virtues also constitute bodhisattva precepts. For instance, as explained in the *Youposai jie jing* 優婆塞戒經 (*Sūtra* on *Upāsaka* Precepts; *T* no. 1488), the bodhisattva practitioner must cultivate the root precepts of the ten virtues. Thus, the first precept of the ten virtues is refraining from killing and the last of the five precepts is refraining from drinking alcohol, both of which constitute the most fundamental precepts for monks and nuns. Thus, Liang Wudi used himself as a model for the promotion of bodhisattva precepts in which he proscribed alcohol and meat. He moreover brought together "regal law" and the "Buddhadharma" and with this corrected the traditional *vinaya* convention concerning the three types of clean meat.

Second, Liang Wudi utilized the "Doxography of the Five Times" (*wushi panjiao* 五時判教) in order to resolve the contradiction between two sources: namely, the three types of clean meat found throughout the *vinaya* and the proscription against meat in scriptures such as the *Da boniepan jing*. Within the doxographical thoughts of the Southern Dynasties, that of the "sudden and gradual over the five times" was the most popular. It is as follows:

I. Sudden Teaching (*dunjiao* 頓教): *Huayan jing* 華嚴經 (*Avataṃsaka-sūtra*).

II. Gradual Teaching (*jianjiao* 漸教):
   - II.1. Specific teaching of three separate vehicles (*sancheng biejiao* 三乘別教): *Āgama Sūtra*s
   - II.2. General teaching of the three vehicles (*sancheng tongjiao* 三乘通教): *Bore jing* 般若經 (*Prajñāpāramitā-sūtra*).
   - II.3. Restraining and Praising Teaching (*yiyang jiao* 抑揚教): *Weimojie jing* 維摩詰經 (*Vimalakīrti-nirdeśa-sūtra*).
   - II.4. Teaching Concerning Same Intention (*tonggui jiao* 同歸教): *Fahua jing* 法華經 (*Lotus Sūtra*).
   - II.5. Teaching of Eternal Abiding (*changzhu jiao* 常住教): *Da boniepan jing* 大般涅槃經 (*Mahāparinirvāṇa-sūtra*).

He was able to resolve the contradiction between the three types of clean meat and the proscription against alcohol and meat through a deep investigation of the *vinaya* canon and the *Da boniepan jing* in relation to their doxographical positions. For instance, we can examine Fachao's reply:

> The teachings in the *vinaya* and those in the *sūtra* are one, and it is readers who take different ideas from the texts. According to Fachao's understanding, although the *vinaya* permits eating three kinds of clean meat, its true purpose is eternal abstinence. How can we know this? First, [the

> *vinaya*] articulates the abstinence from ten kinds of unclean meat, then teaches to eat three kinds of clean meat, and finally teaches to eat nine kinds of clean meat. Such prohibition in a progressive manner means nothing but eternal abstinence.[145]

The three *vinaya* masters Fachao, Sengbian and Baodu all emphasized that the three types of clean meat are from the gradual teachings, while the Buddha's originally intended to permanently forbid alcohol and meat. For instance, Baodu's interpretation as follows:

> The foolish and short interpretation is merely the gradual teaching, which is why the *vinaya* text permits eating the three types of clean meat. If the *Da boniepan jing* ultimately explains the true principle, then we should not permit meat consumption. In the case of someone with sharp faculties, they will all understand with respect to the three types of pure meat that it is never to be eaten. In the case of someone with dull faculties, they will stay with the later teaching.[146]

Baodu assigned the three types of clean meat to the gradual teachings and those with dull faculties, but he did not permit meat consumption as part of the sudden teachings or as a doctrine for those with sharp faculties. Although this interpretation reveals that the proscription against alcohol and meat is ultimate, and meat consumption being expedient, it still offers grounds for the latter. Liang Wudi was still unsatisfied with respect to finding reason and basis for meat consumption.

The *vinaya* canon belongs to the gradual teachings of the five times. What times? The "Duan jiurou wen" states the following:

> Another imperial question asked, "When did the teachings of *vinaya* arise?" Sengbian replied, "[It arose] eight years after the *nirvāṇa* of the Buddha and continued through the time of *Niepan jing*."

---

145 Ibid., 26. 299a22-26:
律教是一，而人取文下之旨不同. 法超所解：律雖許啖三種淨肉，而意實欲永斷. 何以知之？先明斷十種不淨肉，次令食三種淨肉，未令食九種淨肉，如此漸制，便是意欲永斷.

146 Ibid., 26.299b2-6:
愚短所解只是漸教，所以律文許啖三種淨肉. 若《涅槃》究竟明於正理，不許食肉. 若利根者，於三種淨肉教，即得悉不食解. 若鈍根之人，方待後教.

> [The emperor] asked, "If so, the *Niepan jing* contains the idea of abstinence of meat, the *Lengqie jing* has also the idea of the abstinence of meat, the *Yangjuemoluo jing* also teaches the abstinence of meat, and both the *Dayun jing* 大雲經 (*Mahāmegha-sūtra*) and the *Fuxiang jing* 縛象經 (*Sūtra* of Constraining Elephants) teach the abstinence of meat. If indeed the teachings of *vinaya* continued to the time of the *Niepan jing*, why does the *Vinaya* not include the matter of the abstinence of meat." [Sengbian] replied, "The *vinaya* succeeds the Initial Teachings, and that is why it is so."
>
> [The emperor] asked, "Supposing that the *vinaya* succeeds the Initial Teachings and continues to the *Niepan jing*, it ought to have included the abstinence of meat." [Sengbian] replied, "If talking about the Teaching of Restraint, this succeeds the Initial Teaching, common to all Five Periods of Teaching. It never says every kind of teaching is the same."[147]

Sengbian also advocated the "Doxography of the Five Times" with the *Da boniepan jing* being of the fifth time, and the *vinaya* canon ran through five periods from the eighth year after the time of Buddha's enlightenment to the time of the *Da boniepan jing*. Thus, Liang Wudi clearly argued that the *vinaya* and *Āgama sūtra*s were of the same first period of time, but Sengbian's interpretation was that "they continued from the first teachings through to the fifth time period; we do not say that they are all the same."[148] Sengbian still sought a vague response for not proscribing meat. Liang Wudi on the basis of the doxography of the five times regarded the meat proscription of the *Da boniepan jing* as ultimate and on this basis advocated his proscription against alcohol and meat, thereby resolving the contradiction between the three types of clean meat in the *vinaya* and the account of the meat proscription in the *Da boniepan jing*.

Liang Emperor promoted a policy of unifying state and religion, in addition to advocating for Mahāyāna bodhisattva precepts. Employing both royal law and the Buddhadharma, he developed the movement to proscribe alcohol and meat. With respect to the whole implementation of the proscription against

---

147 Ibid., 26. 300a6-14:
制又問：律教起何時？僧辯奉答：起八年已後, 至《涅槃》.
問：若如此,《涅槃經》有斷肉,《楞伽經》有斷肉,《央掘摩羅經》亦斷肉,《大雲經》、《縛象經》並斷肉. 律若至《涅槃》, 云何無斷肉事？答：律接續初教, 所以如此.
問：律既云接續初教, 至於《涅槃》, 既至《涅槃》, 則應言斷肉. 答：若制教邊, 此是接續初教, 通於五時, 不言一切皆同.

148 Ibid., 26.300a13-14: 接續初教, 通於五時, 不言一切皆同.

alcohol and meat, the carefully-designed Dharma service and the "Duan jiurou wen," which was composed based on the discussion by Liang Wudi and Fayun among other eminent monks, demonstrate deep historical traditions and a well-documented basis of theory that "meat eaters destroy the seed of great compassion."

Intellectual integration was carried out via two Dharma services and discussion of two related aspects: namely, Dharmic doctrine and the *vinaya* precepts. In addition, the policy of proscribing alcohol and meat was guaranteed on a practical level through national administrative ordinances and proclamation by contemporary Buddhist leadership.

## 3 Buddhist Societies in the Northern and Southern Dynasties and Philanthropy

Prior to Buddhism's introduction into China, local faith was multidimensional, but lacked unified articles of faith. One clear example are the differences that exist in the order of grades, differences in roles, and sacrificial items. Even though sacrifices to ancestors were universal, there were still a myriad of differences, which lacked any coherence. For example, there were sacrifices for the whole nation, emperor, magistrate, country, prefecture, town, and village.[149] As Buddhist faith was transmitted through society, there was an increase in common elements outside the diversified traditional faiths in China, giving people definite common articles of faith as well as common beliefs and pursuits. With a common faith based upon Buddhism and the devotees under the guidance of the monks, there was common engagement in Buddhist activities such as copying, carving and reciting of scriptures, carving of caves, producing Buddha images and building Buddhist *stūpas*. At the same time, under the popular appeal of ideas of Buddhist merit, people engaged in building infrastructure and philanthropic activities such as aiding the poor and disaster relief.

### 3.1 *Buddhist Societies of the Northern and Southern Dynasties*

Following the flourishing of Buddhism during the Northern and Southern Dynasties, assemblies gradually formed on the basis of common faith. Moreover, virtuous and spiritually charismatic monks who promoted conversion also produced faithful groups centered around monks. This kind of faith community, organization, or assembly is called by various terms such as *she*

149 Hou, *Fojiao xinyang*, 270.

社 (society), *fashe* 法社 (Dharma society), *yi* 邑 (group), *yihui* 邑會 (club), *yiyi* 邑義 (devotional society), or *yihui* 義會 (congregation).

As early as the Eastern Jin period, Huiyuan of Mout Lu actively formed societies. Huiyuan established the *Fashe jiedu* 法社節度 (Regulations of Dharma Societies), in which we can see the organizational system he brought together for "Dharma societies" (*fashe* 法社). The *Da Song sengshi lüe* explains the origin and development of Dharma societies as follows. Between the Jin and Song period, there was a Dharma master called Huiyuan, whose power of moral transformation prevailed in Xunyang 潯陽. Eminent gentlemen and recluses gathered at Donglin Monastery like spokes converging in a hub, all willing to form a Buddhist society. At that time, Lei Cizong 雷次宗 (386-448), Zong Bing 宗炳 (375-443), Zhang Quan 張詮 (d.u.), Liu Yimin 劉遺民 (352-410), and Zhou Xuzhi 周續之 (337-423), among others, formed the White Lotus Society. They erected a statue of Amitābha and sought to be reborn into the Pure Land. They called the society Lianshe 蓮社 (the Lotus Society), which was the origin of the "*she*" naming patterns. Prince Jingling, posthumously known as Prince Wenxuan, rallied clerical and lay Buddhist devotees to engage in the practice of Pure Abode, also regarded as the Pure Abode Society. Sengyou of the Liang dynasty composed the piece "Fashe jian gongde yihui wen" 法社建功德邑會文 (Text of Merit-Making Assembly of Dharma Society). Through the past dynasties, monasteries of achievements took the society as their model. The rationale of a society is that many inconsequential things add up to one consequential issue. Other than a society, nothing else could be more effective in accomplishing an aim. Societies in our time form to collectively facilitate the causation of blessings; the terms of their pledge are so strict and more serious than the governmental regulations. Member practitioners lend incentives to one another and apply themselves assiduously to empirical cultivation; thus so very great is a society's merit in producing good.[150]

Zanning believed that Huiyuan's Dharma Society constituted the earliest Dharma society. Prince Jingling of the Southern Qi gathered together the two assemblies (monks and laypeople) to carry out *poṣadha* and Dharma services. This gathering was also a Society of Pure Abiding, probably because they regularly held *poṣadha*. Pring Jingling always held purification gatherings in the

150 *Da Song sengshi lüe*, *T* no. 2126, 54: 3.250c19-28: 晉宋間有廬山慧遠法師, 化行潯陽, 高士逸人輻湊於東林, 皆願結香火. 時雷次宗、宗炳、張詮、劉遺民、周續之等, 共結白蓮華社, 立彌陀像, 求願往生安養國, 謂之蓮社, 社之名始於此也. 齊竟陵文宣王募僧俗行淨住法, 亦淨住社也. 梁僧祐曾撰《法社建功德邑會文》. 歷代以來成就僧寺, 爲法會社也. 社之法, 以眾輕成一重, 濟事成功, 莫近於社. 今之結社, 共作福因, 條約嚴明, 愈於公法. 行人互相激勵, 勤於修證, 則社有生善之功大矣.

garden of his residence. In his *Qi Taizai Jingling Wenxuan wang faji lu* 齊太宰竟陵文宣王法集錄 (Dharma Record of Prime Minister of Qi Prince Jingling Wenxuan) there are works such as *Shu Yang Chang hongguang zhai* 述羊常弘廣齋 (Shu Yang Chang Great Purification Ceremony), *Huayan zhai ji* 華嚴齋記 (Record of the Huayan Purification Gathering), *Shu fangsheng donggong zhai* 述放生東宮齋 (Purification Ceremony of Life Release at the Eastern Palace), "Bari Chanling si zhai bing song" 八日禪靈寺齋並頌 (Eight-Day Purification Ceremony at Chan-ling si and Verses) and *Longhua hui bing Daolin zhai* 龍華會並道林齋 (Gathering at Longhua and Purification at Daolin Si). With respect to the efficacy of Buddhist societies, Zanning emphasized that they were to "gather the lightness of the many into one heavy weight, succeeding in acts of salvation,"[151] i.e., gather the community's strengths and carry out social philanthropy. Moreover, within Buddhist societies "the articles of conduct were rigid and clear, exceeding those of public law,"[152] which meant that strict regulatory systems existed within the Dharma societies.

The Dharma societies of the Southern Dynasties were primarily "*fashe*" that placed weight upon activities related to so-called "Dark Learning" (*Xuanxue* 玄學), such as lecturing on *sūtras*. The participants were mostly people from high society, which was related to the system of established aristocratic families during the Southern Dynasties. During the Norther Dynasties, however, Buddhism emphasized practice and possessed both popular and secularized characteristics. The process by which Buddhist societies organized in the Northern Dynasties was either through one or several monks facilitating them, who led lay devotees to come together. Otherwise they were organized by devotees who requested a monk to function as a guide for the organization. The members of the groups participated together in Buddha image production, construction of temples, recitation of Buddhist *sūtras* and holding of purification gatherings and rituals. They were spiritually tied together by the Buddhist faith, possessing a common conception of values, belonging, and collective action. As the *Yizhu Sun Niantang deng canke* 邑主孫念堂等殘刻 (Partial Inscription of Society Head Sun Niantang) states:

> On the fifth day of the third month of the second year of the Shengui era 神龜二年 (519) 三月十五日建,
> Confraternity Master Huigan 邑師惠感
> Confraternity Head Sun Niantang, Wu 邑主孫念堂吳
> Great Administrator of Confraternity Wu 都維那吳

151 *Da Song sengshi lüe*, *T* no. 2126, 54: 3.250c25-26: 以眾輕成一重, 濟事成功.
152 Ibid., 3.250c27: 條約嚴明, 愈於公法.

Confraternity Administrator Zhang 維那張
Confraternity Administrator [lacuna] 維那 [ ]
Monk [lacuna] 僧 [ ][153]

It is clear that the community who produced these images was under the leadership of the monk Huigan with Sun Niantang as the "Society Head" (*yizhu* 邑主). These societies also also included jobs such as rector (*duweinuo* 都維那; *weinuo* 維那). In the *Changyue bai yu ren zaoxiang bei* 常岳百餘人造像碑 (Stele for the More than Hundred People Who Produced an Image in Changyue), the roles that appear include (1) *du yizhu* 都邑主; (2) *yuan xin quanhua zhu* 元心勸化主; (3) *quanhua zhu* 勸化主; (4) discipline Master (*zhongzheng* 中正); (5) capital rector (*duweinuo* 都維那); (6) rector (*weinuo* 維那); (7) Purification Gathering Master (*zhaizhu* 齋主); (8) Society Elder (*yilao* 邑老); (9) Society Son (*yizi* 邑子); and (10) Pure Believer (*qingxin* 清信).[154] In the *Zhao Asi timing* 趙阿四題名 (Inscription of Zhao Asi), there also appears the Director of Worship (*dianzuo* 典座), Reciter (*baini* 唄匿) and Burner of Incense (*xianghuo* 香火).[155] These are titles related to management of the Buddhist society. "Society Son" is the most fundamental member of the society, always called Brothers in Dharma.

"Society Head" is the chief of the devotional society (*yiyi* 邑義). The role of rector (*weinuo* 維那) is from the system of monastic management. During the time of Emperor Xiaowen of the Northern Wei (Wei Xiaowen di 魏孝文帝 [r. 471-499]) this role had already become a vice-leader of the monks. The role's responsibility included assisting in the management of the monks' files, seals, and documents while handling the execution and investigation of precepts. Within societies, there were always various rectors. We can see that there were changes in the administrative roles. Within the organization of these societies, renunciate positions included two possibilities: first, personally serving as Society Head, organizing and leading the whole of the society's activities. Second, serving as "Society Teacher" in a role guiding the devotees primarily consisted of carrying out the Dharma services and providing instruction during Buddhist activities. Director of Worship originally meant "the manager of meditation divan." They managed ten matters when the monks did their prostrations: the seats, shelter, robes, fragrances (incense and flowers), fruits, and drinking water as well as the order of precedence. They also managed miscellaneous affairs. From the Sui Dynasty onward, the Elder, Rector and Temple

153 *Baqiongshi jinshi buzheng* 13.74.
154 Ibid 16.94.
155 Ibid 17.98.

Manager constituted the "three cords" (*sangang* 三綱) of the monastery. Thus, Director of Worship in the societies was perhaps a borrowed title from monastic professions. The duty was to manage the relevant matters of the organization when Dharma services were carried out. The *huazhu* 化主 and *quanhua zhu* 勸化主 perhaps recruited people into the society's group or recruited devotees to assist in production of images or execution of ceremonies.[156]

In the societies, there is also the *zhongzheng* 中正 or "Discipline Master," which is borrowed from the Nine-Rank Controller System (*jiupin* 九品) from the Wei-Jin Northern and Southern Dynasties period. For instance, the "Fuhu dudou Yuan Kai deng timing" 伏虎都督元愷等題名 (Tiger Taming Commander Yuan Kai, among Others, Having Their Names Inscribed) reads as follows:

> Confraternity Authority, the Tiger Taming Commander Le/Yue Yuankai
> Confraternity Administrator, the Tiger Taming Commander Zhang Yonggui
> Confraternity Administrator, the Tiger Taming Commander Kai Hanshi
> Benefactor of Bodhisattvas of the Right Chest, Army Controller Shuai Shenghe
> Benefactor of Bodhisattvas of the Right Chest Guo Chang[lacuna]
> Benefactor of Bodhisattva of the Right Chest Wang Yanhuai
> Benefactor of Bodhisattva of the Right Chest Zhang Ziyuan
> Benefactor of Ananda Zhang Xida
> [...]
> Confraternity Head, Chief of the Personel Evaluation Section of the Jiexiu 介休 county, Army Controller, You Daorong [who is depicted as] attending the Buddha
> Person in Charge of Making Offerings, Recorder of the Jiexiu County, Adjunct Commander, Shangguan Yan[lacuna] [who is depicted as] attending the Buddha
> Member of the confraternity Wang [lacuna]gui, member of the confraternity [lacuna] Xian
> Member of the confraternity Le/Yue Shiyuan, member of the confraternity Zhang Dao
> Member of the confraternity Zhai Heier
> Benefactor of the statue of [lacuna] Zhang Hongchang[157]

---

156 Liu, "Huabei xiangcun," 524.

157 *Baqiongshi jinshi buzheng* 17.100.
邑中正伏虎都督樂元愷
維那伏虎都督張永貴
維那伏虎都督開韓仕

It is clear that the position of "Society Discipline Master" was quite high, being both a leadership role and a role for someone in a high secular position. In addition, among these society activities in image production, there were the Image Head (*xiang zhu* 像主), Śākya Head (*Shijia zhu* 釋迦主), Bodhisattva Head (*pusa zhu* 菩薩主) and Vajra Head (*jingang zhu* 金剛主). These are believed to have been donors for the construction of an image or buddha-shrine.

When carrying out purification gatherings or ceremonies, seven different heads could appear: the (1) Head of Lights (*guangming zhu* 光明主); (2) Head of Eye-Opening Ceremony (*kai guangming zhu* 開光明主); (3) Procession Head (*xingdao zhu* 行道主); (4) Purity Head (*qingjing zhu* 清淨主); (5) Hall Head (*daochang zhu* 道場主); (6) Purification Gathering Head (*zhaizhu* 齋主); (7) Eight Purification Precepts Gathering Head (*baguan zhaizhu* 八關齋主). The Procession Head was related to the ceremonies of procession. The Purification Gathering Head, the Eight Purification Precepts Gathering Head and the Purity Head were related to the purification gathering. The Hall Head was related to the halls in which the purification gathering and ceremonies were held. In addition, the Head of Incense (*xianghuo zhu* 香火主) and Head of Lamps (*dengming zhu* 燈明主) were included, which were related to the offerings provided to the produced images.

To conclude, Buddhists during the Northern and Southern Dynasties produced Buddha images and cave-temples, or carried out purification gatherings, copied scriptures, or read them through organized bodies of Buddhist societies. At the same time, these organized bodies also were formed to generate merit through repairing infrastructure, building wells, planting trees, donating to build cemeteries for those without relatives, and providing food to the poor.

### 3.2 *Buddhist Merit Making in the Northern and Southern Dynasties*

Buddhists during Northern and Southern Dynasties were highly active in social philanthropy, influenced by Buddhist ideas of merit making or the "field of

---

右箱菩薩主統軍帥升和
右箱菩薩主郭長口
右箱菩薩主王顏懷
右箱菩薩主張子渕
阿難主張悉達
……
邑主介休縣功曹軍主尤道榮侍佛時
供養主介休縣主簿別將上官延口口佛時
邑子王口貴 邑子口顯
邑子樂仕渕 邑子張道
邑子翟黑兒
口像主張洪昌

merit" (*futian* 福田). During the sixth century, two scriptures exerted a particularly large influence. "Field of merit" refers to acts which bring about fortunate karmic results, similar to how you can obtain a harvest if you plant fields. From the Western Jin onward, some Chinese translations of Buddhist scriptures mentioned this concept of fields of merit, such as the concepts of field of respect (*jingtian* 敬田) and field of compassion (*beitian* 悲田). The former refers to the Triple Gem (Buddha, Dharma and *Saṃgha*). A field of gratitude (*entian* 恩田) is in reference to one's parents, teachers and elders. A field of compassion is in reference to the poor. A field of suffering (*kutian* 苦田) is in reference to animals. The *Foshuo zhude futian jing* 佛說諸德福田經 (*Sūtra* of the Buddha's Teachings on the Virtues and Fields of Merit; *T* 683), which was translated during the Western Jin, mentions the seven types of fields of merit. The practitioner who gains merit will be reborn in Brahma Heaven. These "seven dharmas" include the following:

a. Creating Buddha icons, monastic quarters and halls;
b. Producing gardens, pools, trees and places to wash and purify;
c. Always administering medicine and saving beings from disease;
d. Producing safe boats with which to ferry people across;
e. Building bridges with which to carry across the weak;
f. Digging wells near roads to quench thirst;
g. Producing latrines which people can conveniently use.[158]

Dunhuang Mogao Cave #296, which was built during the Northern Zhou, and the lower level of the pyramidal ceiling of Cave #302, which was built in 584, are both *jingbian* 經變 (scriptural transformation) paintings from the *Foshuo zhude futian jing*. These two paintings are all painted on the basis of the content of the *Foshuo zhude futian jing*. The wall mural from the Northern Zhou in Dunhuang Mogao Cave #269 includes altogether six scenes paintings from west to east starting from the cave's northern top: (a). building Buddha icons, painting the halls (立佛圖、畫堂閣); (b). planting trees and gardens to provide refreshment (種植園果以施清涼); (c). providing medicine (施給醫藥); (d). digging wells along distant roads (曠路作井); (e). building bridges (架設橋樑); and (f). building small shelters along the roadside (道旁立小精舍). The first five scenes clearly depict the seven fields of merit as explained in the *Foshuo zhude futian jing*. With respect to the sixth scene of the roadside shelters, it is one of the fields of merit explained in the *Foshuo zhude futian jing*. The *sūtra* explains that a monk named Tingcong 聽聰 was reborn in heaven as Indra when he died as a result of the merits of building roadside shelters in a past life and providing monks with rations and bedding, as well as offering travelers

158 *Foshuo zhude futian jing*, *T* no. 683, 16: 1.777b2-8.

rest. Later he also took a lower rebirth as a Wheel-Turning Sage King for ninety-one *kalpas*. In the present life he also had the merit to be able to meet Śākyamuni Buddha. On the lower edge of the western half of the pyramidal ceiling of Cave #302, running from north to south is a painting of a scene in which there is chopping of trees, building of a *stūpa* and construction of halls and the production of Buddha icons as well as scenes of gardens and wells being built, medicine being distributed, pontoon bridges being installed, wells being dug and small shelters being constructed.[159]

In the sixth century, there was another popular scripture titled *Xiangfa jueyi jing* 像法決疑經 (*Sūtra* of Resolving Doubts during the Age of the Semblance Dharma; *T* 2870) that explained merit making even further. This *sūtra* is not one translated from Sanskrit, but rather was compiled by monks during the Northern Dynasties. This *sūtra*, however, was not only considerably popular at the time, but it also exerted great influence on the Buddhist world. In the sixth century, eminent monks also cited this *sūtra*.[160] The *Xiangfa jueyi jing*, taking the Bodhisattva of Constantly Giving (Chanshi pusa 常施菩薩) as the audient, emphasizing the importance of generosity to the poor, orphans and elderly. It finally states, "The name of this *sūtra* is *Xiangfa jueyi*, also called *Ji gudu* 濟孤獨. It should be upheld in this manner."[161] The *sūtra* very much emphasizes the merit of generosity as follows:

> Son of a good family! My attainment of Buddhahood is all due to practicing giving since time immemorial, in order to succor impoverished and distressed sentient beings. All the buddhas of the ten directions also attained their Buddhahood by [practicing] giving. This is why giving is placed at the head of the six perfections whenever I have expounded them in the scriptures. [...] Son of good family! This teaching of giving is what all the buddhas of the three times (past, present, and future) have each revered. For this reason, of the four means of conversion (giving, kind speech, benefitting others, and emulation of religious training) the means through wealth is by far the most excellent.[162]

---

159 Shi, "Bihua," 320-22.

160 Liu, "Yicihui shizhu," 4-5.

161 *Xiangfa jueyi jing*, *T* no. 2870, 85:1.1338c15-16: 此經名爲《像法決疑》, 亦名《濟孤獨》, 如是受持.

162 Ibid., 1.1336b19-c01:
善男子, 我今成佛, 皆因曠劫行檀佈施、救濟貧窮困厄眾生. 十方諸佛亦從佈施而得成佛. 是故, 我於處處經中, 說六波羅蜜皆從佈施以爲初首. ...... 善男子, 此佈施法門, 三世諸佛所共敬重. 是故四攝法中, 財攝最勝. (Tokuno [trans.], "Book of Resolving Doubts," 193).

The *sūtra* situates generosity in an important position among the six perfections and four methods of winning people over, explaining that it is a Dharma gate through which one attains buddhahood. At the same time, the *sūtra* further particularly stresses the "field of compassion" that is generosity toward the poor, orphans and elderly as being far superior to the "field of respect" that is giving to the Buddha, Dharma and *Saṃgha*:

> Good Sons! In various *sūtra*s I teach generosity, wanting renunciates and laypeople to cultivate a mind of compassion, giving to the poor, orphans and elderly, and even to the hungry dogs. My disciples have not understood my meaning, exclusively giving to the field of respect, and not giving to the field of compassion. The field of respect is the gems of the Buddha, Dharma and *Saṃgha*. The field of compassion is the poor, orphans, and elderly, and even the ants. Of these two types of fields, this field is supreme.[163]

These directly encouraged Buddhists during the Northern and Southern Dynasties to engage in philanthropy.

### 3.3 *Buddhist Philanthropy in the Northern and Southern Dynasties*

Encouraged by Buddhism's compassionate spirit and conceptions of merit, Buddhists amassed funds and human resource through popular organizations such as *yi* 邑, *yi* 義, and *she* 社, and engaged in aiding the poor, disaster relief, the practice of disease diagnosis and medicine, digging wells, and building bridges and roads. This was how philanthropic projects such as charity wells, charity bridges, and charity tombs were carried on.

Fascicle nineteen of the *Kuaiji zhi* 會稽志 (Chronicle of Kuaiji) by Shi Su 施宿 (1164-1222) in the Song period and others interprets the concepts of charity wells and related activities as follows:

> Well of Yi (public good) [...] The word *yi* is used in the name because [the well's water] was to be drawn by the public. Nowadays, people in society build landed estates as gifts to clan members and name them "estates of *yi*," they establish schools to educate the children of folks of their towns and name them "schools of *yi*," they prepare beverages along the roads for

163 *Xiangfa jueyi jing*, *T* no. 2870, 85: 1.1336a27-b2:
善男子, 我於處處經中, 說佈施者, 欲令出家人、在家人修慈悲心, 佈施貧窮孤老乃至餓狗. 我諸弟子不解我意, 專施敬田, 不施悲田. 敬田者即是佛法僧寶, 悲田者貧窮孤老乃至蟻子. 此二種田, 此田最勝.

passers-by to drink and name it "beverage of *yi*," and they reclaim land to build tombs in groups and inter those bare dead bones which are called "tombs of *yi*."[164]

Philanthropy is always accomplished from people's combined strengths, which is why "*yi*" is called charitable, and on the basis of this people charitably engaged in philanthropic activities such as building infrastructure.

As the biography of Liu Yao 劉繇 (156-197) in the *Sanguo zhi* 三國志 (Record of the Three Kingdoms) records, after Ze Rong 笮融 (?-196) became Buddhist, "He frequently washed the Buddha [image] and often provided feasts, laying out seats on the road for dozens of miles. Ten-thousand people would come to watch and eat at enormous expense."[165] We can clearly see Ze Rong's charitable activities. The nun Lingzong 令宗 (d.u.) of Xisi 西寺 in Sizhou 司州 during the time of Emperor Xiaowu of the Eastern Jin (Dong Jin Xiaowen di 東晉孝武帝 [r. 372-396]), for the benefit of the commoners suffering illness and poverty "begged from people to save them, not avoiding any obstacle of distance, and offering relief wherever appropriate."[166] Daomeng 道猛 (411-475) during the Liu-Song period, "Provided for the poor with whatever he could gain, building temples and shrines."[167] Fagong 法恭 (ca. 387-466), who was revered by the Emperors Xiao, Wen and Ming of Liu Song, "always divided what was donated and to the poor and ill, never keeping any of it for himself."[168] Falang 法朗 (507-581) of Xinghuang si 興皇寺 during the Chen Dynasty, "produced scriptures and images, built and repaired temples and *stūpa*s, and saved those in distress all with all the proceeds from the offerings he gained; thus he had many types of fowl and dogs in his quarters, always taking them in and raising them whenever he saw them."[169] It is clear that monastics and wealthy lay Buddhists with the popular appeal of merit making and Buddhist compassion carried out acts of Buddhist charity and acted to save the poor.

There were frequent natural disasters and wars in the centuries of the Wei-Jin Northern and Southern Dynasties. From cities to rural villages, all

164 *Kuaiji zhi*, SKQS, 486:19.417a8-b3:
義井 …… 義者, 蓋以眾所共汲爲名. 今世俗置產以給族人, 曰義莊；置學以教鄉曲子弟, 曰義學；設漿於道, 以飲行旅, 曰義漿；辟地爲叢冢, 以藏暴骨, 曰義冢.

165 *Sanguo zhi*, 49.1185: 每浴佛, 多設酒飯, 布席於路, 經數十裡. 人民來觀及就食且萬人, 費以巨億計.

166 *Biqiuni zhuan*, *T* no. 2063, 50: 1.936c11-12: 傾資賑給, 告乞人間, 不避阻遠, 隨宜贍恤.

167 *Gaoseng zhuan*, *T* no. 2059, 50: 7.374a27: 隨有所獲, 皆賑施貧乏, 營造寺廟.

168 Ibid., 12.407c12-13: 所獲信施, 常分給貧病, 未嘗私蓄.

169 *Xu Gaoseng zhuan*, *T* no. 2060, 50: 7.478a1-3:
所獲檀嚫, 充造經像, 修治寺塔, 濟給窮厄, 所以房內畜養鵝鴨雞犬, 其類繁多, 所行見者無不收養.

settlements suffered. In the eighth lunar month of the year 575, the provinces of Jizhou 冀州, Dingzhou 定州, Zhaozhou 趙州, Youzhou 幽州, Cangzhou 滄州 and Yingzhou 瀛州 were struck by flooding. The *Bei Qi shu* 北齊書 (Book of the Northern Qi) records, "In 576, it was ordered that from autumn that those at great temples and the wealthy save those many stricken by the floods unable to support themselves."[170] The government mobilized the temples and the wealthy to work together to save the poor masses in the disaster areas. There was also no shortage of persons in the Northern Dynasties societies who actively assisted, under Buddhist influence, in charitable funerals, food distribution, and medicine. Based on the account on the "Biaoyi xiangyi cihui shizhu" 標異鄉義慈惠石柱 (Stone Pillar of Honouring and Distinguishing the Compassionate and Beneficent Work of the Local Philanthropists) from the Northern Qi period, during the later years of the Northern Wei, what is now Hebei province went through disruptions from war. With Wang Xingguo 王興國 as chief of some common Buddhists, they lamented that nobody was present to bury the bones of the dead. They first gathered together the corpses alongside the river of Zhuo 涿 and then made it into a mass grave, which they called a "village burial" (*xiangzang* 鄉葬). Later, there was charitable food offerings made at the grave, to feed refugees that were going back to their hometowns via this area. They also built a charity shelter as a place to make the food offerings. At this time, their relief activities had become long-term. After this, Tanzun 曇遵 (b. after 470, d. after 560) and his disciples joined in and the influence of the relief activities grew even larger, also increasing with new relief projects: they started offering medieval services. In 546, because the official route moved westward, this charitable station also moved accordingly. At this time, the Yan 嚴 family also donated land and fields and the economic strength of the relief increased. In the year 557, they succoured labourers who built the Great Wall. In the year 564, they subsequently saved the people suffering famine due to the floods. The relief activities of these people lasted for forty years.[171]

Buddhists at this time taught that digging wells and repairing bridges is a meritorious act of karma. For example, Sengyuan 僧淵 (519-602) of Fuyuan *daochang* 福緣道場 (Practice Center of Auspicious Conditions) in Sichuan "always gave to the orphans and those alone, never going against the will of people; he assisted them far and wide, like the flow from a spring."[172] He aspired to

170 *Bei Qi shu* 8.108-109: 七月春正月壬辰, 詔去秋以來, 水潦人饑不自立者, 所在付大寺及諸富戶濟其性命.

171 Liu, "Yicihui shizhu," 8-23.

172 *Xu Gaoseng zhuan, T* no. 2060, 50: 18.574b29: 常給孤獨, 不逆人意, 遠近隨助, 泉布若流.

FIGURE 6 *Bhikṣuṇī*-sponsor in the Gong county 鞏縣 grotto complex, dated to the Northern Wei (386-534).

plant meritorious karma and give generously to orphans and those without families. The biography of Sengyuan in the *Xu Gaoseng zhuan* states:

> Seeing that victims drowned by waves of the River Jinshui 錦水 were numerous, [Sengyuan] intended to build a bridge over the southern stream. Shortly after this plan was made, various things needed had been in place. In days of yore, Zhuge Liang 諸葛亮 (181-234), the Marquis of Wu District, pointed to the two rivers (of the Pi 郫 and the Jian 檢) and decided to create the Seven Star Bridges. [Then, he ordered them to] produce three iron hammers of some eight or nine *chi* in length and three *chi* in diameter, which people called "the iron pots." When the pillars of the bridge were to be installed, [the hammers], since they were not needed anymore, were thrown and then sunk into the river. Shortly, a prayer was offered, and thereafter [the hammers] emerged from the water. Now, [Seng]yuan was constructing the bridge; when the pillars were about to be erected, the hammers surfaced by themselves and moved to the ford where the bridge would be standing. When the bridge was completed [...][173]

Sengyuan was shocked at the drownings at the river crossing and as a result vowed to build a bridge.

The biography of Narendrayaśas in the *Xu Gaoseng zhuan* states:

> The offerings he gained were never spent on himself. He enjoyed generating compassion. He delighted in bringing forth meritorious karma. When he set up a feast for the monks, he would give to the destitute. ... He often built charity wells and personally filtered water, and provided it to beings. He also took care of the terminally ill, with men and women in separate residences. All necessaties were by all means supplied.[174]

173 Ibid., 18.574c1-6:
又以錦水江波沒溺者眾, 便於南路欲架飛橋, 則扣此機, 眾事咸集. 昔諸葛武侯指二江內, 造七星橋, 造三鐵鐓, 長八九尺, 徑三尺許, 人號鐵槍, 擬打橋柱, 用訖投江. 頃便祈禱, 方爲出水, 淵造新橋, 將行豎柱. 其鐓自然浮水, 來至橋津, 及橋成也.

174 Ibid., 2.432c17-22:
所獲供祿, 不專自資；好起慈惠, 樂興福業；設供飯僧, 施諸貧乏 ...... 多造義井, 親自漉水, 津給眾生 ...... 又收養厲疾, 男女別坊, 四事供承, 務令周給.

It is clear that Narendrayaśas' philanthropic activities were quite diverse, which included feeding monks, saving the poor, building charity wells and looking after the ill.

Digging wells and repairing bridges requires collective group effort, which is why societies were organized, leading to their primary form in which Buddhists of the Northern and Southern Dynasties engaged in philanthropy. The "Li shi heyi zaoxiang beiwen" 李氏合邑造像碑文 (Stele for the Li Family Collectively Producing an Image) of the year 542 records the following:

> Then, two miles south of the village there was the north bank of the great river, a junction of various routes and a hub for both waterways and landways. Here, travellers from the eastern coast were rushing to and fro, and also visible were guests from valleys of the Yi 伊 and Luo 洛 Rivers in the west. They went through the raging thirst in the warmth of spring and the scorching heat in the sunshine of summer. Pitying the stream of travellers, [members of the society] dug a well on the roadside and planted twenty trees in order to quench their thirst and weariness. […] These society members created a site. The site was by the river, to the southeast of the village. It was a flat and open ground and within the view of passersby. People, at the sight of it, came to pay reverence, and the local government held the site with respect. [Visitors would] intone the inscription and arouse the mind [of intention to pursue enlightenment], setting their mind to repaying [the sentient beings] with benefits.[175]

The Li family was an aristocratic clan that led villagers two miles southeast of the village to the northern bank of a great river, where they produced a charity well and planted twenty trees for the use of travelers who could drink water and rest. These kinds of travelers passing through the village were possibly influenced by the kindness of bodhisattva acts exemplified in the *Fahua jing*, who also went a step further to worship the Buddha and bodhisattva images in the village shrine and sincerely vow to generate *bodhicitta*, thereby gaining even larger merit. The social activities of the *Lotus* Society aimed at public good had an ultimate aim of guiding all beings so that they could all attain rebirth in the Pure Land.[176] The activity and goals of Buddhist philanthropy all

175 Beijing tushuguan jinshizu, *Lidai shike tuoben*, 90:
復於村南二里, 大河北岸, 萬路交過, 水陸俱要, 滄海之濱, 攸攸伊洛之客, 亦屬徑春溫之苦渴, 涉夏暑之炎, 愍茲行流, 故於路旁造石井一口, 種樹兩十根, 以息渴乏. …… 斯等邑人, 置立方處. 方處臨河, 據村南東. 平原顯敞, 行路過逢. 人瞻來仰, 府設虔恭. 唅吼發心, 報福是鍾.

176 For a detailed study of this stele, see Yan, "Fahua yiyi", 167-184.

stemmed from Buddhist faith. In the present life they could deal with disasters and seek merit, while achieving rebirth in the Pure Land at death.

In 549, a group of monks and Buddhist devotees repaired an old bridge at Wude County 武德郡 (southeast of modern Qinyang 沁陽 in Henan) and also built a Buddha image with an accompanying stele inscription. The inscription reads as follows:

> [This stone stele was erected] the eighth day of the fourth month of the seventh year of the Wuding 武定 era of the Great Wei dynasty (549.5.20), when Jupiter was at the station of *jisi* 己巳. The masters from the Yangying si 楊膺寺, Jincheng si 金城寺, Yongcheng si 雍城寺, Heng'an si 恆安寺, Gouzhong si 苟冢寺, Zhuying si 朱營寺, Guanling si 管令寺 realized [that everything was impermanent as] a candle flame in the wind or [as insubstantial as] a bubble, and were disheartened by gloominess. Thus, they shaved off their hair and presented it to the gate of profundity. They removed their hairpins and chose the track of Brahma (i.e. Buddhism). Sighing at the great difficulties of traversing [the Qin 沁 river] and taking pity on the people for the pains they endured to cross it, these monks donated wood and other materials for the construction of the bridge. As the Yangying si initiated this good work, it is regarded as the chief benefactor of the bridge.[177]

The first half of the inscription is the same as an inscription for the production of an image—explaining the essential meaning of Buddhism—while the latter part concerns the origins of the Wude County and its mountains and rivers, as well as the civic virtues of its magistrates and the stele's erection following the repair of the bridge. Right after the verse of the stele inscription is a short text that announces that the organizer behind the repair of this bridge was actually a monk from the monastery. Among the more than 260 names inscribed on the back side of the stele, the first two columns are all regional officials of varying ranks while the third column lists names of commoners, who might have been those laborers who worked to repair the bridge. The monks of the seven monasteries who donated timber to the repair the bridge do not have their

177 "Wude yu fu jun deng yi qiao shi xiang zhi shibei" 武德於府君等義橋石像之石碑, *Jinshi cuibian* 31.5:
大魏武定七季歲次己巳，四月丙戌朔八日癸巳建. 楊膺寺、金城寺、雍城寺、恆安寺、苟冢寺、朱營寺、管令寺諸師等見風燭以生悲，睹泡沫而興嘆，遂乃落髮, 以 [ ] [ ] 門, 抽簪而口梵徹, 嗟往還巨難, 愍揭厲多辛, 咸施材木, 構造橋梁. 楊膺寺發善之源, 以為橋主. (Translation based on Kieschnieck, *Impact of Buddhism*, 200-01)

FIGURE 7 Heads of Buddhist societies (*Yi* 邑) acting as sponsors for the grotto complex at Shuiyu Monastery 水浴寺, dated to the Northern Wei.

names listed. With respect to this anomaly, the author of the *Jinshi cuibian* 金石萃編 (Collection of Bronze and Stone Inscriptions) offers the following penetrating argument:

> At the end of the inscription with the dates follows seven monasteries listed, which records the timber that they offered, and Yangying si was the benefactor of the bridge and is listed first. Nevertheless, the rebuilding of the bridge was connected to various temples, but the stele was erected to glorify the magistrates.[178]

Philanthropic activities such as repairing bridges and building roads are public works by nature, which is why regional governments always participated. However, these projects were easily brought to success thanks to the fundraising efforts of the many devotees of monasteries and their monks. Despite the title of this stele inscription for the bridge building superficially attributing the charitable work to local officials, in reality, the inscription clearly points out the efforts of the monks of the monasteries.[179] Repairing bridges requires people's collective efforts. The stele inscription reads, "On the sixth day of the seventh lunar month (549.8.14), this bridge was started and those who assisted with its fortune stood shoulder to shoulder, and those who donated their charity came with their carriages running side by side."[180] In the verses of praises, it reads, "ever since the planning of the project, volunteers thronged to help; within ten days, the structure was completed."[181] It is clear that the monks of the monasteries presided over the movement to repair the bridge and the regional government participated in it, being brought to completion by the collective efforts of the commoners.

Treatment of illness and injuries was also one of the philanthropic activities in which Buddhist monks engaged during the Northern and Southern dynasties. After Buddhism was introduced into China, the medicine of India and the Western Regions as well as the art of mantras were all widely disseminated into Chinese society. For example, *vinaya* texts such as those of the *Sifen lü*, *Wufen lü* and *Shisong lü* traditions, all refer to various types of disease and pathogenesis as well as treatments and medicines. At the same time, in the process of meditative training, it was easy for monks to become ill as a result of not being seated properly or having brought about an internal disorder, which is why

178 *Jinshi cuibian* 31.5:
文末年月後列七寺, 以紀施材木之功, 而楊膺寺爲橋主, 列於首. 然則建橋乃各寺之緣, 立碑則歸美於守令也.

179 For the detailed analysis of this inscription, see Liu, "Cibei xishe," 17-20.

180 *Jinshi cuibian* 31.5: 七月六日經始此橋, 助福者比肩, 獻義者聯轂.

181 Ibid: 爰始經謀, 義勸競塡, 辰不再浹, 斯構已宣.

FIGURE 8 The inscription of a stele for Buddhist image, constructed in 546.

meditation scriptures such as the *Zhi chanbing miyao jing* 治禪病秘要經 (Secret Essentials for Healing the Maladies of Meditation; *T* 620) record a number of medical treatments. In addition, the chapter on curing illness ("Chubing pin" 除病品) in the *Jin'guangming jing* gives a detailed account on medicine. The catalog of texts in the *Sui shu* attributes to Buddhist monks various medical texts, which demonstrate Chinese Buddhism's level of medical learning.[182]

182 *Sui shu* 34.1041-1046:
1. *Hanshi san duiliao* 寒食散對療 (*Treatment via Cold Food*) in one fascicle by Shi Daohong 釋道洪;
2. *Jie hanshi san fa* 解寒食散方 (*Treatment of Relieving Cold Food*) in two fascicles by Shi Zhibin 釋智斌;
3. *Jie hanshi san lun* 解寒食散論 (*Discussions on Relieving Cold Food*) in two fascicles by Shi Huiyi 釋慧義;
4. *Za san fang* 雜散方 (*Various Treatments*) in eight fascicles;
5. *Yao fang* 藥方 (*Medical Prescriptions*) in twenty fascicles by Shi Sengshen 釋僧深;
6. *Danfu yao yan fang* 單複要驗方 (*Simple and Complicated Prescriptions of Efficacy*) in two fascicles by Shi Moman 釋莫滿;
7. *Shi Daohong fang* 釋道洪方 (*Treatments of Shi Daohong*) in one fascicle;

Monks during the Northern and Southern Dynasties did not only have a command of Buddhist medicine. A significant part of their repertoire was knowledge of traditional Chinese medicine, in addition to religious mantras and repentance rituals, all of which monks used in their treatments. Knowledge of medicine (*yifang ming* 醫方明 or Skt. *cikitsā-vidyā*) is one of the five traditional Buddhist sciences that are necessary for monastics to know, which is why renunciates who hailed from South and Central Asia often possessed rich medical knowledge. For example, Fotucheng 佛圖澄 (233-349) "was adept in reciting mantras, [and] was able to command spirits."[183] Shi Bin 石斌 (?-349), the son of Shi Hu 石虎 (295-349), became suddenly ill and expired, but Fotuchang took a willow branch and recited an incantation and restored him. Shan Daokai 單道開 (?-359+) was able to remedy eye diseases and received the favor of Shi Hu.[184] Zhu Fakuang 竺法曠 (327-402) was skilled in mantra and medicine. At the time when a plague had broken out, Zhu Fakuang travelled to various villages and recited mantras to remedy the disease among the commoners.[185] Yu Fakai 于法開 (fl. 361-365) and Yu Daosui 于道邃 (3rd-4th century) were both disciples of Yu Falan 于法蘭 (fl. 280-289), who were adept in the medical arts, especially Fu Fakai whose "ancestor was said to be Jīvaka, excelling in the Dharma of medicine."[186] As the number of monks practicing medicine increased, Daoheng's fifth-century *Shi bo lun* 釋駁論 (Treatise on the Explication of Arguments) cited a criticism against monks: "Some overly pride themselves in the practice of medicine, making light of cold and heat."[187] The Chinese *Xiangfa jueyi jing*, compiled during the sixth century, also depicts monks using mantras, acupuncture and traditional medicines to heal people.

> Son of a good family! In future generations why will all the worldlings slight and look down upon the Three Jewels? It is precisely because monks and nuns do not conform to the Dharma. … Some will recite magical spells to cure others' illnesses. … Some will practice acupuncture and

8. *Liao baibing za wan fang* 療百病雜丸方 (*Various Pellet Treatments for Treating Many Diseases*) in three fascicles Shi Tanluan 釋曇鸞;
9. *Lun qi zhiliao fang* 論氣治療方 (*Discussions on Treatment of Qi*) in one fascicle;
10. *Yilun beiyu fang* 議論備予方 (*Discussion of Preparation of Treatments*) in one fascicle by Yu Hongkai 于洪開;
11. *Zhenjiu jing* 針灸經 (*Text on Acupuncture*) in one fascicle by Shi Sengkuang 釋僧匡.

183 *Gaoseng zhuan*, *T* no. 2059, 50: 9.383b21-22: 善誦神咒, 能役使鬼物.

184 Ibid., 9.387b21-23.

185 Ibid., 5.356c28-357a2.

186 Ibid., 4.350a14-15: 祖述耆婆, 妙通醫法.

187 *Hongming ji*, *T* no. 2102, 52: 6. 35b9: 或矜恃醫道, 輕作寒暑.

> moxibustion (moxa cautery) and various other types of medicine as a means of getting clothing and food.[188]

Monks engaged in medicine and could be adept in offering treatments with laypeople also studying medicine under monks. In 426 when the states of Song and Wei went to war, Li Liang 李亮 (d.u.), the prefectural governor of Nan'an 南安 in Wei, surrendered to the Song court. Li Liang in the Northern Wei period had read widely in medical science and after surrendering to the Song studied medicine under the monk Sengtan 僧坦 (d.u.) in Pengcheng 彭城 : "He only gained a basic grasp of his art, applying acupuncture and administering medicines, and it was always effective."[189] He then became a widely known physician.

Monks and nuns both studied medicine and regarded it as a field of merit, which promoted the development of the institutions of Buddhist medicine. For instance, in the Southern Qi, Crown Prince Wenhui 文惠太子 (458-493) and Prince Jingling was "fond of Buddhism and established six hospitals to take care of people in distress."[190] This was to treat everyone in distress suffering diseases. "Jingling Wenxuan wang funei [=dinei?] shiyao ji" 竟陵文宣王弗 [= 第 ?] 內施藥記 (Account of Prince Jingling's Donating Medicine from His Princely Residence) ought to have been related to the issues of administering medicine in the six hospitals. The monk Tanyan 曇衍 (503-581) in the Northern Qi "extended his sympathy to saving the world, thus for the entirety of his life, among those who he would save, the destitute and the ill came first."[191] Lingyu 靈裕 (518-605) "over the period of his largesse, his charity reached the venerable and pitiful. The monastic robes he had gifted were over one thousand, and those suffering from illness but cured by him were legion."[192] The philanthropy of medicine by these monks doubtlessly benefited the contemporary people.

Monks engaging in medical activities stored medical materials in monasteries, which was called the "Repository of Medicine" (*yaozang* 藥藏) so as to always be able to provide for those seeking medical attention. The "Repository of Medicine" has its origins in India. King Aśoka constructed "Repositories of

---

188 *Xiangfa jueyi jing*, *T* no. 2870, 85: 1.1337b27-29, 1337c4, 1337c5-6: 何故未來世中一切俗人輕賤三寶？正以比丘比丘尼不如法故, …… 或誦咒術, 以治他病; … 或行針灸種種湯藥, 以求衣食. (trans. Tokuno, "Book of Resolving Doubts," 197; with slight modifications)

189 *Wei shu* 91.1966: 略盡其術, 針灸授藥, 莫不有效.

190 *Nan Qi shu* 21.401: 俱好釋氏, 立六疾館以養窮民.

191 *Xu Gaoseng zhuan*, *T* no. 2060, 50: 8.487b28-29: 情及濟世, 故積散所拯, 貧病爲初.

192 Ibid., 9.497b15-16: 自前後行施, 悲敬兼之. 袈裟爲惠, 出過千領; 疾苦所及, 醫療繁多.

FIGURE 9 The cremation pagoda for Daoping 道憑 (487-559). at Lingquan Monastery 靈泉寺 on Mount Bao 寶山.

Medicine" beside the four gates of Rajgir and therein filled them with medicinal herbs. Every day, ten-thousand coins would be used to purchase medical supplies to treat the ill.[193] Monasteries storied medical supplies while at the same time also have monks who understood medicine. The monasteries no doubt had a hospital-like aspect to them. In the late Song and early Qi, Faying 法穎 (?-482) of Linggen si 靈根寺 on Mount Zhong 鐘山 in Jiankang was venerated by Emperor Xiaowu of the Song and Emperor Wugao of the Qi, who provided him with basic necessities as well as expenses. At the same time, he also received many offerings from devotees. Faying used these offerings to produce images and scriptures as well as to establish a "Great Repository of Medicine."[194] Fascicle Thirteen of the *Chu sanzang ji ji* includes a "Linggen si Lei[=Ying] Lüshi shi zao yaozang ji" 靈根寺類 (= 穎) 律師始造藥藏記 (Account of the First Construction of the Repository of Medicine by *Vinaya* Mas-

193 *Shanjian lü piposha*, *T* no. 1462, 24: 2.682a21-27.
194 *Gaoseng zhuan*, *T* no. 2059, 50: 11.402a13-14.

ter Lei [=Ying] of Linggen si), which was likely an account of the origins and process of Faying's building of a repository of medicine.[195] During the Chen Dynasty, there were outbreaks of disease that caused the death of many commoners. At the time, a monk named Huida 慧達 (?-610) of Mount Tiantai 天臺山 was at Da si 大寺 in the capital Jiankang where he built a "great repository of medicine" in which "anyone who needed it were given [medicine]; those saved were numerous."[196] Monastic medical administration and clinic construction became a fine tradition of Chinese Buddhism.

## 4 The Cult of the *Fahua jing* in the Northern and Southern Dynasties

With respect to Chinese translations of the *Fahua jing*, the account of Zhisheng's *Kaiyuan Shijiao lu* records that "there were six successive translations. Three are extant and three are lost."[197] The extant include the following three translations:

a. Zhu Fahu's 竺法護 *Zheng fahua jing* 正法華經. Twenty-seven chapters in ten fascicles. Translated in 286.
b. Kumārajīva's (Jiumoluoshi 鳩摩羅什 [344-413]) *Miaofa lianhua jing* 妙法蓮華經. Twenty-eight chapters in seven fascicles. Translated in 406.
c. Jñānagupta 闍那崛多 (523-600) and Dharmagupta's 達摩笈多 (?-619) *Tianpin Miaofa lianhua jing* 添品妙法蓮華經. Twenty-seven chapters in seven fascicles. Translated in 601.

The *Fahua jing* flourished and became widespread in China after Kumārajīva's translation. Among those listed in the *Gaoseng zhuan* who taught or recited scriptures, the number of people who taught or recited the *Fahua jing* is greatest. Among the manuscripts of Dunhuang, this one occupies the largest proportion. In the Northern and Southern Dynasties alone, the number of commentators on this *sūtra* reached more than seventy authors. Zhiyi established the Tiantai school on the basis of this *sūtra* during the Chen and Sui periods.

---

195 *Chu sanzang ji ji*, *T* no. 2145, 55: 13.93a15.

196 *Xu Gaoseng zhuan*, *T* no. 2060, 50: 29.694a20-21: 須者便給, 拯濟彌隆.

197 *Kaiyuan Shijiao lu*, *T* no. 2154, 55: 14.629a1-2: 前後六譯. 三存三闕. The three lost translations are (1) Zhi Jiangliangjie's 支疆梁接, *Fahua sanmei jing* 法華三昧經, 6 *juan*, in 256; (2) Zhu Fahu, *Sayunfentuoli jing* 薩芸芬陀利經, 6 *juan*, in 265; and (3) Zhi Daogen 支道根, *Fangdeng Fahua jing* 方等法華經, 5 *juan*, in 335. For Chinese, Tibetan, English, and Japanese translations of the *Lotus Sūtra*, see Yazaki, "Hokekyō denyaku," 227-48; and Gao, "Fahua jing," 25-40.

### 4.1 *The Idea of* Samādhi *in the* Fahua Jing

Zhiyi spared no effort in his commentaries on the *Fahua jing*. He authored the *Fahua wenju* 法華文句 (Textual Explanation of the *Lotus Sūtra*; *T* 1718) and *Fahua xuanyi* 法華玄義 (Profound Meaning of the *Lotus Sūtra*; *T* 1716). He relied upon the translation of the *Fahua jing* by Kumārajīva. The "Miaoyin pusa pin" 妙音菩薩品 (Chapter of Marvelous Sound) in the *Fahua jing* read as follows:

> At that time, in the buddha-world of Vairocanaraśmiprati-maṇḍitā there was a bodhisattva whose name was Gadgadasvara (Wonderful Voice). Having planted many roots of good merit over a long period, he paid homage to and closely attended immeasurable hundreds of thousands of myriads of *koṭis* of Buddhas, and accomplished complete and profound wisdom. He attained the *samādhi*s called *dhvajrā grakeyūra, saddharma-puṇḍarīka* … Thereupon, Bodhisattva Padmaśrī addressed the Buddha, saying: "O Bhagavat! Deep are the roots of the good merit that this bodhisattva Gadgadasvara has planted! O Bhagavat! In what *samādhi* does this bodhisattva dwell, such that he was able to appear in various places in this way, and bring sentient beings to the path?" The Buddha answered Bodhisattva Padmaśrī, saying: "O son of a virtuous family, that *samādhi* was called *sarvarūpa saṃ darśana*. Dwelling in this *samādhi* Bodhisattva Gadgadasvara has benefitted innumerable sentient beings in this way." When this chapter "Bodhisattva Gadgadasvara" was being taught, those eighty-four thousand people who had come with Bodhisattva Gadgadasvara attained the *samādhi* called *sarvarūpa saṃ darśana*.[198]

In the *Fahua jing*, the *Lotus samādhi* (*Fahua sanmei* 法華三昧) is a method of integrated spiritual practice. The text mentions this by name and states of it that there will "manifest all form bodies" but it offers no explanation of the concrete method of practice. The *sūtra* altogether refers to the *Lotus samādhi* in three places and on the basis of these we can infer that there are two conditions upon which the *Lotus samādhi* is obtained. First, that one has achieved "profoundly deep wisdom" and, second, that one has received and upheld the *Fahua jing*. Thus, when we have not yet achieved profoundly deep wisdom, the

198 *Miaofa lianhua jing*, *T* no. 0262, 9: 7.55a24-27, 56b12-18:
爾時一切淨光莊嚴國中, 有一菩薩, 名曰妙音, 久已植衆德本, 供養親近無量百千萬億諸佛, 而悉成就甚深智慧, 得妙幢相三昧、法華三昧 …… 爾時, 華德菩薩白佛言：世尊！是妙音菩薩深種善根. 世尊！是菩薩住何三昧, 而能如是在所變現, 度脫衆生？佛告華德菩薩：善男子！其三昧名現一切色身, 妙音菩薩住是三昧中, 能如是饒益無量衆生. 說是妙音菩薩品時, 與妙音菩薩俱來者八萬四千人, 皆得現一切色身三昧. (trans. Kubo & Yuyama, *The Lotus Sūtra*, 289, 294)

primary method of practice if we want to achieve the *Lotus samādhi* is receiving and reciting the *Lotus Sūtra*.

The "Puxian pusa quanfa pin" 普賢菩薩勸發品 (Chapter on the Encouragement of Bodhisattva Samantabhadra) of the *Fahua jing*, however, describes the method to cultivate the *Lotus samādhi* as follows:

> [Those who] wish to practice this *Fahua jing* should persevere single-mindedly for twenty-one days. After a full twenty-one days I will appear upon a white elephant with six tusks, accompanied by innumerable bodhisattvas who themselves will be surrounded by their retinues, and then manifest myself before sentient beings in whatever form they wish to see.[199]

Here it states that one must diligently train for twenty-one days, whereupon Samantabhadra riding a white six-tusked elephant and immeasurable bodhisattvas will appear before the practitioner. This is the meaning of to "manifest all form bodies" and the *Lotus Samādhi*.

In the *Fahua jing*, the "Anle xing pin" 安樂行品 (Chapter of the Means to Attaining Peace) presents the most practice methods, similar to the Brahma Net Bodhisattva Precepts and Yoga-Bodhisattva Precepts, in which there are extremely strict regulations governing the body, speech, intent and vows of a practitioner.[200] Later, on the basis of said chapter, Huisi 慧思 (515-577) compiled the *Anle xing yi* 安樂行義 (Exegesis on the 'Blissful Practice' Section; *T* 1926) and further systematized the method for cultivating the "*Lotus Samādhi*," becoming an important practice transmitted to his disciples.

Hirakawa Akira 平川彰 (1915-2002) believed that the main components of the *Fahua jing* was to be divided into two parts: from the first to the ninth chapters as well as from chapters ten to twenty-two. The six chapter following the twenty-third chapter were later additions. As for the chapter of "Entrustment," the first nine chapters emphasize a cult surrounding the *stūpa*s of buddhas, whereas the latter thirteen chapters encourage receiving and upholding physical *sūtra*s. Nevertheless, the thirteenth chapter or "Jian baota pin" 見寶塔品 (Chapter of the Vision of the Jeweled *Stūpa*) also emphasizes the *stūpa* cult, which is why *stūpa*s and *sūtra*s cannot be held apart.[201]

---

199 *Miaofa lianhua jing*, *T* no. 0262, 9: 7.61b11-14:
欲修學是法華經, 於三七日中, 應一心精進. 滿三七日已, 我當乘六牙白象與無量菩薩而自圍繞, 以一切眾生所喜見身, 現其人前. (trans. Kubo & Yuyama, *The Lotus Sūtra*, 314)

200 Shi Shengyan, "Xiuxing fangfa," 4.

201 Hirakawa, *Shoki daijō to Hokke shisō*, 327.

According to the Chapter of the Vision of the Jeweled *Stūpa* in fascicle four of the *Fahua jing*, Prabhūtaratna Buddha is chief teacher of the Gem Purity Realm in the eastern direction. Long ago when he was practicing the bodhisattva path, he vowed that after achieving buddhahood and passing away, wherever the *Fauhua jing* is preached in the worlds in the ten directions, his *stūpa* would come forth and appear in that spot to testify the substance of the truth. Thus, when the Buddha taught the *Fahua jing*, a Seven-Gem *Stūpa* emerged from the ground and was suspended in mid-air. Within the *stūpa* was Prabhūtaratna Buddha sitting atop a lion-throne, his posture as if in deep meditation. Half the seat was shared with the World-Honoured One. Thus, Huiguan in his "Fahua zongyao xu" 法華宗要序 (Preface to the *Lotus* Tenets) points out that "the *sūtra* has the true wisdom as its essence, and the 'wondrous oneness' as its title. When the Śākyamuni Buddha's ineffable voice rises, it praises the profundity of the buddhas' wisdom, and when expressing his laudation, Prabhūtaratna praises the great wisdom of equality."[202] The truth of the past and present two buddhas simultaneously teaching the *Fahua jing* expressed the eternal quality of the "True Dharma" from the past to the future. At the same time, the two buddhas dividing the seat in half and sitting cross-legged indicates that the eternal quality of the "True Dharma" is founded on the cult surrounding the *stūpa*s of buddhas.[203] The *Fahua jing* states:

> This Mahākātyāyana in the future will honour, respect, and pay homage to eight thousand *koṭi*s of buddhas with offerings. After the *parinirvāṇas* of these buddhas, he will erect *stūpa*s, each of which will be one thousand *yojanas* in height and five hundred *yojanas* in both width and depth. These *stūpa*s will all be constructed of the seven precious treasures—gold, silver, lapis lazuli, mother-of-pearl, agate, pearls, and rubies. He will pay homage to these *stūpa*s with many flowers and necklaces, fragrant ointments, scented powders, burning incense, canopies, flags, and banners. After this he will also pay homage to two myriads of *koṭis* of buddhas in exactly the same way and, having done so, he will perfect the bodhisattva path and become a Buddha.[204]

202 *Chu sanzang ji ji*, *T* no. 2145, 55: 8.57a18-20:
經以真慧爲體, 妙一爲稱. 是以釋迦玄音始發, 贊佛智甚深；多寶稱善, 歎平等大慧.

203 Hirakawa, *Shoki daijō bukkyō no kenkyū* 2, 207. Yinshun maintains that the Prabhūtaratna Buddha's sharing half the seat with the World-Honoured One comes from the story of Mahākāśyapa; see Yinshun, *Chuqi dacheng fojiao zhi qiyuan yu kaizhan*, 1185.

204 *Miaofa lianhua jing*, *T* no. 0262, 9: 3.21b18-24:
於當來世, 以諸供具供養奉事八千億佛, 恭敬尊重. 諸佛滅後, 各起塔廟, 高千由

The *Fahua jing* elevates worship of the *stūpa*s of buddhas to the highest level of a practice aimed at Buddhahood. This no doubt sparked religious fervor among Buddhists with respect to the cult of *stūpa*s. At the same time, the *Fahua jing* emphasizes the merit of "receiving and upholding the *sūtra*." The two are intimately brought together. The ideas of the "Single Vehicle" or *ekayāna* and the "body of the Buddha permanently abiding" emerged from these two types of practice.

At the same time, the idea of "multiple buddhas" emerges from the Chapter of the Vision of the Jeweled *Stūpa*, in which the light of the Buddha brings together the emanations of buddhas from the ten directions, so many that it is difficult to calculate. "At that time these Buddha Tathāgatas filled four hundred myriads of *koṭi*s of nayutas of lands in each direction."[205] This expresses how many buddhas there are in the worlds of the ten directions, all of which are emanations of Śākyamuni. In his "Fahua jing hou xu" 法華經後序 (Postscript to the *Fahua jing*), Sengrui 僧睿 (373-439) states the following:

> The buddhas' life spans are infinite, and one cannot adequately express such eternity by describing them as "throughout all *kalpa*s." Their emanation bodies are innumerable, and even these myriads of forms cannot make themselves different. Their longevity shows that they are not bound by the fate of the mortal; their emanation bodies display their unreality; "All-embracing Goodness" manifests that the achievement knows no bounds, and Abundant Treasures highlights the quality of being inextinguishable. Travelling through the dark antiquity to show up at the present time means that the period of aeons is the same to that of a day, and from the processes of various transformations one could realize the abstruse ultimate that all courses follow the same track. In this way, the reality of ever begetting does not necessarily mean existence, and timeless stillness could not be regarded as extinction.[206]

---

旬, 縱廣正等五百由旬, 皆以金、銀、琉璃、車磲、瑪瑙、真珠、玫瑰七寶合成, 眾花瓔珞, 塗香、末香、燒香、繒蓋幢幡, 供養塔廟. 過是已後, 當復供養二萬億佛, 亦復如是. 供養是諸佛已, 具菩薩道, 當得作佛. (Trans. Kubo & Yuyama, *The Lotus Sūtra*, 108)

205 *Miaofa lianhua jing*, *T* no. 0262, 9: 4.33b15-16:
一一方四百萬億那由他國土, (分身) 諸佛如來遍滿其中 (trans. Kubo & Yuyama, *The Lotus Sūtra*, 262).

206 *Chu sanzang ji ji*, *T* no. 2145, 55: 8.57c2-8:
云佛壽無量, 永劫未足以明其久也；分身無數, 萬形不足以異其體也. 然則壽量定其非數, 分身明其無實, 普賢顯其無成, 多寶照其不滅. 夫邁玄古以期今, 則萬世同一日；即百化以悟玄, 則千塗無異轍. 夫如是者, 則生生未足以期存, 永寂亦未可言其滅矣.

Sengrui developed the ideas of "multiple buddhas" and the "two buddhas seated together" by pointing out that the immeasurable lifespan of a buddha could not be called long-term, since the lifespan is not fixed in number. Although the emanation bodies of Śākyamuni are innumerable, innumerable emanation bodies cannot be different from his person, since emanation bodies are not truly existent. This is existence but non-existence. Samantabhadra Bodhisattva achieved his vast practices and vows, but in actuality nothing was achieved. Prabhūtaratna Buddha might be a buddha of the past, but in reality he always abides and does not cease. This is non-existence but not non-existent.

The earliest extant commentary on the *Fahua jing*, *Fahua jing shu* 法華經疏 (Commentary on *Fahua jing*; *X* 577), by Zhu Daosheng 竺道生 (355-434), offers the following essential explanation of Prabhūtaratna Buddha's appearance the two buddhas seated together when giving commentary on the Chapter of the Vision of the Jeweled *Stūpa*:

> The reason why the *stūpa* was shown was to testify that the teachings of the *Fahua jing* were clear and correct. One testimony was done through the *stūpa*, and the other testimony was through sound. The mindset of men is not open to reason, and therefore it is unlikely to generate their belief without resorting to divine miracles. The *stūpa* emerged to express proof.
>
> That [the Abundant Treasures Buddha] spared half of his seat and sitting side-by-side [with Śākyamuni Buddha] is meant to convey the idea that in an absolute sense, the extinguished is not extinguished, nor the existent is existent. The distinction between existence and nonexistence arises only in the situation of various sorts of sentient beings, and how could it still be the case in terms of the holy beings. It is also meant to signal that [the Buddha's] *nirvāṇa* was imminent, so as to make more ardent the eagerness for his teachings.[207]

As Kumārajīva and his disciples pointed out, the present and past buddhas in the context of the "non-existence" and "not-non-existence" of *prajñā* are free and unimpeded. This is why they could together sit in the Jeweled *Stūpa* and inquire after one another while teaching the Dharma together, thereby successfully unlocking the mystery of the chapter on the Emergence of the

207 *Fahua jing shu*, XZJ no. 1661, 150:2.823b11-12, 823b14-15, 824a18-b2:
所以現塔者, 證說《法華》, 理必明當. 一以塔證, 二以所出聲證. ...... 夫人情昧理, 不能不以神奇致信, 欲因茲顯證, 故現寶塔. 分半坐, 所以分半坐共坐者, 表亡不必亡, 存不必存. 存亡之異, 出自群品, 豈聖然耶？亦示泥洹不久相也, 使企法情切矣.

Jeweled *Stūpa*. Thus, they made "Śākyamuni and Prabhūtaratna sharing the seat" into an important part of the doctrinal tradition of the Hangu Pass and the River; moreover, from the Sixteen Kingdoms period onward, image production connected to the *Fahua jing* became widespread. Therein the most important icon was that of the two buddhas seated together.

### 4.2 *The Contemplative Method of* "Lotus Samādhi" *in the* Siwei Lüeyao Fa 思惟略要法

In the year 406, after having translated the *Fahua jing* in Chang'an, Kumārajīva also transmitted a meditation manual titled *Siwei lüeyao fa* 思惟略要法 (Abridged Essence of Meditation; *T* 617). Therein the *Fahua sanmei guanfa* 法華三昧觀法 (Contemplation Method of the *Lotus Samādhi*) was based primarily upon the Vision of the Jeweled *Stūpa* chapter in the *Fahua jing*.

> Striving with all one's hearts, practicing what was dictated, and correctly reflecting on the *Fahua jing* throughout a period of twenty-one days means imagining the scenario in which Śākyamuni Buddha, on Vulture's Peak, is sitting side-by-side with Abundant Treasures Buddha inside the seven-jeweled *stūpa*, when the Buddha's transformation bodies are each present in every land of all sentient beings and each of all these buddhas has one bodhisattva in the Position of Aiding for One Life as his attendant, just as Śākyamuni Buddha has Maitreya as his attendant. [Imagine that] each of all these buddhas displays his supernatural powers, with his brilliance illuminating immeasurable lands, and then to authenticate his teachings, he shows his tongue-characteristic and has his voices fill all worlds in the ten directions. The ultimate point in teaching the *Fahua jing* is that all sentient beings in ten directions in the three times, regardless their sizes, will become buddhas as long as they utter "Homage to the Buddha" even once. This is the Single Greater Vehicle, and there is no such idea as Two Vehicles or Three Vehicles. All dharmas have only one characteristic and only one aspect; they "neither arise nor cease," absolutely empty of their own nature. There is only this Greater Vihecle and not a second variation. For those who practice such contemplation, their Five Desires will become extinct by themselves, their Five Obstructions will remove themselves, their Five Faculties will be improved, and thus they can attain meditative concentration. Dwelling in such concentration, they hold profound adoration towards the buddhas. When entering this profound, subtle, wondrous, pure Dharma of Single Characteristic and Single Aspect, one should show reverence towards Samantabhadra, Bhaiṣajyarāja, Mahāpratibhāna, Avalokiteśvara, Mahā-

> sthāmaprāpta, Mañjuśrī, and Maitreya among other great bodhisattvas, which is called "singleminded exertion, practicing as is taught, and correctly reflecting the *Fahua jing*." This is called "melding with meditative concentration," which toughens one's mind. By doing so in a period of twenty-one days, Samantabhadra Bodhisattva, on that white elephant with six tusks will come before them, just as is related in the *sūtra*.[208]

From this method we can see it is based upon the chapters of "Jeweled *Stūpa*" ("Baota pin" 寶塔品), "Springing Forth" ("Yongchu pin" 湧出品), "Expedient Means" ("Fangbian pin" 方便品) and "Encouragement of Samantabhadra" ("Puxian quanfa pin" 普賢勸發品) of the *Fahua jing*, in particular the twenty-one day practice (*sanqi ri xingfa* 三七日行法) of the latter.

The "Contemplation Method of the *Lotus Samādhi*" presents a simple method, in which one venerates the great bodhisattvas Samantabhadra, Medicine King and Avalokiteśvara for twenty-one days intently while reciting the *Fahua jing*. One then visualizes Śākyamuni and Prabhūtaratna Buddha seated together in the *Stūpa* of Seven Gems. Later this is brought together with meditative stabilization, making the mind firm. The primary feature of the contemplative method is that "all phenomena are of one characteristic and one gate, meaning they neither arise nor cease, being ultimately emptiness."[209] This is a characteristic of the contemplation of the true characteristic, i.e., that past, present and future phenomena within the true characteristic are equal. It is through practicing contemplation that one is able to witness Samantabhadra Bodhisattva riding a six-tusked white elephant appearing ahead of oneself, as explained in the Encouragement of Samantabhadra chapter, and moreover be able to do away with the five desires and five obstructions, and increase the five faculties. The foundation of the Contemplation Method of the *Lotus Samādhi* basically

208 *Siwei lüeyao fa*, *T* no. 0617, 15: 1.300b25-c13:
三七日一心精進, 如說修行, 正憶念《法華經》者, 當念釋迦牟尼佛於耆闍崛山與多寶佛在七寶塔共坐, 十方分身化佛遍滿所移眾生國土之中, 一切諸佛各有一生補處菩薩一人爲侍, 如釋迦牟尼佛以彌勒爲侍. 一切諸佛現神通力, 光明遍照無量國土, 欲證實法出其舌相, 音聲滿於十方世界. 所說《法華經》者, 所謂十方三世眾生, 若大若小, 乃至一稱南無佛者, 皆當作佛. 惟一大乘, 無二無三. 一切諸法, 一相一門, 所謂無生無滅, 畢竟空相. 唯有此大乘, 無有二也. 習如是觀者, 五欲自斷, 五蓋自除, 五根增長, 即得禪定. 住此定中, 深愛於佛. 又當入是甚深微妙一相一門清淨之法, 當恭敬普賢、藥王、大樂說、觀世音、得大勢、文殊、彌勒等大菩薩眾, 是名一心精進如說修行正憶念《法華經》也. 此謂與禪定和合, 令心堅固. 如是三七日中, 則普賢菩薩乘六牙白象, 來至其所, 如經中說.

209 *Siwei lüeyao fa*, *T* no. 0617, 15: 1.300c4-5: 一切諸法, 一相一門, 所謂無生無滅, 畢竟空相.

indicates the length of practice, means, techniques, visualization method and the features of enlightenment and merits that follow the practice.

After the "Contemplation Method of the *Lotus Samādhi*" was transmitted, the cult of the *Fahua jing* became popular in China, facilitating the development of meditation caves and production of images and moreover becoming an important practice that monks cultivated.

### 4.3 *Idea of Repentance in the* Puxian Guanjing 普賢觀經

The *Puxian guanjing* 普賢觀經 (*Sūtra* of Meditating on Samantabhadra; *T* 277) is considered the concluding *sūtra* that accompanies the *Fahua jing*, becoming one of the three scriptures upon which Tiantai Buddhism was founded. This *sūtra* explains the twenty-one-day practice in the "Chapter on the Encouragement of Bodhisattva Samantabhadra"—the final chapter of the *Fahua jing*—in greater detail. It introduces a practice of repentance level by level, the most unique part of which is progressively repenting the transgressive karma of the six faculties in order to purify them.[210]

The features of the ideas of repentance in the *Puxian guanjing* are found in the "repentance of the six faculties" (*liugen chanhui* 六根懺悔) and the "repentance of non-arising" (*wusheng chanhui* 無生懺悔). The *Puxian guanjing* states the following:

> When monks, nuns, laymen, laywomen, heavenly beings (*devas*), *nāgas*, others of the eight classes of the ever-present guardian spirits, or any living beings are internalizing the Great Vehicle *sūtras*, practicing in accordance with the Great vehicle, aspiring to a Great Vehicle consciousness, and would be pleased to see an embodiment of the bodhisattva All-embracing Goodness, take joy in seeing the *stūpa* of Abundant Treasures Buddha, be happy to see Śākyamuni Buddha as well as buddhas that emanate from him, and be glad to achieve the purification of the six sense faculties, they should learn this way of contemplation. Beneficial effects of this contemplation are the elimination of encumbrances and the perception of extraordinary and wondrous things. As a result of resolutely internalizing and keeping faith with it, and wholeheartedly pursuing mastery of it, a practitioner will become continuously conscious of the Great Vehicle without immersion into a specialized focus of mind, and he or she will gain the perception of All-embracing Goodness within the course of one to three-times-seven days.[211]

---

210 Shi Shengyan, "Xiuxing fangfa," 8.

211 *Foshuo guan Puxian pusa xingfa jing*, *T* no. 277, 9: 1.389c17-24:
若比丘、比丘尼、優婆塞、優婆夷，天龍八部，一切眾生，誦大乘經者，修大乘

FIGURE 10 The mural featuring Mañjuśrī and Vimalakīrti lecturing in the Gong county 鞏縣 grotto complex, dated to the Northern Wei (386-534).

Comparing the aim of the meditation presented in the *Puxian guanjing* and the "Chapter on the Encouragement of Bodhisattva Samantabhadra" from the *Fahua jing*, it is clear that it emphasizes the "purity of the six faculties" in addition to both texts' emphasis on the merit of recitation. The *Puxian guanjing* has a great deal of explanation concerning the "repentance of the six faculties" and later was cited in the *Fahua sanmei chanyi*.[212]

The greatest influence of the *Puxian guanjing* on later ideas concerning repentance is found in the "repentance of non-arising" and "proper contemplation of the true characteristic" (*shixiang zhengguan* 實相正觀). The *sūtra* states the following:

> Contemplate the nonexistence of what is grasped as mind! Conceptualizations arise based on error that is mistaken for truth; in this way delusion gives rise to the concept of mind. In the same manner that wind has no foundation in the air, aspects of phenomena are without origination or cessation. What is guilt? What is bliss? As one's mind—by nature—is emptiness, guilt and bliss have no owner. All phenomena are the same as this—they neither abide or decay. Amend yourself in this way: Contemplate the nonexistence of what is grasped as mind! A phenomenon does not stay fixed in itself. All phenomena conform to literation, to the truth of the extinguishment of suffering, and to complete tranquility. Grasping things in this way is described as ultimate self-amendment; it is described as fully composing self-amendment; it is described as self-amendment free from aspects of guilt; it is described as destroying the distinction of mind. Those who practice this self-amendment will be as flowing water: pure and clean in body and mind, not staying fixed in themselves. They will be able to discern All-embracing Goodness Bodhisattva, and the buddhas of the ten directions as well, in any moment of concentration.[213]

---

者, 發大乘意者, 樂見普賢菩薩色身者, 樂見多寶佛塔者, 樂見釋迦牟尼佛及分身諸佛者, 樂得六根清淨者, 當學是觀. 此觀功德除諸障礙, 見上妙色, 不入三昧, 但誦持故, 專心修習, 心心相次, 不離大乘, 一日至三七日, 得見普賢. (trans. Kubo, Logan, Abbott, Ichishima, & Chappell, *Tiantai Lotus texts*, 52; with slight modifications)

212 *Fahua sanmei chanyi*, *T* no. 1941, 46: 1.952b4-5:
下所說懺悔章句, 多用普賢觀經意, 若欲廣知懺悔方法, 讀經自見；若不能廣尋, 今取意略說以成行法.
Shi (*Tiantai chanfa zhi yanjiu*, 113-16) has put the sentences from the two texts into tables to make a comparison.

213 *Foshuo guan Puxian pusa xingfa jing*, *T* no. 0277, 9: 1.392c24-393a3:
觀心無心, 從顛倒想起. 如此想心, 從妄想起, 如空中風, 無依止處. 如是法相, 不生不滅, 何者是罪？何者是福？我心自空, 罪福無主. 一切法如是, 無住無壞. 如

The ideas of "contemplating mind and no-mind" (*guanxin wuxin* 觀心無心) and "transgression and merit unowned" (*zuifu wuzhu* 罪福無主) are expressed through a contemplation of principle directed at dharmas, in which one contemplates the quality of transgressions as fundamentally empty and thereby achieves the aim of purity via repentance of transgression. This is explained in the *sūtra* as follows: "If someone should want to practice repentance, then sit up straight and consider the true characteristic: that transgressions are like frost and dew. The sun of wisdom can dissipate them."[214]

Tiantai Buddhism took a deep interest in the concepts described above in the *Puxian guanjing*. They became an important conceptual basis for the production of repentance rites later on.[215]

### 4.4 *The Popularity of the Cult of the* Fahua Jing

After Kumārajīva translated *Fahua jing* and transmitted the Contemplation Method of the *Lotus Samādhi*, various types of cults arose with the *Fahua jing* at their core, which was promoted by its cult of *stūpa*s and the merit-making activities associated with *sūtra* worship.

Sheng Yen 聖嚴 (1931-2009) synthesized practice methods connected to the *Fahua jing* and pointed out that what was most adopted was reception and recitation followed by interpretation and explanation to others. With respect to the practice of meditative *samādhi*, very few people practiced it. The numbers of practitioners based upon those given in the *Hongzan Fahua zhuan* 弘贊法華傳 (Chronicle of the Spread of the *Lotus*; *T* 2067) by Huixiang 慧祥 (d.u.) and the *Fahua chuanji* 法華傳記 (*Lotus* Chronicle; *T* 2068) by Sengxiang 僧祥 (d.u.) in the Tang Dynasty are listed as follows:[216]

---

是懺悔, 觀心無心, 法不住法中, 諸法解脫, 滅諦寂靜. 如是想者, 名大懺悔, 名莊嚴懺悔, 名無罪相懺悔, 名破壞心識. 行此懺悔者, 身心清淨不住法中, 猶如流水, 念念之中, 得見普賢菩薩及十方佛. (Trans. Kubo, Logan, Abbott, Ichishima, & Chappell, *Tiantai Lotus texts*, 69-70)

214 *Foshuo guan Puxian pusa xingfa jing*, *T* no. 0277, 9:1.393b11-12: 若欲懺悔者, 端坐念實相, 衆罪如霜露, 慧日能消除.

215 Yūki, "Chigi," 360-63.

216 Shi Shengyan, "Xiuxing fangfa," 9. Sakamoto Yukio has written an article "Chūgoku bukkyō to Hokke shisō no renkan" by using biographical sources. He lists those who worshiped the *Lotus Sūtra* in *Gaoseng zhuan* (*T* no. 2059), *Xu Gaoseng zhuan* (*T* no. 2060), *Song Gaoseng zhuan* (*T* no. 2061), *Da Ming Gaoseng zhuan* (*T* no. 2062). See Sakamoto, "Hokke shisō," 489-548.

| Practices 行門 | *Hongzan Fahua zhuan* | *Fahua zhuanji* |
|---|---|---|
| Translation 翻譯 | 14 | |
| Expounding 講解 | 45 | 19 |
| Meditative Contemplation 修禪觀 | 3 | |
| Self-immolation 捨身/遺身 | 12 | |
| Chanting from Memory 持誦 | 108 | 90 |
| Selective Recitation 轉讀 | 12 | 16 |
| Hand-Copying Scriptures 書寫 | 12 | 34 |
| Hearing the Dharma 聽聞 | | 22 |
| Making Offerings 供養 | | 17 |
| Total | 206 | 198 |

According to the numbers given in the two historical documents from the Tang Dynasty, there were only 3 out of 404 people who practiced the meditative contemplation. There were comparatively more people who recited and read the *Fahua jing*, altogether comprising 226 people. In addition, there are practices such as reading, copying, and self-immolation, which people have carried out throughout history.

The records of historical documents, however, are ultimately limited. Excavation of caves, images, copied scriptures and their inscriptions constitute an important basis for researching the cult of the *Fahua jing*. After Kumārajīva translated *Fahua jing*, it was quickly spread throughout the north and exercised an important influence on the development of Buddhism there.[217] As the cult of the *Fahua jing* flourished during the Northern and Southern Dynasties period, the number of people who practiced the *Lotus Samādhi* increased. This practice involves visualizing the two buddhas Śākyamuni and Prabhūtaratna seated together. At the same time, the merit of image production also cannot be overlooked, since this encouraged the increased production of images of the buddhas Śākyamuni and Prabhūtaratna seated together. Maitreya included among these formed the group of the buddhas of the three times, which became widely popular in cave images during the Northern and Southern Dynasties.[218]

217 Jia, "Gaochang Fojiao," 146-58.

218 Hou Xudong has studied the production of the images of the Prabhūtaratna Buddha from 400 to 580. He points out that the production and worship of the Prabhūtaratna Buddha's images went through a long process: developing from nothing (400-479); increasing (480-489); declining (489-569). The production and worship of the Prabhūtaratna Buddha's images exerted the greatest and longest influence on the masses, less on the monastics,

FIGURE 11 *Bhikṣu*-sponsors in Shuiyu Monastery 水浴寺 grotto complex, dated to the Northern Wei (386-534).

The earliest images of Śākyamuni and Prabhūtaratna date to 410, when Li Pu 李普 (d.u.) cast a small bronze image four and a half inches tall. On the front are the two buddhas seated together, while on the back is the following dedicative inscription: "Day eleven of the ninth lunar month in the second year of Taiping era. Li Pu produced one image as an offering on behalf of his parents."[219] The earliest statues that were inscribed with the names of Śākyamuni and Prabhūtaratna is seen in Cave 169 of Bingling si 炳靈寺. This cave includes a dedicative inscription for an image produced in the year 420. Shrine 11 includes a painting of a shrine in the same of a *stūpa*, within which are painted two buddhas seated with feet resting on the ground. On the right side beside the buddha is an ink inscription that reads "Śākyamuni Buddha" 釋迦牟尼佛 while on the left side beside the buddha is an ink inscription that reads "Prabhūtaratna ..." 多寶佛 [ ][ ].[220] Shrine 13 also includes a painting of Śākyamuni and Prabhūtaratna seated together as well as an ink inscription.[221] In addition, Shrines 12 and 24 each have a set of one thousand buddhas, which include "Prabhūtaratna and Śākyamuni Seated Together."[222]

Cave 126 of Bingling si on the west wall has an image and Śākyamuni and Prabhūtaratna seated together, to the left and right of which each have a bodhisattva attendant. Above the outer doorway into this cave is a dedicative inscription by Cao Ziyuan 曹子元 (d.u.) from August 2, 513 (Yanchang 延昌 2.6.15).[223] Caves 132 and 128 of Bingling si (Northern Wei) are identical to Cave 126 in cave structure. Both have two accompanying bodhsiattvas alongside Śākyamuni and Prabhūtaratna seated together.[224] Cave 144 of Bingling si (Northern Wei) on the western wall has two accompanying bodhsiattvas alongside Śākyamuni and Prabhūtaratna seated together.[225] Cave 1 of the Gongxian caves 鞏縣石窟 along the bottom part of the eastern wall has four shrines. The first shrine from the south has two accompanying bodhisattvas alongside Śākyamuni and Prabhūtaratna seated together.[226] Cave 10 of Mount Tianlong 天龍山 (Northern Qi) is flat and square in shape, the primary chamber having three shrines along three walls. The shrine in the northern wall includes

and the least on officials. Images with donors' names are mostly seen in Hebei, Henan, Shandong and Shanxi. Cf. Hou, *Fojiao xinyang*, 118-20.

219 Ōmura, *Chūgoku bijitsushi chōso hen*, 174: 太平二年九月十一日李普爲父母造像一軀供養 (cited from He, "Fahua jingbian," 129).

220 Zhang, "Shiku", 188.

221 Ibid. For a study of the Cave 169 of Bingling-si, see Lai, "169 ku," 82; Du, "Shulun," 207-26.

222 Lai, "Qianfo sixiang', 250.

223 He, "Wenti," 12.

224 Ibid., 12-13.

225 Ibid., 13.

226 Ibid., 13.

Śākyamuni and Prabhūtaratna seated together.[227] In addition, in the early-period caves of Yungang, there are images of Śākyamuni and Prabhūtaratna seated together. According to the statistics tallied by He Shizhe 賀世哲, the five caves of Tanyao 曇曜 (?-463+) alone include as many as 120. In the cave of Longmen 龍門, there also appear a number of images of Prabhūtaratna.[228] In the Mogao caves of Dunhuang from the Northern Dynasties, there are four extant images of Śākyamuni and Prabhūtaratna seated together. Inside one is a painted clay model from the Northern Wei, found in the shrine of of *stūpa*-pillar at the western wall in cave 259. There are two wall murals from the Western Wei painted on the southern wall of cave 285 and the western wall of cave 461. One specimen from the Northern Zhou was painted on the western wall of cave 428. Cave 8 of the Western Thousand-Buddhas Cave 西千佛洞 also has an image of Śākyamuni and Prabhūtaratna seated together painted on the northern wall.[229] From the Sui Dynasty onward, there started appearing illustrations of the *Fahua jing* painted on murals at Dunhuang. These appeared in each time period until the time of the Guiyi Army 歸義軍.[230]

The appearance of these images of Śākyamuni and Prabhūtaratna seated together on one hand were required for the cultivations of the *Lotus Samādhi*. This was primarily limited to the level of monks and nuns, especially in the case of caves drilled out for meditation. The caves and images, however, were to a large extent aimed at generating merit and worldly benefits. For instance, the inscription of cave 17 at Yungang 雲岡 reads:

> On the nineteenth day of the ninth month, which was the first day of the moon, in the twelfth year of the Taihe era of the Great Dai dynasty (the Northern Wei) (489), a year of Ji-Si in the sexagenary cycle, the nun Huiding, suffering from a critical illness, made a vow to sponsor the three Buddha statues of Śākyamuni, Abundant Treasures, and Maitreya, hoping that the illness would be eliminated, and that her person would be safe and secure in this life, that her observation of Buddhist precepts would bring about blessings and benefits, and that her spiritual aspiration would grow with each passing day. She swore never to retreat. She hoped that the Dharma merit [she earned] from making these statues could extend to her parents of the past seven lives, and she invited Buddhist teachers of a multitude of past kalpas and boundless sentient beings to

227 Ibid.

228 Sakawa, "Chūgoku no sekkutsu," 293.

229 He, "Fahua jingbian," 129-30.

230 For illustrations of the *Lotus Sūtra*, see He, "Fahua jingbian," 127-217; Nomura, "Hokke sangyōshi," 97-128.

> join her in celebrating [the erection of the statues]. May my hopes become reality from the merit I have accumulated from producing an image.[231]

The above inscription fully emphasizes the meritorious act of producing an image. This is akin to saying, "This sort of veneration of images is not important to any buddha."[232] Regardless, it is through the karmic results of merit that faith in the Buddhadharma is expressed.

As the cult of the *Fahua jing* spread throughout medieval Chinese society, there appeared groups centered on this cult, i.e., "Lotus Dharma Societies." For instance, the buddha-niche on the front of a stele with the title "Lishi heyi zaoxiang bei" 李氏合邑造像碑 (Li Collective's Construction of an Image) has an inscription that reads, "Rector and donor of the Great Image's Stele Li Xianzu, the donor who sponsored an eye-opening ceremony for the two buddhas, Retainer of the Luozhou prefecture Li [lacuna]…."[233] The fifth line of the fourth column on the left side of the stele has a title reading "Head of the *Fahua jing* Lian Jingsong" 法華經主連景嵩. The front of the stele has an inscription and stele text approximating six-hundred characters, all of which incorporate ideas from the *Fahua jing*. In particular, the fourth line reads, "Revealing the Three Vehicles is [done] out of the thought to offer a ladder for those of the Small Vehicle, and expounding the One Vehicle is the principle to guide those of the Great Vehicle… "[234] And this stresses the theme of "Revealing and Uniting," namely "revealing the Three Vehicles and highlighting the One Vehicle." The inscription mentioned above shows that Li[lacuna] was the sponsor of eye-opening ceremony for the two buddhas. The "two buddhas seated together" is a particular type of image that was transmitted from the *Fahua jing*.[235]

The Li Family society's organizational roles included one Temple Head (*sizhu* 寺主), Head of the Lecture Hall (*jiangtang zhu* 講堂主), two Heads of the Heavenly Palace (*tiangong zhu* 天宮主), one Head of Offerings (*gongyang zhu* 供養主), one Head of Procession (*xingdao zhu* 行道主), one Head of the Shrine Hall (*daochang zhu* 道場主), one Head of Purity (*qingjing zhu* 清淨主), and one Head of the Circumambulatory Procession Around the Image (*xingdao simian xiangzhu* 行道四面像主).

---

231 Mizuno & Nagahiro, "Unkō kinsekiroku," 16:
大代太和十二年（ 489 年）, 歲在己巳, 九月壬寅朔十九日庚申, 比丘尼惠定, 身遇重患, 發願造釋迦、多寶、彌勒像三區. 願患消除, 願現世安穩, 戒行福利, 道心日增, 誓不退轉. 以此造像功德, 逮及七世父母, 累劫諸師, 無邊眾生, 咸同斯慶.

232 Satō, "Hokuchō zōzō," 86.

233 Yan, "Fahua yiyi," 171: 都唯那大像碑主李顯族、開二佛光明主洛州從事李口.

234 Ibid: 171-72: 開三爲級小之心, 演一爲接大之則.

235 Ibid: 167-84. See also Yan, "Gongtongti," 233-47.

FIGURE 12 Pagoda of four buddhas with colored stone carvings, dated to the Northern Qi Dynasty (550-557) (The Metropolitan Museum of Art, the United States).

Yan Shangwen pointed out that according to these roles, the Li Family *Lotus* Society was organized likely to carry out sacred tasks such as offerings, preces- sions and purifications in temples, lecture halls and shrine halls.[236] Zhiyi's *Fa- hua sanmei chanyi* is a practical method adapted from the *Fahua jing*, which

236 Yan, "Fahua yiyi," 180.

includes activities such as purification of the shrine hall, precession and recitation of *sūtras*. It is clear that these societies' organization and activities had a deep relationship to the Tiantai traditions that formed later.[237]

The cult of the *Fahua jing* has at its core the cult of buddha-*stūpas* and worship of physical *sūtras*, which is why, in addition to the *Lotus Samādhi* and image production, there are also other elements such as copying *sūtras* and reading/recitation. There are a great number of copies of the *Fahua jing* among the Dunhuang manuscripts, which offer us examples to explore *sūtra* worship as it existed in the cult of the *Fahua jing*. Among the Dunhuang manuscripts, there are all three extant versions of the *Fahua jing*, that of Kumārajīva being the most numerous. The National Library in Beijing holds over 2,000 copies of Kumārajīva's version of the *Fahua jing*. There are also more in England, France, Russia and Japan, totaling around over 5,000.[238]

These many manuscripts include a number of colophons, such as that of fascicle four stored in the Taitō City Calligraphy Museum (Taitō Kuritzu Shodō Hakubutsukan 台東区立書道博物館):

> On the twenty-fifth day of the first month, which was the first day of the month, in the first year [of the reign of Emperor Feidi 廢帝 of the Western Wei], a year of *renshen* in the sexagenary cycle (552), I, your disciple Xin Xingsheng 辛興升 (otherwise unknown), pay homage to all those of the Three Jewels who are constantly abiding in the Three Times. Your disciple Xingsheng thinks to themselves that my conduct prior to this time was impure, and that I am merely of the class of those possessing consciousness. I receive a physical form that is as miserably inferior as the dirt following the tail of the wind. Hopelessly dull, I have been led astray by worldly concerns, and blinded by ignorance, I dived into the flow that leads to endless rebirths. To my humble knowledge, the *sūtra* says that the subtle observation of the great Awakened One, veneration of the Greater Vihecle begets infinite dharmic rewards. For this reason, I, you disciple Xingsheng, was sent by the [Tang] state as an envoy to Turkic area (Tugui [=Tujue] 突貴 [= 突厥],[239] and my children have remained in the east (i.e. the hinterland of China). Thus, called by the concern of my own person but for the sake of my parents, wives, children, and kin of my past seven lives, I spared portion of my subsistence sources to copy by hand the *sūtras* of the *Fahua jing*, the *Wuliangshou* [*jing*] 無量壽 [經]

237 Ibid.

238 Fang, "Dunhuang yishu," 211-32.

239 厥 interchangeable with 貴 due to their phonetical identity.

> (*Sūtra* of the Immeasurable Life), the *Yaoshi* [*jing*] 藥師 [經] (Medicine Master *Sūtra*), and the *Hu shenming jing* 護身命經 (*Sūtra* of Protecting One's Life). I hope that through the merit of my wish to embrace [these *sūtras*] and such a shred of goodness, your disciple I could rise above the mortal coil of the herd and my physical form could ascend to the [real] of Non-Obstruction, and that I could be reborn into the palace of Tuṣita Heaven and rise to the Ten Abodes. I would possess unimpeded eloquence, like Śāriputra; and I would wield unfathomable magical power, like Vimalakīrti. I would be able to practice as Mañjuśrī does and attain the Way and become a Buddha. Again, I your disciple, hope to reunite with my children. May [the Buddha's grace] extend to my families, brothers, friends, nephews and nieces, and cousins. May the children of me, your disciple Xingsheng, be reborn in the time of a buddha and hear the Dharma. May all sentient beings share the divine response.[240]

The aim of copying *sūtras* is required in Buddhism, being a part of attaining the path to awakening. It is, however, more expressive of the actual hopes of laypeople, such as the people's reunion with their children. Such worldly aims are hoped to be achieved through the power of faith.

The *Fahua jing* emphasizes the meritorious acts of worship, recitation and copying of the *sūtra* as well as explaining it to others. These are all part of a uniform goal, in that after having gotten ahold of the *sūtra*, one should worship it and thereafter constantly recite it. When reciting, one should understand the meaning of the *sūtra*. After comprehending the meaning of the *sūtra* clearly, one should teach it widely to others. At the same time, in order to circulate the scripture among the people, copying by hand was the sole and most elegant way of transmitting texts in a time before printing technology had been invented, which is why people are encouraged to personally copy or get others to do so, since both bring about immeasurable merit.

Thus, after Kumārajīva translated *Fahua jing*, there appeared spiritual practices founded upon *Fahua jing*, such as translation, teaching, meditation,

240 Fang, "Dunhuang yishu," 218:
元年（ = 西魏元年 [552] ）歲次壬申正月庚午朔二十五日甲午成, 弟子辛興升南無一切三世常住三寶, 弟子興升自惟宿行不純, 等類有識, 稟受風末塵穢之形, 重昏迷俗, 沈溺有流, 無明所蓋. 竊聞經云：大覺玄監, 信敬大乘, 果報無極. 以是弟子興升, 國遣使向突貴, 兒女在東, 即率單情. 咸（ = 減？）割身分之餘, 爲七世父母、妻子親眷, 敬寫《法華經》一部、《無量壽》一部、《藥師》一部、《護身命經》一部, 願持之功, 一豪之善, 使弟子超纏群俗, 形升無礙. 托生紫宮, 登階十住. 辯才無滯 [如] 舍利弗, 不思議力如維摩詰, 行如文殊, 得道成佛. 又願弟子, 兒女相見, 現家眷、兄弟、知識、子侄、中表, 普及弟子興升兒女得還家. 慶會值佛聞法, 含生等同斯契.

self-immolation, recitation, reading, copying, hearing and ritual offerings, with a cult centered on buddha-*stūpa* worship and worship of physical *sūtras*. In order to facilitate practice of the "*Lotus samādhi*" and accumulation of merit, there appeared things such as construction of caves and the production of images of Śākyamuni and Prabhūtaratna seated together. At the same time, there formed "*Lotus* Societies" with the *Fahua jing* at their core, engaged in relevant Buddhist activities and social philanthropy.

### 4.5 *Huisi's* Fahua Jing Anlexing Yi 法華經安樂行義

The cult of the *Fahua jing* can be divided into a kind of "upward advancement" and "downward permeation." The former is expressed as comprehension of scriptural doctrines and the implementation of meditative practices. After Kumārajīva translated the *Fahua jing*, one of his disciples named Daosheng 道生 (355-434) produced a *Fahua jing shu* 法華經疏 (Commentary on the *Lotus Sūtra*). Later there were continually people who offered their exegeses of it. There were not, however, many works that specifically explained the meditative practice of the *Fahua jing*. The one that was the most influential was Huisi's *Fahua jing anlexing yi* 法華經安樂行義 (Exegesis on the 'Blissful Practice' Section of the *Lotus Sūtra*). When Huisi ordained in his early years, he "recited the *Fahua jing* and those [scriptures] of the Mahāyāna, being diligent in his practice of austerities."[241] Huisi's biography in the *Xu Gaoseng zhuan* records that after Huisi received full monastic precepts he continually sat and and thoroughly engaged in his practices. Everyday he would "recite more than thirty fascicles of *sūtras* such as the *Fahua jing*, doing this thousands of times for several years."[242] Later, he had a meaningful dream and as a result, his diligence and engagement became ever more intense, and his exacting practice of mindfulness became especially devoted. He continued through the day and night without stopping.[243] Seated meditation and recitation of the *Fahua jing* became a daily practice for him. After meeting and being influenced by Huiwen 慧文 (fl. 479-493), a meditation master, "By nature he delighted in hardship, managing the monks as his task. Winter and summer he made offerings. He had no aversion to hard labor. Day and night he remained focused and resolved to penetrate the principle and phenomena."[244] Later, as he was relaxing his body toward the wall, just as his body was about to meet the wall, "He sud-

241 *Nanyue Si da chanshi lishi yuanwen*, *T* no. 1933, 46: 1.787a7-8: 誦《法華經》及諸大乘, 精進苦行.

242 *Xu Gaoseng zhuan*, *T* no. 2060, 50: 17.562c11-13: 誦《法華》等經三十餘卷, 數年之間, 千遍便滿.

243 Ibid., 17.562c19-20: 勤務更深, 克念翹專, 無棄昏曉.

244 Ibid., 562c29-563a1: 性樂苦節, 營僧爲業, 冬夏供養, 不憚勞苦, 晝夜攝心, 理事籌度.

denly became awakened in one mind-moment to the Lotus *Samādhi* and Dharma Gate of the Mahāyāna. With the sixteen superior forms of meditation he abandoned the world, the aggregates and the sense-fields, understanding on his own [these things], not being awakened by another."[245]

Prior to his experience of awakening, Huisi had practiced many forms of meditation, such as the four meditations (*si jinglü* 四靜慮), four formless concentrations (*si kongding* 四空定), sixteen superior forms of meditation (*shiliu tesheng* 十六特勝), and eight abandonments (*ba beishe* 八背捨), but later he was able to "expound, laud, cite, and explain by metaphor the meanings of practices of concentration and insight meditation in both the Mahāyāna and Hīnayāna for himself and others."[246] He became a great meditation master admired by Daoxuan.[247] His meditative practices uniquely flourished in the Jiangnan region.[248] Before passing away, he addressed his disciples and stated:

> If there are ten persons who would give up their lives in the course of regular practices of various *samādhi*s such as *Lotus* [*samādhi*], *Pratyutpanna* [*samādhi*], and *samādhi* of Mindfulness of the Buddha, the *Mahāvaipulya* Repentance, and seated asceticism, I would not spare myself to provide them with whatever they need. If there are no such persons, I will leave the world.[249]

The *Xu Gaoseng zhuan* lists various activities, such as those related to the *Lotus samādhi*, *Pratyutpanna samādhi*, and *samādhi* of Mindfulness of the Buddha, *samādhi* of continuous sitting and the *Mahāvaipulya* Repentance, which constituted the primary components of Huisi's meditative practice. Later they became the "four types of *samādhi* (*sizhong sanmei* 四種三昧) in Zhiyi's *Mohe zhiguan* 摩訶止觀 (The Great Calming and Contemplation).[250]

The Buddhist *sūtra*s upon which Huisi's thought was based were primarily the *Dapin bore jing* 大品般若經 (*Mahāprajñāpāramitā-sūtra*) and *Fahua jing*. He saw the former as the doctrine of gradualism and the latter as complete and

245 Ibid., 17.563a11-13: 霍爾開悟, 法華三昧, 大乘法門, 一念明達. 十六特勝, 背捨陰入, 便自通徹, 不由他悟.

246 Ibid., 17.563a16-17: 以大小乘中定慧等法, 敷揚引喻, 用攝自他.

247 Ibid., 20. 597b21: 思遠振於清風.

248 Jan, "Zaoqi chanfa," 63-99.

249 *Xu Gaoseng zhuan*, *T* no. 2060, 50: 17.563c19-21:
若有十人, 不惜身命, 常修法華、般舟、念佛三昧、方等懺悔、常坐苦行者, 隨有所須, 吾自供給, 必相利益. 如無此人, 吾當遠去.

250 Muranaka Yūshō maintains that inferred from the names of *samādhi* in the biography of Huisi, it is of greater possibility that there were several forms of practice, but Zhiyi just summarized them as four types (see Muranaka, "Shugyōhō no keisei," 42).

subtism in meaning. This is why in terms of practical implementation, the *Sui ziyi sanmei* 隨自意三昧 (*Samādhi* of Following One's Own Thoughts) and *Zhufa wuzheng sanmei famen* 諸法無諍三昧法門 (Dharma-Gate of the Samādhi Wherein All Dharmas are Without Dispute) have implementation of the contemplation of emptiness via *prajñā* at their core, whereas the *Fahua jing anlexing yi* explains a practical path connected to the *Fahua jing*.[251]

The *Fahua jing anlexing yi* is a summary compilation of his experiences after having attained the *Lotus Samādhi* through practice of austerities. The opening lines read as follows:

> *The Fahua jing* is what suddenly awakes one to the teachings of the Greater Vehicle. Enabling one to enlighten without the help of a teacher and attain buddhahood swiftly, this is the hardest to believe among all dharma-gates in the world. For all elementary bodhisattvas who seek the teachings of the Greater Vehicle, aspire to surpass all bodhisattvas, and swiftly attain buddhahood must abide by precepts, develop tolerance, exert themselves, practice diligently meditation, and attentively and diligently study the *Lotus samādhi*.[252]

In the *Fahua jing anlexing yi* Huisi explains that practice should be like the contemplation of all beings akin to buddhas as in the "Changbuqing pusa pin" 常不輕菩薩品 (Chapter on Sadāparibhūta Bodhisattva) in the *Fahua jing*, and that we should cultivate meditative concentration as in the "Anle xing pin" 安樂行品 (Chapter of the Means to Attaining Peace). In actuality, he obtained the image of being "without master and self-awakening" (無師自悟) through practicing the *Fahua jing*. He achieved the *Lotus samādhi* via the *Fahua jing*. This is why all practitioners seeking to cultivate the Mahāyāna and quickly achieve the path to buddhahood the path to buddhahood should also cultivate the *Lotus samādhi* with the *Fahua jing* at the core of their practice.

The *Fahua jing anlexing yi* gives a primary outline of the method for the *Lotus samādhi* as follows:

---

251 Satō, *Zoku Tendai daishi no kenkyū*, 284. Chronologically, the three texts, *Sui ziyi sanmei*, *Zhufa wuzheng sanmei famen*, and *Exegesis on the 'Blissful Practice' Section of the Lotus Sūtra* were written in sequence; see Satō, *Zoku Tendai daishi no kenkyū*, 267-68.

252 *Fahua jing anlexing yi*, *T* no. 1926, 46: 1.697c19-22:
《法華經》者, 大乘頓覺, 無師自悟, 疾成佛道, 一切世間, 難信法門. 凡是一切新學菩薩, 欲求大乘, 超過一切諸菩薩, 疾成佛道, 須持戒、忍辱、精進, 勤修禪定, 專心勤學法華三昧.

> Those who aspire to the Unexcelled Way should learn and practice The *Fahua jing*, having the body and mind attain the wondrous teachings of nectar and purity. Observing the precepts, practicing tolerance, and exercising various kinds of meditative concentration leads to the achievement of the *samādhi*s of various buddhas and purifies the six senses. A bodhisattva learns the *Fahua jing* and perfects two kinds of practice: one is Practice without Characteristics, and the other Practice with Characteristics.[253]

Huisi believed that the *Fahua jing* was a method of practice for bodhisattvas with sharp capacities, its features including "sudden awakening" and "rapid attainment of the path to Buddhahood" (*jicheng Fodao* 疾成佛道). The foundation for practice was the original purity of the six faculties of beings. Practice was merely to return to the "original purity." The *Fahua jing anlexing yi* continually stresses this point. The theory is that of the pure mind of the *tathāgatagarbha*:

> With the markless four means of attaining peace and profound meditative concentration, one observes the six faculties; dharmas are originally pure, beings by nature are without defilement. [With] no basis and also no purity, and no cultivation of rectifying practices, you naturally transcend all sages. Naturally awoken without teacher, you do not follow sequential practice. Your understanding is identical to that of the buddhas, having awoken to profound stillness.[254]

Moreover, when interpreting the title of the *sūtra*, Huisi interpreted *miao* 妙 (profound) as "beings profound" and *fa* 法 (Dharma) as "beings' Dharma," while *zhongshengmiao* 眾生妙 (beings profound) meaning "the six wondrous marks of every human's physical form"[255] and "the pure nature of the 'Six Sovereignty Ruler'".[256] This is founded upon the idea of "the six faculties originally being pure" as in *Tathāgatagarbha* and *Ekayāna*. Finally, one is to reach "one's

253 Ibid., 698a16-21:
欲求無上道, 修學《法華經》, 身心證甘露, 清淨妙法門. 持戒行忍辱, 修習諸禪定, 得諸佛三昧, 六根性清淨. 菩薩學《法華》, 具足二種行, 一者無相行, 二者有相行.

254 Ibid., 698a22-27:
無相四安樂, 甚深妙禪定, 觀察六情根, 諸法本來淨, 眾生性無垢. 無本亦無淨, 不修對治行, 自然超眾聖. 無師自然覺, 不由次第行, 解與諸佛同, 妙覺湛然性.

255 Ibid., 698c19: 一切人身六種相妙.

256 Ibid., 698c19: 六自在王性清淨.

body being the body of beings, and the bodies of beings being the body of the Tathāgata."[257]

Returning to this "original purity," however, requires practicing the "four means of attaining peace." The first is the "means to attaining peace that is freedom from attachments via true wisdom."[258] The second is the "means to attaining peace that is not lightly praising and disparaging"[259] (also called the "means to attaining peace that is turning the *śrāvakas* to attain the wisdom of the Buddha."[260] The third is the "means to attaining peace that is being equanimous without afflictions"[261] (also called the "means to attaining peace that is respect for virtuous friends."[262] The fourth is the "means to attaining peace that is guiding others with compassion"[263] (also called the "means to attaining peace that is attaining supernormal powers, wisdom, the path to buddhahood and *nirvāṇa* in a dream."[264] The "Four Means of Attaining Peace" appears in the *Fahua jing*. Huisi on the basis of the Chapter of the Means to Attaining Peace explained the "Markless Four Means of Attaining Peace":

> Practice without Characteristics is Practice of Peace; without any dharma present, the functional aspects of the mind remain extinct and of absolute non-arising, and thus it is named "practice without characteristics." Once one can constantly remain in the profound and wondrous meditative concentration, he/she would be in accord with awe-inspiring etiquettes whether walking, standing, sitting, lying down, drinking, dining, or speaking, because his/her mind is constantly concentrated. [...] The profound and wonderous meditative concentration, in the case of Practice of Peace, is different. Why so? It is not based on the Realm of Desire, nor on the Realms of Form or the Formless Realms. Practicing such a type of meditation is the Absolute Non-Thought practice by a bodhisattva, and therefore it is called the Practice of Non-Thought.[265]

---

257 Ibid., 699b3: 人身即是眾生身, 眾生身即是如來身.

258 Ibid., 700a13-14: 正慧離著安樂行.

259 Ibid., 700a14: 無輕讚毀安樂行.

260 Ibid., 700a14-15: 轉諸聲聞令得佛智安樂行.

261 Ibid., 700a15-16: 無惱平等安樂行.

262 Ibid., 700a16: 敬善知識安樂行.

263 Ibid., 700a16-17: 慈悲接引安樂行.

264 Ibid., 700a17-18: 夢中具足成就神通智慧佛道涅槃安樂行.

265 Ibid., 700a19-29:
無相行者, 即是安樂行. 一切諸法中, 心相寂滅, 畢竟不生, 故名爲無相行也. 常在一切深妙禪定, 行住坐臥飲食語言一切威儀, 心常定故. …… 安樂行中, 深妙禪定即不如此. 何以故? 不依止欲界, 不住色無色, 行如是禪定. 是菩薩遍行畢竟無心想, 故名無想 (= 相) 行.

On the basis of the ideas explained in the Chapter of the Means to Attaining Peace,[266] Huisi applied the doctrine of emptiness realized via *prajñā* as it is expressed in the idea of the "true characteristic of dharmas" in meditative contemplation. Freedom from all attachments toward all dharmas in the three realms is achieved as a result of realizing the emptiness of all dharmas, whereby one is unmoved by all dharmas connected to sensation, thus in all ritual gravitas and decorum, the mind perpetually abides in the state of meditative concentration. Huisi explained the concrete details of the "markless practice" or "practice without characteristic" (*wuxiang xing* 無相行) with reference to the three kinds of tolerance (*sanren* 三忍), meaning "tolerance toward all beings" (*zhongsheng ren* 眾生忍), "tolerance toward dharma-nature" (*faxing ren* 法性忍) and "tolerance of supernormal powers in the sea of the dharma-dhātu" (*fajie hai shentong ren* 法界海神通忍).

On the basis of the Chapter on the Encouragement of Bodhisattva Samantabhadra in the *Fahua jing*, Huisi established "practice with characteristics," and in contrast to the "practice without characteristics" that is focused solely on meditative concentration, it emphasizes reading and reciting the *Fahua jing* with the ordinary mind:

> As for the Practice with Characteristics, it refers to what is described in the chapter of "Encouragement of Bodhisattva Samantabhadra" as exerting oneself via the ordinary mind when reciting the *Fahua jing*. Such practitioners do not practice meditative concentration nor enter *samādhi*; whether sitting, standing, or walking, they are always single-mindedly reciting the words of the *Fahua jing*, vigorously progressing and never lying down to rest, as if they were in course of saving their burning heads. This is named the Practice with Characteristics of Letters. Such practitioners do not spare their own lives [in the practice], and when gaining success, one will see the physical body of Samantabhadra, riding on a six-tusked white elephant coming before his/her person. [Then the bodhisattva] points at the eyes of the practitioner with a Vajra, eradicating the transgression that impedes his/her's approach to the Way. The faculty of sight purified, he/she is able to see Śākyamuni and the Seven Past Buddhas. Also one can see various buddhas of the ten directions of the three times. [The practitioner] should repent with total sincerity: he/she throws five parts of the body to the ground before the buddhas and

266 *Miaofa lianhua jing*, *T* no. 262, 9: 5.37b12-14:
觀一切法空, 如實相, 不顛倒、不動、不退、不轉, 如虛空, 無所有性. 一切語言道斷.

> then rises with palms joint. [He/She] will gain the power of *dhāraṇīs*. If [the practitioner] cares about the life and is attached to the Four Kinds of Offerings, thus unable to practice assiduously, he/she will never make the achievements even over the course of a *kalpa*. This is why it is named [Practice] with Characteristics.[267]

Huisi used "practice with characteristics" (*youxiangxing* 有相行) to guide beings with dull faculties, in which they could enter "practice without characteristic" (*wuxiang xing* 無相行) through cultivating the former, which was the goal of his advocacy. Although "practice with characteristics" emphasizes that one may recite the *Fahua jing* with an unfocused mind, one must still pay no heed to the body, being fully dedicated to recitation. If you fear for your body, and seek after the four offerings (food, clothing, bedding and medicine), and you cannot remain dedicated to your practice, then you may find success through "practice with characteristics." Succeeding through "practice with characteristics" means the practitioner will be able to witness Samantabhadra Bodhisattva riding a six-tusked white elephant come before themselves and at the same time witness Śākyamuni, the past six buddhas and the buddhas of the three times and ten directions, while gaining three methods of *dhāraṇī*. Moreover, Huisi mentions "prostrating oneself before the buddhas to do the sincerest repentance."[268] This is not found in the *Fahua jing*.

The three methods of *dhāraṇī* are divided as follows:

a. *Dhāraṇī* of Total Retention, the Physical and Heavenly Eyes, the Wisdom of Bodhisattva Path;[269]
b. *Dhāraṇī* Revolving Hundreds of Thousands of Myriads of *Koṭis* of Immeasurable Times, Perfected Wisdom of the Seed of the Bodhisattva Path, the Purity of Dharma Eye;[270]
c. *Dhāraṇī* of Skilful Means in Dharma Voice, Perfected All-Inclusive Wisdom of the Bodhisattva, the Purity of Buddha-Eye.[271]

---

267 *Fahua jing anlexing yi*, *T* no. 1926, 46: 1.700a29-b8, 700b14-15:
復次有相行, 此是《普賢勸發品》中, 誦《法華經》, 散心精進. 如是等人, 不修禪定, 不入三昧, 若坐、若立、若行, 一心專念《法華》文字, 精進不臥, 如救頭然, 是名 " 文字有相行." 此行者不顧身命, 若行成就, 即見普賢金剛色身, 乘六牙象王住其人前, 以金剛杵擬行者眼, 障道罪滅, 眼根清淨得見釋迦, 及見七佛. 復見十方三世諸佛, 至心懺悔, 在諸佛前五體投地, 起合掌立, 得三種陀羅尼門. ...... 若顧身命, 貪四事供養, 不能勤修, 經劫不得, 是故名爲有相也.

268 Ibid., 700b7-8: 至心懺悔, 在諸佛前, 五體投地.

269 Ibid., 700b9: 總持陀羅尼, 肉眼天眼菩薩道慧.

270 Ibid., 700b9-11: 百千萬億旋陀羅尼, 具足菩薩道種慧, 法眼清淨.

271 Ibid., 700b11-12: 法音方便陀羅尼, 具足菩薩一切種慧佛眼清淨.

These three types of *dhāraṇī* are simply called *zongchi tuoluoni* 總持陀羅尼. They are certainly not explained in the *Fahua jing*, but there are references to three types of *dhāraṇī*: the *āvarta-dhāraṇī* (*xuan tuoluoni* 旋陀羅尼), *koṭīśa-tasahasrāvartā-dhāraṇī* (*baiqianwanyi xuan tuoluoni* 百千萬億旋陀羅尼) and *sarvarutakauśalyāvartā* (*fayin fangbian tuoluoni* 法音方便陀羅尼).[272] Huisi turned the *āvarta-dhāraṇī* into the *zongchi tuoluoni*, thus separately establishing these three methods of *dhāraṇī*.

At the same time, when Zhiyi was studying under Huisi as a disciple, he recited the "Yaowang pusa benshi pin" 藥王菩薩本事品 (Chapter on the Original Conducts of the Bodhisattva Bhaiṣajyarāja). His mind was affected by the bodhisattva's austerity practice of self-immolation as an offering to the Buddha. Upon reading the line that reads, "This is the true effort, called Offering True Dharma to the Tathāgata,"[273] he had a vision of Huisi atop Vulture's Peak at the the *Lotus* Assembly. When he requested instructions from Huisi about this experience, Huisi exclaimed, "If not in this way, it is impossible to attain awakening, and no one except me could recognize it. The meditative concentration one entered is preparatory work for the *Lotus samādhi*, and what arose was the first *āvarta-dhāraṇī*."[274] Here the "first *āvarta-dhāraṇī*" is the *zongchi tuoluoni* as taught in the *Fahua jing anlexing yi* by Huisi.

The *Fahua jing anlexing yi* finally refers to the highest practice in meditative contemplation: the contemplation of the true characteristic of dharmas:

> "Perceive various dharmas as they are in actuality" means to understand that the Five Aggregates, the Eighteen Realms, and the Twelve Links of Dependent Arising are all true aspects of thusness: they are of non-essence-function, non-arising-cessation, and non-affliction-liberation. "Neither acts nor discriminates" means to understand that cyclic existence and nirvana are neither the same nor different and that ordinary beings and buddhas are in the Dharma-Realm of Non-Duality. Therefore, a practitioner should make a difference nor does one see non-duality. This is why [the *Huayan jing*] says, "Neither acts nor discriminates"; the

272 *Miaofa lianhua jing*, *T* no. 262, 9: 7.61a28-b9:
是人若行、若立、讀誦此經, 我爾時乘六牙白象王, 與大菩薩眾俱詣其所, 而自現身, 供養守護, 安慰其心, 亦爲供養法華經故. 是人若坐、思惟此經, 爾時我復乘白象王現其人前, 其人若於法華經有所忘失一句一偈, 我當教之, 與共讀誦, 還令通利. 爾時受持讀誦法華經者, 得見我身, 甚大歡喜, 轉復精進, 以見我故, 即得三昧及陀羅尼, 名爲旋陀羅尼、百千萬億旋陀羅尼、法音方便陀羅尼, 得如是等陀羅尼.

273 *Sui Tiantai Zhizhe dashi biezhuan*, *T* no. 2050, 50: 1.191c27-28: 是真精進, 是名真法供養.

274 Ibid., 1.192a5-7: 非爾弗證, 非我莫識, 所入定者法華三昧前方便也, 所發持者, 初旋陀羅尼也.

> characteristic of non-differentiation is unobtainable. Therefore, bodhisattvas who abide in such nameless *samādhi*, though abiding nowhere actually, are able to give rise to various powers of numinous penetration without resorting to skilfull means. Thus, it is named the sphere of the practice of the *bodhisattva mahāsattva*. Upon attaining sagehood one becomes on equal terms with the sage. This would be the Imperturbable True-and-Eternal Dharma-Body, not the Dharma-Body into which contributory conditions coalesce. It could also be named as the Attainment of the Womb of the Tathāgata and even the Womb of Mentation.[275]

The "true characteristic of dharmas" (*zhufa rushi xiang* 諸法如實相) is found in the Chapter of Four Means of Attaining Peace in the *Fahua jing*, but Huisi carried out his interpretation using ideas concerning the contemplation of emptiness via *prajñā*, pointing out that the "true characteristic of dharmas" is indivisible, but also it is not to be made indivisible, since there are no indivisible characteristic that can be obtained, i.e., emptiness via *prajñā*: emptiness is also empty.

Thus, Huisi's method of meditation placed importance on *samādhi*, such as the *Lotus samādhi*, while in terms of meditative contemplation he placed importance on the "true characteristic of dharmas," which became a prototype for the theories of meditation taught by Zhiyi later on. Moreover, Zhiyi adopted the ideas of "Practice without Characteristics" and "Practice with Characteristics." "Practice with characteristics" refers to the later repentance of the six faculties. "Practice without characteristics" refers to the later "Repentance of Contemplation of the Unarisen" (*guan wusheng chanhui* 觀無生懺悔). When Zhiyi produced the *Fahua sanmei chanyi*, he inherited the ideas on meditative practice from Huisi, while at the same time also absorbing the related procedures, which are primarily found in the *Fahua jing anlexing yi*. The *Fahua sanmei chanyi* states, "The features of practice largely stem from the *Puxian guan jing* and 'Four Means of Attaining Peace'. Should the practitioner want to diligently cultivate *samādhi*, they are to practice without fault, and should thoroughly read these two texts."[276] Moreover, it is important to note that the "right

---

275 *Fahua jing anlexing yi*, *T* no. 1926, 46:1.702b29-c9:
觀諸法如實相者, 五陰、十八界、十二因緣, 皆是真如實性. 無本末、無生滅, 無煩惱、無解脫；亦不行不分別者, 生死涅槃無一無異, 凡夫及佛無二法界, 故不可分別. 亦不見不二, 故言不行不分別, 不分別相不可得. 故菩薩住此無名三昧, 雖無所住而能發一切神通, 不假方便, 是名菩薩摩訶薩行處. 初入聖位即與等, 此是不動真常法身, 非是方便緣合法身. 亦得名爲證如來藏乃至意藏.

276 *Fahua sanmei chanyi*, *T* no. 1941, 46: 1.954b27-28:
行法相貌, 多出《普賢觀經》中, 及四安樂行中. 行者若欲精進修三昧, 令行無過失, 當熟看二處經文.

contemplation method of the true characteristic" and "cultivation of realization" of the *Fahua sanmei chanyi* originate in the *Fahua jing anlexing yi*.

## 5 Cults of Bhaiṣajyaguru, Avalokiteśvara and Relics in the Northern and Southern Dynasties

As various scriptures that form the basis for worship of buddhas and bodhisattvas were introduced into China—such as Amitābha, Bhaiṣajyaguru, Maitreya, Avalokiteśvara—related cults connected to salvation via buddhas and bodhisattvas, connected with the pure lands and the aforementioned figures, gradually became popular in China.

### 5.1 *The Cult of Bhaiṣajyaguru in the Northern and Southern Dynasties*

The cult of Bhaiṣajyaguru aimed to cease calamities, extend life, and cure illnesses through worship, production of images, repentance, copying of scriptures and Dharma services, which together express the main feature of that cult: peace in the present lifetime. The cult of Bhaiṣajyaguru is an important part of Chinese Buddhism, for which commentaries were written explaining its ideas after the *Yaoshi jing* 藥師經 (Medicine Master *Sūtra*; *T* 450) was translated, in addition to relevant rites being drafted. This was directly introduced into the daily lives of common people. From the Northern and Southern Dynasities until the modern people, the cult of Bhaiṣajyaguru has continually existed, having become an important cult among Chinese Buddhists.

After the cult of Bhaiṣajyaguru was introduced into China, there were a great many changes to it in order to adapt to Chinese culture, in terms of its developmental process. The cult of Bhaiṣajyaguru, which is characterized by various sorts of wondrous efficacy and the importance it places on peace in the present life, had attracted a great many devotees from the Northern and Southern Dynasties onward. For example, The "*Yaoshi Rulai benyuan gongde jing* xu" 藥師如來本願功德經序 (Preface to the *Sūtra* of Medicine Master Tathāgata's Original Vows and Merit) by Dharmagupta (Damojiduo 達摩笈多, ?-619) states,

> [Scripture on the Original Vows of the Medicine Tathāgata] is the essential teaching for fostering good fortune and eliminating disasters. Mañjuśrī, by the power of his compassion, requested [the Buddha] to discourse upon this holy appellation. The Tathāgata, because of his altruistic mind, extensively laid out the merits and deeds [of the Medicine Tathāgata]. The Twelve Great Vows played up the broadness and profoundness of the causal practices [of his Buddhahood]; the ornamentation by Seven Treasures manifest the purity of the resulted merits. Recollecting him or

> reciting his title strips away various afflictions; praying and making offerings to him fulfills the various wishes of the worshipers. If the sick seek [him] for a cure, and, even if they are facing certain death, they could prolong their lives, and when rulers [resorted to him] to ward off disasters, the misfortunes could turn into a fortune. Belief in this is the magical talisman that disperses hundreds of fiends and the miraculous arts that rules out the nine kinds of unnatural death.[277]

Production of images and paintings of Bhaiṣajyaguru, as well as engravings and reproductions of the *Yaoshi jing* plus accompanying commentaries, served as a foundation for the spread of the Bhaiṣajyaguru cult. At the same time, religious experiences connected to Bhaiṣajyaguru encouraged this movement.

After the appearance of the *Guanding jing* 灌頂經 (Consecration *Sūtra*; *T* 1331), "life extension practices" (*xuming fa* 續命法) became widespread during the Northern and Southern Dynasties, being an important part of the Bhaiṣajyaguru cult. The inscription on fascicle twelve of the *Guanding jing* reads, "Day fifteen of the fifth lunar month in year 12 of Taihe 太和 (488.6.10). *Foshuo guanding zhangju bachu guozui shengsi dedu jing* 佛說灌頂章句拔除過罪生死得度經 (Buddha Teaches the *Sūtra* of Consecration Text: Elimination of Transgressions and Liberation from Birth and Death)."[278]

The "Huangxing ernian Kang Na zaofan fayuan wen" 皇興二年康那造幡發願文 (Kang Na's Aspirational Text of Banner Production of Year 2 of Huangxing) states the following:

> On the eighth day of the fourth month of the second year of Huangxing 皇興 era (468.5.15), a year of *wushen* 戊申 in the sexagenary cycle, the pious layman Kang Na 康那 (d.u.) financed the five-coloured banners, which were forty-nine *chi* long, and offered them to the various buddhas in the ten directions. He made the following ardent vow: The ultimate path is void and dark, too dim and abstruse to explore. The enlightened perception has incubated for long, and the True Passage has thus been blocked. For this reason, those with form are drawn into the cycle of transmigration and maintain delusions, and they are in the bondage of

277 "*Yaoshi rulai benyuan gongde jing* xu" 藥師如來本願功德經序, *T* no. 0449, 14: 1.401a5-11:
致福消災之要法也: 曼殊以慈悲之力, 請說尊號；如來以利物之心, 盛陳功業. 十二大願, 彰因行之弘遠；七寶莊嚴, 顯果德之純淨. 憶念稱名, 則眾苦咸脫；祈請供養, 則諸願皆滿. 至於病士求救, 應死更生；王者攘災, 轉禍爲福. 信是消百怪之神符, 除九橫之妙術矣！

278 Duan (ed.), *Dunhuang wenxian*, 1: 7.

> false views and dwell on desires and profits having no sense of repent. Na was afraid of wallowing [in that situation] and being increasingly removed from the Truth, for [he would be] blinded by the darkness of the eternal night [of birth and death], a cycle never ending by itself. Feeling distressed at that he was among the mortal men, who are deaf [to Buddhist teachings], and that the Way and the world have lost each other. He admired the wondrous teachings, [lacuna]. None of the beings, however humble, will not receive the spiritual response, for [the *sūtra*] is specialized in all-inclusive deliverance. He hoped that his family would be reborn where they could meet a buddha and hear scriptural teachings, that they would believe in the subtle tenets and brightly awaken at the site of practice, that they would forsake the evil and choose the good, [lacuna], and would never form wicked ideas, that he was joined by his parents of the past seven lives, the family of his present life, various kins of both his paternal and maternal sides, as well as boundless beings, in being converted to [the Buddhist teachings], and that they would all attain enlightenment. This was the greatest wish of his kins.[279]

According to the inscription on the *Guanding jing* circulated at Dunhuang, Kang Na in the year 468 produced banners, which ought to have been done according to the said *sūtra*. Although in the year 457, the monk Huijian 慧簡 (fl. 457) of Luye si 鹿野寺 in Moling 秣陵 produced a later-circulated "Life-extension practice" (*xuming fa* 續命法) based upon the *Yaoshi jing*, there is no way of determining whether Kang Na carried out his aspirational practice of banner production based on this.[280]

This "Life extension practice" clearly emerged during the Northern and Southern Dynasties.

The biography of Zhang Yuan 張元 (d.u.) in the *Zhou shu* 周書 (Book of Zhou) records the following:

---

279 Ibid., 2: 105:
皇興二年四月八日, 歲在戊申, 清信士康那造成五色幡卌九尺, 上十方諸佛, 發精誠之願：夫至道虛凝, 幽玄難究, 靈覺久潛, 真途遂塞, 緣使有形, 輪轉昏迷, 邪見縛著, 利慾住而莫還. 那恐沈溺, 去真喻遠, 萇（ = 長）夜翳障, 永不自息. 慨在聾俗, 道世交喪, 仰惟妙門虛空口釋（？）, 微無不感, 精專畢濟. 願眷屬所生, 値遇諸佛, 聽聞經法；信解妙旨, 朗悟道場；棄惡入善, 三寶口天, 更無邪念；與七世父母, 現在眷屬, 內外諸親, 並無邊眾生, 齊均信向, 共成菩提, 是那眷屬之所至願也.

280 Li Xiaorong believes that Kang Na produced the banner based on Huijian's "Life-extension practice." See Li, "Lungao," 191.

> When [Zhang] Yuan turned the age of sixteen *sui*, his grandfather had lost his sight already for three years. Constantly anxious and crying, Yuan recited Buddhist scriptures day and night and offered worship so as to pray for blessings and protection. Later on, he read the *Yaoshi jing* and spotted the line "making the blind person recover the sight." Thus, he invited seven monks and lighted seven lamps, requesting them to ritually recite the *Yaoshi jing* for seven days and nights. Often he said, "Are you the Teacher of Gods and Men? I, Yuan, am an unworthy grandson whose grandfather lost his sight. Now, I offer the light of the lamps to the universe, hoping that my grandfather would regain sight and I would like to suffer the blindness for his sake." The situation continued for seven days, at night Yuan dreamed that an elder cured his grandfather's eyes using a gold scalpel and told Yuan, "Don't be anxious and sad! After three days, your grandfather will definitely recover." Yuan, in the dream, jumped with joy, and woke up. He spread this message to all of his family. After three days, as had been told, his grandfather was able to see again.[281]

Zhang Yuan during the Northern Zhou period requested seven monks to light seven lamps for seven days and seven nights and to read the *Yaoshi jing* in order to cure the blindness of his elder relative. This was actually the "life extension practice."

During the Southern Dynasties, fascicle thirteen of the *Chu sanzang ji ji* by Sengyou 僧祐 (445-518) lists the "Qiceng deng wuse fan fangsheng ji" 七層燈五色幡放生記 (Account of Life Release with Seven Levels of Lamps and Five-Colored Banners), which he notes is adapted from the *Guanding jing*, but unfortunately its content is otherwise unknown.[282] Emperor Wen of the Chen established a large-scale Bhaiṣajyaguru repentance-ritual and energetically proclaimed the merits of Bhaiṣajyaguru related rituals for blessings and the elimination of disasters, which was socially quite influential. Emperor Wen's "Yaoshi zhaichan wen" 藥師齋懺文 (Medicine Master Repentance Text) states the following:

281 *Zhou shu* 46.832. Cf. *Bei shi* 84.2834; *Fayuan zhulin*, *T* 53: 62.761b1-11: 及元年十六, 其祖喪明三年, 元恆憂泣, 晝夜讀佛經, 禮拜以祈福祐. 後讀《藥師經》, 見盲者得視之言, 遂請七僧, 燃七燈, 七日七夜, 轉《藥師經》行道. 每言："天人師乎！元爲孫不孝, 使祖喪明. 今以燈光普施法界, 願祖目見明, 元求代暗." 如此經七日. 其夜, 夢見一老公, 以金鎞治其祖目. 謂元曰："勿憂悲也, 三日之後, 汝祖目必差." 元於夢中喜躍, 遂即驚覺, 乃遍告家人. 居三日, 祖果目明.

282 *Chu sanzang ji ji*, *T* no. 2145, 55: 12.90c9.

According to my humble view, all things are impermanent and dharmas burdensome, and myriads of existence are the result of distorted perception, being the root of afflictions. From the mirage and the mirror reflection one learns that change is incessant, and from the floating grass and the burning straw, one learns that the course from arising to dissolving are fleeting. Blown by the wind of karma, one flows into the sea of sorrow, and chasing after the delusion caused by karmic retribution, one runs into the dark path. In the Three Realms of coming-and-going, no shelter is in sight, and in the middle of transmigrating among the Five Paths, no respite is expectable. The Medicine Tathāgata has great pledges to guide myriads of beings [to the Pure Land] and to save and protect living creatures. [He] directs hundreds of the streams of various beings back into the river of the Dharma which has only one flavor. He is also able to give [the entry into the Flower Forest *ksetra*], and he caters for the needs of worldlings and makes them relieved, happy, and free of fears. As for the Eight Disasters, Nine Kinds of Unnatural Deaths, Five Defilements, Three Calamities, floods, conflagrations, thefts, robberies, plagues, famines, enemies seeking revenge, and involvement in lawsuit—agents of encroachment are myriad, and ways of devastation are of thousands in variety—all sorts of misfortune could be turned into fortune, and crisis into ease. Besides, as for the seeking of wealth, or pursuit of official positions, the need to prolong lifespan or of abundant descendants, all of these are people's major desires and critical issues of the secular world, none would not be satisfied according to people's thoughts. Thus, it could be understood that the skillful means of various buddhas are beyond understanding. We, as a Buddhist disciple, are less than resourceful as the "pastor in office" and have not made achievements in secular governance. Therefore, we resort to the original vows of the Medicine Buddha so as to help various beings obtain enlightenment. Now, we, deferentially following the scriptural teachings, sponsor this Medicine Buddha Repent Retreat of a certain number of days conducted by a certain number of monks at a certain location. The multitude present at this retreat, pay homage with the utmost mind to our original teacher Tathāgata Śākyamuni and to Medicine Tathāgata! [Medicine Buddha] widely extends his compassion and never reneges his original pledges nor does he forsake worlds; he raises the "clouds" of the Four Kinds of Equality and sends the "rain" of the Six Perfections; he quenches the "fire" of birth-and-death and removes the "arrow" of affliction. The circles of lamps symbolize the worlds in the ten directions that are illuminated, and the seven hundred demons and deities approach on invitation guided by the knotted threads. Karmic

> obstructions are burnt upon the burning of the incense, and thus disasters cease to exist. The lifespan is prolonged as the banners are connected, gradually reaching the extent of permanence. May we be able to roam in the infinitely profound Dharma realm and enter the peerless enlightenment. May we could fulfill our vows as perfectly as Medicine Tathāgata.[283]

During Northern and Southern dynasties, various purification gatherings became popular, which primarily consisted of various ritualized actions such as worship, repentance and recitation of scriptures. The *Yaoshi zhaichan wen* had no definite ritualized form. We only know that it consisted of venerating buddhas and producing banners and lamps. Of course, the aim of repentance is to prevent disasters from arising, cure illness, extend life, and attain fortune and wealth, which constitutes prayer for worldly benefits. It is clear that the *Yaoshi zhaichan wen* may have been a prayer text for the Medicine Master Service or for general usage, for it says that "now deferentially we follow the teachings in scriptures and hold this Medicine Buddha repentance ceremony that participated by such-and-such a number of monks and for such-and-such days."[284]

The solumn services of Bhaiṣajyaguru formed through worship of him in addition to recitation of the *Yaoshi jing*, or otherwise through activities such as building of shrines for the "Life-extending practice," life release and charity. These ceremonies for Bhaiṣajyaguru no doubt promoted the establishment of repentance rites connected to him.

### 5.2 *The Cult of Avalokiteśvara in the Northern and Southern Dynasties*

The popularity of the individual chapter "Pumen pin" 普門品 (Chapter of Avalokiteśvara's Universal Gate) was representative of how the ideal of salva-

---

283 *Guang Hongming ji, T* no. 2103, 52: 28.334b14-c6:
竊以諸行無常, 悉爲累法, 萬有顛倒, 皆成苦本. 熱炎鏡像, 知變易之不停; 漂草爨矛, 見生滅之奔迅. 隨業風而入苦海, 逐報障而趣幽途. 去來三界, 未見可安之所; 輪回五道, 終無暫息之期. 藥師如來, 有大誓願, 接引萬物, 救護眾生. 導諸有之百川, 歸法流之一味, 亦能施與花林, 隨從世俗, 使得安樂, 令無怖畏. 至如八難九横, 五濁三災, 水火盜賊, 疾疫飢饉, 怨家債主, 王法縣官, 憑陵之勢萬端, 虔 (= 虐 ?) 殺之法千變, 悉能轉禍爲福, 改危成安. 復有求富貴, 須祿位, 延壽命, 多子息, 生民之大欲, 世間之切要, 莫不隨心應念, 自然滿足. 故知諸佛方便, 事絕思量. 弟子司牧寡方, 庶績未又 (= 乂 ?), 方憑藥師本願, 成就眾生. 今謹依經教, 於某處建如乾僧如乾日藥師齋懺, 現前大眾, 至心敬禮本師釋迦如來, 禮藥師如來！慈悲廣覆, 不乖本願, 不棄世間, 興四等雲, 降六度雨, 滅生死火, 除煩惱箭. 十方世界, 若輪燈而明朗; 七百鬼神, 尋結縷而應赴. 障逐香然, 災無復有; 命隨幡續, 漸登常住. 游甚深之法性, 入無等之正覺. 行願圓滿, 如藥師如來.

284 Ibid., 28. 334b28-29: 今謹依經教, 於某處建如幹僧如幹日藥師齋懺.

tion were produced in the *Fahua jing*. This chapter narrates the aspirational vows of Avalokiteśvara Bodhisattva and the "divine merit" of saving people from various sufferings as well as the "expedient means" manifested via different forms in accord with the differences of beings. At the same time, the "Universal Gate" also explains the methods with which beings may attain salvation through Avalokiteśvara, such as recitation or hearing his name as well as refuge and veneration. The "Universal Gate" Chapter presented the cult of salvation of Avalokiteśvara and sparked its popularity among commoners in China.

As we immediately know, the earliest collection of stories concerning such experiences is the *Guangshiyin yingyan ji* 光世音應驗記 (Accounts of Spiritual Experiences with Avalokiteśvara) by Xie Fu 謝敷 (313-362) during the Eastern Jin. Later, he sent more than ten of the stories of spiritual experiences that he recounted to his good friend Fu Yuan 傅瑗 (d.u.). As a result of Sun En's 孫恩 (?-402) rebellion in the later years of the Eastern Jin, most copies of this book that were preserved in Fu's home in Kuaiji 會稽 were lost. During the Liu-Song period, Fu Yuan's son Fu Liang 傅亮 (374-426) copied out seven of the stories based upon memory, which became the *Guanshiyin yingyan ji* 光世音應驗記 (Accounts of Spiritual Experiences with Avalokiteśvara) that has been handed down until today. Later, Zhang Yan 張演 (fl. 438) also compiled ten stories from what he had heard and carried on after the book of the Fu family, which became the *Xu Guangshiyin yingyan ji* 續光世音應驗記 (Extended Accounts of Spiritual Experiences with Avalokiteśvara). During the Xiao Qi period, Lu Gao 陸杲 (459-532), the grandson of Zhang Yan, also compiled sixty-nine tales of such spiritual experiences based upon contemporary books and hearsay, being the *Xi Guanshiyin yingyan ji* 繫觀世音應驗記 (Connected Accounts of Spiritual Experiences with Avalokiteśvara). These three books altogether constitute the *Guanshiyin yingyan ji san zhong* 觀世音應驗記三種 (Three [Books] on Spiritual Experiences with Avalokiteśvara): eighty-six stories concerning spiritual experiences with Avalokiteśvara. Older handwritten copies of these books were discovered during the twentieth century in Japan and came to the attention of the academic world.[285]

The birth and transmission of these stories no doubt explains the widespread popularity of the cult of Avalokiteśvara during the Six Dynasties period. In the Northern dynasties, the "Universal Gate" was recited by everyone such as Gonghui 功迴 (6-7th c.), who wanted to renounce the home life at age six. His parents "personally recited the *Guanyin jing* 觀音經 (Avalokiteśvara *Sūtra*, i.e.,

285 Makita, *Kanzeon ōkenki no kenkyū*, 1970; Sun (coll.), *Yingyanji sanzhong*, 1994; Dong, *Yingyanji sanzhong yizhu*, 2002.

FIGURE 13 Bodhisattva statues made by Zhang Jingzhang 張景章 (d. after 544) in 544.

Chapter of the Universal Gate of the *Lotus Sūtra*)."[286] Hongman 洪滿 (557-639) "constantly recited the *Guanyin jing* for three years."[287] Fatong 法通 (6-7th c.) "recited the *Guanyin jing* day and night without stopping."[288] Recitation of the "Universal Gate" was an important expression of the cult of Avalokiteśvara. In addition, copying of the *Guanyin jing* also flourished during the Northern Dynasties. For instance, on the eighth day of the fourth lunar month in 530, the lay disciple Yin Bo 尹波 (d.u.) in Dunhuang copied forty scrolls of the *Guanyin jing* and donated them to the temples to recite. The inscribed aspirational text reads as follows:

> May the merciful and judicious Two Sages (i.e. Emperor Xiaoming 孝明 and Empress Dowage Hu) be blessed forever. May the Nine Regions be clear of warfare as soon as possible and the soldiers and chariots hold not any armors. May the steeds scatter in the lush meadow and weapons be abandoned and put to use in farming. May the court be crowded with virtuous civil officials and the palace be filled with sagacious scholars, the assembly looking so massive and solemn, surpassing the circumstances of festival days. May the rulership be august and enlightened and loyal ministers appear generation after generation. May the wheel-gauges within the Eight Margins be ultimately unified. May his Highness Prince Dongyang keep a healthy constitution and a vision as far as beyond the clouds, and enjoy a longevity as infinite as the bamboo or cypress. May his Highness have nothing to worry about in defending the frontiers and pacifying foreign states, and may his splendid prospect appear so that he could return to the capital soon.[289]

In the colophon, Yin Bo expresses his hopes that the country will flourish and that there will be peace while moreover mentioning Yuan Rong 元榮 (6th c.) or Prince of Dongyang 東陽王. Yuan Rong was part of the royal clan, being the Provincial Chief of Guazhou 瓜州 for twenty years (525-545). He believed in Buddhism and as a result, brought the Buddhist faith from the Central Plains to Dunhuang. Yin Bo celebrates that Yuan Rong was able to "quickly return to

286 *Xu Gaoseng zhuan*, *T* no. 2060, 50: 13.528c5: 親口授《觀音經》.

287 Ibid., 25.663a7: 常念《觀音經》三年.

288 Ibid., 25. 663b3: 誦《觀音經》晝夜不捨.

289 Huang & Wu, *Yuanwen ji*, 812:
願使二聖慈明, 永延福祚；九域早清, 兵車息甲. 戎馬散於茂苑, 干戈輟爲農用. 文德盈朝, 哲士溢闕. 鏘鏘濟濟, 隆於上日, 君道欽明, 忠臣累葉. 八表宇宙, 終齊一軌. 願東陽王殿下, 體質康休, 洞略雲表；年壽無窮, 永齊竹柏. 保境安蕃, 更無虞處；皇途尋開, 早還京國.

the capital," which fully expresses the reality and utility of the cult of Avalokiteśvara.

At the same time, image production of Avalokiteśvara and engravings of the "Universal Gate" appear at times, such as the Longmen Cave, which has the "Yin Bocheng qi tiji" 尹伯成妻題記 (Inscription of Yin Bocheng's Wife):

> On the twelfth day of the twelfth month of the fourth year of the Yongping era, the pious laywoman and wife of Yin Bocheng financed the creation of this statue of Guanyin for the sake of her late husband Bocheng. She hoped that he would have the opportunity to be of service to the Buddha and hear the Dharma, and that thereupon he could break away from the three evil destinies. She also hoped that all beings receive the same blessings.[290]

In addition, on October 28, 548 (Wuding 武定 6.9.9), Zhilang 志朗 (d.u.) produced an image (in modern Pingding 平定 in Shanxi), mentioning the inscription the *Guanyin jing*. On the statue stele erected by Li Ronggui 李榮貴 (d.u.) and his brother on March 6th, 559 (Tianbao 天保 10.2.10), the inscription mentions the "Universal Gate" in the twenty-fourth chapter of the *Fahua jing*.[291] These images and inscriptions all reflect the popularity of the cult of Avalokiteśvara in the Northern and Southern dynasties.

Among images produced in the Northern dynasties, those of Śākyamuni, Maitreya and Avalokiteśvara were the most widely influential, but the cult of Avalokiteśvara was stabler. After the Northern Dynasties period, the cult of Amitābha Buddha was popular, and worship of Śākyamuni and Maitreya declined. Following the popularity of the cult of Avalokiteśvara during the Northern and Southern dynasties, it became even more fashionable in various areas and universally known from the Sui-Tang period onward.

### 5.3 *The Cult of Relics during the Northern and Southern Dynasties*

In Sanskrit a relic is called *śarīra*. Normally this refers to a bone fragment of the Buddha. Later, this also referred to the solid bone fragments left behind after the cremation of an eminent monk. There are *stūpa*s and vases that hold relics, as well as services for making offerings to them.

---

290 *Baqiongshi jinshi buzheng* 13.73:
永平四年十二月十二日, 清信女尹伯成妻口, 爲亡夫伯成, 造觀音像一軀, 願使侍佛聞法, 永離三途, 一切眾生, 普同斯願.

291 Hou, *Fojiao xinyang*, 138.

FIGURE 14 Baita Monastery 百塔寺 on Mount Zhongnan 終南山, the patriarchal monastery for the Sanjie Jiao 三階教 (Three-Stages Sect).

In the time of early Buddhism when there were no images, worship of relics and *stūpa*s were important forms within the Buddhist faith. Moreover, the ideas of merit generation that results from circumambulation of *stūpa*s and worship of and offerings to relics became popular and quickly developed.

As to the proliferation of the Buddha's relics, it is related to how the five countries divided up his relics following his *nirvāṇa*. According to the account in the *Youxing jing* 遊行經 (*Sūtra* of the Account of Travels) in Fascicle Four of the *Dīrghāgama*, following the Buddha's cremation, the Mallas' people of Pāvā wanted to possess a portion of the Buddha's relics and to erect a *stūpa* in their land to make offerings; therefore, they rallied four kinds of troops and sent them to the city of Kuśinagara and dispatched envoys to request a share of the relics. The king of Kushinagar believed that the Buddha had died in his country, and that the people of the country should make offerings themselves. He thus prohibited the relics to be divided. At the same time, the Buli people of Allakappa, Koliya people of Rāmagāma, the Brahmins of Vethadīpa, the Śākyas of Kapila, the Licchavī people of Vesālī and King Ajātasattu of Magaha each prepared four armies to cross the Ganges River. After the deliberations, they had Brahmin Dona distribute the relics. The king of Kushinagar still refused to divide the relics. Having heard this, the kings considered using their weapons to seize the relics with all their might. Dona the Brahmin informed the kings that it ought not be like this. As a result, the relics were distributed to the eight countries. The eight kingdoms each took relics and returned to their homes where they built *stūpa*s to which they made offerings.

After the relics were divided into eight, Aśoka opened up the seven *stūpa*s apart from that of Rāmagāma and took the relics and had them deposited into 84,000 vessels, for which 84,000 *stūpa*s were built. According to the Pāli *Mahāvaṃsa* (Great Chronicle), Aśoka's son Mahinda promoted Buddhism in Sri Lanka. Devānajpiyatissa requested from Aśoka some relics, for which an extremely grand ritual was carried out to welcome them. In addition, according to the account of Sri Lanka (師子國 [錫蘭] 條) in the *Gaoseng Faxian zhuan* 高僧法顯傳 (Chronicle of the Eminent Monk Faxian), there was a monastery built in connection with a tooth of the Buddha in the capital of this kingdom.[292] Fascicle eleven of the *Da Tang Xiyu ji* has an identical account. There was a monastery connected with a tooth of the Buddha at the side of the royal palace in Sri Lanka.[293]

Worship of buddha-relics also flourished in India and the Western Regions. As in the account of Faxian 法顯 (338-423), there was a monastery connected

292 *Gaoseng Faxian zhuan*, *T* no. 2085, 51: 1.865a7-8.

293 *Da Tang Xiyu ji*, *T* no. 2087, 51: 11.934a19.

with a skull-bone of the Buddha in the city of Hidda in Nagarahara.[294] The account of the country Kapiśā in fascicle one of the *Da Tang Xiyu ji* records that there was a *stūpa* built by a Nāga-king in this country. Therein were enshrined relics of flesh and bone of the Tathāgata. Northwest of Rajgir on the south bank of a great river was the earlier monastery of old Rajgir and a fragment of the Tathāgata's skull bone was enshrined within.[295] According to the account in fascicle twelve of the *Da Tang Xiyu ji*, Xuanzang brought back 150 relic fragments of the Tathāgata with him to China.[296] Fascicle one of the *Song Gaoseng zhuan* records that the monk Yijing during the Tang Dynasty returned to China carrying 300 relic fragments.[297]

During the Wei-Jin, Northern and Southern and Sui-Tang periods, the cult of relics constituted an important element in middle-ancient political and social icons. When Buddhism was first introduced into China, the monks convinced royalty to convert to Buddhism using displays of miracles with relics. The *Gaoseng zhuan* records that when Kang Sengui 康僧會 (?-280) came to Jianye 建業, Sun Quan 孫權 (182-252) did not believe in the story of the Han emperor Ming 漢明帝 (r. 57-75) having dreamt of a deity as the Buddha and so summoned Kang Senghui. Kang Senghui related the following:

> Soon over one thousand years has flown by since the demise of Tathāgata, and his bodily relics divinely illuminate everywhere without making distinction among different directions. In days of yore, King Aśoka erected eighty-four *stūpas*, and the rise of *stūpa* temples was meant to commend the teachings left by the Buddha.[298]

Sun Quan thus demanded that if Kang Senghui should get a hold of a relic and have some miraculous experience, then he would build for him a temple and *stūpa*, otherwise he would punish him according to the law. Kang Senghui cleansed himself in a quiet room and prayed for twenty-one days when finally, through his sincerity, a relic manifested in a bronze vessel that he had prepared. This miracle convinced Sun Quan, who built a *stūpa* and temple, calling it Jianchu si 建初寺.[299]

294 *Gaoseng Faxian zhuan*, *T* no. 2085, 51: 1.858c9.

295 *Da Tang Xiyu ji*, *T* no. 2087, 51: 1.875a8-9, 875a14-16.

296 Ibid., 12.946c2-3.

297 *Song Gaoseng zhuan*, *T* no. 2061, 50:1.710b20.

298 *Gaoseng zhuan*, *T* no. 2059, 50: 1.325b12-14:
如來遷跡, 忽逾千載; 遺骨舍利, 神曜無方. 昔阿育王起塔, 乃八萬四千, 夫塔寺之興, 以表遺化也.

299 Ibid., 1.325b14-c5.

The cult of relics in Chinese Buddhism originated in the construction of *stūpa* for relics by King Aśoka. In the *Mingfo lun* 明佛論 (Treatise Clarifying Buddhism) by Zong Bing 宗炳 (375-443) during the Liu-Song period, mention is made of Linzi 臨淄 in Shandong and Puban 蒲阪 in Shanxi having ruins from Aśoka.[300] Huida's 慧達 (252-435+) *Gaoseng zhuan* biography records that Huida, who was Liu Sahe 劉薩訶 at birth, followed his teacher's instructions and went south in search of the *stūpa*s and images of Aśoka. Huida went to Changgan si 長干寺 in Jiankang and saw a strange light emanating from the *stūpa*. He drilled underneath it and uncovered vessels of iron, silver and gold place inside one another. Within the gold one were three relics, a fingernail and some hairs from a head. People at the time believed that this was one of the 84,000 *stūpa*s built by King Aśoka. As a result, on the side of the original *stūpa* another new *stūpa* was built to house the relics.[301] The *Shilao zhi* 釋老志 (Monograph on Buddhism and Daoism) in the *Wei shu* 魏書 (Book of Wei) records the following:

> After one hundred years, there was a king called Aśoka, who, using numinous power, divided the relics of the Buddha and drove various demons and deities to build eighty-four thousand *stūpa*s which spread all over the world, and were completed on the same day. Today at each city of Luoyang, Pengcheng 彭城, Guzang 姑藏, and Linzi, there is the Aśokan Buddhist temple, which may have been purposed to accommodate those historical remains.[302]

Later, the number of relic *stūpa*s connected to Aśoka gradually increased. Fascicle Fifteen of the *Guang Hongming ji* lists seventeen *stūpas*.[303] The *Ji Shenzhou sanbao gantong lu* 集神州三寶感通錄 (Record of Collected Spiritual Experiences of the Triple Gem in Shenzhou) lists nineteen *stūpas*.[304] The *Fayuan zhulin* increases this to twenty-one sites.[305] However, among these relic *stūpa*s connected to Aśoka, the sole preserved one is the *stūpa* in the Mao 鄮 county of Kuaiji (Ayuwang si 阿育王寺 in modern Ningbo 寧波, Zhejiang).

---

300 *Hongming ji*, *T* no. 2102, 52: 2.12c15-16.

301 *Gaoseng zhuan*, *T* no. 2059, 50: 13.409b13-28.

302 *Wei shu* 114.3028:
於後百年, 有王阿育, 以神力分佛舍利, 役諸鬼神, 造八萬四千塔, 布於世界, 皆同日而就. 今洛陽、彭城、姑藏、臨淄, 皆有阿育王寺, 蓋承其遺跡焉.

303 *Guang Hongming ji*, *T* no. 2103, 52: 15.201b24-202a22.

304 *Ji Shenzhou sanbao gantong lu*, *T* no. 2106, 52: 1.404a28-b10.

305 *Fayuan zhulin*, *T* no. 2122, 53: 38.584c29-585a9.

Looking at the extant literature, the earliest worship of relics was during the time of Emperor Xiaowen of the Northern Wei (r. 471-499). In 1964, a stone vessel of relics was unearthed in Ding county 定縣 in Hebei. Twelve lines were engraved atop the casket explaining the story behind the building of a *stūpa*. The relics were placed within a small glass jar in the shape of a gourd. A bronze spoon and tweezers made exclusively to handle the relics were inside the stone case. There was also a necklace made from glass, agate, quartz, pearl, coral and ruby as well as bronze coins plus silver coins from Persia. These were what is called the "seven treasures" to be entombed with the relics. Other items such as gold and silver pendant earrings, bracelets, rings and hair-rings were donated contributions. With respect to the seals, bronze arrowheads and fragments of bronze mirrors, it was customary at the time to include these in a tomb. It is clear that these were buried under a five-floor *stūpa* built in 481 by Emperor Xiaowen of the Northern Wei.

The flourishing of the cult of relics in Chinese Buddhism started under Liang Wudi's reign. Liang Wudi's theocratic approach was quite similar to the ideas and practices of King Aśoka. In 512, Liang Wudi ordered the monk Saṃghabhara from Funan 扶南國 (in modern Cambodia) to retranslate the *Ayuwang jing* 阿育王經 (*Sūtra* of King Aśoka; *T* 2043). As a result, Liang Wudi in his later years worshipped relic *stūpa*s connected with Aśoka. The account of Funan in the *Liang shu* 梁書 (Book of Liang) records the following:

> In year 2 of [Datong] [536], the *stūpa* of the Mao county of Kuaiji was rebuilt. The old *stūpa* was opened and the relics extracted. Four monks of Guangzhai si, such as Shi Jingtuo 釋敬脫 (d.u.), and the Serviceman Sun Zhao 孫照 (d.u.), were sent to escort the relics temporarily to the imperial palace. After Gaozu had finished offering worship, the [relics] were sent back to the county and newly set under the *stūpa*. The *stūpa* of this county was also found by Liu Sahe.[306]

In the eighth lunar month of 537, Liang Wudi ordered the rebuilding of the *stūpa*. This reconstruction uncovered relics of the Buddha plus fingernails and hair from its foundation. Liang Wudi convened an "unhindered great assembly" and he granted pardon to all offenders.[307]

---

306 *Liang shu* 54.788:
(大同) 二年, 改造會稽鄮縣塔, 開舊塔出舍利, 遣光宅寺釋敬脫等四僧及舍人孫照, 暫迎還台. 高祖禮拜竟, 即送還縣, 入新塔下. 此縣塔亦是劉薩訶所得也.

307 Ibid.

Liang Wudi in his "Chu gu Yuwang ta xia Fo sheli zhao" 出古育王塔下佛舍利詔 (Order for Uncovering Relics from underneath the *Stūpa* of King Aśoka) states the following:

> In the eighth month of the fourth year of the Datong 大同 era (536), the moon intruded on the Five Chariots (Capella), and the Old Man Star (Canopus) appeared. When, [under the imperial order], the Aśokan *stūpa* in Changgan si 長干寺 was revamped, the relics of the Buddha's hairs and nails were uncovered. Aśoka was a king of Iron Wheel, and his Majesty had unified Jambudvīpa under his ruler and drove demons and deities to complete eighty-four thousand *stūpa*s within one day, of which this was one. [Liang Wudi], riding in a carriage, graced the Changgan si with his presence and arranged a Feast of Joy in Dharma for Undiscriminating Crowd. The decree reads thus,
>
> [The *Yijing* says,] "The [interaction of] heaven and earth is now vigorous and abundant, now dull and scanty, growing and diminishing according to the seasons." The myriads of lives cannot make their first stir at the same moment, and the Two Norms (heaven and earth) cannot keep overspreading and sustaining for all eternity. Thus, some years are more stressful while others more relaxing; some days are more pleasing while others more saddening. Last year was hit by crop failure, and the price of a single *dou* of millets was exorbitant. Driven by distress and scarcity, people turned to various crimes. Details uncovered and guilts analysed, some of the crimes proved to be forgivable. Descending from the chariot and inquiring after the crimes, we were given a presentation of the past imperial announcement. As is indicated, the responsibility falls on the head of the country, indeed on ourselves! If brought to justice, none of them would have the opportunity to reform himself. The [*Shang*] *shu* [尙] 書 (Book of Documents) says, "Rather than put an innocent person to death, you will run the risk of irregularity and error." The *Yi* (Book of Changes) says, "Great indeed is the significance of keeping in tune with times." Now the relics of the Buddha's real form have appeared in the world, and such a rare event rises the awe for the slight chance. Now, we set an Undiscriminating Assembly at the Ayuwang si 阿育王寺, and none of the elders and children are not elated, as those chronically hungry find food or they reunite with their families after a long separation. Beings in both the world of light and the world of darkness turn their hearts towards [the assembly], and people from far and near rush over in admiration. The multitude of gentlemen and ladies is shaped like rosy glows, and caps and canopies of officials gather like clouds. We are spreading

> goodness according to time, and people thus joyfully submit themselves. Criminals under the heaven, no matter their guilts are lesser or greater, are all pardoned![308]

The "year four of Datong 大同" in the *Guang Hongming ji* ought to be year 3, which corresponds to 537—specifically, the twenty-first to the twenty-eighth of the eighth lunar month in that year. Liang Wudi also took a relic and offered it at the imperial shrine. On the fifth day of the ninth lunar month he ordered the princes and ministers to pay their respects to the relic. Altogether tens of thousands of people welcomed the relic.

On October 25, 538 (Datong 4.9.15), Liang Wudi convened an "unhindered great assembly" and built two *stūpa*s for the Buddha, placing the relics and the hair and fingernails of the Buddha in gold and jade jars. The service for making offerings to the relic was extremely grand; the wealth offered up by the aristocracy and commoners was piled up like a mountain.[309] The crown prince Xiao Gang 蕭綱 (503-551) donated a million coins to jointly bring this sacred project to completion and presented the "Feng Ayuwang si qian qi" 奉阿育王寺錢啓 (Text on the Offering to the Ayuwang si) as follows:

> Your subject [Xiao] Gang has the following to state. I, your subject, hear that the eight kingdoms all begged [to own the relics of the Buddha], for this matter was superior to the Dharma texts (i.e. *sūtra*s); the human body is all comprised of *skandha*s, a teaching elaborated in Buddhist scriptures whose teachings are as inexhaustible as the gushing spring. Therefore, relics on the tusk-made bed or under the white canopy could not be seen if there were no purposes; the relics in the gold vase or the treasurable casket appeared only for good reason. In my humble view, Your Majesty hangs the heavenly mirror above the imperial domain and exerts your great authority within the realm. All Three Kinds of Existence are dreamlike, and you bring the wisdom-sun to them; various herbs have

308 *Guang Hongming ji*, *T* no. 2103, 52: 15.203c12-27:
大同四年八月, 月犯五車, 老人星見. 改造長干寺阿育王塔, 出舍利佛髮爪. 阿育鐵輪王也, 王閻浮一天下. 一日夜役鬼神造八萬四千塔, 此其一焉. 乘輿幸長干寺, 設無礙法喜食. 詔曰, "天地盈虛, 與時消息. 萬物不得齊其蠢生, 二儀不得恆其覆載. 故勞逸異年, 歡慘 (=愉 ?) 殊日. 去歲失稔, 斗粟貴騰, 民有困窮, 遂臻斯濫. 原情察咎, 或有可矜. 下車問罪, 聞諸往誥; 責歸元首, 寔在朕躬. 若皆以法繩, 則自新無路. 書不云乎, '與殺不辜, 寧失不經'. 易曰, '隨時之義, 大矣哉'! 今真形舍利, 復現於世, 逢希有之事, 起難遭之想. 今出阿育王寺說 (=設 ?) 無礙會, 耆年童齒, 莫不欣悅. 如積飢得食, 如久別見親. 幽顯歸心, 遠近馳仰, 士女霞布, 冠蓋雲集. 因時布德, 允協人靈. 凡天下罪無輕重, 皆赦除之!"

309 *Liang shu* 54.792.

> withered, and you moisten them by sending merciful rain. Either work or relaxation is not out of your own need, and whether travelling or stopping off is because of the requirement of various affairs. No words are worthy to naming your deeds, and how could I express my admiration? The shining light and the red scripts [which alludes to a yellow dragon which carried the River Chart to Shun 舜] are regarded in history as a numinous omen, while precious ganoderma and fine jade should have been taken as precious in previous times! What is indeed rarely seen are the relics of the Buddha's real body. The relics illuminate like the precious bottle that was suffused with various light, and their radiance floats like that of the waters of merit [in the Lotus Pond of the Pure Land]. They look like the bones hooked together like chains [left by the magical monk] and the pearl under the dragon's jaw. Were it not for your sacred virtue, people would never have had the honour to view such a rarity. Both heavenly beings and humans bow their heads in worship and people from far and near turn the heart towards [the relics]. I humbly hear that the Ayuwang si is about to be decorated, and tons of gold have been given as the gift, resulting in ten treasuries. Treasures are presented by the Bureau of Rivers, and money is allotted by the office of tax and coinage. Monks are carrying earth, and the great mansion is soon constructed; arhats are drawing cords, and the towering *stūpa* is going to be erected. Overcome with joy, I clap my hands, and I deferentially present one million cash. Although my piety equals [that of those who make offerings to the Buddha by] strewing flowers, my feelings are inexhaustible; the offering is as petty as droplets and as humble as nothingness. I discreetly lay out such a trivial matter; in fear and in a sweat, I prostrate myself present the above statements. Deferentially presented.[310]

In the year 539, Liang Wudi dispatched Yunbao 雲寶 (d.u.) to Funan to make a request for the hair of the Buddha.[311] On December 22, 545 (Datong 11.11.2), monks of the Ayuwang si also requested that Liang Wudi produce a foreword

---

310 *Guang Hongming ji, T* no. 2103, 52: 16.209a9-23:
臣諱 (綱) 言：臣聞八國同祈, 事高於法本; 七區皆蘊, 理備於湧泉. 故牙床白傘, 無因不睹; 金瓶寶函, 有緣斯出. 伏惟陛下, 懸天鏡於域中, 運大權於宇內. 三有均夢, 則臨之以慧日; 百藥同枯, 則潤之以慈雨. 動寂非己, 行住因物, 無能名矣. 臣何得而稱焉 ?! 故以昭光赤書, 賤前史之爲瑞; 珥芝景玉, 嗤往代之爲珍. 難遇者乃如來真形舍利, 昭景寶瓶, 浮光德水, 如觀鈎鎖, 似見龍珠. 自非聖德威神, 無以値斯希有. 天人頂戴, 遐邇歸心. 伏聞阿育王寺方須莊嚴, 施巨萬金, 檀豐十藏. 寶陳河府, 泉出水衡. 比丘持土, 大廈方構; 羅漢引繩, 高塔將表. 不勝喜抃, 謹上錢一百萬. 雖誠等散花, 心符不盡, 而微均渧瀝, 陋甚鄰空. 輕以塵聞, 伏啓悚汗. 謹啓.

311 *Liang shu* 54.790.

to the *Bore jing* 般若經 (*Prajñāpāramitā-sūtra*). That night, the two *stūpas* radiated light, the emperor ordering Xiao Lun 蕭綸 (ca. 507-551; i.e., Prince of Shaoling 邵陵王 and the Zhendong General 鎮東將軍) to compose a memorial inscription in celebration of the great merits of the temple.[312]

Liang Wudi in years two (536), three (537), four (538), and eleven (545) during the Datong 大同 reign era spent a great amount of money to rebuild Ayuwang si. He carried out "unhindered great assemblies" and recognized the events of Aśoka and the superb miracles associated with relics of the Buddha. He also pardoned those living in the realm. Thus, the cult of relic worship under Liang Wudi emphasized his own ideal of being a "wheel-turning king" governing a "Buddhist country."

When dynasties changed, relics of the Buddha also acted as a means to unifiy political power. At the same time, propelling political authority also facilitated the popularity of the cult of relics. During the transition of the Liang and Chen dynasties, Emperor Wu of the Chen, Chen Baxian 陳霸先 (503-559), used a tooth of the Buddha as a sign indicating the legitimization of his revolution.

In Khotan, Faxian 法獻 (424-498) obtained the tooth of the Buddha, to which Emperor Wu of the Chen made offerings. After the Buddha's cremation, there were four of his teeth in total left in the world. According to the biography of Faxian in the *Gaoseng zhuan*,[313] Faxian 法獻, influenced by the eminent monks of the Eastern Jin, Faxian 法顯 (338-423) and Zhimeng 智猛 (fl. 404-424), who went west to India to worship the Buddha and to search for the Dharma, aspired to sacrifice himself from a young age by travelling west to see the holy sites for himself. In the year 475, Faxian departed from Jiankang and endured all manner of physical hardships along the way as he crossed the wastelands and desert, finally arriving in Khotan (Yutian county in modern Xinjiang). He had to halt his westward travel as a result of the route being blocked. On his return when passing through Ruirui 芮芮 (an ancient country, Rouran 柔然, a territory in modern Orkhon and Tuul River), he unexpectedly found a relic. According to tradition, this tooth was originally in Udyāna (in modern Orissa in India) before it was later transported to Ruirui. Faxian took the relic into his hand like it was the most precious thing. He felt that even though his trip to the west did not succeed in reaching the holy land, he had still obtained a tooth of the Buddha and considered that his trip had not been fruitless. He took the tooth of the Buddha back to Jiankang but kept it secret, not showing it to anyone for fifteen years. As Faxian was approaching death, he revealed the relic and placed it in the relic pavilion of Upper Dinglin si 上定

312 Ibid., 792.

313 *Gaoseng zhuan*, *T* no. 2059, 50: 13.411b28-412a7.

FIGURE 15 Forest of pagodas at Shaolin Monastery 少林寺 on Mount Song 嵩山, Henan.

林寺, where it was widely worshipped by Buddhists from all over. On a night, during the first lunar month of the year 522 under Liang Wudi, a group of incredibly evil strongmen with torches and staff, using a search for a household slave as a pretext, forced themselves into the temple and barged into the relic pavilion. They snatched away the relic and left. The whereabouts of the relic for a time was unknown. Chen Zuolin 陳作霖 (1837-1920) during the Qing Dynasty in his *Nanchao Fosi zhi* 南朝佛寺志 (Account of Buddhist Temples in the Southern Dynasties) explains, "Now, reading the account of Gaozu in the *Chen shu* 陳書 (Book of Chen), we know that it was Emperor Wu of the Chen who took the tooth of the Buddha. That day, Huixing 慧興 of Qingyun si 慶雲寺 gave excuses."[314] In any case, the tooth of the Buddha finally landed in the hands of Chen Baxian.

In the tenth lunar month of the year 557, Emperor Wu of the Chen proclaimed that he found a relic. The second fascicle of the *Chen shu* records, "On

314 *Nanchao Fosi zhi* 1.158.

November 21, 557,[315] it was declared that the tooth of the Buddha be taken from the estate of Du Lao. The four groups are to be gathered for a 'unhindered great assembly'. Gaozu (i.e. Chen Baxian) himself presented himself to worship."[316] Chen Baxian inherited the Liang dynasty, which venerated and served Buddhism, so he had to gain popular support through Buddhist omens and to proclaim that he had gained Heaven's Mandate. This tooth of the Buddha passed hands throughout time before finally being offered to Lingguang si 靈光寺 in Beijing.

## 6 Concluding Remarks

The introduction of Buddhism into China not only meant the propagation of certain religious notions, but also the introduction of a new form of social organization: the monastic community and the *saṃgha*. The structure of this new social organization and its way of life was "embedded" into the original power structures, social hierarchy and lifestyle. "To the Chinese, Buddhism has always remained a doctrine of monks."[317] According to Erik Zürcher, the "religious community" is made up of monastics, the monastic community and monasteries. This organized religion was embedded in the "Han cultural circle" regions of China. Its forces and counter-forces exhibited a kind of real "life experience" and historical setting. Therefore, apart from the underlying ideological conflict between Indian and Han cultures, there was a more realistic, practical, and living conflict between the Buddhist institution and the Chinese way of life. Buddhist ideologies in China not only embodied Indian Buddhist thought and belief, but also reflected the emotional, understanding and experiential aspects of Buddhists in China. As such, the formation of Han Buddhists' beliefs and lives was the result of the dissemination of Indian Buddhism in China, as well as the self-invention of Han Buddhism. During the Han, Wei and Jin periods, the translation of Buddhist precepts and monastic regulations from India, *Vinaya*-regulated lifestyle, and monastic lifestyle were all transmitted into China from Central Asia. They represented the importation of Indian Buddhist belief, lifestyle and tradition to China. During the Northern and Southern dynasties, there were many conflicts and clashes between Indian Buddhist disciplinary ideology, lifestyle, custom and Han cultural tradition. The "distinctions between Chinese and foreigners" was not only a clash on the

315 I.e., the *gengchen* 庚辰 day of the tenth lunar month of the first year of the Yongding era.

316 *Chen shu* 2.34.

317 Zürcher, *Buddhist Conquest of China*, 2.

perceived civilizational level, but even more so on the practical level of institutions and way of life.

During the Wei, Jin, Northern and Southern dynasties, Chinese Buddhism constructed itself on the foundation of Buddhist belief systems from India and Central Asia. It gradually adopted those systems that suited the Chinese belief systems. Through a processes of assimilation and remodeling, Chinese Buddhists were finally able to have their own Buddhist belief system and way of life.

Repentance is an important practice method in Buddhism.[318] When ideas of Buddhist repentance were transmitted to China, repentance rites were brought into the beliefs and lifestyles of Chinese Buddhists. However, the reason why repentance rites possess characteristics of Chinese Buddhist culture, is because of the influence of native Chinese culture, especially from Confucian and Daoist thought. Buddhist repentance rites were developed by eminent monks. On the basis of repentance rites from India and Central Asia, they absorbed some of the concepts from the debates among the three religious teachings during the Wei, Jin, Northern and Southern dynasties, and gradually adopted practices that were suited to the "ritual" (*li*) culture of China Chinese "ritual" (*li*) culture. An example is the "Monastic Regulations" formulated by Daoan, which has "Procedures for sending envoys and confession of transgressions and so on at *poṣadha*." In the Northern and Southern dynasties, repentance rites including practices of singing hymns, *sūtra* recitation and vegetarian purification services, were continuously refined based on the needs and beliefs of the community. Through the creation of worship and repentance rites, Buddhists in the Northern and Southern dynasties transformed this foreign religion into one that conformed to the the belief systems of the Chinese.[319]

Therefore, the Sinicization of Buddhism, completed at the end of the Northern and Southern dynasties, was based on the criteria of traditional Chinese lineage-centered religion, with the production of the *Lianghuang chan* from the Liang Wudi period as its basis and Tiantai repentance rites by Zhiyi as a representative symbol. The earliest form of the *Lianghuang chan* was the "Section on Repentance" in the *Jingzhuzi jingxing fa*, compiled by Prince Jingling of the Southern dynasty, Xiao Ziliang. The work was also called the *Liugen dachan*. During the Chen dynasty, Zhenguan expanded the *Liugen dachan* to become the current *Lianghuang chan* in ten fascicles. During the Tang and Song

318 About the repentance in Chinese Buddhism, the long-term studies of Shioiri Ryōdō ("Juyō katei"; "Reisan") can be consulted.

319 About the repentance rituals during the 5-10th century, see Kuo, *Confession*. About the latest study of repentance rituals, see Hou, *Yishi yanjiu*.

periods, it was called "Liudao cichan" 六道慈懺 (Compassion for the Sixth Paths Repentance), "Cibei chan" 慈悲懺 (Repentance of compassion) and "Liang Wu chan" 梁武懺 (Repentance of Liang Wudi). As such, Zhenguan is the true author of *Lianghuang chan*, not Baochang.

Vegetarianism is a tradition of Chinese Buddhism. Chinese Buddhist monastic life promotes vegetarianism. The formation of vegetarianism as a tradition was not only based upon Mahāyāna scriptures, since it was also influenced by the trend of thought in Buddhism during the Northern and Southern dynasties. During the Qi and Liang periods, Zhou Yong and Shen Yue strongly promoted vegetarianism. Liang Wudi ruled by combining sovereign and religious authorities. Taking the Buddhist notion of compassion as the core and through the implementation of "Service for Abstaining from Alcohol and Meat," he served as an important promoter in establishing vegetarianism as a tradition in Chinese Buddhism.[320] Therefore, factors contributing to the development of vegetarianism include: "scriptural basis," "political power," "conflicts within the *Saṃgha*," and so on. Through its adoption by monastics, vegetarianism became a distinctive feature of Chinese Buddhism. This kind of "lifestyle assimilation" then further strengthened the "institutional embedment" and "ideology" behind it.

At the same time, as Buddhism became prevalent during the Northern and Southern dynasties, groups were gradually formed following the assembly of those connected by the bonds of the same faith. Monastics possessing inspirational power sparked the development of devotional groups when they spread the faith. These collective bodies, organizations or assemblies based on faith were called: *she* 社 (society), *fashe* 法社 (Dharma society), *yi* 邑 (group), *yihui* 邑會 (club), or *yiyi* 邑義 (devotional society), *yiyi* 義邑 (association), *yihui* 義會 (congruence), and so on. Through these organized bodies, Buddhists of the Northern and Southern dynasties constructed Buddha statues, cave temples or conducted services like vegetarian purification, transcribing *sūtras*, *sūtra* recitation and so on. They also engaged in meritorious activities such as building bridges, roads, digging wells, planting trees, providing burial grounds for the destitute, giving food to the poor and others. These devotional groups, characterized by their appeal of sacredness, practicality, virtue and others, gained much support. They represent the religious and charitable organizations

---

320 Suwa, *Chūsei Bukkyō shi*, 57. The studies on Buddhist vegetarianism are many; see Kieschnick, "Buddhist Vegetarianism," 186-212; Lin, "Beichuan Fojiao," 93-138; Suwa, "Saishoku shugi," 73-99.

during the chaotic times of frequent warfare in the Wei, Jin, Northern and Southern dynasties.[321]

The worship of Mahāyāna scriptures and devotion to Buddhas and Bodhisattvas were prevalent during the Wei, Jin, Northern and Southern dynasties. It was especially so for scriptures like the *Fahua jing*, *Huayan jing* and so on, as well as devotion to Maitreya and Avalokiteśvara Bodhisattva. "Pagoda devotion" and "upholding the text of the *Sūtra*" are two core elements from *Fahua jing* devotion. Kumārajīva and his disciples' interpretation of the *Fahua jing* influenced the later iconography of "two Buddhas sitting together." The doctrines of contemplation of the empty nature of transgression from the *Puxian guanjing*—through contemplating the true characteristic, repentance of the six faculties, and the emphasis on seeing the physical body of Samantabhadra Bodhisattva—became the basis for developing Tiantai repentance rites. As such, the worship of Mahāyāna scriptures like the *Fahua jing*, *Huayan jing* not only provided an "upward method" of meditative practice, but also a "downward method" of seeking the mundane and practicality of merit making. They were influential in the construction of caves and images in the Northern and Southern dynasties. In addition, repentance rituals centered on scriptures became popular. For example, Zhiyi's *Fahua sanmei chanyi* was composed during the popularity of the cult of the *Fahua jing* in the Sixteen Kingdoms, Northern and Southern dynasties. It was modeled on Huisi's *Fahua jing anlexing yi* and incorporated the method of the *Lotus samādhi* of the time to become a complete repentance and meditative contemplation system. Furthermore, scripture worship and the cult of buddhas and bodhisattvas were also combined. For instance, faith in the Medicine Buddha was formed through practices like prostrating to the Medicine Buddha, recitation of the *Yaoshi jing*, or combining the setup of "life extension practice" shrines, conducting life release and charitable activities. These Medicine Buddha Dharma service practices drove the formulation of the repentance ritual of the Medicine Buddha. Furthermore, the devotion to Amitābha, Maitreya and Avalokiteśvara and other buddhas and bodhisattvas as well as Buddha's relics were also popular during the Wei, Jin, Northern and Southern dynasties. When this faith and devotion gradually penetrated Chinese society and their spiritual world, slowly being accepted by the Chinese and expressed through the Chinese's own customary systems, only then, was the Sinicization of Buddhism complete.

321 Michibata, *Shakai fukushi jigyō*.

## Appendix 1.1: The Translation of Avalokiteśvara's Name and the Transmission of Related Scriptures

Avalokiteśvara as a Sanskrit term was phonetically transliterated into Chinese in various ways: Afuluzhidishifaluo 阿縛盧枳低濕伐羅, and Anabolouqudishu 阿那波婁去低輸. Before the Sui-Tang period, it was mostly translated as Guangshiyin 光世音, Guanshiyin 觀世音 and Guanyin 觀音. Xuanzang 玄奘 (602-664) translated it as Guanzizai 觀自在. The earliest confirmed translation was the *Zheng fahua jing* 正法華經 translated by Zhu Fahu in 286, in which the name was rendered Guangshiyin. In 291, Mokṣala's translation of the *Fangguan bore jing* 放光般若經 (*Pañcaviṃśati-sāhasrikā-prajñāpāramitā-sūtra*; *T* 221) translated the named as Guanyinsheng 觀音聲. Between 280-321, Nie Daozhen 聶道真 (fl. 307-316) translated the *Guanshiyin shouji jing* 觀世音受記經 (*Sūtra* of Prophecy of Avalokiteśvara), which is now lost, but among his translations, the *Wenshushili banniepan jing* 文殊師利般涅槃經 (*Sūtra* of the *Parinirvāṇa* of Mañjuśrī; *T* 463) and *Wugoushi pusa yingbian jing* 無垢施菩薩應辯經 (*Sūtra* of the Eloquence of Vimāladattā Bodhisattva), use the translated name Guanshiyin. The *Fahua jing lun* 法華經論 (i.e., *Miaofa lianhua jing youbotishe* 妙法蓮華經憂波提舍, *Saddharmapuṇḍarīkōpadeśa*; *T* 1519), translated in 508 by Bodhiruci, translates the name as Guanshi zizai 觀世自在. The *Da Tang Xiyu ji* 大唐西域記 (Great Tang Record of Travels to the Western Region; *T* 2087) states the following:

> [Avalokiteśvara Bodhisattva] is known as "Guanzizai" in Chinese. When it is pronounced in connected syllables it reads as the above-mentioned Sanskrit form, and when it is read separately it is divided into "avalokita," translated as "guan" or "observe," and "īśvara," translated as "zizai" or "master." Formerly it was translated as "Guangshiyin," "Guanshiyin," or "Guanshizizai," all erroneously.[322]

There are clear differences between the new and old translations.

There is a scriptural basis from the "Universal Gate" for the translation Guanshiyin (in Chinese literally "Observing the Sounds of the World"): "If any immeasurable trillions of beings are suffering and hear of this Guanshiyin [Avalokiteśvara] Bodhisattva, and sincerely call his name, Guanshiyin Bodhisattva will immediately perceive that sound and they shall be liberated."[323] This is a kind of interpretation in which a semantic translation is created based upon the meritorious act of the bodhisattva. However,

322 *Da Tang Xiyu ji*, *T* no. 2087, 51: 3.883b22-24:
唐言觀自在, 合字連聲, 梵語如上. 分文散音, 即阿縛盧枳多, 譯曰觀；伊濕伐羅, 譯曰自在. 舊譯爲光世音, 或云觀世音, 或觀世自在, 皆訛謬也 (Trans. Ji & Li, *The Great Tang Dynasty Record of the Western Regions*, 75).

323 *Miaofa lianhua jing*, *T* no. 0262, 9: 7.56c6-8:
若有無量百千萬億衆生受諸苦惱, 聞是觀世音菩薩, 一心稱名, 觀世音菩薩即時觀其音聲皆得解脫.

is Guanshiyin or Guanyin an erroneous translation? Fazang 法藏 (643-712) of the Huayan school in the Tang Dynasty offers the following interpretation:

> "Guanshiyin" is also called "Guangshiyin" or "Guanzizai." Its Sanskrit form is "Avalokiteśvara." "Avalokita," [The first part of this term], means in Chinese "*guan*" or "observe," and "vairo" means "*guang*" or "light." As the spelling and pronunciation are similar, [the first part] was translated as "*guang*" or "light." [The second part] "īśvara," means "*zizai*" or "master," while "svara" means "*yin*" or "sound." Checking scriptures written in Sanskrit reveals that [the part] is rendered either as "*svara*" or as "*īśvara*," and this is why translations are different.[324]

Fazang points out that the Sanskrit source itself include two different names. The name Avalokiteśvara appeared five times in three fragments of the *Fahua jing* from the late fifth-century that was unearthed in Xinjiang in 1927, which subsequently confirmed Fazang's explanation.[325]

Fazang's interpretation, however, never clearly solved the problem of what was an "erroneous translation." The Japanese scholar of Siddhaṃ or Sanskrit, Myōkaku 明覺 (1056-?), in fascicle three of the *Shittan yōketsu* 悉曇要訣 (*Siddhaṃ* Essentials) offers the following interpretation:

> There are four strategies of translation: exactly matching translation, paraphrasing translation, translation with additional words, and contingent translation. Here, rendering "Avalokita" as "Guan" or "observe" and "iśvara" as "*zizai*" or "master" is a case of exactly matching translation. Since "Avabhāsa" refers to "*guang*" or "light," "*ava*" may also take the meaning of "*guang*"; "*avaloka*" means "*guan*," so "*ava*" may also take the meaning of "*guan*." This is a translation with an additional word for a better explanation. In the case of the new translation, where "*loka*(*i*)*śvara*" is rendered as "Guanzizai," isn't this a translation with an added word? The actual meaning of "Lokita" is "*shi*" or "world"; but "*śvara*" is rendered as "*yin*" or "sound." Why? In Sanskrit the letters "ś" and "s" tend to be used with confusion, and in this case, it results in two different words. It is unknown which spelling is correct, and therefore different translations are given according to the spelling. Xuanying 玄應 (fl. 645), in *Yiqiejing yinyi* 一切經音義 (Pronunciation and Meaning in the Complete Buddhist Canon), says that the version from Kucīna has it as "*svara*," so it was translated as "*yin*" or "sound"; while the Indian

324 *Huayan jing tanxuan ji*, *T* no. 1733, 35: 19.471c7-11:
觀世音者, 有名 " 光世音," 有名 " 觀自在." 梵名 " 逋盧羯底攝伐羅," " 逋盧羯底," 此云 " 觀." " 毗盧," 此云 " 光," 以聲字相近, 是以有翻爲 " 光 "; " 攝伐羅," 此云 " 自在 "; " 攝多," 此云 " 音." 勘梵本諸經中有作 " 攝多," 有 " 攝伐羅," 是以翻譯不同也.

325 Tay, *Guanyin*, 241.

> version has it as "*iśvara*," and therefore it was translated as "*zizai*." Thus, it is clear that in this scriptural text, the translation was made according the version that had it as "*śvara*," as "*zizai*"; if according to a version that has "*svara*," it would have been translated as "*yin*." This is a case of contingent translation. Since there are two possibilities in the meaning, both are kept in the translation, and thus it is rendered as "*yin-zizai*." Here are another two examples. Since the term "*siṃha*" may mean "*shizi*" (the lion) or "*wuwei*" (fearlessness), they are combined in the translation of "*shizi-wuwei*." "Jina" has two meanings; one is "*renzhe*" (the benevolent one), and the other "*shengzhe*" (the conqueror). Therefore, in translation it becomes "*ren-sheng zhe*." [These two examples] are in the same manner. What is wrong with it?[326]

Myōkaku emphasized the different translation methods of Sanskrit. The translation "Guanshiyin" was correct. In addition, Xuanying pointed out the differences between the versions from Kucha and India, and noted that the old translations often were derived from those of the Western Regions. Xuanzang, however, went to India and returned via the Western Regions, so he must have known these differences. The *Da Tang Xiyu ji* mentions that "all these are errors of accented pronunciation."[327] Fascicle two of the *Da Tang Da Ciensi sanzang fashi zhuan* 大唐大慈恩寺三藏法師傳 (Biography of the Tripiṭaka Master of Da Cien Temple; *T* 2053) cites an identical excerpt from the *Da Tang Xiyu ji* and critically states, "They are all accented pronunciations,"[328] but without the character *miu* 謬 ("error").[329] It is clear that this character was added by later people. In light of this "accented pronunciation," the languages of the Western Regions were considered dialects of Sanskrit, and the old translation was carried out with this "accented pronunciation" and was not at all a "mistaken translation."

---

326 *Shittan yōketsu, T* 84: 3.540c21-541a8:
翻有四種：敵對翻、會意翻、增事翻、異事翻也. 今 Avalokita 觀, Iśvara 自在者, 是敵對翻意也. Avabhāsa 此云光, 故 *ava* 亦云光； *avaloka* 云觀, 故 *ava* 亦云觀, 此增字翻意也. 新譯中 loka- （ i ） śvara 云觀自在, 豈非增字翻耶. Lokita 正言世, 但 śvara 云音者, śs 二字梵文多濫, 此字作不同, 不知何形為正, 故隨形而翻歟. 玄應《一切經音義》意云：龜茲本云諷（婆）婆羅, 故翻云音；天竺本云濕婆羅, 故翻為自在. 可見正文, 此意依 *śvara* 本, 云自在；依 *svara* 本, 云音也, 此為異事翻也. 有二義, 故合而言之, 名為音自在. 例如 *siṃha* 言下有師子義、無畏義, 故合云師子無畏； *jina* 言下有二義：仁者義、勝者義, 故合云仁勝者. 此亦如是, 有何過耶！

327 *Da Tang Xiyu ji, T* no. 2087, 51: 3.883b23-24: 皆訛謬也.

328 *Da Tang Da Ci'ensi sanzang fashi zhuan, T* no. 2053, 50: 2.230c10: 皆訛也.

329 Matsumoto, "Kannon no gogi," 5-6.

CHAPTER 2

# Faith and Lifestyle of Buddhists in the Sui, Tang and Five Dynasties

## 1 Buddhist Faith and Rituals in the Sui and Tang

The true establishment of Chinese Buddhist systems of repentance rites began from Tiantai Zhiyi 智顗 (538–597). Based on the Tiantai doctrinal perspective, Zhiyi combined the views and repentances of Mahāyāna Buddhism and composed the four repentance rites of the *Fahua sanmei chanyi* 法華三昧懺儀 (*Lotus Samādhi* Repentance Ritual), *Fangdeng sanmei chanfa* 方等三昧懺法 (*Vaipulyas-samādhi* Repentance Practice), *Qing Guanshiyin chanfa* 請觀世音懺法 (Repentance Ritual of Petitioning Avalokiteśvara), and *Jin'guangming chanfa* 金光明懺法 (*Golden Light* Repentance Practice). The *Fahua sanmei chanyi* in particular influenced the actualization and practice methods of Tiantai adepts, and the style of repentance rites compiled in later generations. From the position of repentance rites and ritual procedures that are popular in contemporary Buddhism, such as the *Shuilu yigui* 水陸儀軌 (Water and Land Ritual Procedure), *Jingtu chan* 淨土懺 (Pure Land Repentance), *Yaoshi chan* 藥師懺 (Medicine Buddha Repentance), *Dizang chan* 地藏懺 (Kṣitigarbha Repentance), *Dabei chan* 大悲懺 (Great Compassion Repentance), and so forth, it seems that they are almost all ritual procedures that have been composed by Tiantai masters. At the same time, the repentance rites of Huayan, Chan, Pure Land, Three Stage teachings, and so forth, also thrived extremely well.

### 1.1 *Zhiyi and the Compilation of Repentance Rites*

The unification of political forces taking place nation-wide in the Sui dynasty also set up a social foundation for the unification of southern and northern Chinese Buddhism. Therefore, Zhiyi systematically integrated the general climate, in which the northern regions emphasized practical actualization, while the southern areas focused on doctrinal principles, as he advocated the parallel practice of doctrines and contemplation, and the dual application of calm and insight, to establish the Tiantai teachings which were a unique creation of China. Broadly viewing the life of Zhiyi, we see that it spanned the three dynasties of the Liang, Chen and Sui, and as such, the influence on the Buddhist climate at the time is immeasurable. At the same time, the background of the transmissions from his own teachers also directly influenced his thinking. The

 | DOI:10.1163/9789004431775_004

formation of Zhiyi's system of repentance rites is inseparably connected with these.

At the age of eighteen, Zhiyi renounced into monasticism under Master Faxu 法緒 (d.u) of Guoyuan si 果願寺 in Changsha 長沙, received full ordination at the age of twenty, and studied monastic discipline under the *Vinaya* Master Huikuang 慧曠 (d.u). At Mount Daxian 大賢山, he recited the three scriptures, *Fahua jing*, *Wuliangyi jing* 無量義經 (*Sūtra* of Innumerable Meanings, *T* 276), and *Puxian guanjing* 普賢觀經 (*Sūtra* of Meditating on Samantabhadra; i.e. *Guan Puxian pusa xingfa jing* 觀普賢菩薩行法經, *T* 277), and cultivated the expansive repentance rites, where he received "auspicious signs" which manifested to him.[1] It is stated in the *Sui Tiantai Zhizhe dashi biezhuan* 隋天台智者大師別傳 (Alternate Biography of Sui Dynasty Master Tiantai Zhizhe, *T* 2050):

> At eighteen years of age, he gave himself over to the *śramaṇa* Faxu of Guoyuansi in Xiangzhou and left home. [Master Fa]xu transmitted the ten [novice] precepts to him, and guided him in monastic discipline and etiquette. He then went north to the *Vinaya* Master Huikuang, and also studied the *vaipulyas* [scriptures], thus serving his seniors. Later, he went to Mount Daxian, where he recited the *Fahua jing*, *Wuliangyi jing*, and *Puxian gua jing*. After twenty days, he completed reciting these three texts. Further cultivating the *vaipulyas* repentance rites, with purified mind and vigorous practice the auspicious signs appeared before him. He saw a place of spiritual practice, vast and broad, adorned with majestic ornamentation, but with *sūtra*s scattered in confusion all around. His body sat on a high seat with his feet upon a divan. He recited the *Fahua* [*jing*] with his mouth, and with his hand he rectified the *sūtra*s. After this, his mind and spirit were melded with purity, serene and tranquil every day. After he received full ordination, he was well versed in the *vinaya-piṭaka*. Clearly knowing the actions of past lives, he still always delighted in the happiness of *dhyāna* joy. But, dissatisfied, there was nowhere east of the [Yangzi] River where he could further study.[2]

1 *Xu Gaoseng zhuan*, *T* no. 2060, 50: 17.564b8-13.

2 *Tiantai Zhizhe dashi biezhuan*, *T* no. 2050, 50: 1.191c6-15:
年十有八,投湘州果願寺沙門法緒而出家焉.緒授以十戒,導以律儀.仍攝以北度,詣慧曠律師.兼通方等,故北面事焉.後詣大賢山,誦《法華經》《無量義經》《普賢觀經》,歷涉二旬,三部究竟.進修方等懺,心淨行勤,勝相現前,見道場廣博,妙飾莊嚴;而諸經像,縱橫紛雜;身在高座,足躡繩床;口誦《法華》,手正經像.是後心神融淨,爽利常日.逮受具足,律藏精通.先世萠動,而常樂禪悅.快快江東,無足可問.

Through his own training and the guidance of Huikuang, Zhiyi took great steps in terms of his Buddhist studies, while he also certainly had a foundation in *dhyāna* meditation. At the same time, when Zhiyi was under the tutelage of *Vinaya* Master Huikuang, he "further cultivated the *vaipulyas* repentance rites", which illustrates that when Zhiyi composed the *Fangdeng sanmei chanfa* he already had his own experiences of actualization. Additionally, in the "Fayuan zayuan yuanshiji mulu xu" 法苑雜緣原始集目錄序 (Preface to the Catalogue of the Original Compilation of the Assorted Conditions of the Dharma Garden) in the *Chu sanzang ji ji* 出三藏記集 (Document Collection from the Translation of *Tripiṭaka*, *T* 2145), there is a record of "Fangguang tuoluoni qizhong hui fa yuan ji" 方廣陀羅尼七眾悔法緣記 (Expansive *Dhāraṇī* Seven-Community Remorses Dharma Condition Record).[3] This should be seen as a repentance and remorse rite of the *Da Fangdeng tuoluoni jing* 大方等陀羅尼經 (*Mahāvaipulya-dhāraṇī-sūtra*, *T* 1339), because in the scriptural catalogues of the time we cannot find any other similar scriptures. Furthermore, in the *Gaoseng zhuan* 高僧傳 (Biographies of Eminent Monks, *T* 2059) compiled by Huijiao 慧皎 (497–554), it is recorded that Fada 法達 (fl. 458) previously cultivated this repentance rite.[4] Yet, in the records of the *Xu Gaoseng zhuan* 續高僧傳 (Extended Biographies of Eminent Monks, *T* 2060) and the *Sui Tiantai Zhizhe dashi biezhuan*, there are even more monks who cultivated the expansive repentance rites.[5] Therefore, Zhiyi should have re-edited the *Fangdeng sanmei chanfa* according to Tiantai doctrinal positions and his own experiences of actualization.

Because there was nobody east of the [Yangzi] River from whom Zhiyi could seek the Dharma to study and train in, he risked his life and went to Mount Dasu 大蘇山 in Guangzhou 光州 to seek guidance from Huisi 慧思 (515-577), under whom he spent eight years. It was only after this that he went to Jinling to propagate the Buddhadharma. Therefore, Zhiyi was greatly influenced by Huisi. Huisi looked very highly upon both the thought and practice of repentance. The "Huisi Biography" in the *Xu Gaoseng zhuan* states that during Huisi's

---

With regard to Zhiyi's life and works the first detailed account in Chinese to recommend is Pan Guiming's 潘桂明 *Zhiyi pingzhuan* 智顗評傳 (Critical Biography of Zhiyi). In Japanese it should be Satō Tetsuei's 佐藤哲英 *Tendai daishi no kenkyū* 天臺大師の研究 (Master Tiantai Studies) and *Zoku Tendai daishi no kenkyū* 續天臺大師の研究 (Further Master Tiantai Studies).

3 *Chu sanzang ji ji*, *T* no. 2145, 55: 12.91b3: 方廣陀羅尼七眾悔法緣記第十二 (出彼經).

4 *Gaoseng zhuan*, *T* no. 2059, 50:11. 398a25-b2:
沙門法達,爲僞國僧正.欽高日久,未獲受業.…… 達頂禮求哀,願見救護.高曰：君業重難救,當可如何？自今以後依方等苦悔,當得輕受.

5 Ōno Hideto has listed these practitioners into tables; see Ōno, "*Tendai shikan seiritsushi*", 91–95.

early years as a monastic he contracted dysentery and "sought to end it through repentance".[6] Before his death he asked the community: "If there are ten people who do not cling to their life and always cultivate the *Lotus samādhi, Pratyutpanna samādhi,* the Buddha recollection *samādhi* (*Nianfo sanmei* 念佛三昧), and *Vaipulyas* repentance (*Fangdeng chanhui* 方等懺悔), always sit and practice austerities, whatever they need I will personally provide it for them, which will certainly be of mutual benefit. If there is nobody like this, I shall leave".[7] In the records of Huisi's biography, it is evident that Huisi greatly valued and actualized the *Lotus samādhi* (*Fahua sanmei* 法華三昧), *Bozhou sanmei* 般舟三昧 (*Pratyutpanna samādhi*), Buddha recollection *samādhi,* and *Vaipulyas* repentance. According to the *Sui Tiantai Zhizhe dashi biezhuan,* Huisi cultivated the *Vaipulyas* repentance for seven years.[8] Within Zhiyi's four types of *samādhi,* the *Samādhi* of Constant Sitting (*Changzuo sanmei* 常坐三昧) is the "Buddha recollection *samādhi*", the *Samādhi* of Constant Walking (*Changxing sanmei* 常行三昧) is the *Pratyutpanna samādhi,* the Half Walking Half Sitting *Samādhi* (*Banxing banzuo sanmei* 半行半坐三昧) is the *Vaipulyas samādhi* (*fangdeng sanmei* 方等三昧) and the *Lotus samādhi,* and the Neither Walking Nor Sitting *Samādhi* (*feixing feizuo sanmei* 非行非坐三昧) is what Huisi refers to as the "According to One's Intents *Samādhi*" (*suiziyi sanmei* 隨自意三昧).[9] Furthermore, Zhiyi took the *Qing Guanshiyin chanfa* and added the complete repentance rite of the "Neither Walking Nor Sitting *Samādhi*", and the *Jin'guangming chanfa* and *Qing Guanshiyin chanfa* are completely similar in terms of their order of ritual procedure. Therefore, we can find the source of Zhiyi's four types of *samādhi* from Huisi himself.

Huisi emphasized *dhyāna* meditation, but at the same time also emphasized psychic powers. However, the attainment of *dhyāna* meditation and psychic powers must be preceded by repentance. The *Zhufa wuzheng sanmei famen* 諸法無諍三昧法門 (Dharma-Gate of the *Samādhi* Wherein All Dharmas are Without Dispute, *T* 1923), fascicle one, states:

---

6 *Xu Gaoseng zhuan, T* no. 2060, 50: 17.562c13-14: 遂顯厲疾, 求誠乞懺.

7 *Xu Gaoseng zhuan, T* no. 2060, 50: 563c19-21:
若有十人, 不惜身命, 常修法華、般舟、念佛三昧、方等懺悔, 常坐苦行者, 隨有所須, 吾自供給, 必相利益. 如無此人, 吾當遠去.

8 *Sui Tiantai Zhizhe dashi biezhuan, T* no. 2050, 50:1.191c15-17:
時有慧思禪師, 武津人也. 名高嵩嶺, 行深伊洛. 十年常誦, 七載方等, 九旬常坐, 一時圓證.

9 About the relationship of the Neither-Walking-Nor-Sitting *samādhi, Samādhi* According to One's Own Intention and Enlightening *Samādhi,* cf. Sakamoto, "Shishu sanmai", 159–77.

> One who wishes to seek liberation for self and others,
> Should universally practice the six perfections everywhere.
> First, aspire to the supreme mind of *bodhi*,
> Cultivate patience and be firm in upholding morality,
> Earnestly perform repentance in six sessions day and night,
> Aspire for the heart of great love, compassion and equality,
> [Practice] the vigour that does not cling to body or life,
> One wishing to seek the Buddha's path upholds pure morality,
> And focuses cultivation of *dhyāna* and wisdom to gain psychic powers,
> Enabling one to subdue the deity Māra and overcome non-Buddhists,
> …
> Uphold pure morality and cultivate *dhyāna* meditation,
> Abandon [clinging to] fame and personal gain,
> Remove oneself from clamour and ignorant companions,
> Recollect the Buddhas of the ten directions and always repent.[10]

Whether it is self-liberation or the teaching of others, the accomplishment of the path to Buddhahood and the attainment of *dhyāna* meditation and psychic powers were believed to be only achieved through the constant cultivation of repentance and the constant practice of the six perfections.

At the same time, Zhiyi absorbed Huisi's "Practice with Characteristics" and "Practice without Characteristics". In his *Mohe zhiguan* 摩訶止觀 (Greater Teaching on Calm and Insight, *T* 1911) he states:

> Master Nanyue said: "Are not 'Joyous Easy Practice with Characteristics' and 'Joyous Easy Practice without Characteristics' so named based upon [the distinction between] phenomena and principle? When people undertake this practice while being connected to phenomena as they cultivate repentance of the six sense faculties in order to realize it and bring it about, it is named 'With Characteristics'. When people directly contemplate all phenomena as empty as an expedient means, it is said to be 'Without Characteristics'. At the time of wondrous realization, both of these are abandoned".[11]

10 *Zhufa wuzheng sanmei famen*, *T* no. 1923, 46: 1.629c4-13:
欲自求度及眾生, 普遍十方行六度, 先發無上菩提心, 修習忍辱堅持戒, 晝夜六時勤懺悔, 發大慈悲平等心, 不惜身命大精進. 欲求佛道持淨戒, 專修禪智獲神通, 能降天魔破外道 …… 持清淨戒修禪定, 捨諸名聞及利養, 遠離憒鬧癡眷屬, 念十方佛常懺悔.

11 *Mohe zhiguan*, *T* no. 1911, 46: 2.14a18-21:
南岳師云：有相安樂行、無相安樂行, 豈非就事理得如是名. 持是行人, 涉事修

Based on Huisi's teachings of "Joyous Easy Practice with Characteristics" and "Joyous Easy Practice without Characteristics", Zhiyi analyzed the "Puxian pusa quanfa pin" 普賢菩薩勸發品 (Chapter on the Exhortations of the Bodhisattva Samantabhadra) and "Anlexing pin" 安樂行品 (Chapter of Comfortable Practices) of the *Fahua jing* as "Practice with Characteristics" (*youxiang xing* 有相行) and "Practice without Characteristics" (*wuxiang xing* 無相行). The practice with characteristics indicates recitation of the *Fahua jing* with a scattered mind. One does not enter into *dhyāna* meditation and, irrespective of walking, standing or sitting, single-mindedly recite the *Fahua jing*. During the six sessions of the day and night, one repents transgressions of the six senses. The practice without characteristics, on the other hand, refers to entering into deep *dhyāna* meditation, and contemplates the six senses by way of knowledge, realizing the correct emptiness of the true characteristics of the three truths.[12] Huisi transmitted the *Lotus samādhi* to Zhiyi at Mount Dasu 大蘇山 in Guangzhou 光州, and subsequently Zhiyi attained realization due to this. We can thus see the importance that both teachers gave to this *samādhi*.

Therefore, the formation of Tiantai repentance rites was due to the influence of both Buddhist repentance rites, as well as the popularity of performance of repentance rituals during Zhiyi's time in the North and South dynasties and the influence of Zhiyi's masters—Huikuang and Huisi. Thus, Zhiyi composed the four repentance rites, pushing the repentance rites of Chinese Buddhism to a new height.

### 1.1.1 Explanation of the Term "Repentance" (*Chanhui* 懺悔)

Following the translation of Buddhist scripture, "repentance" (*chanhui*) gradually became a term commonly appearing in Buddhist scriptures.[13] Chinese patriarchs and eminent monks began explaining the term "repentance" after its translation with great variation in what they said. The earliest explanation of "repentance" was done by Zhiyi in his *Shi chan boluomi cidi famen* 釋禪波羅蜜次第法門 (Explanation of the Gradual Method of the Perfection of *Dhyāna*, also called *Cidi chanmen* 次第禪門 [Gradual *Dhyāna* Method], *T* 1916),[14] in which Zhiyi gave the following explanation:

六根懺，爲悟入弄引，故名有相；若直觀一切法空爲方便者，故言無相. 妙證之時，悉皆兩捨.

12 Pan, "Pingzhuan", 326.

13 About the studies on repentance linguistically and philologically, cf. Sheng, "Chanhui yuanyu".

14 Shioiri, "Sange no Tenkai", 4.

> What is "repentance" (*chanhui*)? *Chan* is to apologize to the Three Jewels and all sentient beings. *Hui* is to have remorse, correct faults and lament: "If I am to eliminate this transgression of mine, in the future I would rather lose my own life than ever create again such painful karma". Just as a *bhikṣu* said to the Buddha, "I would rather embrace this blazing, great fire than ever dare to transgress against the pure precepts of the Thus Come One". Generating this sort of attitude, solely wishing that Three Jewels will bear witness and accept one, is named "repentance" (*chanhui* 懺悔). Furthermore, *chan* is to not externally conceal [ones faults], and *hui* is to internally lay down the blame. *Chan* is to know that the transgression is wrong, and *hui* is to fear its retribution. There are many other [explanations of the meaning], so we will not go into detail here. To speak of the essential point, if one is able to know that phenomena are false, one can forever cease evil karma and cultivate the wholesome path. This is known as "repentance" (*chanhui*).[15]

According to Zhiyi's explanation of repentance (*chanhui*), *chan* is the wish that the Three Jewels and all living beings will act as witness and accept one, and *hui* is seeking to express correction of one's faults due to regret and remorse. *Chan* is externally not concealing and acknowledging the fault of transgression, and *hui* is an inner sense of responsibility and fear of receiving the result of that action. All together, if one is able to know the false nature of all phenomena, one can forever end evil actions and cultivate what is wholesome. This is Zhiyi's fundamental position on repentance.

The above explanation is obviously not the meaning of the original term for repentance. But, in Zhiyi's *Jin'guangming wenju* 金光明文句 (Words and Phrases of the *Golden Light Sūtra*), fascicle three, "Shi chanhui pin" 釋懺悔品 (Explanation of Repentance Chapter), he further adds a number of other meanings to his explanation of "repentance":

1. [In "repentance" (*chanhui*),] *chan* is the leader, and *hui* is to yield. Just as if a secular person offends the king, one is subdued and yields, not daring to rebel or resist. Not resisting is to "yield", one acquiesces to the "leader". The practitioner is likewise. They yield at the feet of the Three Jewels,

---

15 *Shi chan boluomi cidi famen*, *T* no. 1916, 46: 2.485b16-24:
夫懺悔者, 懺名懺謝三寶及一切眾生, 悔名慚愧改過求哀. 我今此罪, 若得滅者, 於將來時, 寧失身命, 終不更造如斯苦業. 如比丘白佛：我寧抱是熾然大火, 終不敢毀犯如來淨戒. 生如是心, 唯願三寶證明攝受, 是名懺悔. 復次, 懺名外不覆藏, 悔則內心剋責；懺名知罪為惡, 悔則恐受其報. 如是眾多, 今不廣說. 舉要言之, 若能知法虛妄, 永息惡業, 修行善道. 是名懺悔.

correcting and acquiescing to the principles, not daring to act wrongly. This is named "repentance".

2. Also, *chan* is bright practices, and *hui* is dark practices. Dark practices should be regretted and not performed, bright practices should be engaged in and done. Combining the notions of what is to be done and forsaken, this is said to be "repentance".
3. Also, *chan* is to cultivate the future, and *hui* is remorse for the past. Those unwholesome, evil practices performed in the past are despised and rejected. This is named "*hui*". Those wholesome practices abandoned in former days one now vows to diligently cultivate. This is named "*chan*". Due to abandoning the past and seeking the future, it is called "repentance".
4. Also, *chan* is to confess many faults, admit mistakes, and not dare to conceal them. *Hui* is to stop the mind which continues [committing transgressions], rejecting and forsaking it. Forsaking both the actor and the action, it is thus known as "repentance".
5. Also, *chan* is regret (*can* 慚), and *hui* is remorse (*kui* 愧). "Regret" is regret to the gods, and "remorse" is remorse for humanity. Humans see what is exposed, and gods see what is hidden. The hidden is subtle, the exposed is coarse. Due to rejecting both the coarse and the subtle, it is known as "repentance".
6. Also, "humans" are sagely people, and "gods" are saintly people. Due to not encountering the stream of the sagely and saintly, it is "repentance" (*chanhui*). Also, the sagely and saintly are both humans and gods. This is "gods" in the highest sense. Gods in the highest sense is principle. Sages and saints are phenomena. By not encountering either phenomena or principle, it is "repentance".
7. Also, "regret" (*can* 慚) for those saintly gods of the three vehicles, "remorse" (*kui* 愧) for the sagely humans of the three vehicles. Due to not encountering these gods and humans, it is known as "regret and remorse" (*cankui* 慚愧).
8. Also, sages and saints of the three vehicles are all human beings. The gods are the principle in the highest sense. It is with respect to the regret and remorse (*cankui*) of these humans and gods that it is called "repentance".
9. Also, the sages and saints of the three vehicles are not even *bodhisattva* sages, let alone *bodhisattva* saints. Now, one has "regret and remorse" (*cankui*) for the thirty states of mind of the sages and ten grounds of the saints, therefore it is known as "regret and remorse repentance" (*cankui chanhui*). Altogether, these sages and saints are all humans, and the gods are called the principle in the highest sense. It is with reference to these

humans and gods that one speaks of "regret and remorse" (*cankui*), and thus it is called "repentance".

10. Also, when the thirty states of mind are eliminated, one is judged a saintly person, and the ten [stages of] faith are sagely people. It is with respect to these [meanings of] sage and saint that one discusses "regret and remorse repentance" (*cankui chanhui*). Altogether, these sages and saints are called human beings, and the gods are the principle in the highest sense. It is with respect to these humans and gods that one speaks of "regret and remorse repentance" (*cankui chanhui*). The name is the combination of the ten explanations.[16]

Above is Zhiyi's ten explanations for repentance: (1) follow and obey without resisting, without daring to do what is wrong; (2) use bright practices contrary to dark practices; (3) cultivate the future and correct the past; (4) confess faults, rejecting and abandoning them; (5) after the fifth type, he uses "regret and remorse" (*cankui*) to understand repentance, a special feature of Zhiyi's explanations. At the same time, Zhiyi pairs humans and gods, and sages and saints, of which the scholar Shioiri Ryōdō assumes that this is an explanation through the Tiantai doxography of *piṭaka*, common, specific and complete teachings (*zang tong bie yuan* 藏通别圓).[17]

Zhiyi's broad explanation of repentance shows his extraordinary ability to create theoretical systems. However, this may also be closely connected with Zhiyi's lack of familiarity with the original meanings of these terms in Sanskrit.[18] Therefore, Zhiyi's explanation of the term "repentance" (*chanhui*) does not relate to the original meaning of the word(s), but makes a creative exegesis

---

16 *Jin guangming jing wenju*, *T* no. 1785, 39: 3. 59a8-b4:
懺者, 首也. 悔者, 伏也. 如世人得罪於王, 伏欵順從不敢違逆, 不逆爲伏, 順從爲首. 行人亦爾, 伏三寶足下, 正順道理, 不敢作非, 故名懺悔. 又懺名白法, 悔名黑法, 黑法須悔而勿作, 白法須企而尙之, 取捨合論, 故言懺悔. 又懺名修來, 悔名改往. 往日所作惡、不善法鄙而惡之, 故名爲悔；往日所棄一切善法, 今日已去, 誓願勤修, 故名爲懺. 棄往求來, 故名懺悔. 又懺名披陳眾失, 發露過咎, 不敢隱諱；悔名斷相續心, 厭悔捨離. 能作所作合棄, 故言懺悔. 又懺者名慚, 悔者名愧；慚則慚天, 愧則愧人；人見其顯, 天見其冥；冥細顯麁, 麁細皆惡, 故言懺悔. 又人是賢人, 天是聖人, 不逮賢聖之流, 是故懺悔. 又賢聖俱是人天, 是第一義天, 第一義天是理, 賢聖是事, 不逮事理, 俱皆懺悔. 又慚三乘之聖天, 愧三乘之賢人, 不逮此天人, 故名慚愧, 慚愧名懺悔. 又三乘賢聖皆是人, 第一義理爲天, 約此人天慚愧, 故名懺悔. 又三乘賢聖尙非菩薩之賢, 況菩薩之聖, 今慚愧三十心之賢, 十地之聖, 故名慚愧懺悔. 總此賢聖皆是人, 第一義理名爲天, 約此人天論慚愧, 故名懺悔. 又三十心去自判聖人, 十信是賢人, 約此賢聖論慚愧懺悔. 總此賢聖皆名人, 第一義理名爲天, 約此人天論慚愧懺悔, 合十番釋名也.

17 Shioiri, "Sange no tenkai", 6.

18 From Zhiyi's life story, there is no sign showing that he had learned Sanskrit. Cf. Pan, "Pingzhuan".

which then provides a foundation for the composition of repentance rites and their actualization.

### 1.1.2 The Reasons for Repentance

In Zhiyi's system of cultivation and realization, the special feature is the dual emphasis on both calm and insight. In order to attain calm and insight, one must first uphold morality. However, ordinary common sentient beings are unable to purely uphold morality as they break precepts and commit transgressions, and, therefore, must repent their negative actions. This is a necessity in terms of both logic and actualization and is the simplest and most original reason for repentance.

In the correct cultivation methods of Tiantai calm and insight practice, in the *Cidi chanmen* and the later *Mohe zhiguan*, which explicate calm and insight as complete and sudden, Zhiyi raises the point that one must first prepare twenty-five preliminary practices. Within these, in the first of a set of five conditions is "upholding morality purely". In the *Cidi chanmen*, "upholding morality purely" is developed into three aspects: one, clarification of the presence of morality or its absence; two, clarification of upholding and transgression; and three, clarification of repentance. The third, "clarification of repentance" is further divided into application of the mind of repentance and clarification of methods of repentance. Zhiyi explains the goals and meaning of repentance as follows:

> What is application of the mind of repentance? If a person by nature does not themselves commit anything evil, then there would be no transgression to repent. Practitioners cannot absolutely uphold morality, and if at some time they encounter bad situations they may thereupon end up breaking [precepts]. Whether it is a serious or a light infraction, due to breaking the precepts their *śīla* is impure, and *samādhi* will not be generated. By analogy, it is like how if a piece of cloth is stained with oil, it will not be able to receive the dye. Therefore, it is appropriate that one must repent, and due to repentance their various precepts will be purified, and [they will be able to] generate *samādhi*.[19]

---

19 *Shi chan boluomi cidi famen, T* no. 1916, 46: 2.485b7-12:
云何名運懺悔之心？若人性自不作惡, 則無罪可悔. 行人既不能決定持戒, 或於中間值遇惡緣, 即便破毀. 若輕若重, 以戒破故, 則尸羅不淨, 三昧不生. 譬如衣有垢膩, 不受染色, 是故宜須懺悔, 以懺悔故, 則戒品清淨, 三昧可生.

Based on the nature of human society, if there is no conscious intention to commit transgression, then there is not any transgression at all which could be repented. However, along the process of cultivation, it is difficult for *practitioners* to avoid encountering bad circumstances upon which they break precepts and transgress against morals. Due to breaking the precepts, *samādhi* will not arise as a result. In this way, because their various categories of precepts will become purified because of repenting, they are subsequently able to bring about *samādhi*.

Zhiyi discusses the meaning of repentance from the relationship between morality, meditation and wisdom, which of course is very different from repentance and rectification, which is merely based on morality and precepts alone. In his *Cidi chanmen*, fascicle two, he cites the ten kinds of morality from the *Da zhidu lun* 大智度論 (Treatise on the Great Perfection of Wisdom, *T* 1509), which subsumes all forms of morality into these ten types.[20] For the sake of convenience, we may represent this pictorially, as follows:

1. Upholding precepts without lack: not transgressing the four serious precepts.
2. Upholding precepts without break: not transgressing the *saṅghavaśeṣa* precepts.
3. Upholding precepts without interruption: not transgressing the lower three categories of precepts.
4. Upholding precepts without flaw: not generating mental states of deception of affliction, being aware of taint. (Not tainting the precepts, morality derived from meditation.)
5. Upholding precepts according to the path: mental engagement in contemplation of the sixteen aspects, developing the knowledge of receptivity into dissatisfaction. (Morality derived from the path.)
6. Upholding precepts without attachment: if an *anāgamin* completely cuts off the nine types of thought of the desire realm, up to completely [cutting off] the various bonds of lust for form and lust for the formless. (Morality which cuts off discipline.)

20 *Shi chan boluomi cidi famen*, *T* no. 1916, 46: 2.484c18-485a5: 一時不缺戒. 謂持初四重不犯. 二持不破戒. 謂對僧殘不犯. 三持不穿戒. 謂對下三篇不犯. 四持無瑕戒. 亦名不雜戒. 謂不起諂心及諸惱覺觀雜念. 亦名定共戒. 五持隨道戒. 即是心行十六行觀. 發苦忍智慧. 亦名道共戒. 六持無著戒. 即阿那含人. 若斷欲界九品思惟盡. 名斷律儀戒. 乃至色愛無色愛等. 諸結使盡. 皆名無著戒. 七持智所讚戒. 發菩提心. 爲令一切眾生. 得涅槃故持戒. 如是持戒. 則爲智所讚歎. 亦可言持菩薩十重四十八輕戒. 此戒能至佛果故. 爲智所讚歎. 八持自在戒. 菩薩持戒. 於種種破戒緣中. 而得自在. 亦可言菩薩知罪不罪不可得故. 但隨利益眾生. 而持戒心. 無所執故. 名自在戒. 九持具足戒. 菩薩能具一切眾生戒法. 及上地戒. 十持隨定戒. 不起滅定現種種威儀戒法. 以度眾生.

7. Upholding precepts which are praised by the wise: upholding precepts due to mental aspiration for *Bodhi*, in order to let all living beings attain *nirvāṇa*. This kind of upholding the precepts can also be called upholding the *bodhisattvas*' ten serious and forty-eight light precepts, because these precepts enable one to reach the fruition of a Buddha.
8. Upholding of precepts with freedom: when *bodhisattvas* uphold precepts, they attain freedom with respect to the many various conditions that cause one to break precepts. This is also said to be because *bodhisattvas* know that transgression and non-transgression are not apprehensible.
9. Upholding precepts with endowment: *bodhisattvas* are able to be endowed with all the types of precepts of living beings, as well as the precepts of the higher stages.
10. Upholding precepts according to meditation: not generating the cessation meditation, they manifest the various practices of deportment and morality.

Zhiyi continued the tradition of thinking from the *Fanwang jing* 梵網經 (*Brahma Net Sūtra*, *T* 1484), "Living beings receive the precepts of the Buddhas, and immediately enter into the status of a Buddha; their status is already the same as great awakening".[21] Therefore, in the seventh, "Upholding precepts which are praised by the wise", it raises the idea of attaining Buddhahood based on upholding morality.[22] At the same time, in his *Miaofa lianhua jing xuanyi* 妙法蓮華經玄義 (Profound Meaning of the *Lotus Sūtra*, *T* 1716), end of fascicle three,[23] he analyses the ten kinds of precepts into the four types of doctrinal classification of *piṭaka*, common, specific and complete, in order to execute his explanation. Later, in the *Mohe zhiguan*, Zhiyi further took the precepts in accord with the path to precepts with endowment out of the ten types of precepts and evolved them into upholding precepts as the real truth, conventional truth and ultimate truth of the middle way, as well as upholding the precepts through the principles of the three contemplations of the three truths. From this we can see that Zhiyi gave an extremely high position to upholding morality purely as a key point in the cultivation of calm and insight, and the development of meditation and wisdom.

However, after obtaining the precepts, if one breaks the precepts and loses them, they will certainly commit a transgression. Repentance is precisely in

21 *Fan wang jing*, *T* no. 1484, 24: 2.1004a20-21: 眾生受佛戒, 即入諸佛位, 位同大覺已.

22 About the variation of the ten categories of precepts, cf. Satō, "kairitsu no kenkyū", 585–89.

23 *Miaofa lianhua jing xuanyi*, *T* no. 1716, 33: 3.717b23-c23.

order to cease the transgression, but in Zhiyi's thought, how does he view transgressing action? In his *Cidi chanmen*, he states:

> There are three kinds of transgression: One, transgression by violation of precepts that gives rise to obstacles on the path. Two, transgressions by nature. Three, fundamental transgressions that are the affliction of ignorance. The term "transgression", is "to destroy". When they appear, they destroy the virtues and wisdom of practitioners, and one experiences their retribution in the three lower destinies in a future lifetime, thus they are capable of destroying and rending the body and mind of the practitioner. Hence, they are known as transgressions.[24]

The three kinds of transgression mentioned by Zhiyi are: First, transgressions by violation of precepts that gives rise to obstacles on the path. This refers to the morality practices of the *śrāvaka* disciples when practitioners violate moral discipline and the transgressing action is set according to the characteristics of the precepts. Second, transgressions by nature. This is the natural transgressing action which dependently generates a result. For example, when a *bhikṣu* transgresses the precept of killing a living being, even if he engages in repentance with formal act to remove the transgression which is an obstacle to the path, this is still unable to remove the natural transgression by which condition the action brings about the retribution of killing. Third, fundamental transgressions which are the affliction of ignorance. This refers to the fact that the root of the transgression comes from the affliction of ignorance.[25]

When a cultivator transgresses the precepts and commits an offense, why is repentance able to remove it? In his *Mohe zhiguan*, Zhiyi states:

> Four, clarification of repentance to purity. Transgressing both phenomena and principle obstruct calm and insight, and meditation and wisdom will not develop. How does repentance allow the transgression to be eliminated and not obstruct calm and insight? If the transgressed event is a medium or light fault, the text of the discipline has practices of repentance. If the repentance practice is accomplished, then it is called pure. With the purification of morality and transformation of the obstacle, calm and insight are easily clarified. If one makes a serious transgression,

---

24 *Shi chan boluomi cidi famen*, *T* no. 1916, 46: 2.486c4-7:
罪有三品：一者違無作起障道罪, 二者體性罪, 三者無明煩惱根本罪. 通稱罪者, 摧也. 現則摧損行人功德智慧, 未來之世三塗受報, 則能摧折行者色心, 故名爲罪.

25 Shi, *Tiantai chanfa*, 59.

> one is a dead person with respect to the Buddha Dharma. There is no repentance practice in the Hīnayāna, but according to the Mahāyāna one is permitted to repent, just as explained above in the four types of *samādhi*, which shall become clearer below. Next, contemplation by principle, for those who have a perverted, inaccurate perception of the truth. Such a person's mental attachment is weak, covered and clouded, but if one applies the mind of right contemplation to refute their view and attachment, with regret and remorse, with a sense of shame, they will lower their head and be responsible for themselves. With a mind pointed and on the right track, the transgressing obstacle can be removed, and they can develop calm and insight. If their view is heavy, they can still cultivate repentance with a contemplative mind, which we shall explain later. Based on the four kinds of *samādhi*, if the transgressed event is of serious offence, one can practice repentance.[26]

Zhiyi believes that transgressing the two aspects of the phenomenal and the principle are both able to obstruct calm and insight and make meditation and wisdom unable to come about. Shioiri Ryōdō thinks that the phenomenal is an attitude expressed from the clear texts of the *sūtra*s and commentaries, whereas the principle is an attitude and understanding expressed from comprehension of the clear texts of the *sūtra*s and commentaries as substantiality.[27] In fact, the phenomenal should refer to the phenomenal characteristics, such as the characteristics of the precepts, and so forth, from which they can be shown and revealed; whereas the principle instead refers to ideas, views and comprehension. Transgressions in terms of phenomenal characteristics are lighter, so using the practices of repentance in the codes of precepts one is able to reach a state of purity. However, if one transgresses in terms of principles, a mind with correct contemplation can refute that opinionated attachment and cause them to generate a sense of regret and remorse wherein they can lower their head and blame themselves. If obstacles of contemplation of principles are heavier and one repents with a mind of contemplation, in the Hīnayāna practices there are no methods by which one can be saved. It is only in the Mahāyāna

---

26 *Mohe zhiguan*, *T* no. 1911, 46: 4.39c3-14:
四明懺淨者, 事理二犯, 俱障止觀, 定慧不發. 云何懺悔令罪消滅, 不障止觀耶. 若犯事中輕過, 律文皆有懺法, 懺法若成, 悉名清淨. 戒淨障轉, 止觀易明. 若犯重者佛法死人, 小乘無懺法；若依大乘, 許其懺悔. 如上四種三昧中說, 下當更明. 次理觀小僻不當諦者, 此人執心若薄, 不苟封滯, 但用正觀心破其見著, 慚愧有羞低頭自責, 策心正轍罪障可消, 能發止觀也. 見若重者, 還於觀心中修懺, 下當說也. 若犯事中重罪, 依四種三昧則有懺法.

27 Shioiri, "Sange no tenkai", 10.

that repentance practices with the four kinds of *samādhi* let one attain purity for the regretted transgression.

Therefore, Zhiyi not only integrated the transgression of precepts and practices of repentance in the *śrāvaka* disciples' teachings, but also discovered methods of repenting transgressions in the Mahāyāna *sūtras* and texts, broadly incorporating transgressions by nature and the fundamental affliction of ignorance. At the same time, he took those repentance practices and ultimately condensed them into the four kinds of *samādhi*, and from this actually constructed the Chinese Buddhist practices of repentance.

### 1.1.3 Three Types of Repentance

Zhiyi raises three kinds of repentance practice based on three types of transgression. He states:

> One, clarification of repentance with formal act, which defeats transgressions by violations of precepts with obstruction to the path. Two, clarification of repentance contemplating characteristics, which defeats the transgression of actions which are evil by nature. Therefore, the *Moheyan lun* 摩訶衍論 (Discourse on Mahāyāna) states: "If a *bhikṣu* transgresses the precept against killing living beings, although they can repent and attain purity of morality, the transgression that obstructs the path will be eliminated, but the result of killing will not be eliminated". This can prove the former and explain the latter. One should understand that the intentional application in repentance which contemplates signs is very great, and is able to remove transgressions by nature. Three, as for the repentance that eliminates transgressions by contemplating the unarisen, it defeats transgressions due to habituation of ignorance and afflictions. Only this can ultimately remove the root source of transgression.[28]

Zhiyi has three kinds of repentance practice: One, repentance with formal act (*Zuofa chanhui* 作法懺悔). This is for transgressions of the *śrāvaka* disciples in breaking and violating moral discipline. Two, repentance contemplating signs (*Guanxiang chanhui* 觀相懺悔). This is for transgressions by nature to defeat the conditions of action. Three, repentance which contemplates the unarisen

28 *Shi chan boluomi cidi famen*, *T* no. 1916, 46: 2.486c7-14:
一明作法懺悔者, 破違無作障道罪. 二明觀相懺者, 破除體性惡業罪. 故摩訶衍論云：若比丘犯殺生戒, 雖復懺悔得戒清淨, 障道罪滅而殺報不滅, 此可以證前釋後, 當知觀相懺悔用功既大, 能除體性之罪. 三觀無生懺悔罪滅者, 破除無明一切煩惱習因之罪, 此則究竟除罪源本.

(*Guan wusheng chanhui* 觀無生懺悔). This defeats the affliction of ignorance, and ultimately eliminates the root source of all transgressions.

In his *Cidi chanmen*, Zhiyi explains in detail the three kinds of repentance practice. Repentance with formal act is when the *Saṃgha* community holds the formal act of *karma*, and according to the specific precept code, one repents the transgressing action in accordance with the Dharma. They do not need to see any kind of auspicious sign, and do not need to contemplate emptiness through wisdom. However, within the moral discipline codes, the four serious transgressions cannot be repented. The *Cidi chanmen* states:

> One, Repentance with Formal Act. This maintains the moral discipline, and most of the previous practices are repentance rites of the Hīnayāna. ... First, clarification of Repentance with Formal Act. Due to performing a wholesome deed to counter an evil deed, it is known as repentance. As in the *Vinaya*, it regularly uses this practice to eliminate transgressions. Why? As repentance in the second category, twenty members of the community enact the *karma* rite of seclusion with the intention of eliminating the transgression, and so forth, to completion. This is known as elimination. This does not mention seeing various signs or omens, and also does not discuss the knowledgeable contemplation of emptiness. Therefore, understand that this is just Repentance with Formal Act, the performance of this *karma* rite. This is the case up until the third category, they are all formal acts, which are easily understood. The meaning is as clarified in detail in the discipline codes, though they do not elucidate repentance of the four serious actions.[29]

Repentance with Formal Act is attaining purification of the transgressing obstruction through the formal act. Repentance with Formal Act in the canon of discipline does not state that the four serious transgressions can be repented. However, in Zhiyi's *Cidi chanmen*, he cites the *Zuimiao chujiao jing* 最妙初教經 (Most Sublime First Teaching *Sūtra*), which is the *Miao shengding jing* 妙勝定經 (Sublime Superior Meditation *Sūtra*) mentioned in the *Xiao zhiguan* 小止觀 (Lesser Teaching of Calm and Insight) (i.e. *Xiuxi zhiguan zuochan fayao* 修習止觀坐禪法要 [Essentials of Practicing *Śamatha* and *Vipaśyanā*

29 *Shi chan boluomi cidi famen*, *T* no. 1916, 46: 2.485c1-12:
一作法懺悔, 此扶戒律. ...... 前一法多是小乘懺悔法. ...... 初明作法懺悔者, 以作善事反惡事故, 故名懺悔. 如毘尼中, 一向用此法滅罪, 何以故？如懺第二篇二十眾作別住下意出罪等羯磨作法成就, 即名爲滅. 此不論見種種相貌, 亦不論智慧觀空. 故知但是作法懺悔, 羯磨此翻作法, 如是乃至下三篇, 並是作法, 此事易知. 義如律中廣明, 但未明懺悔四重法.

Meditation], *T* 1915), and says that based on the teaching of the *sutra*, repentance with formal act is able to eliminate the four serious transgressions.[30]

Repentance contemplating signs is by focusing the mind and thought and seeing various signs with a pacified mind. This is based on the practices of cultivating meditation, and most belong to the Mahāyāna practice methods of repentance. When Indian Buddhism was first transmitted to China, there were repentance methods like that taught in the *Da fangdeng tuoluoni jing*, and the contemplation of signs like the hells, poisonous snakes, the white mark [between the eyebrows] and so forth in the *Āgama sūtra*s. If one accomplishes seeing these signs, this demonstrates that the transgression was eliminated. The *Cidi chanmen* states:

> Two, clarification of repentance by contemplating signs. Based on the repentance methods in the *sūtra*s, practitioners focus their minds, apply their thoughts, and see various signs within a pacified mind. As is taught in the *bodhisattva* precepts, if one repents the ten serious transgressions, one must see auspicious signs, and so forth. That is, signs of elimination. After the Buddha comes and rubs the crown of their head, they see light or flowers, or various other auspicious signs, and then the transgression is eliminated. If one does not see signs, even if they repent, it is useless. In the Mahāyāna expansive *dhāraṇī* methods of practice, many have this kind of repentance rite of contemplating signs. In the three canons and the *Za Ahan jing* 雜阿含經 (Assorted *Āgama*, *T* 99), it also teaches repentance methods of contemplating signs, namely, contemplating the signs of the hells, poisonous snakes, the white mark [between the eyebrows], and so forth. The accomplishment of this is said to be elimination of the transgression. Because all of these are performed in a mental state of meditation, repentance by contemplation of signs is mostly taught based on methods of cultivation of meditation.[31]

---

30 *Shi chan boluomi cidi famen*, *T* no. 1916, 46: 2.485c13-18:
別有《最妙初教經》, 出懺悔四重法. 彼經云：當請三十清淨比丘僧, 於大眾中, 犯罪比丘當自發露, 僧爲作羯磨成就. 又於三寶前, 作諸行法, 及誦戒千遍, 即得清淨. 亦云令取得相爲證, 而說罪滅清淨. 當知律中雖不出, 經中有此羯磨明文. 作法相貌, 如彼經中廣說.

31 *Shi chan boluomi cidi famen*, *T* no. 1916, 46: 2.485c18-27:
二明觀相懺悔者, 行人依諸經中懺悔方法, 專心用意, 於靜心中, 見種種諸相. 如菩薩戒中所說, 若懺十重, 要須見好相, 乃滅相者. 佛來摩頂, 見光華種種瑞相已, 罪即得滅. 若不見相, 雖懺無益. 諸大乘方等陀羅尼行法中, 多有此觀相懺法. 三藏及《雜阿含》中, 亦說觀相懺悔方法, 謂作地獄、毒蛇、白毫等觀相, 成就即說罪滅. 此悉就定心中作故, 觀相懺悔多依修定法說.

In Mahāyāna scriptures, repentance by contemplating signs, such as receiving the bodhisattva precept repentance in the *Fanwang jing*, or repenting to eliminate serious transgressions in the *Da fangdeng tuoluoni jing*, all utilize practice methods of cultivating meditation, and see signs within a meditative mental state.

With regard to the conditions for repentance by contemplating signs, the *Mohe zhiguan* states:

> Causes and conditions are internal and external. The internal: the developed mind of calm and insight, the mind moistened with clarity and purity, illuminating wholesome and evil. If one uses calm to stop evil, evil will soon cease; if one uses insight to contemplate the wholesome, the wholesome will soon arise. Conversely, if one uses calm to stop evil, evil will arise because of pacification; if one uses insight to contemplate the wholesome, the wholesome will cease because of contemplation. Immeasurable characteristics of action come from calm and insight. Just as when a mirror is polished, the myriad images themselves appear. The external: the love and compassion of the Buddhas always responds to all living beings, though without the right circumstances one will be unable to see them. By the power of calm and insight, one is able to bring about the Buddhas' *dhyāna*, which reveals the wholesome and evil, and all actions will be made manifest. It is like holding a floral wreath and showing it to the community. These are known as internal and external causes and conditions.[32]

From the position of the cultivators themselves, when they cultivate calm and insight, within meditation they may manifest wholesome signs or evil signs. Regardless, all signs are manifested due to causes and conditions, just like the myriad images that themselves appear within a mirror. Apart from this, the love and compassion of the Buddhas always responds to living beings, due to the power of calm and insight within the inner mind. The combination of these causes and conditions thus enables a response from the Buddhas to manifest the various wholesome and evil *dhyāna* meditation states.

32 *Mohe zhiguan*, *T* no. 1911, 46: 8.112a3-11: 因緣者, 有內有外. 內者, 止觀研心, 心漸明淨, 照諸善惡. 或可以止止惡, 惡方欲滅；以觀觀善, 善方欲生. 或可以止止惡, 惡因靜生；以觀觀善, 善因觀滅, 無量業相出止觀中. 如鏡被磨, 萬像自現. 外者, 諸佛慈悲常應一切眾生, 無機不能得覩, 以止觀力, 能感諸佛示善惡禪, 諸業則現. 如持花鬘, 示於大眾, 是名內外因緣.

Lastly, Zhiyi discusses repentance on contemplation of the unarisen, an idea based on the *Puxian guanjing*. He considers repentance by contemplating the unarisen to be an explanation of repentance augmented from the aspect of wisdom. The *Cidi chanmen* states:

> Three, clarification of repentance by contemplating the unarisen. As the verses in the *Puxian guanjing* state: … If a practitioner wants to practice great repentance, they should generate the mind of great compassion and have pity on all, deeply fathoming the source of transgression. For what reason? All phenomena are originally empty, pacified. There is not even merit, how could there be transgression? However, living beings' unwholesome thinking and false attachment to the conditioned generates ignorance, as well as desire and aversion. From these three poisons, they broadly commit all immeasurable, boundless serious transgressions, all generated from a single thought of incomprehension. If one wishes to eliminate these, just contemplate back to where this mind comes from. … Contemplating in this way, one does not see signs or omens, it is not in any location. One should know that this mind is ultimately empty, pacified. With neither seeing the mind, nor seeing non-mind, there is not even anything to contemplate, let alone a contemplator. Without subject or object, perverted thinking is cut off. With the cutting off of perversion, there is no ignorance, no desire or aversion. With the absence of these three poisons, from where can transgressions arise?
> Moreover, all methods of practice belong to the mind. Even the nature of mind is empty, let alone myriad phenomena. If there are no myriad phenomena, who commits transgression? If transgression cannot be apprehended, non-transgression is also not apprehended. Contemplating that transgression is unarisen, one defeats all transgressions, because the fundamental nature of all transgressions is empty and always pure … Performing this repentance is known as great repentance … For a practitioner of this repentance, their mind is like flowing water, and in thought after thought they see Samantabhadra Bodhisattva and the Buddhas of the ten directions. Therefore, know that the deep contemplation of the unarisen is known as great repentance. Within all repentances, this is the supreme, the most sublime. All the explanations of repentance rites in the Mahāyāna scriptures take this contemplation as the focus.[33]

---

33 *Shi chan boluomi cidi famen*, *T* no. 1916, 46: 2.486a15-b21:
三明觀無生懺悔者, 如普賢觀經中偈說 …… 夫行人欲行大懺悔者, 應當起大悲心憐愍一切, 深達罪源. 所以者何？一切諸法本來空寂, 尚無有福, 況復罪耶？但衆

The main focus of repentance by contemplation of the unarisen is to concentrate on the ultimate meaning of contemplating the nature of transgressions as empty. Zhiyi primarily argues three aspects for the nature of transgression being empty: One, all phenomena are originally empty and pacified. However, living beings wrongly and falsely attach to the conditioned, and from this give rise to the afflictions of ignorance, greed and desire, and broadly engage in countless serious transgressions. Two, the mind is ultimately empty and pacified. All phenomena belong to the mind, and since the mind is neither internal, nor external, and there is neither subject nor object, therefore, the nature of the mind is fundamentally empty. Three, the fundamental nature of transgression is empty. This is because phenomena and mind are all originally empty. Thus, transgressions that come about within the mind are due to attachment to phenomena and are also originally empty by nature. In this way, only by finding the ultimate condition of transgressions will one reach purity of *śīla* and have the possibility of cultivating meditation.

Accordingly, Zhiyi takes pure upholding of morality as the foundation and matches up repentance by formal rite, repentance by contemplating signs, and repentance by contemplation of the unarisen with the three trainings of morality, meditation and wisdom. This illustrates that all the Buddha Dharma is contained within repentance.

### 1.1.4 Five Dharma Methods of Remorse

Over time there have been two types of repentance rite. The first type is the collation of the ritual procedures for repenting transgressions in the *sūtras*. The other type is the practice method of cultivating calm and insight based on the practice method of the five regrets. Zhiyi's repentance thought and the ritual procedures for repentance that he established include the above two types of repentance.[34] The five regrets are simply five repentances, seeing as Zhiyi calls the five practices of repentance, invitation, rejoicing, dedication and making vows the "five regrets" (*wuhui* 五悔). Five regrets thought is rooted in and developed from the five regrets system in the scriptures, namely the

---

生不善思惟, 妄執有爲而起無明及與愛恚, 從此三毒, 廣作無量無邊一切重罪, 皆從一念不了心生. 若欲除滅, 但當反觀如此心者從何處. ...... 如是觀之, 不見相貌, 不在方所, 當知此心畢竟空寂. 既不見心, 不見非心, 尙無所觀, 況有能觀. 無能無所, 顛倒想斷. 既顛倒斷, 則無無明及以愛恚. 無此三毒, 罪從何生. 復次一切萬法, 悉屬於心. 心性尙空, 何況萬法. 若無萬法, 誰是罪業. 若不得罪, 不得不罪. 觀罪無生, 破一切罪, 以一切諸罪根本性空, 常清淨故. ...... 作是懺悔, 名大懺悔. ...... 行此悔者, 心如流水. 念念之中, 見普賢菩薩及十方佛, 故知深觀無生, 名大懺悔. 於懺悔中, 最尊最妙, 一切大乘經中明懺悔法, 悉以此觀爲主.

34 Pan & Wu, *Tongshi*, 217.

"Pusa wufa chanhui wen" 菩薩五法懺悔文 (Bodhisattva's Five Practices of Repentance Text, *T* 1504), *Ligouhui pusa suowen lifo fajing* 離垢慧菩薩所問禮佛法經 (*Sūtra* on Questions of Vimalamati Bodhisattva with Respect to the Buddhadharma, *T* 487), *Zhancha shan'e yebao jing* 占察善惡業報經 (*Sūtra* on the Divination of the Effect of Good and Evil Actions, *T* 839), and *Guanfo sanmei hai jing* 觀佛三昧海經 (*Sūtra* on the Ocean-Like *Samādhi* of the Visualization of the Buddha, *T* 643).

In his *Mohe zhiguan*, *Fahua sanmei chanyi*, *Guoqing bailu* 國清百錄 (Hundred Records of Guoqing Monastery, *T* 1934), and other works, Zhiyi analyses and interprets the notion of the five regrets. In the eighth of the ten vehicles of Tiantai practice of contemplation—clarification of the order of status in the *Mohe zhiguan*, where the order of status of the complete teaching is emphasized—Zhiyi states that the practitioner knows the stage of status in their own cultivation and realization and is unable to directly contemplate the inconceivable state. This is the method of contemplation cultivated by those of lower faculties.[35] According to the explanation in Zhanran's *Zhiguan fuxing chuanhong jue* 止觀輔行傳弘決 (Guide to Practice Calm and Insight, *T* 1912), the five regrets of the *Mohe zhiguan* are cited from the *Shizhu piposha lun* 十住毗婆沙論 (*Daśabhūmika-vibhāṣā*, *T* 1521) and the *Zhancha shan'e yebao jing*.[36] The *Guoqing bailu*, fascicle one, "*Jingli fa*" 敬禮法 (Practices of Etiquette), also states: "This practice is correctly based on Nāgārjuna's *Vibhāṣa*, further enhanced by the intention of the *sūtras*".[37]

Zhiyi's five regrets thought can be seen in the *Fahua sanmei chanyi* in the earlier period, and in the latter period the *Mohe zhiguan*. The *Mohe zhiguan*, in the second half of fascicle seven, states:

> As for the expedient means for the cultivation of the four kinds of *samādhi*, it is the same as taught above. Only the *Fahua* [*sanmei chanyi*] separately has the five regrets in the six sessions, as a further expedient means. Now we shall clarify the characteristics of its stages with respect to the five regrets. First, know the ten states of minds in accord and resisting, and take the true characteristic as object. This is the first repentance. Constantly repent, let there be no time when one is not repenting. However, the principle of the mind is subtle and close, and the use of contemplation is gentle and distant. Dark evil covers and obstructs, and it is very

35 *Mohe zhiguan*, *T* no. 1911, 46: 7.98a10-99a29.

36 *Zhiguan fuxing chuanhong jue*, *T* no. 1912, 46: 7.382b26-27: 今僧常儀, 前四出《十住婆沙》, 願文在《大涅槃》, 若《占察經》亦但列四.

37 *Guoqing bailu*, *T* no. 1934, 46: 1.794a19: 此法正依龍樹《毘婆沙》, 傍潤諸經意.

> difficult to reveal it clearly. By repeatedly applying body and speech to assist in mental action, connection with it speeds up, further developing the five regrets … Now, at the place of worship for six sessions during each day and night, one practices this repentance, and defeats the transgression of great evil actions. Invitation defeats the transgression of slandering the Dharma. Rejoicing defeats the transgression of jealousy. Dedication defeats the transgression of work for the conditioned. Making vows is in accord with emptiness and the signless. The merit attained from this is immeasurable, and cannot be described by any analogy of calculation. If one is able to earnestly practice the five regrets, it is an expedient means to assist the development of contemplation methods, and the three truths in one mind are also revealed.[38]

Zhiyi thinks that because common people have heavy obstructions it is difficult for them to come into connection when cultivating contemplation. Therefore, they must properly practice the five regrets during six sessions as an expedient means. This eliminates and ceases transgressions and assists in developing contemplation methods, enabling the three truths in one mind to suddenly open and show forth. From this, one attains the factor of rejoicing, the first of the five factors on the status of the disciples. After that, adding recitation, teaching the Dharma, vigorous effort, the six perfections, and so forth, on top of the five regrets, one can advance and ascend through each of the factors.[39]

Furthermore, the *Tiantai sijiao yi* 天台四教儀 (Outline of the Tiantai Four Teachings, *T* 1931) says: "Internally one contemplates the object of the three truths through the three contemplations, and externally one increases vigorous effort through the five regrets"; and "The subsequent statuses all the way up to equal awakening, all use the five regrets".[40] The importance of the five regrets in Tiantai calm and insight can thus be seen.

---

38 *Mohe zhiguan*, *T* no. 1911, 46: 7.98a12-17, 98c13-18:
若四種三昧修習方便, 通如上說. 唯法華別約六時五悔, 重作方便, 今就五悔明其位相, 先知逆順十心而繫緣實相, 是第一懺. 常懺悔無不懺時, 但心理微密, 觀用輕疎, 黑惡覆障卒難開曉, 重運身口助發意業, 使疾相應, 更加五悔耳. …… 今於道場, 日夜六時, 行此懺悔, 破大惡業罪, 勸請破謗法罪, 隨喜破嫉妬罪, 迴向破爲諸有罪, 順空無相願, 所得功德, 不可限量, 譬算校計, 亦不能說. 若能勤行五悔方便, 助開觀門, 一心三諦, 豁爾開明.

39 *Mohe zhiguan*, *T* no. 1911, 46: 7.98a12-99a29.

40 *Tiantai sijiao yi*, *T* no. 1931, 46: 1.779a9-10, 779b4:
內以三觀觀三諦境, 外以五悔勤加精進 …… 下去諸位, 直至等覺, 總用五悔.

### 1.1.5 Ten States of Mind in Repentance

Tiantai repentance uses the repentance rite as the external ritual procedure, but the repentance itself requires internal mental application. Within the internal mind, one contemplates and observes the actions which are conditions for transgressional obstructions, and from this truly generates the mind of repentance. Living beings are more able to recognize transgressing actions of the present when contemplating them, but with respect to transgressions of the past it is very hard for them to observe them if they lack deep wholesome roots. The *Mohe zhiguan* states:

> For one who wishes to practice the four kinds of *samādhi* to repent serious obstructions in the present and past life, they should know the ten mental states that are in accord [with *saṃsāra*] and know their fault. Then they should apply the ten mental states contrary [with *saṃsāra*] and use them as counter agents. These twenty mental states are all the root of repentance.[41]

Repenting heavy obstructions from the past, when one cultivates the four kinds of *samādhi*, one should recognize the suffering of living beings in the cycle of life and death. That is, contemplate the mind that goes against *nirvāṇa* and follows life and death. These are the ten states of mind that are in accord [with cyclic existence], just as the Buddha contemplated the twelve links of dependent origination in forward direction. Contrary to this, one should take the resisting ten states of mind as counter agents, which is contemplation of dependent origination in reverse direction. At the same time, from the deep contemplation of the principles of the three truths, Zhiyi matches up the ten states of mind that resist these and repents with a sincere mind.

The Tiantai repentance rites emphasize the two aspects of principle and phenomena. The ritual procedure of the repentance rite is the external characteristic of phenomena, whereas only the internal ten resisting states of mind and the deep contemplation of the principle of the three truths is the really essential element. Only the internal principle can enable the phenomenal characteristics to produce their true significance. Zhiyi states:

> The ten kinds of repentance are in accord with the path to *nirvāṇa*, and resist the flow of life and death. They are able to eliminate the faults of

---

41 *Mohe zhiguan*, *T* no. 1911, 46: 4.39c23-26: 若欲懺悔二世重障行四種三昧者, 當識順流十心, 明知過失. 當運逆流十心, 以爲對治. 此二十心通爲諸懺之本.

> the four serious and the five heinous [transgressions]. If one does not understand these ten states of mind, one will not be able to recognize right and wrong—how could one repent? Even if one enters the place of worship and engages in austere practices, ultimately there will be no benefit. When applying these ten repentances, one should deeply contemplate the three truths, and also add the phenomenal rite, and with a strong, serious mind, not cling to life and limb. This is known as the second strong hero. This is known as the phenomenal-principle dual repentance, elimination of transgressions which obstruct the path, purity of *śīla*, manifestation of *samādhi*, and the development of calm and insight.[42]

Zhiyi points out that only repentance with the ten kinds of resisting mind is true repentance. If one is unable to understand these ten minds which resist [cyclic existence], but merely follows the external practice of the repentance procedure, that is austerity in vain, which has not the slightest benefit for cultivation and practice. Therefore, both phenomena and principle are to be emphasized. Repentance by Phenomena and Repentance by Principle should be practice together. Only in this way can the transgressions which obstruct the Buddha path be eliminated, the upholding of morality be purified, and ultimately bring about *dhyāna* meditation and accomplishment of calm and insight.

Therefore, Zhiyi's repentance rites are ultimately aimed at the accomplishment of calm and insight, though they are able to take care of the demands of practitioners of differing faculties. The main target audience of Tiantai repentance rites are those of high level faculties. That is, it provides a practice method for fast realization for those of high faculties. Hence, it puts the greatest emphasis on realization through principle, from the angles of *prajñā* knowledge and the true characteristic of the middle way, to accentuate the meaning of repentance by contemplation of the unarisen. This is his fundamental reason for placing repentance rites within the discussion of cultivation of calm and insight.

---

42 *Mohe zhiguan*, *T* no. 1911, 46: 40b29-c3, 41b24-27: 十種懺悔, 順涅槃道, 逆生死流, 能滅四重、五逆之過. 若不解此十心, 全不識是非, 云何懺悔？設入道場, 徒爲苦行, 終無大益. ...... 運此十懺時, 深觀三諦, 又加事法, 以殷重心不惜身命, 名第二健兒. 是名事理兩懺, 障道罪滅, 尸羅清淨, 三昧現前, 止觀開發.

### 1.1.6 Repentance and Calm and Insight: Status of Repentance Ritual in the Tiantai Cultivation and Realization System

From the Wei, Jin, and Southern & Northern Dynasties onwards, through the organization of repentance rites and range of performance of repentance, most of the popular scriptures have benefits in the present life, such as the treatment of illness, as their content, and have the recitation of *mantras*, worship, praise, repentance, and so forth, as their selected methods of practice. Therefore, from the special features of the scriptures upon which they are based, we can likewise reason that peace in the present life and removal of difficulties, combined with repentance to eliminate transgressions, is what conforms to the needs of Chinese people.[43]

The extraordinariness of Zhiyi is evident in his use of ritual worship forms suited to the Chinese, upon which he then adds his methods of contemplation, as he seeks to actualize the practices of Chinese Buddhism.[44] The first special feature of Zhiyi's repentance rites is the removal of elements of secular wishes and prayers, and the inclusion of repentance rites within the first stages of sitting meditation and correct contemplation of true characteristics. The *Mohe zhiguan* states: "Thus know that pure upholding of morality and sincere, despondent repentance are together the first conditions for calm and insight".[45] The Tiantai system of cultivation and realization takes the three kinds of calm and insight and the four kinds of *samādhi* as its centre. Zhiyi places repentance within "pure upholding of morality" of the "twenty-five expedient means", which explains that repentance is merely a method, a kind of aid to the path.

However, Zhiyi matches up the three trainings of morality, meditation and wisdom with the repentance with formal rite, repentance by contemplating signs and repentance by contemplating the unarisen, thus placing repentance within the entire system of Buddhist cultivation. In the *Mohe zhiguan*, Zhiyi raises the use of the ten states of mind in accord and the ten states of mind that resist, and deep contemplation of the principle of the three truths, to engage in cultivating repentance rites. From this, it can be seen that because true repentance is the combination of both phenomena and principle, this intangibly raises the position of repentance within the Tiantai systems of cultivation and realization. The *Mohe zhiguan* states: "Repentance rites are based on the four kinds of *samādhi*",[46] thus subsuming repentance within *samādhi*. That is, the *Fahua sanmei chanyi* and the *Fangdeng sanmei chanfa* are included within the

43 Shioiri, "Sange no juyōkatei", 732–33.
44 Shioiri, "Sange no juyōkatei", 448.
45 *Mohe zhiguan*, *T* no. 1911, 46: 4.41c5-6: 故知持戒清淨, 懇惻懺悔, 俱爲止觀初緣.
46 *Mohe zhiguan*, *T* no. 1911, 46: 4.39c13-14: 依四種三昧則有懺法.

"Half Walking Half Sitting *Samādhi*", and the *Qing Guanshiyin chanfa* is encompassed within the "Neither Walking Nor Sitting *Samādhi*". In the four kinds of *samādhi*, the "Constant Sitting *Samādhi*" and the "Constant Walking *Samādhi*" are not concrete practice methods of repentance. Thus, the four *samādhi*s and repentance rites have definite distinctions. Although, the cultivation of the four kinds of *samādhi* aims for direct contemplation of the principle of true characteristics, which is a description of the character of Tiantai practices of contemplation in specific terms of practice methods of the nature of characteristics. Zhiyi, in his *Mohe zhiguan*, states:

> If one wishes to ascend to the sublime status, it is not by practicing without steps. With the churning of good comprehension, ghee can be made. The *Fahua* [*jing*] states: One also sees the Buddhas' disciples cultivate many practices as they seek the Buddha path. There are a great many practice methods, but they can be stated briefly as four: One, constant sitting. Two, constant walking. Three, half walking half sitting. Four, neither walking nor sitting. They are all considered *samādhi*, which is straightened meditation. The *Da* [*zhidu*] *lun* states: With the mind well established on one object, without moving, this is called *samādhi*. The Dharma element is one object, on which right contemplation can stand, unmoving. With the four practices as conditions, the contemplating mind through these conditions is straightened. Thus, it is called *samādhi*.[47]

Here, the "four practices" refers to the four kinds of *samādhi*. "Contemplating Mind" refers to the "ten objects and ten vehicles contemplation" in the *Mohe zhiguan*, which provides the ten kinds of contemplation as contemplation methods, and the ten objects as conditions. The relationship between the two is "with four practices as condition, the contemplating mind through these conditions is straightened". In other words, the four kinds of *samādhi* are the external condition for the "ten objects and ten vehicles contemplation" in the *Dharma Lotus* complete teaching. The former is the phenomena, the latter is the principle, and only through the combination of principle and phenomena can one accomplish complete and sudden calm and insight. It is because the four kinds of *samādhi* are called *samādhi*, because they are firstly *dhyāna* and secondly meditation, that they can be said to belong to conditions which

47 *Mohe zhiguan*, *T* no. 1911, 46: 2.11a22-28:
欲登妙位, 非行不階, 善解鑽搖, 醍醐可獲. 法華云：又見佛子修種種行以求佛道, 行法眾多, 略言其四：一、常坐, 二、常行, 三、半行半坐, 四、非行非坐. 通稱三昧者, 調直定也. 大論云：善心一處住不動, 是名三昧. 法界是一處, 正觀能住不動, 四行爲緣, 觀心藉緣調直, 故稱三昧也.

develop liberating wisdom. Whereas, the correct cultivation of the method of contemplation of the "ten objects and ten vehicles" can be called the main cause of the development of liberating wisdom. The two merely have a difference in terms of the breadth of their content.[48]

In this way, from "four kinds of repentance rite" to "four kinds of *samādhi*", and then to the "ten objects and ten vehicles (*Shijing shicheng guan* 十境十乘觀)", we can see that the position of Tiantai repentance rites within their entire cultivation and realization system was continuously elevated. In the Tiantai thought of "three contemplations in one mind", the three truths, three contemplations, and three wisdoms are each attained within one mind, not before or after, without any difference in order. Yet the three truths in one mind, the three contemplations in one mind, and the three wisdoms in one mind are also without before or after, they have no difference in terms of their order. Then, contemplation and observation of the fundamental nature of transgressing actions is likewise. The *Jin'guangming jing wenju*, "Shi chanhui pin" 釋懺悔品 (Explanation of Repentance Chapter), states, ""Great repentance" is situated within the middle way. As for "three kinds of distinctions", this is an alternative theory. "Just one, yet three; just three, yet one", this is complete and wondrous repentance".[49] Therefore, from the position of the complete teaching, the three kinds of repentance can be just one, yet three, and just three, yet one. Just this is the ultimate elimination of transgression. Repentance is not only able to purify transgressing action, it is also able to penetrate through to the nature of Dharma, realize the wisdom of receptivity to the unarisen, and completely perfect the three trainings of morality, meditation and wisdom. Within the complete teaching, there is no phenomenon which is not the true characteristic of the middle way. Even the nature of transgression and virtue is the true characteristic of the middle way. Just this is ultimate repentance.

Therefore, Zhiyi locates repentance rites with worldly prayers and wishes within the first requisite for the accomplishment of calm and insight—upholding morality purely. Through setting up four kinds of repentance rites, using specific ritual processes for these repentance rites, one actually attains the goal of elimination of transgression, achievement of meditation, and development of wisdom. However, he also includes the four kinds of repentance rites within the "four kinds of *samādhi*", and the "four kinds of *samādhi*" are the

---

48 Andō, *Tiantai xue*, 223.

49 *Jin guangming jing wenju*, *T* no. 1785, 39: 3.59b21-23:
大懺悔者, 約中道爲處也. 若三種差別者, 此是歷別論處爾. 即一而三, 即三而一者, 此圓妙懺悔也.

external conditions for the "contemplation of the four objects and ten vehicles". In this way, within the entire system of cultivation and realization, repentance rites are elevated from phenomenal characteristics to the Dharma of principles, finally entering into the true characteristic of the middle way. This is the special feature of Zhiyi's repentance rite thought.

### 1.2 *Zongmi and the* Yuanjue Jing Daochang Xiuzheng Yi 圓覺經道場修證儀

The Huayan repentance rite system is represented by Guifeng Zongmi's 圭峰宗密 (780–841) *Yuanjue jing daochang xiuzheng yi* 圓覺經道場修證儀 (Ritual for the Realisation in the Altar of the *Sūtra* of Perfect Awakening, *XZJ* 1454) in eighteen fascicles, and Huijue's 慧覺 (fl. 706–713) *Huayan jing haiyin daochang chanyi* 華嚴經海印道場懺儀 (Repentance Ritual in the Ocean Seal Altar of the *Flower Adornment Sūtra*, *XZJ* 1452) in forty fascicles. These are two of the largest texts of all the various presently extant repentance rites. After these, Jingyuan 净源 (1011–1088) from the Song dynasty, simplified the *Yuanjue jing daochang xiuzheng yi* into the *Yuanjue jing daochang lüeben xiuzheng yi* 圓覺經道場略本修證儀 (Abbreviated Ritual for the Realisation in the Altar of the *Sūtra of Perfect Awakening*, *XZJ* 1455), in one fascicle.

Zongmi spent a lifetime of effort explaining and annotating the *Yuanjue jing* 圓覺經 (*Sūtra* of Perfect Awakening, *T* 842), such as the presently extant *Yuanjue jing da shu* 圓覺經大疏 (Great Commentary on the *Sūtra of Perfect Awakening*, *XZJ* 210), in twenty fascicles, *Yuanjue jing dashu shiyi chao* 圓覺經大疏釋義鈔 (Notes on the Commentary of the *Sūtra of Perfect Awakening*, *XZJ* 211), in thirteen fascicles, *Yuanjue jing lüeshu* 圓覺經略疏 (Abbreviated Commentary on the *Sūtra of Perfect Awakening*, *XZJ* 212), in four fascicles, and *Yuanjue jing lüeshu chao* 圓覺經略疏鈔 (Notes on the Abbreviated Commentary of the *Sūtra of Perfect Awakening*, *XZJ* 213), in twelve fascicles. He also compiled the *Yuanjue jing daochang xiuzheng yi*, in eighteen fascicles, which elaborates the methods to practice sitting *dhyāna* cultivation and to repent and eliminate transgressions for Buddhist practitioners' actual cultivation and religious practices. It also regulates the practice methods for praising, reciting and worshiping, according to the methods of cultivation in the *Yuanjue jing*, as well as cultivation and actualization systems from Daoan of the East Jin up to Zhiyi, and, in particular, Zhiyi's *Xiao zhiguan* and *Fahua sanmei chanyi*.

Taking the union of sudden and gradual, and the union of Chan and teachings as his foundation, Zongmi included Tiantai repentance rites and *dhyāna* methods into his system of cultivation. *Yuanjue jing daochang xiuzheng yi*, fascicle one, "Outline of Capacities", demands the cultivator must first visit "Tiantai, and masters who well comprehend the three contemplations and three

FIGURE 16 Zhixiang Monastery 至相寺 on Mount Zhongnan 終南山.

truths", asking questions on the essential methods in order to let themselves clearly understand and know the nature of mind. Only then can they hear and receive the commentaries on the *Yuanjue jing*.[50] Furthermore, Zongmi's section of calm and insight is also cited from Tiantai calm and insight. From this, it is clear that Zongmi looked very favourably on Tiantai repentance rites and calm and insight practices.

The *Yuanjue jing daochang xiuzheng yi* does not clearly express that its repentance rites are from Tiantai repentance rites. But, in the *Yuanjue jing daochang xiuzheng yi*, fascicle two, "Supplication [to the Holy]", it states: "Question: In the repentance rites of the various schools of thought, they all begin by kneeling, and solemnly holding incense and flowers as offerings".[51] Here, "schools of thought" should be referring to the Tiantai repentance rites. Jingyuan states, in his *Yuanjue jing daochang lüeben xiuzheng yi*, "Zongxu yuanqi" 總敘緣起 (General Outline of Circumstances):

> Dharma Master Mitian of the West Jin (i.e. Daoan) composed a four times daily worship text. Seeing the words of majestic offerings and five regrets, while there are a great many meanings of this worthy scripture,

50 *Yuanjue jing daochang xiuzheng yi*, XZJ no. 1454, 128: 1.723b10-12.

51 *Yuanjue jing daochang xiuzheng yi*, XZJ no. 1454, 128: 2.730b3-4: 諸家禮懺, 皆先胡跪, 嚴持香花供養.

> he selected the essentials. Thus, all the learners of the world delight in studying it. Between the Chen and Sui dynasties, Tiantai Zhizhe wrote the *Fahua* [*Sanmei*] *chanfa*, [*Jin'*]*guangming* [*chanfa*] and [*Guoqing*] *bailu*, showing the ten states of mind in accord and resisting. The procedure is quite detailed, and it is prevalent throughout the area east of the Yangzi River. In the Tang dynasty, my ancestor Chan Master Guifeng followed the brilliance of Mitian and was in line with the rhythm bequeathed by Zhizhe to comprehensively compose the *Yuanjue lichan changuan* 圓覺禮懺禪觀 (Contemplation of the Repentance according to the *Sūtra of Perfect Awakening*, i.e., *Yuanjue jing daochang xiuzheng yi*), in eighteen fascicles.[52] …

Jingyuan points out that Zongmi's *Yuanjue jing daochang xiuzheng yi* is a continuation and development of Daoan and Zhiyi. Not only does the procedure of the *Yuanjue jing daochang xiuzheng yi* imitate the *Fahua sanmei chanyi* in terms of structure, it also has many passages which are direct quotations from it. Its influence from the *Fahua sanmei chanyi* is obvious to see. However, the *Yuanjue jing daochang xiuzheng yi* takes the *Yuanjue jing* as its main theme and the thought of the Huanyan School as its conceptual basis. Thus, its system of repentance methods of course illustrates its own special features.

In fascicle two of the *Yuanjue jing daochang xiuzheng yi*, Zongmi gives three types of repentance: One, Repentance with a Formal Act (*zuofachan* 作法懺); Two, Repentance by Phenomena (*shichan* 事懺); and Three, Repentance by Principle (*lichan* 理懺). He also indicates that Repentance with a Formal Act repents transgressions that are to be restrained, whereas Repentance by Phenomena and Repentance by Principle repents transgressions by nature.[53] Zongmi, in his *Yuanjue jing daochang xiuzheng yi*, fascicle four, gives his own explanation of repentance by phenomena and repentance by principle:

> In general, repentance has Repentance by Phenomena and Repentance by Principle. To repent ignorance, there is only Repentance by Principle. Ignorance is delusion with respect to the real principle. As soon as one realizes the principle, then there is no ignorance. Therefore, one should repent by principle. Ignorance is the root and if one reaches it, then the

52 *Yuanjue jing daochang xiuzheng yi*, XZJ no. 1454, 128: 1.1a18-b5:
西晉彌天法師, 嘗著四時禮文, 觀其嚴供、五悔之辭, 尊經尚義, 多摭其要, 故天下學者悅而習焉. 陳隋之際, 天台智者撰《法華懺法》、《光明》《百錄》, 具彰逆順十心, 規式頗詳, 而盛行乎江左矣. 有唐中吾祖圭峰禪師, 追彌天之餘烈, 貫智者之遺韻, 備述《圓覺禮懺禪觀》. 凡一十八卷.

53 *Yuanjue jing daochang xiuzheng yi*, XZJ no. 1454, 128: 2.739a13-740a06.

three obstructions, which are like the branches and tips, will be transformed and eliminated. Therefore, in the *Weimojie jing*, when Upāli repents for two *bhikṣus* who transgress their monastic discipline, Vimalakīrti scolds him, saying: "Do not increase the transgression of these two *bhikṣus*. You should directly eliminate it, and not harm their minds. Why? The nature of transgression is neither internal, nor external, nor between the two. As the Buddha taught, due to mental taints, living beings have taints; due to mental purity, living beings are pure. The mind is also neither internal, nor external, nor between the two. Just as one's mind, so too are one's transgressions and taints. They are not beyond suchness. …"

Furthermore, the *Puxian guanjing* and the *Huayan jing*, "Suihao pin" 隨好品 (i.e., "Rulai suihao ganging gongde pin" 如來隨好光明功德品 [Chapter of the Buddha's Secondary Marks and Luminous Merits]), also teach two kinds of repentance. The [*Puxian*] *guanjing* explains how one should vigorously form (should read: "worship") the Buddha day and night. This is Repentance by Phenomena. Contemplating the mind as no-mind, arisen from perversion, if one wishes to repent these, one should sit upright and be mindful of the true characteristics. This is Repentance by Principle. In the "Secondary Marks Chapter", equivalent to the realm of living beings, wholesome physical, verbal, and mental actions repent to eliminate obstructions. This is Repentance by Phenomena. Contemplating the nature of actions, that they do not end (should read: "come from") the ten directions, the mind abides in the mind, arisen from perversions, and does not abide externally. This is Repentance by Principle. Repentance by Phenomena removes the branch, Repentance by Principle pulls out the root. Moreover, Repentance by Phenomena removes transgression, while Repentance by Principle removes doubt. Repentance eliminates the three obstructions, the combination of phenomena and principle. Now, one should repent by principle, where Repentance by Principle is the contemplation of its nature as empty.[54]

---

54 *Yuanjue jing daochang xiuzheng yi*, XZJ no. 1454, 128: 4.764a13-b12:
夫懺悔有事懺, 有理懺. 懺無明者, 唯是理懺. 無明者. 迷於實理, 今但悟理, 則無無明, 故當理懺. 然無明是本, 義達其中, 則枝末三障亦展轉除滅. 故《維摩經》中, 優婆離爲二犯律比丘懺悔, 維摩詰呵云：無量增此二比丘罪, 當直除滅, 勿損其心. 所以者何？罪性不在內, 不在外, 不在中間, 如佛所說, 心垢故眾生垢, 心淨故眾生淨. 心亦不在內, 不在外, 不在中間, 如其心然, 罪垢亦然, 不出於如如. …… 又《普賢觀經》及《華嚴隨好品》亦云二種懺, 《觀經》明晝夜精勤形（應爲“禮”）佛等, 即是事懺；觀心無心, 從顛倒起, 若欲懺悔者, 端坐念實相, 即是理懺. 《隨好品》中, 等眾生界, 善身語意業, 懺除諸障, 即是事懺；觀諸業性, 非十方末（應爲“來”）心住於心, 從顛倒生, 無有住處等, 即是理懺. 事懺除末, 理懺拔根. 又事懺除罪, 理懺除疑. 懺除三障, 則兼事理. 今當理懺, 理懺者, 觀其性空.

Zongmi thinks that Repentance by Principle is necessary in order to repent ignorance, because ignorance is delusion with respect to principles. Once one realizes principles, then ignorance is eliminated. In the *Yuanjue jing daochang xiuzheng yi*, Zongmi cites the *Weimojie jing* incident of Upāli repenting for two *bhikṣus* who went against monastic discipline, in order to explain that Mahāyāna repentance differs from Repentance by Formal Act. This is because the reason for Repentance by Principle is in contemplation of the nature of transgression as empty. One contemplates that the nature of transgression is not internal, nor is it external, nor is it in between, and also the mind is neither internal, external nor in between. Because the mind is empty, the transgression is also empty. From this, one reaches the goal of elimination of transgression. Zongmi also cites the *Puxian guanjing* and the Chapter of the Buddha's Secondary Marks and Luminous Merits of the *Huayan jing* to explain the meaning of both Repentance by Phenomena and Repentance by Principle.

Zongmi makes a summary of his own repentance thought in fascicle fifteen of the *Yuanjue jing daochang xiuzheng yi*:

> Evil deeds which violate the truth must be destroyed forever. Wholesome ways which are in accord with principles should be further practiced. Evil is, moreover, of two kinds: the two transgressions by nature and by prohibition, which are like root and branch respectively. Transgressions of prohibitions should first be repented by formal act. [Transgressions] of nature [are repented] by engaging in actions which mutually wax and wane. Actions to be performed are, furthermore, of two kinds: by phenomena and by principle, in accord and resisting, each are based on the *sūtras*. [Repentance] by Phenomena are practices based on the *Vaipulyas* [*sūtras*] and common [teaching]. Repentance by Principle is contemplation of emptiness to enter into the city of awakening. The two methods, in accord and resisting, each have Ten [states of mind]. By engaging in the ten [states of mind] that resist, taints are overturned and destroyed. The ten kinds [of mental state] which are in accord cause transgressions to become overgrown and lush. The ten methods which resist destroy transgressions, making them wither and wilt.[55]

55 *Yuanjue jing daochang xiuzheng yi*, XZJ no. 1454, 128: 15.940b14-941a07: 惡事違真須永斷, 善門順理倍須營. 就惡之中復二種, 性遮二罪似根莖, 遮罪先當作法懺, 性愆起行互虧盈. 起行之中復有二, 事理順逆各依經, 事依方等通諸行, 理懺觀空入覺城. 順逆二門各有十, 以起十逆後飜破, 十種順生罪榮茂, 十門逆破罪枯零.

Zongmi summarizes his own repentance thought into Repentance by Formal Act, Repentance by Phenomena, and Repentance by Principles, as well as the ten states of mind in accord and resisting. All these concepts related to repentance come from Tiantai repentance practices. Moreover, when Zongmi explains these ideas, his terms and phrasing are exactly the same as the vocabulary of Tiantai Zhiyi. We can thus see how Zongmi is "in line with the rhythm bequeathed by Zhizhe".[56] However, from beginning to end, Zongmi takes "repentance" as a way of assisting successful contemplation methods and does not really place repentance methods into his system of contemplation methods. Therefore, within Zongmi's system of cultivation and realization, repentance methods are unable to enter into the practice and realization of contemplation methods in the way in which Tiantai repentance methods do. This is the difference between Zongmi's and Tiantai repentance methods.

Zongmi takes the massive Huayan system of thought and, with the *Yuanjue jing* as its main theme, continues the Huayan thought and methods of actualization of Chengguan and other Huayan patriarchs. He absorbs Tiantai repentance practices and methods of *dhyāna* contemplation and thus composes the eighteen fascicle *Yuanjue jing daochang xiuzheng yi*. He emphasizes the importance of phenomenal characteristics and also gives attention to elevating the principle and the non-obstruction of principle and phenomena. He accentuates comprehension of conceptual principles and also underscores the actualization of cultivation. The dual emphasis on theory and practice highlights the special feature of his complete interfusion.

### 1.3 *Repentance Ritual of Chan Buddhism in the Tang Dynasty*

Early Chan uses the *Lengqie jing* 楞伽經 (*Laṇkāvatāra-sūtra*) as its scriptural basis. As stated in the *Xu Gaoseng zhuan*, "In the beginning, Chan Master [Bodhi]dharma 菩提達摩 (?–535/536) transmitted the *Lengqie* [*jing*] to [Hui]ke, and said, 'As I observe the land of Han, only by relying on this *sūtra* will good people practice and cross themselves over from the world'".[57] At the time, the transmission of the *Lengqie jing* in four fascicles was an actual event, about which there can be no doubt. The *Lengqie jing* deems that the myriad things of the world are all created by mind, and are thus false and unreal, and that living beings all have the treasury of the Thus Come One and can thus all attain liberation. Simultaneously, the *Lengqie jing* also emphasizes self-realization by the inner mind, contrary to attachment to words and texts. Therefore, under

---

56 *Yuanjue jing daochang xiuzheng yi*, *XZJ* no. 1454, 128: 1.1b4: 貫智者之遺韻.

57 *Xu Gaoseng zhuan*, *T* no. 2060, 50:16. 552b20-22:
初, 達摩禪師以四卷楞伽授可曰：我觀漢地, 惟有此經, 仁者依行, 自得度世.

FIGURE 17 Twenty-four Dharma-transmitters at Lingquan Monastery 靈泉寺 on Mount Bao 寶山.

Bodhidharma's tutelage, in the past there was a system of "masters of the *Laṇkā*[*vatāra*]", to which the scholar Hu Shi called the "*Laṇkāvatāra* lineage", the root tenet of which was the advocation of gradual cultivation. This lineage from the start was of the "gradual practice method".[58] Later, it was the fourth patriarch Daoxin 道信 (580–651) who pushed Bodhidharma's *dhyāna* (*chan*) to a new level. He combined "the mind of the Buddhas is foremost" of the *Lengqie jing* and the "one practice *samādhi*" of the *Wenshu bore jing* 文殊般若經 (i.e., *Wenshushili suoshuo mohebore boluomi jing* 文殊師利所說摩訶般若波羅蜜經, *Sūtra* of *Prajñāpāramitā* Taught by Mañjuśrī, *T* 232) to construct the *Rudao anxin yao fangbian men* 入道安心要方便法門 (Essential and Expedient Method for Entering the Path and Settling the Mind). This made a *chan* meditation method that unified the *Laṇkāvatāra* and the *Prajñāpāramitā*. Therefore, within the early writings of the Chan School, while emphasizing the *prajñā* of

58 Hu, *Lengqie zong kao*, 168.

emptiness, there is a return to the inconceivable true nature, the wondrous existence of comprehension of *prajñā* as emptiness.

It was under the guidance of this kind of thought that the early Chan explanations of repentance fully shows the unification of the purity of self-nature and the emptiness of *prajñā*. Simultaneously, they located repentance as an expedient method for Chan practices. The need to properly deal with the relationship between repentance and the contemplative mind in sitting Chan, as well as the matter of how to engage in repentance, were all problems that needed to be resolved by early Chan.

The basic requirements of Bodhidharma's Chan methods were the "two entrances and four practices". This was a Mahāyāna Chan method established based on the *prajñā* middle way and Buddha nature theory. This Chan method is reflected in the presently extant *Er'ru sixing lun* 二入四行論 (Treatise on Two Entrances and Four Practices). Early Chan repentance thought appears in the second section, assorted contents, of the *Er'ru sixing lun*:

> He then said: Allow me, your disciple, to repent.
> He answered: Take out your transgression, and then I shall allow you to repent.
> He then said: Transgression has no form or characteristic that can be known. What thing should I take out?
> He answered: I have already allowed you to repent. Go back to your room.
> Meaning, one must repent if there is a transgression. But if one does not see transgression, there is no need to repent.[59]

This section utilizes the theory of *prajñā* emptiness. Given that transgression is empty of substance, without any form and characteristic that can be found, then there is no need for someone to repent them. Transgressive obstructions are originally formless, and the original mind is also originally pure in its own nature. Therefore, awakening oneself to the empty nature of transgressions is the true method of practice to eliminate transgressions. Repentance initially

59 Suzuki Daisetsu divides the "two entrances and four practices" into three sections and 101 paragraphs. This paragraph is no. 83, cf. Suzuki, "Zen shisōshi kenkyū", 158.
又言："與弟子懺悔."
答："將你罪來. 與汝懺悔."
又言："罪無形相可得, 知將何物來？"
答："我與汝懺悔竟, 向捨去."
意謂有罪須懺悔, 既不見罪, 不須懺悔.
Yanagida Seizan divides this text into 74 paragraphs; so this paragraph is no. 59. See Yanagida, *Daruma no goroku*.

emphasizes religious reflection, so returning to one's original mind is something that should be done. However, this emphasis on the empty nature of transgressions is a continuation and development of of the Mahāyāna Buddhist view of repentance. Later, the *Baolin zhuan* 寶林傳 (Chronicle of the Baolin Monastery) and *Zutang ji* 祖堂集 (Anthology of the Patriarchal Hall) record that the narrative of the questions and answers between Sengcan 僧璨 (ca. 512–606) and Huike 惠可 (487–593) was very similar to the aforementioned.

The Chan apocryphal, *Jin'gang sanmei jing* (Kor. *Geumgang sammae gyeong*) 金剛三昧經 (Diamond *Samādhi Sūtra*, *T* 273), appeared at this time in the early Tang period. It included repentance within the awakened contemplation of sitting Chan.[60] The *sūtra* states:

> [The Buddha said:] Gentlemen! The minds of those who make living beings uphold this *sūtra* will always be in meditation, and they will not lose their original mind. If they lose their original mind they should repent. The practices of repentance are for the sake of reaching cool purity.
> Ānanda said: Are not previous transgressions that are repented considered past?
> The Buddha said: So it is. It is like a dark room, where the darkness instantly disappears when a bright lamp is lit. Gentlemen! I do not teach repenting transgressions of the past, but it is said that they become past.
> Ānanda said: What is the meaning of "repentance"?
> The Buddha said: Entering into contemplation of the truth based upon the teaching of this *sūtra*. As soon as one enters into contemplation, transgressions will all be eliminated and cease.[61]

Repenting all past transgressions, the mind cannot be attached. Yet, when the mind in the present moment, in dependence on the *Jin'gang sanmei jing*, generates the power of contemplative knowledge of true reality, then past transgressions will naturally be eliminated. Therefore, repentance is included within awakened contemplation. The aware contemplation of the present is itself repentance, and there is no other method of repentance apart from this.

60 Mizuno, "Kongō zanmai kyō", 27. Okabe, "Zensō no chūshō", 360–62.

61 *Jin'gang sanmei jing*, *T* no. 273, 9: 1.374b17-24:
善男子！令諸衆生持是經者, 心常在定不失本心. 若失本心, 當即懺悔, 懺悔之法是爲清涼. 阿難言：懺悔先罪不入於過去也？佛言：如是, 猶如暗室, 若遇明燈, 暗即滅矣. 善男子！無說悔先所有諸罪, 而以爲說入於過去. 阿難言：云何名爲懺悔？佛言：依此經教入真實觀, 一入觀時, 諸罪悉滅.

### 1.3.1 Repentance Thought of Northern Chan

Bodhidharma's Chan passed into the south, where it was Daoxin 道信 (580–651) who promoted it in this new environment. His repentance thought is recorded in the *Lengqie shizi ji* 楞伽師資記 (Records of the Laṇka Teachers and Disciples, *T* 2837):

The *Puxian guanjing* states:

> "The entire ocean of obstructing actions,
> Is all generated from deluded thought.
> If one wishes to repent this,
> Sit upright and be mindful of the true characteristic".
> This is known as the foremost repentance, which removes the mental states of the three poisons, mental states which cling to objects, and mental states of perception and reflection. Being mindful of the Buddha continuously, in thought after thought, it suddenly becomes stilled, and there are no other thoughts.[62]

Daoxin made equivalent the three notions of mind, Buddha, and true characteristics. He believed that mindfulness of the mind was just mindfulness of the Buddha and mindfulness of the true characteristics. Since all afflictions are generated due to deluded thoughts, the cultivation of *dhyāna* meditation should begin from cutting off deluded thoughts and scattered states of mind. But, how does one cut them off? One should practice against the run of things, "sit upright and be mindful of the true characteristics", cast away all mental states of the three poisons, mental states which cling to objects, and mental states of perception and reflection, do not discriminate anything at all, and do not think thoughts. This state without any thought is in accord with the true characteristics of phenomena, and the state of the Buddhas. This is the best, the foremost repentance. Daoxin advocated the sitting Chan contemplation method of watching the mind as the most thorough and correct repentance. This is a continuation and development of Zhiyi's thought.

Therefore, ever since Bodhidharma's Chan was brought to China, the Chinese Chan lineage has continued the Mahāyāna Buddhist view of repentance, an explanation of repentance from the perspective of *prajñā* emptiness. At the same time, there was inclusion of repentance within expedient methods of Chan practice, considering that contemplating the mind in sitting Chan is true

---

62 *Lengqie shizi ji*, *T* no. 2837, 85: 1.1287a7-10:
《普賢觀經》云, "一切業障海, 皆從妄相生；若欲懺悔者, 端坐念實相." 是名第一懺, 併除三毒心、攀緣心、覺觀心. 念佛心心相續, 忽然澄寂, 更無所緣念.

repentance, without there being some other form of repentance practice. This is a continuation and development of Tiantai repentance thought.

Daoxin and Hongren 弘忍 (602–675) made great efforts to develop and propagate Bodhidharma's Chan at Shuangfeng 雙峰 and Dongshan 東山 in Huangmei County 黃梅縣 in the middle reaches of the Yangzi River, and the Chan methods flourished. However, the Chan lineage was later divided between Huineng 慧能 (638–713) and Shenxiu 神秀 (605–706) propagating in the south and north respectively, which led to the names Southern lineage and Northern lineage. The Northern lineage was represented by Shenxiu and Puji 普寂 (651–739), and continued the emphasis from the time of Bodhidharma on transformation of the conscious mind through the Chan method of sitting meditation. In particular, it directly continued and developed Daoxin's meditation methods of "maintaining the one" and "watching the mind", and Hongren's "maintaining in the mind". It raised a more systematic Chan method which had "contemplating the mind" and "watching purity" as its themes. It flourished in the northern areas for a time.

Shenxiu and Puji continued the Chan methods from the time of Bodhidharma, as well as being a direct line in terms of repentance thought. In the *Guanxin lun* 觀心論 (Treatise on contemplating mind), P. 4646, it is stated:

> A further question: The three realms and six destinies are vast without boundary. How can one avoid their suffering by merely contemplating the mind?
> Answer: The retribution of action in the three realms is generated by the mind alone. If originally there were no mind, then there would be no three realms. About "three poisons", desire is the desire realm, aversion is the form realm, and ignorance is the formless realm. Due to these three states of mind, evil is formed and accumulated, retribution of action is made, and cyclic existence continues unabated. This is called the "three realms". Furthermore, due to the degree of severity of action created by the three poisons, there are differences in the retributions which are experienced, which may be divided up into the six destinies. This is called the "six destinies".[63]

63 Nishiguchi, "Kanjinron", 137:
又問, " 三界六趣, 廣大無邊, 若唯觀心, 云何免彼之苦 ? "
答曰, " 三界業報, 唯心所生, 本若無心, 則無三界. 三毒者, 貪爲欲界, 嗔爲色界, 痴爲無色界. 由此三心, 結集諸惡, 業報成就, 輪回不息, 故名 ' 三界 '. 又三毒造業輕重, 受報不同, 分歸六處, 故名 ' 六趣 '."

In the *Guanxin lun*, Shenxiu indicates that the fundamental principle of Chan cultivation is in restraint of the six senses, elimination of the six thieves, removal of attachment, destruction of affliction and casting away of the ignorant, tainted mind, letting living beings' pure Buddha-nature manifest forth, and, from this, realization of liberation. However, how can cultivation of Chan through contemplation of mind lead to liberation from birth and death? It is because the six destinies of the three realms and the pain and suffering of birth and death are all due to living beings' inability to recognize the true suchness of Buddha nature which is originally within their own minds, and so they cultivate the ten wholesome ways deludedly and fall into the six destinies of the three realms. If they are able to cultivate Chan by contemplating the mind, they will awaken to and know the true suchness of Buddha nature replete within their own minds. Not letting it be tainted and corrupted and keeping it constantly pure, all the sufferings of life and death will then naturally be avoided, and the six destinies of the three realms will cease forthwith. Therefore, the foundation of cultivation is in the removal of the polluted, tainted mind, and maintenance of the unpolluted, pure true suchness of Buddha nature.

Shenxiu thought that the three *asaṃkhyā kalpa*s of cultivation, the three categories of pure precepts, the six *pāramitā*s, burning incense and lighting candles to offer to the Buddhas, practicing the path in six sessions, circumambulating *stūpa*s, upholding the fasting days, worshiping and so forth, were all conditioned virtues, and none of them were ultimate. Therefore, only reflexive contemplation of one's own mind, cultivation through conditioned phenomenal characteristics to realize the principle of unconditioned true suchness, was true cultivation. Thus, Shenxiu placed repentance within contemplation of mind, because contemplation of mind was capable of eliminating obstructing actions and was the best method of repentance practice. From this, we can see that Shenxiu continued repentance thought from the time of Bodhidharma and included repentance within the expedient means for Chan practice.

In another text of the Northern lineage, *Dacheng wusheng fangbian men* 大乘無生方便門 (Expedient Means for Attaining Birthlessness in the Mahāyāna), one first transmits the *bodhisattva* precepts, and then transmits the methods of Chan. The content concerning the transmission of the precepts is as follows:

> Each of you kneel down and join palms. I shall teach you how to make the four great vows … Next, we shall invite the Buddhas of the ten directions as preceptors, and so forth… Next, I shall teach you to receive the three refuges. Next, I shall ask you about the five capacities … Next, each of you call out your name, and repent your transgressions, saying:

> "In the past, future and present,
> Transgressions of the ten evils of body, speech and mind,
> I now sincerely repent them all,
> Vowing to eliminate transgressions and never perform them again.
> Obstacles of the five heinous crimes and heavy transgressions appear,
> Like a bright pearl submerged in murky water,
> By the power of that pearl, the water becomes clear and pure.
> The awesome virtue of Buddha nature is just like this,
> The murky water of afflictions becomes clear and pure."
> You all have completed repentance. Your three actions are purified, like clear glass, internally and externally transparent, and you are now capable of receiving the pure precepts. The *bodhisattva* precepts are upheld in the mind, with Buddha nature as the nature of the precepts. To activate the mind for even a brief instant is to violate Buddha nature, and this breaks the *bodhisattva* precepts. To maintain the mind which is not activated is to be in accord with Buddha nature. This is the threefold declaration of upholding the *bodhisattva* precepts.
> Next, all cross your legs [to meditate].[64]

In the Northern lineage, after guiding the Chan monastics in performing the three self-refuges and repentance, the abbot who presides over sitting Chan then says to the monastic community that they already "purified their three actions", and can now receive the "pure precepts". The pure precepts are the *bodhisattva* precepts, which are said to be the "Buddha nature precepts", which "take Buddha nature as the nature of the precepts". The nature of the precepts is equivalent to what Daoxuan calls the "precept body". The abbot tells the Chan monastics that they must understand that the Mahāyāna precepts take Buddha nature as the precept body. If they are unable to control their own mind and thoughts, they will violate Buddha nature, which is to transgress against the *bodhisattva* precepts. On the other hand, if the mind is not activated, then that is upholding the *bodhisattva* precepts. At the same time, within repentance, this advocates that the awesome virtue of Buddha nature is like

---

64 *Dacheng wusheng fangbian men*, *T* no. 2834, 85: 1.1273b13-29:
各各蹋跪合掌, 當教令發四弘誓願 ...... 次請十方諸佛爲和尙等 ...... 次教受三歸, 次問五能 ...... 次各稱已名, 懺悔罪言：過去、未來及現在, 身口意業十惡罪；我今至心盡懺悔, 願罪除滅永不起. 五逆罪障、重罪准前. 譬如明珠沒濁水中, 以珠力故, 水即澄清；佛性威德亦復如是, 煩惱濁水皆得清淨. 汝等懺悔竟, 三業清淨, 如淨瑠璃, 內外明徹, 堪受淨戒. 菩薩戒是持心戒, 以佛性爲戒性, 心瞥起即違佛性, 是破菩薩戒；護持心不起, 即順佛性. 是持菩薩戒三說. 次各令結跏趺坐.
Also cf. Suzuki, *Zen shisōshi kenkyū*, 167-68.

a bright pearl which is able to clarify the murky water of afflictions. Therefore, the Northern lineage not only combines contemplation of mind and watching purity with upholding the precepts, it also combines contemplation of mind and repentance. Using contemplation of mind to manifest Buddha nature is the best kind of repentance.

At that time, it was recorded in the *Zongjing lu* 宗鏡錄 (Records of the Source Mirror, *T* 2016), fascicle ninety-eight, that Foku Yize 佛窟遺則 (751–830) of the Ox Head lineage gave the following explanation of repentance:

> Question: What kind of contemplative repentance practice should one do so as to avoid being led by action at the time of death?
> Answer: You must sincerely believe that the things practiced and taught by the Buddhas are not different from what I today teach and practice. All the way up until attaining Buddhahood, do not even grasp at the characteristics of *nirvāṇa*, let alone grasp at the false actions of transgression or virtue along the way. This is true right knowledge and right view, true cultivation, true repentance. Just by not lacking this contemplation in walking, standing, sitting or lying down, at the time of death you will naturally not lack right mindfulness.[65]

Yize continued Ox Head Farong's 牛頭法融 (594–657) Chan practice, which teaches emptiness without characteristics, mindlessness, and no apprehension. Based on the notion of emptiness in the *Prajñā*[*pāramitā*] and the Three Treatises, he argued for abstaining from distinctions such as living beings versus the Buddhas, transgression versus virtue, and so on, to reach the state of equality and non-duality. Since *prajñā* emptiness contemplation is true right view, cultivation of the *prajñā* contemplation of emptiness while walking, standing, sitting or lying down is true cultivation and true repentance.

Therefore, this is a further step and development from the Northern lineage's thought of cultivation of contemplation as repentance, which makes repentance not only included within the original mind, but also makes it

65 *Zongjing lu*, *T* no. 2016, 48: 98.946a27-b3:
問：作何觀行懺悔，臨終免被業牽？答：汝須深信諸佛所行所說處，與我今日所行所說處無別，乃至成佛尚不得涅槃相，何況中間罪福妄業可得．此是真實正知正見，真實修行，真實懺悔，但於行住坐臥不失此觀，臨終自然不失正念．
Yize's biography is in *Song Gaoseng zhuan*, cf. *T* no. 2061, 50: 10.768b13-c17. Yize followed Ox Head Huizhong 慧忠 (683–769) to become a monk. When Huizhong died, Yize was only seventeen. Therefore, though Yize was a disciple of Huizhong, he had his own understanding. Besides Southern Chan, Northern Chan, and the Oxhead Chan, there was also Foku Chan, which shows that Foku Yize had his own Chan. Cf. Yinshun, "Chanzong shi", 337–43.

applicable in the actual practice of the four physical postures. There is thus no need to actually practice some other forms of repentance. This is the reason why the early Chan did not form its own independent repentance rites.

### 1.3.2 Repentance Thought of the Southern Chan

Bodhidharma's Chan explains repentance from *prajñā* emptiness, and also includes repentance within the expedient methods for Chan practice. At the time of Huineng, he then took this kind of thought and made another step in elevating it by bringing up "Formless Repentance" (*wuxiang chanhui* 無相懺悔) or "Self-nature Repentance" (*zixing chan* 自性懺). Although this kind of thought had an intimate connection with the practice methods of Dongshan and the Oxhead Chan methods which were deeply influenced by Sanlun Buddhism (Sanlun zong 三論宗), formless repentance still has its own special features. Formless repentance is one of the important contents of precepts without characteristics, as advocated by Huineng. Formless precepts can also be called Buddha nature precepts or upholding of mind precepts, because Buddha nature is the real characteristic of formlessness, and the mind is also formless. Hence, it is called formless precepts. The content of formless precepts is fourfold: going for refuge to one's own Buddha of three bodies; making the four great vows; formless repentance; and precepts of three natures and three refuges. In the *Tan jing* 壇經 (Platform *Sūtra*), Huineng states:

> Good advisors!
> In past thought, future thought and present thought, when each and every thought is not tainted by ignorance and delusion, all past evil deeds are instantly removed by self-nature. Just this is repentance.
> In past thought, future thought and present thought, when each and every thought is not tainted by ignorance and stupidity, past arrogant mania is removed, and the tainted mind is forever cut off. This is called self-nature repentance.
> In past thought, future thought and present thought, when each and every thought is not tainted by disease and plague, past jealous states of mind are removed, removed by self-nature. Just this is repentance.
> (The above is chanted thrice.)
> Good advisors! What is known as "repentance" (*chanhui*)?
> *Chan* is when one never does [evil]; *hui* is to know ones past wrong, evil actions never leave the mind. Reciting [*sūtras*] with the mouth before the Buddhas is useless. In this practice method of mine, [transgression] is

> forever cut off and never enacted. This is known as "repentance" (*chanhui*).[66]

In Repentance without Characteristics, there is no need to "confess and repent" before a statue of the Buddha or to recite a repentance text. Just "[in] past thought, future thought and present thought, when each and every thought is not tainted by ignorance and delusion", all kinds of arrogant mania, jealousy and other "tainted minds" which bring about evil deeds are eliminated.

However, why is formless repentance also called "Self-nature Repentance"? "Nature" (*xing* 性) is an important technical term in the *Tan jing*, such as "Dharma-nature" (*faxing* 法性), "Original Nature" (*benxing* 本性), and "Self-nature" (*zixing* 自性). Another important technical term is "mind" (*xin* 心), for example "Original Mind" (*benxin* 本心), "Own Mind" (*zixin* 自心), and so on, which is a term that has the same significance. Self-nature as originally pure, as originally empty pacification, is the transcendence of the phenomenal world. Therefore, wholesome and evil, the Pure Land and hell, "past wrong, evil actions" (*qianfei eye* 前非惡業), are all due to "thinking", and manifest from self-nature. The manifestations of all phenomena are not apart from self-nature. All is originally pure, there is nothing to grasp or let go that could be repented. However, living beings are deluded about self-nature, and so self-nature becomes the ego-self (small self) of life and death. Speaking from the position of transforming delusion into awakening, self-nature is the Dharma body, self-nature is replete with the Buddha of three bodies, and therefore, self-nature already possesses repentance. One only needs to remove arrogance, mania, jealousy and so on, the "tainted minds", to do so. Thus, it is called "self-nature repentance", which is a full development and expression of the philosophy of the treasury of the Thus Come One. Because living beings grasp at characteristics, and cling to characteristics, this obstructs their own original nature, just as the clouds and fog block out the clear purity of empty space. If they are freed from characteristics, then they will suddenly see the substance of that nature is originally pure, just as empty space is clear and pure when the clouds part.

---

66 Yang, *Liuzu tanjing*, 24–25:
善知識,
前念後念及今念, 念念不被愚迷染, 從前惡行, 壹時自性若除, 即是懺悔.
前念後念及今念, 念念不被愚癡染, 除卻從前矯誑, 雜心永斷, 名爲自性懺.
前念後念及今念, 念念不被疽疫染, 除卻從前嫉妒心, 自性若除, 即是懺.
已上三唱.
善知識, 何名懺悔？
懺者, 終身不作；悔者, 知於前非惡業, 恒不離心.
諸佛前口說無益, 我此法門中永斷不作, 名爲懺悔.

So, being without characteristics is not just leaving all characteristics, but is the manifestation of the substantial nature of purity due to being freed from characteristics. "Self-nature" is the substance of absence of characteristics. Therefore, self-nature repentance can also be called Repentance without Characteristics.

In the *Dunhuang xinben Liuzu tanjing* 敦煌新本六組壇經 (The Dunhuang New Text of Sixth-Patriarch Platform *Sūtra*), Huineng develops and advances the thought of formless repentance to its fullest. He expands this theme further in the "*Wuxiang song* 無相頌 " (Verses on Formlessness):

> The Master said: Good advisors! Hear me teach the "No-characteristic Verses", which will let those who are deluded eliminate their transgressions. It is also known as the "Miezui song" 滅罪頌 (Verses on Eliminating Transgressions). The verses state:
> "The ignorant cultivate merit and not the path,
> Claiming that cultivating merit is the path.
> The merit of giving and offerings is measureless,
> But the three actions in the mind continue to be made".
> "If one wishes to eliminate transgression through cultivating merit,
> Despite merit in future lives, the transgression is still there.
> To resolve, go to the mind to remove the conditions of transgression,
> And within your own self-nature do true repentance".
> "If one realizes Mahāyāna true repentance,
> Removing the perverse and practicing the straight is the absence of transgression.
> Those who study the path can contemplate themselves,
> And are the same as those people who have realization".
> "The master now transmits this sudden teaching,
> Wishing that students may be of the same substance.
> If one wants in the future to see the original body,
> Cleanse the mind of the three poisons and evil conditions".
> "Do not digress as you vigorously cultivate the path,
> Passing an entire life in vain, doing nothing.
> If one encounters the Mahāyāna sudden teaching Dharma,
> Sincerely join your palms and seek within your mind"![67]

---

67 Yang, *Liuzu tanjing*, 35–36:
大師言：善知識, 聽吾說《無相頌》, 令汝迷者罪滅, 亦名《滅罪頌》, 頌曰：
愚人修福不修道, 謂言修福便是道；布施供養福無邊, 心中三惡元來造.
若將修福欲滅罪, 後世得福罪元在；若解向心除罪緣, 各自性中真懺悔.
若悟大乘真懺悔, 除邪行正即無罪；學道之人能自觀, 即與悟人同壹類.

Because transgression and merit are both manifested from within self-nature, one cannot therefore cultivate merit to eliminate transgression. However, when one "[goes] to the mind to remove the conditions of transgression, and within [their] own self-nature does true repentance", we see a full expression of the idea of self-nature repentance. Self-nature Repentance is a further advance of Mahāyāna repentance methods, which are built on the foundation of the fusion of Buddha nature and *Prajñā[pāramitā]* theories. This is the product of the combination of the *Lengqie jing* and the *Jin'gang jing* 金剛經 (Diamond *Sūtra*), though leans more toward treasury of the Thus Come One Buddha nature thought of the former.

### 1.3.3 Chan Buddhism's Practices of Forms of Repentance in the Tang Dynasty

The opposition between the Southern lineage and the Northern lineage was not only a dispute about the direct and indirect transmission from teachers to disciples, but the opposition of the practice methods of "Southern sudden, Northern gradual" was in fact a reality. The Southern lineage emphasized no-thought, a direct piercing with a single blade that did not have recourse to expedient means and did not favour religious rite and ritual. On the other hand, the Northern school used a variety of expedient means, observing first a succession of gradual means, and only then having realization. Therefore, the Self-nature Repentance of the Southern lineage also did not need expedient means, and so the Chan meditators of the Southern lineage never had any records of actual repentance practices. The Northern lineage, however, differed on this, and included repentance as an expedient means to practice Chan methods, and therefore had actual forms of worship and repentance. Thus, due to the differences in Chan practices, this brought about a discrepancy in the forms of these two lineages.

As it is recorded in the "Songyue si bei" 嵩岳寺碑 (Stele of Songyue si), when Puji of the Northern lineage was at Mount Song 嵩山, "Subsequently there was a shrine to [the Buddha of] Infinite Life, who the masters would extol with worship, repentance and recitation".[68] When Shenhui 神會 (684–758) criticized the essentials of the Chan methods of Shenxiu and Puji of the Northern lineage, he said, "Consolidate the mind to enter meditation; stabilize the mind to watch purity; activate the mind to observe externally; focus the mind to

大師今傳此頓教, 願學之人同壹體；若欲當來覓本身, 三毒惡緣心裏洗.
努力修道莫悠悠, 忽然虛度壹世休；若遇大乘頓教法, 虔誠合掌至心求.

68 *Quan Tang wen* 263.1181: 後有無量壽殿者, 諸師禮懺誦念之場也.

FIGURE 18 Statue of an *Arhat* at Kanjing Monastery 看經寺 in Longmen 龍門, dated to the mid-Tang Dynasty (618-907).

realize internally".[69] The Northern lineage emphasized sitting in Chan meditation, within which one "contemplates the mind", "focuses the mind", and "stabilizes the mind to watch purity", and at the same time they emphasize repentance and recitation. This is just a continuation of the kind of expedient means used in the usual Chan methods of Daoxin with his "be mindful the Buddha's [name] to purify the mind".

When teaching the Dharma and transmitting Chan, Wuxiang 無相 (684–762) of Jingzhong si 浄眾寺, in the system of Zhishen 智詵 (609–702) from Jiannan 劍南, first performed repentance, and after that did sitting meditation. As it is stated in the *Yuanjue jing dashu shiyi chao*, fascicle three:

> Although there are a great range of expedient means when developing an idea or teaching, the main directive returns to these three sentences. Their transmission ritual is, in brief, like the means for transmitting the full precepts at official ordination ceremonies in this country in the present day. That is, the day is selected a month or two before, and notification is posted up to gather together monks and nuns, laymen and laywomen, to erect an Expansive Altar for the performance of repentance, for either three weeks or five weeks. After this, the precepts are transmitted in the course of the night, with the intention to prevent external disruption or interference. Having transmitted the Dharma, they are then instructed in mindfulness of the breath sitting Chan.[70]

The essence of Wuxiang's Chan methods is in the three statements: "No recollection, no thought, do not be deluded".[71] When transmitting this Chan method, they first "erect a *Vaipulyas* Altar for the performance of repentance", where for three or five weeks they cultivate the Expansive repentance rites.

Because Wuxiang's transmission rite is like the "means for transmitting the full precepts at official ordination ceremonies", where the official ceremony is just an Expansive Altar, Hao Chunwen 郝春文 undertook research into the Dunhuang Expansive Altar rites. He thinks that the procedure for transmitting the precepts at the Expansive Altar includes: first, purely entering into the

---

69 Yang, *Yulu*, 29: 凝心入定, 住心看淨, 起心外照, 攝心內證.

70 *Yuanjue jing dashu shiyi chao*, XZJ no. 211, 14: 3.556a5-9: 雖開宗演說, 方便多端. 而宗旨所歸, 在此三句. 其傳授儀式, 略如此此國今時官壇受具足戒方便. 謂一兩月前, 先剋日牒示, 召集僧尼士女, 置方等道場禮懺, 或三七、五七, 然後授法了, 皆是夜間, 意在絕外屛喧亂也. 授法了, 便令言下息念坐禪.

71 *Yuanjue jing dashu shiyi chao*, XZJ no. 211, 14: 3.556a1-2: 無憶無念莫忘.

altar; then, supplicating a public prayer; requesting exhortation from the venerable monastics of Chan and *Vinaya* temples; confession; examination and pondering; prayers to the light; distinctions; faults and penalties; and receiving the precepts.[72] Confession is repentance of transgressions, and examination and pondering is cultivation of Chan meditative contemplation. However, there is a confessional text used when confessing, as in the *Shou bajie fa* 受八戒法 (Ritual for Receiving the Eight Precepts), P. 2849. This preserves the confessional text when a lay disciple receives the eight precepts, though it does not specifically indicate what kind of repentance rite one performs.[73] Even though the Expansive Altar stresses a thorough all-encompassing attitude, according to the Mahāyāna Buddhist spirit of the equality of all things, one only needs to aspire the mind to *bodhi* and the precepts will be received, which pushes aside any fundamental differences in preceptees. However, in order to guarantee the purity of the precepts, confession and repentance became extremely important. When Wuxiang transmitted Chan methods, performance of repentance was a basic fact.

In the "Xuanshi" lineage under the Dongshan tradition, when Xuanshi 宣什 (ca. seventh century) transmitted Chan methods, he also gathered the community and did a short period of cultivation: "He first gathered the community and performed repentance and other rites and rituals, just as under the tutelage of abbot Jin".[74] We can see that performing repentance in the Jingzhong lineage and Xuanshi lineage was a kind of requisite expedient means.

The actual practices of repentance by Puji, the Jingzhong lineage, the Xuanshi lineage and so forth, are simple records. However, two Northern lineage repentance texts are preserved in the Dunhuang texts, the *Jin'gang wuli* 金剛五禮 (Diamond Five Repentances) and "Datong heshang qili wen" 大通和尙七禮文 (Abbot Datong Sevenfold Worship Text), also known as the "Xiu chanshi qili" 秀禪師七禮 (Chan Master Xiu Sevenfold Worship), which are primary sources for understanding the form of repentance in Tang-dynasty Chan Buddhism.[75]

72 Hao, *Sengni de shehui shenghuo*, 25–61.

73 Huang, *Dunhuang baozang*, 124.474-76.

74 *Yuanjue jing dashu shiyi chao*, XZJ no. 211, 14: 3.558a12-13: 其初集眾, 禮懺等儀式, 如金和上門下.

75 When Yanagida Seizan works on the Chan text *Den bōhō ki*, he makes detailed notes on the Dunhuang manuscript P. 3559 that had *Den bōhō ki* on it and suggests that this text has the style of the Northern Chan. He considers the *Diamond Five Repentances* written at the end of the manuscript is a similar repentance text to the "Datong heshang qili wen" by Shenxiu, cf. Yanagida, "Den bōhō ki", 50.

### 1.4 *Daoxuan and the Repentance Ritual of the* Vinaya *School*

The development of monastic precepts in the Tang dynasty took the parallel development of the Hīnayāna *Sifen lü* 四分律 (Four-Part *Vinaya*) and the Mahāyāna bodhisattva precepts as its core. From the point of view of upholding or violating the monastic precepts, irrespective of Hīnayāna or Mahāyāna precepts, they provide their own methods of repentance, which enable those precepts to be upheld purely. Because of the situation of the dissemination of the *Vinaya* canon in the Sui and Tang period, "Now, it is most popular for masters to use the *Shisong lü* 十誦律 (Ten Recitations *Vinaya*)",[76] though there is no standardization in terms of the rituals for repentance for violating precepts, penalties for transgressions, and treatment of transgressions. Daoxuan 道宣 (596–667) said: "The ancient masters all practiced repentance rituals, [but] they added or reduced, hiding or revealing, with much conjecture, explaining the teachings without texts, and making practices which violated the precepts".[77] Yuanzhao believed that the "ancient masters" referred to those who compiled monastic ritual ceremony and procedures (*jiemo* 羯磨).[78] The formal karma rites of the various scholarly traditions reflected their lack of knowledge with respect to the various rituals. They either changed the rites, had discrepancies between their practices, had no scriptural support for their repentance practices, or had practices that were in violation of the characteristics of the monastic discipline. Therefore, establishing regulations for the treatment and penalties for transgressions that were appropriate for the actual circumstances of a transgression, as well as being able to resonate with the psychology of the Chinese proponents of Mahāyāna Buddhism, was of course a desideratum.

In the *Sifen lü shanfan buqüe xingshi chao* 四分律刪繁補闕行事鈔 (Transcript Regarding the Revised [Regulation] of the Practice of the Four-part *Vinaya*; hereafter, *Xingshi chao* 行事鈔), Daoxuan divided repentance into Repentance by Principle (*lichan* 理懺), Repentance by Phenomena (*shichan* 事懺), and Repentance by Precepts (*lüchan* 律懺). He stated: "Now, the practice of repentance is in general of two kinds: the first is Repentance by Principle; the second is Repentance by Phenomena. These two kinds of repentance are found throughout renunciants and laity. But, discussion of Repentance by Precepts is only for the renunciant community".[79] Repentance by Principle and

76 *Sifen lü shanfan buqüe xingshi chao*, *T* no. 1804, 40: 2.59b29-c1: 今諸師盛行多依於《十誦》.

77 *Sifen lü shanfan buqüe xingshi chao*, *T* no. 1804, 40: 2.96a21-22: 邃古之師, 並施悔法, 增減隱顯, 臆課者多, 照教無文, 撿行違律.

78 *Sifen lü xingshi chao zichi ji*, *T* no. 1805, 40: 2.349b28: 古師即指諸家集羯磨者.

79 *Sifen lü shanfan buqüe xingshi chao*, *T* no. 1804, 40: 2.96a27-29: 今懺悔之法, 大略有二：初則理懺, 二則事懺. 此之二懺通道含俗, 若論律懺唯局道眾.

Repentance by Phenomena are not restricted to either monastics or lay people, though Repentance by Precepts is restricted to only the monastic community. Daoxuan had a full explanation of both the audience and meaning of these three kinds of repentance practice. Concerning Repentance by Principle, Daoxuan states in the *Xingshi chao*:

> [Repentance by] Principle is based on sharp wisdom to contemplate the nature of that transgression. Because the deluded thought covers the mind, one forms actions, so one needs to cognize that the original nature of the deluded thought is unarisen, lest in thought after thought the mind is scattered and action proceeds following delusion… To speak of Repentance by Principle, it is for the wise, who use many expedient means according to their performed actions, to constantly contemplate that they have no nature; and by this absence of nature, the false self has no basis. Phenomena are not generated by the self, transgression and merit are unarisen, they are separately seen and separately cognized, separately eliminated and separately ceased, as a person who awakes is not in the stupor of sleep. Whereas the essentials of [Repentance by] Principle are no other than three kinds: One, phenomena are empty of nature and not self. To illuminate the mind through this principle is considered Hīnayāna. Two, the original characteristic of phenomena is empty, merely falsely seen through the emotions. To illuminate using this principle is considered a small *bodhisattva*. Three, phenomena do not originally exist as external elements, in fact, they are only cognition. This principle is the most subtle, an object is known only through the mind. This [illumination] is that of a great *bodhisattva*, the realization and practice of the fruition of the Buddhas. Therefore, the *She* [*dacheng*] *lun* 攝 [大乘] 論 (Compendium of the Great Vehicle Treatise) states that only cognition is equal throughout the four states. By way of these three principles, depending on the strength or weakness of wisdom applied, one accordingly contemplates phenomena as objects and all transgressions are cast forth. Thus, the *Huayan* [*jing*] states: The entire ocean of obstructing actions, is all generated from deluded thought. If one wishes to repent this, one should seek the true real characteristic. This kind of great repentance dissolves the cloud of the accumulated transgressions.[80]

---

80 *Sifen lü shanfan buqüe xingshi chao*, *T* no. 1804, 40: 2.96b3-21:
理據智利觀彼罪性, 由妄覆心便結妄業, 還須識妄本性無生, 念念分心業隨迷遣. …… 言理懺者, 既在智人, 則多方便隨所施爲, 恒觀無性, 以無性故, 妄我無託. 事非我生, 罪福無主, 分見分思, 分除分滅, 如人醒覺則不眠醉. 然理大要不出三種：一者諸法性空無我, 此理照心名爲小乘；二者諸法本相是空, 唯情妄見, 此

Repentance by Principle is a method cultivated by those with sharp faculties. The ritual practice is grounded on the contemplation of emptiness: because phenomena are not self, it is believed that phenomena are also empty. However, realization of this kind of emptiness principle is explained from three aspects by Daoxuan: One, phenomena are empty of nature and have no self. Two, phenomena are characterized by emptiness, and merely falsely perceived through the emotions. Three, phenomena are only cognition, with no object. Although Daoxuan absorbed the thought of repentance by principle, which was commonly practiced in the Sui and Tang Buddhist spheres, namely the theoretical principle of transgressions being empty of nature in the *prajñā* teachings of the *Puxian guanjing*, he gave a further explanation in terms of the theories of mere consciousness without external object. This is related to the consciousness only teachings he learned from Huiyun 慧頵 (564–637), which is the special features of his thought of repentance by principle.

With respect to Repentance by Phenomena, he states:

> Concerning Repentance by Phenomena, it belongs to those with dull faculties. Because they cannot see the principle, they always practice with the notion of self. False action blinds their minds, and they are caught up in accordance with various objects. These movements bring about actions, and by actions they are bound to threefold existence. If one teaches them true contemplation, their minds dim and their knowledge is confused. They only have to adorn and purify an altar to praise, extol and worship; or they may worship, recite or circumambulate using full sincerity to take these superior objects [of worship]. Action may be serious or light, distinguished as fixed or not fixed, which may transform the retribution or experience a light retribution. This is as explained in the *Foming* [*jing*] 佛名 [ 經 ] (*Sūtra* of Buddhas' Names), [*Da*] *fangdeng* [*tuoluoni jing*] 大方等陀羅尼經 (*Mahāvaipulya-dhāraṇī-sūtra*) and other *sūtras*.[81]

---

理照用屬小菩薩；三者諸法外塵本無, 實唯有識, 此理深妙, 唯意緣知, 是大菩薩, 佛果證行. 故《攝論》云：唯識通四位等. 以此三理, 任智彊弱, 隨事觀緣, 無罪不遣. 故《華嚴》云, 一切業障海, 皆從妄想生, 若欲懺悔者, 當求真實相. 如此大懺, 眾罪雲消.

81 *Sifen lü shanfan buqüe xingshi chao*, *T* no. 1804, 40: 2.96b4-10:
若論事懺, 屬彼愚鈍. 由未見理, 我倒常行, 妄業翳心, 隨境纏附, 動必起行, 行纏三有. 爲說真觀心昏智迷, 止得嚴淨道場, 稱歎虔仰. 或因禮拜, 或假誦持旋繞, 竭誠心緣勝境. 則業有輕重, 定不定別, 或有轉報, 或有輕受, 並如《佛名》《方等》諸經所明.

Repentance by Phenomena is also applicable to both monastics and laity, but this is a practice cultivated by those of dull faculties, whose "minds are dim and knowledge is confused". The ritual practice of Repentance by Phenomena is just the various kinds of repentance rites that were commonly used in the Buddhist world, such as the repentance rites based on the *Foming jing*, *Da fangdeng tuoluoni jing*, and other such ritual practices.[82] They just "adorn and purify an altar to praise, extol and worship; or they may worship, recite or circumambulate, use full sincerity to take these superior objects [of worship]",[83] in order to cultivate the repentance rite with actions of body, speech and mind.

Daoxuan not only believed that there were distinctions between the audience capabilities for Repentance by Principle and Repentance by Phenomena, he also felt that there were differences in function. As he says:

> If one's own mind experiences enjoyment at the time of transgression, one must perform Repentance by Phenomena. If one experiences enjoyment at the time of creating merit, one must perform Repentance by Principle. [Repentance by] Principle goes through both the deep and the shallow, as described above. If it is a transgression of one of the five categories [of monastic precepts], then one must use the condition of both the principle and phenomena. The phenomenal is in accord with the teachings, and does not violate consciousness only; the principled reaches the deluded thought, that external objects originally do not exist. As the [*She dacheng*] *lun* states: "The meaning of consciousness only is not faulty. It is not that there is no significance of the subject and the object".[84]

Daoxuan believes that if living beings commit transgressions, they must cultivate Repentance by Phenomena, and if they cling to the results of meritorious deeds, they should cultivate Repentance by Principle. If monastics transgress the five categories of precepts, they should cultivate both phenomena and principle. However, both Repentance by Phenomena and Repentance by Principle can demonstrate the meaning of consciousness only. Of course, the functions of the two are different: Repentance by Principle is able to cease

82 About the repentance rite of the Buddhas' names, cf. Shioiri, "Raisan to butsumyō kyōten", 569–89.

83 *Sifen lü shanfan buqüe xingshi chao*, *T* no. 1804, 40: 2.96b4-10: 嚴淨道場, 稱歎虔仰, 或因禮拜, 或假誦持旋繞, 竭誠心緣勝境.

84 *Sifen lü shanfan buqüe xingshi chao*, *T* no. 1804, 40: 2.96b23-27: 自心若樂罪時, 須修事懺；若樂福時, 須修理觀. 理通深淺, 如上所明. 若是五眾犯罪, 則理事兩緣. 事則順教, 無違唯識；理則達妄, 外塵本無. 故論云：唯識義不失, 亦不無能取所取也.

FIGURE 19 The stone-pillar of the *Da Foding tuoluoni jing* 大佛頂陀羅尼經 (Skt. *Sitātapatroṣṇīṣa dhāraṇī*), constructed in 906 in Longmen 龍門.

transgressions, whereas Repentance by Phenomena is only able to either suppress transgressions, transform the retribution, or lighten the result.

From our proceeding analysis of Repentance by Principle and Repentance by Phenomena, we can see that Daoxuan uses the consciousness only teachings to systematize these two types of repentance practice. In Repentance by Principle, he explains the original emptiness of nature of transgressions through the consciousness only notion that there are no external objects. For Repentance by Phenomena, he deems that it is in conformity with the *sūtras*, and does not run contrary to consciousness only thought. However, when he composed the *Xingshi chao*, his only citations of consciousness only scripture are the five times he cites the *She dacheng lun*.[85] Daoxuan composed the *Xingshi chao* at Chongyi si 崇義寺 in the year 626 CE.[86] It was only in his later years that Daoxuan participated in Xuanzang's translation bureau, and so his citations of the *She dacheng lun* should be from Zhendi's 真諦 (Paramārtha, 499–569) translation. Therefore, Daoxuan's early theories of consciousness only should belong to the consciousness only system of Zhendi.

With respect to Repentance by Precepts, in the *Xingshi chao*, Daoxuan states:

> On the matter of Repentance by Precepts, this is only applicable to the renunciant community. This is because violation is due to receiving [the monastic precepts], tainting the root which should be pure. To return to the state of first receiving [the precepts], they are treated in order, with rites established according to the category [of precept], which the practice of repentance permits.[87]

Repentance by Precepts is limited to the monastic community because it only relates to the violation of the specific precepts in the monastic discipline codes, and the actual practices of repentance rites. Its ultimate aim is the long term preservation of the *saṃgha* and the monastic way of strictly maintaining the monastic precepts. Daoxuan's basic position with respect to Repentance by Precepts is as follows:

> The commentator states: When the Buddha Dharma spread to the East, there were still few who practiced these teachings. Although some

85 Kawaguchi, "Inyōtenseki", 120.

86 Suwa, "Dōsenden", 57.

87 *Sifen lü shanfan buqüe xingshi chao, T* no. 1804, 40: 2.96a29-b2: 若論律懺, 唯局道眾, 由犯託受生, 污本須淨, 還依初受, 次第治之, 篇聚立儀, 悔法準此.

> practiced repentance, they discarded the small [vehicle] and took up the great [vehicle]. As for those who repented based on the *Foming* [*jing*], [*Da*] *fangdeng* [*tuoluoni jing*], my mind is still not at peace. Because their minds harbor rejection and favouring, they do not accord with the great path.[88]

Daoxuan thought that those practicing Repentance by Precepts in the Tang period were extremely few. Even those that did practice Repentance by Precepts used the excuse that because Repentance by Precepts is a Hīnayāna practice they should therefore abandon it, and instead practice the repentance rituals according to the *Foming jing*, *Da fangdeng tuoluoni jing*, and so forth. At the same time, he also thought that they harboured an attitude of rejection toward the teachings of the Hīnayāna and had an attitude of favouritism toward the Mahāyāna Dharma, which is inappropriate for the path to Buddhahood.

The actual specific practices of performing Repentance by Precepts are as described in the *Xingshi chao*:

> Repentance for violation in the *Vinaya* must be understood without any doubt. One must well fit the name to the type, making distinctions in terms of group. Those of the same category may be repented together, those of different groups repented separately. Also, transgressions should be formally recorded in the repentant rite, and should be stated by their number. If one forgets and does not know, it should be said that one does not recall. … Therefore, one must repent by recognizing the transgressions, as clearly as the water-mirror, letting them not conceal one another and emotions not in accord, only then can one be said to be a Buddhist who follows the teachings. Why? It is because the *Vinaya* lineage takes the precepts as the standard. The precepts are violated when both the mind and action are wrong, which is different from the Mahāyāna where the three retributions can all be repented as one.[89]

---

88 *Sifen lü shanfan buqüe xingshi chao*, *T* no. 1804, 40: 2.99b12-15:
鈔者云：佛法東流,行此法者亦少.縱有行悔,則棄小取大,依《佛名》《方等》而懺者,余意所未安,由心懷厭欣,未合大道.

89 *Sifen lü shanfan buqüe xingshi chao*, *T* no. 1804, 40: 2.101a10-22:
律中犯懺,必須識知不疑,善宜名種,依聚歷別,同篇合懺,異聚別悔.又牒罪入法,隨數稱之,若忘不知,乃云不憶.…… 故須照達罪懺明逾水鏡,使彼此無私隱,情事

When performing Repentance by Precepts, one must confirm the name of the transgression and also the kind of transgression. If they are of the same type then they can be repented together, but if they are of different types then they must be separately repented. The name of the transgression is written down and called according to the number of them. If one forgets, then they say, "I do not remember". Therefore, Repentance by Precepts involves performance of repentance based on the characteristics of the transgression that occurred. When compared to the Mahāyāna, which uses a method wherein all transgressional obstructions with present life retribution, next life retribution, or subsequent life retribution are all repented together, it is quite a different situation.

In the *Xingshi chao*, the Repentance by Precepts that Daoxuan advocates is not based on the teaching of "five categories and seven groups (*wupian qiju* 五篇七聚)" that was transmitted from the past, but rather establishes a theory of "six groups (*liuju* 六聚)". He states: "The amount of repentance rites is many, but the outline is only six states".[90] These six are:

> The five categories and seven groups are distinguished in terms of their meanings. It is a precise summary of the classes of transgressions by erecting six practices. Now, based on the six groups, we explain their names: one, *pārājika*; two, *saṃghāvaśeṣa*; three, *sthūlāyaya*; four, *pāyattika*; five, *pratideśanīya*; and six, *duṣkṛta*.[91]

Daoxuan's explanation of the "six groups" emphasizes the continuation of the Buddha's own tradition in the *Vinaya* canon. Setting out from a position of the concrete maintenance of the Dharma, and based on the four complete *Vinaya*s and many *sūtra*s and treatises, he sets up the form of the "six groups" teaching.

Therefore, Daoxuan's three kinds of repentance rite have definite distinctions in terms of their capacities, theories, functions and so forth. Tsuchihashi Shūkō previously made the following comparison:[92]

---

有相應, 則可爲順教佛子矣. 何者以律宗約相, 違相心事俱非, 不類大乘三報同皆一懺.

90 *Sifen lü shanfan buqüe xingshi chao*, *T* no. 1804, 40: 2.96b29-c1: 懺法乃多, 要唯六位.

91 *Sifen lü shanfan buqüe xingshi chao*, *T* no. 1804, 40: 2.46c6-9: 五篇七聚約義差分, 正結罪科止樹六法. 今依六聚, 且釋其名：一、波羅夷, 二、僧伽婆尸沙, 三、偷蘭遮, 四、波逸提, 五、波羅提提舍尼, 六、突吉羅.

92 Tsuchihashi, "Bini to sange", 83.

| | | | | | | |
|---|---|---|---|---|---|---|
| **Repentance by Principle 理懺** | Sharp faculties (laity and renunciants) 利根 (道俗) | Contemplation of emptiness 空觀 | *Prajñā* [*pāramitā*] 般若 | No external object 無境 | Eliminate transgressions 滅罪 | bring about merit 招福 |
| **Repentance by Phenomena 事懺** | Dull faculties (laity and renunciants) 鈍根 (道俗) | Performance of a rite (repentance rite) 行儀 (懺法) | *Vaipulyas* 方等 | Consciousness only 唯識 | Suppress transgressions 伏罪 | remove transgressions 除罪 |
| **Repentance by *Karma* 行懺** | Renunciant community 道眾 | Performance of repentance (*karma*) 行懺 (羯磨) | *Vinaya* texts 律典 | Manifest characteristics 現相 | Suppress transgressions 伏罪 | long abiding of the *saṃgha* 僧寶久住 |

It should be noted that the categories into which these three kinds of repentance rite are divided are not Daoxuan's original creation. Rather, his unique element is in integrating Repentance by Principle and Repentance by Phenomena into the perspective of consciousness only. At the same time, with respect to the then contemporary tide of the Buddhist world, he forcibly advocated Repentance by Precepts and tended toward traditional explanations for repentance from sectarian Buddhism. Although he absorbed the thought of Repentance by Principle and Repentance by Phenomena, which were common in Tang dynasty Buddhism, on one hand, he wanted to respond to the popular direction of the time and combine *Vinaya* discipline from both the Hīnayāna and Mahāyāna to reveal unity between the "small" and "great" vehicles. On the other hand, he felt that Mahāyāna repentance rites ran contrary to the *Vinaya* rules, and somewhat rejected them. This is because he was situated within a very strong conscious awareness of the Dharma ending age, and so his ideal of protecting the teachings and letting the right Dharma abide in the world contains the aspiration to return to the monastic discipline of India. This contradiction is evident through Daoxuan as a *Vinaya* master facing the sinicization of *Vinaya* monastic codes, and the differences between the Hīnayāna and Mahāyāna.

### 1.5 *Shandao and Pure Land Rites of Worship and Praise*

Shandao 善導 (613–681) was a master of the Pure Land lineage in the Tang dynasty. After his own master, Daochuo 道綽 (562–645), passed away, he undertook many Buddhist religious activities in Chang'an. The *Xu Gaoseng zhuan* states:

> Recently we have the mountain monk Shandao. He travelled far and wide, seeking a ford to the path. Traveling to the West River, he encountered the community of Daochuo, and just practiced the pure action of recitation of Amitābha. After he entered the capital, he preached this teaching extensively. He transcribed the [*A*]*mituo jing* [阿] 彌陀經 (*Amitābha-sūtra*) many tens of thousands of times. There were countless ladies and gentlemen who extolled him. He often taught the Dharma at Guangming si 光明寺.[93]

Chang'an was the centre of Tang dynasty Buddhism. With the support of the imperial court and aristocrats, a great many large temples and monasteries were erected, and many lineages and traditions were strongly promoted, such as Sanlun, Tiantai, Huayan, Weishi 唯識 (Consciousness Only), and others. Therefore, during Shandao's process of propagating the Pure Land practice methods, he most certainly was influenced by the Buddhism of Chang'an, as well as the need to fly his own flag with its special features.

Under the influence and prodding of various religious services and repentances that were common in the contemporary Buddhism of that time, Shandao used many concrete practice methods in order to express his own Pure Land religious faith. He shaped rites of worship and praise that were complete and majestic, recording them in the four texts in five fascicles of the "Xingyi fen" 行儀分 (Practice of Rite Section), namely the "Fashi zan" 法事讚 (Praise of Dharma Practice), "Wangsheng lizan" 往生禮讚 (Worship and Praise *Gāthās* of Rebirth), "Guannian famen" 觀念法門 (Method of Contemplation and Mindfulness Practice), and "Bozhou zan" 般舟讚 (Praise of *Pratyuptpanna*). The completeness and actualization of these religious rituals display the combined Buddhist art and architecture of the cosmopolitan city of Chang'an. However, based on the special features of his own religious experiences and Pure Land faith, Shandao composed these solemn and majestic praise and worship rites to draw in greater numbers of the common folk to take refuge in the Pure Land, propagating the Dharma methods of the Pure Land teachings to even greater heights.

93 *Xu Gaoseng zhuan*, *T* no. 2060, 50: 27.684a11-15:
近有山僧善導者, 周遊寰寓, 求訪道津. 行至西河, 遇道綽部. 惟行念佛彌陀淨業. 既入京師, 廣行此化. 寫《彌陀經》數萬卷, 士女奉者, 其數無量, 時在光明寺說法.

FIGURE 20 The statue of Vairocana in Longmen 龍門 (dated 672).

### 1.5.1 Ritual of the *Fashi Zan* 法事讚

The *Fashi zan* in two fascicles is the most complete and solemn among Shandao's worship and praise rituals. The first fascicle is the *Zhuanjing xingdao yuan wangsheng jingtu fashi zan* 轉經行道願往生淨土法事讚 (Praise of Dharma Practice of Turning the *Sūtra*s and Practising the Path to Vow to be Reborn in the Pure Land), and the last fascicle is the *Anle xingdao zhuanjing yuansheng jingtu fashi zan* 安樂行道轉經願生淨土法事讚 (Praise of Dharma Practice of Blissfully Practising the Path and Turning the *Sūtra*s to Vow to be Reborn in the Pure Land). "Turn the *sūtras*" means to recite or chant the *sūtra*s, as the *Nittō guhō junrei kōki* 入唐求法巡禮行記 (Record of a Pilgrimage to the Tang in search of the Law) states, "When a person comes to request recitation of the *sūtra*s, have that person say 'Ascend to the [Dharma] Hall to recite the *sutras*'".[94] "Practice the path" means a ritual wherein people form lines to circumambulate and worship, which was a form of worship in ancient India. These respected and honoured worship rites were forms of worship where one walks clockwise to circumambulate around the Buddha or *stūpa*. Usually one circumambulates once, thrice, seven, or even up to hundreds or thousands of times. The directive and nature of the *Fashi zan* is described in the Japanese

94 *Nittō guhō junrei kōki*, 1.21: 若有人到請轉經時, 亦令人道 " 上堂念經 ".

text the *Shūgyō yōketsu* 修業要決 (Essentials of Cultivation) by Shōkū 證空 (1177–1247) of Japan:

> Explanation: "Turn the *sūtra*s and practice the path" is to turn and praise the *Amituo jing*, which is the path to renunciation. "Vow to be reborn in the Pure Land" means that there are no two Pure Lands, but only the one land of ultimate bliss. Rebirth is only in the western realm, in accord with Amitābha's original vows.
> "Dharma service and praise" is service to the Buddha, service to the Dharma and service to the *saṃgha*. Because this is now the teaching of the *sūtra*s, it is called "Dharma service".
> "Praise," to commend and extol, using *gāthā*s to praise and laud the Buddha, Dharma and *saṃgha*.

*Fashi zan* is a practice method for one night, the [*Wangsheng*] *lizan* is a practice method for a whole day, and the *Bozhou zan* is a practice method for the ninety days of the summer [rains].[95]

Shōkū's explanation of the *Fashi zan* can be summarized into four points: One, this practice rite is designed with the aim of rebirth in Amitābha's Pure Land. Two, this practice rite's main form is the recitation and praise of the *Amituo jing*. Three, this practice rite is performed over the period of one night. Four, this practice rite is considered to be a Dharma service rite in the broad category of "teaching the *sūtra*s". However, we can see that the *Fashi zan* is not a "teaching of the *sūtras*", but rather a religious service that benefits self and others with the aim of rebirth in the Pure Land. At the very start it states: "In general, for those who wish to set up an altar for themselves or for others",[96] and also within the text itself it repeatedly says, "For the present donor so-and-so, etc".[97] Therefore, both monastics and laity participate in the *Fashi zan*, and at times it may be held specifically for a certain donor as a Dharma service where they seek to be reborn in the Pure Land.

---

95 *Shūgyō yōketsu*, *T* no. 2621, 83: 1.371a07-13:
釋曰：轉經行道者，轉讚《阿彌陀經》，即行出離道也. 願往生淨土者，淨土無二，唯究極樂一土，往生限西方，偏在彌陀本願. 法事讚者，有佛事、法事、僧事，今講經故云法事矣. 讚者，稱揚也，以伽陀讚嘆佛法僧. 法事讚一夜行法，禮讚長日行法，般舟讚一夏九十日行法也.

96 *Zhuanjing xingdao yuan wangsheng jingtu fashi zan*, *T* no. 1979, 47: 1.424c25: 凡欲爲自、欲爲他立道場者.

97 *Zhuanjing xingdao yuan wangsheng jingtu fashi zan*, *T* no. 1979, 47: 1.425c23-24: 爲今施主某甲等.

The outline of the Dharma Practice is just the adornment of the altar of worship. When the service starts there must be an adorned altar. The *Fashi zan* states from the beginning:

> In general, for those who wish to set up an altar for themselves or for others, they must first adorn the hall and room. They should fully put up statues of the World Honoured One, banners and flowers. It does not matter how many or how much. One should bathe and don clean clothes in order to enter the altar to hear the Dharma. If one wishes to have petitioners and those praising they should all be standing, with the great community sitting. One person should first light incense, scatter flowers, and circumambulate one round. Then the petitioners should call out in accordance with the Dharma.[98]

Therefore, one must first adorn the altar and set up statues of the Buddha, such as statues of Amitābha Buddha, statues of Avalokiteśvāra Bodhisattva, or statues of Śākyamuni Buddha, and so forth. Then they should use banners, flowers and other adornments to make offerings to the Buddha statues. The *Fashi zan* explains the procedures for the practice of the Dharma service, so Shandao requires that participants must wash and put on clean clothes before they enter the altar. We will now go in detail of the twelve steps of the ritual ceremony.

First, the rector strikes the bell, sits down, and the great community enters into the altar, each going to their place. As stated previously: "One person should first light incense, scatter flowers, and circumambulate one round", so we can see that the petitioners have some ritual actions, such as burning incense, and scattering flowers. The junior leads, kneeling before the statue of the Buddha, and chanting *gāthā* praises like those above. Also, there is someone to scatter flowers in a circle. In this way the Dharma service formally begins.

Second, is the Invitation to the Dharma protectors: When performing the Dharma service, it is necessary to invite the Dharma protecting deities to protect the altar. The rector strikes the bowl bell, and chants: "We invite the four heavenly kings to enter the altar; We invite the king of lions, lions which are rare to encounter; To leap with his robe of fur, that the hoard of Māra retreats;

98 *Zhuanjing xingdao yuan wangsheng jingtu fashi zan*, *T* no. 1979, 47: 1.424c25-29: 凡欲爲自、欲爲他立道場者, 先須嚴飾堂舍, 安置尊像、幡、花竟. 衆等無問多少, 盡令洗浴著淨衣, 入道場聽法. 若欲召請人及和讚者盡立, 大衆令坐, 使壹人先須燒香、散花周匝壹遍竟, 然後依法作聲召請.

We turn to invite the Dharma masters, to take the city of *nirvāṇa*".[99] When the great community is chanting *gāthās* of praise, the senior monastic pays respect to the Buddha with three prostrations in the centre, and ascends to the high seat.

Third, is the brief invitation to the Three Jewels: After the senior monastic ascends to the high seat, he reads the "Preface", up to "At the end of life, ride the platform and go to that country".[100] This is because in the *Fashi zan* it states, "The community together single-mindedly invites the senior monastic", and "The great community with one mind invites the senior monastic",[101] so the *gāthās* in praise for the invitation petition are led by the rector who begins by chanting "The *Pratyutpanna samādhi* joy", and the great community which joins the praise on left and right joins by chanting "vows to be reborn". This alternating chanting on both sides continues up to the junior monastic, who chants "difficult to imagine", and the great community joins with "joy to be reborn". At this point they petition and invite Amitābha, Avalokiteśvāra, Mahāsthāmaprāpta and the others of the holy community of the western Pure Land.

Fourth, is the broad invitation to the Three Jewels: After the senior monastic has read the "Respectful address", the praise begins. At "The junior monastics enjoin the senior in praise",[102] the "junior monastics" refers to those who chant the praise, and the great community are those who continue and join the praise chanted by the senior monastic. "The senior enjoins the junior in praise" is then the opposite, where the senior monastic joins the praise chanted by the junior monastic. There are a few sections which are begun with "Senior enjoins the junior in praise" or "Junior enjoins the senior in praise", where the author considers that it refers to a whole section when the chanting is by the senior monastic or junior monastic. If at the start of a section it states, "The senior enjoins the junior in praise", it means that the senior monastic chants one sentence, and the junior monastic also chants the same sentence in the same tune. Actually, the senior monastic chants a section and the junior monastic chants a section. Then, the senior monastic and junior monastics chant a

99 *Zhuanjing xingdao yuan wangsheng jingtu fashi zan*, *T* no. 1979, 47: 1.424b28-c2: 奉請四天王，直入道場中；奉請師子王，師子亦難逢；奮迅身毛衣，眾魔退散去；回頭請法師，直取涅槃城.

100 *Zhuanjing xingdao yuan wangsheng jingtu fashi zan*, *T* no. 1979, 47: 1.424c24: 壽盡乘臺齊臨彼國.

101 *Zhuanjing xingdao yuan wangsheng jingtu fashi zan*, *T* no. 1979, 47: 1.425b20: 大衆同心請高座.

102 *Zhuanjing xingdao yuan wangsheng jingtu fashi zan*, *T* no. 1979, 47: 1.426a13: 下座接高讃云.

section together at the same time, with tone rising and falling, so that people will not feel that it is tiring. The broad invitation to the Three Jewels is an invitation petition to Śākyamuni Buddha and the Buddhas of the ten directions, the canon of 84,000 *sūtra*s, the Buddha's *sarīra*, *arhat*s, *pratyekabuddha*s, bodhisattvas, jeweled trees of incense and flowers, and so forth, with the aim that they "now accept the invitation of the donor so-and-so, to enter the altar and bear witness to virtue".[103]

Fifth, is the first walking the path: After the invitation petition, next is walking the path. The method for walking the path is as follows:

> Have one person take flowers and stand in the south-west corner. When the representatives to walk the path go there, they completely give the flowers to those walking the path. Having received the flowers, they may not immediately scatter them, but must each await their own vows to make the offering. The representatives to walk the path go before the Buddha, and then scatter [the flowers] as they will. Having scattered them, they go to where the flower carrier is, receive the flowers as explained previously, and continue to do this seven times. When walking the path is finished, they each stand at their original seats, and await the end of the chanting of the scriptures until they then sit down.[104]

From the monastic who scatters the flowers standing in the south-west corner, they then give the flowers to the walkers of the path. The walkers of the path go before the Buddha and scatter the flowers as they like and make vows with the offerings for a total of seven times.

The senior monastic first chants: "Invitation with incense and flowers in offering is complete. All be respectful. May the community of the altar each take incense and flowers and walk the path according to the Dharma".[105] Next, the senior monastic chants the three sentences of, "We invite the World Honoured One Amitābha to enter the altar",[106] and the junior monastic praises with, "The joy of scattering flowers". Then, the rector and the chanter chant: "The altar is

103 *Zhuanjing xingdao yuan wangsheng jingtu fashi zan*, *T* no. 1979, 47: 1.426a10-11: 受今施主某甲及衆生請. 入此道場證明功德.

104 *Zhuanjing xingdao yuan wangsheng jingtu fashi zan*, *T* no. 1979, 47: 1.427c8-14: 使一人將華在西南角立, 待行道人至, 即盡行華與行道眾等. 即受華竟, 不得即散, 且待各自標心供養. 待行道至佛前, 即隨意散之. 散竟, 即過至行華人所, 更受華亦如前法, 乃至七遍亦如是. 若行道訖, 即各依本坐處立, 待唱梵聲盡即坐.

105 *Zhuanjing xingdao yuan wangsheng jingtu fashi zan*, *T* no. 1979, 47: 1.427c16-17: 奉請一切香華供養已訖, 一切恭敬, 道場眾等各執香華, 如法行道.

106 *Zhuanjing xingdao yuan wangsheng jingtu fashi zan*, *T* no. 1979, 47: 1.427c19: 奉請彌陀世尊入道場.

adorned and most pure … Then realize non-regression and enter the Three Jewels".[107] The senior monastic then comes down, and together with the great community in the sound of the praise, silently follows the proceeding method in walking the path. If the number of people is very great, and when chanting a praise *gāthā* once the great community has not yet finished walking the path, the rector and chanter need to chant it again, and continue up until everyone has walked the path. If the people walking the path already finished, they stand by their own place and wait until the chanting has completely finished, and only then sit. After they all sit down, "The junior joins the chanters, standing, and praises",[108] and the senior monastic and junior monastic again begin the praise.

Sixth is the first repentance: Having praised together, "The senior monastic takes the end of the junior monastics chant, and immediately begins the repentance",[109] with the senior monastic reciting the repentance text. After having read a large section, the junior monastic enjoins the senior monastic in praise, saying: "Having repented, sincerely take refuge in Amitābha Buddha",[110] and the senior monastic again immediately beings to recite the repentance text. In this way, the first practices are considered completed.

Seventh, Recitation of the *Amituo jing*: The senior monastic recites the *Amituo jing* by breaking it into seventeen parts. Each time, he recites a part of the *sūtra*, then "The senior monastic enters the text", and the junior monastic and senior monastic again start the praise; or "The junior enjoins the senior in praise", or "The senior enjoins the junior in praise", or "The senior enjoins the junior in praise, the junior enjoins the senior in praise", or "The junior enjoins the senior in praise, the senior enjoins the junior in praise", for a total of four different formats.

Eighth, Repentance: Having finished reciting the *Amituo jing*, "The senior monastic awaits the junior monastic to finish chanting, then performs a general repentance for the great community",[111] which is a repentance with respect to the ten evil [ways of action]. In the process of "repentance", after each kind of transgression the junior monastic only calls: "Having repented,

107 *Zhuanjing xingdao yuan wangsheng jingtu fashi zan*, *T* no. 1979, 47: 1.427c22-428a6: 道場莊嚴極清淨 …… 即證不退入三賢.

108 *Zhuanjing xingdao yuan wangsheng jingtu fashi zan*, *T* no. 1979, 47: 1.428a7: 下接梵人聲立讚云.

109 *Zhuanjing xingdao yuan wangsheng jingtu fashi zan*, *T* no. 1979, 47: 1.428b19: 高座待下座聲盡即懺云.

110 *Zhuanjing xingdao yuan wangsheng jingtu fashi zan*, *T* no. 1979, 47: 1.429b24-25: 懺悔已, 至心歸命禮阿彌陀佛.

111 *Zhuanjing xingdao yuan wangsheng jingtu fashi zan*, *T* no. 1979, 47: 1.435b23: 高座待下座聲盡, 即爲大眾, 總懺悔云.

sincerely take refuge in Amitābha Buddha",[112] while the majority of the content is the senior monastic reading out the repentance text.

Ninth, Walking the path: After the repentance, there is another occasion of walking the path. The *Fashi zan* states:

> Then, having finished reciting the *sūtra* and chanting praises, the senior monastic tells one person to walk with the incense, and the great community to walk with flowers. Then, the praisers go to stand for walking the path. He then tells them to chant offerings and walk the path according to the Dharma. Having chanted, they scatter flowers as described previously. Then, having performed three circumambulations or seven circumambulations, they should stand before the Buddha and chant the final praise.[113]

The rector comes out and walks with incense, and at the same time they start to walk the path and scatter flowers as previously. On finishing walking the path, the senior and junior monastic chant together the praise *gāthās* of the "*Pratyutpanna samādhi* joy".

Tenth, Praising the Buddha and making vows: After walking the path and chanting praises, the rector strikes the bowl bell and the community kneels down, chanting "Homage to the permanent Three Jewels". Then, the senior monastic reads the "Text praising the Buddha and making vows", praying and making vows for the community and donors, which is equivalent to the praying text in a Dharma assembly. This text says:

> Now, the disciples so-and-so, of pure faith, … Therefore, everyone makes vows together to be reborn [in the Pure Land], by each reciting the [*A*] *mituo jing* tens of thousands of times and chanting the name of Amitābha tens of thousands of times. Also, they have performed such-and-such meritorious deeds, very complete and well rounded. Therefore, on such-and-such a date they have adorned the monastery compound, beautified the altar, and invited monks and nuns to spend several days in cultivating

---

112 *Zhuanjing xingdao yuan wangsheng jingtu fashi zan*, *T* no. 1979, 47: 1.435c15: 懺悔已, 至心歸命阿彌陀佛.

113 *Zhuanjing xingdao yuan wangsheng jingtu fashi zan*, *T* no. 1979, 47: 2.437a19-23: 又誦經唱讚已, 高座即令一人行香, 與大眾行華, 次當讚人等向行道處立, 又令小者唱禮供養及如法行道. 唱已, 其散華法用一如上, 或三匝或七匝竟, 即當佛前立, 次唱後讚.

> the path. Also, they have offered a delicious, fragrant, royal banquet to the Buddhas and monastic disciples, letting them all be delighted.[114]

From the vow text above, we can see that the *Fashi zan* does not necessarily have to take place in a temple or monastery. If there is an invitation from a donor, it may take place in the donor's own home, though the Dharma service will be very solemn and majestic.

Eleventh, Chanting the seven-fold worship: After the senior monastic recites the vow text, it passes on to the junior monastic. The rector chants alone the seven-fold worship text, and the great community follows the chanting of the rector in prostrating to the Buddha seven times.

Twelfth, As one wishes: After the seven prostrations, the great community closes their praise texts, and the rector alone chants "As one wishes", and then "Send *Sūtra*s". The monastic in charge of incense collects the praise texts, and the whole Dharma service is ended.

The *Fashi zan* was a new Pure Land religious service that focused on recitation of the *Amituo jing*. In the Dharma service, apart from recitation of the *sūtra*, there were also ritual elements of invitations, repentance, walking the path and scattering flowers, vows for rebirth, and so forth. In the Dharma service, the senior monastic and rector are the presiders, where the Dharma service is made very solemn and majestic through the senior monastic and great community alternating in their chanting and praise.

The *Amituo jing* is one of the three Pure Land *sūtra*s, and an important authority for Pure Land religious faith. Shandao heavily favoured this *sūtra* and transcribed it "many tens of thousands of times".[115] In 1909, an Ōtani 大谷 [University] field work team discovered some of Shandao's transcribed *Amituo jing* fragments at Turfan, so we can see how many of them he copied out. In the transcribed texts from Dunhuang, there are 183 copies of the *Amituo jing*, among which are manuscripts from the eighth century CE. Therefore, it is evident the *Amituo jing* was extremely popular in the Tang period, so recitation of the *Amituo jing* is to be expected.

---

114 *Zhuanjing xingdao yuan wangsheng jingtu fashi zan*, *T* no. 1979, 47: 2.437c16-26: 然今清信弟子某甲等爾許多人 ...... 故人人同願共結往生之業, 各誦《彌陀經》爾許萬遍, 念彌陀名爾許萬遍, 又造某功德等, 普皆周備. 故於某月日, 莊嚴院宇, 瑩飾道場, 奉請僧尼, 宿宵行道. 又以厨皇百味種種甘香, 奉佛及以僧徒, 同心慶喜.

115 *Xu Gaoseng zhuan*, *T* no. 2060, 50: 27.684a14: 寫《彌陀經》數萬卷.

### 1.5.2 Ritual of the *Wangsheng Lizan* 往生禮讚

The *Wangsheng lizan* is known in full as the *Wangsheng lizan ji* 往生禮讚偈 (Worship and Praise *Gāthās* of Rebirth), but is also called the *Yuan wangsheng liushi lizan ji* 願往生六時禮讚偈 (*Gāthās* of Worship and Praise of Vows for Rebirth in six periods), the *Quan yiqie zhongsheng yuansheng xifang jile shijie Amituofoguo liushi lizan ji* 勸一切衆生願生西方極樂世界阿彌陀佛國六時禮讚偈 (*Gāthās* of Worship and Praise of Exhortation to All Living Beings to Vow for Rebirth in the Western Land of Ultimate Bliss of Amitābha Buddha), and the *Liushi lizan ji* 六時禮讚偈 (*Gāthās* of Worship and Praise in Six Periods).

This text is composed of a Preface, Six-Session Worship and Praise, and an Epilogue. The Preface is in turn divided into three parts: One, discussion on pacifying the mind. This is an explanation of the three mental states of the sincere mind, the profound mind, and the mind of dedication and making vows. Two, discussion on initiating action. This is Shandao's developed discussion of initiating action of the five-fold recitation, based on Vasubandhu's *Wangsheng lun* 往生論 (Rebirth Treatise). Three, discussion on tasks to be done. This is a discussion on four methods of the practice of respect, nothing else, uninterrupted, and long duration. Using the basic system of pacification of mind, initiation of action, and tasks to be done to explain the actual methods of practice of those who cultivate Pure Land techniques is related to the actual theories for guidance. At the same time, the Preface tasks a further step in explaining recitation of the Buddha's name, providing details of the meaning of focused calling of the name, single practice *samādhi*, and recitation of the Buddha *samādhi* as taught in the *Wenshu bore jing*. It explains issues such as calling of name as being easy practice, original vows in recitation of the Buddha, and the pros and cons of focused and unfocused cultivation. The Epilogue, on the other hand, is an exhortation of the benefits involved. It gives examples of the five kinds of assisting conditions mentioned in the *Guannian famen*, namely seeing the Buddha, eliminating transgressions, guarding mindfulness, embracing living beings, and realization of rebirth. It also clearly explains the eighteenth vow. Therefore, the Preface begins by giving a set guides to cultivation in terms of theory, and also discusses some important questions in the matter of practice, whereas the Epilogue explains the benefits of such practice and cultivation.

The most important part of the *Wangsheng lizan* should be the worship and praise in six sessions. That is, the six-session time periods of dusk, evening, midnight, pre-dawn, dawn, and midday, when one does prostrations in worship and praise. The *Wangsheng lizan* is a kind of daily practice rite, which is to be performed at these six times each day. The intention behind Shandao's composition of the *Wangsheng lizan* is: "Collating in one place and dividing into six sessions the rites of worship and praise for rebirth, which have been composed based on the *Greater* [*Amituo*] *jing*, and the works of Nāgārjuna, Vasubandhu, and *śramaṇa*s of this country [China]. It is solely with the desire to continue fixing the mind, assisting the beneficial result of rebirth, and with the expectation to make those who have not yet heard aware [of the teachings] and to benefit future generations in the long term".[116]

In order to be able to teach all living beings to be reborn in the Pure Land, Shandao compiled the practice rites of worship and praise related to rebirth from India and China together, and thus resulted with the *Wangsheng lizan* we have today.

The six-session worship and praise has prostrations and chanting, and at the same time it is threaded through with repentances. In the six sessions of chanting repentance, making vows, praise and so on, each session has its own set number of prostrations. The content of praise and worship with each of the six sessions can be shown in the following table:

| Session | Textual authority | Number of prostrations |
| --- | --- | --- |
| Dusk | Twelve bright names from the *Wuliangshou jing* 無量壽經 (Infinite Life *Sūtra*) | 19 |
| Evening | Essential text from the *Wuliangshou jing* | 24 |
| Midnight | Nāgārjuna bodhisattva's *Yuan wangsheng lizan ji* 願往生禮讚偈 (Worship and Praise *Gāthās* of Rebirth) | 16 |
| Pre-dawn | Vasubandhu bodhisattva's *Yuan wangsheng lizan ji* 願往生禮讚偈 (Worship and Praise *Gāthās* of Rebirth) | 20 |
| Dawn | Yancong's 彥琮 (557–610) *Yuan wangsheng lizan ji* 願往生禮讚偈 (Worship and Praise *Gāthās* of Rebirth) | 21 |
| Midday | Shandao's *Yuan wangsheng lizan ji* 願往生禮讚偈 (Worship and Praise *Gāthās* of Rebirth) | 20 |

The *Wangsheng lizan* displays a perfect amalgam of theory and practicality. The Preface teaches the fundamental principles of cultivation, the six-session worship and praise describes the concrete procedures for actualization, and

116 *Wangsheng lizan ji*, *T* no. 1980, 47: 1.438b18-20:
謹依《大經》及龍樹、天親、此土沙門等所造往生禮贊，集在壹處，分作六時.
唯欲相續繫心，助成往益，亦願曉悟未聞，遠沾遐代耳.

the Epilogue then details the benefits of practice. The *Wangsheng lizan* is thus an excellent guidebook for practice.

The *Wangsheng lizan* is also known as the *Liushi lizan*, as it is the actual practice of prostration worship, chanting praise, and repentance through six sessions of the day and night. While the procedure for the six-session worship and praise is the same, the number of prostrations and content of the *gāthā*s of praise differ. Therefore, its procedures are already described in detail in the *Rimo lizan* 日沒禮讚 (Dusk Worship and Praise), and then the worship and praise for the subsequent remaining five sessions just says, "Repentance as previously described".[117]

### 1.5.3 Ritual of the *Guannian Famen* 觀念法門

The *Guannian famen* 觀念法門 is known in full as the *Guannian Amituofo xianghai sanmei gongde famen* 觀念阿彌陀佛相海三昧功德法門 (Method of Contemplation and Mindfulness of Amitābha Buddha's Ocean-like Marks and *Samādhi* Qualities). It contains the *Yijing ming wuzhong zengshangyuan yi* 依經明五種增上緣義 (Elucidation of Five Kinds of Assisting Conditions Based on the *Sūtras*), in one fascicle, which is unrelated to the content of the *Guannian famen*, and so, based on the opinions of previous scholars, it should be considered as a separate book. The *Guannian famen* indicates four parts in its opening passages, namely, "One, clarification of the practice of the *samādhi* of contemplating the Buddha based on the *Guan Wuliangshou jing* 觀無量壽經 (*Sūtra* of the Meditation on the Buddha of Immeasurable Life; i.e., *Guan jing* 觀經, Contemplation *Sūtra*, *T* 365)", "Two, clarification of the practice of the *samādhi* of mindfulness of the Buddha based on the *Bozhou sanmei jing* 般舟三昧經 (*Pratyutpanna-samādhi-sūtra, T* 418)", "Three, clarification of the practice of the *samādhi* of mindfulness of the Buddha while entering the altar based on the *sūtras*", and "Four, clarification of the practice of repentance and making vows in the altar based on the *sūtras*". However, in the "clarification of the practice of the *samādhi* of mindfulness of the Buddha based on the *Bozhou sanmei jing*" and "clarification of the practice of repentance and making vows in the altar based on the *sūtras*", Shandao only cites textual passages from the *Bozhou sanmei jing* and the *Guanfo sanmei hai jing* 觀佛三昧海經 (*Sūtra* on the Ocean-Like *Samādhi* of the Visualization of the Buddha, *T* 643), and does not add any explanation. Therefore, in reality, the *Guannian famen* only deals with two kinds of practice rite, namely, the practice rite of the *samādhi* of contemplating the Buddha and the practice rite of the *samādhi* of mindfulness of

---

117 *Wangsheng lizan ji, T* no. 1980, 47: 1.441a15: 懺悔同前後.

the Buddha. Apart from this, the text appends at the end an explanation called the "Method of visiting the sick".

The practice rite of the *samādhi* of Visualizing the Buddha can be practiced in any place and at any time, and therefore it is a daily type of practice. The concrete method of cultivation of the practice rite of the *samādhi* of visualizing the Buddha is:

> If practitioners wish to sit, they should first cross their legs and sit, with the left heel placed on the right thigh, in line with the outside; and the right heel placed on the left thigh, in line with the outside. The right hand is placed in the palm of the left hand, with the two thumbs' tips touching. Then, straighten the body and sit erect, with mouth barely closed and eyes lightly shut. Then, using the mind's eye, visualize starting from the top-knot on the crown of the Buddha's head.[118]

The practitioner should sit with their legs crossed, body upright, and begin visualization. According to the first thirteen visualizations of the *Guanfo sanmei hai jing* and *Guan jing*, they visualize the thirty-two marks and eighty secondary signs of the Buddha, the lotus seat, and so forth. Also, Shandao emphasizes that when visualizing each particular mark, it has the virtue of eliminating certain transgressions.

At the same time, at the end of the practice rite of the *samādhi* of visualizing the Buddha, Shandao emphasizes recitation of the *sūtra*s, calling the name, worship and praise, and so on:

> Also, if practitioners wish to be reborn in the Pure Land, they must only uphold morality, recite the Buddha's [name], recite the *Amituo jing*. Fifteen times a day for two years gives 10,000 times; thirty times a day for one year gives 10,000 times. Daily, they should recite the Buddha's [name] 10,000 times. Also, at the appropriate time they should praise the Pure Land and its majesty. Those who are very diligent and can achieve 30,000 times, 60,000 times, or 100,000 times will have a rebirth which is the highest of the highest grade. One should know that they should completely dedicate all of their other merits to rebirth.[119]

---

118 *Guan nian Amituofo xianghai sanmei gongde famen*, *T* no. 1959, 47: 1.22c5-9: 行者若欲坐, 先須結跏趺坐, 左足安右髀, 上與外齊；右足安左髀, 上與外齊；右手安左手掌中, 二大指面相合. 次端身正坐, 合口閉眼, 似開不開, 似合不合, 即以心眼先從佛頂上螺髻觀之.

119 *Guan nian Amituofo xianghai sanmei gongde famen*, *T* no. 1959, 47: 1.23b9-14: 又白行者, 欲生凈土, 唯須持戒、念佛、誦《彌陀經》, 日別十五遍, 二年得一

Because visualizing the Buddha is not easy, Shandao acknowledges that calling of the name and recitation of the *sūtra*s for a certain number of times can also lead to rebirth in the Pure Land and can also reach the same wondrous result by a different means as the *samādhi* of visualizing the Buddha, and from this they can return to their original state of a common person.

The textual source for the practice rite of the *samādhi* of mindfulness of the Buddha is the *Bozhou sanmei jing*. Although, Shandao's *samādhi* of mindfulness of the Buddha is evolved from the *Bozhou sanmei jing*. He instead emphasizes mindfulness of reciting the Buddha's name, which is a fundamental difference from the *Bozhou sanmei jing*.

The *Guannian famen* has a very detailed description of the practice rite of the *samādhi* of mindfulness of the Buddha, as follows:

> When one wishes to enter into the *samādhi* altar, according to Buddhist methods of practice, one must first prepare the altar by setting up a statue of the Buddha, and clean it with fragrances. If there is no Buddha shrine but there is an available clean room, then purify it properly, and select a statue of the Buddha to set up on the west wall. Practitioners, from the first to the eighth of the lunar month, or from the eighth to the fifteenth, or from the fifteenth to the twenty-third, or from the twenty-third to the thirtieth, dividing a month into four sessions, should assess the weight of their own domestic matters, and at one of these sessions enter [the altar] and purely practice the path.[120]

The practice rite of the *samādhi* of mindfulness of the Buddha is not a daily practice. It needs to be performed in a *samādhi* altar or in a purified room, and the altar must be adorned. Also, in terms of time, it is to be performed on a specific set of seven days in a month. Therefore, the cultivation is within these set times and spaces where one focuses their thought and cultivates vigorously.

The concrete practice methods to be cultivated in the altar are extremely simple. It is just concentrating the mind in upholding recitation of the name of the Buddha:

---

萬；日別三十遍，一年一萬. 日別念一萬遍佛，亦須依時禮贊凈土莊嚴事，大須精進或得三萬、六萬、十萬者，皆是上品上生人，自餘功德盡回往生，應知.

120 *Guan nian Amituofo xianghai sanmei gongde famen, T* no. 1959, 47: 1.24a26-b3: 欲入三昧道場時，一依佛教方法，先須料理道場，安置尊像，香湯掃灑. 若無佛堂，有凈房亦得，掃灑如法，取一佛像西壁安置. 行者等從月一日至八日，或從八日至十五日，或從十五日至二十三日，或從二十三日至三十日，月別四時佳，行者等自量家業輕重，於此時中入凈行道.

> Whether it is from one day to seven days, it is necessary to have very clean clothing, including clean socks and shoes. Within those seven days, one must maintain the fasting practice of one meal [a day], soft crackers and coarse rice with seasonal sauces and vegetables, simple and in moderation. In the altar, the mind must be continued day and night, focusing the mind on mindfulness of Amitābha Buddha, with the mind and sound [of recitation] uninterrupted. One may only sit or stand, and one may not sleep for the duration of those seven days. Nor should one prostrate to the Buddha, recite *sūtra*s, or use rosary beads during that time. One should only be conscious of joining palms and reciting the Buddha's [name], thinking of seeing the Buddha with each and every thought. The Buddha says to be mindful and think of Amitābha Buddha's body of pure gold, with a radiating brilliance, dignified without equal, before the mind's eye. When correctly being mindful of the Buddha, if standing, one should stand for 10,000 recitations or 20,000 recitations; if sitting, one should sit for 10,000 or 20,000 recitations. It is not permitted to whisper or communicate with one another inside the altar.[121]

Within the altar, one wears new and clean clothes, which shows the sincerity and respect for the cultivation. At the same time, one must reduce intake of food and drink as much as possible, taking just one meal per day, which should be very bland. A pure mind with minimal desires is conducive to concentrating mental energy in practice. Inside the altar, there is no need to prostrate to the Buddha or recite any *sūtra*s, one just single-mindedly joins palms and upholds the name of the Buddha mindfully. However, when reciting the [name of the] Buddha one should visualize the totality of the characteristics of the Buddha, letting the mind and the sound [of recitation] continue uninterrupted.

The *Fashi zan*, *Wangsheng lizan*, *Guannian famen* and the *Bozhou zan* are Shandao's "practice rite section" writings. Shandao was influenced by the various religious services and their procedures of the time, and composed these rites of worship and praise in order to actualize his own Pure Land religious faith.

---

121 *Guan nian Amituofo xianghai sanmei gongde famen*, *T* no. 1959, 47: 1.24b3-12: 若一日乃至七日, 盡須凈衣, 鞋襪亦須新凈. 七日之中, 皆須一食長齋, 軟餅粗飯, 隨時醬菜, 儉素節量. 於道場中, 晝夜束心相續, 專心念阿彌陀佛, 心與聲相續, 唯坐唯立, 七日之間不得睡眠, 亦不須依時禮佛、誦經, 數珠亦不須捉, 但知合掌念佛, 念念作見佛想. 佛言：想念阿彌陀佛真金色身, 光明徹照, 端正無比, 在心眼前. 正念佛時, 若立即立念一萬、二萬, 若坐即坐念一萬、二萬, 於道場內不得交頭竅[=竊]語.

### 1.6 *Sui and Tang Medicine Buddha Altars and the Repentance Ritual of Worshiping the Medicine Buddha*

Following the surge of faith in Medicine Buddha, Dharma services, which specifically focused on the practice method about the Medicine Buddha, were formed since the Tang period and known as the "Medicine Buddha altar (*Yaoshi daochang* 藥師道場)". In the "Medicine Buddha altar", there are of course specialist rites of practice. The "Medicine Buddha altar" is a crystallization and concretization of "life sustaining practices". In particular, there was Yijing's 義淨 (635–713) translation of the *Yaoshi liuliguang qifo benyuan gongde jing* 藥師琉璃光七佛本願功德經 (*Sūtra* on the Merit of the Former Vows of the Beryl Illumination of Master of Medicine Buddha of the Seven Buddhas, *T* 451), which undoubtedly had a huge influence on the development of the tantricization of Medicine Buddha faith. At the same time, the success of Tang dynasty tantric Buddhism also certainly helped push the inception of the "Medicine Buddha altar". Traditionally attributed to Yixing 一行 (683–727), the *Yaoshi liuliguang rulai xiaozai chu'nan niansong yigui* 藥師琉璃光如來消災除難念誦儀軌 (Ritual Procedure for Recitation to the Master of Healing, the Lapis Lazuli Radiance Tathāgata, for Eliminating Disaster and Escaping Hardships, *T* 922) states:

> One must invite seven monastics, erect an altar, construct a statue of the Buddha, transcribe the Yaoshi jing, walk the path in six sessions, light seven levels of lamps, make five-coloured forty-nine feet long banners, turn the *sūtra* forty-nine times a day, and release forty-nine land and water living creatures. At the appropriate time, diligently make offerings of flowers and fruit, invoke the mantra of the five-coloured thread and make vows. Also, mudra must be made on the thread, then the mantra is recited forty-nine times, making forty-nine knots.[122]

Comparing this with the "life sustenance methods" of the *Yaoshi jing*, it adds the making of knots on the thread, *mantra* and *mudra*, and so on.

The building of the "Medicine Master altar" is probably from the mid-Tang onwards. Zanning reports that by 757 CE, Tang Emperor Suzong (r. 756–762) requested Yuanjiao 元皎 (fl.757–764) to set up a "royal Medicine Buddha altar" at Kaiyuan si 開元寺 in Fengxiang 鳳翔, saying "select thirty-seven monastics

---

122 *Yaoshi liuliguang rulai xiaozai chu'nan niansong yigui*, *T* no. 922, 19:1.22b3-8: 須請七僧, 建置道場, 造本尊像, 寫《藥師經》, 六時行道, 燃七層燈, 造五色幡四十九尺, 日轉經四十九遍, 放水陸生命四十九頭. 時花果子般勤供養, 咒五色線發願. 又以印拄於線上, 更咒四十九遍, 結四十九結.

to walk the path in six sessions, light lamps and chant scripture, praise, recite and uphold the *sūtras*".[123] Also, he invoked the propitious response of forty-nine branches on a plum tree, thus receiving the compliments of Emperor Suzong.[124] We can thus see that Tang period "Medicine Master altars" were divided into two kinds: those of the common citizens and those of the imperial house. The "Medicine Master altars" of the imperial house were supported by resources from the emperor, who would invite eminent monastics to recite *sūtras*, and thus call them "royal Medicine Master altars". "Medicine Master altars" for the common people were used for cultivation by laymen and laywomen gathered together by temples and monasteries, because the setting up of the altar, such as the forty-nine lamps, five-coloured banners, releasing of living creatures, offering of fruits, etcetera, all required large amounts of money, and so they needed to first collect financial resources. The *Mengliang lu* 夢粱錄 (Liang Record of Dreams) by Wu Zimu 吳自牧 (fl. 1270) in the Song period, states:

> In the Taiping Xingguo period (976–984), Chuanfa si 傳法寺 had just set up a Pure-Deeds Society (Jingye hui 淨業會). Every month on the seventeenth, the good laymen would gather, and the good laywomen on the eighteenth, entering the temple to recite the *sūtras*, hold vegetarian meals, and listen to the Dharma. At the end of the year, all of the collected money was used to set up a Medicine Master altar for seven days and nights to end the service. These have now been inoperative for some time.[125]

In the Taiping Xingguo period of the Song dynasty, Chuanfa si in Hangzhou established a "Pure-Deeds Society", which attracted good laymen and laywomen to the temple to recite *sūtras*, listen to the Dharma, and organize vegetarian banquets. At the end of the year, the offering money they received was put toward construction of a "Medicine Buddha altar", that ran for a total of seven days and nights. This was the last Dharma service for the year of the "Pure-Deeds Society".

The construction of "Medicine Buddha altars" was not only in the Jiangnan area, but was also as far afield as Yunnan[126] and the Dunhuang area, for which

123 *Song Gaoseng zhuan, T* no. 2061, 50: 24.864b24-25: 擇三七僧, 六時行道, 然燈歌唄, 讚念持經.

124 *Song Gaoseng zhuan, T* no. 2061, 50: 24.864b23-c2.

125 *Mengliang lu*, 19.168:
太平興國傳法寺向者建淨業會, 每月十七日集善男信人, 十八日集善女信人, 入寺誦經, 設齋聽法, 年終以所收貲金, 建藥師道場七晝夜, 以終其會. 今廢之久矣.

126 *Yuding yuanjian leihan*, 34: 滇南大理府, 有放光谷, 云是藥師道場, 四面放佛光.

we all have records. In the extant texts from Dunhuang, we have copies of the *Yaoshi daochang tanfa* 藥師道場壇法 (Ritual Practice of the Medicine Buddha Altar), the *Yaoshi daochang wen* 藥師道場文 (Text of the Medicine Buddha Altar), and so forth, which provide valuable and sufficient source materials for our understanding of Tang and Song period "Medicine Buddha altars".

In the remaining texts from Dunhuang, the Peking D180 manuscript is divided into two parts: One, *Yinzhao lichan wen* 寅朝禮懺文 (Text of the Third-Watch Worship and Repentance); and two, the *Yaoshi daochang tanfa* 藥師道場壇法 (Ritual Practice of the Medicine Buddha Altar). The *Yaoshi daochang tanfa* is a thorough description of the set up and methods of cultivation for the "Medicine Buddha altar".

> *Yaoshi daochang tanfa*
> The altar is the same as the usual Avalokiteśvāra altar platform. On the platform are left {…} seven lotus flowers, and an incense censor with five sticks [of incense]. The holy monastics are seated on five couches, with five banners. In the centre is placed a statue of Medicine Master [Buddha], a collared shirt, 490 gold [coins], and forty-nine measures of rice grain. In front of the platform statue are placed seven levels of lamp wheels, in which forty-nine night and day lamps of ignorance burn non-stop. The sunflower oil for the lamps are lit at the {…}. A banner of five colours, forty-nine feet long, is used to tie the thread for releasing living creatures. Every day the *Yaoshi jing* is turned seven times, and each session the path is walked forty-nine times, reciting [the name of] Medicine Master Beryl Radiance Buddha. Each person [recites] four breaths, and the others prostrate twelve times in worship to the *gāthās* with the sound. If they can follow the method, there is nothing that they cannot bring about. At twilight and the third watch, they worship the Three Jewels, and for the other four sessions, [they] worship the seven Buddhas.[127]

We can see that the setup of the altar platform in the Dunhuang area "Medicine Buddha altar" is the same as that for an "Avalokiteśvāra altar" (*Guanyin*

---

127 Beijing daxue tushuguan, *Dunhuang wenxian*, 2.194-95:
藥師道場壇法
壇與尋常觀音道場壇壹般，壇上蓮花留（？）七只，香爐五枚；聖僧座五，鋪子、幡子五口. 中心置藥師像, 領座衣一件, 錢四百九十, 米四十九升, 當壇像前置七層燈輪, 燃四十九盞無明晝夜燈, 須不絕. 其燈葵油, 於口點. 用五色幡壹口, 長四十九尺, 結線放生. 逐日轉《藥師經》一七遍, 每時行道四十九匝, 念藥師琉璃光佛, 每人各四口, 餘者和聲禮偈子, 十二拜. 若能依法, 無引不從. 黃昏寅朝禮三寶, 餘四時禮七佛.

*daochang* 觀音道場). On the highest point on the altar platform is placed a statue of Medicine Master Buddha. Before the Buddha statue is placed, seven levels of lamp wheels, upon which are lit forty-nine lamps that must use sunflower oil, which burn day and night without being extinguished. After these, one collared shirt, 490 coins, and forty-nine measures of rice are placed. The second level of the altar platform has five seats for the holy monastics, five couches, and banners. The five-coloured forty-nine feet long banner may be hung in the courtyard of the altar platform. Second, inside the altar platform, the "Medicine Master altar" is held for seven days, where daily the *Yaoshi jing* is chanted seven times, and the path is walked in six sessions. However, we are not certain if the *sūtra* is turned at the same time as the walking of the path or not. The six periods are dawn, midday, and dusk (the three day sessions), and early evening, midnight, and pre-dawn. Here, the "third watch" is dusk, and "twilight" is dusk. Third, is the method of practice for walking the path in six sessions: The path is walked forty-nine times in each session, while reciting the name of Medicine Master Beryl Radiance Thus Come One. Each of the holy monastics recites it four times, and the other people enjoin. They then prostrate in worship to the Three Jewels or the seven Buddhas.

The *Yaoshi daochang tanfa* describes the setup of the "Medicine Buddha altar" platform, but only mentions turning the *sūtra*, walking the path, prostrations, etcetera, for the actual rites to be practiced, and lacks specific content. The "Yaoshi daochang wen" 藥師道場文 (Text of the Medicine Buddha Altar), B.8719V, has more detail in its explanation of the ritual practice of the "Medicine Master altar", and we can supplement the missing material from the end of the text with the Peking D180 manuscript (see Appendix 2.1).

This text is divided into two parts, the first part being the *Yaoshi daochang wen*, and the other part the *Yinzhao lichan wen* 寅朝禮懺文 (Third-Watch Worship and Repentance). However, some of the *Yinzhao lichan wen* is fragmented and missing, and we can emend it with Peking D180 and P.3038. From the manuscript of the text, Li Xiaorong 李小榮 considers that the character 民 (*min*) in line forty-eight is missing its last stroke, which may be due to avoiding the taboo of using the character in the name of the Tang Taizong [Emperor], Li Shimin 李世民. However, the character *shi* 世 in line fifty-five does not avoid the taboo, and thus the date of its transcription is somewhat after that of Tang Emperor Taizong.[128] The *Yaoshi daochang wen* shows two long names for Buddhas, "Namo eastern world Lord of Liberation ... Unobstructed King Thus Come One" 南無東方解脫主世界 ... 無障礙王如來 and "Namo Eyebrow Mark ... King Thus Come One" 南無毫相 ... 相王如來, which are from Sui dynasty

128 Li, *Mijiao wenxian*, 195.

Jinagupta's (She'najueduo 闍那崛多, 523–600/601) translations of the *Fo shuo shi'er foming shenzhou jiaoliang gongde chuzhang miezui jing* 佛說十二佛名神呪校量功德除障滅罪經 (*Sūtra* of the Twelve Buddha Names and An Incantation for Scholastic Merit, Dispelling Harm and Extinguishing Sin, *T* 1348), and the *Wuqian wubai foming shenzhou chuzhang miezui jing* 五千五百佛名神呪除障滅罪經 (*Sūtra* of Five Thousand Five Hundred Buddha Names and Dispelling Harm and Extinguishing Sin, *T* 443) fascicle one.[129] Zhisheng's 智昇 (fl. 730–786) *Ji zhujing lichan yi* 集諸經禮懺儀 (Compilation of Worship and Repentance Rituals Contained in Various *Sūtras*, *T* 1982), first fascicle, also has these two Buddha names.[130] These are the two Buddha names which appear the most in the Dunhuang repentance text the *Qijie li* 七階禮 (Seven Steps Worship). It can thus be seen that *Yaoshi daochang wen*, B.8719V, was influenced by the *Qijie li*.

According to the demands of the *Yaoshi daochang tanfa*, Peking D180, the structure of the content of *Yaoshi daochang wen*, B.8719V, is divided into three parts:

(1) "Yaoshi daochang qiqing wen" 藥師道場啓請文 (Inviting the Medicine Buddha): First of all, based on the twelve vows of the Yaoshi jing and transcription of the praise of merit at the back, in total there are twelve prostrations. From the structure of each prostration, the presider of the Dharma service chants the four lines, "The radiance from his body shines upon suffering creatures; The thirty-two marks realize the Buddha's body. May we swiftly achieve such vows as these; As we wish to save living beings. Respectfully worship Medicine Master Beryl Radiance Buddha!",[131] and the others join at "Respectfully worship Medicine Master Beryl Radiance Buddha". In this way, each prostration is four lines, with the presider leading the chanting, and the other participants then joining at "Respectfully worship Medicine Master Beryl Radiance Buddha", then they all prostrate together. The structure of each gāthā verse is the same, with the booming resonance and rhythm of their voices leading the chanting. The use of the "Inviting the Medicine Buddha" is, according to the Yaoshi daochang tanfa, Peking D180: "Every day the Yaoshi jing is turned seven times, and each session the path is walked forty-nine times reciting [the name of] Medicine Master Beryl Radiance Buddha. Each person [recites] four breaths, and the others prostrate twelve times in worship to the gāthās with

129 *Foshuo shi'er foming shenzhou jiaoliang gongde chuzhang miezui jing*, *T* no. 1348, 21:1.860c27-861a3; *Wuqian wubai foming shenzhou chuzhang miezui jing*, *T* no. 443, 14:1. 318b5-9.

130 *Ji zhujing lichan yi*, *T* no. 1982, 47:1.456c27-457a1, 457a2-4.

131 Huang, *Dunhuang baozang*, 111: 289–91.

the sound".[132] Therefore, it may be used when they have returned to their places to prostrate after reciting the *sūtra* and walking the path.

Next, at the last of the twelve prostrations, from "With a single practice and a single vow, one rectifies the path", to "Therefore may the community sincerely worship Beryl Radiance Buddha", there is the function of dedication of merit from making vows, praise of the merit of Medicine Master Beryl Thus Come One's twelve great vows. The merit of making forty-nine prostrations and walking the path forty-nine times is dedicated to all living beings, vowing that all living beings will realize and enter into the unarisen.

Finally, from "We, from immeasurable *kalpa*s in the past", to "May it lead to the altar of the Medicine Master; The holy [...]", has the function of repentance and invitation. Repentance for the depth of one's own obstructing actions, for which one is only able to walk the path in repentance during the six sessions. By lighting lamps, tying threads, releasing living creatures, hanging banners and so forth, the "life sustenance methods", one invites the Medicine Buddha to come to the altar, since only in this way can one reach final liberation.

*Yaoshi daochang tanfa*, Peking D180, regulates that: "At twilight and the third watch, they worship the Three Jewels, and for the other four sessions worship the seven Buddhas".[133] Therefore, after the *Yaoshi daochang wen*, B.8719V, "Inviting Medicine Buddha", it appends the "Huanghun lichan wen" 黃昏禮懺文 (Text of Twilight Worship and Repentance) and the *Yinzhao lichan wen*, to be used at the twilight and third watch sessions. The other four sessions only require prostrations to the seven Buddhas, that is sufficient.

(2) "Huanghun lichan wen": The "Huanghun lichan wen" is the content from "Namo pure Dharma body, Vairocana Buddha", to "Take refuge and worship with joined palms", namely the twilight session. After the "Medicine Master Altar Invitation Text", it continues with prostrations to the Three Jewels. According to the research of Taiwanese scholar Wang Juan, the "Huanghun lichan wen" is divided into three categories: Category I and II both take worship of the seven Buddhas as the main focus, but due to differences in the five regrets, they are in two different categories. Category III, on the other hand, takes worship of the Buddhas of the ten directions as the focus. Manuscripts of Category I include S.5490, S.4293, S.5620, and P.2991; Category II includes B.8313; and Category III includes P.2692 and B.8332.[134] However, B.8719V and P.3038 also

132 Beijing daxue tushuguan, *Dunhuang wenxian*, 2.195: 逐日轉《藥師經》一七遍, 每時行道四十九匝, 念藥師琉璃光佛, 每人各四口, 餘者和聲禮偈子, 十二拜.

133 Beijing daxue tushuguan, *Dunhuang wenxian*, 2.195: 黃昏寅朝禮三寶, 餘四時禮七佛.

134 Wang, *Lichanwen*, 164.

include the "Huanghun lichan wen", which belongs to the Category III manuscript, with the focus on worship of the Buddhas of the ten directions.

The structure of the "Huanghun lichan wen", v.8719V, is as follows: prostrations to the Buddhas, universal worship, and the practice of the five regrets. At the end it may have "Declare the twilight *gāthā* on impermanence",[135] the three refuges, and so forth. However, many of the worship and repentance texts from Dunhuang only have up to the "practice of the five regrets", and so this is the usual situation.

(3) "Yinzhao lichan wen": In the "Yinzhao lichan wen", B. 8719V, end of the fifty-ninth line, the four characters "*yin chao li chan*" indicate that the text after this point belongs to the *Yinzhao lichan wen*. Furthermore, we can emend any missing characters according to the "Yinzhao lichan wen" in Peking D 180 and P. 3038. In this way, the structure of the content of the "Yinzhao lichan wen" B.8719V is: respectful worship of the Three Jewels, universal worship, five regrets, teachings on the third watch pure *gāthā*s, six recollections, and dedication.

Therefore, the worship and repentance rites of the "Medicine Buddha altar" from the Dunhuang area build upon the foundation of the life extension practices (*xuming fa* 續命法) of the *Yaoshi jing*, further emphasize the setup of the altar platform, and absorb the *Seven Step Worship* of worship and repentance rites, which were popular at the time. From this, formed a rich and special Medicine Master worship and repentance rite. Combining the *Yaoshi daochang tanfa* Peking D180 and "Yaoshi daochang wen" B.8719V, apart from the commonly seen five regrets, there are also prostrations in worship, refuge, offerings, contemplation of the true characteristic, chanting of the Buddha's name, and other such repentance rites. This again reveals the original appearance of Tang and Song period "Medicine Buddha altars".

In terms of its ideas, the *Yaoshi jing* emphasizes peace and happiness in the present life, the removal of calamity, and the prolonging of life. Yet "Yaoshi daochang wen" B.8719V not only shows the spirit of the *Yaoshi jing*, it also shows some features of the then contemporary society. For example, it contains prayers for blessings in "the emperors, that their holy teachings be boundless", "the crown prince and kings, that their blessings be extended 10,000 generations", and "peace at the borderlands, the end to all battle and war". Secondary to this, the *Yaoshi jing* focuses on levels of religious faith, whereas the

135 Cf. The Dunhuang edition collected by Fusetsu Nakamura, which is compiled in the *Taishō* canon. *Lichan wen*, *T* no. 2856, 85: 1.1303c26-29:
白衆等聽説黄昏無常偈：西方日以暮, 塵勞有微塵, 老病死時至, 相看不久居. 念念催年足, 猶如少水魚, 勸諸行道衆, 懃學至無畏.

"Yaoshi daochang wen" has special characteristics of Chinese Mahāyāna Buddhist repentance rites, such as realization of the original empty nature of transgression, and contemplation of the true characteristic of phenomena. It also takes as its core the "unarisen repentance", original empty nature of transgression, and dual focus on both repentance by phenomena and repentance by principle.[136] Therefore, the "Yaoshi daochang wen" displays a sinicization of Medicine Buddha faith, and at the same time shows changes in the form of Medicine Buddha faith as it entered deeply into Chinese culture and society.

### 1.7 *Maitreya Faith and Ritual of Maitreya Worship and Repentance*

During the Zhenguan period (627–649) of the Tang dynasty, Maitreya worship and religious faith reached a highpoint due to Xuanzang's 玄奘 (602–664) propagation.[137] As stated in the *Da Tang gu sanzang Xuanzang fashi xingzhuang* 大唐故三藏玄奘法師行狀 (Account of the conducts of the late "Master of Tripartite Canons", Dharma Master Xuanzang of the Great Tang, *T* 2052):

> From a young age, the Master always vowed to be reborn with Maitreya Buddha and travel to the west. On hearing that the bodhisattva brothers Asaṅga [and Vasubandhu] also vowed to be reborn in the palace of the Tuṣita heaven and serve upon Maitreya, that they attained their wishes, and there was proof thereof, he further increased his efforts. Personally going to Yuhua [Temple], every time he translated, he would perform worship and repentance, always making vows to be reborn in the Tuṣtia heaven and see Maitreya Buddha. Apart from translating the scriptures, whether day or night, this attitude continued unabated without even the shortest period of respite. After he translated the Da bore [jing], he did no further translations, and only cultivated the path with worship and repentance.[138]

Xuanzang's Maitreya faith was mainly based on his own religious beliefs and system of thought. Moreover, during his own travels in the west to seek the

136 About the theories of Chinese Buddhist repentance rites, cf. Sheng, *Chanfa yanjiu*, 395–403.

137 About the Maitreya belief of Xuanzang, cf. Wang, "Mile xinyang", 192–231.

138 *Da Tang gu sanzang Xuanzang fashi xingzhuang*, *T* no. 2052, 50: 1.219a6-12: 法師從少以來, 常願生彌勒佛所, 及遊西方. 又聞無著菩薩兄弟, 亦願生睹史多天宮, 奉事彌勒, 並得如願, 俱有證驗, 益增克勵. 自至玉花, 每因翻譯, 及禮懺之際, 恒發願上生睹史多天, 見彌勒佛. 除翻經以外, 若晝若夜, 心心相續, 無暫休廢. 從翻《大般若》訖後, 即不復翻譯, 唯行道禮懺.

Dharma, there were numerous occasions of efficacious spiritual responses, which further strengthened his faith.

The *Da Tang Da Ci'en si sanzang fashi zhuan* 大唐大慈恩寺三藏法師傳 (Biography of the "Master of the Tripartite Canon", Dharma Master (Xuanzang) of Da Ciensi under the Great Tang, *T* 2053), fascicle ten, provides an even more detailed description of the circumstances of his passing:

> He happily bade farewell to the community of the monastery, the venerable translators, and his disciples, saying: "This poisonous body of Xuanzang is deeply repulsive. As my work has been completed, there is no need for me to live any longer. I wish to share the merits and wisdom I have cultivated with all living beings, that I together with all living beings, may be reborn in the inner circle of Tuṣita heaven to serve upon the Kind Lord. When he descends to the world as a Buddha, we shall also descend with him to perform the deeds of the Buddhas, until we attain unsurpassed bodhi". ...

He then taught a *gāthā* and instructed everyone there to recite it:

> "Namo Maitreya the Thus Come One, the Perfectly Awakened One!
> May all living beings swiftly be in the presence of your kind visage
> Namo the inner community abiding with Maitreya the Thus Come One!
> May after I shed this life I be reborn among them"![139]

Xuanzang's religious faith did not only take ascending to the inner court of Tuṣita heaven as its goal, but also to follow Maitreya in his rebirth and to perform the vast deeds of a Buddha. This is the true positive spirit of entry into the world of a Mahāyāna bodhisattva. Therefore, Xuanzang, "the master, spent a lifetime performing the deeds of Maitreya".[140] Furthermore, according to the records of our sources, Xuanzang's service to Maitreya included translation of *sūtras*, worship in repentance, making vows, building *stūpas*, erecting statues,

139 *Da Tang gu sanzang Xuanzang fashi xingzhuang*, *T* no. 2052, 50: 10.277a11-23:
因從寺眾及翻經大德並門徒等, 乞歡喜辭別云：玄奘此毒身, 深可厭患, 所作事畢, 無宜久住. 願以所修福慧回施有情, 共諸有情同生睹史多天彌勒內眷屬中, 奉事慈尊；佛下生時, 亦願隨下廣作佛事, 乃至無上菩提 ...... 復口說偈教傍人云：
南無彌勒如來應正等覺, 願與含識速奉慈顏；
南無彌勒如來所居內眾, 願捨命已, 必生其中.

140 *Zhujing yaoji*, *T* no. 2123, 54:1.7a3: 法師一生已來常作彌勒業.

providing bathing for the *Saṃgha* community, making charitable donations to the poor, dedicating merit, and so forth.[141]

What draws the attention of most people is that not only did he recite a *gāthā* and instruct everyone to recite it too, there is also a translation by him of the *Zan Mile sili wen* 讚彌勒四禮文 (Praise of Maitreya in Four Worships), which is preserved in the *Fayuan zhulin* 法苑珠林 (Pearl Forest of the Dharma Garden, *T* 2122), fascicle sixteen. The complete version is as follows:

*Zan Mile sili wen*
Translated by Master Xuanzang based on the *sūtras*.

Sincerely take refuge for life to Maitreya the future Buddha!

The Buddhas have all realized the substance of the unconditioned,
True suchness, the principle of reality, is originally without object.
In order to persuade the gods to reveal Tuṣita,
That those gentlemen, like illusions, will manifest in the assembly.
Originally people and horses do not exist, they only exist through delusion,
One who comprehends knows the illusion, that things have never been so.
The original purity of the Buddha's body is also like this,
The foolish, not understanding, claim it is just as the profane.
To know that the Buddha does not come, is to see the true Buddha,
For this, one certainly attains the eternal rejoicing.
I therefore prostrate in worship to Maitreya Buddha,
And wish that the Kind Lord will liberate living beings.

May I, together with all living beings, be reborn in the Tuṣita heaven, and see and serve Maitreya Buddha!

Sincerely take refuge for life to Maitreya the future Buddha!

The Buddha has the inconceivable power of autonomy,
He is able to move the elements of many *kṣetras*.
How much more so manifest the abode of the Tuṣita palace,
Sitting cross legged on the lion's divan.
With his body like the most refined gold, without equal,

141 Wang, "Mile xinyang", 196.

His precious hue, signs and marks, shine and blaze.
The bodhisattvas of psychic power are also immeasurable,
To assist the Buddhas in propagating and rescuing sentient beings.
If living beings merely worship with sincerity,
Transgressive actions from time without beginning will certainly not arise.
I therefore prostrate in worship to Maitreya Buddha,
And wish that the Kind Lord will liberate living beings.

May I, together with all living beings, be reborn in the Tuṣita heaven, and see and serve Maitreya Buddha!

Sincerely take refuge for life to Maitreya the future Buddha!

In the jewelled crown of the Kind Lord are many manifestation Buddhas,
Their numbers passing beyond hundreds and thousands.
The bodhisattva assembly of this world and the other lands,
Fully show their psychic transformations in the precious portal.
Eighty thousand rays of light shine from the Buddha's white eyebrow mark,
He always teaches the causes of the wheel of the Dharma which cannot be turned back.
If living beings are merely able to cultivate meritorious actions,
In the time to stretch out their arm they encounter the Kind Lord.
As many Buddhas as sands of a river manifest due to this,
How much more so my original teacher Śākyamuni.
I therefore prostrate in worship to Maitreya Buddha,
And wish that the Kind Lord will liberate living beings.

May I, together with all living beings, be reborn in the Tuṣita heaven, and see and serve Maitreya Buddha!

Sincerely take refuge for life to Maitreya the future Buddha!

The Buddhas always dwell in a pure *kṣetra*,
Experiencing their retribution, boundless in size.
Incognizable to profane beings with their physical eyes,
They manifest a golden frame, a thousand feet tall.
Living beings that see it never reject it,
Letting them know the results of action manifest in Jambudvīpa.

If one just hears the *sūtra*, and recites the Dharma,
From afar they will definitely go to the Tuṣita palace.
One is forever removed from the three lower destines,
And in the future one will also realize the singular Dharma body.
I therefore prostrate in worship of Maitreya Buddha,
And wish that the Kind Lord will liberate living beings.
May I, together with all living beings, be reborn in the Tuṣita heaven, and see and serve Maitreya Buddha![142]

With the evidence of the above content, we can deduce that Xuanzang translated the text of these *gāthā*s based on the *Fo shuo guan Mile pusa shangsheng doushuaitian jing* 佛說觀彌勒菩薩上生兜率天經 (*Sūtra* of Contemplation of Maitreya's Ascent to Tuṣita Heaven, *T* 452; hereafter, *Shangsheng jing* 上生經). Just as in the content of the first round of worship, it should be as stated in the *sūtra*: "Previously in the *Vinaya* and the *sūtra piṭaka*, the Blessed One stated that Aśita would be next to attain Buddhahood. This Aśita is presently an ordinary, common person, and has yet to cut off the influxes. At the end of his life, where will he be reborn? Although he has presently again renounced lay life, he does not cultivate *dhyāna* meditation and does not abandon the afflictions.

142 *Fayuan zhulin*, *T* no. 2122, 53: 16.403c27-404a29:
讚彌勒四禮文 (玄奘法師依經翻出)
至心歸命當來彌勒佛
諸佛同證無爲體, 真如理實本無緣, 爲誘諸天現兜率, 其猶幻士出眾形.
元無人馬迷將有, 達者知幻未曾然, 佛身本凈皆如是, 愚夫不了謂同凡.
知佛無來見真佛, 於茲必得永長歡, 故我頂禮彌勒佛, 唯願慈尊度有情.
願共諸眾生上生兜率天奉見彌勒佛
至心歸命禮當來彌勒佛
佛有難思自在力, 能以多剎內塵中, 況今現處兜率殿, 師子床上結跏坐.
身如檀金更無比, 相好寶色曜光暉, 神通菩薩皆無量, 助佛揚化救含靈.
眾生但能至心禮, 無始罪業定不生, 故我頂禮彌勒佛, 唯願慈尊度有情.
願共諸眾生上生兜率天奉見彌勒佛
至心歸命當來彌勒佛
慈尊寶冠多化佛, 其量超過數百千, 此土他方菩薩會, 廣現神變寶窗中.
佛身白毫光八萬, 常說不退法輪因, 眾生但能修福業, 屈伸臂頃值慈尊.
河沙諸佛由斯現, 況我本師釋迦文, 故我頂禮彌勒佛, 唯願慈尊度有情.
願共諸眾生上生兜率天奉見彌勒佛
至心歸命禮當來彌勒佛
諸佛常居清凈剎, 受用報體量無窮, 凡夫肉眼未曾識, 爲現千尺壹金軀.
眾生視之無厭足, 令知業果現閻浮, 但能聽經勤誦法, 逍遙定往兜率宮.
三途於茲必永絕, 將來同證一法身, 故我頂禮彌勒佛, 唯願慈尊度有情.
願共諸眾生上生兜率天奉見彌勒佛

The Buddha has predicted that this man will attain Buddhahood, without any doubt".[143]

The *Zan Mile sili wen* combines together prostrations in worship with praises and invocations. Moreover, at the start of each worship is stated, "Sincerely take refuge for life to Maitreya the future Buddha", and at the end is stated, "May I, together with all living beings, be reborn in the Tuṣita heaven, and see and serve Maitreya Buddha", for a total of four acts of worship. The form of the *Zan Mile sili wen* is reminiscent of the form of Shandao's *Wangsheng lizan*, where at the start of each worship is "Namo sincere refuge in the western Amitābha Buddha", and "May I, together with all living beings, be reborn in the land of ease and joy" at the end. Using the Dunhuang manuscript of the "Wangsheng lizan ji" 往生禮讚偈 (*Gāthā*s of Worship and Praise of Rebirth), Hirokawa Gyōbin contemplates that at the time of Shandao's writing of these *gāthā*s, there was no "Namo", but that it was added at the time of Zhisheng. The *gāthā*s in the "Wangsheng lizan ji" contained in Zhisheng's *Ji zhujing lichan yi* also in fact do not have "Namo".[144] Therefore, we can consider that Shandao's "Wangsheng lizan", written in Chang'an, imitated the form of the "Zan Mile sili wen", and thus provides new evidence for the formation of the "Wangsheng lizan ji".

It has always been difficult to understand Maitreya worship and repentance rites during the Tang and Five Dynasties period due to limits on the resources available. However, due to the discovery of the Dunhuang manuscripts, we now have the three preserved *Shangsheng li* 上生禮 (Ascension Worship) manuscripts: S.5433, S.4451, and P.3840.[145] The order of the ritual procedure of the *Ascension Worship* can be basically divided into the following elements: invitations to the Buddhas, extolling the Buddhas, worship of the Kind One, determined repentance, determined making of vows, recollection of the Kind One, Brahmās abiding in the world, dedication, three refuges, Kind One rebirth *gāthā*, all constructions are impermanent *gāthā*, *nirvāṇa* of the Thus Come One *gāthā*, and so forth. Within this are inserted seven *mantra*s. The organization and structure of the *Shangsheng li* and the *Qijie li* are completely identical. There are merely alterations of the repentance text according to the Dharma teaching of Maitreya, such as changing the worship of the Buddhas in seven steps to "worship of Maitreya" and changing "six session *gāthā* on

143 *Foshuo guan Mile pusa shangsheng doushuaitian jing*, *T* no. 452, 14: 1.418c5-9: 世尊往昔於毗尼中及諸經藏說阿逸多次當作佛，此阿逸多具凡夫身未斷諸漏，此人命終當生何處？其人今者雖復出家，不修禪定，不斷煩惱，佛記此人成佛無疑.

144 Hirokawa, "Raisan", 445.

145 Wang, *Lichan wen*, 235-88.

impermanence" to "Kind One rebirth *gāthā*".[146] Therefore, the composition of the rebirth worship was formed according to the contemporary, commonly practiced Buddhist repentance rites. Furthermore, in the *Shangsheng li*, within "worship the Kind One" has the harmony of "May I, together with all living beings, be reborn in Maitreya's land", and the recollection of the *bodhisattva* Kind One is also in four rounds. Therefore, its entire form has a great similarity with the *Zan Mile sili wen*.

The *Shangsheng li* is mainly a method of cultivation practice based on the *Shangsheng jing*, which is constructed out of a set of worship and repentance rites about seeking rebirth in the Tuṣita inner court. However, the sung praises of the *gāthā* text includes the hope of the three Dragon Flower assemblies (*Longhua sanhui* 龍華三會) and transmission of the prediction from Maitreya, which are taught in the *Xiasheng jing* 下生經 (i.e., *Mile xiasheng jing* 彌勒下生經, *Sūtra* on the Descent of Maitreya). Therefore, it is evident the *Shangsheng li* and *Shangsheng jing* and *Xiasheng jing*[147] all have a very close relationship.

After the composition of the *Shangsheng li* in the middle of the eighth century, it was popular in about the ninth and tenth centuries. The *Shangsheng li* was likely a kind of repentance rite used by the public during rebirth services, though it is unknown whether or not they were connected with Song and Qi period Dragon Flower assemblies. According to the teachings of the *Fozu tongji* 佛祖統紀 (Complete Chronicle of the Buddha and Patriarchs, *T* 2035), Bai Juyi 白居易 (772–846) previously encouraged 148 people to form a rebirth assembly and practice mindfulness of the name of the Kind One, vowing to be definitely reborn in Tuṣtia in future lives.[148] Other than this, Bai Juyi also wrote "Hua Mile shangsheng zhenzan bing xu" 畫彌勒上生幀讚並序 (Praise of Paintings of Maitreya's Ascension with a Preface) and the "Hua Mile shangsheng zhenji" 畫彌勒上生幀記 (Records of Paintings of Maitreya's Ascension).[149] The "Hua Mile shangsheng zhenzan bing xu' states:

146 Hirokawa, "Shichikai butsumyōkyō", 95.

147 The *Shangsheng jing* is generally referring to *Foshuo Mile xiasheng jing* (*T* no. 453) translated by Zhu Fahu 竺法護 (Dharmarakṣa, 239–316), *Foshuo Mile laishi jing* (*T* no. 457) by an unknown translator, *Foshuo Mile xiasheng chengfo jing* (*T* no. 454) translated by Jiumoluoshi 鳩摩羅什 (Kumārajīva, 334–413), *Foshuo Mile da chengfo jing* (*T* no. 456) translated by Kumārajīva, and *Foshuo Mile xiasheng chengfo jing* (*T* no. 455) translated by Yijing 義淨 (635–713).

148 *Fozu tongji*, *T* no. 2035, 49: 28.282b23-25: 勸一百四十八人結上生會, 行念慈氏名, 願當來世必生兜率.

149 *Quan Tang wen* 676.3059.

> In the southern continent of Jambudvīpa, in the eastern regions of the nation of the Great Tang, at Changshou si 長壽寺, the great bhikṣus Daosong 道嵩 (d.u), Cunyi 存一 (d.u), Huigong 惠恭 (d.u) and others, sixty people in total, as well as the *upāsaka*s Shiliang 士良 (781–843), Weijian 惟儉 (d.u), etcetera, eighty-one people in total, in the summer of the eighth year of the Taihe period (834), received the eight precepts, cultivated the ten wholesome actions, made Dharma offerings, gave away pure wealth, and painted a set of Maitreya bodhisattva in the Tuṣita palace and inner circle, surrounded by his retinue, adorned with his marks and signs. Toward this, [Dao]song and others bowed and joined their palms, lit incense and made prostrations, and made great vows wishing to be reborn in the inner palace, in life after life, age after age, being blessed to serve and make offerings. ... The disciple of Maitreya, Letian (i.e. Bai Juyi), made these vows and encountered these conditions, and at that time prostrated his head to the feet of the Blessed One, the Kind One, who shall in the future descend to the world. With immeasurable respect he intoned these words of praise: The one hundred and forty states of mind unite in singular sincerity; The one hundred and forty acts of speech all make the same sound. We entrust to the form of the Kind One and call out the Kind One's name; Vowing that we shall in the future, ascend in rebirth together.[150]

Bai Juyi, in the eighth year of the Taihe period (834), made vows at the ascension service to be reborn in the inner court of Tuṣita, and painted a set of images of the ascension of Maitreya. Subsequently, in the fifth year of Kaicheng (840), he once again made vows in witness in front of his own image of the ascension of Maitreya. This tells us that in the ninth century, Changshou si in Luoyang had organized the activity of an ascension religious service. I am afraid that other areas did not lack this situation of forming an ascension service, and the *Shangsheng li* was a form of worship and repentance rite used at the time of ascension services by the common people.

---

150 *Quan Tang wen* 677.3064-65:
南贍部州, 大唐國東都長壽寺大苾芻道嵩、存一、惠恭等六十人, 與優婆塞士良、惟儉等八十一人, 以太和八年（ 834 ）夏受八戒、修十善、設法供、捨淨財, 畫兜率陀天宮彌勒菩薩上生內眾一鋪, 眷屬圍繞, 相好莊嚴. 於是嵩等曲躬合掌, 焚香作禮, 發大誓願, 願生內宮, 劫劫生生親近供養. ...... 有彌勒弟子樂天, 同是願, 遇是緣, 爾時稽首當來下生慈氏世尊足下, 致敬無量, 而說贊曰：百四十心, 合爲一誠；百四十口, 發同一聲. 仰慈氏形, 稱慈氏名, 願我來世, 一時上生.
In *Sibu congkan chubian*, this text is slightly different. For example, it is eighty people instead of "eighty-one", inner and outer circles instead of "inner circle", etc. Cf. *Sibu congkan chubian* 41.340.

## 2 *Neidaochang* 內道場 and *Śarīra* Worship in the Sui and Tang

When Buddhism was transmitted into China, the earliest transmission was at the higher strata of society. Also, as a foreign introduced religion, it received the protection of the highest governing bodies. With the emperor as the governor of the nation, he naturally understood Buddhism's special governing functions in encouraging the good of the populace and putting financial support under royal power. Likewise, the prosperity of Buddhism could not be found apart from the support of feudal emperors and kings, and throughout historical times there were many eminent monastics who proactively sought affiliation with imperial power, interaction between state and religion, and royal donations and offerings. With the emperor as the principle power within a centralized power structure, their religious faith and practices were the ideal point of intersection between nation and Buddhism. The best example that shows this is the *neidaochang* 內道場 (palace chapels) and *sarīra* worship.

### 2.1 *Origins of the* Neidaochang 內道場

The establishment of the *neidaochang* was founded on the personal needs of the emperor and royal household for making prayers and seeking merit. Because the royal family is unable to participate in any Buddhist religious rituals that would be held in other temples or monasteries outside of the forbidden city, they must therefore use the system of the *neidaochang* and hold these events directly within the palace. With respect to the origins of the *neidaochang*, Zanning 贊寧 (919–1001) of the Song dynasty states in the *Da Song sengshi lüe* 大宋僧史略 (Great Song Topical Compendium of Monks, *T* 2126):

> Why did the *neidaochang* originate in the Late Wei, yet receive its name around the Sui dynasty? The Emperor Yang was revolutionary with respect to the past, changing Buddhist monasteries (*sengsi* 僧寺) to *daochang* 道場, and changing *daoguan* 道觀 (Daoist temples) to *fangtan* 方壇 (local platforms). Matters of monastics in the inner palace were known as the *neidaochang*.[151]

The *neidaochang* is the altar inside the palace compound, where a statue is erected in a shrine of the imperial palace, and Buddhist services and cultivation take place. Zanning thinks that the *neidaochang* has its origins in the

151 *Da Song sengshi lüe*, *T* no. 2126, 54: 2.247b8-10:
內道場起於後魏, 而得名在乎隋朝何邪. 煬帝以我爲古, 變革事多, 改僧寺爲道場, 改道觀爲方壇. 若內中僧事, 則謂之內道場也.

Zhishen *daochang* 至神道場 (Altar of the Gods), of the Northern Wei second year of Shiguang 始光 (425), and the Shengri *daochang* 生日道場 (Birthday altar), of the fourth year of Shenjia 神䴥 (431), which was where the emperor held religious services for birthday celebrations. After Zanning cites the "*neidaochang*", and then also the "*shengri daochang*", we can see that these two are not the same thing.

The *Fozu tongji* records that in the sixth year of Tianjian (517), the Liang Wudi ordered Huichao 慧超 (fl. 517–526) to gather the community of monastics to teach and explain the *sūtras* and treatises to the intelligentsia of the Shouguang Hall 壽光殿, and that they would dwell inside the imperial palace, which is "the start of the *neidaochang*".[152] Concerning this, Zanning has the following record, "The Northern dynasties sometimes had nuns inside [the palace] upholding the services. Also, the monks and Dharma were gathered in the Shouguang Shrine, either scholars, or lecturers, or explaining the text of the *sūtras*, or demonstrating the essentials of *Chan*. In general, all that occurred within the forbidden [city] was considered the *neidaochang*."[153] In the first year of Dacheng (579) in the Northern Zhou, Emperor Xuan (r. 578–579) revived Buddhism and instructed seven monastics of lofty virtue and pure practice to organize the walking of the path in the west wing of the Zhengwu Hall 政武殿, which Zanning strongly claimed to be the "start of the *neidaochang*".[154] *Guang Hongming ji*, fascicle ten, has "Zhou Gaozu xun ye chutian fofa you qianseng Ren Daolin shangbiao qingkai fashi" 周高祖巡鄴除殄佛法有前僧任道林上表請開法事 (Emperor Gaozu of Zhou inspected the Capital Ye to Eradicate the Buddhadharma, the former Monastic Leader Daolin Presented a Petition to [Re]open the Dharma), which is this very event.[155]

However, by setting up a *neidaochang* within the palace compound, there was a merging of religion and royal power, which was sourced from the traditions of Chinese religion. In the Han dynasty, the Dao of the Yellow Emperor was popular within the palace, following the entrance of the Buddha Dharma, and many people looked upon Buddhism as of the same type as the Yellow Emperor teachings.[156] For example, the prince of Chu, Liu Ying 劉英 (?–71), liked the Yellow Emperor and also studied Buddhism, making offerings at fasting days and taking precepts. The Han Emperor Huan (r.146–167) made

152 *Fozu tongji*, *T* no. 2035, 49:37. 350a1-3: 此內道場之始.

153 *Da Song sengshi lüe*, *T* no. 2126, 54: 2.247b17-20: 南朝或以尼在內中持課. 又壽光殿中群僧法集, 或充學士, 或號講員, 或註解經文, 或敷揚禪要. 凡存禁中, 並內道場也.

154 *Da Song sengshi lüe*, *T* no. 2126, 54: 2.247b14-17: 此內道場之始也.

155 *Guang Hongming ji*, *T* no. 2103, 52: 10.156c22-24.

156 Yokoi, "Uchidōjō", 196.

offerings to the Yellow Emperor and the Buddha in the palace. Xiang Kai 襄楷 (ca. fl. 166–184) said to the emperor:

> I have heard that there are altars to the Yellow Emperor and Buddha in the palace. This path is clear and in vain, it brings about evil and killing, decreasing desire and removing excess. Your lowly servant will not speak of lusting desires, the punishment for killing is beyond reason, it runs contrary to the path, let alone could it reap some good reward. Some say that Laozi went to the barbarians as Buddha.[157]

When Buddhism was first transmitted into China, the emperor made sacrificial offerings to the Buddha and the Yellow Emperor. This was the original form of the *neidaochang*.

By the time of the Eastern Jin period, Emperor Ai (r. 361–365) favoured the Yellow Emperor and Buddhism and was poisoned by taking alchemical *dan* elixirs. Zhu Daoqian's 竺道潛 (286–374) *Gaoseng zhuan* biography states:

> Emperor Ai (r.361–365) heavily favoured the Buddha Dharma, frequently sending emissaries to earnestly beseech them. Due to the important requests, Qian was temporarily active in the imperial palace, where he taught the Dapin [bore jing] on the imperial banquet, which was praised as excellent by those even as high as the courtiers.[158]

Emperor Ai of Jin invited Zhu Daoqian to the forbidden palace to lecture on and teach the *Bore jing*, but it is hard to determine whether or not Zhu Daoqian lived in the palace. However, Emperor Jianwen (r. 372) constructed a *daoshe* 道舍 (house of the way)[159] inside the palace, and thus we can see that religious sites were erected in the palace, which was a very common phenomenon.

As far as we now know, the earliest construction of a chapel inside the palace was in the sixth year of Taiyuan (381) during the reign of Emperor Xiaowu of the Eastern Jin (r. 372–396). The *Jin shu* 晉書 (Book of Jin) states: "On the first month of spring in the sixth year, the emperor first served the Buddhadharma. Erecting a chapel inside the hall, he brought in *śramaṇa*s to dwell

157 *Hou Han shu* 30.1082:
又聞宮中立黃老、浮屠之祠. 此道清虛, 好生惡殺, 省欲去奢. 今陛下嗜欲不云, 殺罰過理, 既乖其道, 豈獲其祚哉！或言老子入夷狄爲浮屠.

158 *Gaoseng zhuan*, *T* no. 2059, 50: 4.347c27-348a1:
至哀帝好重佛法，頻遣兩使殷勤徵請，潛以詔旨之重，暫遊宮闕，即於禦筵開講《大品》, 上及朝士並稱善焉.

159 *Biqiuni zhuan*, *T* no. 2063, 50: 1.936b14-16.

there".[160] Liang Wudi often lectured on and taught *sūtras* and treatises in the imperial palace and ordered Huichao 慧超 (?–526) to live within the palace.

Therefore, the origins of the *neidaochang* had a very close connection with the Buddhist religious faith of the emperors and are also related to the form of offerings and worship of the Yellow Emperor within the Han dynasty palace. Therefore, the *neidaochang* is a point of union in the relationship between Buddhism and the nation state, which not only shows the personal religious faith of the governor, but also reveals the status of monastics in society and politics.

### 2.2 *Yang Guang's Huiri* Daochang *and Riyan Monastery*

Yang Guang's 楊廣 (569–618; r. 604–618) religious faith during his life took place throughout Yangzhou 揚州, Chang'an 長安 and Luoyang 洛陽, where he constructed the Huiri *daochang* 慧日道場 (Huiri Temple) in Jiangdu 江都 (near Yangzhou), the Riyan si 日嚴寺, and the Huiri *daochang* 慧日道場 in Dongdu 東都 (the eastern capital of Luoyang). These three monasteries that belonged to him were places to gather renowned monastics from afar, and to revere the Buddha and propagate the Dharma.

#### 2.2.1 Jiangdu Huiri *Daochang* and Fayun *Daochang*

Yang Guang was put in charge of Yangzhou in the eleventh month of the tenth year of Kaihuang (590). In order to increase the level of control over the sphere of religious thinking south of the Yangzi river, he erected four *daochang* 道場 (temples), namely the two Buddhist *daochang*, Huiri 慧日 and Fayun 法雲, and the two *daoguan* 道觀 (Daoist temples), Yuqing 玉清 and Jindong 金洞. He broadly gathered together eminent monastics and Daoist masters from south of the Yangzi River in Jiangdu 江都 in order to draw them closer for control and employment. Daoxuan said of this: "At the start of the reign of Jin, he established Huri and Fayun *Daochang* to broadly congregate the Śākyan monastics, and Yuqing and Jindong to draw in the [Daoist] lineage of Li".[161] After building these temples, they were funded by resources from the national treasury, and the most outstanding and talented monks and Daoist masters were specially selected to live in the *daochang*. Jizang's 吉藏 (549–623) *Xu Gaoseng zhuan* biography states: "When Emperor Yang (i.e. Yang Guang) was Prince of Jin, four temples were set up and subsidized from the national coffers, for both the Śākyans [Buddhists] and Li [Daoists], and all were fully supported and

160 *Jin shu* 9.231: 六年春正月, 帝初奉佛法, 立精舍於殿內, 引諸沙門以居之.

161 *Xu Gaoseng zhuan, T* no. 2060, 50: 15.549b1-2: 自爰初晉邸即位, 道場慧日、法雲, 廣陳釋侶；玉清、金洞, 備引李宗.

promoted".[162] After Emperor Yang of the Sui was enthroned, he changed *fosi* 佛寺 (Buddhist Monasteries) to *daochang*, and *daoguan* to *xuantan* 玄壇 (altars of the mysteries), starting from the establishment of these four *daochang*. The *Ji gujin Fodao lunheng* 集古今佛道論衡 (Collection of the Past and Present Treatises of Buddhists and Daoists, *T* 2104) states:

> After Yangdi succeeded as an emperor, the previous political administration became even more prosperous. The former inhabitants of the Jin royal residences gathered together the grizzled heroes. Huiri 慧日 and Fayun 法雲 were named as "temple altars", and Yuqing and Jindong were entitled "altars of the mysteries". Selected and chosen from across the four seas, they were brought back to the Jin capital. Offerings of the four requisites were based on the three actions. Worshipped as jiaseng 家僧 (household monks), they did not belong to any province or state. Until the end of ages, they will be a model to which none will compare.[163]

Yang Guang revered the eminent monastics at Huiri and Fayun as "*jiaseng*", meaning that they were monastics who were supported by him and were not regulated by any particular province or state. As to the exact times of the construction of Huiri and Fayun *daochang*, it has never been clear throughout history. The *Guoqing bailu*, fascicle two, has "Wang chongqian Kuangshan canshu" 王重遣匡山參書 (Prince Sends Emissary again to Mount Kuang [i.e. Mount Lu]), a letter sent by an emissary of Yang Guang to Zhiyi, who was at Mount Lu 廬山 at that time. The letter says:

> I, [your] disciple, crossed the [Yangzi] River. Last month moved to a new residence. Due to my own negligence, I have not yet been able to settle down. You, my master, have sent me a letter encouraging me with dharma, which only embarrassed and frightened me. [I] have started to construct the Huiri Temple at the outer area (waiyuan 外援) of my residence to accommodate Chan Master Zhao 照 and others. Dharma Master Lun 論 from Jiangling 江陵 also has come from afar. At the inner area

162 *Xu Gaoseng zhuan*, *T* no. 2060, 50: 15.514a8-9: 煬帝晉蕃, 置四道場, 國司供給, 釋李兩部, 各盡搜揚.

163 *Ji gujin fodao lunheng*, *T* no. 2104, 52: 2.379b7-10:
大業嗣曆, 彌隆前政. 昔居晉府, 盛集英髦；慧日、法雲, 道場興號; 玉清、金洞, 玄壇著名. 四海搜揚, 總歸晉邸；四事供給, 三業依憑. 禮以家僧, 不屬州省. 迄於終歷, 徵訪莫窮.

> (neiyuan 內援) [of my residence], [I] have set up the Fayun Temple to accommodate Chan Master Jue 覺 from Tanzhou 潭州 and others.[164]

The letter of correspondence is dated the tenth day of the tenth month of the twelfth year of Kaihuang (592.11.19). Yang Guang returned to Yangzhou in the ninth month, moving into a new general office. But, how do we understand *neiyuan* and *waiyuan*? There is one explanation that claims "*waiyuan*" means support for matters external to the general office, in particular the care of monks; and "*neiyuan*" is set up for the internal office and the prince's concubines. Perhaps Fayun *daochang* was a nunnery.[165] From presently extant sources, there are no records about the monastics residing in the Fayun *daochang* except the "Chan Master Jue 覺 from Tanzhou" that we do not know who he was. "Chan Master Zhao" is Xinzhao 信照 (d.u), the disciple under the tutelage of Huisi. "Dharma Master Lun" is Falun 法論 (ca. 536–608), who has a biography in fascicle nine of the *Xu Gaoseng zhuan*.[166] Therefore, the time of the construction of the Huiri and Fayun *daochang* is some time between the eleventh month of the tenth year of Kaihuang (590) and the tenth month of the twelfth year (592).

The eminent monastics attracted to Huiri *daochang* all passed as "skilled and talented in various arts, chosen and selected from ocean to mountain",[167] "a selection of the greatest elites",[168] and "specially selected masters".[169] They were the most famous Monks of their time. Among them, the "Yijie pian" 義解篇 (Explainers of Doctrine Section) includes Zhituo 智脫 (541–607/608), Hongzhe 洪哲 (d.u.), Facheng 法澄 (ca.534–608), Daozhuang 道莊 (ca. 533–608), Falun, Zhiju 智矩 (535–606/607), Jizang, and Huijue 慧覺 (554–606). The "Practitioners of *Dhyāna* Section" has Huiyue 慧越 (ca. 510–605). The "Hufa pian" 護法篇 (Protectors of the Dharma Section) featured Huicheng 慧乘 (555–630/631); the "Gantong pian" 感通篇 (Displayers of Psychic Power Section) incuded Fa'an 法安 (518–615/616); and the "Zake shengde pian" 雜科聲德篇 (Section on Other Miscellaneous Worthies) has Lishen 立身 (ca. 569–617) and Facheng 法稱 (ca. 565–605).[170] According to the types of eminent monas-

164 *Guoqing bailu*, *T* no. 1934, 46: 2.806a3-8:
弟子渡江還, 去月初移新住. 多有造次, 未善安立. 來旨勖以法事, 實用慚悚. 始於所居外援, 建立慧日道場, 安置照禪師以下, 江陵論法師亦已遠至；於內援, 建立法雲道場, 安置潭州覺禪師已下.

165 Yamazaki, *Zuitō bukkyōshi*, 94–95.

166 Ikeda, *Kokusei hyarroku*, 309.

167 *Xu Gaoseng zhuan*, *T* no. 2060, 50: 9.499a2: 盛搜異藝, 海岳搜揚.

168 *Xu Gaoseng zhuan*, *T* no. 2060, 50: 11.509c3: 採拔英靈.

169 *Xu Gaoseng zhuan*, *T* no. 2060, 50: 17.568c25: 搜選英異.

170 Yamazaki, *Zuitō bukkyōshi*, 90–93.

tics at Huiri *daochang*, we do not see any monastics who are translators of scripture or specialists of the *Vinaya* monastic codes. It thus appears that Huiri *daochang* took explanation of doctrinal principles as its mainstay. Apart from this, we see things illustrating Yang Guang's own personal favourites. For example, Fa'an was "short and ugly, with light speech and laughter".[171] After living at Huiri *daochang* "it was inspected by the prince, whom he certainly obeyed."[172] Facheng "mastered the language of the *sūtra*s, and his clear resonance moved the community."[173] Yang Guang "revered, honoured and respected"[174] him, and after he entered into Huiri *daochang*, he "patted his shoulder as a friend, and appreciated his council."[175] In addition, Lishen, Zhiguo 智果 (ca. 553–617) and Zhiqian 智騫 (d.u.) were all accomplished in the areas of chanting, calligraphy, literature and so forth. Zhiguo, the monk from Yongxin si 永欣寺 in Kuaiji 會稽, worked in calligraphy and engraving, being of comparable fame to the calligrapher Zhiyong 智永 (d.u.). His calligraphy was of the tradition of the loose cursive form of Wang Xizhi 王羲之 (303–361), slim and lithe in style, with great accomplishment. Yang Guang heard of his renown and called him to enter into the four temples.[176] Also, most of these eminent monastics originally lived in the areas of Jiangdu, Wujun 吳郡, Jianye 建業, Danyang 丹陽 and Jianghuai 江淮. We can thus see that Yang Guang was primarily instigating control and management of the Buddhist world south of the Yangzi River.

At the same time, Yang Guang also managed the monastics in Jiangdu to organize the Buddhist *sūtra*s. At the time of the conquest of Chen, Yang Guang ordered his armies from afar to collect the Buddhist statues, images and scriptures. After constructing the *neidaochang* in Jiangdu, he set up the *Baotai jingzang* 寶台經藏 (Treasure-Platform Scriptural Canon) at Huiri *daochang*, and had the eminent monastic Huijue and others organize the amassed scriptures. "The wonderful classics of the five times are all included here"[177] in four canons, with "one hundred thousand scrolls".[178] Yang Guang personally wrote the "Baotai jingzang yuanwen" 寶台經藏願文 (Votive Text of Treasure Platform Scriptural Canon).[179] In the Tang dynasty, Falin 法琳 (571–639/640) recorded:

171 *Xu Gaoseng zhuan*, *T* no. 2060, 50: 25.651c28-29: 形質矬陋, 言笑輕舉.
172 *Xu Gaoseng zhuan*, *T* no. 2060, 50: 25.652a2: 王所遊履, 必齎隨從.
173 *Xu Gaoseng zhuan*, *T* no. 2060, 50: 30.7701b25: 通諸經聲, 清響動眾.
174 *Xu Gaoseng zhuan*, *T* no. 2060, 50: 30.701c8: 彌崇敬愛.
175 *Xu Gaoseng zhuan*, *T* no. 2060, 50: 30.701c9: 把臂朋從, 欣其詞令.
176 *Taiping guangji* 207.370.
177 *Xu Gaoseng zhuan*, *T* no. 2060, 50: 12.516b21-22: 五時妙典, 大備於斯.
178 *Guang Hongming ji*, *T* no. 2103, 52: 22.257b28: 將十萬軸.
179 *Guang Hongming ji*, *T* no. 2103, 52: 22.257b17-258a8.

"After the conquest of Chen, the scriptures were emended and bound in Yangzhou. New copies were transcribed, in total 612 volumes, with 29,173 texts, and 903,580 fascicles."[180]

However, there were some eminent monks who refused Yang Guang's authority and were not willing to live at Huiri *daochang*. Jingsong's 靖嵩 (537–614/615) *Xu Gaoseng zhuan* biography tells us:

> Emperor Yang of the Sui previously ruled over Yangyue 楊越, and established four daochang. With the repeated announceemnt of imperial edicts, [Jing]song ultimately declined and refused. Even when he ascended the imperial palace, and there were further imperial summons, he still turned them down. His disciples asked why, and he answered, "the imperial city is restricted, and it is difficult to come and go. Although they are *neidaochang*, it does not compare to the non-material world."[181]

The renowned monk Zhiyan 智琰 (564–634) from Mount Huqiu 虎丘 in Suzhou 蘇州 was invited to Huiri *daochang* by Yang Guang due to "the splendour of his path and height of his fame",[182] but he also "on the pretext of illness returned back to the mountain".[183] Although Zhiyi had already been invited to Jiangdu, he also steadfastly resisted entering Huiri *daochang*.

Emperor Wen of Sui (r. 581–604) worshipped Buddhism, and the emperor's sons each had a group of eminent monks in their orbit: "The Sui imperial prince [Yang] Yong [ 楊 ] 勇 (?–604) drew renowned worthies together in the imperial capital."[184] The Prince Qinxiao 秦孝, Yang Jun 楊俊 (571–600), received the precepts from Huikuang 慧曠 (534–613/614), and at Taiyuan 太原 invited Yancong 彥琮 (557–610/611) to enter and dwell in the royal palace. To Zhenguan 眞觀 (538–611), Zhiyi and other eminent monastics in the south Yangzi area, he also had some degree of courtesy interaction. The Prince of Shu 蜀, Yang Xiu 楊秀 (573–618), built and managed Konghui si 空慧寺, Faju si 法聚寺, and Da Jianchang si 大建昌寺, and also supported Xiaojing si 孝敬寺. At these four locations, he summoned well known monastics, such as Zhishen 智

180 *Bianzheng lun*, *T* no. 2110, 52: 3.509c8-11:
平陳之後, 於揚州裝補故經, 并寫新本, 合六百一十二藏, 二萬九千一百七十三部, 九十萬三千五百八十卷.

181 *Xu Gaoseng zhuan*, *T* no. 2060, 50: 10.502a6-9:
隋煬昔鎭楊越, 立四道場, 教旨載馳, 嵩終謝遣. 及登紫極, 又有敕徵, 固辭乃止. 門人問其故, 答曰：王城有限, 動止嚴難, 雖內道場, 不如物外.

182 *Xu Gaoseng zhuan*, *T* no. 2060, 50: 14.532a8: 道盛名高.

183 *Xu Gaoseng zhuan*, *T* no. 2060, 50: 14.532a10: 以辭疾, 得返舊山.

184 *Xu Gaoseng zhuan*, *T* no. 2060, 50: 28.687b17-18: 隋太子勇, 召集名德, 總會帝城.

詵 (539–618). "In Chang'an, he promoted the *Vinaya* canon. At Yizhou 益州, the Prince of Shu [Yang] Xiu was chief administrator. After the invitation, he returned to Shu and the prince personally came to welcome him to dwell at Fajusi.[185]

Yang Xiu also invited Shanzhou 善胄 (550–620) to approach Chengdu 成都, and requested Daoxian 道仙 (ca. 480–601) to live at Jingzhong si 靜眾寺.[186] Emperor Wen of Sui built Shengguang si 勝光寺 at Chang'an for Yang Xiu, and positioned Tanqian 曇遷 (543–608) to live there. The Prince of Han, Yang Liang 楊諒 (575–605), constructed Chandingsi 禪定寺 in Chang'an, and had respectful social interaction with Zhinian 志念 (535–608/609), Faleng 法楞 (d.u.), Jingduan 靜端 (544–607), and other famous monks there. According to Zhinian's *Xu Gaoseng zhuan* biography, when he was at Taiyuan, "[Zhi]nian and four hundred others from his group paid respect, moved to the west, and followed the tradition of the princely offerings. When [Yang] Liang was in the imperial palace, he further constructed a secondary city where he erected spiritual *stūpa*s and built shrines. Known as the Neicheng si 內城寺, he brought [Zhi] nian to dwell there, that is, Kaiyi si 開義寺."[187] Yang Liang built a monastery inside the imperial city, and so Kaiyi si should also be considered a *neidaochang*.

The sons of the emperor believed in and followed Buddhism, and their requests to important monastics not only came from the traditions of the royal family, but were also tools in balancing state and religion between the imperial sons. Huicheng's 慧乘 (555–630) *Xu Gaoseng zhuan* biography states:

> When Gaozu (i.e. Emperor Wen of Sui) toured to lordly Mount Dai 岱, his carriages drove to [the rivers] Yi 伊 and Luo 洛, where he commended monks from Wu, south of the Yangzi, and venerable monastics from Guandong 關東, to ascend to the shrine and explain the meaning [of scriptures]. Cheng was the first to ascend and respond. ... Gaozu was pleased and praised him as being exceptional among elites.[188]

---

185 *Xu Gaoseng zhuan*, *T* no. 2060, 50: 21.613b13-15: 即於長安敷揚律藏, 益州總管蜀王秀, 奏請還蜀, 王自出迎, 住法聚寺.

186 *Xu Gaoseng zhuan*, *T* no. 2060, 50: 25.651b26-29.

187 *Xu Gaoseng zhuan*, *T* no. 2060, 50: 11.509a13-16:
念與門學四百餘人, 奉禮西並, 將承王供. 諒乃於宮城之內, 更築子城, 安置靈塔, 別造精舍, 名爲內城寺, 引念居之, 開義寺是也.

188 *Xu Gaoseng zhuan*, *T* no. 2060, 50: 24.633c4-8:
暨高祖東巡岱宗, 鑾駕伊洛, 敕遣江南吳僧與關東大德升殿豎義, 乘應旨首登 ...... 高祖目屬稱揚, 群英嘆異.

This happened in the twelfth month of the fourteenth year of Kaihuang (594). At Luoyang, he called together monastics from Wu, south of the Yangzi, as well as eminent monks from Hebei and Shandong, in order to hold a great debate about the meaning of various aspects of the Dharma. At that time, Huicheng was the representative of the monastics from Wu, south of the Yangzi, meaning that he was the delegate of the community at Huiri *daochang*. When the Empress Wenxian 文獻 (544–602) passed away in 602, the princes entered Chang'an to pay their respects. The Prince of Han, Yang Liang, brought Zhinian with him to come to Chang'an with the intention that: "The Dharma Master is the one person with the highest of all spiritual comprehension who is thus permitted to enter the imperial capital along with the king. He shall make argument in debate in the splendid capital, passing on the recitation to renunciants and laity alike."[189] The expectations and standards of the eminent monastics were able to provide greater glory to their own political power. Therefore, Yang Guang's construction of Huiri *daochang* also had the purpose of being a means by which he could contend for power with the princes.

### 2.2.2 Chang'an Riyan Monastery

Riyan si 日嚴寺 in Chang'an was an important intermediary between Huiri *daochang* in Jiangdu and Huiri *daochang* in Dongdu [Luoyang]. It was not entirely of the nature of a *neidaochang*, but it was Yang Guang's "donors' temple" in Chang'an, the same as Shengguang si 勝光寺 and Chanding si 禪定寺. The "donors" were the princes.

Riyan si was built by the Prince of Jin, Yang Guang, and located in the Qinglong Ward 青龍坊 in the south eastern corner of Chang'an city. It was the most renowned and excellent Buddhist monastery in the Sui dynasty. The *Chang'an zhi* 長安志 (Chang'an Gazetteer), fascicle eight, states: "The Qinglong Ward … in the south west corner is situated the abandoned Riyan si. When Emperor Yang of Sui was the Prince of Jin, in the first year of Renshou era (601), he donated the lumbers for his own residence to construct the temple, so that renowned monastics could be brought together to live there. In the sixth year of Zhenguan, it was abandoned."[190] According to this report, Riyan si was constructed in Renshou one (601), and was abandoned in Zhenguan six (632). Zhiju's 智炬 (535–606) *Xu Gaoseng zhuan* biography records that: "In the nineteenth year of Kaihuang, he moved his residing place to Guanrang 關壤

189 *Xu Gaoseng zhuan*, *T* no. 2060, 50: 11.509a29-b1: 今須法師一人神解高第者, 可共寡人入朝, 擬抗論京華, 傳風道俗.

190 *Chang'an zhi* 8.294-95:
青龍坊 …… 西南隅廢日嚴寺. 隋煬帝爲晉王, 仁壽元年, 施營第材木所造, 因廣召名僧以居之. 貞觀六年廢.

and on imperial command dwelt in the capital city at Riyan si. With offerings provided by the state of Jin, his teaching and studies flourished. Furnished in a beautiful abode, he was friends with the wise and virtuous. An outstanding leader of that time, he was acclaimed throughout the four seas."[191] Huiyun's 慧賱 (564–637) *Xu Gaoseng zhuan* biography records that Huiyun went to Riyan si in the last year of Kaihuang.[192] Daoxuan renounced under Huiyun and also originally dwelt at Riyan si. After Riyan si was abandoned, he was relocated to Chongyi si 崇義寺, which was built by the Princess Guiyang 桂陽 for her husband in the Changshou ward 長壽坊. The *Ji Shenzhou sanbao gantong lu* 集神州三寶感通錄 (Collection of Records of Miraculous Responses of the Three Jewels in China, *T* 2106) states that: "Others lived at Riyan si in Quchi 曲池 of the capital city, a monastery constructed by Emperor Yang of Sui. … By the seventh year of Wude (624), Riyan si was abandoned, the monastics and disciples scattered and gone, the buildings and facilities taken by government officers."[193] Daoxuan very clearly notes the time of the abandonment of Riyan si as the seventh year of Wude (624), and not the sixth year of Zhenguan (632), when the Buddhist monasteries which belonged to the imperial house of the Sui dynasty were confiscated as religious wealth by the Tang Dynasty.[194] Furthermore, Yancong 彥琮 (557–610) also previously lived at Riyan si, as his *Xu Gaoseng zhuan* biography states:

> On the twelfth year, he was ordered to enter the capital and be in charge of translation activities, living in Daxingshan [Monastery] 大興善寺 with ongoing and abundant support. … At the time, emperor Yang was the Prince of Jin, and at Quchi 曲池 of the capital city, he built Riyan si. Yancong was formally invited to stay there in perpetuity.[195]

Therefore, the *terminus post quem* for the construction of Riyan si was the twelfth year of Kaihuang (592). Also, in the Sui period, Fei Zhangfang's 費長房 (fl. 572–578) *Lidai sanbao ji* 歷代三寶記 (Record of the Three Jewels throughout Successive Dynasties) gives Yancong's works as the *Damojiduo zhuan* 達摩

191 *Xu Gaoseng zhuan*, *T* no. 2060, 50: 11.509c6-8:
開皇十九年, 更移關壤, 敕住京都之日嚴寺. 供由晉國, 教問隆繁, 置以華房, 朋以明德. 一期俊傑, 並是四海搜揚.

192 *Xu Gaoseng zhuan*, *T* no. 2060, 50: 14.534a2-3.

193 *Ji Shenzhou sanbao gantong lu*, *T* no. 2106, 52: 1.405c27-406a4: 余本住京師曲池日嚴寺, 寺即隋煬所造. …… 至武德七年, 日嚴寺廢, 僧徒散配, 房宇官收.

194 Wang, *Shilun*, 173–74.

195 *Xu Gaoseng zhuan*, *T* no. 2060, 50: 2.437a20-26:
至十二年, 敕召入京, 復掌翻譯, 住大興善, 厚供頻仍. …… 煬帝時爲晉王, 於京師曲池營第林, 造日嚴寺, 降禮延請, 永使住之.

笈多傳 (Biography of Dharmagupta) in four fascicles, the *Tongji lun* 通極論 (Realization of the Utmost Treatise) in one fascicle, the *Bianjiao lun* 辯教論 (Defense of the Teachings Treatise) in one fascicle, the *Tongxue lun* 通學論 (Realization of Training Treatise) in one fascicle, the *Shancai tongzi zhuzhishi lu* 善財童子諸知識錄 (Records of the Spiritual Guides of the Youth Sudhāna) in one fascicle, the "Xinyi jing xu" 新譯經序 (Preface to the New Translation of *Sūtras*) also in one fascicle, and other works, stating: "Six texts totalling nine fascicles, composed by the *śramaṇa* of Riyan si, Yancong."[196] The *Lidai sanbao ji* was written in the seventeenth year of Kaihuang (597), so we can see that the *terminus ante quem* for the construction of Riyan si is also the seventeenth year of Kaihuan (597).[197] The *Sui shu* 隋書 (Book of Sui), fascicle two, records that in the second month of the nineteenth year of Kaihuang (599), "the Prince of Jin [Yang] Guang made an official visit."[198] On the eleventh month of the twentieth year of Kaihuang (600), Yang Guang was the crown prince of the empire. Japanese scholars have taken these dates to also be the dates of the construction of Riyan si.[199] However, the evidence for the period from the twelfth year of Kaihuang (592) to the seventeenth year (597) is more obvious and complete.

Based on our present sources and evidence, there were over fifty people living at Riyan si. In the second year of Renshou (602), the Empress Wenxian passed away, and "Over fifty nobles from Riyan were called to the Chengming Inner Hall 承明內殿 to perform continuous walking of the path."[200] Zhinian's *Xu Gaoseng zhuan* biography records that: "Over forty people were called from the venerables of Riyan, all of whom were lineage leaders throughout the four seas, the most exceptional of the age", "at that time there were the *śramaṇa*s Zhiju, Jizang, Huicheng and others, over thirty people, all revered by the emperor Yang, who lived together at Riyan."[201] Furthermore, when Emperor Wen of Sui requested these venerables to enter the capital, his order permitted them to also bring their disciples along, and in this way, the monks living at Riyan si must have numbered over two hundred. Among them, the majority were monastics who moved north from Jiangnan.

In the presently extant *Xu Gaoseng zhuan*, there are about seventeen people who dwelt at Riyan si. Those who went to Riyan si from Huiri *daochang* in

196 *Lidai sanbao ji*, *T* no. 2034, 49: 12.106b16: 若六部, 合九卷, 日嚴寺沙門釋彥棕撰.

197 Wang, *Shilun*, 173.

198 *Sui shu* 2.44: 晉王廣來朝.

199 Hanazuka, "Nichigonji", 673–74.

200 *Xu Gaoseng zhuan*, *T* no. 2060, 50: 9. 499a14-15: 召日嚴英達五十許人, 承明內殿連時行道.

201 *Xu Gaoseng zhuan*, *T* no. 2060, 50: 11. 510b28-c5: 時有沙門智矩、吉藏、慧乘等三十餘人, 並煬帝所欽, 日嚴同止.

Jiangdu included six people, namely Zhituo, Facheng, Daozhuang, Falun, Jizang and Zhiju. Apart from Yancong, Faxian 法顯 (ca. 520–617) and Huichang 慧常 (ca. 564–614), the three renowned monks from northern China, others came from the area of the Jiang and Huai [rivers] 江淮 near Yangzhou 揚州 and Jinling 金陵, such as Bianyi 辯義 (541–606/607), Fakan 法侃 (551–623), Huiyun, Shanquan 善權 (ca. 561–608), Fayan 法琰 (ca. 546–636/637), Zhikai 智凱 (ca. 555–646/647), Tanxie 曇瑎 (ca. 544–620) and others. Riyan si was built after Huiri *daochang* in Jiangdu and thus mainly had monastics from south of the Yangzi, though there was a small minority of eminent monks from northern China. Therefore, Riyan si maintained the interpretative traditions of Jiangnan Buddhism, and upon the Buddhism of the southern dynasties, it added an important avenue of transmission and dissemination. In Riyan si, there were those of the Chengshi 成實 group such as Zhituo 智脫 (541–607/608), Falun, Huiyun, Tanxie, Shanquan and so on; representatives from the Sanlun Buddhism like Jizang, Facheng, Daozhuang, Zhiju and others; and apart from this, there was Bianyi of the Abhidharma group, Mingshun 明舜 (547–606/607) of the *Prajñāpāramitā* and Sanlun traditions, and Fakan with his *Mahāyāna-saṃgraha* tradition, all of whom were masters standing tall within their respective fields of discipline.

At the same time, some Buddhist cultural relics from the southern Chen were also brought to Chang'an, where they were stored at Riyan si. There were *sarīra* from the Changgan *stūpa* in Jinling, what was believed to be Liang Wudi's hair and finger nails, and an Indian stone picture from Xilin si 西林寺 at Mount Lu.

### 2.2.3 Huiri *Daochang* in Dongdu Luoyang

According to the records of Zanning, *neidaochang* began in the Northern Wei. However, the formulation of their name and regulation began under Emperor Yang of Sui, as recorded in the *Sui shu*, "Jingji zhi" 經籍志 (Gazetteer of Classic Texts): "During the time of Daye 大業 (605–618), the *śramaṇa* Zhiguo 智果 (ca. 553–617) was ordered to compose a *sūtra* catalogue at the Dongdu *neidaochang*, distinguishing into various categories. The *sūtras* taught by the Buddha were divided into three types: one, Mahāyāna; two, Hīnayāna; three, assorted *sūtras*."[202] The "Dongdu *neidaochang*" 東都內道場 is the earliest recorded appearance of the term "*neidaochang*".

202 *Sui shu* 35.1099:
大業時，又令沙門智果，於東都內道場，撰諸經目，分別條貫，以佛所說經爲三部：一曰大乘，二曰小乘，三曰雜經.

On the twenty-first day of the eleventh month in the fourth year of Renshou (604.12.17), Emperor Yang of Sui announced construction in the eastern capital Luoyang. On the seventeenth of the third month of the first year of Daye (604.4.10), he requested Yang Su 楊素 (544–606) and Yuwen Kai 宇文愷 (555–612) to formally start construction at Dongdu. In the four months in between, Emperor Yang of Sui personally visited Luoyang to provide direct supervision and participate in the planning phase. The new capital was entrusted with Emperor Yang of Sui's ideals and ambitions, and thus four *daochang* were built in Luoyang. In the Tang period, Du Bao 杜寶 (d.u.) wrote in the *Daye zaji* 大業雜記 (Annals of Daye): "On entering the Jingyun Gate 景運門, through the main road to the left were the offices of the metropolitan superintendent 內史內省, offices of the secretariat 秘書內省, ..., to the main road on the right were the Hall of the Ladies 命婦朝堂, the two *daochang* Huiri and Fayun, and the two *xuantan* Tongzhen 通真 and Yuqing 玉清."[203] Based on this evidence, the four *neidaochang* in the forbidden palace were placed in parallel positions on the right, and the offices of the director and offices of the secretariat on the left. The *neidaochang* of Dongdu were the extension of the *neidaochang* of Jiangdu, with the Buddhist ones called the Dongdu Inner Huiri and Fayun *daochang*, and the Daoist called the Tongzhen and Yuqing *xuantan*.

Of the four *neidaochang* of Dongdu, there are more extant sources for the Huiri *daochang*. Many of the monastics came directly from the Huiri *daochang* in Jiangdu, and some also came from Riyan si in Chang'an. However, the monastics came from places throughout the entire empire to Huiri *daochang* in Luoyang. As shown in Appendix 2.2, the thirty-four monastics are connected with the *neidaochang* constructed by Yang Guang. In terms of the types of monastics here, there were twenty-three who explained the meaning of the texts, which shows that Emperor Yang of Sui placed importance on the doctrines of Buddhism and enjoyed abstract theoretical discussion. This is related to his personality being influenced by the southern style [of Buddhism]. Emperor Wen of Sui served Buddhism throughout his life, though he favoured building monasteries, *stūpas*, statues and the like as works in the field of merit. This displays the special feature of emphasizing creation of merit in the Buddhism of the northern dynasties. Thus the father and son had differences in their contributions to Buddhism.

Furthermore, there were seven monastics who were skilled in a variety of disciplines. This demonstrates that apart from giving emphasis to those with

203 Yuan, *Yangdi*, 383:
入景運門, 入道左有內史內省、秘書內省 …… 道右命婦朝堂, 慧日、法雲二道場, 通真、玉清二玄壇.

talent in the areas of doctrinal teachings and abstract discussion, Yang Guang's bringing together of monks also sought to include those with other arts and talents. Among those eighteen eminent monks from the Dongdu Huiri *daochang*, there were six who came over from Huiri *daochang* in Jiangdu. Moreover, Zhituo, Facheng, Daozhuang and Falun previously lived at Riyan si. Comparing the Luoyang Huiri *daochang* and that at Jiangdu, approximately half of the worthy monastics at Luoyang were from northern China. Because the Jiangdu Huiri *daochang* was built when Yang Guang was the Prince of Jin, his power at that time was limited to south of the Yangzi. However, the Luoyang Huiri *daochang* was built after Yang Guang ascended to the throne, so his power extended throughout north and south.

From the point of view of Buddhist doctrinal learning, the Jiangdu Huiri *daochang* and Riyan si were mainly from the Chengshi and Sanlun groups. Yet Xuanzang's *Xu Gaoseng zhuan* biography states: "At that time, Huiri in Dongdu was glorious as a seat of the Dharma, connecting through the [*Da bo*]*niepan* [*jing*] and the *She* [*dacheng*] *lun*."[204] Huiri *daochang* in Dongdu took the *Nirvāṇa* and *Mahāyānasaṃgraha* groups as the mainstay of its Buddhist doctrinal learning. This was because Daoji 道基 (ca. 576–637/638), Fahu 法護 (576–643), Daozong 道宗 (563–623/624), and others were well known *Mahāyānasaṃgraha* teachers, and Bianxiang 辯相 (ca. 556–632), Zhihui 智徽 (560–638), Zhikuan 志寬 (566–643/644), Sanhui 三慧 (ca. 566–650) and so forth promoted the *Da boniepan jing*.

Therefore, the transformations in Huiri *daochang* and Riyan si in Jiangdu, and Huiri *daochang* in Luoyang, were not only intimately connected with Yang Guang's political career, but were also closely related to his own personal interests. At the same time, following Yang Guang's own movement from Yangzhou to Chang'an, and then to Luoyang, the construction of these three *neidaochang* undoubtedly furthered interaction and exchange between northern and southern Chinese Buddhism. This in turn directly influenced the birth of the various Buddhist sects and schools of the Sui and Tang periods.

### 2.3 Neidaochang *in the Tang Dynasty*

With the Tang dynasty following after the Zhou and Sui, *neidaochang* continued to be erected inside the palace, and quickly flourished. In Zanning's *Da Song sengshi lüe*, he briefly describes the situation of *neidaochang* during the Tang period. From this we can see that in the imperial palaces of Chang'an and

---

204 *Xu Gaoseng zhuan*, *T* no. 2060, 50: 4.446c21-22: 時東都慧日,盛弘法席,《涅槃》、《攝論》,輪馳相繫.

Luoyang, the Tang emperors continued to set up *neidaochang* with a range of functions.[205]

When Xuanzang returned to China from India in 644, the Emperor Taizong (r. 626–649) told him to dwell at Hongfa yuan 弘法院 and engage in the translation of Buddhist scriptures. The *Da Tang Da Ci'en si sanzang fashi zhuan* states: "The emperor ordered to build another [temple] named Hongfa yuan to the west of the Ziwei Hall 紫微殿 at the northern side [of the imperial palaces]. Xuanzang moved in there as soon as he arrived. During the day, the emperor remained to talk with him, and in the evening he returned to the [Hongfa] yuan to translate the scriptures."[206] Hongfa yuan was located to the west of the Ziwei Hall at the northern side inside the Xuanwu Gate 玄武門. Hongfa yuan was considered a *neidaochang* and functioned as a temporary translation office while Da Cien si was under construction.

In the first year of Xianzhuang (658), Emperor Gaozong (r. 649–683) erected a *neidaochang* known as Helin si 鶴林寺 in the forbidden garden for the nun Baocheng 寶乘 (fl.656). The *Da Tang Da Ci'ensi sanzang fashi zhuan*[207] records that when Gaozong was a child, he received an education with the daughter of Xue Daoheng 薛道衡 (540–609), the Supervisor of Xiangzhou 襄州總管, Lord of Linhe 臨河公 during the Sui dynasty. When he ascended to the throne, he wished to repay the aid of his master, and gave her the title of "Lady of Hedong Prefecture" (河東郡夫人). After the lady renounced into monastic life, Gaozong then specially built Helin si in the forbidden garden, and daily requisites were provided from the state treasury. Also, he had Xuanzang and other eminent monks enter Helin si to transmit the full ordination precepts to the nun Baocheng, and thus the very first "*neilintan*" 內臨壇 (Receiving ordination in the inner palace) appeared.[208] Helin si was located in the imperial garden grounds very near to the south gate of the garden, the Jingyao Gate 景曜門. At the same time, next to Helin si was Deye si 德業寺, a *daochang* where several hundred nuns received the precepts. We can thus see that nunneries certainly existed inside the imperial palace of the Tang dynasty.

### 2.3.1 Wu Zetian's *Neidaochang*

During the time of Wu Zetian 武則天 (r. 690–705), Da Biankong si 大遍空寺 was the *neidaochang* established in Dongdu Luoyang, in the first year of Zhengsheng 證聖 (695). Here, Wu Zetian invited Putiliuzhi 菩提流志 (Bodhiruci,

205 Zhang, "Neidaochang".

206 *Da Tang Da Ci'ensi sanzang fashi zhuan, T* no. 2053, 50: 7.259a29-b2: 敕所司於北闕紫微殿西別營一所, 號弘法院. 既到居之, 晝則帝留談說, 夜乃還院翻經.

207 *Da Tang Da Ci'ensi sanzang fashi zhuan, T* no. 2053, 50: 7.266b22-c11.

208 *Da Song sengshi lüe, T* no. 2126, 54: 3.252a27-29.

572–727), Yijing 義淨 (635–713), and others to translate the *Avataṃsaka-sūtra*.[209] The *Da Song sengshi lüe* records:

> Tang Empress Zetian ordered the venerables Sengfa 僧法 (d.u.), Chuyi 處一 (fl.689–692), Huiyan 慧儼 (fl. 689–690), [Leng]xing [稜] 行 (d.u.), [De]gan [德] 感 (fl. 689–703), Xuanzheng 宣政 (d.u.), and others to perform recitation in the *neidaochang*, with Xue Huaiyi 薛懷義 (662–694) participating at times. In the great palace of Luoyang, Zetian set up a *neidaochang*.[210]

Not only did Wu Zetian translate *sūtra*s in the *neidaochang*, she also had the monks recite texts there. This kind of monastic community in the *neidaochang* was completely for Wu Zetian's personal service. They also participated in the making of the *Dayun jing* 大雲經 (Great Cloud *Sūtra*), which became an important element in the "Wu Zhou Revolution".

Between the years of Guangzhai and Chuigong (684–685), the princess Qianjin 千金 recommended Xue Huaiyi to Wu Zetian. According to Huaiyi's biography in the *Jiu Tang shu* 舊唐書 (Old Book of Tang), "From this, the Luoyang venerables Faming (fl. 689–690), Chuyi, Huiyan, Lengxing, Degan, Ganzhi 感知 (d.u.), Jinggui 靜軌 (d.u.), Xuanzheng and others did recitation in the *neidaochang*".[211] These eight people, Faming and so on, plus Xue Huaiyi, were the most important members of the *neidaochang* monastic community. In the first year of Tianshou (690), the matter of the *Dayun jing* shows the formation of the *neidaochang* monastic community.

At that time, those who were invited into the *neidaochang* by Wu Zetian, apart from Xue Huaiyi, also included some eminent monastics. For example, Wanhui was often requested to enter the *neidaochang*, where he was bestowed with silk brocade robes, and had palace servants assigned to him.[212] In the first year of Jiushi (700), Wu Zetian invited Shenxiu to stay at the capital from Mount Dangyang 當陽山, and "the *neidaochang* lavished him with offerings, and constantly asked him about the Way".[213]

---

209 *Song Gaoseng zhuan*, *T* no. 2061, 50: 2.718c24-28.

210 *Da Song sengshi lüe*, *T* no. 2126, 54: 3.247b20-22: 唐則天令大德僧法、處一、慧儼、行、感、宣政等在內道場念誦, 以薛懷義參雜其間. 則天又於洛京大內, 置內道場.

211 *Jiu Tang shu* 133.4741: 自是與洛陽大德法明、處一、惠儼、稜行、德感、感知、靜軌、宣政等在內道場念誦. *Jiu Tang shu* mistakes "Degan" as "Gande".

212 *Song Gaoseng zhuan*, *T* no. 2061, 50: 18.824a8-10.

213 *Song Gaoseng zhuan*, *T* no. 2061, 50: 8.756a15: 內道場豐其供施, 時時問道.

### 2.3.2 Tang Zhongzong's *Neidaochang*

After Wu Zetian, Tang Emperors Zhongzong (r. 683–684; r. 705–710), Ruizong (r. 684–690; r. 710–712) and Xuanzong (r. 712–756) continued the system of the *neidaochang*.

Emperor Zhongzong used Da Biankong si as a *neidaochang* for the translation of scripture. In the first year of Shenlong (705), when Yijing "at the *neidaochang* of the Eastern Capital Luoyang translated the *Kongquewang jing* 孔雀王經 (Peacock King *Sūtra, T* 988)",[214] it was at Da Biankong si. Another of Zhongzong's *neidaochang* was at the Linguang Cloister 林光院, within the Imperial Palace in the Eastern Capital (Luoyang). In the second year of Shenlong (706, or the first year), the south Indian *śramaṇa* Bodhiruci (Putiliuzhi 菩提流志, 572–727), translated the *Mahāratnakūṭa-sūtra* into Chinese as *Da baoji jing* 大寶積經 (Great Collection of Treasures *Sūtra, T* 310) at the Linguang Cloister, and Fazang 法藏 (643–712) was invited to certify the meaning.[215] In the third year of Shenlong (707), the *Vinaya* Master Daoan 道岸 (654–717) was invited into the palace to transmit the refuges and precepts to concubines, which took place at the Lin'guang Hall.[216] In the fourth year of Shenglong (708), when Bodhiruci lectured on the newly translated *sūtra*s, Tang Emperor Zhongzong prepared a vegetarian offering at the Lin'guang Hall and watched *śramaṇa*s debate on doctrinal principles.[217] Wen'gang 文綱 (636–727), known as the imperial teacher for four dynasties, was invited into the *neidaochang* by Zhongzong to walk the path in the second year of Jinglong (708). He transmitted the precepts to the nuns in the Qianling Palace 乾陵宮, and also completed the summer rains retreat in the palace, where he once taught the *Sifen lü* to the nuns there. In the first year of Xiantian (712), he transmitted the *bodhisattva* precepts to Ruizong in a secondary palace.[218] In the third year of Jinglong (709), Hengjing 恒景 (634–712) requested to go into mountain retreat, and so Zhongzong prepared a vegetarian banquet for him at the *neidaochang* in the Lin'guang Hall, which was attended by [prime minister] Li Qiao 李嶠 (645–714), Daojun 道俊 (ca. fl. 660–709), Xuanzang, and others.[219] We can thus see that, on one hand, the Lin'guang Hall or Lin'guang Palace was a site for translation of scripture, and on the other hand, it was a *neidaochang* for holding vegetarian and precept events, and arranging meetings. Vegetarian banquets in the

214 *Song Gaoseng zhuan, T* no. 2061, 50: 1.710c5-6: 於東洛內道場譯《孔雀王經》.

215 *Tang Tae Ch'ŏnboksa kosaju pŏn'gyŏng taedŏk Pŏpjang hwasang chŏn, T* no. 2054, 50:1.282b6-7.

216 *Song Gaoseng zhuan, T* no. 2061, 50: 14.793b21-24.

217 *Fozu tongji, T* no. 2035, 49: 40.372c21-22.

218 *Song Gaoseng zhuan, T* no. 2061, 50: 14.792a21-b1.

219 *Song Gaoseng zhuan, T* no. 2061, 50: 14.732b21-25.

*neidaochang* were known as "*neizhai*" 內齋 (inner banquets), and originated in offerings of food in the Northern Wei palace shrines. The *Da Song sengshi lüe* states: "On the emperor's birthday, eminent venerable monastics were selected and invited to enter the shrine to be given food and extravagant offerings. On examining the texts, this is found to have originated in the Latter Wei, to prolong the virtue of the lords, in order to bring about fortune and long life".[220] Zanning emphasized that Daizong arranged vegetarian banquets in the *neidaochang*, which were the start of Tang dynasty "inner banquets". However, Zhongzong's vegetarian banquet in the Lin'guang Palace should have itself already been an "inner banquet".

Emperor Ruizong, in the first year of Jingyun (710), moved the translation work from the Dongdu *neidaochang* back to the North Garden in Chang'an. Bodhiruci's *Song Gaoseng zhuan* biography records, "The filial and harmonious passed away, and Ruizong ascended to the highest, he ordered that translation work continue at the Ganlu Pavilion 甘露亭 by the White Lotus Pond in the North Garden".[221] The North Garden is just the West Inner Garden at Chang'an, in which was the North Garden White Lotus Pond with Ganlu Pavilion for the new translation site. This became yet another *neidaochang* for the translation of scripture in Chang'an after Hongfa yuan. In the first year of Kaiyuan (713), Emperor Xuanzong "ordered the establishment of a *neidaochang*, honouring [Śubhakarasiṃha (Shanwuwei 善無畏, 637–735)] as the head of the congregation",[222] and here the function of the Chang'an *neidaochang* was equivalent to the Lin'guang Palace in Dongdu. Xuanzong valued Daoism, and did not have many Buddhist activities, and so the program at the *neidaochang* was rather more subdued and quiet.

### 2.3.3 Tang Daizong's *Neidaochang*

After the "An Shi Rebellion" (An Shi zhi luan 安史之亂), *neidaochang* flourished even more following the frequency of the rebel battles. In particular, during the period of Emperor Daizong (r. 762–779), *neidaochang* reached their historical peak. By the second month of the second year of Zhide (757), Emperor Suzong (r. 756–762) set up a *neidaochang* in Fengxiang 鳳翔, "at that time they provided for the monks in the *neidaochang* to recite the Buddha's names day and night, using several hundred people, with the sounds reaching outside

220 *Da Song sengshi lüe*, *T* no. 2126, 54: 3.248b19-20: 皇帝誕日, 詔選高德僧, 入內殿賜食加厚嚫, 尋文起於後魏之間, 多延上達, 用僥福壽.

221 *Song Gaoseng zhuan*, *T* no. 2061, 50: 3.720b14-15: 屬孝和厭代, 睿宗登極, 敕於北苑白蓮池、甘露亭續其譯事.

222 *Xuanzong chao Fanjingsanzang Shanwuwei zeng Hongluqing xingzhuang*, *T* no. 2055, 50: 1.291b6: 飾內道場, 尊爲教主.

the palaces".[223] After reclaiming Chang'an, in the twelfth month of that same year, "he requested the Buddha's bone [relic] from Famen si 法門寺 in Fengxiang to enter the forbidden palace to establish a *neidaochang*, ordering the *śramaṇa*s to worship and praise it from dawn to dusk".[224]

During the time of Emperor Daizong, Bukong's 不空 (Amoghavajra, 705–774) tantric monastic community was extremely active. At that time, many shrine halls inside the palace compound constructed *neidaochang*. In the first year of Yongtai (765), Amoghavajra re-translated the *Renwang huguo bore boluomiduo jing* 仁王護國般若波羅蜜多經 (*Prajñāpāramitā Sūtra* for Humane Kings who Protect Their Countries, *T* 246, abbreviated as *Renwang jing* 仁王經), to which the *Xu Kaiyuan shijiao lu* 續開元釋教錄 (Extended Record of Śākyamuni's Teachings Compiled during the Kaiyuan period, *T* 2156), fascicle two, states: "It was translated in the Nantao Garden 南桃園, from the new moon of the month to the full moon of the month, at the Consecration Altar in the Chengming Hall 承明殿. His majesty held the old [*Renwang*] *jing* and read it, comparing it with the new text".[225] Moreover, he also lectured on the *Miyan jing duiyu ji* 密嚴經對御記 (Imperial Comparative Records of the Secret Adornment *Sūtra*) in one fascicle. The Nantao Garden was also a *neidaochang*, as referenced in the "*Dasheng Wenshushili pusa zanfo fashen li xu*" 大聖文殊師利菩薩讚佛法身禮序 (Preface to the Rite of the Great Sage Mañjuśrī Bodhisattva's Praising of the Buddhas' Dharma Body): "Order the gathering of the sixteen *śramaṇa*s of doctrinal interpretation such as Liangbi 良賁 (717–777), etcetera, translate the *Renwang huguo bore* [*boluomiduo jing*], *Dacheng miyan* [*jing*] 大乘密嚴經 (Mahāyāna Secret Adornment *Sūtra*, *T* 682), and other texts, at the *neidaochang*".[226] In the same year, at the *neidaochang* of the Chengming Hall, Hanhui yuan 含暉院, Amoghavajra translated and lectured on the *Jin'gangding yuqie lüeshu sanshiqi zun xinyao* 金剛頂瑜伽略述三十七尊心要 (Heart Essentials of the Thirty Seven Figures of the Brief Description of the *Vajraśekhara* Yoga, *T* 871).[227] In the twelfth year of Daizong's Dali (777), Amoghavajra's disciple Huixiao 惠曉 (fl. 757–779) stated in his "Wang Wutaishan xiu gongde cixie sheng'en biao" 往五臺山修功德辭謝聖恩表 (Letter of Gratitude to the Emperor, Farewell before Traveling to Mount Wutai to

223 *Jiu Tang shu* 111.3327: 時供奉僧在內道場晝夜念佛, 動數百人, 聲聞禁外.

224 *Fozu tongji*, *T* no. 2035, 49: 40.376a16-17: 詔迎鳳翔法門寺佛骨入禁中立道場, 命沙門朝夕贊禮.

225 *Da Tang Zhenyuan xu Kaiyuan shijiao lu*, *T* no. 2156, 55: 2.758b4-5: 於南桃園翻譯, 起自月朔, 終乎月望, 於承明殿灌頂道場, 禦執舊經, 對讀新本.

226 *Dasheng Wenshushili pusa zanfo fashen li xu*, *T* no. 1195, 20: 1.936c15-17: 令集上都義學沙門良賁等一十六人, 於內道場, 翻《仁王護國般若》及《大乘蜜嚴》等經畢.

227 *Jin'gangding yuqie lüeshu sanshiqi zun xinyao*, *T* no. 871, 18: 1.291c23-25.

Cultivate Merit): "Following and serving the visage of the Tripiṭaka Master Da Guangzhi 大廣智三藏和尙 (i.e., Amoghavajra) for over thirty years, receiving personal transmission of the five major *mantra*s, I have not left his side. Under the direct presence of the son of heaven, every occasion at the halls of Hanhui 含暉, Yanying 延英, Changsheng 長生 and so forth, merit has been cultivated".[228] Therefore, *neidaochang* in the imperial palace include the Hanhui hall, Yanying hall, Changsheng hall, Nantao Garden, Chengming hall and others. These halls were mainly in the Taiji Palace 太極宮, Xingqing Palace 興慶宮 and Daming Palace 大明宮 of the city of Chang'an, and the Yanying hall, Changhsheng hall, Hanhui hall and Chengming hall were probably in the Daming Palace.[229] The Daming Palace was the palace used for political governance and dwelling for many emperors over the course of years since the time of Gaozong's third year of Longshuo (663). It was for this reason that most *neidaochang* were erected in the Daming Palace.

Amoghavajra had a great many disciples. Before his time in the country of Siṃhala (Śrī Lanka), he already had the disciples Han'guang 含光 (fl. 741–766), Huibian 惠辯 (d.u.), and others. Among these disciples, apart from the two who passed away quite early on, there were only six people who Amoghavajra considered to be capable of receiving the full transmission of the Dharma of the five types of *abhiṣeka*, who were known as the "six wise men" (*liuzhe* 六哲). They were Han'guang from Jin'ge si 金閣寺, Huichao 惠超 (fl. 774) from Silla, Huiguo 惠果 (746–805/806) from Qinglong si 青龍寺, Huilang 惠朗 (fl.774–778) from Chongfu si 崇福寺, and Yuanjiao 元皎 (fl.757), and Juechao 覺超 (fl.764–777) from Baoshou si 保壽寺. The tantric monastic community with Amoghavajra at its head also centred its activities around these "six wise men".

Below are the *neidaochang* activities related to Amoghavajra's monastic community.

1. As previously done, Huixiao cultivated merits at the Hanhui hall, Yanying hall and Changsheng hall. The Nantao Garden was a place for translation of scripture, were Liangbi, Zilin 子隣 (fl. 713–765), Qianzhen 潛真 (718–788/789), and others participated in translation works.
2. In the twelfth year of Dali (777), the letter to the emperor, "Qingci neidaochang chenqing biao" 請辭內道場陳情表 (Letter of Sentiment on Retiring from the *Neidaochang*) begins with: "The *śramaṇa*s Juechao, Huihai 惠海 (748–812/813), and so forth who practice recitation in the

228 *Daizong chao zeng Sikong Dabianzheng Guangzhi sanzang heshang biaozhi ji*, *T* no. 2120, 52: 6.858b28-c2:
承順大廣智三藏和尙顏色三十餘年, 五部真言親被指授, 不離左右. 得對天顏, 每於含暉、延英、長生等殿常修功德.

229 Iwasaki, "Naidōjō", 67.

Changsheng hall *daochang* state";[230] and in the address line for the "He qiyu biao" 賀祈雨表 (Letter of Celebration for the Praying of Rain) it says: "Presented to the emperor by the *śramaṇa*s of the Changsheng hall *daochang*, Juechao, and others".[231] Therefore, there were other monastics at the *neidaochang* of the Changsheng hall apart from Juechao and Huihai.

3. In the thirteenth year of Dali (778), in the letter to the emperor, "Shamen Yuanjiao qing duseng biao" 沙門元皎請度僧表 (Request to Ordain Monastics by the *Śramaṇa* Yuanjiao), the address line states: "Former recitation monastic of the Changsheng hall *daochang* and abbot of Baoshou si, Yuanjiao".[232] From this, we can see that Yuanjiao was also a recitation and chanting monastic for the Changsheng hall.
4. The *Da Tang Qinglongsi sanchao gongfeng dade xingzhuang* 大唐青龍寺三朝供奉大德行狀 (Account of the conduct of Palace Chaplain of Three Reigns [i.e. Huiguo], a Venerable Monk of Qinglongsi of the Great Tang, *T* 2057) records the works and accomplishments of Huiguo. In the fifth year of Dali (770), Huiguo was twenty-five years of age, and had received the special privilege of being requested into Changsheng hall, where he received Daizong's decree. In the thirteenth year of Dali (778), "Declaration of the passing of the *Tripiṭaka* Abbot, anointed Dharma transmitter through the three dynasties at the *neidaochang* of the Changsheng hall".[233] In the sixth year of Zhenyuan (790), on the fourth month, Huiguo was ordered into the Changsheng Hall to practice recitation for the good of the country, for over seventy days.[234] We can see that Huiguo was also a recitation monk in the Changsheng Hall.

Apart from these, Amoghavajra's tantric community also had activities in unnamed *neidaochang* in the palace chapel:

5. In the second year of Zhide (757), there was the imperial order, "Suzong enming sanzang dizi Huixu ru neidaochang niansong zhi" 肅宗恩命三藏弟子惠肝入內道場念誦制 (Decree from Suzong to Gratefully Request Tripiṭaka Disciple Huixu to Enter the *Neidaochang* and Perform Recitation): "The decree stated that the personnel of the Yintai Gate 銀台門

230 *Daizong chao zeng Sikong Dabianzheng Guangzhi sanzang heshang biaozhi ji*, *T* no. 2120, 52: 5.854c2: 長生殿道場念誦沙門覺超、惠海等言.

231 *Daizong chao zeng Sikong Dabianzheng Guangzhi sanzang heshang biaozhi ji*, *T* no. 2120, 52: 5.854c28: 長生殿道場沙門覺超等上表.

232 *Daizong chao zeng Sikong Dabianzheng Guangzhi sanzang heshang biaozhi ji*, *T* no. 2120, 52: 6.856c9-10: 前長生殿道場念誦僧保壽寺主沙門元皎.

233 *Da Tang Qinglongsi sanchao gongfeng dade xingzhuang*, *T* no. 2056, 50: 1.295b11-12: 勅長生殿內道場三朝傳法灌頂歿故三藏和上.

234 *Da Tang Qinglongsi sanchao gongfeng dade xingzhuang*, *T* no. 2056, 50: 1.295c3-5.

asked the four disciples of Tripiṭaka Master Amoghavajra, Huixu 惠肝 (d.u.), Qu'na 瞿那 (d.u.), Huixiao and Huiyue 惠月 (d.u.) to enter into [the palace chapel]".[235]

6. In the seventh year of Dali (772), there was the imperial order, "Xie fuzeng wangshi Huijian wu biao" 謝賻贈亡師惠堅物表 (Letter of Gratitude for Giving the Deceased Master Huijian's Gifts), in which the address line wrote: "Letter presented by Changqing 常清 (d.u.), etc., the disciples of the *neidaochang* recitation monk Huijian 惠堅 (ca.?–772)".[236]
7. In the ninth year of Dali (774), "*daochang śramaṇa* Huichao" presented the "He Yunütan qiyu biao" 賀玉女潭祈雨表 (Letter of Celebration for the Praying of Rain at the Jade Lady Pond).[237]
8. In the twelfth year of Dali (777), "*Neidaochang* of Baoshou si *śramaṇa* Juechao, etcetera", presented the "He po Tubo biao" 賀破吐蕃表 (Letter of Celebration for Defeating Tibet).[238]
9. In the thirteenth year of Dali (778), Huixiao presented the letter, "Enming ling yu Huilang tongxiu gongde xiebiao" 恩命令與惠朗同修功德謝表 (Letter of Gratitude for the Imperial Order of Cultivating Merit with Huilang), which states: "On the tenth day of this month, one receives the grace of the son of heaven, whenever Huilang cultivates merit, he has the special favoured permission to repeatedly enter into the Golden-Gate Precious Hall 金門寶殿 to cultivate".[239]

Amoghavajra's "six wise men" disciples, Juechao, Huichao, Yuanjiao, Huilang, and Huiguo, apart from Han'guang, were the most important and central people in the *neidaochang*. At the same time, Amoghavajra, Juechao, Yuanjiao, Huiguo, Huixiao, Huihao and others, were the eminent monastics who cultivated meritorious practices in the *neidaochang* of the Changsheng hall. Therefore, as Zhao Qian 趙遷 (fl. 770–777) states: "Fourteen monks often entered

235 *Daizong chao zeng Sikong Dabianzheng Guangzhi sanzang heshang biaozhi ji*, *T* no. 2120, 52: 6.858b6-7: 奉敕語有銀臺門家喚不空三藏弟子惠肝、瞿那、惠曉、惠月等四人入內.

236 *Daizong chao zeng Sikong Dabianzheng Guangzhi sanzang heshang biaozhi ji*, *T* no. 2120, 52: 6.856c19-20: 內道場故念誦僧惠堅弟子常清等上表.

237 *Daizong chao zeng Sikong Dabianzheng Guangzhi sanzang heshang biaozhi ji*, *T* no. 2120, 52: 6.855a18-28.

238 *Daizong chao zeng Sikong Dabianzheng Guangzhi sanzang heshang biaozhi ji*, *T* no. 2120, 52: 5.855a5-14.

239 *Daizong chao zeng Sikong Dabianzheng Guangzhi sanzang heshang biaozhi ji*, *T* no. 2120, 52: 6.858c27-29: 今月十日蒙天恩, 令每與惠朗同修功德, 殊私曲照, 再入金門寶殿修持.

into assemblies in the heavenly palace".[240] We can see the very active role of Amoghavajra's tantric monastic community in the *neidaochang*. Amoghavajra advocated tantric Buddhism to protect the country, which further promoted cooperation between imperial and religious power. This in turn furthered the flourishing of *neidaochang* during the time of Daizong.

After Daizong, *neidaochang* continued their activities unabated. However, following the arrival of "Wuzong's (r. 840–846) prohibition of Buddhism", *neidaochang* in Tang dynasty palaces came to a halt.

### 2.4 Śarīra *Worship of Emperor Wen of Sui*

Due to promotion by successive emperors and participation by the public, *Śarīra* worship in the Sui and Tang dynasties became a religious activity for the entire society. Emperor Wen of Sui's (Yang Jian) Buddhist faith and ideals of governance were tightly connected. In the four years of the Renshou period, he mobilized people and material nationwide on three occasions to construct *stūpa*s in all provinces across the empire.

According to the records in Wang Shao's 王劭 (fl. in the turn of the seventh century) *Sheli ganying ji* 舍利感應記 (Records of Miraculous Responses from *Śarīra*), before Emperor Wen of Sui ascended to the throne, a *śramaṇa* previously gifted a packet of *śarīra*. Emperor Wen and Tanqian 曇遷 (543–608) counted together, but it was difficult to determine how many. So, Emperor Wen gave it special attention and tied together the *śarīra*, the premonition of the nun Zhixian 智仙 (ca. sixth century), and the fate of the Sui royal household, and came to the conclusion: "my success is due to Buddhism".[241] This fact is also recorded in Tanqian's *Xu Gaoseng zhuan* biography. On the thirteenth day of the sixth month of the first year of Renshou (601.7.18), the metropolitan superindependent, Prince of Yuzhang announced the imperial decree:

> I have taken refuge in the Three Jewels, and raised up the holy teachings. I wish that together with all the people within the four seas we may aspire to bodhi and all cultivate meritorious actions. May the present, now, support the future times in always performing wholesome deeds, and together ascend to the most sublime result. We shall invite thirty śramaṇas who are conversant and knowledgeable in the characteristics of the Dharma, and are capable of declaring it and guiding others, to each take two attendants and one itinerant official, one hundred and twenty pounds of

240 *Da Tang gu dade zeng Sikong Dabianzheng Guangzhi Bukong sanzang xingzhuang*, *T* no. 2056, 50: 1.294b28: 二七僧人, 常入天宮之會.

241 *Guang Hongming ji*, *T* no. 2103, 52: 17.213b26-c7.

milk incense, and five horses, to each travel on different roads to deliver *śarīra*, travelling to the provinces to erect *stūpa*s. Those without designated attendants who have mountain and water temples, will build *stūpa*s based on their former mountains. Those originally without attendants will, at pure and quiet monasteries in their respective provinces, construct their *stūpa*s, constructing in like manner and travelling to that given province. First to those with three hundred and sixty monastics, then those with two hundred and forty monastics, and then those with one hundred and twenty monastics. If the monastics are less than that, then for the amount of monastics, for the sake of myself, the empress, the imperial princes, the royal children and grandchildren, and so forth, as well as all officials internal and external, and all the population, sentient beings seen and unseen, each for days will walk the path and perform repentance. There is no need to ask the same or other provinces as to the day or monastery to start the practice of walking the path and performing rites. People may make donations, the value of which is restricted to ten strings of coins. It must not exceed ten strings. All money donated will be offered to the construction of the *stūpa*. If there is not enough, it is not permitted to mobilize able bodied men or use stores. All monks and nuns within the area will be universally invited to a vegetarian banquet for the *śarīra*. It is limited to midday on the fifteenth of the tenth month. They will also enter the stone container. Those below the general provincial inspector and those above the county officers will cease military affairs and stop their usual responsibilities for those seven days. They will solely supervise the walking of the path and perform rites, and so forth. Ending those responsibilities and being sincere and respectful will conform to my wishes. Those in charge will execute this.[242]

---

242 *Guang Hongming ji, T* no. 2103, 52: 17.213b5-23:
朕歸依三寶, 重興聖教, 思與四海之內一切人民俱發菩提, 共修福業, 使當今現在爰及來世, 永作善因, 同登妙果. 宜請沙門三十人諳解法相兼堪宣導者, 各將侍者二人, 並散官各一人, 薰陸香一百二十斤, 馬五匹, 分道送舍利, 往前件諸州起塔；其未註寺者, 就有山水寺所起塔依前山；舊無寺者, 於當州內清靜寺處建立其塔, 所司造樣送往當州. 僧多者三百六十人, 其次二百四十人, 其次一百二十人, 若僧少者, 盡見僧, 爲朕、皇後、太子廣、諸王子孫等及內外官、壹切民庶、幽顯生靈, 各七日行道並懺悔. 起行道日打刹, 莫問同州異州, 任人布施, 錢限止十文已下, 不得過十文. 所施之錢以供營塔, 若少不充, 役正丁及用庫物. 率土諸州僧尼, 普爲舍利設齋, 限十月十五日午時, 同下入石函. 總管刺史已下、縣尉已上, 息軍機、停常務七日, 專檢校行道及打刹等事, 務盡誠敬副朕意焉, 主者施行.

Emperor Wen of Sui imitated the story of King Aśoka's distribution of *śarīra* and construction of *stūpas* by ordering thirty eminent monastics and accompanying palace officials to travel to Buddhist monasteries in the thirty provinces to give *śarīra*. If they went to any province that did not have a monastery, they needed to build a local *śarīra stūpa*, which had to be finished by the fifteenth day of the tenth month. On that day, the entire nation would place the *śarīra* into stone containers, and the monks and nuns at each monastery would have an altar for seven days, performing repentance for Emperor Wen, the imperial household and family members, and hold a vegetarian banquet for the *śarīra*. Furthermore, Emperor Wen instructed the commoners to give donations, and ordered the local officials to stop carrying out their official responsibilities for those seven days. This kind of distribution of *śarīra* activity, which was nationwide, even reaching out across provinces to remote areas, helped to create a religious fervour toward Buddhism throughout the whole country. Also, the area over which *śarīra* were bestowed was not limited to China, but "representatives from the three nations of Goryeo [Korea], Baekje and Silla returned, each requesting *śarīra* for their countries so as to make offerings and build *stūpas*. These requests were all granted".[243]

Following the sensational effects of *śarīra* worship, each location sent in its reports as to the spiritual experiences that occurred, which were, according to tradition, extremely protracted and lengthy. Emperor Wen of Sui then again distributed more *śarīra*. The *Guang Hongming ji*, fascicle seventeen, records that on twenty-third day of the first month of the second year of Renshou (602.2.20), Emperor Wen again gifted *śarīra* to fifty-one provinces,[244] and also "ordered all those beneath the general provincial inspector and above the county officers to put aside their usual works for seven days", "just as the previous method, the period of work was up to midday of the eighth day of the fourth month".[245] In the fourth year of Renshou (604), he also divided *śarīra stūpas* among over thirty provinces. Hongzun's 洪遵 (530–608) *Xu Gaoseng*

243 *Guang Hongming ji*, *T* no. 2103, 52: 17.217a17-18: 高麗、百濟、新羅三國使者將還, 各請一舍利於本國起塔供養, 詔並許之.

244 About the numbers of prefectures in which *stūpas* were erected, different texts record differently. In *Guang Hongming ji*, it is recorded that there are fifty-one prefectures, but fifty-two prefecture names are listed. In *Ji Shenzhou sanbao gantong lu*, it is recorded that *śarīra* are distributed to fifty-three prefectures. The one added prefecture is Shenzhou, but the time is mistaken as in the third year of the Renshou reigning period. In *Fayuan zhulin*, it is also recorded as fifty-three prefectures. Cf. *Guang Hongming ji*, *T* no. 2103, 52: 17.217a25-26; *Ji Shenzhou sanbao gantong lu*, *T* no. 2106, 52: 1.412c3-20; *Fayuan zhulin*, *T* no. 2122, 53: 40.604a10-11.

245 *Guang Hongming ji*, *T* no. 2103, 52: 17.217a27-29: 令總管刺史已下、縣尉已上, 廢常務七日 …… 一如前式, 期用四月八日午時.

FIGURE 21 The painted Bodhisattva bust in the 21st Cave on Mount Tianlong 天龍山, dated to the Tang Dynasty (618-907) (The Metropolitan Museum of Art, the United States).

*zhuan* biography states: "In the fourth year of Renshou, he put forth a decree, saying: … I have already divided them near and far, and all have erected religious *stūpa*s. There are no provinces that have not been covered. We now further invite the venerables to respectfully deliver the *śarīra*, each travelling to the provinces, building *stūpa*s as previously. … They were all simultaneously sent to thirty provinces".[246]

Emperor Wen built *śarīra stūpa*s three times. According to the records of the *Jinshi cuibian* 金石萃編 (Collection of Bronze and Stone Inscriptions), fascicle forty, and the *Baqiongshi jinshi buzheng* 八瓊室金石補正 (Supplement to the stone and metal inscriptions from the Chamber of Eight Jewels), fascicle twenty-six, steles of the *śarīra stūpa*s that were extant at the time include those that were built in Tongzhou 同州, Qingzhou 青州, Dengzhou 鄧州, Xinzhou 信州, and Jingzhao 京兆. From this fervour of constructing and erecting *stūpa*s nationwide three times, the welcoming and seeing off of the emissaries, and the reports of the spiritual experiences, we can see the massive accomplishments of the deep sentiment of Buddhist worship and Buddhist activities.

## 2.5 Śarīra *Worship of the Emperors in the Tang Dynasty*

Under the imperial decrees of Emperor Wen of Sui, *śarīra* worship in the Sui dynasty spread throughout all corners of the country. Tang dynasty *śarīra* worship was focused in the imperial household, in particular, with Famen si 法門寺 as the center of worship. In the *stūpa* of Famen si was enshrined the *śarīra* of a joint bone from Śākyamuni's middle finger. Textual sources from the Tang and subsequent dynasties had different names for this, such as "Buddha's bone", "Buddha's finger joint", "true body", "gold bone", and so forth. The shape of the Buddha's finger *śarīra* is recorded in the *Ji Shenzhou sanbao gantong lu*, fascicle one: "That *śarīra* was shaped like the first bone of a little finger, one and a fifth inches in length, with a square hole inside, and likewise outside, flat below and round above, bright and clean inside and outside. The smaller finger bone fit well into a slot, which was a good holder for it, to show to the congregation. It would show when the light fell upon it, which could not always be prepared".[247] In 1987, the "Da Tang Xiantong qisong qiyang zhenshen zhiwen" 大唐咸通啓送岐陽真身志文 (Stele Inscription of Sending the True Body to

---

246 *Xu Gaoseng zhuan*, *T* no. 2060, 50: 21.611c11-21:
仁壽四年, 下詔曰 …… 朕已分布遠近, 皆起靈塔, 其間諸州, 猶有未遍. 今更請大德, 奉送舍利, 各往諸州, 依前造塔. …… 三十餘州, 一時同送.

247 *Ji Shenzhou sanbao gantong lu*, *T* no. 2106, 52: 1.407b2-6:
其舍利, 形狀如小指初骨, 長寸二分, 內孔正方, 外楞亦爾, 下平上圓, 內外光淨. 余內小指於孔中恰受, 便得勝戴, 以示大眾. 至於光相變現, 不可常準.

the South Face of Mount Qi in the Xiantong Years of the Great Tang) was discovered in the Tang dynasty underground vault in Famen si, which records:

> On the nineteenth day of the eighth month of the twelfth year of Xiantong (871.9.7), the *śarīra* were received at the north west corner of the old tunnel. The old records states: It is one and a fifth inches in length, narrow above and flat below, not equal across its length, flat on its three sides, with one face higher, and a mark in the middle. Its colour is like that of jade, slightly green. Fine and delicate, with gloss. The marrow hole is large and square, open from top to bottom. There are marks on two edges, but the marks are not deep. Tracing all classical records, it has efficacious powers, which are a true model that past generations have previously heard of. Its marvellous characteristics harmonize the right and brilliant.[248]

In 1987, archeologists again discovered four true body finger bone *śarīra* in the Tang dynasty underground vault beneath the *stūpa*. On inspection, the Buddha's finger bone is 40.3mm long, 17.55 to 20.11mm wide, with the body diameter of 13.75 to 16.5mm, and a weight of 16.2g. This completely conforms with the records in Daoxuan's *Ji Shenzhou sanbao gantong lu* and the "Da Tang Xiantong qisong qiyang zhenshen zhiwen".

The Buddha bone *śarīra* at Famen si came from two or three monks from Taibai, and was a *śarīra* gifted by King Aśoka to the entire country. In the thirteenth year of Dali in the Tang dynasty, the "Da Tang shengchao Wuyouwang si dasheng zhenshen baota beiming" 大唐聖朝無憂王寺大聖真身寶塔碑銘 (Inscription of the Treasure *Stūpa* for the Great Sage's True Body in Wuyouwang si in the Holy Dynasty of Great Tang) records:

> There were the two or three monks from Taibai who focused his mind, steadfastly maintained it, and achieved purity of {…}. His origins were distant, but looked to and {…}. He seldom approached, yet {…} and believed in it. He travelled all around one area. Of broad visage {…} town {…} colour {…} righteous light throughout the night, ever more courageous until the morning, those who did not leave stayed long. Offering his own life, pulverized into dust, vigorous, sincere, in strong faith,

248 Li, *Famensi zhi*, 248–49:
以咸通十二年八月十九日得舍利於舊隧道之西北角. 按舊記云：長一寸二分, 上齊下折, 高下不等, 三面俱平, 一面稍高, 中有隱跡. 色白如玉少青, 細密而澤, 髓穴方大, 上下俱通, 二角有文, 文並不徹. 徵諸古典, 驗以靈姿, 貞規既叶於前聞, 妙相克諧於端彩.

> this result was as clear as the palm of his hand. Verifying the inscription he declared: It was built by King Aśoka, and so it shall be named.[249]

The Buddha's finger *śarīra* at Famen si was believed to be one of those *śarīra* allegedly sent by Aśoka.

According to historical records, in the second year of Emperor Gong (555) of the Western Wei (Xi Wei Gongdi 西魏恭帝 [r. 554–556]), the former grand governor of Qizhou 岐州, Tuoba Yu 拓跋育 (d.u.), renovated Ayuwang si 阿育王寺. This was thus the first occasion when underground vaults were used to house offerings of the Buddha's bone relics. In the fourth year of Renshou (604), the western metropolitan superintendent and commander of Fufeng, Li Min 李敏 (d.u), petitioned the emperor for opening the underground vault and rebuilding the "Chengshi daochang" 成實道場. In order to attack the rebel army of the Xue clan of Longxi, Li Yuan 李淵 (566–635; i.e. Tang Gaozu 唐高祖 [r. 618–626]) went to the area of Fufeng to observe. The monk Puxian 普賢 (d.u.) sent a request to the emperor to renovate the monastery, and Li Yuan renamed it "Famen si". In the second year of Wude in the Tang dynasty, Li Shimin (598–649, r. 626–649) pacified the rebel army of the Xue clan. Li Shimin then went to Famen si and invited eighty renowned monastics to preside over an ordination ceremony. In the fifth year of Zhenguan (631), the provincial inspector of Qizhou, Zhang Deliang 張德亮 (d.u.), reported to the emperor that Famen si collapsed and was in ruin and requested further repair work. In the *Ji Shenzhou sanbao gantong lu*, Daoxuan records:

> In the fifth year of Zhenguan, the provincial inspector of Qizhou, Zhang Liang, out of his longstanding belief, came to pay worship at the monastery. He only saw the ancient foundations without a roof, and reported the wish of building a shrine to cover the foundation of the *stūpa*, to which permission was given in reply. Due to this work on the *stūpa*, its majesty became apparent. It was said since olden days that: After the closing of the *stūpa*, thirty years had passed, once it is shown to people they become wholesome. When [Zhang] Liang heard this, in the middle of the year Zhenguan, he wanted to request to have it opened, to take out the *śarīra* to show people, but was afraid that it would cause a great crowd and so did not dare to open the *stūpa*. The imperial reply permitted it,

249 *Jinshi cuibian* 101.1:
厥有太白二三沙門, 攝心住持, 得 [ ] 清淨. 其始遠也, 望而 [ ] 之. 其少近也, [ ] 而信之. 周流一方, 磅礴 [ ] 裹 [ ] [ ] [ ] 色 [ ] [ ] 瑞光通宵, 更雄達曙, 不散者久之矣. 咸請奉以身命, 碎於微塵, 精誠克孚, 指掌斯獲. 驗其銘曰：育王所建. 因以名焉.

> and so they opened it, and excavating to the depth of over a fathom, they found two ancient steles, which were erected in the Zhou and Wei periods. The text was unreadable, so there is no record of that. It was bright and radiant like the *śarīra*. The *śarīra* were thus immediately excavated, and shown to both the monastics and laity. Countless thousands of people all saw it at the same time.[250]

From this, the regulation was determined where the Famen si underground vault was opened once every thirty years and began the historical occurrence of a total of eight emperors in the Tang dynasty receiving and making offerings to the *śarīra*.

In the fourth year of Xianqing (659), Gaozong invited Zhicong 智琮 (d.u.) and others to come to Famen si to receive the *śarīra*, and also mentioned that they must see "auspicious signs" before they were able to open the *stūpa* and welcome them. On the third month of the fifth year of Xianqing (660), they received the Buddha's bone relic as it entered into the eastern capital Luoyang to the *neidaochang* to make offerings. The "Da Tang shengchao Wuyouwangsi dasheng zhenshen baota beaming" states: "(From Zhenguan) to the fifth year of Xianqing, thirty frosts have passed. The eight-fold [Dharma protectors] earnestly receive it, and again {...} open it up. That is, on the eighth day of the second month of that year, {... ... ...} received and guarded the *śarīra*. The two sages personally made nine-layered treasured containers".[251] It was only in the second year of Longshuo (662), that Emperor Gaozong finally returned the *śarīra* back to Famen si.

In the seventh month of the first year of Wu Zetian's Jiushi period (700), there was a western foreign monk who requested of the empress to open up the underground vault to view the Buddha's finger bone *śarīra*, which due to Di Renjie's 狄仁傑 (630–700) forceful remonstrations, had been temporarily discontinued. In the fourth year of Chang'an (704), Wu Zetian sent the Vice Director of the Phoenix Hall, Cui Xuanwei 崔玄暐 (639–706), the *śramaṇa*s, Fazang 法藏 (643–712) and Wen'gang 文綱 (636–727), and others, to go to Famen si to

---

250 *Ji Shenzhou sanbao gantong lu*, *T* no. 2106, 52: 1.406c5-14:
貞觀五年,岐州刺史張亮素有信向,來寺禮拜,但見古基曾無上覆.奏敕望云宮殿以蓋塔基, 下詔許之. 因構塔上尊嚴相顯. 古老傳云：此塔一閉經三十年, 一示人,令生善.亮聞之,以貞觀年中請開剖出舍利以示人,恐因聚眾,不敢開塔.有敕並許,遂依開發,深一丈余獲二古碑,並周魏之所樹也.文不足觀,故不載錄.光相照燭,同諸舍利.既出舍利,通現道俗,無數千人,一時同觀.

251 *Jinshi cuibian* 101.1:
(貞觀) 至顯慶五年蓋三十霜矣,八部瞻仰,再 [ ] 開發,即以其年二月八日 [ ] [ ] [ ] [ ] [ ] [ ] [ ] [ ] 奉迎護舍利. ...... 二聖親造九重寶函.

receive the Buddha's bone relic. The *Tang Tae Ch'ŏnboksa kosaju pŏn'gyŏng taedŏk Pŏpchang hwasang chŏn* 唐大薦福寺故寺主翻經大德法藏和尚傳 (Biography of the Preceptor Fazang, the Late Venerable Translator and Abbot of Great Jianfusi of the Tang, *T* 2054), states:

> At the very end of the fourth year of Chang'an, at the *neidaochang*, because the pronouncement had spread around that the Qizhou *śarīra* were the spiritual legacy of king Aśoka, namely the Fufeng *stūpa* as recorded in the annals of Wei, Zetian gave a special order to the gentleman in attendance at Fengge, Cui Xuanwei, to go together with [Fa]zang to Famen si to receive it. At that time, [Fa]zang was the abbot of Dachongfu si, and along with the ten other welcoming venerables, such as the *Vinaya* Master [Wen]gang and others, they went to the *stūpa*. Walking the path for seven days and nights, they then opened it to spiritual light and splendour. In the past, [Fa]zang had burnt off his finger in offering, and he now displayed his courage and raised up his hand to make a vow, showing it to the monastics and laity. In his palm, the *śarīra* blazed with light, which shone forth pervading near and far. …
>
> On the eve of the new year, he went to Chongfu si in the western capital. On that day, the Regent [of Chang'an], that is, Prince of Kuaiji, associated ministers and five-fold community threw themselves down to prostrate on the left side of the road, making various offerings and donations of beautiful incense, flowers and music of drums, which even the blind and deaf could see and hear. By the first month of the new year, one day he entered Shendu [Luoyang], and had the king and ministers and the surrounding officials of the city of Luo[yang] make efforts to put up banners, flowers and flags, and even had the grand master of ceremonies prepare music to receive it, setting up the Ming Hall. On lantern day [of the full moon,] Zetian maintained purity of body and mind, and with the deepest sincerity invited [Fa]zang to bear it aloft, and make universal prayers for the good of all.[252]

---

252 *Tang Tae Ch'ŏnboksa kosaju pŏn'gyŏng taedŏk Pŏpjang hwasang chŏn, T* no. 2054, 50: 1.283c25-284a12:
長安四年冬杪於內道場, 因對揚言及岐州舍利是阿育王靈跡, 即魏冊所載扶風塔是. 則天特命鳳閣侍郎博陵崔玄暐, 與藏偕往法門寺迎之. 時藏爲大崇福寺主, 遂與應大德綱律師等十人俱至塔所, 行道七晝夜, 然後啓之, 神輝煜爚. 藏以昔嘗煉指, 今更隳肝, 乃手擎興願, 顯示道俗. 舍利於掌上騰光, 洞照遐邇. …… 歲除日, 至西京崇福寺. 是日也, 留守會稽王率官屬及五部眾投身道左, 競施異供, 香華鼓樂之妙, 蒙瞶亦可睹聞. 咱新年端月孟旬, 有一日入神都, 敕令王公已降, 洛城近事之眾, 精事幡華幢蓋, 仍命太常具樂奏迎, 置於明堂. 觀燈日, 則天身心護凈, 頭面盡虔, 請藏捧持, 普爲善禱.

The Buddha's finger *śarīra* first stopped at Chongfu si in the western capital, and then began its journey to be delivered to the eastern capital Luoyang, to be enshrined in the Ming Hall 明堂 inside the Palace of Dongdu. In the first year of Shenlong (705), Wu Zetian suffered serious illness, and so the prime minister Zhang Jianzhi 張柬之 (625–706) took the opportunity to instigate political change in the palace court. Zetian also died in that same year. The Emperor Zhongzong Li Xian 李顯 (r. 683–684; 705–710) thereupon ascended to the throne and enshrined the Buddha's bone relic in the palace for three years. Only in the second year of Jinglong (708) did he finally send Wengang to deliver and return the Buddha's bone relic to back to Famen si. In the fourth year of Jinglong, Li Xian honoured Famen si with the title of "Shengchao Wuyouwang si'" 聖朝無憂王寺 (Aśoka Monastery in the Holy Dynasty), called the *śarīra stūpa* the "Dasheng zhenshen baota" 大聲真身寶塔 (Treasure *Stūpa* for the Great Sage's True Body), and also held a ceremony to ordain forty-nine monastics. Later, archeologists discovered at the chambers of the Famen si underground vaults a large quantity of gold threaded silk, embroidered dresses of Wu Zetian making offerings to the Buddhas, and also gold *kaśayas*.[253] Furthermore, in the middle chamber they found a white jade funerary cloth 164cm in length, upon which was written: "This is a record to state that the fifteenth day of the second month of the second year of the Jinglong era (708.3.11) in the Great Tang, Fazang and others made this white stone funerary cloth, to place the *śarīra* into the *stūpa*".[254] This particular event to receive the Buddha's finger *śarīra* took some four years from start to finish. Subsequent receptions of the Buddha's bone relics mostly took just two or three years in total.

In the first year of Shangyuan (760), Emperor Suzong (r.756–762) sent Fadeng 法燈 (d.u.), the mid-rank official Song Heli 宋合禮 (d.u.), and governor of the capital Cui Guangyuan 崔光遠 (?–761), to go to Famen si to open the underground vault, receive the Buddha's bone *śarīra*, and make offerings to it at the *neidaochang* in the forbidden palace of the capital. On the first day of the seventh month (760.8.16), it was put on display and extravagant offerings were made to it. 300 taels (*liang* 兩) of sandalwood incense were given in worship as an offering by the great ministers of the imperial court. This occasion of the reception of the Buddha's bone relics was a period of two months. Due to the chaos of war at that time, it was not of large scale and the offerings were not particularly bountiful.

By the time of Emperor Dezong (r. 779–805), the *Zizhi tongjian* 資治通鑑 (Comprehensive Mirror in Aid of Government), fascicle 233, records:

253 Shaanxi sheng kaogu yanjiuyuan et al., *Fajue baogao*, 1: 270.

254 Shaanxi sheng kaogu yanjiuyuan et al., *Fajue baogao*, 1: 236-44.

> In the sixth year [of Zhenyuan] (790), [in] spring, the Buddha's finger relic was invited from Wuyouwang si on Mount Qi 岐山 and taken to the forbidden palace. It was also taken around the monasteries and shown to the community. In the capital, it was worshipped and honoured, with many tens of thousands in wealth offered to it. On the second month, day of yihai (790.2.27), emissary officials again interred it in its original location.[255]

The "Dezong ji xia" 德宗紀下 (Chronicle of Dezong, Two) in the *Jiu Tang shu* 舊唐書 (The Old Book of Tang) records that in the second month, in spring, of the sixth year of Zhenyuan, "Wuyouwang si on Mount Qi had a Buddha's bone relic, over one inch in length. It was first taken to the forbidden palace where it was enshrined and worshipped. On the *yihai* day, it was returned back to its original monastery".[256]

In the history of the Tang dynasty, both admiring worship and rejecting remonstrations toward the Buddha's bone relics were simultaneously present. In Han Yu's 韓愈 (768–824) "Jian Fogu biao" 諫佛骨表 (Remonstration against the Buddha's Bone Relics) was a letter presented to Emperor Xianzong (r. 805–820), which vehemently pointed out the faults of receiving the Buddha's bone relic. The *Zizhi tongjian*, fascicle 250, records that on the eleventh month of the thirteenth year of Yuanhe (818):

> The Commissioner of Merit and Virtue (gongde shi 功德使) reports above, saying: "There is a finger bone relic of the Buddha in the *stūpa* at Famen si, which by tradition is opened once every thirty years. The year when it is opened is bountiful and the populace is at peace. It should be opened next year and the relic greeted [into the palace]". On the twelfth month, "middle officials" (enunchs) as emissaries should be sent and it should be welcomed by the community of monastics.[257]

In the first month, in spring, of the fourteenth year (819):

---

255 *Zizhi tongjian* 233.7520:
(貞元) 六年, 春, 詔出岐山無憂王寺佛指骨迎置禁中, 又送諸寺以示眾. 傾都瞻禮, 施財巨萬. 二月, 乙亥, 遣中使復葬故處.

256 *Jiu Tang shu* 13.368: 岐州無憂王寺有佛骨寸餘, 先是取來禁中供養. 乙亥, 詔送還本寺.

257 *Zizhi tongjian* 240.7756:
功德使上言："鳳翔法門寺塔有佛指骨, 相傳三十年一開, 開則歲豐人安, 來年應開, 請迎之" 十二月, 上遣中使帥僧眾迎之.

> The Eunuch Manager received the Buddha's bone relic to the capital. It remained at the forbidden palace for three days. Then it was sent on tour to the monasteries. When the court officials and people worshipped it with extravagant offerings, they were afraid of missing this opportunity. There were those who are bankrupt yet gave, and there were those who burnt their arms and heads with incense as offerings.[258]

During the time period when the Buddha's finger relic was worshipped in the inner courtyard of the imperial palace, Emperor Xianzong served upon the Buddha with great piety. Every day he dressed simply, upheld the vegetarian fast, and held the precepts. He wrote an untitled seven word rhyme poem (七律・無題), showing his unsurpassed adoration of the Buddha's *śarīra*.

During the period of "Huichang Anti-Buddhist Persecution" (Huichang fa'nan 會昌法難), Emperor Wuzong (r. 840–846) of Tang issued an order that did not permit worship of the Buddha's bone relic in the underground vault at Famen si. In the eighth month of the twelfth year of Xiantong (871), Emperor Yizong (r. 859–873) repaired the Famen si underground vault, and searched for the abandoned Buddha finger bone relic, enshrining it in the underground vault for respectful worship. In the fourteenth year of Xiantong (873), Yizong sent official emissaries and several dozen venerable monastics from the Left and Right Streets in the capital to Famen si to receive the Buddha's bone relic. After entering the forbidden palace for three days, it was sent to An'guo si 安國寺 and Chonghua si 崇化寺 in the capital for worship and adoration. The "Da Tang Xiantong qisong qiyang zhenshen zhiwen' records:

> On the twenty-second day of the third month of the fourteenth year (873.4.22), on imperial order, the Officer For Court Service (gongfengguan 供奉官) Li Fengjian 李奉建 (d.u.), [Eunuch of] High Rank (gaopin 高品) Peng Yanlu 彭延魯 (d.u.), Storehouse Commissioner (kujia 庫家) Qi Xunjing 齊詢敬 (d.u), Academician Recipient of Edicts (chengzhi 承旨) Wan Luwen 萬魯文 (d.u), Monastic Registrars from the Left and Right Streets, Qinglan 清瀾 (d.u.) and Yanchu 彥楚 (d.u.), senior monastics Sengche 僧澈 (d.u.), Weiying 惟應 (d.u.), masters Chongqian 重謙 (d.u.), Yünhao 雲顥 (d.u.) and Huihui 慧暉 (d.u.), and others, all solemnly took lamps and incense to sincerely invite the True Body. At that time, the Military Inspector of Fengxiang (Fengxian Jianjunshi 鳳翔監軍使), Wang Jingxun

258 *Zizhi tongjian* 240.7758:
中使迎佛骨至京師, 上留禁中三日, 乃歷送諸寺, 王公士民瞻奉餘施, 惟恐弗及, 有竭產充施者, 有然香臂頂供養者.

> 王景珣 (d.u.), and Surveillance Administrative Assistant (guancha panguan 觀察判官) Yuan Chong 元充 (d.u.) came to watch over the delivery. On the nineteenth day of the twelfth month (874.1.11), the True Body was guarded as it was sent back from the capital city to the original monastery. … … On the fourth day of the first month of the fifteenth year (874.1.25), it was returned and placed in the stone chamber beneath the *stūpa*. In a jade casket, a golden case, it was the most majestic in the world; with cicada wings and dragon ripples, it was the greatest beautiful glory of humanity. Reflecting with six layers of beads, shining with encrustments of jewels, the fortune and wealth of the imperial family is boundless, the good causes of favourable ages will not wilt. This let the High Rank Peng Yanlu and the Eunuch (neiyang 內養) Feng Quanzhang 馮全璋 (d.u.) give gifts of gold, silver, silk cloth and other items.[259]

Emperor Yizong considered this occasion of the invitation for the Buddha's bone relics as being particularly important, and the period of the entire event took nearly one whole year from start to finish. The *Xin Tang shu* 新唐書 (New Book of Tang), fascicle 181, states:

> In the spring of the fourteenth year of Xiantong (873), [the Emperor Yizong] issued a decree to invite the Buddha's bone relic to Fengxiang, saying, "In the past, Emperor Xianzong performed offerings in this way, and shortly after that passed away". The emperor said, "If I see it in my life, I can die without regrets!" The guts take gold and silver as the flagstaff, pearl and jade as the flag, embellished with peacock and crane. The smallest is nearly a fathom long, the highest twice that. A sandalwood engraving is the pillar, the stairs are covered with gold. Each flagstaff is raised up by several hundred people. The paths are lined with incense, and canopies and banners covered in beads and jewels. There are pennants of many bright colours. There is no limit to the costs involved. By summer, the fourth month, it went to Chang'an, and the road was bedecked to welcome it, with devotees leading the way. The son of heaven was at the Anfu Tower 安福樓 to respectfully welcome it with tears. By

259 Li, *Famensi zhi*, 249–50:
十四年三月廿二日, 詔供奉官李奉建功、高品彭延魯、庫家齊詢敬、承旨萬魯文與左右街僧錄清瀾、彥楚, 首座僧澈、惟應, 大師重謙、雲顥、慧暉等, 同嚴香火, 虔請真身. 時鳳翔監軍使王景珣, 觀察判官元充咸來護送. 以十二月十九日自京都護送真身來本寺. …… 以十五年正月初四日歸安於塔下之石室. 玉棺金篋, 窮天上之莊嚴；蟬翼龍紋, 極人間之煥麗. 疊六銖而斥映, 積秘寶以相鮮, 皇家之厚福無涯, 曠劫之良因不朽, 仍令高品彭延魯、內養馮全璋頒賜金銀絹等.

> decree, the monastics of court and city were given gold coins, the old officials of the capital and servants were all given to generously. Dissatisfied lowly people cut off their arms and fingers, and blood flowed throughout the streets. Approaching the towns and villages, earth was heaped up and people stood on them to see from afar, competing with decorations in gold and green. Many stories spread around of the earth shaking and quaking, and lights in the clouds. The capital officials praised these signs and gathered the city guards, who made decorated platforms and bedecked the gates, with pools of mercury and trees of gold and jade. Gathering the monastics, the drums were struck and the conch was blown throughout day and night, and it was led with an adorned carriage, with song and dance following behind it.[260]

Within the underground vault was engraved the "Da Tang Xiantong qisong qiyang zhenshen zhiwen" and the "Jiansong zhenshenshi sui zhenshen gongyang daoju ji jinyin baoqi yiwu zhang" 監送真身使隨真身供養道具及金銀寶器衣物帳 (Accounts of Paraphernalia for Offerings to the True Body of Gold, Silver, Treasures, Items, Clothings and Goods by the Emissary of Escorting the True Body). This was an inventory statement recording the gold, silver, jewels, treasures and so forth for offerings throughout the process of the occasion of the reception of the *śarīra*, from which we can see how stupendous the whole situation was.

At the time, due to the worship of the imperial household, the fame of the Famen si Buddha's finger *śarīra* spread throughout the whole land. However, during the Tang period there were four Buddha's tooth relics in the city of Chang'an, which were individually kept at Da Zhuangyan si 大莊嚴寺, Chongsheng si 崇聖寺, Jianfu si 薦福寺 and Xingfu si 興福寺. These monasteries themselves each held "Gatherings of Worshipping the Buddha's Tooth". With respect to the resplendent nature of these Buddha tooth services and the pious and sincere devotion of the Buddhist community, Ennin's *Nittō guhō junrei kōki* provides an even more detailed description:

---

260 *Xin Tang shu* 181.5354:
咸通十四春,詔迎佛骨鳳翔,或言:"昔憲宗嘗爲此,俄晏駕."帝曰:"使朕生見之,死無恨!"乃以金銀爲刹,珠玉爲帳,孔鷸周飾之,小者尋丈,高至倍,刻檀爲檐註,陛墄塗黃金,每一刹,數百人舉之.香與前後系道,綴珠瑟瑟幡蓋,殘彩以爲幢節,費無貲限.夏四月,至長安,彩觀夾路,其徒導衛.天子禦安福樓迎拜,至泣下.詔賜兩街僧金幣,京師耆老及見元和事者,悉厚賜之.不逞小人至斷臂指,流血滿道.所近鄉聚,皆裒土爲刹,相望於途,爭以金翠拉飾.傳言刹悉震搖,若有光景雲.京師高貲相與集大衛,作繒臺縵闕,註水銀爲池,金玉爲樹木,聚桑門羅像,考鼓鳴螺繼日夜,錦車繡輿,載歌舞從之.

> From the eighth day to the fifteenth day at Lantian county 藍田縣, tea and rice were prepared for all, for which monastics and laity all came from all directions to eat. The Monastic Registrar of the Left Street Venerable Tixu 體虛 (d.u.) presided over the service. Monastics from the monasteries gathered and all prepared precious offerings, medicinal food of one hundred kinds, wondrous fruit and flowers, many fragrances and adornments, all to offer to and worship the Buddha's tooth. The preparations to decorate the buildings and walkways for worship were uncountable. The Buddha's tooth was in the courtyard amidst the buildings, and the venerables of the city were all there in the buildings praising and exclaiming as they wished. The whole city came to worship and pay respects. Some people donated ten thousand catties of rice, and two thousand catties of millet. Some people donated as much food as people could eat. Some people donated sundry monies as much as people needed. Some people donated as many flat breads as people wanted. Some people donated as much accommodation as the monastics needed. In this way, everyone made vows to donate to adorn the Buddha's tooth service, and scattered money like rain toward the tower which housed the Buddha's tooth.[261]

At the same time, Ennin also recorded that during the Tang, the Wutai mountains also had relics of *pratyekabuddha* teeth and skull bone.

Therefore, the worship services for the *śarīra* were not just splendid events for the Buddhist world, but included the participation of the whole of society. This helped to further aid in the acceptance of Buddhism within secular society.

## 3 Buddhist Social Philanthropy in the Sui and Tang Periods

Under the influence of Buddhist notions such as the merit field, loving kindness and compassion, and so forth, Buddhist engagement in social welfare and charitable activities during the Sui and Tang included the establishment of

261 *Nittō guhō junrei kōki* 3.148:
藍田縣從八日至十五日, 設無礙茶飯, 十方僧俗盡來吃. 左街僧錄體虛法師爲會主. 諸寺赴集, 各設珍供, 百種藥食, 珍妙果花, 眾香備嚴, 供養佛牙, 及供養樓廓下敷設, 不可勝計. 佛牙在樓中庭, 城中大德盡在樓上隨喜贊嘆. 舉城赴來, 禮拜供養. 有人施百石粳米、廿石粟米；有人施無礙供餤頭足；有人施無礙供雜用錢足；有人供無礙薄餅足；有人施諸寺大德老宿供足. 如是各各發願, 布施莊嚴佛牙會, 向佛牙樓散錢如雨.

institutions such as the compassion-field infirmaries and guest lodges, and the development of poverty and disaster relief, civil construction and so forth.

### 3.1 *Buddhist Philanthropy in the Sui Dynasty*

Sui dynasty Buddhism, under the support of Emperor Wen of Sui, Emperor Yang of Sui, and others, put much effort into various types of charitable works and activities. After renowned monastics held Dharma services or transmitted the precepts and taught the Dharma to the emperors and royalty, devotees and the imperial family would give large amounts of money as offerings, which would be used by those monastics to undertake charitable and relief activities. For example, as stated in Jizang's 吉藏 (549–623) *Xu Gaoseng zhuan* biography, "[Ji]zang was inexhaustible in his teaching of Dharma and accumulation of material giving, establishing merit fields wherever he went. The excess was used to fill the immeasurable treasury, with intermediaries to perform the giving, which went into the [fields of] compassion and respect".[262] Demei's 德美 (575–637/638) *Xu Gaoseng zhuan* biography states: "From the end of Kaihuang up to the tenth year of Daye, annual donations were made, each of them like this. … The two fields of compassion and respect were given to once each year. Sometimes clothing was given, or stocks of food".[263] Poverty relief work for the suffering masses not only gave money, as giving of clothing and food were commonly seen. Moreover, during the chaos of war at the end of the Sui, monasteries and temples often became centres for social relief and rescue work. Daozong's 道宗 (563–623/624) *Xu Gaoseng zhuan* biography tells us, "During the seasons of Daye, there was continuous famine. The funeral mounds ever gathered more bones, and the populace ate one another. Only [Dao]zong spread the teachings of the four gratitudes, and taught the suffering masses. Whatever things could be given were given to them in full. Thus Daoxun 道愻 (556–630/631) from Puzhou 蒲州, Daozong from Tongzhou 同州, … went to aid them out of compassion, and their good names spread far and wide".[264] In addition, monasteries took in refugees, such as in the *Ji Shenzhou sanbao gantong lu*, fascicle one: "In the last years of Daye, groups of bandits roamed around. The monastery was on Mount Xigelü 西葛屨山 on the Sanjuetai 三爵臺, where

262 *Xu Gaoseng zhuan*, *T* no. 2060, 50: 11.514a20-22: 藏法化不窮,財施填積,隨散建諸福田. 用既有餘,乃充十無盡藏,委付曇獻,資於悲敬.

263 *Xu Gaoseng zhuan*, *T* no. 2060, 50: 29.697a22-25: 故自開皇之末,終於大業十年,年別大施,其例咸爾. …… 悲敬兩田,年常一施,或給衣服,或濟糇糧.

264 *Xu Gaoseng zhuan*, *T* no. 2060, 50: 29.534b18-22: 大業季曆,薦餒相尋,丘壑填骸,人民相食. 惟宗偏廣四恩,開化氓隸. 施物所及,並充其供. 故蒲州道愻、同州道宗 …… 情同拯濟,騰實廣焉.

four villages came as refugees, fortifying the city and defending it. The people were crammed in, and there was not a foot of free space. Even above and below the *stūpa* were filled up".[265] We can thus see some of the types of charitable activities of these monasteries and temples.

At the same time, there were circumstances when the government would release prisoners and the monastics would preach the Dharma to them to bring about a change of heart and turn over a new leaf. For example, a document in the *Guoqing bailu*, fascicle three, "Zhiyi da fangtuliu shu" 智顗答放徒流書 (Zhiyi's Answers to Released Convicts), states:

> The Academician Opening An Office (Kaifu xueshi 開府學士) Liu Guyan 柳顧言 (537–605) declared: The practice of the Jin'guangming [jing] has been enacted to its fullest. On the pure full moon of the fifteenth of the month, an amnesty will be given to convicts. Out of pity, they will avoid flogging. ... When the hinges of the gates of the prison were opened and they were released, not a single convict given amnesty did not dance with joy. The grace of the imperial court further increased with this. They were farewelled with victory banners, which were hung from the treasure *stūpa*, and those on high strewed flowers, burnt incense and lit candles. Also it was arranged that there was a Dharma sermon, to encourage them to turn to the righteous.[266]

Emperor Wen and Emperor Yang of Sui were influenced by Buddhism in their amnesty for criminals, and after releasing the convicts provided "a dharma sermon, to encourage them to turn to the righteous". Also, the monastics gave clothes and goods to the convicts, and exhorted them with dharma teachings, assisting in the education of society.

At the same time, monastics in the Sui dynasty also used their own power to draw people and set up communes and societies, under which they raised funds in order to carry out activities for the benefit of society. For example, in the *Baqiongshi jinshi buzheng*, fascicle twenty-four, in the sixth year of Kaihuang (586), the "Zhongsina deng zaoqiao bei" 仲思那等造橋碑 (Stele for Bridge Construction by Zhong Sina and Others), records:

---

265 *Ji Shenzhou sanbao gantong lu*, *T* no. 2106, 52: 1.410a2-5:
大業末歲, 群盜互陣. 寺在三爵臺西葛屨山上, 四鄉來投, 築城固守. 人物擁聚, 尺地不空, 塔之上下, 重復皆滿.

266 *Guoqing bailu*, *T* no. 1934, 46: 3.808c8-21:
開府學士柳顧言宣教：金光明行法究竟, 如十五月清凈圓滿, 恩放徒流, 矜免鞭罰 ...... 爰開獄門, 杻械解脫, 徒流原宥, 莫不蹈舞. 殿庭稱恩, 感戴加復. 送以勝幡, 仍懸寶塔, 登高散華, 燒香朗燭, 並留供設, 說法開示, 咸令向善.

> The shape of the canopy is like a spark of flint, suddenly appearing then disappearing, just as life is like a floating bubble, coming into existence then ceasing. If one does not fully commit to giving up their life, like the great being casting forth his body, overcoming oneself through vigour and sincerity. … Now, the head of the society Zhong Sina 仲思那 (d.u) and others, thirty people in total, have seen the south of the village and divided up the land. … Departing at the main road, it brought Yang Zhu 陽朱 (ca. fourth century BCE) to weep at the parting. … Now at this site they respectfully construct this stone bridge.[267]

The Sui dynasty continued this special feature of civic societies from the Northern Qi and Northern Zhou. There were no hard restrictions on the numbers of monasteries and monastics, and monastic officials were used to manage and regulate the monastics. Exchange and interaction between monastics and laity was quite free, and so monastics and laity together formed communes and societies through the cities and down to the farming villages.

### 3.2 *Compassion-Field Infirmaries in the Tang Dynasty*

Compassion-field infirmaries were places for the treatment of illness inside monasteries, which were half government and half public. Later, they evolved into a kind of charitable program for the monasteries, which included such functions as relief for the impoverished, treatment of illness, distribution of medicine, consolation for widows and orphans, and so forth. Early on in ancient China, there already were homes for widows and orphans and infirmaries for the ill which had similar qualities to these. The *Guanzi* 管子, "Ruguo pian" 入國篇 (The Nation Chapter), states: "All nations support orphans. They are whatever orphaned children are themselves not old enough to have children. Their relatives should raise them. If there is one child, there is no military service. If there are two children, then the second child has no military service. This is the ancient rule. On the second year of Putong (521), Liang Wudi ordered the establishment of orphanages".[268] There are also records of those who had difficultly surviving due to illnesses being taken in by the official institutions, which are similar to infirmaries. "In the Southern Qi, Prince Wenhui

267 *Baqiongshi jinshi buzheng* 24.150:
蓋形同石火, 忽有便無, 命似浮泡, 攸存還滅. 若不傾心捨命, 如薩埵之投骸, 剋己精誠 …… 今大邑主仲思那等卅人, 謹見村南分派成地 …… 阻隔長衢, 遂使陽朱泣分岐之淚 …… 謹於此處敬造石橋.

268 *Shiwu yuanhui* 6.4:
凡國都有掌孤, 舉凡孤幼不能自生者, 屬之其親戚故人. 養一孤者, 一子無徵；二孤者, 二子無徵. 本古制也. 至梁武帝普通二年辛丑, 詔置孤獨院.

(458–493) established six illness lodges. Emperor Xuanwu (r. 499–515) of the Late Wei ordered the grand master of ceremonies to set up lodges, allowing those sick and unwell both within and outside the city to dwell there, so that they could be treated".[269] Therefore, compassion-field infirmaries in the Tang dynasty were an extension of the older orphanages and infirmaries. The difference between the two was that the controlling authorities for the compassion-field infirmaries in the Tang period were a tightly connected combination of government offices and Buddhist monasteries.

Compassion-field infirmaries were created in the Tang dynasty, during Wu Zetian's Chang'an period (701–704). The *Tang Huiyao* 唐會要 (Institutional History of the Tang), fascicle forty-nine, records:

> In the fifth year of Kaiyuan (717), Song Jing 宋璟 (663–737) declared: "Compassion-field infirmaries, from the Chang'an period onwards, have been specially taken charge of by an official appointed [by the court]. The state provides for orphans and relieves the poor, respects elders and cares for the ill, each has their own arrangements and responsible people. Now, nameless people are beginning to meet there, and receive such benefits as these, and in truth these places become places where felons gather together, places of secret debauchery…".

In the fifth year of Huichang (845), in the eleventh month, Li Deyu 李德裕 (787–850) memorialized the emperor: "Relief for the poor, and help for the sick, are found in the *Regulations of Zhou*. Those without legal recourse, who are constantly in hunger, are to be cared for—this is recorded in the Chapter of Wangzhi [in the *Liji* 禮記 ]. The present government establishes compassion-field infirmaries, which are specially taken charge of by an official appointed [by the court]".

In the fifth year of Kaiyuan, Song Jing memorialized the emperor: "The compassion-field [infirmary] is the providence of the Śākyan religion, this is the vocational responsibility of the monks and nuns. It is inappropriate that government officials are responsible for it". Emperor Xuangzong did not approve it. By the twenty-second year (734), he removed all beggars from the capital, and had them all managed by the infirmaries. The officials used the basic funds to finance these benefits.[270]

---

269 *Shiwu yuanhui* 6.4: 南齊文惠太子立六疾館；後魏宣武帝詔太常立館, 使京畿內外疾病者咸令居處, 使醫治之.

270 *Tang huiyao* 49.1010:
開元五年, 宋璟奏, " 悲田養病, 從長安以來, 置使專知. 國家矜孤恤窮, 敬老養病, 至於安庇, 各有司存. 今驟聚無名之人, 著收利之便, 實恐逋逃爲藪, 隱沒成奸."

Compassion-field infirmaries were started in Chang'an and Luoyang, and later spread to further cities and provinces, then eventually the entire country. Song Jing felt that the government should not be in charge of these religious organizations where "nameless people are beginning to meet", and that such organizations should be immediately disbanded. However, his suggestion was not accepted by Emperor Xuanzong. In order to increase the amount of control over them, in the twenty-second year of Kaiyuan (734), Emperor Xuanzong issued an order that "removed all beggars from the capital and had them all managed by the infirmaries. The officials used the basic funds to finance these benefits". Infirmaries became government operated orphanages, which, although they were run by the monasteries and monastics, were funded by the accumulated interest from lending of the state finance. The very first establishment of compassion-field infirmaries during the Tang dynasty was, according to Song Jing's explanation, "The compassion-field [infirmary] is the providence of the Śākyan religion, this is the vocational responsibility of the monks and nuns".[271] We can thus see that they were operated by the Buddhists, but received support from the government. In the *Zizhi tongjian*, fascicle 214, in the twelfth month of the twenty-second year of Kaiyuan, Emperor Xuanzong also "prohibited beggars in the capital city, and established infirmaries to look after them".[272] This demonstrates that Xuanzong set up infirmaries and changed their management to the government offices. However, the Hu Sanxing's 胡三省 (1230–1302) commentary to the *Zizhi tongjian* states: "At that time, infirmaries were affiliated with different monasteries, as compassion field infirmaries originally were of the Śākyan religion".[273] This shows that they were later affiliated with different monasteries.

In the second year of Zhide (757), Emperor Suzong also established universal-relief infirmaries in the two capital cities, which were operated by government offices. After the Huichang Anti-Buddhist Persecution, almost all the monasteries and temples throughout the whole country were destroyed, and the monks and nuns were forced into laicization. This created the problem of "nobody to lead the compassion-field infirmaries",[274] causing huge problems for the relief of the poor, sick, and those without legal recourse. Li Deyu

...... 會昌五年十一月,李德裕奏云,"恤貧寬疾,著於"周典";無告常餒,存於《王制》. 國朝立悲田養病,置使專知." 開元五年,宋璟奏,"悲田乃關釋教,此是僧尼職掌,不合定使專知." 玄宗不許. 至二十二年,斷京城乞兒,悉令病坊收管,官以本錢收利給之.

271 *Tang huiyao* 49.1010: 悲田乃關釋教,此是僧尼職掌.

272 *Zizhi tongjian* 214.6809: 禁京城丐者,置病坊以廩之.

273 *Zizhi tongjian* 214.6809: 時病坊又分署於諸寺,以悲田養病,本於釋教也.

274 *Tang huiyao* 49.1010: 悲田坊無人主領.

applied to the emperor to prepare to construct infirmaries, as stated in the "Lun liangjing ji zhudao beitianfang Zhuang" 論兩京及諸道悲田坊狀 (Discussion on the Condition of the Compassion-Field Infirmaries in the Two Capitals and Other Provinces):

> In present circumstances, the monks and nuns of the monasteries have all been laicized, and there is nobody to lead the compassion-field infirmaries. This is certainly a concern for the sick and poor, creating further difficulties. The ministers have discussed the matter, that the compassion fields originally were under the Śākyan religion, and hope that they can become infirmaries (yangbingfang 養病坊). In the two capitals and all the provinces, each is to go through the records of senior elders, and select one person who is most trustworthy, praised and admired in their village and neighbourhood, and have them take over in position. The two capitals will give ten qing [sixty-seven ha.] of the monasteries' fields, the larger provinces will be given seven qing [forty-seven ha.] of the monasteries' fields, and the other provinces will set up a commission to inspect the number of fields to give for the poor and sick, whether it be five qing [thirty-three ha.], or three or two qing [twenty or thirteen ha.]. They will also be provided with rice porridge. If provinces have any fiscal supplus of official funds, they can weigh up the benefits and decide what is appropriate.[275]

Li Deyu's application to change the names of "compassion-field infirmaries" to "infirmaries", is just the removal of the Buddhist term "compassion field". In order for the infirmaries to have a stable source of funding and supplies, Li Deyu also requested that each infirmary be given five to ten *qing* [thirty-three to sixty-seven ha.], with other provinces inspecting the numbers of poor and infirm people to determine how much to give, so that the produce from the fields could provide porridge for those in need of relief. After Li Deyu's request was approved, the management of the infirmaries was passed from vocational monks and nuns to the hands of individuals of high moral character. They would continue to be run as before, with the expenses covered by the state. The *Quan Tang Wen*, fascicle seventy-seven, contains Emperor Wuzong's "Xuan

---

275 *Quan Tang wen* 703.3201:
今緣諸道僧尼盡已還俗, 悲田坊無人主管, 必恐病貧, 轉致困窮. 臣等商量, 緣悲田出於釋教, 並望更爲養病坊. 其兩京及諸州, 合於子錄事, 耆年揀一人, 有名行謹信爲鄉閭所稱者, 專令勾當. 其兩京望給寺田十頃, 大州鎮望給寺田七頃, 其他諸州望委觀察使量貧病多少給田五頃、三二頃, 以充粥飯. 如州鎮有羨餘官錢, 量與置本, 收利最爲穩便.

qishou goudang beitian yangbingfang chi" 選耆壽勾當悲田養病坊敕 (Decree for Selection of Elders to Manage the Compassion-Field Infirmaries), which states: "As the monks and nuns have been laicized, the compassion-field infirmaries have no managers. I fear that the sick are not being provided for. In the two capitals, give them monastery fields to support them, each province giving seven *qing* to ten *qing* [forty-seven to sixty-seven ha.], for them to manage; and select a senior elder to be in charge. Provide them with porridge and grain".[276]

In this way, the compassion-field infirmaries were yet again passed over to government officials' management. For example, Duan Chengshi's 段成式 (ca. 803–863) *Youyang zazu* 酉陽雜俎 (Miscellaneous Morsels from Youyang) states: "The beggar of Chengdu Yan Qishi 嚴七師, squanderers and profligates, covered in dirt and stinking filth, unapproachable; their speech incomprehensible, their replies nonsensical. They should live in the compassion-field infirmary in the west of the city".[277] By the time of Emperor Yizong (r. 859–873), the infirmaries were yet again under the management of the monastics. Emperor Yizong's "Jiyu tuien chi" 疾愈推恩敕 (Decree on Grace for Treatment of Illness) states:

> I had ongoing illness over the winter and summer, which continued unabated. Now, during these weeks, I can eat and sleep. I have received the grace and blessings of heaven and earth, the kindness and favour of ancestors and spirits. Now that the pain of sickness has been cured, I think of the weak and vulnerable who have no sanctuary. As mother and father, we cannot but pity them. I worry that if amnesties are too frequent, the villains will have their way. Perhaps the grace of giving from afar will somehow aid these poor refugees.
>
> All those of the common populace, Buddhist monks and nuns, Daoist masters and ladies, and so forth, who are over seventy years of age, afflicted by illness and disease, weak and vulnerable, bedridden and immobile, will each be gifted two *pi* [about forty m.] of silk cloth.
>
> Soldiers who during military operations were injured by the enemy on arm, or leg, or their eyes, now unable to make a living, will each also be given four *pi* [about eighty m.] of silk cloth. The poor in the city and county infirmaries should be gifted 1,000 catties of rice where they are many, or 700, 500 or 300 where they are few.

276 *Quan Tang wen* 77.351:
悲田養病坊, 僧尼還俗無人主持, 恐殘疾無以取給, 兩京量給寺田賑濟, 諸州府七頃至十頃, 各於本管, 選耆壽一人勾當, 以充粥料.

277 *Youyang zazu* 3.225: 成都乞兒嚴七師, 幽陋凡賤, 塗垢臭穢不可近, 言語無度, 往往應於未兆. 居西市悲田坊.

According to the original decree, those infirmaries each have excess funds. The regional inspectors are to make record of military affairs, the county administrator is to audit them, and in an auxiliary role, a virtuous monastic will be in charge of these for a term of three years.

In times of wind or snow, the infirm are unable to beg. Then take the interest of funds of the infirmaries and go to the market to buy rice to make porridge, giving equally to all who are hungry. If the illness is treatable, then go to the market to buy medicine to treat them. The silk cloth, rice, and so forth that are used will all be covered by the funds from the ministry of households.

Quickly report to inform of the exact numbers, so that local officials can manage the expenditure for the materials needed to treat these illnesses.

Once this decree is received, may all cities and counties make a written record of this decree and post it on the city and town gates, and also have it put up on the entrances to the roads of the villages and neighbourhoods. Aware that the silk and rice distributed by the cities and counties may be embezzled by lower officials, regional inspectors and local leaders must establish public notifications, and not allow the goods to not reach the people. After goods are distributed, each and every one must be reported to the emperor in detail. Quickly providing for relief from illness of the people is what accords with my will.[278]

Throughout the whole country, those compassion field infirmaries that took in more of the poor were given 1000 catties of rice, and those with less given 700, 500 or 300 according to the ratio. Management continued as previously, selected from monastics with virtuous conduct, and rotated every three years. If there were days of snowstorms, the infirm were unable to go out onto the streets to beg for food, and so the interest of funds from the infirmaries were

278 *Quan Tang wen* 84.386:
朕比寒暑致疾, 綿滯經時. 今旬朔之間, 寢膳已復. 蒙天地保右, 宗社寵靈, 既疾痛之有瘳, 念疲羸之無告, 爲之父母, 得不憫傷. 慮赦令之或頻, 則奸人之得計; 倘恩惠之遠布, 冀窮氓之稍蘇. 應天下百姓僧尼道士女冠等, 有年七十以上, 疾病癥痼, 委頓床榻者, 宜各賜絹兩匹. 在軍旅行陣, 經敵傷害手足眼目, 不能營生, 亦各賜絹兩匹. 應州縣病坊貧兒多處, 賜米十石, 或數少處, 即七石、五石、三石. 其病坊據元敕各有本利錢, 委所在刺史錄事參軍縣令糾勘, 兼差有道行僧人專勾當, 三年一替. 如遇風雪之時, 病者不能求丐, 即取本坊利錢, 市米爲粥, 均給饑乏. 如疾病可救, 即與市藥理療. 其所用絹米等, 且以戶部屬省錢物充. 速具申奏, 候知定數, 即以藩鎮所進賀疾愈物支還所司. 此敕到, 仰所在州縣寫錄敕, 榜於州縣門, 並坊市村閭要路. 其州縣所給恤絹米, 恐下吏之所隱欺, 仍委刺史縣令設法頒布, 不得令不到本身. 所在給恤之後, 一一分析聞奏, 俾令速濟疾病, 稱朕意焉.

taken to cook porridge from rice grain to give to the unwell who were hungry. With respect to those with chronic illness, they were given medicines to treat them, with the expenses taken from the extra funds of the ministry of households.

However, there were also monastics who established their own infirmaries to take in the poor and sick. The *Taiping guangji* 太平廣記 (Extensive Records of the Taiping Era), fascicle 95, cites the Tang dynasty Niu Su's 牛肅 (ca. fl.804) *Jiwen* 紀聞 (Threads of Stories Heard), which says, "With its dawn in the city of Shaan, an open undeveloped area of land was selected, Longguang si 龍光寺 was built there, and an infirmary was also constructed, which always cared for many hundreds of sick people".[279] But, by the end of the Tang dynasty, the compassion-field infirmaries managed by Buddhist monasteries were already starting to deteriorate, and were unable to show the full extensive nature they previously had.

### 3.3 *Monastery Boarding Houses in the Tang Dynasty*

Monasteries and temples are the homes of the Buddhist community, the four assemblies of disciples, and itinerant monastics can stay and board at any Buddhist monastery. However, following the deep penetration of Buddhism into general society, monasteries gradually started to have laity come to live and eat there. In order to provide convenience to government officials and the educated classes, they slowly developed the social function of boarding houses.

During the period of the Northern and Southern dynasties, temples began accepting outside guests. In the time of Yongchu (420–422) during the Liu Song dynasty, the hermit from Mount Lu, Zhou Xuzhi 周續之 (377–423), entered the capital, "lodging at Anle si 安樂寺".[280] During the Liang dynasty, the grandson of Emperor Gaodi (r. 479–482) of the Southern Qi, Xiao Zifan 蕭子範 (486–549), had no residence in which to live, and so dwelled at the monastics' quarters of Zhaoti si 招提寺 in Jiankang. Another grandson, Xiao Ziyun 蕭子雲 (487–549), also dwelled at Xianyun si 顯雲寺 in Jinling during the chaotic period of Hou Jing 侯景 (503–552), where he starved to death.[281] During the Northern Qi, Li Gai 李概 (ca. fl. 554) sent emissaries to the Chen dynasty, and saw that "south of the Yangzi there are many guests who stay at monasteries",[282] from which we can see that in the last years of the southern dynasties it was a very common phenomenon that officials and the public lodged at Buddhist

279 *Taiping guangji* 95.508: 昉於陝城中, 選空曠地造龍光寺, 又建病坊, 常養病者數百人.

280 *Song shu* 93.2280: 館於安樂寺.

281 *Nan shi* 42.1071, 1076.

282 *Bei shi* 33.1212: 江南多以僧寺停客.

FIGURE 22 The scriptural hall at Qinglian Monastery 青蓮寺 in Jincheng 晉城, Shanxi, dated to the Tang (618-907).

monasteries. During the time of Northern dynasty Emperor Xiaowu (r. 532–534) of Wei, the Chief Administrator (*puye* 僕射) Wei Lan'gen 魏蘭根 (486–545) was afraid of committing an offense, and "left his house to take sanctuary at a monastery".[283] Emperor Wenxuan (r. 550–559) of the Northern Qi indulged in drinking alcohol. But the Director of the Chancellery (*shizhong* 侍中) Gao Dezheng 高德正 (d.u.) often rebuked him, which made Emperor Wenxuan displeased. Gao Dezheng "was very anxious and afraid and very quickly moved to seclude himself away in a Buddhist monastery to train in sitting meditation as his back up plan".[284] Non-monastic residents who dwelled at Buddhist monasteries during the northern dynasties were mainly high officials and from politically influential families. Monasteries thus had a function of serving as sanctuaries and retreats, which was rather different from the function of housing guests as seen in the southern dynasties.

In the rapid development of Buddhism during the Tang dynasty, monasteries served as one of the centres for the entire society and carried many social and community functions. With monasteries acting as lodges, the greatest source of guests were scholars and literati. Following the popularity of the imperial examination system, a great number of candidates dwelled for a while at

283 *Bei Qi shu* 23.331: 去宅避於寺.
284 *Bei shi* 31.1139: 甚憂懼, 乃移疾, 屏居佛寺, 兼學坐禪, 爲退身之計.

monasteries in various locations as they participated in the imperial examination process. The *Tang Huiyao*, fascicle seventy-six, states:

> Decree of the third month of the third year of Yuanhe (808): Those with plans to return by night, but [who] are unable to go back, will stay the night at Guangzhai si. Once the examinees have finished their tasks, officials who have been invigilators for the examinations, and those accompanying, etcetera, will also stay the night at Baoshou si 保壽寺. All of them will rely on the imperial insignia guards for inspection of the officials to deliver them to their quarters. These matters should be done without talking and disturbance.[285]

Because the imperial examinations often ran into the night, those students who were unable to return to their dwellings spent the night at the Guangzhai si lodge. Examiners, other officials, and those who accompanied the students had to wait until the examination was finished. It was arranged for them to spend the night at Baoshou si. Nobody was permitted to talk or make noise.

From the period of Dali (766–779) up until the end of the Tang, it was very popular for the lettered classes to stay at Buddhist monasteries, and there was the fashion of poetry and poetic repartee. In the *Quan Tang shi* 全唐詩 (Complete collection of Tang poems) there are several hundred "Poems of Dwelling at Monasteries", which shows the literati scholars' travels of "reflections roaming rivers and lakes", their wandering around and interconnecting paths, wherein they very often used Buddhist monasteries as chalets.[286] "I often sojourn at the mountain temple when I wander; A brief spell from the city lasts over a week".[287] This is a classic example of the practice of staying at monasteries. In addition, sometimes artists and friends would all dwell together in a monastery, which was called a "lodging party". During these "lodging parties", the scholarly friends would toast each other beneath the moon, recite poems, and hum verses, sharing their friendship and sentiments. Tang dynasty "Buddhist monastery lodging parties" were a kind of cultural phenomenon which drew the attention of people in the Song dynasty. In the *Wenyuan yinghua* 文苑英華 (Finest Blossoms in the Garden of Literature) there is a special

285 *Tang huiyao* 76.1649:
元和三年三月敕：制舉人試訖, 有逼夜納策, 計不得歸者, 並於光宅寺止宿. 應巡檢勾當官吏, 並隨從人等, 待舉人納策畢, 並赴保壽寺止宿. 仍各仰金吾衛使差人監引, 送至宿所, 如勾當, 勿令喧雜.

286 Zhang, *Wenhua shi*, 1020.

287 *Quan Tang shi* 459.1168: 山寺每遊多寄宿, 都城暫出即經旬.

collection of "Lodging Party Poems".[288] The collection shows the particular kind of atmosphere and sentiment of these educated artists. For example, Liu Deren's 劉得仁 (fl. 823–838) "Dongye yu Cai Jiaoshu su Wuke shangren yuan" 冬夜與蔡校書宿無可上人院 (Lodging Together with Editor Cai at the Place of Master Wuke over a Winter's Night):

> Buddhist and Confucian lodge for the night together,
> The freezing winter window ever clearer.
> Forgetting our artifices too long in the world,
> Talking and conversing until the dawn.
> The moon upside down, the tall pine's shadow,
> The wind blows a chime on the bell bowl.
> Even the gate to the truth is illusion,
> There is no need to awaken to this gliding life.[289]

Liu Deren was "in and out of the examination hall for thirty years",[290] but was unable to ascend to a position. During a winter's night at Tianxian si 天仙寺 in the capital, the two of them mutually discussed the ups and downs of their lives' journeys.

The officials, examination candidates, literati, and even the common population, often lodged at monasteries for various shorter and longer periods of time. As Yancong's 彥琮 (557–610/611) *Xu Gaoseng zhuan* biography records, Yancong returned to Zhaojun 趙郡 to teach the *Wuliangshou jing*, and at the time Wang Shao 王邵 (d.u.) was in charge of the military at Zhaojun: "Staying for the night at the monastery halls, heard of and admired, respect in friendship deepened".[291] The *Zizhi tongjian* records that in the fourth year of Kaiyuan (716), "Yao Chong 姚崇 (651–721) had no residence to stay in and so lodged at Wangji si 罔極寺, taking leave on the pretext of illness. The emperor sent messengers—dozens of them each day—to inquire of his living and eating conditions".[292] Wangji si was a monastery built in the first year of Shenglong (705) by Wu Zetian for the Taiping Princess at Daning ward 大寧坊, and was famous for its peony flowers.

288 *Wenyuan yinghua* 217.1080-1086.

289 *Wenyuan yinghua* 217.1084:
儒釋偶同宿, 夜窗寒更清. 忘機於世久, 晤談恐天明.
月倒高松影, 風旋一磬聲. 真門猶是幻, 不用覺浮生.

290 *Tang Zhiyan* 10.108: 出入舉場三十年.

291 *Xu Gaoseng zhuan*, *T* no. 2060, 50: 2.436b24-25: 寓居寺宇, 聽而仰之, 友敬彌至.

292 *Zizhi tongjian* 211.6723: 姚崇無居第, 寓居罔極寺, 以病痁謁告, 上遣使問飲食起居狀, 日數十輩.

At the same time, Buddhist monasteries spread throughout the entire nation, naturally became pilgrimage stops for both monastics and lay devotees, and simultaneously served as boarding houses for itinerant guests. Huixu's 慧序 (d.u.) *Xu Gaoseng zhuan* biography records that Huixu was travelling between Liang (present day Hanzhong in Shaanxi) and Yi (present day Chengdu in Sichuan), and saw conflict at Bailao Keep, "where everyone returned to",[293] but there was no monastery. "The monastics and laity had nowhere as refuge, coming and going with nowhere to stay".[294] After this, Huixu built Puti si 菩提寺 at the entrance to the keep, which was "used to receive guests from afar, so travellers relied on it".[295] Ennin's *Nittō guhō junrei gyōki* records that during the late Tang period, a "*Putong yuan*" 普通院 (universal courtyard) in Ji 冀 and Jin 晉 was laid out as a travellers' rest stop. The so-called "universal courtyard" was a place where "there was always rice and porridge, whether monastics or laity came to gather, there was a monastic dormitory. Rice was given immediately when there was any, but not given when there was none. But that did not stop monastics and laity lodging there".[296] This was a kind of free and open rest stop. The eastern route was a road over the mountains, starting from Xingtang county 行唐縣 in Hengzhou 恆州 (present day Hebei, Xingtang), one then progresses through Mount Huang 黃山 Bahui si 八會寺 with universal courtyard (twenty-five miles), to (another twenty miles) the universal courtyard in Liushi 劉使, and eventually reach the final stop universal courtyard, entering the area of Mount Wutai. The starting point of the southern route was the universal courtyard at Daxian Peak 大賢嶺, then at each point along the way through Wutai county 五臺縣 Jian'an si 建安寺, Dingxiang county 定襄縣 Qiyan si 七岩寺, then straight through to the universal courtyard at the old city; then from the old city "travelling fifteen miles, one reaches the halls of Taiyuan", which was the road out of the mountains. Therefore, in famous mountains and ancient temples, Buddhist monasteries had systematic layouts of guest houses, showing the enormous scope of Buddhist monasteries housing and benefitting guests. Universal courtyards were still prevalent in the Song dynasty, and the *Da Song sengshi lüe* states: "There are many universal [courtyards] now on Mount Wutai".[297]

Staying at Buddhist monasteries became an impressive fashion, but with both monastics and laity dwelling there it was easy for problems to arise.

293 *Xu Gaoseng zhuan, T* no. 2060, 50: 24.638c20: 四方所歸.

294 *Xu Gaoseng zhuan, T* no. 2060, 50: 24.638c20: 道俗栖投, 往還莫寄.

295 *Xu Gaoseng zhuan, T* no. 2060, 50: 24.638c21: 用接遠賓, 故行侶賴之.

296 *Nittō guhō junrei kōki* 2.102: 常有飯粥, 不論僧俗來集, 便僧房宿. 有飯即與, 無飯不與, 不防僧俗赴宿.

297 *Da Song sengshi lüe, T* no. 2126, 54: 1.237a11: 普通, 今五臺山有多所也.

Daoxuan said: "With laity enjoying and using monastic quarters and dormitories, there is shameless damage and destruction done".[298] Moreover, with the increase in numbers dwelling there, itinerant monastics often had no place to hang their kit and lodge. Ennin, in his *Nittō guhō junrei kōki,* recorded that at Kaiyuan si 開元寺 in Dengzhou 登州, Shandong province: "Filled with official guests in place, there were no empty rooms. When monastics came, there was nowhere for them".[299] In the eighth month of the first year of Baoying (762), Emperor Daizong of Tang issued the "Jinduan gongsi jie siguan juzhi zhao" 禁斷公私借寺觀居止詔 (Decree to Forbid Public or Private Dwelling in Monasteries and Temples):

> For the two religions of the Dao and the Śākyans, their function is in skillful guidance, their destination is in the forming of images, their essence is in worship of the icon. It has been heard that many dwell and stay in public and private Buddhist monasteries and Daoist temples in the cities and counties, which has caused corruption and debasement. This needs to be forbidden, and must be made clean and proper. At these monasteries and temples, apart from the three mainstays, and the old and sick who are unable to support themselves, the remainder must walk the path and perform worship daily at the two times. If any are lax in this, they are to be equally punished.[300]

In the third month of the fifth year of Zhenyuan (789), Emperor Dezong issued the "Xiuqi siguan zhao" 修葺寺觀詔 (Decree to Repair Monasteries and Temples): "The two religions of the Śākyans and Daoists benefit and aid living beings, so their accommodation buildings and practices must be dignified and clean. From now, monasteries and temples in the cities may not have guests staying the night. Damage to buildings are all to be repaired".[301] The *Fozu tongji,* fascicle forty-two, records that in the third year of Dazhong of Emperor Xuanzong (r. 846–859), regional inspector Pei Xiu 裴休 (791–864) said: "Monasteries and temples all over the country are trampled and encroached upon by official

298 *Sifen lü shanfan buqüe xingshi chao, T* no. 1804, 40:3.135a2: 僧房堂諸俗受用,毀壞損辱,情無所愧.

299 *Nittō guhō junrei kōki* 2.86: 盡安置官客,無閑房,有僧人來,無處安置.

300 *Quan Tang wen* 46.219:
道釋二教,用存善誘,至於像設,必在尊崇.如聞州縣公私,多借寺觀居止,因茲褻黷.切宜禁斷,務令清肅.其寺觀除三綱並老病不能支持者,餘並仰每日二時行道禮拜.如有弛慢,並量加科罰.

301 *Quan Tang wen* 52.244: 釋道二教,福利群生,館宇經行,必資嚴潔.自今州府寺觀,不得宿客居住.屋宇破壞,各隨事修葺.

guests. From now on, they are not permitted to dwell at the monasteries and temples. Transgressors will be heavily punished. So it is regulated".[302] The "Jin tianxia siguan tingke zhi" 禁天下寺觀停客制 (Edict of Forbidding lodging at all Monasteries and Temples) drafted by Chang Gun 常衮 (729–783) on behalf of the imperial court describes in detail the state of things at the time:

> Decree:
> The Śākyan religion takes beneficial teaching as its root, The Daoist tradition takes managing the country as primary. They prevent evil, encourage good, and make death and birth equal. With loving humaneness, they beautify and benefit all beneath heaven. Many are protected, and benevolence is profound. Therefore, they have been venerated over dynasties, which have not been changed. I list out my virtuous ancestors from ancient times, celebrating the grand fate of the nation. The holy sages of the west have come to bless this land, to whom we are forever most grateful, and dare not forget our sincerity. To reach the substance of the truth requires refined purity, and that admired by vulgar fashions is not worthy of any pride. As we have heard, many of the nation's monasteries and temples have military men and government officials dwelling there, their familiarity has tainted those places, which they have never feared. The Buddhist monks in black and the Daoist priests in yellow are secluded away, their shrines and halls in ruins, their beds in public spaces, their kitchens in empty corridors. Thinking of the long term consequences, one cannot help but be exasperated. From now on, this must be stopped. Those military men, head officers of the cities and counties, should discuss with the generals, and move to another secluded location. Any place where sacred statues have been damaged should be repaired and mended. In any location that houses the gods, that hosts ritual services, that draws religious effects, that benefits human lives, if there is damage it must also be repaired. The ruler uses purity to regulate the law, the sages use the spiritual path to establish the teachings. Where there is vigorous intent, the aim will be reached. It is not by seeking blessings for myself, that will bring the auspicious to the people. The proclamation of the sagely directive is to be constantly kept in mind.[303]

302 *Fozu tongji*, *T* no. 2035, 49: 42.387a10-11: 天下寺觀, 多爲官僚寄客蹂踐, 今後不得在寺居止, 違者重罰, 制可.

303 *Quan Tang wen* 410.1861:
敕：釋教本以助化, 道家先於理國, 懲惡勸善, 以齊死生, 薰然慈仁, 美利天下, 所庇者大, 所益者深, 故歷代崇尙而弗易也. 朕以元元烈祖, 慶我昌運；西方聖人, 福茲下土. 常所盡敬, 敢忘致誠. 且至真之體, 尙於精潔, 流俗所尊, 不宜褻慢. 如

The demands of the Buddhist world and the policies of government both reflect the extreme popularity of government and private guests staying at Buddhist monasteries at that time, which had already seriously affected the image of dignity and purity of Buddhism.

## 4 Public Lectures and Illustrative Narrative in the Tang and Five Dynasties

### 4.1 *Ritual Procedures for Lecturing on* Sūtras *in the Tang and Five Dynasties*

Ritual procedures for lecturing on *sūtra*s (*jiangjing* 講經) in the Tang dynasty had there origins in chanting (*fanbai* 梵唄), reading aloud (*zhuandu* 轉讀), preaching (*changdao* 唱導) and intoning (*changdu* 唱讀) of the texts, as developed in the Jin and Liu Song periods.[304] When Daoan was setting up the monastic regulations during the Jin dynasty, "The regulations and rules set up for the monks and nuns, the constitution of the Buddha Dharma, are given in three items: One, methods for walking the incense, ascending to the seat, setting up the *sūtra*, and starting the lecture".[305] Here, there are regulations for lecturing *sūtra*s. However, due to limits in resources, scholars always had difficulties in precisely determining the actual regulations for lecturing on *sūtras* in historical times. Discovered among the manuscripts of Dunhuang were large quantities of texts of lecturing on *sūtra*s and rituals for public lectures, which have enabled us to go back to the ritual procedures for Dharma services that lecture on *sūtras*. From this, we can return to the actual scenes of Dharma services in those ancient times.

Due to differences in audiences and function, *sūtra* lecturing in the Tang period can be divided into monastic lectures (*sengjiang* 僧講) and public lectures (*sujiang* 俗講). In the *Guan Puxian pusa xingfa jing ji* 觀普賢菩薩行法

---

聞天下寺觀, 多被軍士及官吏諸客居止, 狎而黷之, 曾不畏忌. 緇黃屏竄, 堂居毀撤, 寢處於眾設之門, 庖廚於廊廡之下. 緬然遐想, 慨嘆良深, 自今已後, 切宜禁斷. 其軍士委州縣長吏與本將商量, 移於穩便處安置. 其官吏諸客等, 頻有處分, 自合遵承, 仰敕到當時發遣. 應尊像有損壞處, 俾隨事修補; 其有諸神所居, 載在祀典, 靈跡昭著, 福及生人者, 如有毀廢, 亦宜增葺. 且王者以清凈統法, 聖人以神道設教, 精意所在, 感而遂通. 非僥福於朕躬, 斯降祥於黎庶, 申明詔旨, 用悉勞懷.

304 Zhang Gong (*Wenhua shi*, 459) believes that the texts and intonations belonging to the categories of lecturing and singing constitute the origin of public lectures and the beginning of public lectures in the Tang Dynasty was chanting in medieval Buddhism.

305 *Gaoseng zhuan*, *T* no. 2059, 50: 5.353b24-25: 所製僧尼軌範, 佛法憲章, 條爲三例：一曰行香上座, 上經上講之法.

FIGURE 23 *Da Boniepan Jing* 大般涅槃經 (Skt. *Mahāparinirvāṇa sūtra*), carved in the Xiaonanhai 小南海 grotto complex, Anyang 安陽.

經記 (Accounts on the *sūtra* of Meditating on Samantabhadra Bodhisattva, *T* 2194), Enchin 円珍 (814–891) states:

> As for "lecture" (*jiang* 講), there are two types of lecture in the land of Tang.
> One, public lecture. That is, prepared on the third month of the year, with men and women in attendance. An exhortation to give things, the provision of monastic items. Thus it is called a public lecture (as the monastics do not attend). And so forth.
> Two, monastic lecture. A specialist lecture at the month of the summer retreat. (Lay people do not attend, and if they do, the monastics will be reprimanded by the officials.)
> The above two types of monastery event are applied for from management, who judge on whether to carry it out or not. (That is, through imperial request, external request to the city. Length of one day.)
> If it is not done in this way, the monastery will be reprimanded by the officials. And so forth.[306]

Therefore, public lectures are specifically for the lay household devotees, whereas the monastic lectures strictly prohibit the laity from entering. The two are thus complementary names with respect to their target audiences, though certainly they were never quite so absolute in their divisions. Although the audiences of the two were different, the ritual procedure for them was quite similar. Thus, we can use the Dunhuang manuscripts and other records in order to examine the steps of the ritual procedure for lecturing on *sūtra*s.

Following the discoveries of the Dunhuang manuscripts, the international academic community has already achieved some excellent research results concerning the system of public lectures in the Tang period. This was previously studied by Ōtani Kōshō 大谷光照 (1911–2002), Naba Toshisada 那波利貞 (1890–1970), Fukui Fumimasa 福井文雅 (1934–2017), Michibata Ryōshū 道端良秀, Xiang Da 向達 (1900–1966), Sun Kaidi 孫楷第 (1898–1986), Wang Caiwen

306 *Foshuo guan Puxian pusa xingfa jing ji*, *T* no. 2194, 56: 1.227c23-27:
言講者,唐土兩講：
一俗講,即年三月就緣修之,只會男女,勸之輸物,充造寺資,故言俗講（僧不集也）云云；
三僧講,安居月傳講是 (不集俗人類,若集之,僧被官責).
上來兩寺,皆申所司 (就經奏,外申州也.一日爲期),蒙判行之.若不然者,寺被官責云云.

王文才, Jiang Boqin 姜伯勤, and Zhang Gong 張弓.[307] However, compared to public lectures, the research on monastic lectures has been extremely weak, and so we intend to reconstruct the system for lecturing the *sūtras* to monastics. In the *Nittō guhō junrei kōki*, Ennin records that on the twenty-second day of the eleventh month of the fourth year of Kaicheng (839.12.31), he describes in detail the situation for three types of *sūtra* lecture rites, namely the "*Chŏk san wŏn kang kyŏng ŭi sik*" 赤山院講經儀式 (Jeoksan Court *sūtra* lecture ritual, Chin. *Chishanyuan jiangjing yishi*), the "*Sin la il il kang ŭi sik*" 新羅一日講儀式 (Silla one day lecture ritual, Chin. *Xinluo yirijiang yishi*), and the "*Sin la song kyŏng ŭi sik* 新羅誦經儀式" (Silla *sūtra* recitation ritual, Chin. *Xinluo songjing yishi*).[308] Following the discoveries of P.3849, *Sujiang yishi* 俗講儀式 (Ritual for Public Lectures)[309] (S.4417 is basically similar), and various texts on *sūtra* lecturing from Dunhuang,[310] we can further supplement any inadequacies of Ennin's records (Appendix 2.4).

Other than this, in the *Sifen lü xingshi chao zichi ji* 四分律行事鈔資持記 (Supporting Notes on the *Sifen lü xingshi chao*), "Shi daosu pian" 釋導俗篇 (Section of Explanation on Guiding the Laity), Yuanzhao 元照 (1048–1116) describes the "ten steps" of lecturing the *sūtras*:

> One, prostrations to the Three Jewels.
> Two, ascending to the high throne.
> Three, striking the bell bowl to silence the community (now many strike wood).
> Four, chant of praise. (The text is written by oneself, though now some include those written by others. When the chanting stops, hold the censor and chant the *gāthās* for beseeching, etc.)
> Five, the teaching proper.
> Six, proceed and stop according to the situation, with questions and listening according to the Dharma, delighting in listening and replying. (If the text is not clear, the junior monastic will now recite it.)

---

307 Ōtani, *Bukkyō girei*; Naba, *Shakai bunkashi*; Fukui, "Soshiki naiyō"; Michibata, *Bukkyōshi*; Xiang, *Sujiang*; Sun, "Tangdai sujiang"; Wang, "Sujiang"; Jiang, *Dunhuang*; Zhang, *Han Tang Fosi*.

308 *Nittō guhō junrei kōki* 2.73-74.

309 Huang, *Dunhuang baozang*, 131: 304.

310 In Huang Zheng & Zhang Yongquan's *Dunhuang bianwen jiaozhu*, several *sūtra* lecture texts are included: *Changxing sinian Zhongxingdian Yingshengjie jiangjingwen*, *Jin'gang bore boluomi jiangjingwen*, Fo *shuo Amituo jing jiangjingwen* (3 fascs.), *Miaofa lianhua jing jiangjingwen* (4 fascs.), *Weimojie jing jiangjingwen* (7 fascs.), *Shuang'en ji*, *Fo shuo guan Mile pusa shangsheng Doushuaitian jing jiangjingwen*, *Fumu enzhong jiangjingwen* (2 fascs.), *Yulanpen jing jiangjingwen*. Cf. Huang & Zhang, *Bianwen*.

Seven, after teaching, the dedication.
Eight, again chant of praise.
Nine, descending from the seat, and prostrations in farewell. The [*Xu Gao*]*seng zhuan* states: When the Zhou monk Sengmiao 僧妙 (ca. 466–581) lectured, the junior monastics had to join palms and repent, saying: The Buddha's meaning is difficult to understand, it is not fathomable by ordinary common people. Now it is being taught, we receive it from the ancient teachers, and dare not break the transmission. I beg the community that with respect to the meaning of this Dharma, whether they agree or disagree, it will give happiness.
At the very start, the bell is struck to assemble the community.
This gives a total of ten steps.
Now, when lecturing, one should use this method.[311]

Because Yuanzhao only raises a couple of items for an overview of the ritual procedure, it is thus difficult to understand the detailed steps of the ritual. However, combining all the textual sources together, we are able to have some comprehension of these Tang dynasty ritual procedures for lecturing the *sūtras*.

### 4.1.1 Principle Members in *Sūtra*-Lecturing Dharma Services

From Ennin's records, we can see that in the *sūtra* lecturing Dharma service, apart from the venerable who actually lectures on the *sūtra*, there are certainly other monastics, such as the reciter, the rector, the chanter, and others, who are there to preside over the Dharma service. In Ratnamati's (Lenamoti 勒那摩提, ca. 477–569) *Xu Gaoseng zhuan* biography, it states: "Although the personnel of the Dharma service cannot perform it alone, the reciter, the incense and fire master, the rector, and the chanter, are all necessary".[312] In Sengyi's 僧意 (ca. fifth century) biography, it mentions that at the time of Sengyi's death, "The reciter lived in Guangzhou, and apart from this the incense and fire

311 *Sifen lü xingshi chao zichi ji*, *T* no. 1805, 40: 3.404b4-12:
初禮三寶；二升高座；三打磬靜眾（今多打木）；四贊唄（文是自作, 今並他作, 聲絕秉爐, 說偈祈請等）；五正說；六觀機進止, 問聽如法, 樂聞應說（文中不明, 下座今加續之）；七說竟回向；八復作贊唄；九下座禮辭. 僧傳云：周僧妙每講下座, 必合掌懺悔云：佛意難知, 豈凡夫所測, 今所說者, 傳受先師, 未敢專輒. 乞大眾, 於斯法義, 若是若非, 布施歡喜. 最初鳴鐘集眾, 總爲十法, 今時講導宜依此式.

312 *Xu Gaoseng zhuan*, *T* no. 2060, 50: 1.429a22-23: 雖然法事所資, 獨不能建, 都講、香火、維那、梵唄咸亦須之.

master and the chanter were scattered in other cities".[313] Therefore, in the *sūtra* lecture Dharma service, the most important members are the *jiangshi* 講師 (lecturer), the *dujiang* 都講 (reciter), the *weino* 維那 (rector), the *baishi* 唄師 (chanter), the *xianghuo* 香火 (incense and fire master), the *sanhua shi* 散花師 (flower scatterer), and so forth.

During the *sūtra* lecture Dharma service, of course the most important person involved is the lecturer. However, the title given to the lecturer is not standardized across the various textual sources. In the *Nittō guhō junrei kōki*, fascicle one, Ennin states:

> There is also a venerable who is a *huasu fashi* 化俗法師 (teacher of the public), which is the same as that called the "flying teacher" in this country. They teach the principles that the world is impermanent, dissatisfactory and empty, guiding gentleman and lady disciples, which is why they are called the teacher of the public. They lecture on the *sūtra*s, treatises, *Vinaya*, records, commentaries, and so forth, so they are called the *zuozhu* 座主 (chairman), *heshang* 和尚 (abbot), or *dade* 大德 (virtuous venerable). If they gather the mind, they are called a Chan master, or man of the path. One who focuses on upholding the *Vinaya* is named a virtuous *Vinaya* venerable, and if they teach it, are called a *lü zuozhu* 律座主 (*Vinaya* chairman). Other titles follow in a similar way.[314]

Therefore, the *sūtra* lecturer can also be called a *huasu fashi*, *zuozhu*, *heshang*, or *dade*. However, to be called a "*huasu fashi*" does not mean that they have lower status than a venerable who specializes in the *sūtra*s or *Vinaya*.[315]

The reciter is a special position within the *sūtra* lecturing Dharma service, with the job of turning, or reading aloud, the *sūtra* text. Wang Wencai believes that the reading of the *sūtra* by the reciter is in accordance with the convention of the Confucian tradition.[316] In the discipleship traditions of the Han

---

313 *Xu Gaoseng zhuan*, *T* no. 2060, 50: 25.647a19-20: 其都講住在光州, 自餘香火、唄匿散在他邑.

314 *Nittō guhō junrei kōki* 1.21:
又有化俗法師, 與本國道 " 飛教化師 " 同也. 說世間無常、苦、空、之理, 化導男弟子、女弟子, 呼道化俗法師也. 講經、論、律、記、疏等, 名爲座主、和尙、大德. 若納衣收心, 呼爲禪師, 亦爲道者. 持律偏多, 名律大德, 講爲律座主, 餘亦準爾也.

315 Wang Wencai ("Sujiang", 102) maintains that *huasu fashi* is a similar honorific title to other titles, so it is not inferior. It is not very possible that there are monks who only preach to the public and monks that only lecture to the monastics. "*huasu*" and "*fashi*" both indicate respect.

316 Wang, "Sujiang", 102.

period, masters of the classics (*jing* 經) had lecture transmissions by reciters of the classics who assisted the classics masters themselves. Hou Ba's 侯霸 (?–37) biography in the *Hou Han shu* 後漢書 (Book of Later Han) states, "The master served the grand governor of Jiujiang 九江, Fang Yuan 房元 (d.u.) to study the *Guliang chunqiu* 穀梁春秋 (Guliang Commentary on the Spring and Autumn Annals), and was the reciter of [Fang] Yuan".[317] Sun Quan's 孫權 (182–252) biography in the *Sanguo zhi* 三國志 (Records of the Three Kingdoms) states, "In the first month of the second year [of Huanglong] (230), the Wei State constructed the new city of Hefei 合肥 and invited a reciter and *jijiu* 祭酒 (libationer) to teach and educate his sons".[318] The reciter is the assistant of the libationer. Since the six dynasties period, the reciter is always on the lecturing podium chanting the classic text (*jing*). Zu Ying's 祖瑩 (?–535) biography in the *Wei shu* 魏書 (Book of Wei) states:

> When the academician Zhang Tianlong 張天龍 (d.u) lectured on the Shang shu 尙書 (Book of Documents), he was chosen as the reciter. The student disciples all gathered. [Zu] Ying read through the night to exhaustion and did not realize that the dawn had come. The lecture was hurried at pace, and thus he took the Quli 曲禮 (i.e., first fascicle of the Liji) [which] belonged to his roommates Zhao Jun 趙郡 (d.u) and Li Xiaoyi 李孝怡 (d.u) by mistake to his seat. The academician was strict on decorum, so [Zu Ying] dared not return [to get the book]. He placed the [Qu]li before him, and recited the Shang shu three times, without missing a single character.[319]

We can see from this that Zu Ying's position was as a reciter, and his job was to recite the *Shang shu* that was to be lectured before the classics lecturer began the actual lecture itself. After this, both Buddhism and Daoism utilized this system of having a reciter from the Confucian tradition.

However, seeking the origins of the term "*dujiang*" from the perspective of linguistics can also give us some important insights.[320] In the *Da mingdu jing* 大明度經 (*Sūtra* on the Transition by Way of the Great Enlightenment, *T* 225),

317 *Hou Han shu* 56.884: 師事九江太守房元, 治《穀梁春秋》, 爲元都講.

318 *Hou Han shu* 47.1203: （黃龍）二年春正月, 魏作合肥新城, 詔立都講、祭酒, 以教學諸子.

319 *Wei shu* 82.2376:
博士張天龍講《尙書》, 選爲都講. 生徒悉集, 瑩夜讀書勞倦, 不覺天曉. 催講既切, 遂誤持同房生趙郡李孝怡《曲禮》卷上座. 博士嚴毅, 不敢還取, 乃置《禮》於前, 誦《尙書》三篇, 不遺一字.

320 Fukui, "Tokō".

fascicle one, we can see the translation idiom "*dujiang*": "Śāriputra said: Just as Subhūti is a *fa dujiang* 法都講 (Dharma reciter), the greatest who cannot be matched".[321] Corresponding with this, in alternate translation by Kumārajīva, in fascicle one of the *Xiaopin bore boleomi jing* 小品般若波羅蜜經 (Shorter Version of the *Mahāprajñāpāramitā-sūtra*, *T* 227), we have: "Śāriputra said: Excellent! Excellent! Subhūti, you are foremost among those people who are *shuofa ren* 說法人 (speakers of the Dharma)".[322] So "*fa dujiang*" is another translation for "*shuofa ren*". The *Da mingdu jing* is a version of the *Prajñā*[*pāramitā*] in 8,000 verses family, of which in the Sanskrit text we can find the original term is "*dharma-kathika*".[323]

The term "*fa dujiang*" can first be seen in Zhu Fahu's translation of the *Zheng fahua jing*[324] in the Western Jin period, for which Kumārajīva's corresponding translation term is "*shuofa ren*", which was originally "*dharma-kathika*".[325] The "*shuofa ren*" is a person who speaks and lectures on the Buddha Dharma, which in Han Chinese translation is usually "*fashi*" 法師 (Dharma master). In fact, as speakers of the Dharma, Dharma masters and reciters do have definite distinctions. "*Fashi*" originally was "*dharma-bhāṇaka*", which means to chant out the Buddha Dharma. The phrase "*dujiang*" corresponds to the Han Chinese word "*chang*" 唱 (chant). Therefore, in the *Fanyi mingyi daji* 翻譯名義大集 (Great Compendium of Translation Terms and Meanings), "*dharma-kathika*" is translated into Han Chinese as "*xuanfazhe*" 宣法者 (preacher of Dharma), and "*dharma-bhāṇaka*" is translated into Han Chinese as "*shuofa*" 說法 (speaker of Dharma).[326]

Therefore, because the "*dujiang*" (reciter) in the Confucian tradition is also one who lectures on the meaning of the classic texts, it is very appropriate to be the translation of "preacher of Dharma" (*dharma-kathika*) in Chinese. Thus, "*dharma-kathika*" is translated as "*dujiang*". However, this is just a borrowing of this term at the time of translation, and does not entail taking the Confucian system of reciters into Buddhism itself.[327]

During the *sūtra* lecturing Dharma service, when the reciter reads aloud the *sūtra* for the lecturer, they use a particular tone to turn the *sūtra*. The *Xu Gaoseng zhuan*, fascicle fifty, states: "In olden times, after the illustrious Shi

321 *Da mingdu wuji jing*, *T* no. 225, 8: 1.481c26-27: 秋露子曰：如善業爲法都講, 最不可及.

322 *Xiaopin boreboluomi jing*, *T* no. 227, 8: 1.539c20-21: 舍利弗言：善哉, 善哉！須菩提, 汝於說法人中, 最爲第一.

323 Vaidya, "*Aṣṭasāhasrikā-Praiñāpāramitā*".

324 *Zheng fahua jing*, *T* no. 263, 9: 8.95b29-c1.

325 Karashima, *Shiten*, 120.

326 Sakaki, *Siyiduijiao*, 199.

327 Fukui, "Soshiki naiyō", 378.

Daoan had stationed himself on his seat whenever he lectured, the ever present reciter, and others, turned the *sūtra* for sentient beings in three aspects".[328] Because reading the text out loud required the use of a specific tune, the term often used is "*changjing*" 唱經 (chant the *sūtra*), as stated in the above mentioned *Sin la il il kang ŭi sik*: "the south seat chants the title of the *sūtra*, that is, chanting the *sūtra* drawing it out long, with the tune taking many twists and turns".[329] In the *Xu Gaoseng zhuan*, we can see "the gods and deities and so forth, all solemnly turn their ears to all lecturing and chanting of texts",[330] and that "he (i.e., Lingzhi 靈智, 560–634) was always [Ling]yu's 靈裕 (518–605) reciter, clearly chanting the text, aptly looking to the sentiment".[331] Sometimes in the *sūtra* lecturing Dharma service, the reciter also acts as an "exegete", making queries and issuing questions to the lecturer. In Zhidun's 支遁 (314–366) *Gaoseng zhuan* biography, it is stated:

> Going out in the evening to lecture on the Weimo[jie] jing, [Zhi]dun was the Dharma master, Xu Xun 許詢 (?–361/362) was the reciter. If [Zhi]dun penetrated the meaning of a given term, the audience all said Xun had not posed any questions. If Xun gave a question, they then said that Dun would be unable to answer. It continued on in this manner until the end, neither side having exhausted their ability.[332]

Xu Xun was the reciter, who directed queries to Zhidun, which Zhidun must answer. Back and forth in this way would bring about a high point in the *sūtra* lecturing Dharma service.

The rector is an important position within the monastery. They manage various tasks of the *saṃgha* within the monastery, as described in the *Xingshi chao*:

> In the Shisong [lü], at times nobody knew the time limits in the *saṃgha* quarters. When chanting, they went up to the striking of the gaṇṭā [wooden board]. Also, nobody swept, mopped or wiped down the eating area of the lecture hall. Nobody continued to prepared the seat or teach people

328 *Xu Gaoseng zhuan*, *T* no. 2060, 50: 5.463b6-7: 昔彌天釋道安, 每講於定坐後, 常使都講等爲含靈轉經三契.

329 *Nittō guhō junrei kōki* 2.74.

330 *Xu Gaoseng zhuan*, *T* no. 2060, 50: 15.542b24: 然都講唱文, 諸天神等皆斂容傾耳.

331 *Xu Gaoseng zhuan*, *T* no. 2060, 50: 20.588c6-7: 常爲裕之都講, 辨唱明衷, 允愜望情.

332 *Gaoseng zhuan*, *T* no. 2059, 50: 4.348c25-28:
晩出山陰講《維摩經》, 遁爲法師, 許詢爲都講, 遁通一義, 眾人咸謂詢無以昔難；詢設壹難, 亦謂遁不復能通. 如此至竟, 兩家不竭.

> to clean the fruits and vegetables, leaving insects inside when eaten. When eating and drinking, nobody served water. When the community was chatting and babbling, nobody snapped their fingers [to silence them]. The Buddha established the rector (*karmadāna*), who would chant to preserve order in the community. That is, the proper order of actions for the monastic staff. Traditionally, it is said to mean "one who delights the community (*yuezhong* 悅眾)".[333]

The rector position was originally established by the Buddha. Ancient Chinese monasteries set up three mainstays, namely, the *shangzuo* 上座 (senior monk), the *sizhu* 寺主 (monastery abbot), and the rector, with the rector directing the *saṃgha*. Therefore, the rector knows that striking the bell is an important responsibility when chanting. "The rector chimes the bell and holds the stick himself",[334] and "the rector on this day strikes the bell".[335]

Therefore, during the *sūtra* lecture Dharma service, it is the rector's job to strike the bell for lecturing the *sūtra*. Though, in the *Nittō guhō junrei kōki, Chŏk san wŏn kang kyŏng ŭi sik*, it is said: "… the rector comes forth, and before the high throne reads the reasons for requesting the assembly, as well as the individual names of the donors, and the items which have been donated. This request being completed, he then passes the form over to the lecturer".[336] The form which is read by the rector is the benediction text for the *sūtra* lecture, which explains the conditions and names of the patrons for the *sūtra* lecture Dharma service. During the Dharma service, the rector also has to proclaim aloud the benediction text.

The chanter mainly does the liturgical chanting. As the *Chŏk san wŏn kang kyŏng ŭi sik* says, "Then, a junior monastic does liturgical chanting, another maintains the Tang tune", "a monastic chants the *gāthā* on 'Dwelling in the world is like empty space'", and "a monastic chants the three prostrations".[337] Wang Wencai thinks that the monastic doing the liturgical chanting is the rector,[338] but this does not really describe the situation. This is because in the ritual the name for the rector is already given, so if it was the rector doing the

333 *Sifen lü shanfan buqüe xingshi chao, T* no. 1804, 40: 1.6b24-29: 十誦中, 時僧坊中無人知時限、唱時至及打犍稚. 又無人灑掃塗治講堂食處, 無人相續鋪床及教人凈果菜食中蟲, 飲食時無人行水, 眾亂語時無人彈指等, 佛令立維那. 聲論翻爲次第也, 謂知事之次第, 相傳云悅眾也.

334 *Xu Gaoseng zhuan, T* no. 2060, 50: 18.577b24: 維那鳴鐘而杵自折.

335 *Xu Gaoseng zhuan, T* no. 2060, 50: 25.646b2-3: 維那此日打鐘.

336 *Nittō guhō junrei kōki* 2.73.

337 *Nittō guhō junrei kōki* 2.73.

338 Wang, "Sujiang", 106.

liturgical chanting, it should just say that it is the rector, rather than stating "a monastic". Therefore, we think that here the "monastic" refers to the chanter. In S.2073, *Lushan Yuangong hua* 廬山遠公話 (Words of Master [Hui]yuan of Mount Lushan), it says, "the rector does liturgical chanting",[339] showing that the rector leads the chanting of praises and knows the order of procedures for such chanting, which is understandable.

The incense and fire master holds the incense and lights it during the Dharma service, and is equivalent to the modern monastery role of the *xiangdeng* 香燈 (incense and lamp [master]). Because there is also the scattering of flowers during the Dharma service, there is another who is the flower scatterer.

Therefore, in the *sūtra* lecture Dharma service, the principal actors are the lecturer, the reciter, the rector, the chanter, the incense and fire master, and the scatterer of flowers. Only by everyone performing their job can the *sūtra* lecturing Dharma service be carried out and successfully accomplished.

#### 4.1.2 Steps in the Ritual Procedures for *Sūtra* Lecturing in the Tang Dynasty

Ennin's records and the discoveries of Dunhuang manuscripts have brought about the possibility of recovering the original Tang dynasty ritual procedures for lecturing on the *sūtras*. Therefore, by generalizing the records of these textual sources and taking Ennin's notes as the base source, but comparing it to the Dunhuang manuscripts, we can reconstruct the steps of the ritual procedures for Tang dynasty *sūtra* lectures.

1. Striking the bell, entering the hall, prostrating to the Buddha, ascending to the seat.

The rector strikes the *sūtra* lecture bell, the community goes to the hall, and with the chanter leading the chanting, they invoke the Buddha's name together in unison. At the same time as the recitation of the Buddha's name, the lecturer and rector simultaneously ascend to their seats. After ascending to their seats, the chanter strikes the bowl bell to silence the community, and the chanting of the Buddha's name ends. Regarding the seats of the lecturer and reciter, the *Sin la il il kang ŭi sik* states: "The lecturer ascends to the north seat, and the reciter ascends to the south seat".[340] From this we can see that the seats set out for the Dharma service are separated into north and south. Tansui's 曇邃 (fl. 417) *Gaoseng zhuan* biography mentions that when Tansui and a disciple were invited by a *wu* spirit (*wushen* 塢神) to lecture on the *sūtras*,

339 Huang & Zhang, *Jiaozhu*, 264: 維那作梵.

340 *Nittō guhō junrei kōki* 2.73.

"there were two high thrones, with [Tan]sui at the north and the disciple to the south".[341] If the hall has a Buddha statue enshrined within, then the seats are set out to the south-east and south-west, just as stated in Enchin's *Guan Puxian pusa xingfa jing ji*, fascicle one: "In the lecture hall, the Buddha statue was placed at the north. The lecturer's seat was high and placed to the east of the Buddha statue. The rector's seat was smaller and placed in the southwest corner or facing the statue. Thus, when donors set the theme of the lecture, the [lecturer in the] north seat said, 'all people your join palms and listen to the south seat chant the title of the *sūtra*'".[342] Due to the influence of Chinese Confucian culture, Buddha statues in halls are usually placed at the north and facing the south, so it is common that people sit at the east and west, just as when Emperor Wu of Liang made the collective agreement on prohibiting meat and alcohol. In the *Guang Hongming ji*, it is stated,

> At dawn on the twenty-third day (519.7.5), acting as the Dharma master, Fayun 法雲 (467–529) from Guangzhai si ascended the high throne facing east before the Hualin Hall 華林殿, and acting as the reciter, Huiming 慧明 (ca. fifth to sixth century) from Waguan si ascended the high throne facing west. They chanted the first of four parts of the "Chapter on Characteristics" of the *Da [bo] niepan jing*, which describes the idea that those who eat meat destroy the seeds of great loving kindness, which Fayun explained. The emperor personally attended, and a seat on the floor was placed to the south of the high thrones. The two communities of the monks and nuns then sat lined up from here.[343]

Therefore, the lecturer's and reciter's ascent to the high thrones is divided into two sides, either south and north, or east and west. The size of their seats also has a slight difference.

2. Liturgical chanting (*zuofan* 作梵).

After the lecturer and reciter have ascended to the high thrones, the chanter begins the liturgical chanting. The rector and the chanter are both on the

341 *Gaoseng zhuan*, *T* no. 2059, 50: 12.406c3-4: 有兩高座, 邃在北, 弟子在南.

342 *Foshuo guan Puxian pusa xingfa jing ji*, *T* no. 2194, 56: 1.227c29-228a01: 講堂時正北置佛像, 講師座高閣, 在佛東向；於讀座短狹在西南角, 或推在佛前. 故檀越設開題時, 北座言：大衆處心合掌聽南座唱經題.

343 *Guang Hongming ji*, *T* no. 2103, 52: 26.299a1-6: 二十三日旦，光宅寺法雲於華林殿前登東向高座爲法師，瓦官寺慧明登西向高座爲都講, 唱《大涅槃經》四相品四分之一, 陳食肉者斷大慈種義, 法雲解釋. 輿駕親禦, 地鋪席位於高座之北, 僧尼二眾各以次列坐.

lower seats, so it is said "a junior monastic does the liturgical chanting".[344] In Daoxuan's *Xingshi chao*, it states: "When the sound of the *gaṇṭā* [wooden board] ends, first praise by chanting *gāthās*".[345] In Tang dynasty Fazhao's 法照 (746–838) *Jingtu wuhui nianfo lüe fashi yi zan* 淨土五會念佛略法事儀讚 (The Brief Praise Rite of Dharma Service for the Pure-Land Five Stage Progression for Chanting the Buddha's Name, *T* 1983), there is the liturgical chanting of praise *gāthās*:

> What is "liturgical chanting" (*fan* 梵)?
> How does one achieve longevity, the adamantine indestructible body?
> Also, through what conditions does one attain great strength and power?
> How, through this *sūtra*, does one ultimately reach the other shore?
> May the Buddha reveal the subtle meaning and teach living beings in detail.[346]

According to the explanation in Tang dynasty Daoshi's 道世 (?–683) *Fayuan zhulin*, fascicle thirty-six, "Fanbeipian zantan bu" 唄讚篇讚嘆部 (Chanting Praise Section, Praise Portion), this *gāthā* comes from the *Niepan jing*.[347] This *gāthā* can be seen in both the Northern Liang translation of Tanwuchan 曇無讖 (Dharmarakṣa, 385–433), and also the Liu Song translation of Huiyan 慧嚴 (363–443), whereas only the first two lines can be seen in the Eastern Jin translation of Faxian.[348]

According to Ennin's notes, the *gāthā* chanted in the liturgical style by the chanter is the latter portion of the above described: "How, through this *sūtra*, does one ultimately reach the other shore? May the Buddha reveal the subtle meaning and teach living beings in detail".[349] This is chanted by the chanter alone. After they have chanted this, the community together chants the *gāthā*, "The incense of morality, incense of meditation, incense of liberation", and so

---

344 *Nittō guhō junrei kōki* 2.73: 下座一僧作梵.

345 *Sifen lü shanfan buqüe xingshi chao*, *T* no. 1804, 40: 3.138b4: 鍵稚聲絕, 先贊偈唄.

346 *Jingtu wuhui nianfo lüe fashi yi zan*, *T* no. 1983, 47: 1.475b27-c2:
云何梵？
云何得長壽, 金剛不壞身,
復以何因緣, 得大堅固力.
云何於此經, 究竟到彼岸,
願佛開微密, 廣爲衆生說.

347 *Fayuan zhulin*, *T* no. 2122, 53: 36.575c14-15.

348 *Da boniepan jing*, *T* no. 374, 12: 3.379c14-15; *Da boniepan jing*, *T* no. 375, 12: 3.619b22-23; *Da bonihuan jing*, *T* no. 376, 12: 2.863c9-10.

349 *Nittō guhō junrei kōki* 1.20.

forth. In the Tang period *Ji zhujing lichan yi* of Zhisheng, we can see the *gāthās* which are chanted in the liturgical style:

> What is "liturgical chanting" (*fan*)?
> How does one achieve longevity, the adamantine indestructible body?
> Also, through what conditions does one attain great strength and power?
> How, through this *sūtra*, does one ultimately reach the other shore?
> The incense of morality, the incense of meditation,
> The incense of liberation, the incense of knowledge and vision of liberation.
> The cloud platform of brilliant light pervades the world,
> Making offerings to immeasurable Buddhas in the ten directions,
> Those who see and hear it are suffused to realize peaceful cessation.
> May the Buddha reveal the subtle meaning, and teach living beings in detail.[350]

However, the three texts from canons of the Song, Yuan and Ming periods all place the line "May the Buddha reveal the subtle meaning, and teach living beings in detail", after "ultimately reach the other shore".[351] Likewise, in the Dunhuang manuscript S. 2580 we see the "Text to Walk with Incense and Proclaim the *Gāthā*": "The incense of morality, the incense of meditation, The incense of liberation, the incense of knowledge and vision of liberation. The cloud platform of brilliant light pervades the world, Making offerings to immeasurable Buddhas in the ten directions, Those who see and hear it are suffused to realize peaceful cessation".[352] This is the same as in the *Ji zhujing lichan yi*, where the community sings together: "The incense of morality, the incense of meditation, The incense of liberation, the incense of knowledge and vision of liberation. The cloud platform of brilliant light pervades the

350 *Ji zhujing lichan yi*, *T* no. 1982, 47: 1.464a12-14:
云何梵？
云何得長壽, 金剛不壞身, 復以何因緣, 得大堅固力.
云何於此經, 究竟到彼岸.
戒香、定香、慧香、解
脫香, 解脫知見香,
光明雲臺遍法界,
供養十方無量佛,
見聞普熏證寂滅.
願佛開微密, 廣爲眾生說.

351 *Ji zhujing lichan yi*, *T* no. 1982, 47: 1.464, note 6.

352 *Ru busatang shuo jiwen deng*, *T* no. 2852, 85: 1.1301a18-19: 戒香、定香、解脫香, 光明雲臺遍法界, 供養十方無量佛, 見聞普熏證寂滅.

world, making offerings to immeasurable Buddhas in the ten directions. Those who see and hear it are suffused to realize peaceful cessation". This proves that Ennin's records are correct, and that the *Ji zhujing lichan yi* has this error, perhaps due to issues at the time of printing.

When the liturgical chanting is performed, if there are donors, they should also have the donor hold incense, and the community chants in unison the "two lines of the *gāthā* of the Thus Come One Body of Marvellous Form", and not "The incense of morality, the incense of meditation, the incense of liberation". In S.6551, the "*Foshuo Amituo jing* jiangjing wen" 佛說阿彌陀經講經文 (Text for Lecturing the *Amitābha-sūtra* Taught by the Buddha), it states: "Having ascended to the seat, first recite the *gāthā*, light incense, invoke the names of the Buddhas and bodhisattvas".[353] The *gāthā* for walking with incense is from the *Shengman jing* 勝鬘經 (Skt. *Śrīmāla Sūtra*, *T* 353), "*Rulai zhenshiyi gongde zhang diyi*" 如來真實義功德章第一 (Chapter One, Qualities of the True Meaning of the Thus Come One): "The body of marvellous form of the Thus Come One, is unequalled in the whole world; Incomparable, inconceivable, therefore we now worship it. The Thus Come One's form is inexhaustible, and so too is his wisdom; All Dharma constantly abides, therefore we take refuge in it".[354]

3. Chanting the *sūtra* title and scattering flowers.

For ordinary public lectures, before the reciter chants the title of the *sūtra*, there is a passage to settle on the seat. But this is not mentioned in Ennin's notes. In monastic lectures in the monastery, because the ritual is very solemn and formal, there is no need to have a passage to settle the audience on their seats and to calm down the community.[355] After the liturgical chanting, the *sūtra* title is chanted by the reciter. The *Sin la il il kang ŭi sik* states: "… the south seat chants the title of the *sūtra*, that is, chanting the *sūtra* drawing it out long, with the tune taking many twists and turns. During the chanting of the *sūtra*, the community strews flowers three times, and there is a verse sung for each

353 Huang & Zhang, *Bianwen*, 679: 升坐已了, 先念偈, 焚香, 稱諸佛菩薩名.

354 *Shengman shizihou yicheng dafangbian fangguang jing*, *T* no. 353, 12: 217a24-27; *Ji zhujing lichan yi*, *T* no. 1982, 47: 1.456b13-16:
如來妙色身, 世間無與等, 無比不思議, 是故今敬禮. 如來色無盡, 智慧亦復然, 一切法常住, 是故我歸依.

355 Jiang Boqin (*Dunhuang*, 409) points out that the most obvious difference between an ordinary public lecture and a non-ordinary public lecture is that there is a passage to settle the audience on the seat which is not seen in the canon and an explanation of the context chanted in vernacular language.

time. Having chanted the *sūtra*, then the title is chanted in the short form".[356] The reciter has a set form of rhythm and length for the chanting of the *sūtra*. At the same time as chanting the *sūtra*, the flower scatterer throws flowers three times. However, sometimes the lecturer themselves chants the title of the *sūtra*, such as in the *Chŏk san wŏn kang kyŏng ŭi sik*, which says, "the lecturer chants the title of the *sūtra*",[357] and P. 3849 states, "The chanting venerable himself reads the title of the *sūtra*".[358] Fayun's 法韻 (570–604) *Xu Gaoseng zhuan* biography states: "Whenever there were the overnight fasting precepts, he was responsible for the tasks of both chanting the *sūtra* and preaching".[359]

4. Revealing the title and lecturing the *sūtra*.

Only after having gone through the above mentioned formal and solemn preparation does the actual lecturing of the *sūtra* begin. First, the lecturer reveals the title, and divides the text of the *sūtra* into three parts. The three parts of the *sūtra* text are typically seen in the written fascicles of the *sūtra* text. For example, in P. 2133, *Jin'gang bore boluomi jiangjing wen* 金剛般若波羅蜜講經文 (Text for Lecturing the Diamond *Prajñāpāramitā Sūtra*), after the explanatory passages for the text of the *sūtra*, it finally states: "Above there are three: one, the preface; two, the main meaning; three, the ongoing continuation".[360] Dividing up the scriptural text into the "preface, main meaning, and ongoing continuation" began with Daoan in the Eastern Jin, as stated in Sengmin's 僧旻 (467–527) *Xu Gaoseng zhuan* biography:

> In olden times, after the illustrious Shi Daoan had stationed himself on his seat whenever he lectured, the ever-present reciter, and others, there was turning of the *sūtra* for sentient beings in three aspects. This matter has long been abandoned. That is, the superior work which is performed as a preliminary, wishing to tame the community, each recites the Guanyin jing one time. From this, those sitting are delighted, those near and far become mutually familiar. Afterwards, both monastics and laity

356 *Nittō guhō junrei kōki* 2.74: 南座唱經題目, 所謂唱經長引, 音多有屈曲. 唱經之會, 大眾三遍散花；每散花時, 各有所頌. 唱經了, 更短音唱題目.

357 *Nittō guhō junrei kōki* 2.73: 講師唱經題目.

358 Huang, *Dunhuang baozang*, 131.304: 唱日法师自说经题了.

359 *Xu Gaoseng zhuan*, *T* no. 2060, 50: 30.703c12-13: 每有宿齋, 經導兩務, 並委於韻.

360 Huang & Zhang, *Bianwen*, 646: 上來有三：一序分, 二正宗, 三流通.

donate goods. The recitation of the *sūtra* before the lecture was started for this reason.[361]

The same record can also been seen in the *Nanhai jigui neifa zhuan* 南海寄歸內法傳 (Record of Buddhist Practices Sent Home from the Southern Sea, *T* 2125), fascicle four, "Zanyong zhi li" 讚詠之禮 (Ritual of Praise and Chanting):

> The *sūtras* recited are mostly recited in three commencements (sanqi 三啓), which were established by the Venerable Aśvaghoṣa. First, one can recite ten or more stanzas, to grasp the main idea of the *sūtra*, and praise the three icons. Next, recite the *sūtra* proper, which is that personally taught by the Buddha. Having finished reciting the *sūtra*, one further goes through the ten remaining stanzas, and discusses the dedication and making of vows. The parts and sections are broken up into three, so it is said to be "three commencements".[362]
>
> The method set up by Daoan came from India. But in the presently extant *sūtra* lecture texts, apart from the revealing of the title, we do not see the *sūtra* text in three parts.
>
> Since being "distinguished into three parts" comes from India, apart from Daoan's commonly mentioned "method of three parts", there is another "method of three parts" still extant. It is stated in P. 2064, *Sifen jieben shu* 四分戒本疏 (Commentary on the Four-Part *Pratimokṣa*), fascicle one:
>
> In general, one who wishes to reveal the *sūtra* title should first distinguish the text into three gates. Then explain following the text. The so-called "three gates": first, raising the key principle which encapsulates the summary of the teachings; second, knowing the summary of the teachings; third, formal explanation of the title of the *sūtra*.[363]

The first is raising the key principles which encapsulate the summary of the teachings, which refers to summarizing which of the three baskets of *sūtra*, *vinaya* and treatise that the text in question belongs to. The second is knowing

361 *Xu Gaoseng zhuan*, *T* no. 2060, 50: 5.463b6-10:
昔彌天釋道安每講, 於定坐後, 常使都講等爲含靈轉經三契, 此事久廢. 既是前修勝業, 欲屈大眾各誦《觀世音經》一遍. 於是合坐欣然, 遠近相習. 爾後道俗舍物, 乞講前誦經, 由此始也.

362 *Nanhai jigui neifa zhuan*, *T* no. 2125, 54: 4.227a13-17:
所誦之經, 多誦三啓, 乃是尊者馬鳴之所集置. 初可十頌許, 取經意而贊嘆三尊. 次述正經, 是佛親說. 讀誦既了, 更陳十餘頌, 論回向發願. 節段三開, 故云三啓.

363 *Sifen jieben shu*, *T* no. 2787, 85: 1.567a5-7:
凡欲開發經題, 先作三門分別, 後乃隨文解釋. 言三門者, 第一舉宗攝教旨歸, 第二知教旨歸, 第三正釋戒經題目.

the summary of the teachings, which means deciding on which *vinaya* text it belongs to. The third is formal explanation of the title of the *sūtra*, being an explanation of the title name of the *sūtra* text. The origins of this kind of "distinguishing into three gates" will require some further research by future scholars. However, in the Tang dynasty there were at least two kinds of "distinguishing into three gates" methods.

5. Making vows.

After the lecturer has explained the title of the *sūtra*, the rector comes forward and proclaims aloud the benediction text. Following the different motivations of the donors, the content of the benediction text also differs. For example, the *Sin la il il kang ŭi sik* is a *sūtra* lecturing Dharma service held for the sake of the deceased, and so "This includes the principle of impermanence, the contributions of the deceased, and the dates of the deceased".[364] If one does charity giving to monasteries for the sake of generating merit, after the rector reads aloud the donors names and the items they have given, it is passed over to the lecturer. The lecturer holds the fly-whisk in their hand and gives the names of the donors, and then donors make vows alone in front of the lecturer. In the *sūtra* lecture Dharma service, there are many strong exhortations to practice giving. For example, in Baoyan's 寶巖 (ca. 556–632) *Xu Gaoseng zhuan* biography, it states:

> Then Yan ascended to his seat, and at the table he looked out, but did not speak a word. Throwing things to scatter the clouds, in an instant the seat disappeared. Only then did he instruct someone to remove it. He talked about the method of cultivating merit, first commending the path of wholesomeness to be appreciated, then describing how repulsive are the dark ways, and finally using teachings on impermanence to spur the audience to ultimately return to the long road. With ears pricked and applauding hands, their minds awakened in that moment. There were none who did not shave their heads and change their robes, with their names being written down.[365]

Due to the lecturer's excellent skill in teaching the dharma, he taught the audience about giving, which is a common situation during Dharma services.

364 *Nittō guhō junrei kōki* 2.74: 其狀中具載無常道理、亡者功能、亡逝日數.

365 *Xu Gaoseng zhuan*, *T* no. 2060, 50: 30.705b27-c2:
及巖之登座也, 几案顧望, 未及吐言, 擲物雲崩, 須臾坐沒, 方乃命人徒物, 談敘福門. 先張善道可欣, 中述幽途可厭, 後以無常逼奪, 終歸長逝. 提耳抵掌, 達晤時心, 莫不解發撤衣, 書名記數.

6. Discuss the meaning, as stated in the *Chŏk san wŏn kang kyŏng ŭi sik*.
Having made the vows, the questioner raises up questions. When raising questions, the lecturer raises the fly-whisk, and listens to the words of the question. Having raised the questions, he then inclines the fly-whisk, then returns to raise it again, thanking the questioner and beginning to answer. Each question is raised by topic and then answered in turn by topic, as it is in this country, but the ritual for the challenge is slightly different. After inclining the hand three times, they explain and clarify, then suddenly explain the challenge, with a booming voice. Finishing, there is silence. The lecturer then receives the challenge, and only answers without refuting the challenge.[366]

The discussion of the meaning starts from the reciter posing questions, the lecturer holding up the fly-whisk while listening. After having posed the questions, the lecturer puts down the fly-whisk.[367] The purpose of the discussion of the meaning is to further clarify the meaning of *sūtras* through question and answer.

The *Da Song sengshi lüe*, "Tasks of the Reciter", states:

> The proclaimer is the instigator, who raises faults without ad hominem, who challenges the chair alone. In olden times, when Liang Wudi lectured the *sūtras*, Fabiao 法彪 (d.u) of Zhiyuan si 枳園寺 was the reciter. Master [Fa]biao would first ask one question, and Liang Wudi would then drum the tip of his tongue. One goes forth, and another responds, each answer following each question. This is the main substance of the reciter. … The reciters of today do not listen but issue questions, and chant aloud the text of the *sūtra*, which is an imitation of the ancient reciters.[368]

Therefore, the tasks that the reciter is responsible for are not only the chanting aloud of the *sūtras* text, but the functions of setting up challenges, resolving doubts, and assisting in promoting the meaning of the lecture are even more important.

---

366 *Nittō guhō junrei kōki* 2.73:
誓願訖, 論義者論端舉問. 舉問之間, 講師舉麈尾, 聞問者語. 舉問了, 便傾麈尾, 即還舉之, 謝問便答. 貼問貼答, 與本國同, 但難儀式稍別. 側手三下後, 申解白前, 卒爾指申難, 聲如大嗔人, 盡音呼諍. 講師蒙難, 但答不返難.

367 About the objects such as fly-whisks and *ruyi* used during Dharma services, cf. Fukui, "Shubi"; idem, "Fukugu".

368 *Da Song sengshi lüe*, *T* no. 2126, 54: 1.239c21-240a4:
敷宣之士, 擊發之由, 非旁人而啓端, 難在座而孤起. 故梁武講經, 以織園寺法彪爲都講. 彪公先一問, 梁祖方鼓舌端, 載索載徵, 隨問隨答, 此都講之大體也. …… 今之都講不聞擊問, 舉唱經文, 蓋似像古之都講耳.

7. Lecturing of the *sūtra* proper.
The above mentioned discussion on the meaning still only belongs to the revealing of the title. The *Chŏk san wŏn kang kyŏng ŭi sik* states: "Discussing the meaning, he enters into chanting the *sūtra*".[369] Only in this way do they formally enter into the explanatory lecture on the *sūtra* text proper. Yuanzhao's "ten steps" states: "Five, the teaching proper (*zhengshuo* 正說). Six, proceed and stop according to the situation, with questions and listening according to the dharma, delighting in listening and replying. (If the text is not clear, the junior monastic will now recite it)".[370] This includes the discussion on the meaning and the lecture on the *sūtra* itself, combined as the "lecture proper".

An explanatory lecture on the text of the *sūtra* first begins with the reciter chanting one portion of the *sūtra* text, then the lecturer immediately explains the meaning of the *sūtra*, and finally forms the *sūtra* lecture text. Therefore, the *sūtra* lecture text is the lecture notes for the lecturer to use to lecture the *sūtra*.[371] For example, the *Weimojie jing jiangjingwen* 維摩詰經講經文 (Lecture Text of the Vimalakīrti *Sūtra*), S. 4571 and S. 3872, have "Chang jianglai" 唱將來 (please chant [the *sūtra* text]) after every section of the *sūtra* lecture text. Following that phrase is a section of the *sūtra* text, which is what the rector chants.[372] In P. 2955, the *Fo shuo Amituo jing jiangjing wen*, there are chanted words in fragmented parts of the text:

> The reciter *ācārya* has lofty virtues,
> Their voice and rhythm are clear and flexible.
> With good meter they use a graceful tune,
> They chant with a high voice.[373]

These are the words for the lecturer's exhorting chant of the *sūtra* text, which is followed by, "The *sūtra* states", which is the *sūtra* text chanted by the reciter. In the *Sujiang yishi*, P. 3849, there is a mention of the *Wenshi jing* as "stating the basic text of the *sūtra*", and references the *Weimojie jing* as "teaching of the *sūtra* through analogies".[374] Because during the *sūtra* lecturing Dharma service

369 *Nittō guhō junrei kōki* 2.73: 論義了, 入文讀經, 講訖.

370 *Sifen lü xingshi chao zichi ji*, *T* no. 1805, 40: 3.404b6-7: 五正說, 六觀機進止, 問聽如法, 樂聞應說 (文中不明下座今加續之).

371 About the details of the *sūtra* lecture text, such as the relationship between the *sūtra* lecture text and commentaries, and the authors of the *sūtra* lecture texts, cf. Hirano, "Kōkyōbun".

372 Huang, *Dunhuang baozang*, 36.583-609; 32.71-83.

373 Huang & Zhang, *Bianwen*, 704: 都講閣梨道德高, 音律清冷能宛轉. 好韻宮商申雅調, 高著聲音唱將來.

374 Huang, *Dunhuang baozang*, 131.304.

there will be profound and deep principles in the *sūtra* being taught, the lecturer must cite some analogies and stories, which is the guiding chanting. Even in the *sūtra* lecturing Dharma service of the present, this is a common occurrence.

8. Dedication liturgical chanting.
The *Chŏk san wŏn kang kyŏng ŭi sik* states: "Having lectured, the community praises it in unison, and the words of praise include the phrases of the dedication".[375] Yuanzhao's "ten steps" also says: "Seven, after teaching, the dedication. Eight, again chant of praise".[376] This refers to after the lecturer has finished lecturing the *sūtra*, they together chant the words of the dedication. Dedication means to take the merit from the *sūtra* lecture and listening to the lecture, and giving it in dedication to the donors and living beings of the dharma realm, a prayer and blessing for these living beings. As in the *Huixiang wen* 迴向文 (Dedication Text), S. 1164, there are vows and a dedication for the holy lord of the Great Tang, the six abbots, the director-general abbot, the secretary Gui Li 貴禮, the two imperial attendents An 安 and Yao 姚, the secretary Gai Zi 姟子, professors from the Śākya school, Śākya school Dharma and *Vinaya* masters, the lord city inspector, city emissary for the clans, elder venerables, all Dharma general venerables, virtuous nuns, gentleman officials, abbot Li 李, and spirits born of some mother and father.[377]

9. Leaving the seat.
In the *Chŏk san wŏn kang kyŏng ŭi sik* it says: "The lecturer descends from the seat, and a monastic chants the *gāthā* on "Dwelling in the world is like empty space", and the tune is similar to that of this country. The lecturer rises to the worship dais, and a monastic chants the three prostrations. With the lecturer and community in the same tune, he leaves the hall and returns to his quarters".[378] Yuanzhao's "ten steps' also states:

> Nine, descending from the seat, and prostrations in farewell. The [Xu Gao]seng zhuan states: Whenever the Zhou monk Sengmiao 僧妙 (d.u) lectured, the junior monastics must join palms and repent, saying: The Buddha's meaning is difficult to understand, it is not fathomable by

---

375 *Nittō guhō junrei kōki* 2.73: 講訖, 大衆同音長音贊嘆, 贊嘆語中有回向詞.

376 *Sifen lü xingshi chao zichi ji*, *T* no. 1805, 40: 3.404b7-8: 七說竟迴向, 八復作贊唄.

377 *Huixiang wen*, *T* no. 2848, 85: 1.1299a5-c6.

378 *Nittō guhō junrei kōki* 2.73:
講師下座, 一僧唱 ' 處世界如虛空 ' 偈, 音勢頗似本國. 講師升禮盤, 一僧唱三禮了, 講師大衆同音, 出堂歸房.

> ordinary common people. Now it is being taught, we receive it from the ancient teachers, and dare not break the transmission. I beg the community that whether the meaning of this Dharma is true or not, they will give happiness.[379]

After the Dharma service is finished, the lecturer, as well as the reciter and others, get down from their seats. At this time, the chanter alone chants the *gāthā* on "Dwelling in the world is like empty space". This is mentioned in the *Ji zhujing lichan yi*, fascicle one, as: "Dwelling in the world is like empty space; like a lotus flower that does not need water. The pure mind transcends even this. Bow your head in prostration, to the unsurpassed sovereign".[380] After chanting this *gāthā*, the chanter also begins to chant the "three worships", namely, the three refuges:

> As I go to the Buddha for refuge, may all living beings realize the great way, and aspire to the unsurpassed mind.
> As I go to the Dharma for refuge, may all living beings deeply enter the canon of scripture, with wisdom vast as the ocean.
> As I go to the *Saṃgha* for refuge, may all living beings administer the community, without any obstacle.[381]

After the three refuges, the lecturer may say some words to leave the seat. For example, as previously said by Sengmiao, to show one's own humility.

After the *sūtra* lecturing Dharma service is completed, sometimes in order to further develop lecturing venerables, there may be a system of a review lecture. That is, a review of the day's lecture content by a younger venerable. As stated in Daoan's *Gaoseng zhuan* biography:

---

379 *Sifen lü xingshi chao zichi ji*, *T* no. 1805, 40: 3.404b8-11:
九下座禮辭. 僧傳云：周僧妙每講下座, 必合掌懺悔云：佛意難知, 豈凡夫所測, 今所說者, 傳受先師, 未敢專輒. 乞大眾, 於斯法義, 若是若非, 布施歡喜.

380 *Ji zhujing lichan yi*, *T* no. 1982, 47: 1.457b2-3: 處世界, 如虛空；如蓮花, 不著水；心清淨, 超於彼；稽首禮, 無上尊.

381 *Ji zhujing lichan yi*, *T* no. 1982, 47: 1.465a28-b5:
自歸依佛, 當願眾生, 體解眾生, 發無上心.
自歸依法, 當願眾生, 深入經藏, 智慧如海.
自歸依僧, 當願眾生, 統理大眾, 一切無礙.
In the three refuges in the morning and evening chantings in modern days, "respect the sacred *Saṃgha*" is added at the end of the third refuge. In Dunhuang manuscripts, "may all living beings create no evil, cultivate all good, and purify the mind. These are the teachings of the Buddha. Respect all sacred *Saṃgha*" is added at the end of the third refuge.

> [Fotu]cheng would lecture, and each time [Dao]an would review, the community would not be satisfied, but say: It must wait until the next time. One should pose a killer question to this swarthy boy. After that, [Dao]An would repeat the lecture, to the many questions posed to him, [Dao]an answered them with ease.[382]

The system of having a lecturer review was an actual practice in China from early on. At the same time, the Confucian tradition also had review lectures. This was an excellent pedagogical method from ancient China. In the present, due to the practices of modern university education, such methods have long since been discontinued.[383]

### 4.2 *Public Lectures in the Tang and Five Dynasties*

Public lectures were a development from the formal *sūtra* lectures and were prevalent during the Tang and Five Dynasties periods. Complementing "monastic lectures', "public lectures" were popularized *sūtra* lectures, with a large amount of the content expressed in narrative and story form. The speakers for the public lectures were almost all monastics, who at the time were called "public lecture monastics" (*sujiang seng* 俗講僧). On one hand, public lecture monastics must have deep training and knowledge in Buddhism, be masterful in Buddhist doctrinal thought, have studied "vocalization, argumentation, oratory and erudition", and be able to adapt and respond to the actual needs and situation of the audience; and on the other hand, the public lecture monastics must be thoroughly familiarized with the requisite skills and techniques.[384] From these points, we can see that they are already different from the usual *sūtra* lecturers, and are more like regular performers. Wenxu 文漵 (ca. early ninth century) was an extremely famous public lecture monastic, with excellent speaking and singing skills. Emperor Jingzong (r. 824–826) of Tang in the second year of Baoli (826), "made an imperial visit to Xingfu si 興福寺, and watched the *śramaṇa* Wenxu give a public lecture".[385] The common people also enjoyed his public lectures, and "uneducated men and illiterate women liked listening to his talks. The audiences packed the halls of the monasteries,

---

382 *Gaoseng zhuan*, *T* no. 2059, 50: 5.351c17-20:
澄講, 安每覆述, 眾未之愜, 咸言：須待後次, 當難殺昆侖子. 即安後更覆講, 疑難紛起, 安挫銳解紛, 行有餘力.

383 The system of a review lecture is called "*fukuen*" in Japanese which was also an actual practice in Japan from early on. Cf. Michibata, "Bukkyōshi", 216–17.

384 Zhang, *Dunhuang dianji*, 643.

385 *Zizhi tongjian* 243.7850: 幸興福寺, 觀沙門文漵俗講.

revering and worshipping him, and called him the "Opera House Abbot" (*heshang jiaofang* 和尙教坊)".[386]

The ritual for public lectures should be about the same as that for the formal *sūtra* lectures. However, due to the cultural background and tastes of the audiences for public lectures which favour popularized and entertaining content, the *sūtra* lecturing venerables commonly used a more colloquial tone to lecture, sing and explain the text of the *sūtra*, and expand out for the textual passages under discussion. In the presently extant *sūtra* lecture texts from Dunhuang, at the revealing of the title before the lecturing of the *sūtra* proper, there is the "passage to settle on the seat" (*yazuowen* 押座文). Presently extant passages to settle on the seat that exist in individual manuscripts include the "Baxiang yazuo wen" 八相押座文 (Eight Junctures Passage to Settle on the Seat), "Sanshen yazuo wen" 三身押座文 (Three Bodies Passage to Settle on the Seat), "*Weimo jing* yazuo wen" 維摩經押座文 (*Vimalakīrti Sūtra* Passage to Settle on the Seat), "*Wenshi jing* yazuo wen" 溫室經押座文 (Lecture and Chant Passage to Settle on the Seat of the *Sūtra on the Saunas and Baths*), "Er'shisi xiao yazuo wen" 二十四孝押座文 (Passage to Settle on the Seat of the Twenty Four Filial Sons), "Zuojie Senglu dashi yazuo wen" 左街僧錄大師押座文 (Passage to Settle on the Seat of the Left Street Monastic Registrar Master), and so forth. "Settle on the seat" (*yazuo* 押座) is in imitation of popular folk lecture chanting. Han and Wei music had preludes, which in the Tang period was known as "settling the hall" (*dingchang* 定場), with a singer using words to guide the hall into a settled state. This had the same intent as the *sūtra* lecturer chanting words to settle the audience on their seats. As stated at the end of the "Baxiang yazuo wen", S. 2440: "I wish to invite the Buddha, but am afraid that people will sit for too long, and will then lecture the *sūtra*. Are you willing? Those who are willing, introspect and join your palms as we wait".[387] The "Sanshen yazuo wen", S.2440, states at the end:

> Since you are able to come to this place of the way,
> You must be willing to listen to the sublime Dharma.
> Those who want to, single-mindedly join your palms,
> Chant the title of the *sūtra*.[388]

386 *Yinhua lu* 4.154: 愚夫冶婦, 樂聞其說. 聽者塡咽寺舍, 瞻仰禮拜, 呼爲和尙教坊.

387 Huang & Zhang, *Bianwen*, 1140: 我擬請佛, 恐人坐多時, 便擬說經. 願不願 ? 願者檢心 (合) 掌待.

388 Ibid: 既能來至道場中, 定是願聞微妙法. 樂者一心合掌著, 經題名字唱 (將) 來.

We thus know that the passage to settle on the seat was before revealing the title and chanting the *sūtra*.

During the mid to late Tang period, public lectures were often held at monasteries. Ennin's notes in his *Nittō guhō junrei kōki* describe the situation of public lectures:

> (Sixth year of Kaicheng, first month,) ninth day (841.2.4), … the name of the regnal year changed to the first year of Huichang (841). There was again an edict that seven monasteries on the Left and Right Streets hold public lectures. On the Left road there were four locations: Zisheng si 資聖寺 was instructed to have Master Hai'an 海岸 (ca. ninth century), holder of the purple robe from Yunhua si 雲華寺 lecture the Huayan jing. Baoshou si 保壽寺 was instructed to have the monastic administrator Master Tixu 體虛 (d.u.), treatise lecturer for the three teachings, holder of the purple robe, lecture on the Fahua jing. Puti si 菩提寺 was instructed to have Master Qigao 齊高 (d.u.), the inner sacrificer and treatise lecturer of the three teachings from Zhaofu si 招福寺, lecture on the Niepan jing. Jinggong si 景公寺 was instructed to have venerable Guangying 光影 (d.u) give a lecture. On the Right road there were three locations: Huichang si 會昌寺 was instructed to have Master Wenxu, inner sacrificer, treatise lecturer and holder of the purple robe, lecture on the Fahua jing. He is the foremost venerable who can give a public lecture in the city. As for Huiri si 惠日寺 and Chongfu si 崇福寺, the names of the lecturing venerables have not yet been given. … Lectures were stopped in the ninth year of Dahe (835), but they will now resume anew. The first will be on the fifteenth day of the first month, the last on the fifteenth day of the second month.[389]

Public lectures had previously been terminated in the ninth year of Dahe (835), and the edict of the first year of Huichang (841) resumed the lectures. They took place simultaneously over the period of one month in seven major

389 *Nittō guhō junrei kōki* 4.147:
(開成六年正月) 九日 …… 改年號, 改開成六年爲會昌元年. 又敕於左、右街七寺開俗講. 左街四處：此資聖寺, 令雲花寺賜紫大德海岸法師講《華嚴經》；保壽寺, 令左街僧錄、三教講論、賜紫、引駕大德體虛法師講《法華經》；菩提寺, 令招福寺內供奉、三教講論大德齊高法師講《涅槃經》；景公寺令光影法師講. 右街三處：會昌寺令內供奉、三教講論、賜紫、引駕起居大德文漵法師講《法華經》. 城中俗講, 此法師爲第一. 惠日寺、崇福寺講法師未得其名. …… 從大和九年以來廢講, 今上新開. 正月十五日起首至二月十五日罷.

monasteries in the city of Chang'an, which was a previously unseen splendour. Subsequently, on the first day of the ninth month of the first year of Huichang (841.9.19), there were two public lectures at monasteries on the two roads. On the first day of the first month of the second year of Huichang (842.2.14), monasteries held even more public lectures.

Public lectures were religious events for the general secular public. With talks and singing inside the monasteries that easily drew people's ridicule. Government officials therefore often banned them. It is only following the discovery of Dunhuang manuscripts of *sūtra* lecturing texts that we have the opportunity to ascertain their basic features.

### 4.3 *Illustrative Lecture and Illustrative Narrative in the Tang and Five Dynasties Period*

During the Tang and Five Dynasties periods, simultaneously popular with the public lectures among the common masses was the art of speaking and singing known as "*zhuanbian*" 轉變 (illustrative lectures). Illustrative lectures are the speaking and singing of *bianwen* 變文 (illustrative narratives), which were incredibly popular at the time, being held from the palace to the market place, and leading to the specific performance location known as the "*bianchang*" 變場 (illustrative court).

Illustrative narratives are abbreviated as "*bian*" 變 (illustratives), which are the basic texts for the illustrative lectures. "*zhuan*" 轉 / 囀 (lecture), [literally "turn"], refers to twisting to make a sound, leading to singing or lecturing a chant. Illustrative narratives made their first appearance in Buddhist temples, when public lecture monastics told stories of mystical transformations (*zhuan*) full of literary connotations to their audiences. Later, there were also specialist artists in the community who sung and talked about folk legends, historical stories and real examples from daily life using illustrative narratives, at locations not limited to Buddhist temples. Illustrative lectures appeared at the latest by the time of Emperor Xuanzong of Tang. Proof of this is found in the presently extent text *Xiangmo bianwen* 降魔變文 (Defeating Māra Illustrative Narrative), S. 5511, S. 4398, which begins by stating: "Beneath the emperor, my Han holy lord of the great Tang, founder of the age, the divine treasure, the sacred text, holy marshall, who is in accord with the way".[390]

The *Taiping guangji*, fascicle 269, "Song Yu 宋昱 (fl.742–756) and Wei Xuan 韋儇 (fl.759–761)", cites the *Tan Bin lu*'s 譚賓錄 (Tan Bin's Record) events of the tenth year of Emperor Xuanzong's Tianbao period (751):

---

390 Huang & Zhang, *Bianwen*, 552: 我大唐漢聖主開元天寶聖文神武應道皇帝陛下.

> As the Military Commissioner of Jiannan 劍南, Yang Guozhong 楊國忠 (ca. 700–756) gathered men who went afar to Lu'nan 瀘南. With few provisions on a dangerous road, none would return. [To gather] those travellers to Jiannan, he ordered Song Yu and Wei Xuan to be the imperial representatives each year, forcing them to recruit in the cities and counties. The people knew that they would certainly die, and in the cities and counties none followed those orders. So they devised a trap, deceiving the monastics to organize a vegetarian banquet, or perform an illustrative lecture by the side of the road. Any solitary poor people among the crowd were captured, and taken to a hidden room, where they were given quilted clothes, shackled together into gangs, and quickly sent into military service as conscripts.[391]

Monastics by the side of the road holding an illustrative lecture would be able to attract quite a sizable crowd. Actually using this with capturing people as the aim shows us just how appealing illustrative lectures were.

The performer of an illustrative lecture was usually a single person, either monastic or lay, male or female. For example, at the end of the *Pinposuoluo wang hougong cainü gongdeyi gongyangta shengtian yinyuan bian* 頻婆娑羅王後宮綵女功德意供養塔生天因緣變 (Illustrative Narrative of the Causes and Conditions for the Palace Lady of Bimbisāra's Queen Reborn in the Heavens from the Merit of Making Offerings to a *Stūpa*), S.3491, P.2187, it states:

> The Buddha Dharma is vast and broad, and its depths cannot be fathomed. For one who sincerely seeks the path, they will surely reap the results. However, Baoxuan 保宣 (d.u) is lacking in skills in the way of emptiness, and is inadequate in ability in the divine mansions, with learning in the *sūtras* not reaching the source, and knowledge of the treatises not touching the front. [I] just articulated my shallow views by making a patchwork of subtle explanations, not afraid of feeling shamed and embarrassed by collecting the profound allegories.[392]

---

391 *Taiping guangji* 269.35:
楊國忠爲劍南, 召募使遠赴瀘南, 糧少路險, 常無回者. 其劍南行人, 每歲令宋昱、韋儇爲禦史, 迫促郡縣徵之. 人知必死, 郡縣無以應命. 乃設詭計, 詐令僧設齋, 或於要路轉變, 其眾中有單貧者, 即縛之；置密室中, 授以絮衣, 連枷作隊, 急遞赴之.

392 Huang & Zhang, *Bianwen*, 1083:
佛法寬廣, 濟度無涯, 至心求道, 無不獲果. 但保宣空門薄藝, 梵宇荒才, 經教不便於根源, 論典罔知於底漠. 輒陳短見, 綴秘密之因由; 不懼羞慚, 緝甚深之緣喻.

We can see that Baoxuan was a monastic who was a performer of illustrative lectures. He was the author of the illustrative narrative and also the performer of the illustrative lecture.

Illustrative lectures and public lectures are both a combination of speaking and singing, though public lectures required two monastics, whereas illustrative lectures just needed a single person, either monastic or lay. Furthermore, public lectures only took place in monasteries, but illustrative lectures could be performed in the busy market or on the streets. Lastly, in terms of content, the public lectures were entirely sourced from Buddhism, whereas illustrative lectures could also speak and sing about secular stories. Therefore, illustrative lectures were looser than public lectures. Due to the excessive entertainment value content of illustrative lectures, illustrative narratives transformed from material for religious propagation to vulgar folk literature. The form of illustrative narratives was a blend of rhyme and prose, using a style of speaking and singing interspersed with poetry, or coupled with pictures, such as the "Xiangmo bianwen" 降魔變文 (Defeating Māra Illustrative Narrative) and the "Pomo bianwen" 破魔變文 (Destroying Māra Illustrative Narrative), which can be said to be a kind of integrated art. For example, the "*Weimojie jing* bianwen" 維摩詰經變文 (*Vimalakīrti Sūtra* Illustrative Narrative) and *Xiangmo bianwen* lecture through prose, and sing poems. The "Damuqianlian mingjian jiumu bianwen" 大目乾連冥間救母變文 (Illustrative Narrative of Mahāmaudgalyāyana's Saving of His Mother from the Nether World) uses prose as a prelude, then uses rhyme to describe in detail. The "Wu Zixu bianwen" 伍子胥變文 (Wu Zixu [d. 484 BCE] Illustrative Narrative) has both prose and verse alternating throughout.

Presently extant Dunhuang illustrative narrative texts can be divided into four types based on their style and content: One, religious illustrative narratives which lecture and sing Buddhist stories, such as the "Baxiang bian" 八相變 (Eight Junctures Illustrative Narrative), "Pomo bianwen", "Xiangmo bianwen", and "Damuqianlian mingjian jiumu bianwen". Two, historical illustrative narratives which lecture and sing historical stories, such as the "Wu Zixu bianwen", and "Zhuo Ji Bu bianwen" 捉季布變文 (Arrest of Ji Bu [d.u.] Illustrative Narrative). Three, legendary illustrative narratives which are about folk legends, such as the "Shunzi bian" 舜子變 (Shunzi Illustrative Narrative), "Meng Jiangnü bianwen" 孟姜女變文 (Lady Meng Jiang Illustrative Narrative), and "Wang Zhaojun bianwen" 王昭君變文 (Wang Zhaojun [54 BCE–19 BCE] Illustrative Narrative). Four, illustrative narratives which take as their topic important local events or people of the time, such as the "Zhang Yichao bianwen" 張義潮變文 (Zhang Yichao [799–872] Illustrative Narrative), and "Zhang

Huaishen bianwen" 張淮深變文 (Zhang Huaishen [831–890] Illustrative Narrative), and so forth.

The influence of illustrative narratives on later Chinese literature mainly appears in the development of literary styles and forms: One, the lecture narrative part influenced the form of script that people in the Song used for telling stories. Two, the performance of the song part evolved into the common folk literature types of treasure scrolls, string songs, and drum songs. Three, concerning the text and words, long novels sometimes have various poems or songs, or have parallel narratives, which are the legacy of illustrative narrative.

## 5 Conclusion

Having passed through the chaos brought to China by the five barbarian tribes and the chronic disorder of the North and South dynasties, in the subsequent unification of the Sui dynasty, various different types and forms of Buddhism from India and other areas of northern and southern China gathered together in Chang'an. This brought about contention between the many traditions of thought and the most splendid period of Sui and Tang Buddhism. Buddhism, which had already Sinicized its religious faith, went through the process of blending into daily life, and then slowly seeped into Chinese systems of thought and regulation. Actualizing an unprecedented development and transformation, it produced the greatest accomplishment of Chinese Buddhism, the various traditions, in particular Sanlun, Tiantai, Huayan, Chan, Pure Land, and Esoteric. These traditions held the exchange and transformation between Indian thought and Confucian and Daoist thought, to reflect the richness and changes of Buddhist thinking. This manifested the successes of Buddhism in terms of conceptual thought and novelty of regulatory systems, another high peak in the convergence between the heights of Chinese and Indian thought. The establishment of these traditions represented the completion of the Sinicization of Buddhist thought, taking the ideas of Zhou Yi and Lao Zhuang as its standards, lecturing and commentary on *sūtra*s as its method, the Buddhist philosophical schools of the Northern and Southern dynasties as its foundation, and the Buddhist sects of the Sui and Tang dynasties as its representative characteristic.

Unification of the nation state, stability and prosperity of society, and development of the economy provided an excellent atmosphere for Buddhist faith and lifestyle in the Sui and Tang periods. The religious faith and lifestyles of Buddhists had closer relationships with the politics of the imperial court and the philosophies of the Buddhist schools of thought. The actual establishment

FIGURE 24 Statue of Bodhisattva Guanyin 觀音 in Wangfo Cave 萬佛洞 (cave # 543), Longmen 龍門, constructed by Nun Zhenzhi 真智 of Yifeng Monastery 儀鳳寺 in Xuzhou 許州, dated to the Tang (618-907).

of the Chinese Buddhist systems of repentance started from Tiantai Zhiyi. Based on the doctrinal viewpoints of Tiantai, he combined Mahāyāna Buddhism principles of contemplation and repentance to compose four repentance practices, the *Fahua sanmei chanyi*, *Fangdeng sanmei chaofa*, *Qing Guanshiyin chanfa*, and *Jin'guangming chanfa*. Within these, the *Fahua sanmei chanyi* in particular influenced the Tiantai scholars in their actual practice methods, as well as the style of composition in later repentance practices.

The repentance practices of Huayan, Chan, Pure Land, Three Stages Teaching and other traditions were also very popular. Zongmi took the vast system of Huayan thought, and using the *Yuanjue jing* as the main substance, continued Chengguan and others' Huayan thought and methods of practical application, absorbing the repentance rites and meditation methods of Tiantai. From this he composed the *Yuanjuejing daochang xiuzheng yi* in eighteen fascicles. He emphasized the importance of the characteristics of phenomena, and also gave attention to promoting the principle, and the mutual non-obstruction of phenomena and principle. He emphasized realization and understanding of theoretical principles, but also gave weight to the practical actualization of cultivation practice. The dual weight of theory and practice shows the special features of his perfect interpenetration.

The Tang dynasty Chan Buddhism also developed its own methods of repentance. In terms of repentance thought, both the southern and northern traditions continued the foundational ideas of Bodhidharma's Chan and developed it to different degrees. Bodhidharma's Chan interpreted repentance through *prajñā* emptiness, classifying repentance as an expedient means for Chan practice, and advocated cultivating contemplation in sitting meditation as the best form of repentance. The northern Chan Buddhism also included repentance within contemplation of the mind, and believed that the spiritual power of buddha-nature is naturally able to clarify the murky waters of the afflictions. Foku Yize of the Oxhead Chan system merged repentance into the four ways of deportment, applying *prajñā* emptiness principles to argue the original emptiness of the nature of transgression. While continuing the repentance thought of Bodhidharma, the southern Chan raised the notions of "self-nature repentance" and "formless repentance", making a union of Buddha nature theory and *prajñā* teachings to interpret repentance in their own way.

*Vinaya* practice in the Tang dynasty took as their central core the parallel development of both Mahāyāna and Hīnayāna precepts. Therefore, there was common popularity of both Mahāyāna repentance by principle and Hīnayāna repentance by precepts in terms of repentance thought in ethical precepts. Mahāyāna repentance by principle was formed by taking the transmission and unbroken upholding of the bodhisattva precepts as its foundation, combined with Mahāyāna *sūtras* such as the *Puxian guanjing*. Based on the *Sifen lü*, Daoxuan faithfully continued the traditional standpoint of the ethical precepts, but at the same time imbued them with the spirit of Mahāyāna. Therefore, through an integration of Mahāyāna and Hīnayāna, Daoxuan divided repentance into Repentance by Principle, Repentance by Phenomena, and Repentance by Precepts. However, he placed more emphasis on Repentance by Precepts, and strongly expressed the spirit of a *vinaya* master protecting the teachings. Daoshi, an ordination brother of Daoxuan, only emphasized Repentance by Principle and Repentance by Phenomena. This was due to the differences between the two in their views about ethical precepts.

Shandao's "*xingyifen*" compositions included the *Fashi zan*, *Wangsheng lizan*, *Guannian famen* and *Bozhou zan*. Shandao was influenced by the stimuli of various kinds of ritual procedures for Dharma services in Tang dynasty Buddhism. He received inspiration from and blended together earlier Chinese "ritual worship" culture to express his own Pure Land faith through a range of concrete practice methods, forming complete and majestic worship and praise rituals. The *Fashi zan* was the most complete and solemn ritual of his worship and praise rites. The *Wangsheng lizan* was a worship and praise rite for daily use. The *Guannian famen* and *Bozhou zan* were rituals for specialized cultivation and training. Moreover, the devotion to the Buddhas and bodhisattvas during the Tang and Five dynasties periods was popular. For example, the "Medicine Buddha altar" was a Dharma service specialized in Medicine Buddha practices. It formalized and fixed the practice of "life extension methods". In particular, Yijing's translation of the *Yaoshi liuliguang qifo benyuan gongde jing* has no doubt made great steps in the esoteric transformation of the devotion to Medicine Buddha. Simultaneously, the strength of Esoteric Buddhism during the Tang dynasty definitely promoted the production of "Medicine Buddha altars". Repentance rituals that took Maitreya as their object of worship included the *Zan Mile sili wen* and the Dunhuang text *Shangsheng li*. The latter was a kind of worship and repentance ritual used by the common populace at the time during services for rebirth ascent.

Due to the preservation of texts left behind at Dunhuang, knowledge of the well-developed worship rites in Tang dynasty Buddhism is supported. From the discovery of various kinds of texts that discuss the *sūtras*, such as Ennin's *Chŏk san wŏn kang kyŏng ŭi sik* in the *Nittō guhō junrei kōki*, and the Dunhuang manuscript P. 3849 *Sujiang yishi*, we now have the opportunity to discuss the Tang dynasty Dharma service rituals for lecturing the *sūtras*. The main people involved in Tang dynasty *sūtra* lecturing rituals were the lecturer, the preacher, the rector, the chanter, the incense officer, and the flower officer. Among them, the Buddhist "preacher" did not come from the Confucian preacher system, as the term was merely borrowed during the time of translation. Other than these, through "narrative performance" and "public lecture" activities, the Buddhist faith permeated into common society and finally integrated to become part of people's daily life.

During the Sui and Tang periods, particularly during the time of Emperor Wen of Sui and Empress Wu Zetian, Buddhism became an ideological tool for the construction of the imperial state, to bring together the different levels of society in the imperial state and act as a medium between ethnic groups. As such, *neidaochang* appeared during the Sui and Tang dynasties, such as Yang Guang's construction of three *neidaochang*, the Huiri *daochang* and Riyan si in Jiangdu, and the Huiri *daochang* in Dongdu. These were used to draw well known monastics from afar and to act as centers for worshipping the Buddha and propagation of the dharma. This helped make considerable progress in exchange between Buddhism in the north and south, directly influencing the rise of different Buddhist traditions in the Sui and Tang periods. The most famous of Tang dynasty *neidaochang* were Empress Wu Zetian's Luoyang *neidaochang* and Tang Daizong's *neidaochang*, led by Amoghavajra, which fully displayed the cooperation between imperial and religious power. Hence, *neidaochang* were the point of intersection in the relationship between Buddhism and the state, not only embodying the personal religious faith of the ruler, but also showing the status of monastics in society and politics. During the regnal period of Renshou, Emperor Wen of Sui bestowed *śarīra* on the nation, established *śarīra* pagodas, and held Dharma services for the installation and receiving of *śarīra* at many locations throughout the land. This fixed the ideology of imperial governing power as well as the emperor's personal will to implement it within the foundational levels of society. Through this method, acceptance for the emperor's governing authority was strengthened in different areas, ethnic groups and all strata of society. The offerings to *śarīra* at Famen si by the Tang emperors also displayed the depth of unification of royal power and the Buddhist religion. Buddhism aided the emperor in educating the populace, and also helped in gaining the people's acceptance to the emperor's political power.

Finally, Sui and Tang dynasty Buddhism was an important force in society, actively participating in charity and philanthropic works. Together with the government, it set up compassion-field infirmaries, developed disaster relief for the poor, and did civil engineering works. Buddhist temples and monasteries were living spaces for public society, and through providing short term dwelling accommodation for scholars and literati, they further advanced the influence of Chinese Buddhism on the learned classes.

Sui and Tang dynasty Buddhism was the "golden age" for the Sinicization of Buddhism. With the creative thinking of its different traditions and the regulatory innovations of Baizhang's pure rules, it completed the Sinicization of Buddhist thought and regulations. Buddhism became the standard for how a system could embed itself within political power and social life. Its religious expression received the support of political power from the imperial household, which was reflected in phenomena such as *neidaochang* and activities like *śarīra* offerings. Moreover, due to the *Da Tang Kaiyuan li* 大唐開元禮 (Ritual Canon of the Kaiyuan Period in the Great Tang) being the representative standard for ritual regulations, this aided the Buddhist world in setting up even more formal rites for Buddhist services. This further demonstrates the wisdom and accomplishments of the Buddhist monastic community during the Sui and Tang dynasties in terms of religious way of life and regulatory standards. Furthermore, many more intellectuals and literati became Buddhists, and to a certain extent the expression of Buddhist rational faith replaced folk religion to become common spiritual values of Sui and Tang dynasty society.

## Appendix 2.1: An English Translation of the *Yaoshi Daochang Wen* 藥師道場文 (*Text of the Medicine Buddha Altar*; B. 8719V), Based on Li Xiaorong's Critical Edition

《藥師道場（文）》
身光照耀苦眾生，三十二相證佛身；
速疾成就如斯願，斯願救眾生.
敬禮藥師琉璃光佛！
出牢困厄苦眾生，淨除羅　網證佛身，速疾成就如斯願. 云云
邪心顛倒苦眾生，皆成正覺證佛身. 云云
盲聾喑啞苦眾生，皆成具生證佛身. 云云
困毒熱惱　苦眾生，咸蒙甘露證佛身. 云云
已成男相苦眾生，皆成相好證佛身. 云云
諸魔外道苦眾生，捨邪歸正證佛身. 云云
系閉枷鎖苦眾生，茲令離苦證佛身. 云云
飢渴憂惱苦眾生，飲食充滿證佛身. 云云
寒風裸露苦眾生，珍寶具足證佛身.（云云）
戒律口犯苦眾生，還令清淨證佛身.（云云）
生淫妄語苦眾生，皆令智慧　證佛身.（云云）
一行一願正其道，弟子常將不退心，十二行願救眾生，一一遙登無畏岸.
頭頂禮足七七滿，行道四十九亦圓，願回圓滿救群生，遍沾六道塵沙界.
唯願蠢動諸含識，聞此立刻悟（無）生.

是故眾等各虔心禮敬琉璃光佛！
一齊道：
至心懺念！
我等自從無量劫，久處輪回五濁中，
塵沙業障被系纏，有幸得逢微妙法.
過去無明宿冤對，六時行道滅災殃，
七層燈焰照如來，結線放生求解脫.
神幡五色隨風轉，徘徊刹上已高懸，
唯引藥師降道場，聖

*Text of the Medicine Buddha Altar*
The radiance from his body shines upon suffering creatures,
The thirty two marks realize the Buddha's body.
May we swiftly achieve such vows as these,
As we wish to save living beings.
Respectfully worship Medicine Master Beryl Radiance Buddha!

May suffering living beings trapped in prison,
Purify the net and realize the body of a Buddha.
May we swiftly achieve such vows as these, etc!
May suffering living beings of evil and perverse thoughts,
All accomplish right awakening, and realize the body of a Buddha, etc.
May suffering living beings who are blind, deaf and mute,
All accomplish full faculties, and realize the body of a Buddha, etc.
May suffering living beings hurt by the poison of the afflictions,
Receive the deathless ambrosia, and realize the body of a Buddha, etc.
May suffering living beings who have already gained a male form,
All accomplish the marks and signs, and realize the body of a Buddha, etc.
May suffering living beings who are Māras and heretics,
Abandon evil and return to the right, and realize the body of a buddha, etc.
May suffering living beings locked in fetters and shackles,
Be freed from suffering, and realize the body of a buddha, etc.
May suffering living beings afflicted by hunger and thirst,
Be satiated with food and drink, and realize the body of a buddha, etc.
May suffering living beings naked and exposed in the freezing winds,
Be fulfilled with precious jewels, and realize the body of a buddha. (Etc.)
May suffering living beings who have … violated the precepts,
Return to a state of purity, and realize the body of a buddha. (Etc.)
May suffering living beings who have fornicated and lied,
All become wise, and realize the body of a buddha. (Etc.)

With a single practice and a single vow one rectifies the path,
Disciples should always retain an attitude of never regressing.
With twelve practices and vows to liberate living beings,
One by one they reach the fearless state of the far shore.
Having made seven times seven prostrations of the head to his feet,
And completed forty nine circuits of walking the path,
Vow to return to completely liberate the mass of creatures,
Fully permeating the six destinies and worlds as many as sands.

May all animals, sentient beings, hear this and immediately realize the (un)arisen.
May the community sincerely worship Beryl Radiance Buddha!
Say together:
Give thought to heartfelt repentance!

We, from immeasurable *kalpa*s in the past,
Have long dwelt in the five turbidities of cyclic existence,
Bound and tied by as many obstacles from actions as grains of sand,
Yet fortunately have now encountered the sublime dharma.
Enemies from ignorance of past lives,
May disaster and calamity be extinguished by practicing the path in six sessions.
Seven layers of blazing lamps shine upon the Thus Come One,
The binding of threads and release of beings to seek liberation.
The spiritual banner of five colours flaps in the wind,
Floating above the monastery it hangs high.
May it lead to the altar of the Medicine Master,
The holy [… … … … … …]

（黃昏禮懺）
南無清淨法身毗盧遮那佛！
南無圓滿報 身盧捨那佛！
南無千百億化身同名釋迦牟尼佛！
南無東方阿閦佛！
南無東南方那羅延佛！
南無南方普滿佛！
南無西南方持地佛！
南無西方無量壽佛！
南無西北方月光面佛！
南無北方難勝佛！
南無東北方寂諸根佛！

南無上方虛空藏佛！
南無下方實行佛！
南無東方十二上願藥師琉璃光佛！
南無西方四十八願阿彌陀佛！
南無當來下生彌勒尊佛！
南無東方解脫主 世界，彼世界有佛號虛空功德，清淨微塵，等目端正，功德相光明，華波頭摩、琉璃光、寶體香、最上香供養訖，種種莊嚴，頂髻無量無邊日月光明，願力莊嚴，變 化莊嚴，法界出生，無障礙王如來！
南無毫相日月光明 焰寶蓮華，固如金剛身，毗盧遮那，無障礙眼圓滿，十方放光普照一切佛刹相王如來！
南無過現未來盡十方（虛）空界一切諸佛！
普爲上界諸天龍梵八部、帝主民生、累劫師僧、所生父母、道場施主及法界眾生，並願斷除諸障，歸命禮懺念！
至心懺念：
一切業障海，皆從妄想 生，
若欲懺念者，端坐觀實相.
眾罪如霜露，慧日能消除.
是故應至心勤懺六根罪.
懺念已，歸命禮三寶.
至心發願：願
眾等生生值諸佛，世世恆聞解脫因，
弘誓平等度眾生，畢竟速成無上道.
發願已，歸命禮三寶.
眾罪皆懺念，諸佛盡隨喜，
禮佛及功德，願成無上道.
去來現在佛，於諸眾生最勝，
無量功德海，歸依合掌禮.

(Twilight Worship and Repentance)[393]

Namo pure Dharma-body, Vairocana Buddha!
Namo perfect Retribution-body, Rocana Buddha!
Namo hundreds of thousands of millions of manifestation bodies, Śākyamuni Buddha!
Namo eastern Akṣobhya Buddha!
Namo south-eastern Nārāyana Buddha!
Namo southern Universal Completion Buddha!

---

393 The sentences below are the same with the Dunhuang repentance text "*Huanghun chanwen*".

Namo south-western Upholding the Earth Buddha!
Namo western Immeasurable Life Buddha!
Namo north-western Moon Light Face Buddha!
Namo northern Hard to Conquer Buddha!
Namo north-eastern Pacifying Faculties Buddha!
Namo zenith Empty Space Treasury Buddha!
Namo nadir True Practice Buddha!
Namo eastern twelve higher vows Medicine Master Beryl Radiance Buddha!
Namo western forty-eight vows Amitābha Buddha!
Namo future rebirth Maitreya honoured Buddha!
Namo eastern world Lord of Liberation. That world has a Buddha named Empty Space Virtue, Purifier of Dust, Even-Eyed Righteousness, Radiance of the Marks of Virtue, *Padma* Lotus Flower, Beryl Radiance, Treasured Fragrance, Who Has Made Offerings with Superior Incense, Greatly Adorned, Immeasurable Boundless Light of Sun and Moon Top-knot, Adorned with the Power of Vows, Adorned with Transformation, Born in the Dharma realm, Unobstructed King Thus Come One!

Namo Eyebrow Mark Sun Moon Radiance Blazing Treasure Lotus Flower, Whose Body is as Strong as Diamond, Vairocana, Unobstructed Visual Perfection, Radiant Light which Universally Illuminates all Buddha Worlds in the Ten Directions King Thus Come One!
Namo all Buddhas in all the worlds throughout all directions of space, in past and future!
May all the gods, dragons, *brahmās* and eight divisions [of protectors], the lords of living beings, teachers and monastics throughout the ages, all birth mothers and fathers, patrons of the temples and living beings in the world, eliminate their obstructions and give thought to refuge, worship and repentance!
Give thought to heartfelt repentance:
The ocean of all obstructing actions, arises from deluded thoughts,
If one wishes to repent, sit upright and contemplate the true characteristics.
The many transgressions are like frost and dew,
That are melted and evaporated by the sun of wisdom.
Therefore, one should sincerely and vigorously repent transgressions of the six faculties.
Having repented, take refuge in and worship the Three Jewels.
Sincerely make vows: May, living beings
meet the Buddhas in life after life,
hear the causes of liberation in existence after existence,
make pledges to save living beings without discrimination,

Ultimately and swiftly attain the unsurpassed path.
Having made vows, take refuge in and worship the Three Jewels.
When repenting the mass of transgressions,
The Buddhas all fully rejoice,
Worship the Buddhas and their virtues,
Vow to attain the unsurpassed path.
The Buddhas of past, present and future,
Are foremost of all living beings,
With an ocean of virtuous qualities,
Take refuge and worship with joined palms.

寅朝禮懺：
敬禮 毗盧遮那佛！
敬禮盧捨那佛！
敬禮釋迦牟尼佛！
敬禮當來下生 彌勒尊佛！
敬禮東方一切諸佛！
敬禮南方一切諸佛！
敬禮西方一切諸佛！
敬禮北方一切諸佛！
敬禮上方一切諸佛！
敬禮下方一切諸佛！
敬禮過現未來一切諸佛！
敬禮舍利形像無量寶塔！
敬禮十二部尊經甚深法藏！
敬禮諸尊菩薩摩訶薩眾！
敬禮聲聞緣覺一切賢聖僧！
爲二十八天釋梵王等，
敬禮常住三寶！
爲諸龍神等，風雨順時，
敬禮常住三寶！
爲皇帝聖化無窮，
敬禮常住三寶！
爲太子諸王，福延萬葉，
敬禮常住三寶！
爲道場施主，六度圓滿，
敬禮常住三寶！

Third-Watch Worship and Repentance:
Respectfully worship Vairocana Buddha!

Respectfully worship Rocana Buddha!
Respectfully worship Śākyamuni Buddha!
Respectfully worship the future born Maitreya honoured Buddha!
Respectfully worship all the Buddhas in the east!
Respectfully worship all the Buddhas in the south!
Respectfully worship all the Buddhas in the west!
Respectfully worship all the Buddhas in the north!
Respectfully worship all the Buddhas in the zenith!
Respectfully worship all the Buddhas in the nadir!
Respectfully worship all the Buddhas of past, present and future!
Respectfully worship the immeasurable treasured *stūpa*s of *sarīra*, images and statues!
Respectfully worship the twelve-fold canon of *sūtra*s, the profound Dharma treasury!
Respectfully worship the honoured bodhisattva, *mahāsattva*s!
Respectfully worship all the holy and sagely *saṅghin*s, the disciples and *pratyeka-buddha*s!

For the sake of the twenty-eight gods, Śākras, *Brahmā* kings, and so forth,
respectfully worship the eternally abiding Three Jewels!
For the sake of the dragon spirits that the winds and rains be good and timely,
respectfully worship the eternally abiding Three Jewels!
For the sake of the emperors, that their holy teachings be boundless,
respectfully worship the eternally abiding Three Jewels!
For the sake of the crown prince and kings, that their blessings be extended 10,000 generations,
respectfully worship the eternally abiding Three Jewels!
For the sake of the patrons and donors of the altar, that their six perfections be complete,
respectfully worship the eternally abiding Three Jewels![394]

（下依北大 D180 補）
爲師僧父母及善知識 ，
敬禮常住三寶！
爲邊方無事，永息干戈，
敬禮常住三寶！（後殘）
爲四威儀中誤傷含識，
敬禮常住三寶！

394 Huang, *Dunhuang baozang*, 111: 289-91.

爲三途八難，受苦眾生，
願皆解脫，歸命禮懺念.
至心懺念：
普懺六根三業罪，願令除滅不復生.
勸請十方諸如來，留身久住濟含識.
隨喜稱贊諸善根，回向菩提證常樂.
願諸眾生入佛慧，生滅永寂證無餘.
懺念、勸請、隨喜、回向、發願已，
至心歸命禮三寶！
白眾等聽說，寅朝清淨偈：
欲求寂滅樂，當學沙門法，
衣食支身命，精粗隨眾等.
諸眾等，今日寅朝清淨，各記六念.
四禮奉報四恩，散周法界. 和南一切賢聖！
南無舍利形像此界他方無量寶塔！
南無十二尊經大藏十輪！
南無諸尊菩薩摩訶薩！
南無聲聞緣覺一切賢聖僧！
普爲四恩三有道場施主及法界眾生（後殘）

(Below is supplemented from Peking D 180.)

For the sake of teachers and monastics, mother and father, and spiritual mentors,[395]
respectfully worship the eternally abiding Three Jewels!
For the sake of peace at the borderlands, the end to all battle and war,
respectfully worship the eternally abiding Three Jewels!
For the sake of not accidentally harming sentient beings while in any physical posture,
respectfully worship the eternally abiding Three Jewels!

For the sake of living beings experiencing suffering in the three lower destinies and eight places of difficulty, may they all be liberated, and give thought to refuge, worship and repentance.

Give thought to heartfelt repentance:
Universally repent transgressions of the six faculties and three actions,
May they be eliminated and never occur again.

---

395 Added according to P. 3038.

Invite the Thus Come Ones of the ten direction,
To remain and abide long to save sentient beings.

Rejoice and praise all wholesome roots,
Dedicate them to *bodhi*, realization of eternal happiness.
May living beings enter into the buddhas' wisdom,
Forever pacifying life and death, realizing non-thought.

After the thought of repentance, invitation, rejoicing, dedication, and making vows,
sincerely take refuge in and worship the Three Jewels!

May the community listen to these words,
The pure *gāthā*s of the third watch:
Those who wish to seek the happiness of pacification,
should train in the Dharma of the *śramaṇa*s.
With fine and coarse robes and food,
to sustain the physical body of those of the community.

Today, at the third watch, the community is pure, and each should recall the six recollections.
The four forms of worship repay the four gratitudes, spread throughout the Dharma realm.
Prostrate to all the holy sages!

Namo immeasurable precious *stūpa*s of *sarīra*, images and statues in this and other worlds!
Namo twelve-fold canon of honoured *sūtra*s, the great treasury of ten wheels!
Namo honoured bodhisattva *mahāsattva*s!
Namo all the holy and sagely *saṃgha*, the disciples and *pratyekabuddha*s!
Universally for the sake of those of the four gratitudes and three forms of existence, the donors to the monastery, and the living beings of the Dharma realm! (Thereafter fragmented.)

## Appendix 2.2: 34 Monastics Affiliated with Yang Guang's Palace Chapels

| Monastic Name | Native Province | Jiangdu Huiri Temple | Riyan Monastery | Luoyang Huiri Temple | Destination | Category |
|---|---|---|---|---|---|---|
| Yancong 彥琮 | Zhaojun 趙郡 | | Daxingshan Monastery 大興善寺 →√ | | Luoyang Translation Bureau 洛陽翻譯館 | *Sūtra* translation 譯經 |
| Zhituo 智脫 | Jiangdu 江都 | √ | √ | √ | | Explanation of meaning 義解 |
| Hongzhe 洪哲 | Xiangyang 襄陽 | √ | | | | Explanation of meaning |
| Facheng 法澄 | Wujun 吳郡 | √ | √ | √ | | Explanation of meaning |
| Daozhuang 道莊 | Jianye 建業 | √ | √ | √ | | Explanation of meaning |
| Falun 法論 | Nanjun 南郡 | √ | √ | √ | | Explanation of meaning |
| Zhiju 智炬 | Wujun 吳郡 | Jianchu Monastery 建初寺 →√ | √ | | | Explanation of meaning |
| Jizang 吉藏 | Jinling 金陵 | √ | √ | | Chang'an Yanxing Monastery 長安延興寺 | Explanation of meaning |
| Bianyi 辯義 | Qinghe 清河 | | √ | | | Explanation of meaning |
| Mingshun 明舜 | Jianye 建業 | | √ | | | Explanation of meaning |
| Fakan 法侃 | Xingyang 滎陽 | | Jiangdu Anle Monastery 江都安樂寺 →√ | | Chang'an Daxingshan Monastery 長安大興善寺 | Explanation of meaning |
| Huiyun 慧頵 | Jianye 建業 | | Jiangdu Hualin Monastery 江都華林寺 →√ | | Chang'an Chongyi Monastery 長安崇義寺 | Explanation of meaning |

APPENDIX 2.2 34 Monastics Affiliated with Yang Guang's Palace Chapels (*cont.*)

| Monastic Name | Native Province | Jiangdu Huiri Temple | Riyan Monastery | Luoyang Huiri Temple | Destination | Category |
|---|---|---|---|---|---|---|
| Huijue 慧覺 | Danyang 丹陽 | Qixia Monastery 棲霞寺 →√ | | | | Explanation of meaning |
| Zhirun 智閏 | Wujun 吳郡 | | | √ | Chang'an Chanding Monastery 長安禪定寺 | Explanation of meaning |
| Daozong 道宗 | Laizhou 萊州 | | | √ | Chang'an Shengguang Monastery 長安勝光寺 | Explanation of meaning |
| Zhiqian 智騫 | | | | √ | | Explanation of meaning |
| Jingtuo 敬脫 | Jijun 汲郡 | | | √ | | Explanation of meaning |
| Bianxiang 辯相 | Yingzhou 瀛州 | | | √ | Chang'an Shengguang Monastery 長安勝光寺 | Explanation of meaning |
| Fahu 法護 | Zhaojun 趙郡 | | | √ | Luoyang Tiangong Monastery 洛陽天宮寺 | Explanation of meaning |
| Daoji 道基 | Henan 河南 | | | √ | Yizhou Fucheng Monastery 益州福成寺 | Explanation of meaning |
| Sanhui 三慧 | Loufan 婁煩 | | | √ | Linghua Monastery 靈化寺 | Explanation of meaning |
| Zhihui 智徽 | Zezhou 澤州 | | | Zezhou Qinghua Monastery 澤州清化寺 →√ | | Explanation of meaning |
| Zhikuan 志寬 | Puzhou 蒲州 | | | √ | Puzhou Renshou Monastery 蒲州仁壽寺 | Explanation of meaning |

APPENDIX 2.2 34 Monastics Affiliated with Yang Guang's Palace Chapels (*cont.*)

| Monastic Name | Native Province | Jiangdu Huiri Temple | Riyan Monastery | Luoyang Huiri Temple | Destination | Category |
|---|---|---|---|---|---|---|
| Huiyue 慧越 | Lingnan 嶺南 | √ | | | | Cultivation of *dhyāna* 習禪 |
| Huicheng 慧乘 | Xuzhou 徐州 | √ | | | Chang'an Shengguang Monastery 長安勝光寺 | Protection of Dharma 護法 |
| Fa'an 法安 | Anding 安定 | √ | | √ | Luoyang Baoyang Monastery 洛陽寶揚寺 | Miraculous responses 感通 |
| Faxian 法顯 | Yongzhou 雍州 | | Jingzhou Wang Monastery 京兆王寺 →√ | | Shamen Monastery 沙門寺 | Miraculous responses |
| Lishen 立身 | Jinling 金陵 | √ | | √ | | Worthy of various skills 雜科聲德 |
| Facheng 法稱 | Jiangnan 江南 | √ | | | Chang'an Dingshui Monastery 長安定水寺 | Worthy of various skills |
| Shanquan 善權 | Yangdu 揚都 | | Yangdu Baotian Monastery 揚都寶田寺 →√ | | | Worthy of various skills |
| Fayan 法琰 | Jinling 金陵 | | √ | | Xuanfa Monastery 玄法寺 | Worthy of various skills |
| Huichang 慧常 | Jingzhao 京兆 | | √ | | | Worthy of various skills |
| Zhiyi 智顗 | Yangdu 揚都 | | √ | | | Worthy of various skills |
| Zhiguo 智果 | Kuaiji 會稽 | | | √ | | Worthy of various skills |

## Appendix 2.3: Monastics Involved in the Construction of *Stūpa*s During the Renshou Era (601-604)[396]

| Province | Prefecture | Monastery | Source | Monastic distributing *śarīra* |
|---|---|---|---|---|
| Gansu 甘肅 | 1 Guazhou 瓜洲 | Chongjiao Monastery 崇教寺 | *Ex 1*, *Co 1* | Zhining 智凝, *Bio* 26 |
| | 2 Liangzhou 涼州 | | *Ex 2*, *Co 2* | |
| | 1 Kuozhou 廓州 | Fajiang Monastery 法講寺 | *Ex 1*, *Co 1* | |
| | 2 Lanzhou 蘭州 | | *Ex 2*, *Co 2* | |
| | 1 Qinzhou 秦州 | Jingnian Monastery 淨念寺 | *Ex 1*, *Co 1* | |
| | 2 Qinzhou 秦州 | Yongning Monastery 永寧寺 | *Ex 2*, *Co 2* | Zhijiao 智教, *Bio* 26 |
| | 1 Jingzhou 涇州 | Daxingguo Monastery 大興國寺 | *Ex 1*, *Co 1* | |
| Shaanxi 陜西 | 4 Longzhou 隴州 | Yaowang Monastery 藥王寺 | | Faxian 法顯, *Bio* 26 |
| | 1 Qizhou 岐州 | Fengquan Monastery 鳳泉寺 | *Ex 1*, *Co 1* | Tanqian 曇遷, *Bio* 18 |
| | 1 Yongzhou 雍州 | Xianyou Monastery 仙遊寺 | *Ex 1*, *Co 1* | Tongzhen 童真, *Bio* 12 |
| | 1 Chang'an 長安 | Daxingshan Monastery 大興善寺 | *Ex 1*, *Co 1* | |
| | 1 Huazhou 華州 | Sijue Monastery 思覺寺 | *Ex 1*, *Co 1* | Baoji 寶積, *Bio* 26 |
| | 1 Tongzhou 同州 | Daxingguo Monastery 大興國寺 | *Ex 1*, *Co 1* | Daomi 道密, *Bio* 26 |
| | 2 Liangzhou 梁州 | | *Ex 2*, *Co 2* | |
| | 1 Puzhou 蒲州 | Qiyan Monastery 棲岩寺 | *Ex 1*, *Co 1* | Sengtan 僧曇, *Bio* 10 |
| | 4 Jiangzhou 絳州 | Juecheng Monastery 覺成寺 | | Juelang 覺朗, *Bio* 21 |
| | 2 Jinzhou 晉州 | Fahou Monastery 法吼寺 | *Ex 2*, *Co 2* | Tansui 曇邃, *Bio* 26 |
| | 2 Cizhou 慈州 | Shiku Monastery 石窟寺 | *Ex 2*, *Co 2* | Mingfen 明芬, *Bio* 26 |

396 *Guang Hongming ji*, fasc. 17, record of construction of *stūpa*s on the 10th month of the 1st year of Renshou (abbreviated as "*Ex 1*") and record of construction of *stūpa*s on the 4th month of the 2nd year of Renshou (abbreviated as "*Ex 2*"); *Ji Shenzhou sanbao gantong lu*, fasc. 1, record of construction of *stūpa*s on the 10th month of the 1st year of Renshou (abbreviated as "*Co 1*") and record of construction of *stūpa*s on the 4th month of the 2nd year of Renshou (abbreviated as "*Co 2*"). At the same time, citing *Extended Biographies of Eminent Monks* for the distribution of *śarīra* by eminent monastics (1 refers to *stūpa*s that were constructed on the 10th month of the 1st year of Renshou; 2 refers to *stūpa*s that were constructed on the 4th month of the 2nd year of Renshou; 4 refers to *stūpa*s that were constructed on the 4th month of the 4th year of Renshou; *Extended Biographies of Eminent Monks* is abbreviated as "*Bio*"). See Yamazaki, *Shina chūsei bukkyō*, 333-36.

APPENDIX 2.3 Monastics Involved in the Construction (*cont.*)

| Province | Prefecture | Monastery | Source | Monastic distributing *śarīra* |
|---|---|---|---|---|
| Shanxi 山西 | 1 Bingzhou 並州 | Wuliangshou Monastery 無量壽寺 | *Ex 1*, *Co 1* | Yancong 彥琮, *Bio* 2 |
| | 4 Zezhou 澤州 | Jingjing Monastery 景淨寺 | | Lingcan 靈璨, *Bio* 10 |
| | 2 Luzhou 潞州 | Fanjing Monastery 梵淨寺 | *Ex 2*, *Co 2* | Daoduan 道端, *Bio* 26 |
| | 4 Hanzhou 韓州 | Xiuji Monastery 修寂寺 | | Fazhou 法周, *Bio* 26 |
| | 4 Liaozhou 遼州 | Xiasheng Monastery 下生寺 | | Fazong 法總, *Bio* 10 |
| Hebei 河北 | 2 Mingzhou 洺州 | | *Ex 2*, *Co 2* | |
| | 4 Xingzhou 邢州 | Fan'ai Monastery 泛愛寺 | | Baoxi 寶襲, *Bio* 12 |
| | 2 Zhaozhou 趙州 | Wuji Monastery 無際寺 | *Ex 2*, *Co 2* | Xuanjing 玄鏡, *Bio* 26 |
| | 4 Lianzhou 廉州 | Huacheng Monastery 化城寺 | | Yuanchao 圓超, *Bio* 26 |
| | 2 Hengzhou 恆州 | Nengzang Monastery 能藏寺 | *Ex 2*, *Co 2* | Lingda 靈達, *Bio* 26 |
| | 1 Dingzhou 定州 | Hengyue Monastery 恆嶽寺 | *Ex 1*, *Co 1* | Huihai 慧海, *Bio* 10 |
| | 2 Youzhou 幽州 | Hongye Monastery 弘業寺 | *Ex 2*, *Co 2* | Baoyan 寶岩, *Bio* 26 |
| | 2 Beizhou 貝州 | Baorong Monastery 寶融寺 | *Ex 2*, *Co 2* | Bianyi 辯義, *Bio* 26 |
| | 2 Weizhou 魏州 | Kaijue Monastery 開覺寺 | *Ex 2*, *Co 2* | Zhikui 智揆, *Bio* 26 |
| | 2 Jizhou 冀州 | Jueguan Monastery 覺觀寺 | *Ex 2*, *Co 2* | Sengfan 僧範, *Bio* 26 |
| | 2 Yinzhou 瀛洲 | Hongbo Monastery 弘博寺 | *Ex 2*, *Co 2* | Huiqian 慧遷, *Bio* 12 |
| | 2 Guanzhou 觀州 | Ta Monastery 塔寺 | *Ex 2*, *Co 2* | Huizang 慧藏, *Bio* 26 |
| | 2 Cangzhou 滄州 | | *Ex 2*, *Co 2* | Senggai 僧蓋, *Bio* 26 |
| Henan 河南 | 2 Shaanzhou 陝州 | Daxingguo Monastery 大興善寺 | *Ex 2*, *Co 2* | Falang 法朗, *Bio* 26 |
| | 2 Huaizhou 懷州 | Changshou Monastery 長壽寺 | *Ex 2*, *Co 2* | Lingcan 靈璨, *Bio* 10, Lingrun 靈潤, *Bio* 15 |
| | 4 Xiongzhou 熊州 | Shishan Monastery 十善寺 | | Huihai 慧海, *Bio* 11 |
| | 2 Luozhou 洛州 | Hanwang Monastery 漢王寺 | *Ex 2*, *Co 2* | Linggan 靈乾, *Bio* 12 |
| | 1 Songzhou 嵩州 | Songyue Monastery 嵩嶽寺 (Xianju Monastery 閑居寺) | *Ex 1*, *Co 1* | Baoxi 寶襲, *Bio* 12 |
| | 1 Ruzhou 汝州 | Xingshi Monastery 興世寺 | *Ex 1*, *Co 1* | Fayan 法彥, *Bio* 10 |
| | 4 Yinzhou 殷州 | Zhidu Monastery 智度寺 | | Sengtan 僧曇, *Bio* 10 |
| | 2 Weizhou 衛州 | Fuju Monastery 福聚寺 | *Ex 2*, *Co 2* | Hongzun 洪遵, *Bio* 21 |

APPENDIX 2.3 Monastics Involved in the Construction (*cont.*)

| Province | Prefecture | Monastery | Source | Monastic distributing *śarīra* |
|---|---|---|---|---|
| | 4 Huazhou 滑州 | Xiude Monastery 修德寺 | | Sengcan 僧粲, *Bio* 9 |
| | 2 Lizhou 黎州 | | *Ex 2*, *Co 2* | Fakan 法侃, *Bio* 11 |
| | 1 Xiangzhou 相州 | Daci Monastery 大慈寺 | *Ex 1*, *Co 1* | |
| | 1 Zhengzhou 鄭州 | Dingjue Monastery 定覺寺 | *Ex 1*, *Co 1* | |
| | 2 Zhengzhou 鄭州 | | *Ex 2*, *Co 2* | |
| | 4 Zhengzhou 鄭州 | Jin'an Monastery 晉安寺 | | Daomi 道密, *Bio* 26 |
| | 2 Xuzhou 許州 | Bianxing Monastery 辨行寺 | *Ex 2*, *Co 2* | Daocan 道璨, *Bio* 26 |
| | 2 Bianzhou 汴州 | | *Ex 2*, *Co 2* | Jingning 靜凝, *Bio* 26 |
| | 2 Songzhou 宋州 | Jinliang Monastery 津梁寺 | *Ex 2*, *Co 2* | Sengshun 僧順, *Bio* 26 |
| | 2 Shenzhou 瀋州 | | *Co 2* | |
| | 2 Yuzhou 豫州 | | *Ex 2*, *Co 2* | Jingduan 靜端, *Bio* 18 |
| | 2 Dengzhou 鄧州 | Daxingguo Monastery 大興國寺 | *Ex 2*, *Co 2* | Baoru 寶儒, *Bio* 10 |
| | 2 Xianzhou 顯州 | | *Ex 2*, *Co 2* | |
| Shandong 山東 | 2 Caozhou 曹州 | Fayuan Monastery 法元寺 | *Ex 2*, *Co 2* | Fakai 法揩, *Bio* 26 |
| | 2 Maozhou 毛州 | Hufa Monastery 護法寺 | *Ex 2*, *Co 2* | Sengting 僧聽, *Bio* 26 |
| | 4 Bozhou 博州 | Longsheng Monastery 隆聖寺 | | Fazun 法遵, *Bio* 21 |
| | 2 Dezhou 德州 | Huitong Monastery 會通寺 | *Ex 2*, *Co 2* | Daogui 道貴, *Bio* 26 |
| | 2 Jizhou 濟州 | Chongfan Monastery 崇梵寺 | *Ex 2*, *Co 2* | Mingyu 明馭, *Bio* 26 |
| | 4 Shenzhou 莘州 | | | Zhiyin 智隱, *Bio* 26 |
| | 1 Taizhou 泰州 | Daiyue Monastery | *Ex 1*, *Co 1* | Huichong 慧重, *Bio* 26, Sengtan 僧曇, *Bio* 10 |
| | 2 Qizhou 齊州 | Taishan Shengtong Monastery 泰山神通寺 (Langgong Monastery 朗公寺) | *Ex 2*, *Co 2* | Fazan 法瓚, *Bio* 10 |
| | 2 Mouzhou 牟州 | Jushenshan Monastery 巨神山寺 | *Ex 1*, *Co 1* | Huichang 慧暢, *Bio* 10 |
| | 2 Gunzhou 袞州 | Pule Monastery 普樂寺 | *Ex 2*, *Co 2* | Faxing 法性, *Bio* 26 |
| | 4 Yizhou 沂州 | Shanying Monastery 善應寺 | | Fayan 法彥, *Bio* 10 |

APPENDIX 2.3 Monastics Involved in the Construction (*cont.*)

| Province | Prefecture | Monastery | Source | Monastic distributing *śarīra* |
|---|---|---|---|---|
| | 2 Juzhou 莒州 | Dingling Monastery 定林寺 | *Ex 2, Co 2* | Tan'guan 曇觀, *Bio* 10 |
| | 4 Mizhou 密州 | Maosheng Monastery 茂勝寺 | | Sengshi 僧世, *Bio* 26 |
| | 2 Laizhou 萊州 | Hongzang Monastery 弘藏寺 | *Ex 2, Co 2* | Sengshi 僧世, *Bio* 26 |
| | 1 Qingzhou 青州 | Shengfu Monastery 勝福寺 | *Ex 1, Co 1* | Zhineng 智能, *Bio* 26 |
| Hubei 湖北 | 1 Xiangzhou 襄州 | Shangfenglin Monastery 上鳳林寺 | *Ex 1, Co 1* | Mingdan 明誕, *Bio* 26 |
| | 4 Yingzhou 郢州 | Baoxiang Monastery 寶香寺 | | Zhifan 智梵, *Bio* 11 |
| | 1 Suizhou 隨州 | Zhimen Monastery 智門寺 | *Ex 1, Co 1* | Fazong 法總, *Bio* 10 |
| | 2 Anzhou 安州 | Jingzang Monastery 景藏寺 | *Ex 2, Co 2* | Jingye 淨業, *Bio* 12 |
| | 4 Fuzhou 復州 | Fangle Monastery 方樂寺 | | Yancong 彥琮, *Bio* 2 |
| | 4 Qizhou 蘄州 | Futian Monastery 福田寺 | | Mingshun 明舜, *Bio* 11 |
| | 2 Jingzhou 荊州 | Kaiyi Monastery 開義寺 | *Ex 2, Co 2* | Yancong 彥琮, *Bio* 2 |
| | 2 Jingzhou 荊州 | Daxingguo Monastery 大興國寺 | *Ex 2, Co 2* | Huizui 慧最, *Bio* 10 |
| Anhui 安徽 | 2 Shouzhou 壽州 | | *Ex 2, Co 2* | |
| | 4 Xizhou 熙州 | Huan'gu Monastery 環谷寺 | | Tanjie 曇瑎, *Bio* 26 |
| | 1 Haozhou 亳州 | Kaiji Monastery 開寂寺 | *Ex 1, Co 1* | Tanliang 曇良, *Bio* 26 |
| | 4 Luzhou 廬州 | Liangjing Monastery 梁靜寺 | | Bianyi 辯義, *Bio* 11 |
| | 4 Yizhou 宜州 | Yong'an Monastery 永安寺 | | Fakan 法侃, *Bio* 11 |
| Hunan 湖南 | 1 Hengzhou 衡州 | Hengyue Monastery 衡嶽寺 | *Ex 1, Co 1* | Jingbian 淨辯, *Bio* 26 |
| | 2 Yingzhou 營州 | Fanchuang Monastery 梵幢寺 | *Ex 2, Co 2* | Bao'an 寶安, *Bio* 26 |
| | 2 Tanzhou 潭州 | Lushan Monastery 麓山寺 | *Ex 2, Co 2* | Jingyuan 淨願, *Bio* 10 |
| Jiangxi 江西 | 2 Jiangzhou 江州 | Lushan Donglin Monastery 廬山東林寺 | *Ex 2, Co 2* | Huizang 慧藏, Fashun 法順, *Bio* 26 |
| | 2 Hongzhou 洪州 | | *Ex 2, Co 2* | Baoxian 寶憲, *Bio* 26 |
| | 4 Jizhou 吉州 | Fameng Monastery 發蒙寺 | | Huizui 慧最, *Bio* 10 |
| | 1 Jiangzhou 蔣州 | Qixia Monastery 棲霞寺 | *Ex 1, Co 1* | Mingcan 明璨, *Bio* 26 |
| | 2 Xuzhou 徐州 | Liujiang Monastery 流講寺 | *Ex 2, Co 2* | Bianji 辯寂, *Bio* 26 |

APPENDIX 2.3 Monastics Involved in the Construction (*cont.*)

| Province | Prefecture | Monastery | Source | Monastic distributing *śarīra* |
|---|---|---|---|---|
| Jiangsu 江蘇 | 2 Chuzhou 楚州 | | *Ex* 2, *Co* 2 | Daosheng 道生, *Bio* 26 |
| | 4 Haizhou 海州 | Anhe Monastery 安和寺 | | Huiqian 慧遷, *Bio* 12 |
| | 1 Suzhou 蘇州 | Huqiushan Monastery 虎丘山寺 | *Ex* 1, *Co* 1 | Daosong 道嵩, *Bio* 26 |
| | 1 Yangzhou 揚州 | Xi Monastery 西寺 | *Ex* 1, *Co* 1 | |
| Zhejiang 浙江 | 2 Hangzhou 杭州 | Tianzhu Monastery 天竺寺 | *Ex* 2, *Co* 2 | Huidan 慧誕, *Bio* 26 |
| | 1 Yuezhou 越州 | Dayu Monastery 大禹寺 | *Ex* 1, *Co* 1 | Bianxiang 辯相, *Bio* 12 |
| Guangxi 廣西 | 1 Guizhou 桂州 | Yuanhua Monastery 緣化寺 | *Ex* 1, *Co* 1 | Daoyan 道顏, *Bio* 26 |
| Guangdong 廣東 | 1 Guangzhou 廣州 | Guoshi Monastery 果實寺 | *Ex* 1, *Co* 1 | Senglang 僧朗, *Bio* 10 |
| | 2 Xunzhou 循州 | Daochangta Monastery 道場塔寺 | *Ex* 2, *Co* 2 | Daoguang 道光, *Bio* 26 |
| Fujian 福建 | 2 Quanzhou 泉州 | | *Ex* 2, *Co* 2 | |
| Annan 安南 | 2 Jiaozhou 交州 | Chanzhong Monastery 禪眾寺 | *Ex* 1, *Co* 1 | |
| Sichuan 四川 | 2 Lizhou 利州 | | *Ex* 2, *Co* 2 | |
| | 4 Longzhou 隆州 | Chanji Monastery 禪寂寺 | | Huichong 慧重, *Bio* 26 |
| | 1 Yizhou 益州 | Faju Monastery 法聚寺 | *Ex* 1, *Co* 1 | Zhiyin 智隱, *Bio* 26 |
| | 4 Zhezhou 浙州 | Faxiang Monastery 法相寺 | | Senggai 僧蓋, *Bio* 26 |
| | 1 Zizhou 梓州 | Hualin Monastery 華林寺 | *Co* 1 | Shanzhou 善胄, *Bio* 12 |
| | 2 Xinzhou 信州 | | *Ex* 2, *Co* 2 | |

## Appendix 2.4: A Comparison of Descriptions of the *Sūtra* Lecturing by Ennin and Other Sources

| ***Chŏk san wŏn kang kyŏng ŭi sik* 赤山院講經儀式 (Jeoksan Court *Sūtra* Lecture Ritual)** | ***Sin la il il kang ŭi sik* 新羅一日講儀式 (Silla One Day Lecture Ritual)** | ***Sin la song kyŏng ŭi sik* 新羅誦經儀式 (Silla *Sūtra* Chanting Ritual)** | **P. 3849 *Sujiang yishi* 俗講儀式 (Ritual for Public Lectures)** |
| --- | --- | --- | --- |
| At dawn, the *sūtra* lecture bell is struck. The various warning bell signals having been struck, for the long service, the community ascends to the hall, and then there is the bell to settle the community. The lecturer ascends to the hall, and reaching the high throne, the entire community intones the Buddha's name in unison. The tune is one from Silla, which is not the same as that of the Tang. When the lecturer has ascended to the throne the chanting of the Buddha's name then stops. Then, a junior monastic does liturgical chanting, another maintains the Tang tune, that is, the line of the *gāthā* "How does this *sūtra*," and so forth. Reaching the sentence "May the Buddha reveal the subtle meaning," the community in unison chants "fragrance of morality, fragrance of meditation, fragrance of liberation," and so forth. Having sung the liturgical chanting, the lecturer chants the title of the *sūtra*. There are three parts that the *sūtra* title is divided into. Having explained the title, the rector comes forth, and before the high throne reads the reasons for requesting the assembly, as well as the individual names of the donors, and the items which have been donated. This request being completed, he then passes the form over to the lecturer. The lecturer holds the fly-whisk, and gives the names of the donors one by one, alone making vows. Having made the vows, the questioner raises up questions. When raising | At dawn, the *sūtra* lecture bell is struck. After the long strike, the lecturer and reciter both enter the hall. The community first enters in lines and sits, then the lecturer and reciter join and enter the hall. The community in unison recites the Buddha's name, drawing it long. The lecturer ascends to the north seat, and the reciter ascends to the south seat. The praise of the Buddha ends. Then, a junior monastic does the liturgical chanting, "How does this *sūtra*," the lines of the *gāthā*. After the liturgical chanting, the south seat chants the title of the *sūtra*, that is, chanting the *sūtra* drawing it out long, with the tune taking many twists and turns. During the chanting of the *sūtra*, the community strews flowers three times, and a verse sung each time. Having chanted the *sūtra*, then the title is chanted in the short | The Great Tang calls it "chanting the *sūtra*": The bell is struck to settle the community. A junior monastic strikes it and chants "Everyone venerate and worship the eternally abiding Three Jewels." Then, a monastic chants liturgical style the two lines of the *gāthā* "Thus Come One Body of Marvelous Form," with the tune and rhyme the same as that of the Tang. During the liturgical chanting, one person holds an incense tray, and walks around in front of the community's seats, walking quickly then resting, and the community in unison chants the title "*Mahāprajñā[pāramitā]*" several dozen times. One venerable describes the reasons for the chanting of the *sūtra*, and the community together recites the *sūtra*, at times either walking with the *sūtra* text or at times not walking with the *sūtra* text. Having recited the *sūtra*, the guides alone chant "Take refuge in the Buddha, take refuge in the Dharma, take refuge in the *Saṃgha*," then intone the names of the *bodhisattvas*. The guide chants: "Namo twelve great vows…," and the community chants: | For the public lecture, first is liturgical chanting. Next is chanting the names of the *bodhisattvas* in two utterances, and the passage to settle into their seats. Linking with this [they chant] the *Wenshi jing* 溫室經 (*Sūtra* on the Saunas and Baths of the *Saṃgha*), and the venerable chants an explanation of the *sūtra* title. They recite the Buddha's name once, then explain each and every character in the *sūtra* title, then state the basic text of the *sūtra*. They then teach the ten *pāramitās*, and so forth, then recite the praise of the Buddha. Next they make vows, then again recite the Buddha's name for a time. Next is the dedication vows, then everyone leaves, and so forth. After this the *Weimojie jing* is begun. Lecturing the *Weimojie* [*jing*], first |

APPENDIX 2.4 A Comparison of Descriptions of the *Sūtra* (*cont.*)

| ***Chŏk san wŏn kang kyŏng ŭi sik* 赤山院講經儀式 (Jeoksan Court *Sūtra* Lecture Ritual)** | ***Sin la il il kang ŭi sik* 新羅一日講儀式 (Silla One Day Lecture Ritual)** | ***Sin la song kyŏng ŭi sik* 新羅誦經儀式 (Silla *Sūtra* Chanting Ritual)** | **P. 3849 *Sujiang yishi* 俗講儀式 (Ritual for Public Lectures)** |
|---|---|---|---|
| questions, the lecturer raises the fly-whisk, and listens to the words of the question. Having raised the questions, he then inclines the fly-whisk, then returns to raise it again, thanking the questioner and beginning to answer. Each question is raised by topic and then answered in turn by topic, as it is in this country, but the ritual for the challenge is slightly different. After inclining the hand three times, they explain and clarify, then suddenly explain the challenge, with a booming voice. Finishing, there is silence. The lecturer then receives the challenge, and only answers without refuting the challenge. Discussing the meaning, he enters into chanting the *sūtra*. Having lectured, the community praises it in unison, and the words of praise include the phrases of thededication. The lecturer descends from the seat, and a monastic chants the *gāthā* on "Dwelling in the world is like empty space." The tune is similar to that of this country. The lecturer rises to the worship dais, and a monastic chants the three prostrations. With the lecturer and community in the same tune, he leaves the hall and returns to his quarters. There is also a person who is the repeat lecturer. They sit on a seat below and to the south of the high throne, and talk about the text that the lecturer lectured on the previous day, up to the sentence "as the implied meaning." After the lecturer explains the meaning of the text, the repeat lecturer also reads it out. After finishing reading out the | form. The lecturer begins with the *sūtra* title, which is distinguished into three parts, to describe the main meaning of the *sūtra*. Finishing the explanation of the *sūtra* title, the rector reads out the reasons for the event. This includes the principle of impermanence, the contributions of the deceased, and the dates of the deceased. | "Medicine Master *Vaidūrya* Light Buddha." The guide chants: "Namo Medicine Master…," and the community chants: "*Vaidūrya* Light Buddha." The guide chants: "Namo Great Compassionate…," and the community chants: "Avalokiteśvāra Bodhisattva." The rest of the names are also done in this manner. Having worshipped the Buddha, the guides alone finish the vows with a dedication, which is somewhat lengthy. After the dedication, the guide chants: "Aspire," and the community chants: "Aspire." Next, the guide having finished chanting the vows of aspiration, makes prostrations to the Three Jewels. Then, the donors hold aloft the gifts and sit, the guides bestow *mantra* vows, and everyone leaves. | is liturgical chanting, next is reciting the name of Avalokiteśvāra Bodhisattva is three or two utterances. Then the passage to settle the audience on their seats. Next is linking to chanting the text of the *sūtra*. The chanting venerable himself reads the title of the *sūtra*, then states the opening praises, then the adornment, then recites the Buddha's name once or two. The venerables analyse the text of the *sūtra* into three parts, recite the Buddha's name once or twice, then state each and every character of the title of the *sūtra*. Next they enter the teaching of the *sūtra* through analogies. Then they read the praise of chanting the Buddha's name. Next the names of the donors and making vows. Then the dedication vows, and everyone leaves. |

APPENDIX 2.4 A Comparison of Descriptions of the *Sūtra* (*cont.*)

| *Chŏk san wŏn kang kyŏng ŭi sik* 赤山院講經儀式 (Jeoksan Court *Sūtra* Lecture Ritual) | *Sin la il il kang ŭi sik* 新羅一日講儀式 (Silla One Day Lecture Ritual) | *Sin la song kyŏng ŭi sik* 新羅誦經儀式 (Silla *Sūtra* Chanting Ritual) | P. 3849 *Sujiang yish* 俗講儀式 (Ritual for Public Lectures) |
|---|---|---|---|
| lectured text from the day before, the reciter immediately reads out the next textual passage. It is done like this each day. | | | |
| 辰時，打講經鐘，打驚眾鐘訖，良久之會，大眾上堂，方定眾鐘. 講師上堂，登高座間，大眾同音稱嘆佛名，音曲一依新羅，不似唐音. 講師登座訖，稱佛名便停. 時有下座一僧作梵，一據唐音，即「云何於此經」等一行偈矣. 至「願佛開微密」句，大眾同音唱云「戒香、定香、解脫香」等. 頌梵唄訖，講師唱經題目，便開題分別三門. 釋題目訖，維那師出來，於高座前讀申會興之由，及施主別名，所施物色申訖，便以其狀轉與講師. 講師把麈尾，一一申舉施主名，獨自誓願，誓願訖，論義者論端舉問. 舉問之間，講師舉麈尾，聞問者語. 舉問了，便傾麈尾，即還舉之，謝問便答. 貼問貼答，與本國同，但難儀式稍別. 側手三下後，申解白前，卒爾指申難，聲如大嗔人，盡音呼諍. 講師蒙難，但答不返難. 論義了，入文讀經. 講訖，大眾同音長音贊嘆，贊嘆語中有回向詞. 講師下座，一僧唱「處世界如虛空」偈，音勢頗似本國. 講師升禮盤，一僧唱三禮了，講師大眾同音，出堂歸房. 更有覆（同「復」）講師一人，在高座南下座，便談講師昨所講文，至「如含義」句. 講師牒文釋義了，覆講亦讀. 讀盡昨所講文了，讀師即讀次文，每日如斯. | 辰時打鐘，長打擬了，講師、都講二人入堂. 大眾先入列坐，講師、讀師入堂之會，大眾同音稱嘆佛名長引. 其講師登北座，都講登南座了，贊佛便止. 時有下座一僧作梵，「云何於此經」等一行偈也. 作梵了，南座唱經題目，所謂唱經長引，音多有屈曲. 唱經之會，大眾三遍散花；每散花時，各有所頌. 唱經了，更短音唱題目. 講師開經目，三門分別，述經大意. 釋經題目竟，有維那師披讀申事興所由. 其狀中具載無常道理、亡者功能、亡逝日數. | 大唐喚作「念經」：打鐘定眾了，下座一僧起打揰，唱「一切恭敬禮常住三寶」. 次一僧作梵，「如來妙色身」等兩行偈，音韻共唐一般. 作梵之會，一人擎香盆，歷行眾座之前，急行行便休，大眾同音誦摩訶般若題數十遍也. 有一師，陳申誦經來由了，大眾同音誦經，或時行經本，或時不行經本. 念經了，導師獨唱「歸依佛、歸依法、歸依僧」，次稱佛菩薩號. 導師唱云：「南無十二大願」，大眾云「藥師瑠璃光佛」. 導師云：「南無藥師也」，大眾同音云：「瑠璃光佛」. 導師云：「南無大慈悲也」，大眾同音云：「觀世音菩薩」. 餘皆如是. 禮佛了，導師獨結願回向，回向稍長. 回向之後，導師云：「發心」，大眾同音亦云：「發心」. 次導師唱發願已竟，頂禮三寶. 次施主擎施物坐，導師與咒願，便散去. | 夫為俗講，先作梵了；次念菩薩兩聲，說押座了；素舊（唱）《溫室經》，法師唱釋經題了，念佛一聲，便一一說其經題字了，便說經本文了；便說十波羅密等了，便念念佛贊了；便發願了，便又念佛一會；便回[向]發願取散云云.<br>已後便開《維摩經》. 講維摩，先作梵，次念觀世音菩薩三兩聲；便說押座了；便素唱經文了；唱日法師自說經題了，便說開贊了，便莊嚴了，便念佛一兩聲了，法師科三分經文了，念佛一兩聲，便一一說其經題名字了，便入經說緣喻了，便說念佛贊了，便施主各發願了，便回向發願取散. |

CHAPTER 3

# Buddhist Faith and Activities in the Song and Yuan Dynasties (960–1368)

It was through processes of maturation and harmonization during the late Tang and Five Dynasties periods that Buddhism in the Song and Yuan periods emerged with a new face and form. In particular, the emergence and development of Chan Buddhism in the regions south of the Yangzi River facilitated the popularization and socialisation of Buddhism itself. As Buddhist repentance practices, Pure Land faith, and charitable activities flourished, Song-Yuan Buddhism and Chinese society established a deeper relationship.

## 1 Buddhist Faith and Rituals in the Song and Yuan Periods

Buddhism in the Song dynasty was to a large extent oriented toward practice, with Chan and Pure Land traditions by far the most widespread. At the same time, following the reacquisition of important scriptures from Korea and intensive study of doctrine, there appeared eminent Buddhist figures, known for their lofty practice, such as Zhili 知禮 (960–1028), Zunshi 遵式 (964–1032), Zhiyuan 智圓 (1005–1062) and Renyue 仁嶽 (a.k.a. Jingjue Renyue 淨覺仁嶽, 992–1064). Tiantai Buddhism in the Song dynasty was thus able to be revived. The tradition was influenced by the flourishing of Pure Land doctrine and the ideas of practicing repentance as a means of achieving rebirth in the Pure Land. It was also under the impact of the activities of Zhili, who, aiming for the restoration of Tiantai, particularly emphasized the practice of analytical meditation in addition to spreading doctrines. Moreover, the tradition was particularly in compliance with what Zhiyi 智顗 (538–597) established: the concept of eliminating past karmic transgressions and realizing *samādhi* by means of practicing repentance ceremonies. Consequently, repentance practices prevailed widely among Tiantai members during the Song Dynasty, while repentance ritual procedures different from those of the Sui-Tang period were produced.[1] The emphasis on the practice of repentance ceremonies by Tiantai in the Song dynasty had a major impact on later Buddhism in the Ming and

1 Shi, *Chanfa*, 284–85.

 | DOI:10.1163/9789004431775_005

FIGURE 25 Painted wood-carved Bodhisattva statue, dated to the Northern Song (960-1127) (The Metropolitan Museum of Art, the United States).

Qing periods. The impact was also seen in the Republic period when the practices combining *sūtra* recitation and repentance rituals were quite popular.

During the Song dynasty, the majority of monks laid equal emphasis on lecturing and repentance. Zhili authored the *Xiuchan yaozhi* 修懺要旨 (Essentials on Practicing Repentance). Zunshi was called the "Ciyun chanzhu" 慈雲懺主 (Repentance Master of the Ciyun) and the "Tianzhu chanzhu" 天竺懺主 (Tianzhu Repentance Master). The Song dynasty was a time when the practice of repentance flourished. If we take a look at the extant Buddhist repentance rituals from the Song dynasty, Zhili's works include the *Dabei chan* 大悲懺 (Great Compassion Repentance), *Jin'guangming zuisheng chanyi* 金光明最勝懺儀 (Supreme Repentance Ritual of Golden Light) and *Li Fahuajing yishi* 禮法華經儀式 (Ceremony of Venerating the *Lotus Sūtra*). Zunshi's works include the *Jin'guangming chan buzhu yi* 金光明懺補助儀 (Supplementary Ritual for the *Golden Light* Repentance), *Qing Guanyin chan* 請觀音懺 (Repentance of Inviting Avalokiteśvara), *Chishengguang daochang niansong yi* 熾盛光道場念誦儀 (Recitation Ritual for the Site of *Tejaprabhā*), *Wangsheng jingtu chanyuan yi* 往生淨土懺願儀 (Ritual of Repentance and Aspirations for Rebirth in the Pure Land), *Xiao jingtu chan* 小淨土懺 (Short Pure Land Repentance), and "Zhizhe Dashi zhaiji lizan wen" 智者大師齋忌禮贊文 (Veneration Verses on the Feast for Zhiyi's Death Anniversary). Zhiyuan, Renyue and Yunkan 允堪 (1005–1062) together produced the "Nanshan zushi lizan wen" 南山祖師禮贊文 (Veneration Verses of the Nanshan Patriarch). Renyue also produced the "Shijia jiangsheng lizan wen" 釋迦降生禮贊文 (Veneration Verses for Śākyamuni's Birth) and "Shijia niepan lizan wen" 釋迦涅槃禮贊文 (Veneration Verses for Śākyamuni's *Nirvāṇa*). Zhipan's 志磐 (of Southern Song) work includes the *Shuilu yigui* 水陸儀軌 (Water and Land Ritual Procedure). Zhigong's 智肱 (d.u.) work includes the "Huayan Qingliang Guoshi lizan wen" 華嚴清涼國師禮贊文 (Veneration Verses for the Qingliang National Teacher of Huayan). Jingyuan's 淨源 (1011–1088) works include two versions of the *Huayan Puxian xingyuan yi* 華嚴普賢行願儀 (Ritual for Avataṃsaka Samantabhadra's Practices and Vows), the *Yuanjue jing daochang lüeben xiuzheng yi* 圓覺經道場略本修證儀 (Abbreviated Ritual for the Realisation in the Altar of the *Sūtra* of Perfect Awakening), and the *Shoulengyan tanchang xiuzheng yi* 首楞嚴壇場修證儀 (Ritual of Practice and Realisation for the *Śūraṃgama* Altar). There were abundant materials of various types, extending to Tiantai, Huayan, Pure Land, and the *Vinaya*.

### 1.1 *The Creation and Practice of Tiantai Repentance Rituals in the Song Dynasty*

Ciyun Zunshi, as a practitioner of Tiantai repentance rituals in the Song Dynasty, might not have been as successful in doctrinal studies as Zhili, but made a great contribution in terms of the practice of repentance rituals. Zhiyi formulated four repentance rituals, but as a result of the Huichang persecution in 845, and the disorder of the late Tang and Five Dynasties period, the literature related to Tiantai repentance was largely lost. That which did survive suffered scribal errors and tampering. Besides, there were new requirements in terms of practice in the new time period. Therefore, it was necessary to formulate new repentance practices. In addition, repentance rituals were considered important Buddhist practices that benefited oneself and others. It was necessary for Tiantai scholars to promote them.

#### 1.1.1 The Organization and Formulation of Repentance Rituals

Zunshi perfected Tiantai repentance rituals by organizing and revising the original rituals. He inherited and also reinterpreted the tradition. A body of literature of repentance rituals could once again enjoy new light following the return of Tiantai literature during the Northern Song period. The organization and revision of such literature became an important task. Many of the extant documents were brought together by figures such as Zunshi.

As for the history of Tiantai texts in the early Song being returned to China, there are two theories which believe they were brought back from either Korea or Japan.[2] However, we know that the *Fangdeng sanmei xingfa* 方等三昧行法 (*Vaipulyas-samādhi* Practice) was brought by the Japanese monk Jakushō 寂照 (964–1034) when he visited Song China, the account of which is given by Zunshi in a preface.[3] The *Fangdeng sanmei xingfa* states the following:

> The documents of the teachings of our monasteries were often spread to foreign countries under the Tang. Some are still recorded in the text catalogues, but those texts are not to be found. The scholars considered and felt [that the texts] are too remote on the other side of the sea. The *Fangdeng sanmei xingfa* was carried by Japanese monks such as Jakushō in year six of Xianping (1003) in the Imperial Song. … In the present time, although the altars have grown to vast and lofty proportions, the practices are carried out in a half-arbitrary fashion, while the regulations are entirely manufactured. … Though it is said that too many images are poor, [the practice] must agree with conventions of expressing the Dharma. The fear is that it does not eliminate old karma, but rather it produces new afflictions, just like dyeing clothing: the cloth gets coloured

2 Shen, "Tiantai jiaoji", 187–205.

3 Japanese literature records that Zunshi once wrote a "postscript" (*houxu* 後序). It is not found in the *Taishō* canon. See Kimiya, "Jiaotong shi", 164.

> while made filthy. Truly, how lamentable it is! Still yet, among the six chapters of this practice, the latter two were not copied. For the purposes of practice and [precepts], they employed [elements of the] [*Guoqing*] *bailu* [國清] 百錄 (Hundred Records of Guoqing Monastery, *T* 1934), and [*Mohe*] *zhiguan* [摩訶] 止觀 (Greater Teaching on Calm and Insight, *T* 1911). The [ceremonies] for receiving precepts were based on these scriptures. From the extant chapters and table of contents [of the *Fangdeng sanmei xingfa*], we can know that the Dharma has both its initiation and fulfillment.[4]

There are three versions of the *Fangdeng sanmei chan* 方等三昧懺 (*Vaipulyas-samādhi* Repentance). First, the Half-Walking-Half-Sitting *Vaipulyas-samādhi* (*fangdeng sanmei* 方等三昧) from the *Mohe zhiguan*. Second, the *Vaipulyas-samādhi* included in the *Guoqing bailu*. Third, a separately transmitted *Fangdeng sanmei xingfa*. The former two are relatively identical in terms of their ritual forms and thought.[5] Although we cannot securely determine that the *Fangdeng sanmei xingfa* is a work of Zhiyi and its transmission history is unclear, it is still thought to be a work of Zhiyi in light of its concepts of "discerning virtuous and evil characteristics" (*jian shan'e xiang* 見善惡相), "fulfilment of six conditions" (*ju liuyuan* 具六緣) and "harmonization" (*tiaoshi* 調適), as well as its interpretation of repentance all bearing resemblance to material in the *Shi chan boluomi cidi famen* 釋禪波羅蜜次第法門 (Explanation of the Gradual Method of the Perfection of *Dhyāna*, also called *Cidi chanmen* 次第禪門 [the Gradual *Dhyāna* Method], *T* 1916).[6]

In 1003 (Xianping 6), Zunshi asked Jakushō to have this practice printed and circulated. Zunshi perceived the issues of the *Vaipulyas-samādhi* repentance practice at that time. The practice had been arbitrarily reduced in quantity and established in shrine halls not in accordance with the ritual form, in reality having lost its original confessional purpose. The *Fangdeng sanmei xinfa* originally included six methods, the latter two concerning practice and precepts only appearing in the table of contents, though not actually being present in the extant text. In actuality, in terms of the development of the repentance

4 *Fangdeng sanmei xingfa*, *T* no.1940, 46: 1.943a6-20:
山門教卷, 自唐季多流外國, 或尙存目錄, 而莫見其文. 學者思之, 渺隔滄海. 《方等三昧行法》者, 皇宋咸平六祀, 日本僧寂照等齎至. ...... 今時或壇場延袤, 形像巍峨, 行法則半任臆裁, 律範則全由心匠. .... 雖曰像多無妙, 要符表法之便, 將恐未除故業, 更貽新戚, 染衣增垢, 良用悲夫 ! 然此行法六篇, 後二不載者, 修行備《百錄》、《止觀》. 受戒具出本經, 存篇目者, 令知法有始終也.

5 Ōno, *Seiritsushi*, 392.

6 Satō, *Daishi*, 190–220.

practice, the essence is focused in practice and precepts. However, these were discarded in favour of supplementary features at that time. It is unsurprising that Zunshi lamented these later developments.

The most influential of the four repentance practices of Zhiyi within Chinese Buddhism was the *Fahua sanmei chanyi* 法華三昧懺儀 (*Lotus Samādhi* Repentance Ritual). During the Song and Ming periods, various repentance rituals were often formulated based on its organization of the "ten divisions" (*shike* 十科) and its principle of practicing repentance.[7] The extant version of this text is Zunshi's critical edition. Zunshi surveyed a number of contemporary editions and found that some "cited *sūtra* passages at the very end of the fascicle" while others "have lavish chapters, problematic annotations, and mistaken content".[8] He, therefore, critically surveyed various editions before printing his version. Zunshi, in his "Fahua sanmei chanyi kanding yuanben xu" 法華三昧懺儀勘定元本序 (Preface to the Critical Original Edition of the *Lotus Samādhi* Repentance Ritual), discusses these issues.

Among the circulated versions in his time there appeared the system of "observing the mind with five phrases" (*wuju guanxin* 五句觀心), yet Tiantai had always taught "observing the mind with four phrases". Zunshi cited the *Zhiguan puxing chuanhong jue* 止觀輔行傳弘決 (Commentary on Zhiyi's *Mohe Zhiguan, T* 1912) by Zhanran 湛然 (711–782) as proof.[9]

---

7 Shi, *Chanfa*, 130–133.

8 *Fahua sanmei chanyi, T* no. 1941, 46:1.949b3-4: 引經文繫乎卷末, 濫回麁注, 錯其篇內.

9 "Fahua sanmei chanyi kanding yuanben xu", *X* no. 951, 57: 23a2-7:
There are some people adding the contemplation methods of mediation into five phrases. Now I list them here. It says: 有於坐禪觀法加成五句者，今列示之。文云：
1. Because of the mind, thus it is the mind 爲因心故心;
2. Not because of the mind, thus it is the mind 爲不因心故心;
3. Because of the mind and not because of the mind, thus it is the mind 爲亦因心亦不因心故心;
4. Neither because of the mind nor not because of the mind, thus it is the mind (original text) 爲非因心非不因心故心 ( 元文);
5. Neither not because of the mind nor not not because of the mind, thus it is the mind (added recently) 爲非非因心非非不因心故心 ( 近加).

Furthermore, when summarizing the phrases about contemplation, the Mountain School [of Tiantai] always uses four phrases. It is not known from which text the fifth phrase stems. Besides, if examined closely, in the fifth phrase, what is the object of contemplation and how it should be contemplated? In the [*Zhiguan*] *fuxing* [*chuanhong jue*], it says that it (i.e. *Fahua sanmei chanyi*) has a section [on calm and contemplation] and gives [the essentials] in four phrases, so here it (i.e., *Mohe zhiguan*) elaborates more on the practice of image contemplation to expand that [section] (direct quotation from [*Zhiguan*] *fuxing* [*chuanhong jue*]). Moreover, the image contemplation is still going through phenomena, but the essential contemplation is all in the four phrases. 且山家凡約句法、用觀, 只但至四, 未知五句出自何文. 又當推檢之際, 第五句下准何爲境？如

The Japanese Kanazawa Bunko 金澤文庫 edition[10] includes the system of "observing the mind with five phrases". It is clear that this was indeed present in contemporary editions in circulation. The two editions are compared as follows.

| **Taishō T46/954a** | **Kanazawa Bunko Edition** |
| --- | --- |
| 云何名觀一切法空?行者當諦觀現在一念妄心隨所緣境, 如此之心, 爲因心故心, 爲不因心故心, 爲亦因心亦不因心故心,爲非因心非不因心故心. | 云何名觀一切法空?行者當諦觀現在一念妄心隨所緣境, 如此之心, 爲因心故心, 不因心故心, 亦因心亦不因心故心, 非因心非不因心故心, 非非因心非非不因心故心. |
| What is the observation that all dharmas are empty? The practioners should observe that the current single consciousness is a false mind that is provoked by its object. Does this mind arise from minds? Does it not arise from minds? Does it arise from minds and also not from minds? Does it not arise from minds and not not arise from minds? | What is the observation that all dharmas are empty? The practioners should observe that the current single consciousness is a false mind that is provoked by its object. Does this mind arise from minds? Does it not arise from minds? Does it arise from minds and also not from minds? Does it not arise from minds and not not arise from minds? Does it not not arise from minds and not not not arise from minds? |

We can clearly see that during Zunshi's time there existed a number of circulated editions of the *Fahua sanmei chanyi*. What confuses people is that the Tiantai compilation of the Sui dynasty, the *Guoqing bailu*, actually did not include *Fahua sanmei chanyi* among the practices established by Zhiyi. However, in fascicle thirty-three of the *Fozu tongji* 佛祖統紀 (Complete Chronicles of Buddhas and Patriarchs, *T* 2035), we find an account that states, "The Wise One [Zhiyi] compiled the *Fahua sanmei yi* (included in the *Guoqing bailu*). Jingxi [Zhanran] taught the *Buzhu yi* (Supplementary Ritual) to assist with visualization".[11] Zhipan believed that the *Guoqing bailu* recorded the existence of the

何用觀？《輔行》自云, "彼別行文, 但推四句. 故今文中廣修象觀, 以廣於彼." (《輔行》正文) 況彼象觀, 猶是歷事, 而正觀一門全今四句.

10 One edition dates to lunar month 8/14 of 1286 (Kōan 弘安 9) by Jōe 靜慧 at Jōraku ji 常樂寺. Another edition dates to lunar month 10/13 1317 (Bunpō 文保 1) by Kenkai 劍海 at Kanazawa ji 金澤寺. See Satō, *Daishi*, 142.

11 *Fozu tongji*, *T* no. 2035, 49: 33.319a11-12: 智者製《法華三昧儀》(《國清百錄》載), 荊溪述《補助儀》以資觀想.

*Fahua sanmei yi*. It is possible that the *Guoqing bailu* that he surveyed and the presently extant version differed. Based on Ikeda Rosan's research, in addition to the extant edition of the *Guoqing bailu*, there also, in fact, exists a *Guang bailu* 廣百錄 (Extensive Hundred Accounts).[12]

In the process of critically editing the repentance practice texts, Zunshi not only corrected the scribal errors, he also criticised the trend of ignoring the "contemplation of principle" (*liguan* 理觀) as a part of repentance activities. He states, "I lament their small changes to the earlier chapters, or forgetting their essentials. Moreover, contemplation of the principle is primary for the practice procedures of the 'ten divisions'. If there are any mistakes in one, the [other] nine practices are carried out in vain".[13] The practice of repentance not only requires concrete rituals, it also further requires "contemplation of principle". If this is lost, then the repentance practice is just a formality. In his organization of repentance literature, Zunshi not only established a reliable edition for future generations, he simultaneously hoped to be able to return to the original intention behind such practices, to the position of Zhiyi on repentance, which was purification of transgressions, attainment of *samādhi*, and liberation through the production of wisdom.

Zunshi not only organized and critically edited the repentance methods, he also formulated a new repentance method based on immediate needs. The account of Zunshi's relevant works differ. They are clearly outlined as follows.

| ***Shanjia Jiaodian Zhi*· 山家教典志 in *Fozu tongji* 佛祖統紀** | ***Famen Guangxian Zhi*· 法門光顯志 in *Fozu tongji* 佛祖統紀** | ***Taishō*** |
|---|---|---|
| *Jin'guangming huguo yi* 金光明護國儀 (based on *Guoqing Bailu* edn.) | *Jin'guangming huguo yi* 金光明護國儀 (based on *Bailu* supplement) | *Jin'guangming chanfa buzhu yi* 金光明懺法補助儀 (also *Buzhu yi* 補助儀) |
| *Qing Guanyin chanyi* 請觀音懺儀 | *Qing Guanyin chanyi* 請觀音懺儀 | *Qing Guanshiyin Pusa xiaofu duhai tuoluoni sanmei yi* 請觀世音菩薩消伏毒害陀羅尼三昧儀 (abbreviated as *Qing Guanyin chanyi* 請觀音懺儀) |

12 Ikeda, *Kokusei hyakuroku*, 15–16.

13 *Fahua sanmei chanyi*, *T* no. 1941, 46: 1.949a21-23: 患其稍易舊章, 或亡精要. 且十科行軌, 理觀爲主, 儻一以誤, 九法徒施.

| *Shanjia Jiaodian Zhi*· 山家教典志 in *Fozu tongji* 佛祖統紀 | *Famen Guangxian Zhi*· 法門光顯志 in *Fozu tongji* 佛祖統紀 | *Taishō* |
|---|---|---|
| *Wangsheng jingtu chanyi* 往生淨土懺儀 | *Jingtu chanyi* 淨土懺儀 | *Wangsheng jingtu chanyuanyi* 往生淨土懺願儀 (abbreviated as *Da jingtu chan* 大淨土懺) |
| *Xiao Mituo chanyi* 小彌陀懺儀 | *Mituo chanyi* 彌陀懺儀 | *Xiao jingtu chan* 小淨土懺 (originally *Wangsheng jingtu jueyi xingyuan men lichan men* 往生淨土決疑行願門·禮懺門 |
| *Chishengguang chanyi* 熾盛光懺儀 | *Chishengguang chanyi* 熾盛光懺儀 | *Chishengguang daochang niansong yi* 熾盛光道場念誦儀 (abbreviated *Chishengguang chanyi* 熾盛光懺儀) |
| *Fahua sanmei chanyi* 法華三昧懺儀 | | "Zhizhe Dashi zhaiji lizan wen" 智者大師齋忌禮贊文 |

The *Fahua sanmei chanyi* is a repentance ritual critically edited by Zunshi, but it is not his work. As to the *Zhizhe Dashi zhaiji lizan wen*, there is no account of it in various materials. According to its preface, it was due to a lack of religious rituals and eulogies when contemporary Tiantai scholars celebrated the anniversary of Zhiyi's passing that Zunshi produced these verses of praise to express his sincerity.

The *Buzhu yi* was created by Zunshi, who expanded the *Jin'guangming chanfa* 金光明懺法 (*Golden Light* Repentance Practice) in the *Guoqing bailu*. The original ritual was based on the *Jin'guangming jing* 金光明經 (Golden Light *Sūtra*; *T* 663) translated by Dharmakṣema 曇無讖 (385–433) in the Northern Liang 北涼 (398–439), but the ceremony was brief and lacked details.[14] Yijing's 義淨 (635–713) translation of this *sūtra*, the *Jin'guangming zuisheng wang jing* 金光明最勝王經 (Golden Light of the Ever-Victorious King *Sūtra*; *T* 665), was able to address the insufficiencies of the earlier ritual. In addition to the issues of the ceremony, there was also a problem with carrying it out:

14 *Jin'guangming chanfa buzhu yi*, *T* no.1945, 46: 1.957b12-14, explains that the earlier *Jin'guangming chanfa* lacks four parts: (1). It lacks a clear offering of food and drinks to the goddesses. (2). It lacks a sprinkling for the gods. (3). It lacks a clear place for eating. (4). The sequence of mantras seems out of order. 一、缺別明奉飲食供施天女, 二、缺分灑散別施諸神, 三、缺明散食處所, 四、誦咒時節似未次第.

FIGURE 26 Bodhisattva Guanyin 觀音 in the water moon form, dated to the Southern Song (960-1279) (Princeton University Museum, the United States).

> People in our time usually consider this practice the same as the *Fahua* [*sanmei chanyi*] or *Fangdeng* [*sanmei xingfa*]. From the start of the first day [of the ritual], they abandon [ritual] invitation to the Triple Gem (Buddha, Dharma and *Saṃgha*), going straight to recitation of mantras. It truly lacks order. Also, the [*Guoqing*] *bailu* does not go beyond the five regrets. Later people erroneously employ them. Now they have been supplemented, and no longer done in vain.[15]

When practitioners carry out the "Repentance Method of *Golden Light*", it is based on the ritual procedures for the *Fahua sanmei chanyi* and *Fangdeng chanfa*, having lost the features of the "Repentance Method of *Golden Light*". Based on the former, they invite the Triple Gem on the first day only. However, according to "Repentance Method of *Golden Light*", mantras are recited following the invitation ceremony, so the Triple Gem should be invited every day. In addition, earlier rituals did not include the "five regrets" (*wuhui* 五悔). Zunshi added them to the *Buzhu yi*.

At that time, Zhili also produced the *Jin'guangming zuisheng chanyi*. Its main content is identical to that of the *Buzhu yi*. After Xianping 咸平 2 (999), Zhili focused on teaching repentance, remaining seated upright without lying down or going outside. It was in this period that he practiced the "Repentance of *Golden Light*" twenty times over the course of seven days. In Xianping 3 (1000), Zhili and Zunshi both practiced the "Repentance of *Golden Light*" to pray for rain.[16] The *Jin'guangming zuisheng chanyi* was based on the *Jin'guangming zuisheng wang jing*. The period in which it was produced should be before 999.

In Qianxing 1 (1022), Empress Dowager Zhangyi 章懿太后 (987–1032) requested Zunshi to carry out a repentance ritual for the state. Zunshi wrote the *Jin'guangming huguo daochang yi* 金光明護國道場儀 (Hall Ritual of the *Golden Light* for Protecting the State).[17] The *Shimen zhengtong* 釋門正統 (The True Lineage of Buddhism, XZJ 1490) records this event. It also states, "Whenever the master started retreat, he would encourage his disciples to practice the [*Golden*] *Light* Repentance ritual for seven days and nights. He also supplemented the teachings of the [*Golden*] *Light Samādhi* practice of the [*Guoqing*]

15 *Jin'guangming chanfa buzhu yi*, *T* no.1945, 46: 1.957b27-c1:
今時行事, 多將此法, 准同《法華》、《方等》. 初日已後, 廢請三寶, 直爾誦咒, 甚缺次第. 又《百錄》不出五悔, 後人濫用, 今並補助, 非徒然也.

16 *Fozu tongji*, *T* no. 2035, 49: 8.192a24-27.

17 *Fozu tongji*, *T* no. 2035, 49: 10.208a21-24.

*bailu* to correct scholars".[18] In Tiansheng 天聖 2 (1024), Zunshi presented a memorial with respect to the *Tiantai jiao suihan mulu* 天臺教隨函目錄 (Catalogue of Tiantai Teachings), an account of Tiantai canonical texts. Therein is only the *Jin'guangming huguo daochang yi* in one fascicle. He explained the title as follows.

> *Huguo daochang yi* is a text compiled by Zunshi. It, along with the *Guoqing bailu*, and the practice of Yijing's new translation [of the *Jin'guangming jing*], are rituals for monarchs to pray for merit. The practice is derived from sacred teachings, not a personal teaching; thus, it is compiled and printed here.[19]

Shi Darui examined the above two documents and regards the *Jin'guangming huguo daochang yi* and *Buzhu yi* as two types of repentance practices. She believes that the *Buzhu yi* was produced after 1024.[20] However, upon careful analysis of these two documents, especially the interpretation of the *Daochang yi* within the *Tiantai jiao suihan mulu*, the *Huguo daochang yi* was produced by Zunshi who compiled it from the new and old translations of the *Jin'guangming jing* plus the *Guoqing bailu*. This interpretation agrees with Zunshi, who holds the same view in the chapter of "Origination" (*yuanqi* 緣起) in the *Buzhu yi*. In addition, the "Repentance of *Golden Light*" itself not only constitutes a ritual to eliminate individual transgressions and karma, but at the same time, with particular concern in the background for "State Buddhism" (*Guojia Fojiao* 國家佛教), it transformed into a ritual of eliminating karma aimed at protecting the state.[21] In reality, the two are not mutually exclusive. In China in particular with its concept of "everywhere being crown land", Zunshi practicing the repentance ritual for the state of course encouraged him during retreat to continue carrying out the "Repentance of *Golden Light*". At the same time, the production of a repentance practice required constant perfection, which is why after Zunshi wrote the *Jin'guangming huguo daochang yi*, it was again supplemented. This was normal. This is why we believe that the *Buzhu yi* is the *Jin'guangming huguo daochang yi*. In 1022, after Zunshi finished compiling this

18 *Shimen zhengtong*, XZJ no. 1490, 130: 5.836a12-14:
師凡遇安居之初, 則勵其徒行光明懺法, 以七晝夜爲程. 又補《百錄》光明三昧行法之說, 以正學者.

19 *Tianzhu bieji*, XZJ no. 949, 101: 1.265b8-10:
《護國道場儀》者, 即遵式纂集本經, 並《國清百錄》、義淨新譯行用之法, 以備人王祈福之儀也. 事出聖教, 文非臆說, 故編付之.

20 Shi, *Chanfa*, 299.

21 Fujitani, "Girei", 565–67.

repentance text, he supplemented it once again, finally making it into the *Buzhu yi*.

The *Chishengguang chanyi* 熾盛光懺儀 (*Tejaprabhā* Repentance Ritual, *T* 1951) was produced by Zunshi based on *Chishengguang daweide xiaozai jixiang tuoluoni jing* 熾盛光大威德消災吉祥陀羅尼經 (Great Venerable Disaster Eliminating Auspicious *Dhāraṇī Sūtra* of *Tejaprabhā*, *T* 963) translated by Amoghavajra (Bukong 不空, 705–774) of the Tang dynasty. According to the account in the preface by Lingjian 靈鑒 (d.u.) for Zunshi's text, when Lingjian was organizing Zunshi's work, he discovered that the *Chishengguang chanyi* had not been put into circulation, so he brought together and supplemented various documents to ensure it was entirely complete. Moreover, he added two sections on "revealing methods" (*shi fangfa* 示方法) and "dissolving doubts" (*shiyi* 釋疑) to the five chapters; it thereby came to constitute seven sections.[22] It is clear that the *Chishengguang chanyi* was not fully developed during Zunshi's lifetime.

The *Da jingtu chan* 大淨土懺 (Great Pure Land Repentance) was revised in Dazhong Xiangfu 大中祥符 8 (1015) by Zunshi, though the postscript states the following:

> Since this practice was compiled, it has been revised twice by now. The earlier version was already printed and circulated by the Yue 越 monk Qi'ning 契凝 (d.u.). The beginning of his postscript states, "This text is what I have learned from the teachings of the patriarchs". The fruit of the sacred teaching is diverse. Recently [I] notice that practicing prostrations is tiring. Therefore, the sections of "Confession" and "Chan meditation" are abridged, while other sections remain the same. Now this version has been expanded and abridged properly, so it may be able to be circulated. [I ask] later wise men to not blame me for the trifling details. [I] have edited it carefully before the print. Who would resent precise formulation! The date of this postscript is year eight of Dazhong Xiangfu.[23]

This repentance practice underwent two revisions. The earlier version was previously printed and circulated. Compared with the present edition, the two

22 *Chisheng guang daochang niansong yi*, *T* no.1951, 46: 1.978b6-15.

23 *Wangsheng jingtu chanyuan yi*, *T* no.1984, 47: 1.494c27-29:
此法自撰集, 於今凡二改治. 前本越僧契凝已刊刻廣行. 其後序首云：予自濫沾祖教等是也. 聖位既廣, 比見行者拜起易勞, 懺悔禪法皆事攻削, 餘悉存舊. 今之廣略既允, 似可傳行, 後賢無惑其二三焉. 刊詳刪補, 何嫌精措, 時大中祥符八年, 太歲乙卯二月日序.

sections on confession (*chanhui* 懺悔) and Chan meditation (*chanfa* 禪法) were abridged. The ten sections of the present edition are complete. The *Da jingtu chan* should therefore have been produced before 1015, but was not compiled by Ma Liang 馬亮 (fl. 980).

The *Xiao jingtu chan* is a "Repentance Method" (*lichan men* 禮懺門) by Zunshi in 1017, being the first method of practices and vows (*xingyuan* 行願) included in the *Wangsheng jingtu jueyi xingyuan ermen* 往生淨土決疑行願二門 (Two Methods of Practices and Vows for Resolving Doubts about Rebirth in the Pure Land) compiled by the Assistant Minister (*shilang* 侍郎) Ma Liang.

The *Qing Guanyin chanyi* 請觀音懺儀 (Repentance Ritual of Petitioning Avalokiteśvara) was first compiled at Guoqing si 國清寺 on Mount Tiantai by Zunshi in Duan'gong 端拱 1 (988). It was revised in Xianping 4 (1001) at Mount Dalei 大雷山 in Cixi 慈溪.[24] The cause behind this was that Baoyun 寶雲 passed away, and Zunshi returned to Mount Tiantai, whereupon he practiced so hard he became ill and vomited blood. He therefore went to the Great Hall of the Compassionate Buddha 大慈佛室 and practiced a "*dhāraṇī* practice for eliminating [obstacles]" 消伏咒法, which was the *Qing Guanshiyin chanfa*, for forty-nine days. There was a significant spiritual response to this. In the process of practicing this method, Zunshi discovered that the ritual in the *Guoqing bailu* was too simple, even including a number of unclear parts. Moreover, contemporaries had arbitrarily edited the ritual. Some had, on their own accord, added supplementary text. Someone added the "four confessions" in the *Fahua sanmei chanyi*, while another edited the text on the contemplation of wisdom (*guanhui* 觀慧). He thus reformulated it with "the text on contemplation of wisdom all being placed at the end of the ritual"[25] so as to facilitate recollection and contemplation when practicing the repentance.

Some of the repentance rituals produced by Zunshi are perfections and formulations of Tiantai repentance practices, such as the *Buzhu yi* and *Qing Guanyin chanyi*. At the same time, in order to meet the needs of faith and be in accord with the trends of the time, he produced materials such as the *Da jingtu chan*, *Xiao jingtu chan* and *Chishengguang chanyi*. This was related to the popularity of the Pure Land faith in the Northern Song period and the many translations of Tantric scriptures. Finally, one type of text he produced was repentance for immediate needs, such as the *Zhizhe dashi zhaiji lizan wen*.

---

24 *Fozu tongji*, *T* no. 2035, 49: 10.207b20-21.

25 *Qing Guanshiyin pusa xiaofu duhai tuoluoni sanmei yi*, *T* no. 1949, 49: 1.968a27-28: 盡取觀慧諸文安於事後.

### 1.1.2 The Practice and Spread of Repentance Practices

Zunshi not only organized and edited existing repentance literature while producing and expanding new ones, he also did his utmost in practicing and spreading them. In Yongxi 1 (984), he arrived at Baoyun si 寶雲寺 in Siming 四明, where he comprehensively studied Tiantai doctrine under Yitong 義通 (927–988). On the anniversary of Zhiyi's passing, he spent a day with a flame burning atop his head, while vowing to diligently cultivate *samādhi*. In Duangong 端拱 1 (988), at the Great Hall of the Compassionate Buddha at Guoqing si of Mount Tiantai, he practiced the "Repentance of Welcoming Avalokiteśvara". In Xianping 3 (1000), Siming was suffering a great drought. Together with Fazhi 法智 (960–1028) and Yiwen 異聞 (d.u.), they led the assembly to practice the "*Samādhi* for Requesting Avalokiteśvara" (*Qing Guanyin sanmei* 請觀音三昧). In Xianping 5 (1002), he returned to Mount Dongye 東掖山, where he built a temple in the western corner of the settlement. He constructed an Amitābha Buddha image, and together with the assembly practiced the Buddha recollection *samādhi* (*nianfo sanmei* 念佛三昧). In Dazhong Xiangfu 4 (1011), he convened a repentance ceremony at Mount Dong 東山. In Qianxing 乾興 1 (1022), he practiced a repentance ceremony for the country at the mountain.

Zunshi was extremely dedicated to his practice of repentance. He would die for it. The *Fozu tongji* states the following:

> He constantly practiced *samādhi* for a period of ninety days. He placed an iron pan on flaming charcoals in each of the four corners of his path [around the hall]. When he felt fatigue, he would soak his hands in the iron pan. Of his ten fingers only three remained. In building the Hall of Luminous Repentance 光明懺殿, for every rafter he hung and tile he installed, he would recite the *Dhāraṇī of Great Compassion* seven times to show the blessings of the sacred Dharma could not be destroyed.[26]

This is pointing out that when Zunshi was practising *pratyutpanna-samādhi* (*bozhou sanmei* 般舟三昧) for a period of ninety days, he placed an iron pan on hot charcoals in each of the four corners of the shrine hall. If he felt tired, he would place his hand in the iron pan to eliminate his fatigue, leading him to lose all but three fingers. When he built the Hall of Luminous Repentance, he would recite the *Dhāraṇī of Great Compassion* seven times for every beam and

---

26 *Fozu tongji*, *T* no. 2035, 49: 10.208c22-26: 常行三昧, 以九十日爲期, 於行道四隅置鐵熾炭, 遇困倦則漬手於鐵, 十指唯存其三. 其建光明懺殿, 每架一椽甃一甓, 輒誦大悲咒七遍以示聖法加被, 不可沮壞之意.

wall built to reveal the blessings of the sacred Dharma. It is clear that he was greatly dedicated and pious with respect to the practice of repentance. As a result of his cultivation, the Empress Dowager Zhangyi had him perform repentance for the state.

He not only led the monks in practicing repentance, he also convened repentance gatherings, ensuring that such practices would become popularised amongst the people. This can be known via the last line in the *Chishengguang chanyi*, which states that his aim was to "encourage devotees". At the same time, following the spread and popularisation of repentance practices, there gradually emerged a chaotic situation in the process of their implementation, as they became a kind of commercial activity. This inevitably damaged its religious sanctity. Zunshi states the following:

> Recently, I have seen that the households of benefactors possess deep convictions, and so invite monks to visit, preparing meals and having them read *sūtra*s hoping for merit and wisdom. Though they are powerful and willing to spend money, the rituals and regulations are not applied properly. They see no difference between being esteemed and haughtiness; how do they distinguish between right and wrong? Some rely on the wealthy, while others immerse themselves in feelings of self-importance. Conversely, they say that the monks are protected by their clothing and food, and should be honoured, and invited to their religious sites. They have lost their decorum in [daily actions such as] walking and gazing. They criticize [the monks] loudly and condemn [them] clearly. When setting up the Dharma banquet, they order about [the monks] at will at their own convenience. The beggar monks are ignorant, and fear losing their sponsor. They are devoted to hard work in order to not bother their benefactor. Even if there are regulations, who dares to speak of them? If benefactors do not ask, the beggar monks do not tell. The signs of their errors are becoming increasingly apparent from here. They do not sweep the hall before spreading out the Dharma mats. They do not refrain from the defilements of garlic and meat, but still regularly call for the three refuges. When welcoming images and venerable masters, they even do not stand up or turn back to offer their greetings.[27]

27 *Chisheng guang daochang niansong yi, T* no.1951, 46: 1.982b20-29:
近見檀越之家, 深有信向, 請僧歸舍, 設食讀經, 望其福慧. 勢力損財, 無善儀則. 敬慢不分, 是非寧別. 或倚恃豪富, 或放縱矜高. 反言衣食庇蔭門僧, 請喚道場便言恩幸, 趨瞻失節朗責明訶. 鋪設法筵, 穩便驅使. 門僧無識, 恐失依棲, 苦事先爲免勞施主, 縱有法則, 豈敢輒言. 檀越不詢, 門僧不說, 訛謬之跡, 自此滋彰. 不掃廳堂, 便張法席; 未斷葷穢, 輒請聖賢; 至於迎像延尊, 殊不避座, 旋踵致敬.

In the Northern Song period, repentance practices were carried out in the homes of benefactors. This is why the issues that Zunshi mentioned appeared. Some wealthy families not only failed to show respect to the monks, they would also request monks to carry out ceremonies, which was done as a kind of favour to the monks. Some monks were ignorant and feared that they might lose clothing, food and shelter, and therefore ignored the arrogance and negligent habits of their benefactors, hence they yielded to indulgences. This sort of ceremony not only lacked the contemplative spirit of repentance practice, but even on the surface it was careless and chaotic.

Through his own efforts and appeals, Zunshi hoped to be able to regulate the system of repentance, purify the centres where it was practiced, and have the practices sincerely respected. He established five regulations as the standards for practice of repentance:

> First, if wanting to arrange a ceremony, young and old in the household must be of the same mindset, doing away with things such as alcohol, meat and the five pungent herbs. The benefactor will daily follow the *Saṃgha* and pay homage to the Buddha while uttering their confessions. Second, they should feed the monks according to their monastic age. They must humbly serve them. They must not sit ahead of the *Saṃgha*, be called master, or in a silly fashion talk and laugh. Third, when making offerings before the Buddha, they must offer double of what has been offered to the *Saṃgha*. With a mindset regarding the sacred and mundane as equal, they will be careful about all matters. Fourth, to the utmost give to the Buddha and *Saṃgha*. Do not hide fine things, and use coarse things instead, for it will invite the karmic retribution of frustration in future lives. Fifth, whether relaxed or in a hurry in the shrine hall, one must not use the monks. They are a field of merit. How could you turn them into servants?[28]

These five regulations of Zunshi were primarily to safeguard the sanctity of Buddhism, the solemnness and purity of the shrine hall, and the integrity and noble quality of the *Saṃgha*. In the process of Buddhism influencing society and leading the people, it was not to lose its sanctity while guiding them. It was

---

28 *Chisheng guang daochang niansong yi*, *T* no.1951, 46: 1.982c18-25: 第一、欲陳法會, 家中長幼, 盡須同心, 去其酒肉五辛等物, 施主每日隨僧禮佛, 陳吐懺悔. 第二、當齋僧次, 躬須給侍, 不得坐於僧上, 稱是主人, 放縱談笑. 第三、佛前供養, 須倍於僧, 凡聖等心, 事事精細. 第四、盡其所惜, 施佛及僧, 勿得隱細用粗, 世世招失意果報. 第五、道場緩急, 不得使僧, 此是福田, 翻爲僮僕, 豈得然乎？

also not to lose its regulations when adapting. This was the key to Buddhist development. In terms of the implementation of repentance rituals, preserving their practical spirit was especially important. Zunshi hoped to be able to return to the original intent behind repentance practice. However, after the Ming-Qing period, such ceremonies were formalized, commodified and made superstitious, having brought great shame to the repentance practice.[29]

Zunshi not only emphasized the sanctity and transcendence of repentance practice, he also proposed strict requirements for copying Tiantai repentance texts, thereby protecting their sanctity. In the *Buzhu yi* he encourages future scholars as follows:

> Whenever you want to copy something, you must copy the entire document from start to finish. Be clear when examining both documents. Do not allow for any errors. Having looked at many of the repentance texts, such as the *Fahua* [*sanmei chanyi*] and [*Qing*] *Guanyin* [*chanfa*], they often omit the beginning and end, as well as the text on the contemplation of wisdom. Only the text on Buddhahood, repentance and rituals are copied. It is quite pitiful. If unable to do this, it would be better to not copy anything, so as to avoid destroying the entirety of the practice text. If not fully completed, the quality of the practice is made deficient. Be very careful! Be very careful![30]

As a result of the popularity and spread of repentance practices, there was a need for a greater volume of such texts, so they could be practiced among the masses. However, the rituals were arbitrarily added or abridged, and copied without careful attention. In this way, the quality of the practice suffered. These flaws subsequently became an obstacle that harmed the practice. Zunshi sincerely cautioned later scholars to be especially careful.

### 1.2 *The Practice of Repentance in the Song Huayan Buddhism*

Jingyuan 淨源 (1011–1088) is called the "master of revival" of Huayan in the Song dynasty. He worked diligently with Huayan doctrine to interpret other, more popular, Buddhist scriptures, encouraging Huayan studies throughout the whole of Buddhist scholarship. He once studied the *Lengyan jing* 楞嚴經 (*Śūraṃgama-sūtra, T* 945), *Yuanjue jing* 圓覺經 (Sūtra of Perfect Awakening,

---

29 Sheng, "Li'nian", 9–18.

30 *Jin'guangming chanfa buzhu yi, T* no.1945, 46: 1.958c27-959a3: 凡欲傳寫, 並須首尾全寫, 對勘分明, 勿令脫誤. 多見《法華》、《觀音》等懺文, 多削前後, 及觀慧之文. 但抄佛位及懺悔文, 單題禮文, 深可悲痛. 若不能者, 寧可莫寫, 免得毀散行法全文. 一事不周, 便虧行相. 深誡, 深誡！

*T* 842), and the *Qixin lun* 起信論 (Awakening of Mahāyāna Faith, *T* 1666, *T* 1667) under Changshui Zixuan 長水子璿 (965–1038). He placed special importance on Zixuan's *Lengyan jing yishu* 楞嚴經義疏 (Commentary on the *Śūraṃgama-sūtra, T* 1799). Addressing the shortage of practices for Huayan, Jingyuan specifically compiled the *Huayan Puxian xingyuan xiuzheng yi* 華嚴普賢行願修證儀 (Ritual for the Realisation of Huayan Samantabhadra's Vows and Practices, *XZJ* 859, *XZJ* 860), *Yuanjue jing daochang lüeben xiuzheng yi* 圓覺經道場略本修證儀 (Abbreviated Ritual for the Realisation in the Altar of the *Sūtra of Perfect Awakening, XZJ* 1455), and *Lengyan xiuzheng yi* 楞嚴修證儀 (Ritual for the Realisation of *Śūraṃgama*).

Jingyuan abridged the *Yuanjuejing daochang xiuzheng yi* 圓覺經道場修證儀 (Ritual for the Realisation in the Altar of the *Sūtra of Perfect Awakening, XZJ* 1454) by Zongmi 宗密 (780–841). Jingyuan states the following with respect to why he composed his work, "Zongxu yuanqi" 總敘緣起 (Reason for the General Exposition):

> Our Buddha promulgated the Perfect Awakening. He established One Dharma Mind, which covers "three capacities" (*sangen* 三根 : superior, medium, and low capacities). The obstructive coverage differs in depth [according to each individual]. The intellectual capacities [to understand it] differ [according to each individual]. This is why there are general and distinct contemplation methods, which are separated as two. Repentance in the shrine hall comes third in order. It is like sending a good colt out of the stable: the shadow of the whip is already shaking, and this great treasure is going to be buried in filth. There must be established corrective methods [to guide the people]. That being so, the meaning of repentance encompasses principle repentance and phenomenal repentance. Phenomenal repentance is announcing the aspects of one's sins while sincerely taking responsibility and feeling shame for them. Principle repentance is contemplating the true characteristics [of phenomena] to be at ease [like] the brilliant sun of wisdom on frost and dew. Nobody now hears of anyone promoting repentance practices from the Han and Wei periods, but in actuality the origin of the teachings was from before the *sūtras* and *śāstras* were produced (Mahāyāna *sūtras* and treatises such as the *Vibhāṣā*). During the Western Jin, Master Mitian 彌天 (i.e., Daoan 道安; 314–385) composed the veneration verses for the four times. From his wordings about the solemn offerings and the five confessions, he showed esteem for scripture and doctrine, and selected essential elements [for practice]. Hence scholars all over the realm rejoiced and studied it. During the Chen and Sui dynasties, the Wise Man of Tiantai [Zhiyi]

compiled the *Fahua* [*sanmei*] *chanfa*, [*Jin*]*'guangming chanfa* and [*Guoqing*] *bailu*, in which there were concretely presented the ten minds contrary or in line [with *saṃsāra*]. The rituals and regulations were quite detailed, and the [practice] flourished throughout the south of the lower reaches of the Yangtze River. During the middle Tang, our patriarch Meditation Master Guifeng 圭峰 (i.e., Zongmi), following the legacy of Mitian (i.e., Daoan), and, connecting with the inherited works of Zhiyi, wrote the *Yuanjue lichan changuan* 圓覺禮懺禪觀 (Repentance and Meditative Contemplation of the *Sūtra of Perfect Awakening*). Altogether eighteen fascicles, it includes encouragement and practice, explaining the realisation of the characteristics [of awakening]. Hence there are seven methods for ceremonies in the shrine hall, but eight methods for repentance rituals and venerating the Buddha. It was extended and developed (using text from *Foming* [*jing*] and the ideas of the *Huayan jing*). The practice was perhaps to just cover the practice during the three periods. At the end of this Semblance Dharma Age of Buddhism, I encountered these last teachings and have been recollecting them for several years to purify my karma. Therefore, I have abridged the larger edition and produced this separate practice. Since the Dharma teachings are all relative, this [text] could be a small cart [that might lead people to Buddha's teaching]. Briefly examining the words, although they might differ from Mitian, reciting the sounds seems to harmonize with the Wise One. If later students should continue to practice it, they will reciprocate a small portion of the virtue of Guifeng's labour.[31]

In the section "Reason for the General Exposition", Jingyuan primarily explains three issues. First, the status of repentance and its types. As the capacities of

31 *Yuanjue jing daochang lüeben xiuzheng yi*, XZJ no. 1455, 129: 1.1a11-b11:
吾佛之唱圓覺也, 開一心法而被乎三根者, 斯蓋障之有深淺, 機之有利鈍矣. 是故通別觀門, 離之爲二, 道場懺悔次其第三；亦猶出廄良駒, 已搖鞭影, 蘊廛大寶, 須設治方耳. 然則懺之爲義, 有理懺焉, 有事懺焉. 若陳罪相以精勤, 責妄心而愧切, 此事懺也; 念實相以宴安, 耀慧日以霜露, 此理懺也. 漢魏以來, 崇茲懺法, 蔑聞其有人者, 實以教源初流, 經論未備 ( 方等諸經 、婆沙等論). 西晉彌天法師, 嘗著四時禮文, 觀其嚴供、五悔之辭, 尊經尙義, 多摭其要, 故天下學者悅而習焉. 陳隋之際, 天臺智者撰《法華懺法》、《光明》、《百錄》, 具彰逆順十心, 規式頗詳, 而盛行乎江左矣. 有唐中吾祖圭峰禪師, 追彌天之餘烈, 貫智者之遺韻, 備述《圓覺禮懺禪觀》. 凡一十八卷, 包並勸修, 撲敘證相, 故道場法事之門有七, 而禮佛懺儀之門有八, 其所伸引, 沖邃澣漫 ( 多用《佛名》文及《華嚴經》等意), 蓋被三期限內修證耳. 余以像法之末, 遇茲遺訓, 緬懷淨業, 其亦有年. 由是略彼廣本, 爲此別行, 法類相從, 蓋盡一席之軌矣. 既而觀其辭, 雖異於彌天；唱其聲, 似協於智者. 後之末學, 繼而修之. 則圭峰劬勞之德, 亦報之之萬一也.

beings differ, there are also different methods, and repentance suits those who possess low capabilities. Repentance is divided into Repentance by Phenomena and Repentance by Principle. Repentance by Phenomena is revealing the characteristics of transgression and producing a mental state of great remorse and accountability. Repentance by Principle is contemplating the characteristics of reality and employing wisdom to observe the emptiness of transgression. Second, the development of repentance practices of Chinese Buddhism commenced from when Daoan established the veneration verses of the four times. Thereafter, it spread throughout the realm. During the Chen-Sui period, Zhiyi established the Tiantai repentance practice, and the ceremonies were brought to completion. Third, the production and abridgment of the *Yuanjuejing daochang xiuzheng yi*. The *Yuanjuejing daochang xiuzheng yi* in eighteen fascicles often cites the confession text of the *Foming jing*, and the ideas of the *Huayan jing*. It thus seems so deep and extensive. Jingyuan abridged the original practice into one fascicle and circulated it in order that beings might be able to practice this repentance practice in the latter years of the Semblance Dharma age.

Jingyuan simplified the twenty-three ceremonies of the three methods of the *Yuanjuejing daochang xiuzheng yi* into the following ten: (1) Reason for the General Exposition 總敘緣起; (2) Ornamenting and Purifying the Hall 嚴淨道場; (3) Requesting the Holy and Wise 啓請聖賢; (4) Offerings and Contemplation 供養觀門; (5) Right Seating and Reflection 正坐思惟; (6) Praise for the Tathāgata 稱讚如來; (7) Venerating the Triple Gem 禮敬三寶; (8) Practicing the Five Confessions 修行五悔; (9) Circumambulation and Chanting 旋繞念誦; (10) Admonishment and Encouragement to Practice 警策勸修. In this way, he largely simplified a number of ceremonies. Therein, the most important feature was taking out the verses of the *Yuanjue jing*, the repentance verses of the *Foming jing*, the verses related to impermanence and the material from other texts, thus ensuring that the *Yuanjuejing daochang lüeben xiuzheng yi* would become a daily ceremony.

Jingyuan's abridgement of the *Yuanjuejing daochang xiuzheng yi* in this manner was also greatly related to the popularity of Buddhist repentance practices in the Song period, in addition to the *Yuanjuejing daochang xiuzheng yi* itself actually being difficult to implement. In particular, the Tiantai repentance rituals caused a stir in society as a result of the efforts of Ciyun Zunshi and Siming Zhili. Jingyuan, as a revivalist scholar of Huayan, also had to make efforts to implement the ideas of his own school, yet Huayan itself lacked a practical aspect. The only ceremonial practice that could be carried out was the *Yuanjuejing daochang xiuzheng yi*. As a result, Jingyuan had to edit eighteen fascicles into one. However, this virtually reduced the characteristics of emphasising contemplation and thought within Huayan repentance itself.

At the same time, Jingyuan produced the *Lengyan xiuzheng yi*. He had a high opinion of the *Lengyan jing*, believing it to be the "essential guide for the convergence of the nine realms; the profound path for the inner insight of the Single Vehicle".[32] In terms of phenomenal characteristics, one could recite *dhāraṇīs*. In terms of the fruits of realisation of meditative contemplation, one might sit in meditation while observing the mind. When Jingyuan studied the *Lengyan jing* under Zixuan, he only studied doctrine, putting together a digest.[33] In year four of Xining 熙寧 (1071), at the temple at the jewelled pavilion of Qingdun 青墩, he taught the *Lengyan jing*, and combined the commentaries and digests of Zixuan, Zhiyuan 智圓 (976–1022) and Renyue, investigating in detail the altar requirements, *dhāraṇīs* and methods of repentance.[34] He thus produced the *Lengyan xiuzheng yi*.

The *Lengyan xiuzheng yi* is a practice of repentance based on ten methods. They are compared as follows with those of the *Yuanjuejing daochang lüeben xiuzheng yi*:

| *Lengyan xiuzheng yi* 楞嚴修證儀 | *Yuanjuejing daochang lüeben xiuzheng yi* 圓覺經道場略本修證儀 |
|---|---|
| 1. Measures for the Altar 壇場方軌 | 1. Reason for the General Exposition 總敘緣起 |
| 2. Requesting the Holy and Wise 啓請賢聖 | 2. Ornamenting and Purifying the Hall 嚴淨道場 |
| 3. Offerings and Contemplation 供養觀門 | 3. Requesting the Holy and Wise 啓請聖賢 |
| 4. Praise for the Tathāgata 稱讚如來 | 4. Offerings and Contemplation 供養觀門 |
| 5. Venerating the Triple Gem 禮敬三寶 | 5. Right Seating and Reflection 正坐思惟 |
| 6. Circumambulating the Altar and Reciting Dhāraṇī 圍壇誦咒 | 6. Praise for the Tathāgata 稱讚如來 |
| 7. Cleansing Karma and Correcting Faculties 滌業規品 | 7. Venerating the Triple Gem 禮敬三寶 |
| 8. Repentance and Vows 懺悔發願 | 8. Practicing the Five Confessions 修行五悔 |
| 9. Circumambulation and Chanting 旋繞念誦 | 9. Circumambulation and Chanting 旋繞念誦 |
| 10. Contemplation of Avalokiteśvara's Method 析通觀法 | 10. Admonishment and Encouragement to Practice 警策勸修 |

32 *Shoulengyan tanchang xiuzheng yi*, XZJ no. 861, 95: 1.1074a3-4: 九界交歸之要門, 一乘冥會之妙道.

33 *Shoulengyan tanchang xiuzheng yi*, XZJ no. 861, 95: 1.1074a7-9.

34 *Shoulengyan tanchang xiuzheng yi*, XZJ no. 861, 95: 1.1074a10-15.

The repentance rituals in both these works are largely identical in structure. The former includes "Contemplation of Avalokiteśvara's Method" as the tenth method, while the latter includes "Right Seating and Reflection" as the fifth method. In actuality, Zongmi's *Yuanjuejing daochang xiuzheng yi* places "Right Seating and Reflection" behind "Circumambulation and Chanting". This is identical to the *Lengyan xiuzheng yi*. In addition, the *Lengyan xiuzheng yi* includes the practice of circumambulation and chanting. This is a result of the distinct *dhāraṇī* practices of the *Lengyan jing*.

1. "Measures for the Altar" refers to the requirements and methods behind setting up the altar. This is based on the instructions given to Ānanda by the Buddha in the *Lengyan jing*.[35] One is to form out of fragrant earth an octagonal altar sixteen feet in radius. At the centre of the altar, one is to place a lotus made of gold, silver, bronze and wood. Within the lotus, one is to place a bowl. Within the bowl, one is to fill it with the dew water of the eighth lunar month (otherwise use pure water). In the water, scatter petals. Take eight round mirrors and place them around the flower bowel. Behind the mirrors, place sixteen lotuses, and sixteen incense burners between the flowers. As offerings, provide sixteen vessels of milk from a white cow, and other assorted offerings. In the altar room, place around the four walls images of the Tathāgatas of the Ten Directions and bodhisattvas. In the middle of the regal position [i.e., in the centre, facing south], hang images of Vairocana, Śākyamuni, Maitreya, Akṣobhya, Amitābha and various emanations of Avalokiteśvara, together with Vajragarbhas placed to the left and right. At the doorway, place Dharma Guardian Deities, such as Indra and Brahmā, to the left and right. Suspend eight mirrors in the space above, so that they all face one another in the shrine hall, making them reflect one another.

This arrangement of the altar space is definitely intended to express the Dharma. Zixuan gives the following explanation:

> If the practitioner is made accustomed to this state, then they will easily realise the principle of the *dharmadhātu* as comprised of unimpeded phenomena. In the present time and place, in a single moment, they will pervade the ten directions, extensively observe buddhas, carry out the deeds of the Buddha, and extensively be able to make offerings. Since it is accomplished in one single moment, it will be accomplished in all phenomena.[36]

35 *Da Foding rulai miyin xiuzheng liaoyi zhu pusa wanxing shou lengyan jing*, *T* no. 945, 19: 7.133b1-c13.

36 *Shoulengyan yishu zhu jing*, *T* no. 1799, 39: 7.916b26-29: 欲使行人熟此境界, 則於事事無礙法界之理易得證耳. 若時若處, 一念之中, 遍遊十方, 遍見諸佛, 遍行佛事, 遍得供養. 一念既爾, 塵塵皆然.

Zixuan interpreted the *Lengyan jing* from a Huayan standpoint, which is why he understood the arrangement of the altar through the principle of the *dharmadhātu* as comprised of unimpeded phenomena. He considered the mutual reflections of light in the mirrors to express the principle of the *dharmadhātu*.

In terms of the ceremony of *dhāraṇī* recitation, for the first seven days one must prostrate to the Tathāgatas and Great Bodhisattvas of the Ten Directions. Throughout the six periods of the day, one constantly walks around the altar, continually reciting the *Śūraṃgama-dhāraṇī* 108 times. In the second week, one makes bodhisattva aspirations sincerely. Starting in the third week, full attention is given to reciting the *Śūraṃgama-dhāraṇī*. The Tathāgatas of the Ten Directions will then be able to appear in the intersecting beams of light from the mirrors. After a hundred days, those practitioners with superior capacities will be able to realise the first fruit.

2. "Requesting the Holy and Wise". Requesting Vairocana, Śākyamuni, Maitreya, the *Lengyan jing*, great Bodhisattvas, and the holy and wise *Saṃgha*, as well as Dharma Guardians, to descend unto the altar.

3. Offerings and Contemplation. Visualization of these incense and flowers being offered to the Triple Gem, buddhas, and noble *Saṃgha* of the three vehicles of the ten directions so as to be able to prompt a compassionate response from them.

4. "Praise for the Tathāgata". These are the verses praising the Buddha from the *Lengyan jing*.[37]

5. "Venerating the Triple Gem". Venerating the Triple Gem and Dharma Guardian deities in front of oneself who were invited.

6. "Reciting *Dhāraṇī* and Circumambulating the Altar". Reciting the *Śūraṃgama-dhāraṇī*. Jingyuan proposed that "the method of reciting the *dhāraṇī* be as in the recitation ritual of Master Ciyun Zunshi. This text is also to be recited with a stern voice; the voice must not have any pauses".[38] The "recitation ritual" probably refers to the *Chishengguang daochang niansong yi*. Zunshi's requirements for *dhāraṇī* recitation included several points. At one time it must be done 108 times. If there is an emergency, then, after returning, one must continue. When reciting the *dhāraṇī*, one should not talk with anyone, nor shall one's hands be engaged in some other activity. One must not leave the altar space when the *dhāraṇī* is being recited. One must kneel or sit within the altar space. One must bring together body and mind, paying attention to food and

37 *Da Foding rulai miyin xiuzheng liaoyi zhu pusa wanxing shou lengyan jing*, *T* no. 945, 19: 3.119b12-20.

38 *Shoulengyan tanchang xiuzheng yi*, *XZJ* no. 861, 95: 1.519a12-13: 誦呪方法具如慈雲式師念誦儀，此文亦厲聲誦之，令聲不得有間.

drink.[39] The repentance methods of Huayan came from Tiantai in terms of their structure and thought. Zongmi's *Yuanjuejing daochang xiuzheng yi* was produced based on the *Fahua sanmei chanyi* and Tiantai meditation (*zhiguan* 止觀).

7. "Cleansing Karma and Correcting Faculties". There are eighteen lines missing from the section of the sixth method of the *Lengyan xiuzheng yi* edition in the *Manji Zokuzōkyō* 卍續藏經 after the line "if able to recite …" 若能讀誦. Each line includes nineteen characters, the result being that the seventh method of "Cleansing Karma and Correcting Faculties" is incomplete. This method primarily explains the types of karma related to transgressions, and the varieties of repentance (see Appendix 3.1 and 3.2).

The relative superiority of the types of transgressions are based on the severity of the mental state preceding, during and following the act, as well as if there was any recognition of the Dharma and the transgressive nature of the act. The relative superiority of the types of repentance is divided into three types. These differ in their respective features, as indicated above, such as the elimination of karma, subduing the karma, compensation for past acts, and complete elimination of the transgression.

With respect to the types of repentance, Zhiyi of Tiantai proposed three repentance methods based on the three types of transgressions.[40] First, repentance according to established *vinaya* conventions (*zuofa chanhui* 作法懺悔), which is to eliminate transgressions by *śrāvaka*s of the *vinaya* precepts. Second, repentance via the witness of signs (*guanxiang chanhui* 觀相懺悔), such as seeing falling flowers or the buddhas rubbing one's head, which eliminates the essential transgression of the karmic conditions. Third, repentance via contemplation of the unborn (*guan wusheng chanhui* 觀無生懺悔), which ultimately does away with the root of transgressions by eliminating ignorance (*avidyā*) and afflictions (*kleśa*). Zhiyi understood purity of precepts as foundational. He associated these three types of repentance with the three practices, namely, precepts, meditative contemplation, and wisdom, showing that all Buddha dharma is found within the practice of repentance.[41] However, Daoxuan 道宣 (596–667) proposed that phenomenal repentance and principle repentance differed in terms of capacities:

> However, there are many varieties of repentance practice. In the case of Repentance by Phenomena, it can only subdue karma and that which is

39 *Chisheng guang daochang niansong yi*, *T* no.1951, 46: 1.979b28-c22.

40 *Shi chan boluomi cidi famen*, *T* no.1916, 46: 2.485c1-3.

41 Sheng, "Tiantai chanfa", 105–108.

> easily removed. In the case of Repentance by Principle, it can burn and destroy karma. First, we will discuss the elimination of karma based on principle [for those possessing] superior capacities. As the [*Da bo*]*niepan* [*jing*] states, if someone cultivates precepts via the body, and wisdom via the mind, they can observe that dharmas are like space; contemplating negative karma, they can turn over the karma, which would otherwise result in hell, and thereby experience it in a lighter form during the present lifetime. In the case of minor transgressions, if people do not themselves reveal them; their minds from the start are without remorse and do not cultivate virtue; and if they conceal flaws, then, even if they do have positive karma, the minor karmic results, which should be experienced during the present lifetime, are turned into the unfortunate extreme result of falling into hell due to the defilement of the transgression. This is due to ignorance. … As to the second, which is repentance based on phenomena [for those possessing] low capacities, if relying on the Mahāyāna, then the rituals are laid out in the *Foming* [*jing*] and [*Da*] *fangdeng* [*tuoluoni jing*]. One must witness signs via phenomenal repentance, prompting a spiritual experience in line with the teachings. If relying on the *Vinaya* Buddhism, one must carry out the scriptural repentance with an awareness of the name of the transgression, and its type and features. If someone has any doubts or is lacking awareness [of the characteristics of a transgression], then he is not in the preparatory stage yet. Except for those who do not study [the *vinaya*], who has committed the crimes that are wrong by itself, this [practice] could eliminate the transgressions against the precepts.[42]

Daoxuan believed that Repentance by Phenomena could subdue karma and prevent it from arising, which corresponds to what Jingyuan called "Repentance of Subduing Karma", while principle repentance could burn karma (equivalent to "repentance of turning karma") and destroy karma (equivalent to "repentance of destroying karma"). Through "Repentance by Principle", one meditates on the emptiness of dharmas, understanding that the nature of

42 *Tanwude bu sifenlü shanbu suiji jiemo*, *T* no.1808, 40: 2.506c3-10:
然懺法多種, 若作事懺, 但能伏業易奪；若作理懺, 則能焦業滅業. 先論利根依理斷業, 如《涅槃》云：若有修習身戒心慧, 能觀諸法由如虛空, 設作惡業思惟觀察, 能轉地獄重報現世輕受；若於小罪, 不能自出, 心初無悔, 不能修善, 覆藏瑕玼, 雖有善業, 爲罪垢汙, 現世輕報, 轉爲地獄極重惡果, 是爲愚癡 …… 二者鈍根依事懺者, 若依大乘, 則《佛名》、《方等》具列行儀, 依法懺悔要須相現, 准教驗心；若依律宗, 必須識於罪名、種、相, 隨有牒懺. 若疑不識, 不合加法, 唯除不學者, 隨犯結根本, 此但滅犯戒罪也.

transgressions is essentially empty. It is through this that one can turn heavy karmic retribution into a lighter form, or even eliminate the transgressive karma altogether. Phenomenal repentance includes repentance of witnessing signs, and repentance according to established *vinaya* conventions. The former is based on the aforementioned *Foming jing* and *Vaipulya* repentance methods, requiring that auspicious signs appear. The latter is the *karma* proceedings based on the *vinaya*. There are different ways to eliminate transgressions based on the different types of transgressions. Thus, Jingyuan's methods of repentance (repentance through subduing, turning and eliminating), inheriting Tiantai's idea of three confessions, were produced after Daoxuan's interpretation.

8. Repentance and Vows is where one repents the transgressive karma that they produced, whereupon making the vow to eliminate it. At the same time, one makes the vow to perfect the merit of having purified the six faculties. The repentance method is merely an external ritual. The practice requires inner visualization. Jingyuan proposed the following method of "carrying the mind":

> There are three methods of repentance, just as we know there are three types of transgression. Next, with a focused mind, proper decorum, reverently kneeled, and offering fine incense, one visualizes Avalokiteśvara Bodhisattva with immeasurable solemnness, surrounded by retainers. [One should confess with] the master of repentance, as if he were right before your eyes. One should confess all negative karma created from the immeasurable past [to him]; sever the stream of the [afflicted] mind, and do not create [such negative karma] any longer. With true wisdom contemplating the emptiness of transgressions, being neither internal nor external; respectfully generate great *bodhicitta*, destroying afflictions as numerous as grains of sand in the Ganges River. One should with a focused mind say, "All obstacles related to transgressions were created by myself and sentient beings from the beginningless past! May the Triple Gem save us out of compassion and [lead us to] realise sudden enlightenment, to see the true reality, and to become one with the Buddha's *dharmakāya*. May the three karmic transgressions be transformed into the three liberations. May the six major obstacles of the faculties be transformed into the six supernormal powers".[43]

---

43 *Shoulengyan tanchang xiuzheng yi*, XZJ no. 861, 95: 1.1079a4-9: 既知罪有三品,懺有三門.次端一心,正身威儀,虔敬互跪,燒諸名香,存想觀音菩薩,無量莊嚴,眷屬圍繞.爲懺悔主,如對目前,發露無量劫來,所造一切惡業,斷相續心,更不復造.而以正慧,觀罪性空,不在內外,敬發大菩提心,摧滅洹沙煩惱.

One is to confess with Avalokiteśvara Bodhisattva as repentance master. At the same time, one meditates on the emptiness of transgressions with *prajñā* wisdom: it is neither internal nor external. One is to generate *bodhicitta*, eliminate all obstacles related to transgressions, realise the *dharmakāya*, turn the three karmas of body, speech, and mind into the three liberations related to emptiness, marklessness and the uncreated, and turn the six faculties into the six supernormal powers.

At the same time, Jingyuan placed a great deal of emphasis on the ten minds contrary or in line with *saṃsāra* (*nishun shixin* 逆順十心), a repentance practice of Tiantai.[44] This practice is the root of the Tiantai repentance practice of "carrying the mind" (*yunxin* 運心). Jingyuan in the *Lengyan xiuzheng yi* states the following:

> One should "carry" these ten minds which are contrary or in line [with *saṃsāra*]. Recollect the "Qingliang ji" 清涼偈 (Verses of Qingliang): Ignorance having arisen from the beginningless past; like an evil friend, it increases the attachment to self. Virtue forever ceased because I did not rejoice; evil gradually grew because I indulged my speech and will. The mind spread out all over, defiling whatever it touched, while succession of thoughts remained active day and night. I did not want people to know, thus I concealed my faults. I did not fear the evil realms, thus I was indulgent. Shameless, I [was caught] in Māra's net. Doing away with cause and effect, I [fell into] the pit of the *icchantika*. Like this, I went along with the flow, and turned my back on the origins [of *saṃsāra*]. I was overwhelmed in the vast expanse of the sea of *saṃsāric* suffering. Fortunately, I came to know of the sons of the elders. I now wish to go against the flow, and abandon the impoverished village. I rightly believe in cause and effect, thereby destroying [the causes for being] an *icchantika*. Ashamed of [having followed the vehicle of] men and gods, I will destroy shamelessness. Fearing the evil realms, I will eliminate my lack of fear of them. I reveal my transgressive karma, and eliminate faults. I sever the stream

---

應一心念言：我與眾生, 無始所作, 一切罪障, 惟願三寶哀滑拔濟, 頓見真性, 等佛法身, 三業罪愆, 成三解脫, 六根重障, 翻作六通.

44 *Mohe zhiguan*, *T* no.1911, 46: 4.39c23-26: If someone wishes to repent [and remove] heavy obstacles from this and past lives, and practice the four types of *samādhi*, they should be aware of the ten minds that are either contrary or in line [with *saṃsāra*], clearly understanding faults. They should carry out these ten minds as a corrective approach. These twenty minds pass throughout and constitute the root of various types of repentance. 若欲懺悔二世重障行四種三昧者, 當識順流十心, 明知過失. 當運逆流十心, 以爲對治. 此二十心通爲諸懺根本.

> of mind, and eliminate conceptions of permanence. I generate *bodhicitta*, and eliminate confusion. I will cultivate merit, correct faults, and eliminate indulgence. I will protect the True Dharma, and eliminate dissatisfaction. I will recollect the Buddhas of the Ten Directions, and do away with evil friends. I will contemplate the emptiness of transgressions, and eliminate afflictions. As to the above six verses, the first three pertain to the ten minds in line with *saṃsāra*, constituting what is to be corrected. The latter three pertain to the ten minds contrary to *saṃsāra*, in which [the minds] are transformed and eliminated.[45]

The "ten minds following the flow" (*shunliu shixin* 順流十心) refers to the following ten "minds" or mental states produced by beings in which one follows afflictions and transmigrates through *saṃsāra*: minds constituted by ignorance, and minds or mental states in which one associates with evil friends, do not follow virtue, produce the three types of negative karmas, "spread the negative mind"; as well as mental states in which there is continuity of the negative mind, the concealment of faults, a lack of fear of the evil realms, shamelessness, and abandonment of cause and effect. The "ten minds which run contrary to the flow" (*niliu shixin* 逆流十心) refer to the following ten "minds" of the practitioner in which they are able to remove the negative developments produced from the earlier ten minds which follow the flow of *saṃsāra*. They are constituted by deep belief in cause and effect, the generation of shame, the generation of great fear, repentance, severance of the continuity of mind, generation of *bodhicitta*, elimination of evil plus the cultivation of virtue, protection of the True Dharma, recollection of the Buddhas of the Ten Directions, and contemplation on the emptiness of transgressions. These ten minds later became core to the practice of repentance within Chinese Buddhism, being cited by Chengguan and Zongmi.[46] This is why Jingyuan also employed them in the *Lengyan xiuzheng yi*.

---

45 *Shoulengyan tanchang xiuzheng yi*, XZJ no. 861, 95: 1.1079a11-16:
當運逆順十心, 即念《清涼偈》云：自從無始起無明, 亦值惡友增我情, 無隨喜心善永滅, 縱自語意惡漸生. 心心遍佈觸處染, 念念相續日夜營, 不欲人知藏過失, 不畏惡道任縱橫. 無慚無愧魔羅網, 拔因拔果闡提坑, 如是順流背本已, 生死苦海浩然盈. 幸識由來長者子, 今欲逆流捨貧里, 正信因果破闡提, 慚愧人天破無恥. 恐怖惡道破不畏, 發露罪業破覆疵, 斷相續心破常念, 發菩提心破徧起. 修功補過破縱恣, 守護正法破無喜, 念十方佛破惡友, 觀罪性空破結使. 上之六偈, 初三順生死十心, 以為所治；後三逆生死十心, 從後翻破.

46 *Da Fangguangfo huayan jing shu*, *T* no.1735, 35: 48.867c28-868a10; *Da Fangguangfo huayan jing sui shu yanyi chao*, *T* no.1736, 36: 78.611b4-6; *Yuanjue jing dashu shiyi chao*, XZJ no. 211, 15: 13.55a3-17.

9. “Circumambulation and Chanting” is walking around the altar while reciting the names of the buddhas, bodhisattvas, and other Buddhist holy figures. Jingyuan explains the method for chanting, and other noteworthy points as follows:

> Go around clockwise in an orderly fashion. One should not stare into the distance. Like this one may go around three times or a hundred times, as there is no fixed number. Next recite the *Guanyin yuantong* 觀音圓通 ([Chapter of the] Perfect Wisdom of Avalokiteśvara). Those with a good voice may recite the “Dharma Gate of Perfect Wisdom of Avalokiteśvara Bodhisattva” (Guanshiyin pusa yuantong famen 觀世音菩薩圓通法門) from the *Lengyan jing*. They may also practice the ritual in a seat, and just recite *sūtra* in the shrine hall. If it is to be for a period of seven days, there must be a meditation hall set up outside the shrine hall. When entering the altar space, the form for *sūtra* recitation is like that of the *Xingyuan yi* 行願儀 (Ritual for [Avataṃsaka Samantabhadra’s] Practices and Vows).[47]

Circumambulation and chanting require that one go clockwise. At the same time, the number of times to go around is not fixed. Afterward, one must recite the “Guanshiyin pusa yuantong famen” of fascicle six of the *Lengyan jing*. This is a result of Avalokiteśvara Bodhisattva being the repentance master in the *Lengyan xiuzheng yi*. The widespread popularity of his cult was also one reason.

10. “Xitong guanfa” 析通觀法 (Contemplation of Avalokiteśvara’s Method) primarily refers to the analysis and practice of the causes and importance of Avalokiteśvara Bodhisattva’s “Method of Perfectly Penetrating Wisdom” for the faculty of hearing. Jingyuan states the following:

> Some say that we focus our attention on counting breaths, for it is actually the root of inner practice, and the essential path of the Three Vehicles. Now as to this repentance, how is it not in accord with tradition? I reply that in the creation of contemplation methods, there are provisional and true methods. As to the provisional, they are limited to that which is inclined towards practice. As to the true, they penetrate into perfect realisation. The present *sūtra* might include the provisional

47 *Shoulengyan tanchang xiuzheng yi*, XZJ no. 861, 95: 1.1080b2-4:
夫右繞者, 順向殷重, 瞻望不足也. 如是三匝乃至百匝, 亦無定數. 次誦《觀音圓通》, 聲德者舉云《首楞嚴經》觀世音菩薩圓通法門. 其或修一席之儀, 只於道場諷經. 如以七日爲期限者, 須於道場外置禪觀堂, 將入壇場, 諷經規式, 亦如《行願儀》辨之.

> method of counting breaths, but it is limited and does not penetrate [into true realisation]. It is snatched up and done away with by Mañjuśrī. Thus, the *sūtra* states, "Meditation on the nose was originally for those with tentative capacities. It just lets them collect their mind in one place. How could they acquire perfect realisation where the mind has come to abide"? In the case of true complete realisation, it is penetrative and not limited; it is given by Marvellous Virtue (i.e., Mañjuśrī). Thus, the *sūtra* states, "The essence of the true teaching here is purity in sound; if wanting to advance in *samādhi*, it is actually entered via hearing". As Avalokiteśvara's single method is supreme, the others are provisional. They are not to be practiced for long. Understanding this was the cause for me to not carry out the counting of breaths.[48]

Jingyuan brought out the features of the *Lengyan xiuzheng yi*, pointing out that the contemplation method of this repentance is Avalokiteśvara Bodhisattva's "Method of Perfectly Penetrating Wisdom" for the faculty of hearing. According to general methods of contemplation, the first method is always observation of thoughts or counting breaths as a form of training. However, the *Lengyan jing* rejects these two methods due to their limited natures, since they are unable to bring about perfect realisation. This is why Jingyuan stresses that one should practice the method of perfect penetration.

Finally, Jingyuan points out the relationship between the repentance ritual and *śamatha-vipaśyanā* (*zhiguan* 止觀):

> Is it not beyond words—that one who would demonstrate the model through cultivation of the practice, guide and benefit those with karmic connections, and respectfully make offerings [to the Buddha], is truly equivalent in terms of merit with bodhisattvas as numerous as grains of sand in 6,200,000,000 Ganges Rivers! If one applies the true [methods] to the expedient [method], then one could reach the two gates of practicing *śamatha-vipaśyanā* even by counting breaths. In the present *sūtra*, one could certainly practice through *śamatha* by the method of liberating the ties of the faculties and their cognitive objects; one could

48 *Shoulengyan tanchang xiuzheng yi*, XZJ no. 861, 95: 1.1080b6-15:
或謂：繫念數息, 實乃內行根本, 三乘要道, 今茲懺儀, 何不遵稟？答曰：夫觀法之設, 有方便門, 有稱實門；方便則局乎偏修, 稱實則通於圓證. 今經雖有數息方便, 局而不通, 乃爲文殊所奪. 故經云：鼻想本權機, 只令攝心住, 住成心所住, 云何獲圓通. 若乃稱實圓證, 通而不局, 即爲妙德所與. 故經云：此方真教體, 清淨在音聞, 欲趣三摩提, 實以聞中入. 既宗觀音一門爲最, 自餘諸方便, 非是長修習. 吾之所以不取數息者, 識此也.

> definitely practise through *vipaśyanā* by the methods of [observing] the similarity and dissimilarity of causes and effects. One who cultivates this, carrying out various Dharma services in the shrine hall, will err in *śamatha* should they give rise to delusional thoughts for a moment. If they lose their focus for a short time, they will be at a loss in *vipaśyanā*. Thus, true practice is only when stillness and focus flow together, and *śamatha* and *vipaśyanā* are equally employed together. The various rituals will all be of assistance to practice![49]

Jingyuan first emphasizes the merit and virtue of the various rituals included among the practices of repentance, while later stressing that in such practices one ought to be free from delusional thoughts. As one enters a state of *vipaśyanā* while reading the text, *śamatha* and *vipaśyanā* are employed together, as stillness and contemplation come to flow together. This is the unification of "phenomenal characteristics" and "contemplation of principle". It is also a feature of repentance practice within Chinese Buddhism.

### 1.3 *Buddhist and Pure Land Communes in the Song-Yuan Periods*

In the Song and Yuan periods, Buddhist communes or societies (*sheyi* 社邑) continued to develop, bringing together various beliefs and becoming a type of community united around faith. After the mid-Tang period, there gradually appeared "Communities of the Western Land" (*xifang she* 西方社) and "Communities for the Nine Grades of Rebirth" (*jiupin wangsheng she* 九品往生社). The monk Shenhao 神皓 (715–790) from Fuyuan si 福願寺 of Mount Bao 包山 in Wu County 吳郡 during his later years established a "Society of the Western Land", in which the community prayed for rebirth in Amitābha's Pure Land.[50] In the fifth lunar month of year five of reign era Kaicheng (840) under Emperor Wenzong 文宗 (r. 826–840), Jiyu si 稽禹寺 of the Zhejiang assembly requested the Dharma Master Xuanying 玄英 (d.u.) to teach the *Jin'gang jing* at the Pingyuan si 平原寺 at Yuyao 余姚. He brought together 250 people and formed the "Society for the Nine Grades of Rebirth". There was an account engraved in stone. The monk Chu'na 處納 (d.u.) in his "Jie jiupin wangsheng she bing xu"

---

49 *Shoulengyan tanchang xiuzheng yi*, XZJ no. 861, 95: 1.1080b15-1081a3: 矧以修法垂範, 導利有緣, 而禮覲供養, 其福與六十二億河沙菩薩正等, 豈勝言哉！若以稱實, 攝於方便, 則數息亦修止觀二門. 今經根塵結解門, 決定修乎止；因果同異門, 決定修乎觀. 厥或造修者, 於道場中, 行諸法事, 暫起妄念, 則失於止也；暫時忘照, 則缺於觀也. 夫然, 則寂照雙流, 止觀齊運, 方爲正修, 其諸事儀, 皆爲助行耳！

50 *Song Gaoseng zhuan*, *T* no. 2061, 50: 15.802c17-803a13; *Quan Tang wen* 918.4242.

結九品往生社並序 (Exposition for Founding of the Society for the Nine Grades of Rebirth) states the following:

> The virtuous are confused about where they are destined, but never cease recollecting the Buddha of Immeasurable Life. The hermit (i.e., Feng Meng 逢萌, d.u.) hung the official hat [and left the court], and Kangle 康樂 (Xie Lingyun 謝靈運, 385–433) threw the hair pin [and resigned from an official position]. The historians praise them. Their ways do not vanish. The masters of Wu study our true teaching and inherit their spirit. The benefactors differ, for nine grades are arranged.[51]

The grades are arranged here based on how much members contributed. Although the inscription states that the Dharma Master gathered 1,250 people, in actuality those named include only 125 people. Therein thirteen are *bhikṣus*, while fourteen are *bhikṣuṇīs*.

During the Song dynasty, the formation of Buddhist fellowships for reciting *sūtras* was quite widespread. There was a "*Diamond Sūtra* Society" (*Jin'gang jing hui* 金剛經會) in which the benefactor provided the *sūtra* texts, and then invited the monks to teach. There were also "*Sūtra* Reading Communities" (*kanjing hui* 看經會) and "*Sūtra* Recitation Communities" (*songjing hui* 誦經會). The former society's members were primarily officials and gentlemen, such as Li Gang 李綱 (1085–1140) and the abbot Cangong 璨公 (Liaocan 了璨, fl. early twelfth century) from Taiping Xinguo si 太平興國寺 in the capital, who collaboratively formed a "*Sūtra* Reading Society".[52] The poem, "You Tianwang si" 游天王寺 (Wandering Tianwang Temple), by Shu Yuexiang 舒岳祥 (1219–1298) from the Song dynasty reads as follows:

> A thousand people assembled at the *sūtra* society
> The Burning lamps shine [just as] the profound [wisdom] of the seven buddhas lightens
> The pine lines bustle with a great many sounds
> Not any sound is perceived by the monks in meditation.[53]

Yao Mian 姚勉 (1216–1262) in the "Chongjian Guanyin'ge yuanhua bangyu" 重建觀音閣緣化榜語 (Account of the Rebuilding of the Guanyin Pavilion) tells

51 *Baqiongshi jinshi buzheng* 73.506:
夫爲善者, 迷於所趣, 無量壽佛, 返念不息. 遺民掛冕, 康樂投簪, 史氏稱之, 其風不泯. 吳公學我真教, 挹其遺蹤, 施有等差, 階陳九品.

52 *Liangxi ji* 108.307.

53 *Langfeng ji* 3.362: 經社千人會, 燃燈七佛深. 松行喧萬籟, 僧定不知音.

us about their activities: "With this pavilion completed, is it merely for its beautiful sight? The monks, and spiritual friends of the '*sūtra* society': some study meditation here, others recite *sūtras*. There are various means for whatever is to be practised".[54] It is clear that this pavilion was an activity site for a "*Sūtra* Recitation Society".

During the Song dynasty, communities organized for Pure Land practice were most representative. The *Fozu tongji* (fascicle forty-three) states the following:

> The *śramaṇa* Xingchang 省常 (959–1020) of Zhaoqing si 昭慶寺 in Xihu 西湖 of Hangzhou, copied out with his own blood the "Chapter on Pure Conduct" of the *Huayan jing*. He formed a society to carry out Pure Land practices. Prime Minister Wang Dan 王旦 (957–1017) acted as chief. One hundred and thirty-two gentlemen, including vice Councillor Su Yijian 蘇易簡 (958–997), were at one time all called disciples of the Pure Land Society. A thousand *bhikṣus* participated. It was said that even the Lotus Society of Mount Lu had never been so glorious as this day.[55]

Xingchang admired the legend of Huiyuan of Mount Lu, who established societies and formed one dedicated to purifying karma. He adopted ideas from the "Chapter on Pure Conduct" of the *Huayan jing* and called it the "Society of Pure Practice" (Jingxing she 淨行社). Prime Minister Wang Dan was made chief, while around 132 Han Lin Academy scholars, such as Su Yijian, participated in the society, writing poems and calling themselves disciples of the Pure Practice Society. There were also more than a thousand devotees who participated. At the time, people thought this society was even more glorious than the one at Mount Lu.

Su Yijian compiled his "Shi *Huayan jing* Jingxing pin xu" 施華嚴經淨行品序 (Preface to the Implementation of the Chapter on Pure Conduct of the *Huayan Jing*) on the twenty-fourth of autumn in year two of the Chunhua 淳化 reign era (991). Xingchang's establishment of the "Society of Pure Practice" was during this year. This preface states the following:

---

54 *Xuepo ji* 46.327-28: 此閣成就, 豈徒美觀？禪衲律僧, 經社道友, 或此習定, 或此誦經, 隨所修爲, 種種方便.

55 *Fozu tongji*, *T* no. 2035, 49: 43.400c19-23:
杭州西湖昭慶寺沙門省常, 刺血書《華嚴 · 淨行品》, 結社修西方淨業. 宰相王旦爲之首, 參政蘇易簡百三十二人, 一時士夫皆稱淨行社弟子. 比丘預者, 千眾人. 謂廬山蓮社, 莫如此日之盛.

> There is nothing sincerer than drawing blood. There is no greater way to send a letter than in official woodblock printing. We printed this *sūtra*, a total of one-thousand scrolls, bringing together a *Saṃgha* fellowship of eighty monks. May the offerings and recitations be limitless.[56]

Song Bai 宋白 (933–1009) in his "Da Song Hangzhou Xihu Zhaoqing si jieshe beiming bing xu" 大宋杭州西湖昭慶寺結社碑銘並序 (Inscription and Preface for the Fellowship Founding at Zhaoqing si of West Lake in Hangzhou during the Great Song) states the following:

> There is a monk at Zhaoqing si in Hangzhou named Xingchang. When at ease and times are bright, he vowed a great aspiration heartily: in order to follow the imperial career and repay four types of kindness, I will draw blood and mix it with ink to copy true scripture—what was copied? It was the "Jingxing pin" 淨行品 (Chapter on Pure Conduct) of the *Huayan jing*. For every letter written, one had to prostrate three times, circumambulate [the shrine] three times, and recite the Buddha's name three times. A skilled artist carved this [text into a woodblock print], before it was printed as a thousand scrolls. Whether monks or laymen, it was given out to a thousand persons. An image of Vairocana was produced also with sandalwood incense. They joined eighty monks as one fellowship.[57]

Xingchang extracted some of his own blood and mixed it with ink to copy the "Chapter on Pure Conduct" of the *Huayan jing*. For every letter that he copied, he would prostrate, circumambulate the shrine, and recite the Buddha's name three times each. The text was printed into a thousand scrolls and distributed to a thousand people.

The *Xihu jingshe lu* 西湖淨社錄 (Record of the Pure Land Society of West Lake), compiled by Xingchang, is not extant. Song Bai in his aforementioned "Da Song Hangzhou Xihu Zhaoqing si jieshe beiming bing xu" states the following:

---

56 *Wŏnjong munryu*, XZJ 1010, 103: 22.851b14-16: 以爲瀝懇莫若刺血, 傳信莫若篆版. 乃印是經, 凡一千卷, 結八十僧社. 散施念誦, 期於無窮.

57 *Wŏnjong munryu*, XZJ 1010, 103: 22.853a8-13:
杭州照慶寺僧曰省常, 身樂明時, 心發洪願 : 上延景祚, 下報四恩. 刺血和墨, 書寫真經. 書之者何 ? 即《華嚴經 · 淨行》一品也. 每書一字, 必三作禮, 三圍繞, 三稱佛名. 良工雕之, 印成千卷, 若僧若俗, 分施千人. 又以栴檀香, 造毗盧像, 結八十僧, 同爲一社.

> At the time when the scriptures and images were complete, he touched his knees to the earth, placed his palms together, and spoke thus: "May I and eighty *bhikṣus*, and the great assembly of one thousand, starting from this day, generate *bodhicitta*, practising bodhisattva practices into the limitless future. May we devote this retributed life to produce support for the country; may we immediately enter the *dharmadhātu*, perfectly awaken to birthlessness, practice the ten *pāramitās*, associate with innumerable true and virtuous friends; may the luminosity of [dharma] body illuminate widely, making all sentient beings attain the *samādhi* of Buddha recollection like Mahāsthāmaprāpta. May we make all sentient beings acquire the fourteen forms of fearlessness, like Avalokiteśvara who hears people's voices and liberates them from suffering; May we cultivate the great limitless sea of practices and vows like Samantabhadra. May we open the subtle profound gate of wisdom like Mañjuśrī. May we be filled with extreme wisdom, taking the place of the next buddha, like Maitreya. When we achieve buddhahood, may we be like Amitābha, be it in body or realm. Eighty *bhikṣus*, and the great assembly of one-thousand, having received prophecies of their buddhahood one after another, will all achieve perfect awakening. I now make this vow extensively for all sentient beings: they are limitless, and so too are my vows like this". Was it not excellent? The words and aspirations of the superior man were like this.[58]

This is the text of aspirations for the Society of Pure Practice, demonstrating that it was founded with the *Huayan jing* as its core, combining the ideas of *nianfo* (Buddha recollection) and rebirth in the Pure Land.

After Xinchang, in year six of reign era Dazhong Xiangfu (1015), Zhili started the "Society of Buddha Recollection, Generosity and Precepts" (*nianfo shijie hui* 念佛施戒會) at Yanqing si 延慶寺 of Siming County. It was convened on an annual basis. Zhili himself composed a commentary.[59] Lingzhao 靈照 (?–1090/1091), the disciple of Renyue, lived at Chaoguo si 超果寺 in Huating 華亭

58 *Wŏnjong munryu*, *XZJ* 1010, 103: 22.853a13-b5: 爾時經像成,乃膝地合掌,作是言曰：我與八十比丘、一千大眾,始從今日,發菩提心,窮未來際,行菩薩行.願盡此報已,生贍養國,頓入法界,圓悟無生,修習十種波羅蜜多,親近無數真善知識,身光遍照,令諸有情得念佛三昧,如大勢至;聞聲救苦,令諸有情獲十四無畏,如觀世音;修廣大無邊行願海,猶如普賢;開微妙甚深智慧門,猶如妙德;邊際智滿,次補佛處,猶如彌勒;至成佛時,若身若土,如阿彌陀.八十比丘,一千大眾,轉次授記,皆成正覺.我今立此願,普為諸眾生.眾生不可盡,我願亦如是.偉矣哉！上人之言如是,志如是.

59 *Siming zunzhe jiaoxing lu*, *T* no.1937, 46: 1.857c25-28.

between 1068 and 1077 (the years of reign era Xining). He started a "Pure Karma Society" from the Yuanfeng 元豐 period (1078–1085). Annually, at the start of every spring, they would do *nianfo* practice for seven days. There were always as many as twenty-thousand people who participated in the society.[60] Wen Yanbo 文彥博 (1006–1097), a man of Fenzhou 汾州, over the course of around fifty years—going through the four imperial reigns of Renzon 仁宗 (r. 1022–1063), Yingzong 英宗 (r.1063–1067), Shenzong 神宗 (r. 1067–1085) and Zhezong 哲宗 (r. 1085–1100)—achieved the position of Grand Teacher (*taishi* 太師), and translated scriptures, as well as annotating literary and historical texts. He was given title of "Duke of Luguo" (*Luguo gong* 潞國公). In the time of Renzong (1022–1063), he established a "Pure Land Society" (*jingtu hui* 淨土會) in the capital with the Meditation Master Jingyan 淨嚴 (ca. eleventh century), bringing together ten-thousand monks and laypeople to chant the Buddha's name.[61]

During the Xuanhe 宣和 period (1119–1125), Qiyu 齊玉 (1071–1129) resided at Baozang si 寶藏寺 in Tiaoxi 苕溪. At the end of every year, he would arrange a "Pure Karma Society". Sijing 思淨 (1068–1137), the disciple of Zeying 擇瑛 (1045–1099), resided at Beiguan 北關 in Qiantang 錢塘, where he gathered ten-thousand people for a Pure Land Society. Figures such as Sizhao 思照 (1119–1120) and Zongli 宗利 (1055–1144) established Pure Land centres in various places. In the Song dynasty, Jiangsu and Zhejiang were the very popular centres in which societies devoted to *nianfo* practices were established.

### 1.4 Niepan Hui 涅槃會 (Nirvāṇa *Gatherings*) *and the* Niepan Lizan Wen 涅槃禮贊文 (*Veneration Verses of the* Nirvāṇa)

Various holidays related to Buddhism first appeared in China following the introduction of Buddhism. At the end of the Eastern Han dynasty, there appeared services for the Buddha's birth. On this holiday, they would parade an image of the Buddha, in addition to washing the Buddha statue. However, checking the holidays preserved in the present literature, it seems one will not see any activities related to commemorating the day of the Buddha's *nirvāṇa*. Investigating the Dunhuang temples of the late Tang and Five Dynasties periods through Dunhuang documents, the better detailed accounts of Buddhist holidays include lamp lighting (*randeng* 燃燈) on the fifteenth of the first lunar month, image procession (*xingxiang* 行像) on the eighth of the second lunar month, the Great Assembly (*dahui* 大會) on the eighth of the fourth lunar month, Ullambana, and the celebration of the Buddha's awakening on the

60 *Fozu tongji*, *T* no. 2035, 49: 21.242b16-19.
61 *Fozu tongji*, *T* no. 2035, 49: 53.469b26-28.

FIGURE 27 Bodhisattva Guanyin 觀音 in the water moon form, dated to the Jin Dynasty (1115-1234) (Yale University Museum).

eighth day of the twelfth lunar month.[62] However, we still find some documents related to *Nirvāṇa* Gatherings, proving that during the Tang and Five Dynasties period, the temples at Dunhuang carried out such an event.

However, following the spread of the *Da bo niepan jing* in China, the teaching, recitation and commentary on this *sūtra* greatly flourished, leading to "masters of the *niepan* [*jing*]" (*Niepan shi* 涅槃師). At the same time, there appeared a "*Nirvāṇa* Repentance" (*Niepan chan* 涅槃懺), which is based on this *sūtra*. In the section on repentance in fascicle twenty-eight in the *Guang Hongming ji* 廣弘明集 (An Expansion of the Collection for Glorifying and Elucidating [Buddhism] *T* 2103) there are included the "Xiechi wei jian *Niepan* chan qi" 謝敕爲建涅槃懺啓 (Imperial Report on the Founding of the *Nirvāṇa* Repentance) by Emperor Jianwen of the Liang (Liang Jianwen di 梁簡文帝 [r. 549–551]) and the "Suoluo zhai chanwen" 娑羅齋懺文 (Repentance Text of the *Śāla* Feast) by Emperor Wen of the Chen (Chen Wendi 陳文帝 [r. 559–566]). These are commentaries on ceremonies that could be commonly used in various places. The function of practicing repentance is for worldly benefits such as removing obstacles and diseases, while also praying for the protection of the realm, and increasing one's field of merit. This met with the requirements of the Chinese, therefore bringing together worldly peace, freedom from difficulties and the elimination of transgressions through repentance.[63] Moreover, in the winter of year two in reign era Zhenming 禎明 (588), when the monk Huibu 慧布 (509–587) of Mount She 攝山 or Mount Qixia 棲霞山 was nearing his end, Xu Xiaoke 徐孝克 (527–599) established a "*Nirvāṇa* Repentance".[64] Due to a paucity of literature, we are unable to determine the details of this "*Nirvāṇa* Repentance", but based on the *Suoluo zhai chan wen* by Emperor Wen of Chen, we might infer that it was the "Great Assembly of No Obstacles" (*wuai dahui* 無礙大會) carried out on the day commemorating the Buddha's *nirvāṇa*:

> For one who seeks true liberation, originally nothing was born; for one capable of true wisdom, now there was also no cessation. Thus, understand that the change of colours of the Crane Forest (in Kuśīnagar where the Buddha died) is not text concerning transformation. Vulture's Peak is always present [like the] true perpetually abiding Dharma. … At the side of the Hiraṇyavatī River, the colours of early morning suddenly shone. Between the *śāla* trees, the sounds of the middle period of night went silent. The final merit was to be roused here on this day. I [honorably]

62 Hao, *Dunhuang sengni*, 229–35.

63 Shioiri, "Sange no juyōkatei", 733.

64 *Guang Hongming ji*, *T* no. 2103, 52: 30.357a20-22.

> have the karmic conditions [to be present in] Jambudvīpa to meet with great responsibility. I have pity for those beings with inverted views, and sigh for those creatures with their delusions. I always wish to build a vessel of the Six Perfections to cross them over to the other shore, and ride in the transmission of the Single Vehicle and drive it along the Middle Way. Now in the Taiji Hall 太極殿 we establish the Great Assembly of No Obstacles. A hundred monks in one evening [to enjoy] the Great *Śāla* Feast.[65]

The reason for Emperor Wen of the Chen to establish the *Śāla* Feast was to accumulate merit, carry on the spiritual legacy (i.e., "wisdom life", *huiming* 慧命) of the Buddha, and to extensively liberate sentient beings. Although there is no clear statement that this "Great Assembly of No Obstacles" was carried out on the day commemorating the *nirvāṇa* of the Buddha, it does say "the final merit was to be roused here on this day". This possibly is in reference to the "day of *nirvāṇa*". However, "*Nirvāṇa* Repentance" is just a type of repentance ritual. It might not be limited to the day of the Buddha's *nirvāṇa*. The "*Śāla* Feast" might have been carried out on the day of *nirvāṇa*. The accounts in this literature are not so clear.

However, it is the Chinese custom of having the Cold Food Festival (*hanshi jie* 寒食節) on the fifteenth day of the second lunar month that draws our attention. The Cold Food Festival is on the two days before Qingming 清明 on the Chinese lunar calendar, in which people eat cold food and refrain from lighting fires. The *Nittō guhō junrei kōki* 入唐求法巡禮行記 [The Record of a Pilgrimage to China in Search of the Dharma], by the Japanese monk Ennin 圓仁 (794–864), has three accounts of the Cold Food Festival. Ennin observed these festivals respectively at Kaiyuan si 開元寺 in Yangzhou 揚州 (year four of Kaicheng = 839), at the Silla Cloister 新羅院 on Mount Chi 赤山 in Wendeng 文登 (year five of Kaicheng = 840), and at Zisheng si 資聖寺 in Chang'an (year two of Huichang = 842).[66] This indicates that temples in the late Tang already acknowledged Chinese customs, and moreover, such festivities met with the approval of both commoners and officials. An account in Dunhuang document S. 381, "Longxing si Pishamen tianwang lingyan ji" 龍興寺毗沙門天王靈驗記 [Account of Auspicious Experiences with Vaiśravaṇa at Longxing si]

---

65 *Guang Hongming ji*, *T* no. 2103, 52: 28.334c8-19:
尋夫真解脫者, 本自不生；實智能者, 今亦無滅. 故知鶴林變色, 非變易之文；鷲山常在, 實常住之法. ...... 熙連河側, 晨朝之色忽明；娑羅樹間, 中夜之聲便寂. 最後功德, 是日茲辰. 弟子有緣閻浮, 屬當重任. 滑群生之顛倒, 嗟庶類之愚迷. 常願造六度之舟, 濟之於彼岸；駕一乘之傳, 驅之於中道. 今謹於太極殿, 設無礙大會, 百僧一夕, 娑羅大齋.

66 Bai, *Jiaozhu*, 113, 216, 396.

states, "On the fifteenth day of intercalary lunar month two, officials and commoners held festivities at Longxing si since it was the Cold Food [Festival]".[67] There appeared on the central plains of China sacrifices at tombs during the period of the Cold Food Festival. This was the origin of what would later become the Qingming tomb sacrifice (*Qingming jimu* 清明祭墓).[68]

As Ennin records, during the Cold Food Festival in 842, everyone went to pay respects at their ancestral tombs.[69] On the fifteenth day of the second lunar month, the temples would simultaneously hold feasts with no limit on the number of people attending.[70] At the same time, Ennin also records that between the eighth and fifteenth in the second lunar month (3.4–11) of 841 (Kaicheng six), the temples of Chang'an would arrange feasts, and carry out offerings to the Buddha tooth:

> Also, Da Zhuangyan si 大莊嚴寺 held an offering ceremony for the tooth of Śākyamuni Buddha. From the eighth to the fifteenth of the second lunar month, Jianfu si 薦福寺 held an offering ceremony for the Buddha tooth. Lantian 藍田 county runs a "Feast of No Hindrances" from the eighth to the fifteenth. Monks and lay people come from all over to eat. Monastic Recorder of the Left Street, Dharma Master Tixu 體虛 (d.u.), was chief of the gathering. The monasteries all came together. Each provided precious offerings, a hundred types of foods, and fine fruits and flowers, as well as carefully preparing incense, and making offerings to the Buddha's tooth. The spread of offerings beneath the veranda is incalculable. When the Buddha's tooth is in the central courtyard of the tower, the eminent monks of the city all go upstairs and sing praises with appropriate delight. [People] come to the capital to prostrate and make offerings. ... Like this, people make various aspirations and offerings. At the solemn "Buddha Tooth Gathering", coins fall down like rain towards the Buddha's tooth in the tower. On the tenth, [we] pilgrim monks went there and rejoiced, going up to the tower [housing] the Buddha's tooth and seeing it for ourselves. We sincerely prostrated ourselves before it.[71]

67 Huang, *Dunhuang baozang*, 3.281.

68 Zhang, *Wenhua shi*, 944–45.

69 Bai, *Jiaozhu*, 396.

70 Bai, *Jiaozhu*, 209.

71 Bai, *Jiaozhu*, 373–374:
又大莊嚴寺開釋迦牟尼佛牙供養. 從二月八日至十五日, 薦福寺開佛牙供養. 藍田縣從八日至十五日設無礙茶飯, 十方僧俗盡來吃, 左街僧錄體虛法師爲會主, 諸寺赴集. 各設珍供, 百種藥食, 珍妙果花, 衆香嚴備, 供養佛牙. 及供養樓廊下, 敷設不可勝計. 佛牙在樓中庭, 城中大德盡在樓上, 隨喜讚歎. 舉城赴來, 禮拜供

From the above account, we can see that from the eighth to the fifteenth in the second lunar month, the great monasteries of Chang'an carried out offerings for the Buddha's tooth. The feasts were quite a grand occasion. Although Ennin does not clearly indicate any "*Nirvāṇa* Society", this ought to have been associated with it.

Among the Dunhuang documents, there are some preserved that were used when the *Saṃgha* at Dunhuang carried out the *Nirvāṇa* Gathering, from which we can see features of these assemblies in the Tang-Song period. S. 2832 and P. 2631 include accounts of the time of year: "In the second month during spring, on the fifteenth day, which is [related to] the time of [the Buddha's] *nirvāṇa* among the paired trees, and phenomenal impermanence. Men and gods cried out. From old times we have lamented [the passing of the Buddha]; the world is empty, and the pain lasts till now"![72] Here "paired trees" refers to the site of Śākyamuni's *nirvāṇa* among the *śāla* trees in Kuśīnagar in Magadha. This indicates that at Dunhuang this anniversary of the Buddha's death was included among annual activities.[73] S. 2832, *Eryue shiwu wen* 二月十五文 (Text for the Fifteenth of the Second Month)[74], clearly demonstrates that the fifteenth of the second lunar month (*kongcun jiri* 空存忌日) already included activities commemorating the *nirvāṇa* of Śākyamuni, which was the *Nirvāṇa* gathering. Moreover, this document explains the weather and scenery on this day, and moreover indicates that the aim of the *Nirvāṇa* gathering is to pray for rebirth in the Pure Land, realisation of the tolerance of birthlessness, the liberation of beings, and that the True Dharma may long abide in the world.

Also, P. 2940, *Zhai wanwen* 齋琬文 (Jade Text of the Feast) includes a *Tan Fo de xian gui jimie* 歎佛德・現歸寂滅 (Praising the Virtue of the Buddha—Display of the Return to Cessation) has the following:

> The fifteenth of the second lunar month: this is the order of the Green Deity—its rhythm beat and [the things] are moved. The wave of the Eight Liberations swells in the golden river, and the adornment of the Seven Flowers is presented in the Jewelled Land. At that time, one sound vibrated distantly, hundreds and millions of roarings of the thunders follow. The flashing lights with five colors shine and illuminate all sentient beings. To bathe in the virtue water of the pool with the mandarin duck,

---

養. ...... 如是各各發願佈施, 莊嚴佛牙會, 向佛牙樓散錢如雨. 求法僧等十日往彼隨喜, 登佛牙樓上, 親見佛牙, 頂戴禮拜.

72 Huang, *Dunhuang baozang*, 23.653 & 123.18: 仲春二月, 十五半旬, 雙林入滅之歲, 諸行無常之日. 人天號哭, 自古興悲；世界虛空, 於今尚痛！

73 Tan, *Daolun*, 92.

74 Huang, *Dunhuang baozang*, 23.649.

> to mark in the auspicious wood with crane trees.... we may say that, at this evening when the Well-Come One [Śākyamuni] teaches those who possess capacities, during the time when the Benevolent [Śākyamuni] reaches *nirvāṇa*, the gate of skilful means is opened, revealing the superior track of practice.[75]

"Green Deity" (*qingqi* 青祇) refers to the "Green Emperor" (*qingdi* 青帝). This is spring, in which the first day of spring is celebrated with sacrifices to the "Green Emperor" in the eastern side of the capital. "Seven Flowers" (*qihua* 七花) refers to "Seven Pure Flowers" (*qi jinghua* 七淨花), in which the flower is a metaphor for the seven types of pure virtue, the seventh being the purity of *nirvāṇa*. One is free from defilements after having attained *nirvāṇa*. The later reference in this text to the "Crane Trees" (*heshu* 鶴樹) refers to the Tathāgata achieving *parinirvāṇa* among the twin *śāla* trees, which all turned to white like the colour of a crane, hence the name.[76] We can see from this document that Dunhuang monasteries on the fifteenth of the second lunar month carried out a sacrifice, "during the time when the Benevolent [Śākyamuni] reaches *nirvāṇa*, the gate of skilful means is opened, revealing the superior track of practice", while furthermore carrying out mourning services for the departed and praying for merits.

Thus, in Chinese Buddhist history, it was during the Tang and Five Dynasties period that the *Nirvāṇa* gathering clearly appears, rather than the Northern Song period.[77] We can infer that the emergence of the *Nirvāṇa* gathering was significantly related to the Cold Food Festival, since the day of the Buddha's *nirvāṇa* and the Cold Food Festival were both on the fifteenth day of the second lunar month. Moreover, the Chinese people had the tradition of worshipping at tombs during the Cold Food Festival. This was done to recollect one's ancestors. Thus, Buddhists in China were able to carry out remembrance and veneration of the Buddha in accord with popular custom, which is why the date of the *Nirvāṇa* gathering was always carried out on this same day. The *Shishi yaolan* 釋氏要覽 (Manual of Buddhist Practices, *T* 2127), compiled by

---

75 Huang, *Dunhuang baozang*, 125.346:
二月十五, 斯乃青祇式序, 彼律驚辰, 金河泛八解之瀾, 寶地秀七花之藻. 於時一音遐震, 吼百億而雷奔；五色光飛, 照三千而電發. 藻 (= 澡) 鴛池之德水, 標鶴樹之祥林 .... 可謂善逝調機之夕, 能仁控 (= 空) 寂之辰, 啓方便之幽關, 示薰修之勝軌.

76 Tan, *Daolun*, 92.

77 Nagai Masashi 永井政之 ("Sanbutsuki", 149) arugues that the first appearance of the *Nirvāṇa* gathering in Chinese Buddhist history was in the Northern Song.

Daocheng 道誠 (d.u.) in year three of Tianxi 天禧 (1019), has the following explanation:

> The fifteenth day of the second lunar month is the day of the Buddha's *nirvāṇa*. Monks and lay people around the realm gather together to make offerings, which is a taboo [commemorative] day. Those gentlemen among the lay people promise to develop their filial piety unto death, hence it is called a taboo day. Furthermore, it is called a day of no festivities since there is to be no drinking or festivities.[78]

The *Shishi yaolan* reveals to us that Confucian gentlemen placed emphasis on filial piety and reverence for one's ancestors. As a disciple of the Buddha, one is also supposed to commemorate the Buddha on the day of his *nirvāṇa*, which is why offerings for the *Nirvāṇa* gathering were established. Moreover, this service during the Song Dynasty became a common practice in temples across China. It is clear that it flourished at the time. The *Shishi yaolan* also indicates that the funerary rituals for the *Saṃgha* at the time primarily included readings of the *Da bo niepan jing* and the *vinayas*, while the mourning garments completely followed Chinese Confucian culture.[79]

Later, the *Fozu tongji*, published in the year seven of Xianchun 咸淳 (1271), records that the "the Tathāgata passed away on the fifteenth day of the second lunar month in year fifty-three of King Mu of the Zhou (Zhou Muwang 周穆王 [c. tenth century BCE]). All monasteries must carry out rituals. It is called the commemoration of the Buddha".[80] Fascicle three of the *Chanyuan qinggui* 禪苑清規 (Pure Rules of the Chan Park, *XZJ* 1234), published in year two of Chongning 崇寧 (1103) of the Northern Song dynasty, mentions under the "monastic superintendent" article (*jianyuan* 監院) that the superintendent should arrange a feast halfway through the second lunar month. This possibly refers to the *Nirvāṇa* gathering.[81] The "Ruzhong xuzhi" 入衆須知 (Necessary Knowledge for the *Saṃgha*, *XZJ* 1236), produced in year four of Jingding 景定 (1263), clearly records that at the *Nirvāṇa* gathering the assembly is to carry out rituals such as presenting incense, praising the Buddha and announcing proclamations.[82]

---

78 *Shishi yaolan*, *T* no. 2127, 54: 3.309c17-20: 二月十五日佛涅槃日, 天下僧俗, 有營會供養, 即忌日之事也. 俗禮君子, 育終身之孝, 忌日之謂也. 又謂不樂之日, 不飲樂故.

79 *Shishi yaolan*, *T* no. 2127, 54: 3.307c23-308a11.

80 *Fozu tongji*, *T* no.2035, 49: 33.319b19-21: 如來於周穆王五十三年 ( 壬申) 二月十五日入滅. 凡在伽藍必修供設禮, 謂之佛忌.

81 *Chanyuan qinggui*, *XZJ* no. 1234, 111: 3.890b16-17.

82 *Ruzhong xuzhi*, *XZJ* no. 1236, 111: 1.964b12-18.

FIGURE 28 Pagoda at Yunju Monastery 雲居寺, Beijing, dated to the Liao Dynasty (916-1125).

The *Jiaoding qinggui* 校定清規 (Revised Pure Rules, *XZJ* 1238), produced in 1293, records that on the day of the Buddha's *nirvāṇa*, the abbot is to take his high seat, while at the same time there are incense offerings, Dharma teachings, chanting practice and Dharma talk.[83] The *Beiyong qinggui* 備用清規 (Backup Pure Rules, *XZJ* 1239), produced in 1311, also includes a detailed record of the ritual procedures for the *Nirvāṇa* gathering.[84] Over time, the ritual procedures for the *Nirvāṇa* gathering became more complete and ceremonious. They were finally fixed with *Chixiu Baizhang qingggui* 敕修百丈清規 (Imperial Revision of Baizhang's Pure Rules, *T* 2025), produced in 1336.[85]

These "Pure Rules" (*qinggui* 清規) record the order of the ritual proceedings for the *Nirvāṇa* gathering, but there is no "Dharma talk" (*fayu* 法語), which is why there is no way to understand the reasons and intention behind the establishment of such a gathering in Chan monasteries. However, after the Song Dynasty, preserved within records of Meditation Masters are a number of "Dharma talks" carried out as lectures during the *Nirvāṇa* gatherings that provide materials to help deepen our investigation.

The "Fo yuanji ri shangtang" 佛圓寂日上堂 (Lecture on the Day of the Buddha's Complete Cessation), included in fascicle three of the *Cishou Huaishen chanshi yulu* 慈受懷深禪師語錄 (Record of Meditation Master Cishou Huaishen, *XZJ* 1433) of Cishou Huaishen 慈受懷深 (1077–1132) of Yunmen 雲門, is an early example of such a "Dharma talk":

> On the day of the Buddha's complete cessation, [Cishou Huaishen] addressed the hall [of monks] and said, "The Great Awakened World Honoured One, two thousand years ago on the fifteenth day of the second month, entered *parinirvāṇa*. Disciples now every time shall generate sorrowful reverence. I venture to question: have you actually attained *nirodha-samāpatti*? Or have you not got it? If you could get it, then you have realized the essence of the Buddha's teaching. If you could not get it, then even the Pāpīyas will frown ..."[86]

This "Dharma talk" not only displays grief over the Buddha's *nirvāṇa*, but it primarily deals with experientially knowing the existence of the "Buddha", and thereafter realising the path of the Buddha.

83 *Conglin jiaoding qinggui zongyao*, *XZJ* no. 1238, 112: 2.606c21.

84 *Chanlin beiyong qinggui*, *XZJ* no. 1239, 112: 1.64a13-b14.

85 *Chixiu Baizhang qinggui*, *T* no. 2025, 48: 1.1116a21-22.

86 *Cishou Huaishen chanshi guanglu*, *XZJ* no. 1433, 126: 3.606a16-b1:
佛圓寂日, 上堂云：大覺世尊, 二千年前, 二月十五日, 入般涅槃. 今之弟子, 每至斯辰, 而生悲仰. 敢問諸人, 且道：果曾入滅耶？不曾入滅耶？若定當得, 方明佛法旨趣；若定當不得, 任是波旬也皺眉.

Fascicle one of the *Jingci Huihui chanshi yulu* 淨慈慧暉禪師語錄 (Record of Meditation Master Jingci Huihui, XZJ 1409) of Jingci Huihui 淨慈慧暉 (1097–1183) of the Caodong sect 曹洞宗 includes a "Eryue wangri Fo niepan shangtang" 二月望日佛涅槃上堂 (Lecture on the Buddha's *Nirvāṇa* on the Full Moon of the Second Month):

> On the full moon of the second month, there was a lecture on the Buddha's *nirvāṇa*. [Jingci Huihui] said, "The Great sage of the Indian went to *nirvāṇa* on this day [many years ago]. The seeds of the crane wood already shrivelled now. You say: are they the same or not the same? … Common people see cessation, whereas the monks see production; common people see production, whereas the monks see death".[87]

Jingci Huihui used the Buddha's *nirvāṇa* as a means to explain the truth of transcending *saṃsāra*, and the truth of non-production and non-cessation.

However, lectures on the Dharma in the hall very easily became a type of regular service, lacking much in the way of innovation. As Xutang Zhiyu 虛堂智愚 (1185–1269) said in the lecture during the *Nirvāṇa* Gatherings:

> Lecture in a *Nirvāṇa* Gathering, "[Our] father, Śākya, had a dream two thousand years ago, and is still not awakened yet. This makes [us] sons and grandsons talk about dreaming in the dream and deludes [our] descendants. [Master] Baoen 報恩 (d.u) was outnumbered, therefore he could only thump his chest and say, 'Oh My Heaven, Oh My Heaven'"![88]
> Lecture in a *Nirvāṇa* Gathering, "There is today, but there is no tomorrow. [Our] father, Śākya, sold himself all his life, and before his death, he looked for trouble. This makes [us] sons and grandsons all [follow him just as jellyfish] use shrimps as its eyes. Master Wansong 萬松 (1166–1246), saved and took care of a crew on the rooftop. He took up his staff and blew on it".[89]

---

87 *Jingci Huihui chanshi yulu*, XZJ no. 1409, 124: 1.915a3-6:
二月望日, 佛涅槃上堂云：竺士之大仙, 今日告涅槃. 鶴林之米子, 當下得枯偏. 且道是同是別 … 時人見滅, 山僧見生; 時人見生, 山僧見死.

88 *Xutang heshang yulu*, *T* no. 2000, 47: 1.987a22-25:
佛涅槃上堂, "釋迦老子二千年前做一個夢, 至今未醒. 引得兒孫, 向夢中說夢. 狐魅後人, 報恩寡不敵眾, 只得換手椎胸道, '蒼天、蒼天 !'"

89 *Xutang heshang yulu*, *T* no. 2000, 47: 1.993a:
佛涅槃上堂, "今日則有, 明日則無. 釋迦老子, 一生賣峭, 臨死自納敗缺. 致令後代兒孫, 個個以鰕為目. 萬松丈人, 屋上之烏, 與之救看, 拈起主杖, 吹一吹".

In Southern Song Chan Buddhism, "Wordy Chan" (*wenzi Chan* 文字禪) was quite popular. If the lectures in the hall did not actually grasp the true meaning of the Buddha's *nirvāṇa*, then there would have been no way to experience the spirit of the *Nirvāṇa* gathering like this.

On the day commemorating the Buddha's *nirvāṇa* in the Northern Song, the abbots of Chan temples would give lectures in the hall, as well as carry out rituals such as incense offerings, proclamations and scripture recitations, but we still lack a detailed understanding of the *Nirvāṇa* gathering. Fascicle one of the *Meng Liang lu* 夢梁錄 (Liang Record of Dreams) gives the following account:

> On the fifteenth day of the mid-spring ... at Changming si 長明寺 by the Congxin Gate 崇新門, there was held a superior gathering for the Buddha's *nirvāṇa* with the monks and nuns of various monasteries. They spread out banners, and made offerings of various incense, flowers and special fruits. They suspended images of famous sages. They set up fine vessels and ornamented the hall. People gathered to see it and did not stop coming all day.[90]

The *Meng Liang lu* provides good materials that aid us in understanding the popularity of the *Nirvāṇa* gathering at the time, revealing its solemnness and grandness.

The popularity of *Nirvāṇa* gatherings during the Song Dynasty prompted the Tiantai scholar-monk Jingjue Renyue of the Northern Song to specialize in carrying out such events, producing the *Shijia Rulai niepan lizan wen* 釋迦如來涅槃禮讚文 (Veneration Verses for the *Nirvāṇa* of the Tathāgata Śākyamuni, *T* 1947). He once studied under Zhili and Zunshi. Both of these men placed great emphasis on repentance, and produced a great number of Tiantai repentance rituals.[91] In addition to this work, Renyue also produced the *Shijia jiangsheng lizan wen* 釋迦降生禮讚文 (Veneration Verses for the Birth of Śākyamuni, *XZJ* 1479), *Nanshan zushi lizan wen* 南山祖師禮讚文 (Veneration Verses for the Patriarchs of Nanshan, *XZJ* 1483), *Lengyan chanyi* 楞嚴懺儀 (*Śūraṃgama* Repentance Ritual, not extant), and *Luohan lizan wen* 羅漢禮讚文 (Veneration Verses for the Arhats, not extant). The latter two are not extant.[92] Renyue produced veneration verses to be carried out at the *Nirvāṇa* gathering based

---

90 *Mengliang lu* 1.7:
仲春十五日 ... 崇新門外長明寺, 及諸教院僧尼, 建佛涅槃勝會. 羅列幡幢, 供養種種香花異果, 掛名賢書畫, 設珍異玩具, 莊嚴道場. 觀者雲集, 竟日不絕.

91 For discussion of the Tiantai repentance rituals of Zhili and Zunshi, see Shi, *Tiantai chanfa*, 279–284.

92 *Fozu tongji*, *T* no. 2035, 49: 25.260a3-4.

on Tiantai repentance rituals. The sequence of procedures in the *Shijia rulai niepan lizan wen* runs as follows: chanting while kneeling, sincere requests, sincere prostrations (twelve prostrations) and the "five regrets" (sincere confession, petitions, rejoicing, merit dedication, and aspirations).[93]

The *Shijia rulai niepan lizan wen* focuses on praising the Buddha's merit through telling the Buddha's *nirvāṇa*. The characteristic of Chinese Buddhist rituals of veneration is combining Buddhist doctrine into rituals of veneration and praise, in particular the twelve prostrations, in which every prostration illustrates a part of the Buddha's *nirvāṇa*, and thereafter follows a verse of praise. During the first prostration, one "sincerely prostrates to Śākyamuni Buddha, the master of *nirvāṇa*, he who endured the world, and manifested sound and light in the assembly". The second prostration primarily elucidates the "receiving of the meal by Cunda". The verse reads as follows:

> The Tathāgata, long having realised the body of Vairocana,
> Provisionally manifested, towards his death, was to be made an offering;
> Able with his tip-of-hair transformation body,
> To receive these foodstuffs of Pāṭaliputra.
> Although the six sensory fields are empty and featureless,
> The five fruits should be known, with connections established;
> I now send off and give an offering of grains;
> May I realise the true and constant profound principle.
> Hence, I with full sincerity take refuge and prostrate.[94]

The Buddha's body became unwell as a result of accepting the offering of food by Cunda, but Jingjue Renyue believed that this was a manifestation of the Buddha; it was his manifest body accepting the offering of Cunda.

The themes of the other prostrations from the third relate to Śākyamuni's displaying illiness while lying down on the precious seat, entering the moon-praising *samādhi* (*yue'ai sanmei* 月愛三昧), displaying auspicious marks to men and gods, contemplation of the world, liberation through entry into the four *dhyānas*, and entry into the gold coffin and white wool, as well as the display of the Drinker of Light at the coffin, the cremation of Śākyamuni, the assembly of the noble *pratyekabuddha Saṃgha* at the *Nirvāṇa* gathering, and the assembly of noble *śrāvaka Saṃgha* at the *Nirvāṇa* gathering. The process of

93 *Shijia rulai niepan lizan wen*, *T* no.1947, 46: 1.964a10-965c23.

94 *Shijia rulai niepan lizan wen*, *T* no.1947, 46: 964b17-21:
如來久證遮那體, 權現臨終應供養；能與毛端變化身, 受茲華氏粳糧食.
六塵雖謂空無相, 五果當知結有緣；我今追遠奉粢盛, 願證真常同妙義.
故我一心歸命頂禮.

FIGURE 29 Three-colour glazed statue of an *Arhat*, dated to the Liao Dynasty (916-1125) (The Metropolitan Museum of Art, the United States).

the Buddha's *nirvāṇa* is told through these verses of veneration, while the true meaning of *nirvāṇa* is explained, and thereafter one realises the principle of non-birth and non-cessation. The *Shijia Rulai niepan lizan wen* illustrates the popularity of *Nirvāṇa* gatherings during the Northern Song period since repentance rituals were specifically produced to be employed for them.

The creation and development of *Nirvāṇa* gatherings in China were closely related to the popular Chinese custom of the "Cold Food Festival". However, these gatherings were limited to the confines of Buddhist temples. It produced no great influence within popular society. In particular, the lectures carried out in halls during these gatherings not only commemorated the Buddha's *nirvāṇa*, they also used the *nirvāṇa* as a way of instructing people within a Chan context.

### 1.5 *The Development of the "Water and Land Rite"*

The full name of the "Water and Land Rite" (*shuilu fahui* 水陸法會) is *fajie shengfan shuilu pudu dazhai shenghui* 法界聖凡水陸普度大齋勝會 (Superior Gathering of the Great Feast where the Holy and Mundane of the *Dharmadhātu* Extensively Liberate Beings). It is abbreviated as *shuiluhui* 水陸會 (Water and Land Gathering). It is also called *shuilu daochang* 水陸道場 (Hall of Water and Land) and *beiji hui* 悲濟會 (Gather of Compassionate Salvation). This ceremony is one of the grandest among repentance ceremonies in Chinese Buddhism. According to fascicle one of the *Shuilu yigui* 水陸儀軌 (Water and Land Ritual Procedures) re-edited by the Ming dynasty master Lianchi 蓮池 (1535–1615)[95], *dharmadhātu* (*fajie* 法界) here refers to the equality of basic nature between buddhas and beings. They are together called "*dharmadhātu*". "Holy and Mundane" (*shengfan* 聖凡) refer to the four nobles (buddhas, bodhisattvas, *śrāvakas* and *pratyekabuddhas*), six mundane beings (devas, people, asuras, hell beings, pretas and animals). In actuality, this term refers to all beings. "Water and Land" (*shuilu* 水陸) refers to the places where beings experience the fruits of their karma: the realms of water, land and air. Beings of the water and land in particular suffer severely, which is why the ritual's name includes "Water and Land". "Extensively Liberate" (*pudu* 普度) means to help all beings of the six paths to achieve liberation from *saṃsāra*. "Great Feast" (*dazhai* 大齋) refers to the offering of food. "Superior Gathering" (*shenghui* 勝會) refers to how the liberators and those being saved gather in one hall, in which food and Dharma come together; beings subject to suffering are all embraced.

The primary goal behind the creation of the "Water and Land Rite" is to save all beings through the great power of the Buddhadharma, by means of

95 *Fajie shengfan shuilu shenghui xiuzhai yigui*, XZJ no. 1475, 129: 1.533a16-b4.

offerings of food and Dharma. In particular, the community must save beings of the six realms who suffer severely, having fallen into places comprised of water and land. This ceremony was the most important in Chinese Buddhism for centuries, given its superior merit.

According to an account in fascicle four of the *Shimen zhengtong* by Zongjian 宗鑑 (fl. 1237) in the Song Dynasty,[96] the "Water and Land Rite" was a result of Liang Wudi meeting with a mysterious monk in a dream who said to him, "The beings of the six paths are suffering immeasurably—why not carry out a great Water and Land feast to save them?" When Wudi woke, he asked a number of eminent monks about this, but none of them knew of any "Great Water and Land Feast". Only the monk Baozhi 寶誌 (418–514) encouraged the emperor to search extensively through the canon, for if he did, then he would surely be able to know the cause behind this dream. Wudi subsequently carried out such a search, reading morning and evening in the Fayun Hall 法雲殿. Later, he came across the story of Ānanda meeting with the "Burning Face Preta King". A vessel bearing equal portions of food as an offering to the pretas was prepared. A ritual was produced from this, and carried out at Jinshan si 金山寺 in Runzhou 潤州 (Zhenjiang 鎮江). Wudi personally visited the shrine, and ordered the monk Sengyou 僧祐 (445–518) to read aloud the text. Extant literature has differing accounts of when Wudi devised this ceremony. The *Shiwu jiyuan* 事物紀原 (Accounts of Events and Things) believes it was in Tianjian 天監 7 (508), whereas the *Fozu tongji* believes it was in Tianjian 4 (505).[97]

The ritual procedures for the "Water and Land Rite" created by Wudi were already lost by the Chen-Sui period. Fascicle three of the *Shishi jigu lüe* 釋氏稽古略 (An Outline of Historical Researches into the Śākya Family Lineage, *T* 2037) records that in the Xianheng 咸亨 period (670–673) of the Tang dynasty, Meditation Master Daoying 道英 (d.u.) of Fahai si 法海寺 in the western capital (Chang'an) obtained the ritual manual from monk Yiji 義濟 (d.u.) of Dajue si 大覺寺. As a result, the ceremony was restored at Shanbei si 山北寺.[98] However, according to the account in the *Guang Hongming ji*, Liang Wudi in year three of Tianjian (504) abandoned Daoism to serve Buddhism, so it is not possible that before 505 he already spent three years reading through the canon.[99] The writing of the *Shuilu yigui* was compiled based entirely on Tiantai theory. The *dhāraṇīs* of the work are derived from the *Bukong juansuo shenbian zhenyan jing* 不空羂索神變真言經 (Infallible Lasso's Mantra and Supernatural

96 *Shimen zhengtong*, *XZJ* no. 1490, 130: 4.802a3-8.

97 Lan, *Bubian*, no. 103, 19: 19.575b7; *Fozu tongji*, *T* no. 2035, 49: 33.321b25-26.

98 *Shishi jigu lüe*, *T* no. 2037, 49: 3.818b19-23.

99 *Guang Hongming ji*, *T* no. 2103, 52: 4.111c25-112c7.

Transformations: King of Ritual Manuals, *T* 1092), translated by Bodhiruci (Putiliuzhi 菩提流志, 572–727) in year four of Shenlong 神龍 (707). This is not something that Liang Wudi could have read. It also would have been unknown to Daoying in the Xianheng period. The present "Water and Land Rite" is divided into the "inner altar" (*neitan* 內壇) and the "outer altar" (*waitan* 外壇). The former is carried out based on the ritual procedures. The latter includes practice of the *Lianghuang chan* 梁皇懺 (Emperor Liang Repentance) and recitation of various *sūtras*. The ritual procedures said to have been personally compiled by Liang Wudi, and Daoying's regular implementation of this feast, perhaps refer to the *Cibei daochang chanfa* 慈悲道場懺法 (Repentance Ritual of the Compassion Altar, *T* 1909). The ritual procedures for the "Water and Land Rite" were first produced in the Song dynasty.

The earliest creation of a "Water and Land Rite" was probably the manual (also called *Yang Tuiguan yiwen* 楊推官儀文; Ritual Manual of Official Yang) compiled by Yang'e 楊鍔 (d.u.) of Dongchuan 東川 in the Xining period (1068–1077), which was popular in Sichuan. This was an early complete form of the ritual procedure for the "Water and Land Rite", but it is not extant. The *Shishi tonglan* 施食通覽 (Survey of Alms, *XZJ* 959) by Zongxiao 宗曉 (1151–1214) in the Song Dynasty cites this work in the sections concerning the meaning behind the first establishment of the "Water and Land Rite", the procedure for summoning into the hall the eight noble assemblies, and the postscript of the ritual manual for the "Water and Land Feast".[100] From these, we can get a general outline of the three fascicles of the *Yang Tuiguan yiwen*.

The *Shuilu yuanqi* 水陸緣起 (The Origin of the Water and Land Rite) by Zongze 宗賾 (fl. 1089–1103) offers a great many details in its explanation of the "Water and Land Rite". Zongze states that the objects of offerings during the rite are divided into top, middle and lower types. The "top offerings" are offered to the buddhas of the *dharmadhātu*, bodhisattvas, *pratyekabuddhas*, *śrāvakas*, *vidyārājas*, eight divisions of beings, and *brahmin* sages. The "middle offerings" are given to Brahma, Indra, and all the gods of the twenty-eight heavens throughout space, including the *nakṣatra* and *graha* astral deities. The "lower offerings" are made to the *nāgas* of the five peaks, rivers, seas and the great earth, ancients, asuras, officials and retainers of hell, hell realm beings, ghosts, pretas and deities with no master or anything to rely on, and animals of the *dharmadhātu*. The four noble and six mundane types of beings of the six paths are therefore all provided with offerings. It is through these offerings that those who have not yet generated *bodhicitta* can generate it as a result of this "Superior Gathering of the Water and Land Rite". It is through this ritual that those

100 *Shishi tonglan*, *XZJ* no. 959, 101: 1.417b10-12.

who are not yet liberated from the cycle of suffering will attain the state non-retrogression, and those who have yet to master the path of the Buddha, will be able to do so.

In year eight of Yuanyou 元祐 (1093), Su Shi 蘇軾 (1036–1101) built a shrine hall for the "Water and Land Rite" for his departed wife of the Song clan 宋氏, and also compiled the *Shuilu faxiang zan* 水陸法像贊 (Praise of the Image of Dharma in the Water and Land Rite) in sixteen chapters. In the preface of this work, he states that the shrine space for the "Water and Land Rite" expanded over time, and it was only in Sichuan that the old way was preserved. Moreover, their various painted images and facilities still preserved the original style.[101] As he was originally from Mount Mei in Sichuan, this work of his was called the "Water and Land Rite of Mount Mei".

Between years seven and eight of reign era Yuanfeng 元豐 (1084–1085) in the Song, when Foyin 佛印 (1032–1098, also named Liaoyuan 了元) resided at Jinshan, a maritime merchant came to the temple, and a "Water and Land Ceremony" was held. Foyin personally presided over it. It was quite magnificent, and it subsequently got the name of "Jinshan Water and Land Rite", otherwise called the "Northern Water and Land Rite". In year three of reign era Shaosheng 紹聖 (1096), Zongze critically edited what was compiled by various authors, producing the *Shuilu yiwen* 水陸儀文 (Text of Ritual Procedure of the Water and Land Rite) in four fascicles. The four assemblies were encouraged to practice it accordingly. At present, this work is lost. We can only know part of its contents from his *Shuilu yuanqi*.

In year nine of reign era Qiandao 乾道 in the Southern Song (1173), Shi Hao 史浩 (1106–1194) of Siming 四明 once passed through Jinshan si in Zhenjiang. He admired the popularity of the "Water and Land Feast", and as a result donated a hundred fields. On Mount Yuebo 月波山 in Donghu 東湖 in Siming, he specifically held "Water and Land Rite of Four Times" as a way of repaying the four types of kindness (*sien* 四恩). He also personally produced commentaries and compiled ritual manuals. Emperor Xiaozong of Song (Song Xiaozong 宋孝宗 [r. 1162–1189]) heard of this news, and bestowed unto the temple a plaque reading "Altar of the Water and Land Rite Unimpeded" (*shuilu wu'ai daochang* 水陸無礙道場). Near to Mount Yuebo was a Zunjiao si 尊教寺, with monastic and lay followers totalling three-thousand people. They offered wealth, bought them land, and venerated the Mount Yuebo practice of carrying out the ceremony four times. The assembly also sincerely requested Zhipan to extend the practice into a text titled *Shuilu xinyi* 水陸新儀 (New Ritual for the Water and Land Rite) in six fascicles. They diligently promoted this

101 *Dongpo houji* 19.625–627.

practice, while encouraging all monasteries of the realm to place special emphasis on it as a superb way of broadly liberating sentient beings.

After the "Water and Land Rite" became popular following the Song Dynasty, it quickly spread across the entire country, in particular becoming a type of memorial service carried out by the court after a war. Zongze, in the *Shuilu yuanqi*, states that making offerings to the Buddha and feeding a single monk brings about unlimited merit, so how much more so making extensive offerings to the Triple Gem of the Ten Directions and all beings on the six paths? Not only can it ensure that one gains benefits, but this will also benefit all one's relatives.[102] This is why in the areas around the Huai and Yangzi rivers, Sichuan, Guangdong and Fujian, the "Water and Land Rite" remained considerably popular since ancient times. If someone should pray for protection and peace, but not carry out the rite, then some will think him not virtuous. If the rite is not carried out when mourning for an elder, then some will think him not filial. If the rite is not carried out when seeking to save the lowly and young, then it would be thought of as a lack of compassion. These areas therefore have wealthy people independently carry out the rite, while the poor bring together their funds to have it done. This was the origin of the later terms "Water and Land Rite by a single family" (*duxing shuilu* 獨姓水陸) and "Water and Land Rite by several families" (*zhongxing shuilu* 眾姓水陸).

After the Song Dynasty, the "Water and Land Rite" became quite popular, with many of them becoming famous. For instance, in year eight of reign era Yuanyou (1093), Su Dongpo built an altar hall for the rite to mourn his departed wife of the Song clan (see fascicle nineteen of the *Dongpo houji* 東坡後集).[103] In year twenty-one of reign era Shaoxing 紹興 (1151), Empress Dowager Cining 慈寧太后 provided funds for Zhenxie Qingliao 真歇清了 (1089–1151) to carry out the rite at Chongxian Xianxiao si 崇先顯孝寺 in Hangzhou (see his memorial stele: "Zhenxie Qingliao Chanshi taming" 真歇清了禪師塔銘 [The Inscription of Meditation Master Zhenxie Qingliao] by Zhengjue 正覺).[104] Fascicle five of the *Ying'an Tanhua chanshi yulu* 應庵曇華禪師語錄 (Record of Meditation Master Ying'an Tanhua, XZJ 1343) includes a record of Meditation Master Tanhua 曇華 (1103–1163) when he was building Taiping Xingguo si 太平興國寺 on Mount Kangjiang 康蔣山, as well as one from when he was at Baoen Guangxiao si 報恩光孝寺 in Pingjiang prefecture 平江府, both of which deal with the "Water and Land Rite".[105] Tanhua lived during the reign of Emperor

102 *Shishi tonglan*, XZJ no. 959, 101: 1.442a4-12.

103 *Dongpo houji* 19.625–627.

104 *Zhenxie Qingliao chanshi yulu*, XZJ no. 1408, 124: 1.634b10-14.

105 *Wang jiyi wei di shumi xianggong she Shuilu shengtang fayu* 王機宜爲弟樞密相公設水陸升堂法語 and *Ciji hui Shuilu shengtang fayu* 悲濟會水陸升堂法語 in *Ying'an Tanhua chanshi yulu*, XZJ no. 1343, 120: 5.846b05-847a3; 843a11-b1.

Gaozong of Song (Song Gaozong 宋高宗 [r. 1127–1162]). It is clear that the "Water and Land Rite" was quite widespread at the time.

In year three of reign era Yanyou 延祐 (1316), the court held a "Water and Land Rite" at Jinshan si. They ordered that the various teachers of the three schools (doctrine, meditation and *vinaya*) of Jiangnan teach the Dharma. There were 1,500 *saṃgha* members who participated. There is a relevant account of Yuansou Xingduan 元叟行端 (1255–1341) of Mount Jing 徑山 in the *Chaoting Jinshan zuo Shuilu shengzuo fayu* 朝廷金山作水陸升座法語 (Record of the Lecture on Imperial Water and Land Rite at Jinshan).[106] Fascicle twenty-eight of the *Yuan shi* 元史 (History of Yuan) records that Emperor Ying of Yuan (Yuan Yingzong 元英宗; r. 1320–1323) in year three of reign era Zhizhi 至治 (1323) ordered that Wan'an si 萬安寺, Qingshou si 慶壽寺, Sheng'an si 聖安寺 and Puqing si 普慶寺 in the capital, Jinshan si on the Yangzi River, and Wansheng Youguo si 萬聖祐國寺 on Mount Wutai 五臺山, all carry out the "Water and Land Rite" for seven days and nights.[107] At this time Meditation Master Yuejiang Zhengyin 月江正印 (d.u.) was abbot of Jinshan. The record of his lectures includes *Chaoting Jinshan si jian shuilu fahui pushuo* 朝廷金山寺建水陸法會普說 (The Story of the Court Holding the Water and Land Rite at Jinshan si), which describes the event.[108] The scale of it was quite large. There were forty-one eminent teachers, and 1,500 *bhikṣus*. In addition, a number of temples in the north and south, including Haotian si 昊天寺 of Dadu 大都 (present day Beijing), Mount Wutai, and Upper Tianzhu si 上天竺寺 in Hangzhou, all held grand "Water and Land Rites". Fascicle one of the *Da Ming Gaoseng zhuan* 大明高僧傳 (Biographies of Eminent Monks in the Great Ming, *T* 2062) records that in the Yuan Dynasty, Chi'an Zujue 癡庵祖覺 (1087–1150), a Huayan scholar of Sichuan residing at Zhongyan si 中巖寺 in Meizhou 眉州 produced the *Shuilu zhaiyi* 水陸齋儀 (Ritual of the Water and Land Feast), which was widely practiced in Sichuan.[109]

From years one to five of reign era Hongwu 洪武 (1368–1372), Mount Jiang in Nanjing hosted in succession the "Ceremony of Extensive Offerings", which was the "Water and Land Rite", the largest of which was carried out in the first lunar month of 1372. These rites requested the eminent monks of the realm to participate, such as Chushi Fanqi 楚石梵琦 (1296–1370), Jitan Zongle 季潭宗泐 (1318–1390), Laifu Jianxin 來復見心 (1319–1391), Dongming Huiri 東溟慧日 (1291–1379) and Mengtang Tan'e 夢堂曇噩 (1285–1373), all of whom accepted

106 *Yuansou Xingduan chanshi yulu*, *XZJ* no. 1399, 124: 4.26b1-5.
107 *Yuan shi* 28. 630.
108 *Yuejiang Zhengyin chanshi yulu*, *XZJ* no. 1389, 123: 2.275a03-276b15.
109 *Da Ming Gaoseng zhuan*, *T* no. 2062, 50: 1.902a6-13.

invitations to come and teach. The number of *Saṃgha* members participating always reached a thousand persons. Ming Emperor Taizu 太祖 (r. 1368–1398) once ordered Zongle to compose eight pieces of musical movements praising the Buddha (*Zanfo yuezhang* 贊佛樂章) and had the officials in charge of sacrifices (*taichang* 太常) perform it. Taizu and his ministers all went to the Dharma service to venerate the Buddha. This ceremony is discussed in detail by Song Lian 宋濂 (1310–1381) in his "Jiangshan si guangjian fohui ji" 蔣山寺廣薦佛會記 (Account of the Ceremony of Extensive Offerings at the Temple of Mount Jiang).[110]

In the eastern areas of China, around Jiangsu and Zhejiang province, during the Ming Dynasty, the "Water and Land Rite" was divided into northern and southern types. During the late Ming, Yunqi Zhuhong 雲棲袾宏 (1535–1615) believed that the *Shuilu yiwen* of Jinshan si had become corrupted. It was very difficult to sort out its complete form. Moreover, practitioners also arbitrarily modified it, which is why it was not so suitable. However, Zhipan's *Shuilu xinyi* was not only concise, but also succinct. Its conciseness did not impede the solemnness of the ceremony. Its succinctness did not produce any deficiencies.[111] Yunqi Zhuhong, therefore, revised Zhipan's work, and widely circulated it. This is the present six fascicle edition of the *Shuilu yigui*.

## 2 Buddhist Philanthropy in the Song and Yuan Periods

Buddhist philanthropy developed a great deal during the Song Dynasty. There appeared various types of charitable institutions including institutes for shelter and care (*juyang yuan* 居養院) and nursing homes (*anji fang* 安濟坊) that looked after the poor, ill and elderly. Orphanages (*ciyou ju* 慈幼局) looked after abandoned children. Grain subsidies (*juzi cang* 舉子倉) helped the destitute look after children. Public cemeteries (*louze yuan* 漏澤園) also existed. Monks in society could take on great responsibilities, owing to their originally playing decisive roles and leading positions in society as virtuous figures, in addition to the vast monastic economy. Regional fiscal administration in the Song faced problems. Public charity, therefore, had no way of smoothly developing. This required the cooperation of gentlemen and Buddhist groups in the countryside, of which the effort and contributions of the Buddhists are evident. Buddhism actively participated in public charity. They had numerous projects. They built bridges and waterworks. They worked tirelessly and spent money on

110 Lan, *Bubian*, no. 160, 29: 3.88a18-90a2.
111 *Fajie shengfan shuilu shenghui xiuzhai yigui*, XZJ no. 1475, 129: 6.604b5-14.

things from highway maintenance to regional safety patrols. With respect to regional philanthropic activities—such as caring for elderly people, paupers, the starving, orphans, and providing medical services—officials often gave monks in monasteries administrative tasks, helping the state to smoothly carry out such beneficial social projects.

### 2.1 *Buddhist Social Programs during the Song Dynasty*

The systems of compassion-field infirmaries (*beitian fang* 悲田坊) and infirmaries (*yangbing fang* 養病坊) from the Tang Dynasty were carried on into the early Song. In Kaifeng, the eastern and western "field of merit institutes" (*futian yuan* 福田院) were established. In the time of Song Emperor Yingzong (r. 1063–1067), they also established these in the north and south, there altogether existing four in Kaifeng.[112] The "field of merit institutes" were also the responsibility of monks. This is based on the remarks of Fan Zuyu 范祖禹 (1041–1098) in year two of Yuanyou (1087):

> I have seen the regulations of the "merit institutes". Each institute annually bestows unto one monk a purple robe. Three practitioners are tonsured, there being the utmost grace displayed… I also beg that there be careful selection of their numbers. For every certain number of persons they supported, [we] allowed the tonsured by one man. For every certain number of persons who died, [we] reduce the tonsured by one man.[113]

At the time, each "field of merit institute" was limited to three-hundred persons. Each institute could annually bestow unto one monk a purple robe, and tonsure three men. Fan Zuyu therefore petitioned the court in the hope that the number of people not be limited, but instead that they establish a standard of examination, and like this they could control those who administrated the institutes. Meditation Master Wuzu Jie 五祖戒 (d.u.) of Qizhou 蘄州 mentions poor children housed at these institutions.[114] It is clear they were similar to orphanages today. In year one of Chongning (1102), the "field of merit institute" was renamed to "institutes for shelter and care" (*anyang yuan* 居養院), in other words, welfare shelters, but their responsibilities did not change to any great extent. The latter were spread across the country. They were also called "insti-

---

112 For relevant research, see Jin, "Fuli zhidu", 127–69; Wang, "Yanglao yu ciyou", 371–401; Huang, "Gongyi shiye".

113 *Fan taishi ji*, *SKQS* 14:6-9:
臣竊見四福院條例, 逐院每年特與僧一名紫衣, 行者三人剃度, 推恩至厚. …… 亦乞詳酌立定分數, 每存活若干人即與剃度一名, 如死損及若干人即減剃度一名.

114 *Chanzong songgu lianzhu tongji*, *XZJ* no.1295, 115: 32.409a1-4.

tutes to benefit beings" (*Liji yuan* 利濟院) and "care institutes" (*Yangji yuan* 養濟院). The *Emituo jingshu chao wenbian* 阿彌陀經疏鈔問辯 (Commentary on the *Amitābha-sūtra*, XZJ 328) by Zhuhong states, "The present 'care institutes' are popularly called 'institutes for orphans and the elderly'" (*gulao-yuan* 孤老院).[115] These institutes actively provided Buddhist welfare. Many regions in the countryside also established orphanages dedicated to looking after abandoned and destitute children.

In year one of Shaoxing (1131), governor Xu Yi 徐誼 (1144–1208) in Huizhou 徽州 built an institute for shelter and care. Its system was largely identical to the Yuanfu 元符 system. There was a small *araṇya* (temple) with three-hundred fields providing for it. The monks were ordered to manage it. Wuxing 吳興 County in Shaoxing three (1133) established a care institute and provided some fields for it. The crops that were taxed were sent to the monks. There was a supervisor that looked after the financial matters.[116] In addition, Jiankang 建康 established a care institute, which was built by Huang Gongdu 黃公度 (1109–1156) in year five of reign era Jiading 嘉定 (1212). It was of a small scale and did not take in many people. During the Jingding era (1260–1264), two institutes for shelter and care were built in the north and south of the capital. Each institute ordained one monk overseer. The number of destitute people that they cared for was limited to five-hundred. They also received the abandoned plaque and quota of Songxing si 宋興寺. One monk was selected to supervise the related issues. Regional governments put more than 590 *mu* of uninherited fields and 519 *mu* of uninherited mountain land under the control of the *Saṃgha*. It also provided more than a thousand strings of cash to Songxing si to build a pawnshop. It was from the surplus funds of the pawnshop that the temple could buy ordination certificates from the bureau of sacrifices every three years to ordain virtuous practitioners and manage the affairs of the two institutes.[117] It is clear that regional governments not only supported the charitable activities of shelters, they also provided cash to build pawnshops for practitioners of the temple to get ordination certificates. These figures later ensured that the shelter could operate properly. Practitioners played an important role in Buddhist charity during the Song Dynasty. Although monks could manage the farmlands and finances of shelters and orphanages, the actual administration was still largely the responsibility of these lay practitioners. This is why regional governments set up pawnshops as a way of providing practitioners with a means to purchase ordination certificates.

115 *Amituo jing shuchao wenbian*, XZJ no.328, 33: 1.518a18: 今養濟院, 俗曰孤老院.

116 *Hongzhi Huizhoufu zhi*, 5.51a.

117 *Kaiqing siming xuzhi*, 4.26.

However, these aforementioned institutes were managed by the monks of temples entrusted by the state, for which there were particular forms of organization and regulations, and a considerably systematized model of charity. For instance, fascicle eighteen of the *Mengliang lu* by Wu Zimu 吳自牧 (fl. 1270) in the Song Dynasty records that funds and other resources were provided for wet nurses of orphans and children abandoned in the street. After they became adults, they would no longer be under control of the state. It was permitted for commoners to adopt children, for which the state would provide three years of support in the form of cash and rice. Resources were also provided for the elderly and lone widows.[118] It is clear that government administration existed behind the philanthropic organization of orphanages and shelters, but regional governments also entrusted temples to carry out affairs, which was done by monks.

Also, looking after the homeless, such as beggars, was another charitable enterprise of the monasteries. When Li Ruogu 李若谷 (970–1049) was serving in Jiangning 江寧, "the beggars out in the streets were divided to labour in the monasteries and assist with cooking".[119] After monasteries took in beggars, they would help the monasteries with various tasks, such as pounding and cooking rice.

At the same time, monks practiced medicine for the benefit of people. Temples built pharmacies to dispense medications. These were also philanthropic activities of Buddhism during the Song Dynasty. For instance, the physician monk Hongyun 洪蘊 (963–1004) from Changsha during the Northern Song, ordained and then "studied medical textbooks, later wandering to the capital, where he became famous for his medical practice".[120] Song Emperor Taizong 宋太宗 (r. 976–997) in the reign era of Taiping Xingguo 太平興國 ordered a search for new medicines. Hongyun "offered dozens of ancient methods that he recorded".[121] When Emperor Zhenzong 真宗 (r. 997–1022) was still living in a frontier estate as a seignior, Hongyun visited him with medicines. Hongyun's best expertise was decoction. The aristocracy would always get examined by him when they fell ill.[122] Monasteries during the Song Dynasty also built pharmacies. For instance, when Meditation Master Yibian 一辨 (1081–1149) of Qingzhou 青州 arrived at Taiping Xingguo si 太平興國寺 on Mount Yang 仰山 in Jiangxi, he heard the area had a certain Xin Gong 新公 who was proficient in medicine. Yibian ordained him as a monk, wanting to invite him to become

118 *Mengliang lu*, 18.161-62.

119 *Song shi* 291.9739.

120 *Song shi* 461.13510: 習方技之書, 後遊京師, 以醫術知名.

121 *Song shi* 461.13510: 錄古方數十以獻.

122 *Song shi* 461.13510.

administrator of the monastery's pharmacy. After Xin Gong passed away, his son took over the pharmacy. The "Shaolin yaoju ji" 少林藥局記 (Record of the Shaolin Pharmacy) by Yuan Haowen 元好問 (1190–1257) records the following:

> Meditation Master [Xing]ying of Shaolin also said, "Long ago in Qingzhou, when Master Bian first opened the hall on Mount Yang, [he] went fifteen miles downhill carrying rice to give it to the great assembly. Afterward, [Xingying] came to know of the physician Xin Gong. He ordained him as a monk and put him in charge of the pharmacy. He forbade making extra money from it, fearing that the idea of making profit may harm the virtuous career. After Xin [Gong] died, his son Neng succeeded him. For twenty years, the [charitable] feast was supported by [the pharmacy] and meanwhile the patients had been taken care of." Thus, it has been over a hundred years that Chan monasteries have had pharmacies, which started in Qingzhou.[123]

The operating expenses for these pharmacies primarily came from donations of devotees, rather than the monastery operating the budget and taking in any profits. These pharmacies not only treated the resident Chan monks, they also served laypeople outside the monastery. In the later years of the Xingding 興定 reign era (1217–1222) of Emperor Xuan of the Jin Dynasty (Jin Xuanzong 金宣宗 [r. 1213–1224]), Meditation Master Donglin Long 東林隆 (d.u.) was abbot of Shaolin si 少林寺. He received a great offering from a devotee, and emulated Yibian of Qingzhou. His successor, abbot Meditation Master Xingying 性英 (d.u.), asked Yuan Haowen to record this event.[124]

Institutes for shelter and care and nursing homes were all managed by monasteries during the Song Dynasty. The monks who acted as managers rotated every three years. While they were in office, they could collect a salary. As their achievements clearly indicate, they could have bestowed upon them a purple robe from the state, a master's title, or an ordination certificate. Tasks within the institutes, such as managing money and registering grains, were the responsibilities of officials in each province and prefecture. Some regions made troops cook, clean and do other tasks. Officials gave confiscated land for the expenditures of shelters. They could hire people to till and harvest. In case of

---

123 Yao, *Yuan Haowen*, 35.730:
少林英禪師爲余言：昔青州辨公初開堂仰山，自山下十五里負米以給大眾. 其後, 得知醫者新公, 度爲僧, 俾主藥局, 仍不許出子錢致贏餘, 恐以利心而妨道業. 新歿, 繼以其子能. 二十年間, 齋廚仰給, 而病者亦安之. 故百年以來, 諸禪剎之有藥局自青州始.

124 Yao, *Yuan Haowen*, 35.730.

any insufficient harvest, support would be provided from the public granaries. It is clear that monasteries were the main body for this system while monks were the leaders, and running between the officials and people was a quite complete and integrated establishment in operation.

## 2.2 *Song Dynasty Buddhism and Regional Charity*

The development of many regions of Song China came to be the necessary responsibility of gentlemen and religious groups as a result of the financial hardship of regional governments. As an example, the Anpu Bridge 安浦橋 in Le'an 樂安 prefecture of Fuzhou 撫州 was repeatedly built and destroyed. In year two of Ruiping reign era (1235) under Emperor Li 理宗 (r. 1224–1264), it again collapsed into the water. The county prefect Huang Wei 黃烓 (d.u.) advised rebuilding it as a stone bridge. The responsibility for this fell onto the monk Rizhang 日章 of Lüyuan si 綠源寺, while the cost of 1,500 strings of money came from the government.[125] There were twelve bridges built by monks in Wukang prefecture 武康縣 in Huzhou 湖州 during the Song Dynasty.[126] When monks participated in the building of bridges, they received regional government support, but also help from devotees.[127] The stone bridge at Wan'andu 萬安渡 was built under government leadership, the monks Yibo 義波 (d.u.)

125 For details, see *Fuzhou fuzhi*, 25.

126 For details, see Huang, *Lunji*, 415.

127 As an example, see "Wan'an du shiqiao ji" 萬安渡石橋記 (Account of the Stone Bridge at Wan'an *Du* [Ford]) from the year 1060. See Zheng & Dean, *Beiming huibian*, 14: The stone bridge of Wanan in Quanzhou started to be constructed on the day of *gengyin* in the fourth month of the fifth year of Huangyou 皇祐 Era (1053), and the construction was completed on the day of *xinwei* in the twelfth month of Jiayou (1059). The piers are built of stone from deep in the valley, dividing the river into forty-seven streams. The arch stretches above in the air, running a length of three thousand six hundred *chi*, with a width of five *chi*. It is flanked by handrails, which are twice as long as the bridge. The project cost fourteen million cashes, which came from donors. From then on, people, in order to travel to Ocean Shizhi 實支, stopped taking boats and began to walk on foot instead. The perilous journey becoming a safe one, none of the people does not benefit from it. Those taking responsibility for the construction included Lu Xi, Wang Shi, Xu Zhong, [the monk] Futu Yibo, and [the monk] Zongshan, and others, fifteen persons altogether. With the bridge completed, the prefecture chief Cai Xiang 蔡襄 (1012–1067), a native of Puyang 莆陽 (present-day Putian 莆田, Fujian), arranged banquet with a concert performance, as a completion celebration. In the autumn of the next year, I received an imperial order to return to the capital city, and my journey started from this point. Thus, I compose this piece commemorative writing, to be inscribed on the east bank. 泉州萬安渡石橋, 始造於皇祐五年四月庚寅, 以嘉祐四年十二月辛未訖功. 絫趾於淵, 釃水爲四十七道. 梁空以行, 其長三千六百尺, 廣丈有五尺. 翼以扶欄, 如其長之數而兩之. 靡金錢一千四百萬, 求諸施者. 渡實支海, 去舟而徙. 易危而安, 民莫不利. 職其事, 盧錫、王寔、許忠、浮圖義波、宗善等十有五人. 既成, 太守莆陽蔡襄爲之合樂, 讌飲而落之. 明年秋, 蒙召還京, 道繇是出, 因紀所作, 勒於岸左.

FIGURE 30 Dining hall of Tiantong Monastery 天童寺, Ningbo 寧波.

and Zongshan 宗善 (d.u.) participated. Perhaps it was easier for them to become leading figures through appealing to benefactors. They possessed great influence.

However, lay Buddhists, driven by the appeal of Buddhist doctrine, also could participate in Buddhist philanthropy. For example, the Well Railing Inscription of Gujing Market 顧逕市 from year two of reign era Ruiping (1235) has the following account:

> West of the Longwang shrine in Gujing Market there lived a devout Buddhist disciple Zhang. He was diligent and sincere. He provided the funds to purchase bricks. He ordered a craftsman to build a public well. He sought to dedicate that merit to his late wife of the Tao clan, and his other women, [hoping that] they might be cleansed of impurities and swiftly achieve rebirth in the Pure Land.[128]

128 *Baqiongshi jinshi buzheng* 119.842-43: 顧逕市龍王廟西居住, 奉佛弟子張 [], 謹發誠心, 施財收買磚灰, 命工砌造義井一口, 所將功德專用追薦亡妻陶氏三四娘子, 洗滌穢塵, 早超淨土, 成就往生者.

This Buddhist disciple of the Zhang family dedicated the merit of building a well to his wife, so that she might be reborn in the Pure Land. It is clear that Buddhist philanthropy was done with religious significance. Monasteries in the Song Dynasty also provided food and lodging for travelers and, in particular, constructed lodges (Jiedai yuan 接待院) to receive travelling monks. There were also lodges that received pilgrims, both noble and common, visiting holy Buddhist sites, such as the Common Temple (Putong yuan 普通院) on Mount Wutai.

Monasteries of Song Buddhism had a close relationship with charitable activities in the countryside, which furthermore affirmed the active role played by these monasteries in society, while at the same time illustrating the function and significance of Buddhism in this period.

## 3 The Practice of Life Release in Buddhism from the Song to Yuan Periods

The practice of life release became an important tradition after the Song Dynasty when Buddhism became deeply rooted in society. The formation of this practice has its roots in the Buddhist ideas of protecting life and forbidding killing, while at the same time it was also encouraged by the Confucian idea of cherishing life. From the Northern and Southern Dynasties period (420–589), natural bays treated as life release ponds under imperial and aristocratic support gradually formed into the Chinese Buddhist practice of life release. After the Song Dynasty, monks built life release ponds inside monasteries, and provided this service to the people, which ensured that the practice became deeply rooted among the people.

### 3.1 *The Origins of the Life Release Practice*

In the period before the Qin Dynasty (221–207 BCE), Confucius (551–479 BCE) held Shun 舜 (d.u.) as an example for cherishing life, emphasizing protection of the environment. Mencius (372–289 BCE) emphasized empathy and inspired King Liang Hui 梁惠王 (400–319 BCE) with his ideas of benevolence. The chapter "Yiyong" 異用 (The Difference of Uses) of *Lüshi chunqiu* 呂氏春秋 (Master Lü's Spring and Autumn Annals) and the chapter "Shuofu" 說符 (The Discussion of Signs) of *Liezi* 列子 developed the practice of restraining from killing and life release. After Buddhism arrived in China, a theoretical basis for Buddhist life release was provided through the "Liushui zhangzhe zi pin" 流水長者子品 (Merchant Son Udakaśrotas Chapter) of the *Jin'guangming jing*, translated by Dharmakṣema (Tanwuchen 曇無讖; 385–433).

The armed success of Tang of Shang 商湯 (ca.1675–1587 BCE), the founder of the Shang Dynasty, not only came from his good use of resources, but also from his cherishing of life. He did not allow for everyone to be massacred. His state governed with benevolence, hence the precedent for him undoing the net (*Cheng Tang jiewang* 成湯解網), where Tang opened a hunting net to free captured birds, for which forty other nations recognized this as an act of benevolence extending to animals.[129] This example of Tang showing benevolence to people and love for animals emphasizes the point that life release is in line with the mind of Heaven above, and the will of people below. The benevolent lord will not tolerate a hunter using a four-sided net with which to catch everything, for it runs contrary to the virtue of Heaven's cherishing of life. Tang, therefore, removed three sides of the net, and only left one side remaining. He also altered the prayer, transforming the sorrow of killing into an auspicious scene. This reveals that a leader will find it easier to capture the heart of the people through life release than killing. The example of Tang had a great impact on later generations. In the Ming Dynasty, Lianchi still cites this story in his *Jiesha fangsheng wen* 戒殺放生文 (Text on Life Release and the Proscription of Killing).

The *Liezi* includes an account of Jianzi 簡子 (d.u.) of Zhou doing an act of life release at dawn:

> On the dawn of the new year, the people of Handan 邯鄲 offered some doves to Jianzi. Jianzi was quite delighted and generously rewarded them for this. A retainer inquired after the reason behind this. Jianzi said, "The act of life release at dawn displays kindness". The retainer said, "The

129 *Lüshi chunqiu* 10.156–57: Tang observed a man blessing his net. Spreading out the four sides of the net, he uttered this prayer: "Let whatever falls from Heaven, whatever emerges from Earth, whatever arrives from the four directions, be caught in my net". Tang exclaimed, "Alas! That would be everything. Who but a Jie would do that?" Tang gathered three sides of the net and laid out only one side. He then instructed the man in another prayer: "In the past, the spider invented the net, men of today have learned to use it. If I want what is on the left, I spread it to the left. If I want what is on the right, I spread it to the right. If I want what is high above, I spread it high above. If I want what is down below, I spread it down below. I catch whatever has violated its destiny". When the states south of the Han River heard of this, they said, "Tang's acts of kindness extend even to the wildfowl and beasts". Forty states changed over their loyalties to him. When the man spread out all four sides of the net, he could not be certain he would catch a bird. Tang spread out only one of the four and thereby caught forty states, not merely a bird. 湯見祝網者置四面, 其祝曰 :"從天墜者, 從地出者, 從四方來者, 皆離吾網." 湯曰 :"嘻 ! 盡之矣, 非桀其庸爲此 ?" 湯乃解其三面, 置其一面, 更教之祝曰 :"昔蛛蝥作網, 今之人循序, 欲左則左, 欲右則右, 欲高則高, 欲下則下, 吾取其犯命者." 漢南之國聞之曰, "湯之德及禽獸矣." 四十國歸之. 人置四面, 未必得鳥; 湯去三面, 置其一面, 以網四十國, 非徒網鳥也 (Knoblock & Riegel, *Annals of Lü Buwei*, 237).

> people know of your desire to release them. They compete with one another to catch them. Many of them die! If you should like that they survive, you might prohibit the people from catching them. If they are caught and released, the kindness does not make up for the damage done". Jianzi said, "So be it"![130]

It is clear from this that the specific practice of catching fish and fowl to release already emerged in Handan during the Spring and Autumn period; the act of life release among the people was primarily a way of showing kindness towards living beings. First, they would catch the creature, and then release it, which itself was contradictory. At the time, Jianzi of Zhou heard from his retainers, who advised that the act of "catching creatures and releasing them" be reformed to an outright ban on people catching them. This is an early account in China prohibiting slaughtering and fishing.

In springtime, life flourishes. Ancients had measures to protect life. The sixth chapter "Yueling di liu" 月令第六 (On Months) of the *Liji* 禮記 (Book of Rites) states, "During the first month of spring, … orders are handed down to offer sacrifices to the mountains, forests, streams and creeks. Do not use female victims. It is prohibited to chop down trees. Do not destroy nests. Larvae are not to be killed, nor young in the wombs, birds [only recently] taking to flight. Dawns and eggs are not to be harmed".[131] In the springtime when life is undergoing renewal, one is not to chop wood as a livelihood, nor damage nests and frolic around, or harm young animals and sprouts, otherwise the Way of myriad creatures of the Great Earth is lost.

The stories of Tang and Jianzi illustrate that the practice of life release possesses a rich intellectual background within Chinese culture. The "Liushui zhangzhe zi pin" of *Jin'guangming jing*, translated by Dharmakṣema, provides its own resources with respect to Buddhist life release. The relevant content is summarized as follows:

> Udakaśrotas would not allow for the fish to be dried out by the sun, so he sought out the king. He would bring water with twenty great elephants to hydrate the fish and save them. The king approved his request. Udakaśrotas then requested two sons to go to the elephant stable and fetch at will twenty great elephants. The pair were to borrow a number of water skins from the wine maker. They quickly went to a pool of water

130 Yang, *Jishi*, 172:
邯鄲之民, 以正月元旦獻鳩於簡子. 簡子大悅, 厚賞之. 客問其故. 簡子曰：" 正旦放生, 示有恩也." 客曰：" 民知君之欲放之, 競而捕之, 死者眾矣. 君如欲生之, 不若禁民勿捕. 捕而放之, 恩過不相補矣." 簡子曰：" 然."

131 *Liji*, 201.

> and filled up the skins, which the elephants carried to the pond. They emptied the water into the pond. The water level rose back to its original level. Udakaśrotas saved the fish that nearly died, providing them with water and food. He also preached Mahāyāna scriptures for their liberation. The fishes listened to the scriptures and they were reborn in Trāyastriṃśa Heaven.[132]

The "Liushui zhanzghe zi pin" had an important impact on Buddhist practices of life release, such as the dharma of the twelve links of dependent origination, holy names for buddhas and bodhisattvas, verses concerning the merit of life release, as well as procedures and rituals for life release. The story of Udakaśrota's saving of the fish increased Chinese understanding of the Buddhist idea of life release and made it more readily accepted and disseminated.

Confucian ideas of life release are rooted in a mentality of pity, such as the story in *Menicus* ("Wanzhang" 萬章 I) about Zichan 子產 (?–522 BC) saving a live fish he received, which was quite influential. The Buddhist practice of life release, therefore, combined with the Confucian appeal, and was able to be smoothly carried out among the common people.

### 3.2 *Life Release Practices Before the Song Period*

The practice of life release gradually became popular from the Northern and Southern Dynasties period. Emperor Xianwen of the Northern Wei (Bei Wei Xianwen di 北魏獻文帝 [r. 465–471]) ordered that no animals be sacrificed to Heaven and Earth on the altars of the ancestors and state. Annually seventy-five thousand victims survived from this order. Emperor Wenxuan of the Northern Qi (Bei Qi Wenxuan di [r. 550–559]) implemented the Buddhist teachings of compassion by actively stopping meat consumption. During the fifth lunar month of year seven of Tianbao 天保 reign era (556), Emperor Wenxuan came to believe that meat eating was contrary to compassion, and thus stopped eating it. During the fourth lunar month of year eight (557), he ordered that all collection of shrimps, crabs and clams stop; only collection of fish was permitted. During the same month, all hunting with hawks, be it public or private, was forbidden. During the second lunar month of year nine (558), it was ordered that the burning of fields would only be permitted during lunar months eleven and one; all other times the use of fire was not permitted.[133]

---

132 *Jin'guangming jing*, *T* no. 664, 16: 4.352c22-353b17 ：
流水長者子不忍魚爲日所曝, 乃求其國王, 與以二十大象, 暫往負水, 濟彼魚命, 王允其請. 長者子乃及請二子, 至象廄中, 隨意取二十大象, 雙從酒家多借皮囊, 往決水處, 以囊盛水, 象負至池, 瀉至池中, 水即彌滿, 還復如故. 流水長者子救起瀕死之魚, 予之水、食, 爲其解說大乘經典, 諸魚聞經後, 皆生忉利天.

133 *Bei Qi shu* 4. 61, 63, 64.

Liang Wudi wrote the "Duan jiurou wen" 斷酒肉文 (Proscription of Alcohol and Meat). He ordered that fruits be used as sacrificial items on the ancestral altar. Moreover, he built thirteen inexhaustible treasuries (*wujin zang* 無盡藏). He implemented both life release and charitable giving. He ordered Zhang Wenxiu 張文休 (early sixth century) to go to the slaughterhouse on a daily basis to purchase animals that were to be killed before releasing them.[134] The aristocracy and commoners were influenced by Emperor Wu, and actively participated in and promoted the practice of life release. Emperor Yuan of the Liang 梁元帝 (r. 551–554) also ordered the construction of a life release pavilion (*fangsheng ting* 放生亭) and composed a stele inscription for it.[135] He

134 For details, see "Yu jiang Mohebore jing xu" 御講摩訶般若經序 by Xiao Zixian 蕭子顯, in *Guang Hongming ji*, *T* no. 2103, 52: 19.237c19-28:
[Emperor Wu of Liang] ordered the *zhidao* 至到 Zhang Wenxiu 張文休 (d.u.) to go to the abattoirs every day, ordering them to do away from the crucible and chopping block. The number of animals that were immediately saved by him exceeded one hundred million. This practice became a routine. [Zhang] Wenxiu was originally a transport clerk. He distributed the [official] transport of rice to the poor people, so he was sentenced to death. The emperor took pity on him and rejected his death penalty. Not only did [the emperor] remit him of his felony, but he even gave him the official title of *zhidao*. [Zhang Wenxiu] was not like Feng Xuan 馮煖 (d.u), who bought his reputation of righteousness [for Lord Mengchang 孟嘗君 (?–279BCE)], nor was he like Ji An 汲黯 (?–112BCE), who asked for punishment [because he delivered a false imperial order to open the state granary to aid the victims of natural calamities]. [Zhang] was a petty person, but the forgiveness [he received] was much greater than in past times. After [Zhang] Wenxiu received benevolent forgiveness, he did not slack off even for a moment. Sometimes he did not have time to eat at noon, and he did not stop running all over the capital city. He ran like he was flying. With the drums beating and banners flying, he carried loads and rushed to [save animals]. Fowls and beasts, all creatures of the four kinds of birth were released [by him]. At that time, both the government officials and the common people all shared his [dharma] joy. 張文休別敕 "至到" 張文休, 日往屠肆, 命切鼎俎, 即時救贖, 濟免億數, 以此爲常. 文休者, 先爲運吏, 輒散運米與貧民, 應入大辟. 上愍其一分, 惻然不許. 非唯赦其重辜, 乃加以 "至到" 之目. 既非憑暖之市義, 又無汲黯之請罪. 人微宥重, 過於昔時. 文休既荷嘉貸, 未嘗暫怠. 日中或不得食, 而足不得息. 周遍京邑, 行步如飛. 擊鼓揚幢, 負擔馳逐. 家禽野獸, 殫四生之品, 無不放捨焉. 是時朝臣, 至於民庶, 並各隨喜.

135 See "Jingzhou fangsheng ting bei" 荊州放生亭碑 (Stele for the Jingzhou Life Release Pavilion), included in *Gujin tushu jicheng—Bowu huibian shenyi dian* 古今圖書集成·博物彙編神異典, fasc. 212 (*fangsheng bu* 放生部). See Lan, *Bubian*, 16.822:
While the fish follows the stream, its home is in the paradise of the Peach-Blossom; although a dragon resides in grand woods, it always takes the path leading up towards the floating clouds. How would one be as stupid as to regard Ziming 子明 of Mount Lingyang 陵陽, who loved angling, as losing his life in the clouds or in the water, or to regard Zhuangzi, who was holding a fishing rod, as taking the bait [of power and position]. The great tortoise, which appeared in the midnight dream of Lord Yuan of the Song, was eventually killed and used by him; the red egret that was marvelously flying in the morning

revised and sorted out the literary items related to the ancient cherishing of life, demonstrating that he sought to rule the realm with benevolence while educating the populace in a beneficial manner.

In year thirteen of Taijian 太建 reign era (581) under Emperor Xuan of the Chen (Chen Xuandi 陳宣帝 [r. 568–582]), Zhiyi petitioned the emperor to forbid the catching of wildlife. Zhiyi witnessed people using fishnets over an area of over four-hundred miles. He therefore purchased some suitable parts of the river and bays to build life release ponds, and he lectured to the fishermen on the *Jin'guangming jing*. The fishermen, having heard the Dharma, changed their professions and came to cherish life and follow virtue. They offered as tribute sixty-three places on waterfronts along the bridge at Huxi 滬溪 for life release ponds, totalling more than three or four hundred miles. The stele by Xu Ling 徐陵 (507–583) explains the story behind this.[136]

The practice of life release became very popular during the Tang dynasty. Daozhou's 道胄 (575–659) *Xu Gaoseng zhuan* biography records that Daozhou built more than one hundred life release ponds in various provinces, which proved to be quite spiritually efficacious.[137] After the An Shi Rebelllion (755–763), the state faced unrest and people became unsettled and depressed, while famines sprung up everywhere. Emperor Suzong of Tang (Tang Suzong 唐肅宗 [r. 756–762]) in year two of Qianyuan 乾元 reign era (759) ordered that eighty-one life release ponds be constructed along various highways.[138] The life release ponds mentioned in the imperial order, placed every five miles up and down the coast, were identical in form to the screens for life release ponds in natural bays that Zhiyi set up.

---

was still netted by the empress of the Han dynasty. When a lurking yellow bird is watching a cicada, it is unaware that a stone is about to shoot it. When a grey buzzard is chasing after a rabbit, it has no idea that it is going to be cooked in a boiling cauldron as well. Staying in the North Sea, the parrot is extremely picky about food, so much so that it is not necessarily regarded as inhuman; Queen Mother of the West sent [the three birds] to deliver letters, and who would call them lowly birds? Thus we can learn from this that fish and birds should be viewed all as the same, for their nature all lies in the desire for life. May the wild geese to be cooked for the feast before glamorous seats return to their flocks back in their winter habitat, Hengyang 衡陽, and the deer from the snow mountain cease to be eaten at the banquet given to friends. 魚從流水, 本在桃花之源; 龍處大林, 恆捻浮雲之路. 豈謂陵陽垂釣, 失雲失水; 莊子懸竿, 吞鈎吞餌？雖復玄龜夜夢, 終見取於宋王; 朱鷺晨飛, 尙張羅於漢后. 譬如黃雀伺蟬, 不知隨彈應至; 青鷂逐兔, 詎識扛鼎方前？北海之飡鸚鵡, 未始非人; 西王之使傳信, 誰云賤鳥？故知鳥魚一觀, 俱在好生. 欲使金牀之鴈, 更返衡陽之侶; 雪山之鹿, 不充食萍之宴.

136 *Sui Tiantai Zhizhe dashi biezhuan*, *T* no. 2050, 50: 1.193c8-10.

137 *Xu Gaoseng zhuan*, *T* no. 2060, 50: 22. 623a5-22.

138 See *Fangsheng beiwen* 放生碑文 (*Inscription on the Life Release Ponds*) by Yan Zhenqing 顏真卿 (709–784). In Lan, *Bubian*, 16.822–23.

### 3.3 *The Popularity of the Life Release Practice in the Song Dynasty*

Life release became increasingly popular as the court promoted it and people participated in it. Emperor Taizu of Song (Song Taizu 宋太祖 [r. 960–976]) ordered that no catching or shooting of wildlife would be permitted amongst the people from the second to ninth lunar months. During year three of reign era Tianxi (1019) under Song Emperor Zhenzong, Ciyun Zunshi of Lingshan si 靈山寺 in Tianzhu 天竺 in Hangzhou petitioned the court to turn the West Lake into a life release pond. He also personally produced the "Fangsheng ciji famen" 放生慈濟法門 (Practice of Compassionate Saving via Life Release). The *Fozu tongji* includes the following account:

> Prime Minister Wang Qinruo 王欽若 (962–1025) took up his position in Qiantang. He led a group of bureaucrats and retainers on a visit to Mount Tianzhu, visiting the Dharma Master of Ciyun, Zunshi, requesting that he lecture on the *Fahua jing*. He praised [Zunshi] saying, "Until now I had never heard of this Way, nor seen this man". He petitioned the court to grant Tianzhu its former name. The Master requested that the West Lake be made into a life release pond. Annually on the eighth day of the fourth lunar month the regional peoples would gather to release fish and fowl, while praying for the long life of their superiors.[139]

Life release was a Buddhist practice of compassion, in which the people prayed for the longevity of the emperor, which is why there was a petition to the emperor to carry out a large scale gathering for life release on the Buddha's birthday on the eighth day of the fourth lunar month on an annual basis. They received the blessing to do this from the emperor.

The *Jinyuan ji* 金園集 (Collection of the Golden Park; *XZJ* 948) includes Zunshi's "Fangsheng ciji famen". The opening of the preface states, "Benevolence is one of the five constant virtues advocated by Confucians; and compassion is one of the four immeasurables advocated by Buddhists. Both despise cruelty and do away with killing, instead promoting blessings and cherishment. Then, one gains the five blessings including longevity and the four virtues including constancy. Actually, it is refraining from killing that is the main essence of life release".[140] Here life release combines the Confucian idea of "five constant vir-

139 *Fozu tongji*, *T* no. 2035, 49: 44.406b6-10:
宰相王欽若出鎮錢唐. 率僚屬詣天竺靈山, 謁慈雲法師遵式, 請講《法華》. 歎曰：此道所未聞, 此人所未見也. 即爲奏錫天竺舊名. 師奏請西湖爲放生池, 每歲四月八日, 郡人會湖上縱魚鳥, 爲主上祝壽.

140 *Jinyuan ji*, *XZJ* no. 948, 101: 2.231a12-14:
儒冠五常謂之仁, 釋御四等謂之慈, 皆惡殘去殺, 推惠廣愛之謂也. 然後果五福之

tues" (*wuchang* 五常) with the Buddhist "four immeasurables" (*si wuliang xin* 四無量心). Zunshi produced the ritual for life release with a narrative, blessing of the water, petition, refuge, recitation of the Buddha's name, Dharma talk, and seven chapters of repentance and vows.

The popularity of life release not only received government support, it also gained a kind of spiritual efficacy in terms of religious faith. Take "Mengyu ji" 夢魚記 (Record of the Fish Dream) by Pan Hua 潘華 (d.u.), who was the Magistrate of Zhuji County of Yue Prefecture 越州諸暨縣事 and acting vice director of the State Farms Bureau of the Department of State Affairs 尙書屯田員外郎, as an example. In year four of reign era Jingde 景德 (1007), Pan Hua was ordered by the court to return to the capital. According to *Meng yu ji,* he dreamed of fish weeping in the rivers and lakes. So he ensured that people would not take fish from rivers and bodies of water following the instruction of the *Puxian guanjing* 普賢觀經 (*Sūtra* of Meditating on Samantabhadra).[141] The popularity of this kind of spiritual story illustrates the fervent state of the practice of life release during the Song Dynasty.

In year three of Tiansheng 天聖 reign era (1025), Zhili of Yanqing si on Mount Siming also petitioned for life release ceremonies to be carried out on the Buddha's birthday as a way of praying for the longevity of the emperor. He also requested that Nanhu 南湖 be designated in perpetuity as a life release pond. Zhili produced a ritual for life release in order to ensure that the ceremony would proceed smoothly. He established the "Fangsheng wen" 放生文 (Text on Life Release) that he compiled as his ritual. At the time, The Military Affairs Commissioner 樞密使 Liu Jun 劉均 (d.u.) composed a stele inscription for this compilation following the imperial order to record this grand affair.[142]

Zunshi and Zhili petitioning the emperor to provide life release ponds reveals that monks actively influenced the emperor. In year one of Tianxi 天禧 reign era (1017), Emperor Zhenzong of Song ordered the renovation of life release ponds, while furthermore forbidding fishing within five miles up or down the Huai River 淮水 in the provinces and counties of Huai. This was possibly influenced by the contemporary situation, in which the life release ponds were being renovated. Ouyang Xiu 歐陽修 (1007–1072) composed a postscript to an inscription for a life release pond ("Ba fangsheng chi bei" 跋放生池碑), which praises Zhenzong's benevolence towards creatures:

---

曰壽, 證四德之曰常, 實唯不殺, 放生之大統也.

141 *Siming zunzhe jiaoxing lu, T* no. 1937, 46: 1.864b3-9.

142 "Fangsheng wen" and "Chi Yanqing-yuan fangshengchi beaming" 敕延慶院放生池碑銘 in *Siming zunzhe jiaoxing lu, T* no. 1937, 46: 1.863a24, 864b21.

> The stele for the above-mentioned life release pond does not name a composer. In Tang times, life release ponds were everywhere. Royal benevolence extended toward vegetation and insects, ensuring that each single creature would certainly flourish in life, but was not subject to any personal favour. … It is the teaching of the Buddha that those who kill beings are guilty of transgression, but those who release beings gain blessings. If this be so, then [the mythical creator of fishing and trapping] Fu Xi became a sage among men, but a sinner below the earth.[143]

The practice of life release during the Song was carried over from the Tang, and moreover extended into the lives of common people. The rise and decline of life release ponds in various regions also followed the prosperity or decline of Buddhist development in the same regions. Starting from the first life release pond created by Zhiyi, which was when Buddhism rose in prominence.

## 4 Conclusion

After the mid-Tang period, Buddhism became an important resource in Chinese lifestyle and society. However, due to the destructions brought by the An Shi Rebellion and the Huichang Persecution, Buddhism was forced out of central cities such as Chang'an and Luoyang, and moved to mountainous areas and local communities. This was precisely why Buddhism was able to shift from the philosophical enquiries of the intellectual elites to the everyday life of the common people, spreading to all corners of China and throughout all levels of society. Buddhist traditions like Tiantai, Huayan and Chan became the most important carriers in East Asian cultural exchanges, which were developed and culminated in various countries. Although much scholarship on Buddhist history stressed the decline of Buddhism in the Song period, from the perspective of the history of Buddhist societies and lifestyle, it is actually to the contrary. The introduction of *Buddhism in the Sung*, edited by Gregory and Getz, attests that the claim of decline of Song Buddhism originated from three biased factors. First, Song Buddhism (especially the Song Chan school) undervalued itself and deified the Tang patriarchs. Second, the prejudice of sectarianism and nationalism from Japanese Buddhism. The third factor was prejudice

---

143 Lan, *Bubian*, 16.823:
右放生池碑, 不著書撰人名氏. 放生池唐世處處有之. 王者仁澤, 及於草木昆蟲, 使一物必遂其生,而不爲私惠也. ... 浮屠氏之說,乃爲殺物者有罪,而放生者得福, 苟如其言,則庖犧氏遂爲人間之聖人,地下之罪人矣.

from the Chinese Confucian tradition. In reality, after the mid-Tang period, the Chan and Pure Land schools were prevalent, and Buddhist faith penetrated deeply into the common populace. Monasteries in the Song period were organized in a system of "Five Mountains and Ten Monasteries" (*Wushan shicha* 五山十刹). This demonstrates that Song Buddhism was a period of prosperity and permeation.[144]

After the mid-Tang period, Buddhism shifted from "State Buddhism" to being more involved in maintaining social order and constructing the spiritual world on a local level. Along with obtaining important texts from Goryeo, and the emergence of Dharma leaders who were masters of doctrine and lofty in practice, like Zhili, Zunshi, Zhiyuan and Renyue, the Tiantai school was revived in the Song dynasty. During the process of reviving the Tiantai school, Master Zhili, influenced by the popularity of Pure Land teachings and the notion of repentance practices to seek rebirth in the Pure Land, not only expounded doctrines, but also gave more emphasis to contemplative practices. He especially relied on Zhiyi's teachings on eradicating transgression and attaining *samādhi* through the practice of repentance rites. As such, repentance practices were popular in the Song Tiantai school, and repentance ritual procedures which differed from the Sui and Tang periods were formulated.[145] Actualizing Song Tiantai repentance practices, Ciyun Zunshi revised and produced a collection of new repentance rites, hence he was called the "Ciyun Master of Repentance" by later generations. Jingyuan's *Lengyan xiuzheng yi*, for *Śūraṃgama* repentance practice, was based on the structure and thought of repentance practice from Zongmi's *Yuanjuejing daochang xiuzheng yi*. He adopted Tiantai repentance ritual procedures and ideas like the "ten minds contrary or in line with *saṃsāra*", to develop the practice system of the Huayan school. Furthermore, Jingyuan's own special characteristics were displayed through his proposition of the three repentance methods: repentance of subduing karma, repentance of turning karma, and repentance of eliminating karma, and through taking the Avalokiteśvara bodhisattva perfect penetration practice method as the practice method for calm and insight.

During the Song and Yuan dynasties, Buddhist devotional societies continued to develop. Combining with other faiths, various devotional groups were formed. Since the mid-Tang period, with the popularity of Amitābha Pure Land devotion, groups like the "Communities of the Western Land" and "Communities for the Nine Grades of Rebirth" gradually emerged. Shengchang (959–1020) followed the example of the society for recollection of the Buddha,

144 Gregory & Getz, *Buddhism in the Sung*, 1–20.
145 Shi, *Chanfa*, 284–85.

supposedly established by Lushan Huiyuan, and formed a group for practicing purification of karma called the Society of Pure Practice. It was named after the Chapter on Pure Conduct from the *Huayan jing*. After the Song dynasty, monasteries held *Nirvāṇa* Gatherings to commemorate the Buddha's *pariṇirvāna*. The Water and Land Rites began with Liang Wudi. Since the Song dynasty, elaborate ritual procedures for Dharma services were developed. Yang'e, Sushi, Foyin Liaoyuan, Zongze, Zhipan and others were important figures in contributing to the making of the ritual procedures for the Water and Land Rites.[146]

Buddhist charitable activities were very well-developed in the Song dynasty. There were charitable institutions such as organizations for shelter and care, nursing homes for taking in sick and destitute elderly, orphanages for taking in abandoned infants and children, grain subsidies to assist indigent families in raising their children, and public cemeteries providing professional funeral services for the poor and unidentified deceased. Buddhist organizations were actively involved in many public welfare works. They provided funding and labor for affairs such as building bridges, water works, roads and local security patrols. In addition, monastics set up life release ponds in the monasteries. The development of life release customs later became an important tradition in Buddhism's penetration into society after the Song dynasty.[147]

Although Buddhism in the Song period may have lacked innovation, in terms of creating systems, merging ritual protocols, and deepening and influencing Buddhist faith and lifestyle in society, Song Buddhism was no doubt at a peak throughout Buddhist history. Thus, when we observe and understand Buddhism in the Song and Yuan dynasties through the perspectives of faith and lifestyle, we will see a "prosperous and vibrant" Song and Yuan Buddhism.

146 The studies on the Water and Land Rites are many; see Makita, "Suiroku'e shōkō", 14–33; Stevenson, "Text, Image, and Transformation", 30–70.

147 Michibata, "Hōjō shisō", 228–30.

FIGURE 31 Main hall of Tiantong Monastery 天童寺, Ningbo寧波.

## Appendix 3.1: Three Transgressions 三品罪

**High Level Transgression 上品罪**

The mind, [driven by] intention to carry out the act, is weighty [with afflictions]; all three times, including the moment of the act and after the act having been completed, are all weighty, while the mind and the object are in union. Alternatively, this is a heinous transgression (ānantarya-kārin), the slandering of Mahāyāna scriptures, and

**Mid Level Transgression 中品罪**

The intention [to act] and the action [in the moment of being carried out] are at both times [characterized] by the mind weighty [with afflictions]; having carried out the act, the mind is light. The [perceived] object was weighty while the mind was sparsely [afflicted]; [actions which] are also not the three

**Low Level Transgression 下品罪**

The mind is weighty [with afflictions] before and after, but when the act is carried out [the mind is] light, while the object and mind are in opposition. A low level [transgression] is defined as also not any crime for which one leaves the assembly, or where there is calculated [gains] but no actual benefit,

APPENDIX 3.1 Three Transgressions 三品罪 (*cont.*)

| **High Level Transgression 上品罪** | **Mid Level Transgression 中品罪** | **Low Level Transgression 下品罪** |
|---|---|---|
| [actions resulting in becoming an] icchantika. [Actions characterized] by the creating of karma for many gains, misunderstanding cause and effect, unawareness of the violation, and unawareness of Dharma are defined as high level [transgressions]. 方便心重, 作時作已, 三時皆重, 心境相應；複是逆罪, 謗方等經, 一闡提等, 作業數利, 迷因謬果, 不識於犯, 又不識法, 名爲上品. | extremes, or there are few benefits, or no misunderstanding of cause and effect, are defined as mid-level [transgressions]. 方便正作, 二時心重, 作已心輕, 境重心微；又非三極, 利而不數, 不迷因果, 名爲中品. | or where there is awareness of Dharma and crime, or where there is clear faith in cause and effect. 前後心重, 正作是輕, 境與心違；又非出眾之犯, 數而不利, 識法識犯, 明信因果, 名爲下品. |

## Appendix 3.2: Three Methods of Repentance 三種懺門

| **Repentance of Subduing Karma (*Fuye chan* 伏業懺)** | **Repentance of Turning Karma (*Zhuanye chan* 轉業懺)** | **Repentance of Eliminating Karma (*Mieye chan* 滅業懺)** |
|---|---|---|
| According to the limited teachings of the Three Vehicles, during the first four sections of confession, [the karma] is subdued, and will not arise. This is what we call repentance. Once [the karma] has been disclosed, the original transgression will not increase and there is no transgression of concealing. What would have arisen [i.e., karmic fruits] will not arise. This is subduing. 依三乘局教, 悔初四篇, 但伏而不起, 名之爲懺；既經發露, 本罪不增, 無隱過覆藏等罪, 應生不生, 名之爲伏. | Repentance of turning karma is defined as the turning a long time (dīrgha-kālam) into a short time (alpam-kāla); employing light suffering to eliminate severe suffering; one who should be subject to rebirth among the three unfortunate paths aspires to compensate for it in the present life, and [thereby] not be subject to rebirth among the unfortunate paths. 以促時換長時, 用輕苦償重苦；於三惡道中, 若應受報, 願於今身償, 不入惡道受, 此名轉業懺也. | There must be clear observation and understanding, and deep generation of great bodhicitta; [recognizing that] from the beginningless past, there have been committed transgressions. It is like being in a dark room. Repentance and true wisdom are like a bright lamp. One shine of the lamp and the darkness all dissipates. There is much darkness when the lamp is rejected. Having misunderstood cause and effect, and made numerous faults, buddha-nature glows latent, thus it is like being in a dark room. Generating the fire of true wisdom, things are clearly illuminated; the illumination removes darkness, and one dispels |

APPENDIX 3.2 Three Methods of Repentance 三種懺門 (*cont.*)

| **Repentance of Subduing Karma (*Fuye chan* 伏業懺)** | **Repentance of Turning Karma (*Zhuanye chan* 轉業懺)** | **Repentance of Eliminating Karma (*Mieye chan* 滅業懺)** |
| --- | --- | --- |
| | | the production of confusion and faults. All karma is thereby eliminated. 必須觀解明白, 深發大菩提心；無始以來, 所造諸罪, 猶如暗室；懺悔正慧, 喻如明燈；明燈一照, 昏暗皆除, 不以暗多, 能拒燈也. 迷因謬果, 具造諸愆, 佛性潛輝, 故如暗室；發真慧火, 事等明燈, 燈起暗除, 解生惑喪, 業無不滅也. |

CHAPTER 4

# Buddhist Faith and Lifestyles in the Ming and Qing Dynasties

Following the division of temples into three types (dealing with meditation, doctrine, and monastic rules) under Emperor Taizu of the Ming dynasty (Ming Taizu 明太祖 [r.1368-1398]), Buddhist services dealing with scripture and repentance flourished during the Ming and Qing periods. Various types emerged one after another. At the same time, the Buddhist faith became deeply integrated into common society common society. The lifestyle of commoners was also heavily influenced by Buddhism. We can observe Buddhist influence in marriage and seasonal festivals.

## 1 Mount Jiang Dharma Services and the Consolidation of Yoga Teachings under Emperor Taizu of Ming

Emperor Taizu of the Ming divided Buddhist temples into three types while consolidating and regulating Yoga teachings (*Yuqie jiao* 瑜伽教), which facilitated the flourishing and development of Buddhist practices of scriptural recitation and repentance during the Ming and Qing periods. Ming Taizu's regulation and promotion of such Buddhist practices was was not only done out of the necessity to uncover malpractice, but his goals also included ideals related to proper government and appeasing eminent monks, the most important expression of which was the Mount Jiang Dharma Service (*Jiangshan fahui* 蔣山法會).

### 1.1 *The Creation and Procedures of the Mount Jiang Dharma Service*

Ming Taizu reunited the nation from the eleventh day of the ninth lunar month in the first year of the Hongwu period (1368.10.22). Until the fifth year of the Yongle period of the Emperor Chengzu (1407), Ming Taizu and Ming Chengzu both visited Mount Zhong in succession in order to request eminent Buddhist monks to carry out the "Unhindered Water and Land Rite" (*wuzhe shuilu* 無遮水陸), which historical records refer to as the "Mount Jiang Dharma Service." This rite was primarily meant to aid the passing of the war dead and innocent souls, through which he placated popular sentiments and eased the political situation.[1]

1 Shiga, "bukkyō seisaku", 199-237.

 DOI:10.1163/9789004431775_006

FIGURE 32 Yao Guangxiao's 姚廣孝 (1335-1418) funerary pagoda (1418).

The Mount Jiang Dharma Service, as a service promoted by the court, was grand in scale and a had a deep impact on Buddhists of the Ming dynasty. The times, locations, and eminent monks who participated in the service are described in Hasebe's book (Appendix 4.1).[2] Fascicle Twenty of the *Chushi Fanqi Chanshi yulu* 楚石梵琦禪師語錄 (Recorded Sayings of Chan Master Chushi Fanqi, *XZJ* 1400) provides an account of a "Water and Land Lecutre" (*shuilu shengzuo* 水陸升座) on the eleventh day of the ninth lunar month in 1368. Chushi Fanqi 楚石梵琦 (1296-1370) lectured on the Dharma at the Land and Waters rites at the Chan temple of Mount Jiang, mentioning that Ming Taizu "provided funds and ordered [the staff of] the national Buddhist bureau, the Shanshi yuan 善世院, to go to the Chan monastery of Mount Jiang and hold the Ceremony of Distributing Food to Beings of on Water and Land and in Both of the Worlds of Light and Darkness. For one day and night, the various ceremonies were conducted, including offerings to the sages and worthies, the deities above and below, and ghosts and spirits of the Three Realms."[3] Moreover, Fanqi was called upon to "preach on Buddhist tenets and the merits accumulated; and to pray for the deliverance of sentient beings of the four births on the sixth paths, that the innocent and mistreated be freed from the darkness and be reborn in a buddha-realm."[4]

On the thirteenth day of the third lunar month in the second year of the Hongwu period (1369.4.19), Chushi Fanqi again lectured on the Dharma at the Water and Land Rite at the Chan temple of Mount Jiang.

Ming Taizu's "Yuzhi Jiangshan si guangjian Fohui wen" 御製蔣山寺廣薦佛會文 (Imperial Account of the Ceremony of Extensive Offerings at Jiangshan Si) records that "on the fifteenth day of the first lunar month in year 3 of Hongwu (1370), I honored the buddhas and made offerings to the monks at a temple on Mount Jiang."[5] The concrete details of the Dharma service, however, are unclear.

In spring of year four of Hongwu (1371), Ming Taizu ordered the assembly of ten famous monks that dealt with meditation, lecturing, and doctrine, and two-thousand of their disciples, to carry out Service of Extensive Offerings (*Guangjian fahui* 廣薦法會) at Mount Zhong 鍾山. Lijin 力金 (1328-1374) of Tianjie si 天界寺 was ordered to carry out *dhāraṇī* recitations and a purifica-

---

2 Hasebe, *Kyōdanshi*, 18-20.

3 *Chushi Fanqi chanshi yulu*, *XZJ* no. 1400, 124: 20.292b8-10:
特賜銀帑, 命善世院, 就蔣山禪寺, 修建冥陽水陸, 大齋一晝夜, 於中作諸佛事, 供佛賢聖、天地神祇、三界鬼神.

4 Ibid., 20.292b10-11: 舉唱宗乘, 所集功勛, 並用超度四生六道, 無辜冤枉悉脫幽冥, 往生佛土.

5 *Jinling fancha zhi* 3.312: 洪武三年正月十五日, 朕於鐘山前蔣山寺奉佛供僧.

tion gathering, but he nominated Zongle 宗泐 (1318-1390) to do this on account of his mother being advanced in age.[6]

In the eleventh lunar month in the winter of 1371, ten people including Jianxin Laifu 見心來複 (1319 -1391) were ordered to Nanjing, where they carried out a Dharma service at Taiping Xingguo Chansi 太平興國禪寺 on Mount Jiang.

The largest Mount Jiang Dharma service in terms of scale, however, lasted several months from winter of 1371 until spring of the following year. This was the Water and Land Rite as a national sacrifice, which was carried out with the most extreme solemn rights. The primary literature in this case is the aforementioned comments by Ming Taizu. Song Lian 宋濂 (1310-1381) in the "Jiangshan guangjian Fohui ji" 蔣山廣薦佛會記 (Account of the Ceremony of Extensive Offerings at the Temple of Mount Jiang) gives a detailed account of the service.

However, the Buddhist ceremony of the Water and Land Rite differs from the court rites to Heaven and Confucius. The emperor presided over the service for the spirits. Much consideration was given to the structure of the rites, which is why it was necessary to combine and make compromises with the two rituals. The biography of Ruqi 如玘 (1320-1385) in fascicle two of the *Xu Fozu tongji* 續佛祖統紀 (Extended Chronicle of the Buddha and Patriarchs, XZJ 1492) gives the following account:

> In the year of *gengshu*, the emperor intended to carry out devotional observances. Considering that the way of ghosts and spirits was nebulous, [the emperor] summoned eminent monks for discussion and an investigation, and the master presented a commentary which met with the emperor's appreciation. In the fourth year, a year of *xinhai*, the national Buddhist bureau dismissed the administrator of the Tianjie si 天界寺. The master was promoted to the Yanfu si 演福寺, and learners, out of admiration, followed him like his shadow. In the fifth year, a year of *renzi*, the emperor bestowed grace upon those removed from office and convened all eminent monks across the country to Mount Zhong. An expanded devotional assembly was held, and the the Dharma rites were quite spectacular. The Imperial Chariot (i.e. the emperor) granted his brilliance presence, and leading monks took their turns to give sermons.[7]

6 *Fozu gangmu*, XZJ no. 1570, 146: 41.861a17-2.

7 *Xu Fozu tongji*, XZJ no. 1492, 131: 2.735a18-b4:
庚戍, 上將修釐事, 以鬼神之道茫昧, 召高僧講究, 師奏疏稱旨. 四年辛亥, 善世院罷天界領事者, 以師升演福, 學者慕之, 羸糧景從. 五年壬子, 上將覃恩幽滯, 召天下高僧畢集鍾山, 設廣薦會, 法儀甚盛, 大駕親臨, 沙門上首分番說法.

This text makes clear that Ming Taizu placed great importance on the Mount Jiang Dharma Service. In 1370, he brought together officials of Ministry of Rites and eminent Buddhist monks to discuss the procedures for executing the rites. In 1371, they tried out the ritual procedures and then in 1372 their final form was formulated.

As the biography of Chan Master Bai An [Li]jin 白庵 [力] 金 in the *Buxu Gaoseng zhuan* 補續高僧傳 (Supplement to the Extended Biographies of Eminent Monks, *XZJ* 1501) states, "The entire system and [its] forms can be transmitted long into the future."[8]

Song Lian's "Jiangshan guangjian Fohui ji" cites Ming Taizu's *Qin luji* 欽錄集 as follows:

> In the fifth year of the Hongwu era, a year of *renzi*, spring, [the emperor] came to the Jiangshan si to organize a Dharma Assembly of Extensive Offerings. [The emperor] ordered the renowned and worthy monks coming from various regions to first collate the Buddhist canon, and then ordered Zongle to compose *Xianfo yuezhang* 獻佛樂章 (Lyric Poems Offered to the Buddha). Upon completion, the piece was presented to the throne, [and the emperor] added a title to every one of the tunes with his own handwriting, which, to be enumerated, were *shanshi* 善世 (benefiting the world), *zhaoxin* 昭信 (illuminating the belief), *yanci* 延慈 (extending mercy), *faxi* 法喜 (dharmic joy), *chanyue* 禪悅 (*dhyāna* joy), *bianying* 遍應 (rounded response), *miaoji* 妙濟 (wondrous relief), *shancheng* 善成 (well establishment), eight sections in all. [The emperor] decreed the Court of Imperial Sacrifices to synchronize the rhymes of the song and dance, and they were adopted and established as an institution. On the twenty-first of the eleventh month in the fourth year, an imperial order was received, saying, "'The Imperially Composed Bulletin for Broad Offering Buddhist Assembly' will be posted by the Department of State Affairs to inform the whole country, both officials and civilians, both the gentry and the commoners."[9]

8 *Buxu Gaoseng zhuan*, *XZJ* no. 1501, 134: 14.254a10-11: 凡儀制規式, 皆堪傳永久.

9 Lan, *Bubian*, 28: 118:
洪武五年壬子春, 即蔣山寺建廣薦法會, 命四方名德沙門, 先點校藏經, 命宗泐撰《獻佛樂章》. 既成進呈, 御署曲名, 曰《善世》, 曰《昭信》, 曰《延慈》, 曰《法喜》, 曰《禪悅》, 曰《遍應》, 曰《妙濟》, 曰《善成》, 凡八章. 勅太常諧協歌舞之節, 用之, 著爲定制. 四年十一月二十一日, 欽奉聖旨 "《御製廣薦佛會榜文》, 命都省出榜, 曉諭天下, 官民士庶人等. "

This was how the Eight Lyric Poems were composed: first, canonical materials were assembled. Zongle was ordered to compile and pen the lyric poems. Ming Taizu formulated the titles. Later, the Ministry of Ceremonies set a melody to the song for performance. Also, Ming Taizu had the "Yuzhi Guangjian Fohui bangwen" 御製廣薦佛會榜文 (Imperial Notice on the Ceremony of Extensive Offerings) posted across the realm so that it would be understood by all. The notices for the ordinary Water and Land Rites were only posted when the rites were carried out, but the notice for the Mount Jiang Dharma Service was posted across the realm. Therefore, it is clear that this rite was uniquely a national sacrifice.

Below, according to Song Lian's "Jiangshan Guangjian Fohui ji",[10] there was a restoration of the ritual procedures for the Mount Jiang Dharma Service at the time:

1. Publishing a notice. On the twenty-first day of the eleventh lunar month in year 4 of Hongwu (1371.12.28), the "Yuzhi Guangjian Fohui bangwen" was posted in every region of the realm.
2. Buddhist purification. In the winter of 1371, Ming Taizu lodged in quarters designed for this and spent a month abstaining from pungent herbs and meat as well as the company of his wives and consorts.
3. Dispatching officials. The Middle Secretaries Wang Guangyang 汪廣洋 (?-1379) and Hu Weiyong 胡惟庸 (?-1380) were dispatched to proclaim the text at the shrines of city gods. "Let words reach the various Realms of Darkness so that all beings will all gather together."[11]
4. The sacrifice text was announced. On the thirteenth day of the first lunar month in spring of year five of Hongwu (1372.2.17), Ming Taizu draped himself in formal robes and went before the Shrine of Heaven with his ministers and attendants. The Chief of Directorate of Palace Seals Liang Zizhong 梁子忠 (d.u.) initiated the text compiled by Ming Taizu, and marked [the commentary piece] with the Emperor's seal. Ming Taizu prostrated and after burning incense at the cauldron prostrated again. Ming Taizu personally read the text and bestowed it unto Secretary Tao Kai 陶凱 (d.u.) of the Bureau of Ties. Tao Kai held it and went out from the North Gate on the Yellow Road and placed the text within the Dragon Carriage, which was accompanied by a music-playing Dharma procession that led the carriage to Mount Jiang. Bai'an Lijin of Tianjie si and the abbot of Jiangshan si, Xingrong 行容 (d.u.) and others, carried incense and flowers to receive the procession of Tao Kai. Later, Wanjin took the

10 Ibid., 116-118.

11 Ibid., 116: 俾神達諸幽冥, 期以畢集.

text and entered into the Jeweled Shrine of the Great Hero (i.e., the shrine to the Buddha) and started reciting scriptures. He recited the text before the image of the Buddha and burnt it after. The eminent monks moved back and recited from the *tripiṭaka* for several days.

5. Welcoming the Buddha. On the fifteenth day (1372.2.19) after the eminent monks carried out the dharma service, Ming Taizu put on his robes and jade ornament, going before the Shrine of the Great Hero of Mount Jiang and stood facing north toward the image of Śākyamuni. The ministers wore Buddhist robes and stood at his sides. When worshipping at the Shrine of Heaven, the ministers wore court robes. At the temple of Mount Jiang, the ministers wore Buddhist robes. It is clear that they were conforming to Buddhist conventions. The conductor raised the baton, and the "Buddhist Tune of Benefiting the World" (*Shanshi qu* 善世曲) was played. Ming Taizu and various officials paid obeisance to show welcome. And then the "Tune of Illuminating the Belief" (*Zhaoxin qu* 昭信曲) was played, and Taizu kneeled down and presented incense and offerings.
6. First ritual offerings. Ming Taizu and his ministers bowed, and the band played "Song of Extending Mercy" (*Yanci qu* 延慈曲). At the same time they paired this with a "Dance of Pleasing the Buddhas (*Yuefo zhi wu* 悅佛之舞)." There were twenty people who danced. Above their hands they carried offerings of clothing, foods and other items, including incense, lamps, pearls and jades, clear water, blue lotuses, water peaches, and fine teas. They danced with accompanying music. Ming Taizu bent a knee and offered pure food and historical annals. He made his vows and again bowed.
7. The middle offerings: The Song of Dharma Joy (*Faxi qu* 法喜曲) was played and the Dance of Pleasing the Buddhas (*Yuefo wu* 悅佛舞) was given. The head of Court of Imperial Entertainment Xu Xingzu 徐興祖 (1327-1402) offered the meal.
8. The final offerings: The Song of *Dhyāna* Pleasure (*Chanyue qu* 禪悅曲) was played and the dance of Pleasing the Buddhas was performed. The head of Court of Imperial Entertainment Xu Xingzu offered the meal. The three rituals of offerings were accompanied by the same dance, although the tune and music differed. When it came to the latter two occasions, the historical annals were not offered, and Xu Xingzu, on Taizong's behalf, served the meals. Upon the completion of the three rituals, Taizong turned back to the rest quarters, and the officials left the scene.
9. Recitation of mantras. The eminent monks circumambulated the Shrine of the Great Hero while reciting mantras three times.

10. Summoning spirits. "First, dig sixty holes in mountainous and rocky land, and apply chalk to each of them. Then, have five hundred of soldiers carry hot water to fill the holes. The water will emit a cloud of vapour, and the monks invite spirits and ghosts to take a bath. Then burn the garment of rites, and lead them with a colorful umbrella and Dharma music to the gate of Three Liberations. Fifty steps into the gate a square altar is built, four *chi*s high. Ascend the altar and sit facing east, and the Imperial Attendant shall kneel down facing west; having received the imperial decree, they gather the spirits and ghosts, and provide an admonishing speech."[12] This illustrates the process of summoning spirits. First they dig a hole and fill it with white earth with steam vapors rising into clouds. This is summoning departed souls into the bath. "Burning robes" means making the departed souls wear the garments of rites and then lead them into the Three Gates of Liberation with painted banners and Dharma instruments. Within the Three Gates of Liberation was constructed a tall altar. Ming Taizu ascended the altar and decreed for the spirits that they be freed from wrongdoings and bindings.
11. Preaching of Dharma, reception of precepts, and offerings of food. After Ming Taizu made decrees, the departed souls were led to hear the Dharma preached by Zongle. Then, they were led to Huiri 慧日 (1291-1379) to take the precepts, and finally they were led to receive the food offerings. A cleric said mantras over the meal and altogether forty-nine meals were laid out.
12. Withdrawing the food. The "Jiangshan Guangjian Fohui ji" refers to "withdrawing the beans", which means taking away the offered items. At this time, it was already midnight. Ming Taizu went into the Shrine of the Great Hero with his ministers following behind. The band played *Song of Universal Response* (*Bianying qu* 遍應曲). The attendants withdrew the offerings of food, and then Ming Taizu and his ministers bowed.
13. Sending off the Buddha. The band played "Song of Marvelous Salvation" (*Miaoji qu* 妙濟曲), and then Ming Taizu and his ministers bowed.
14. Burning of texts and paper money. The band played "Song of Benevolence Perfected" (*Shancheng qu* 善成曲). Ming Taizu and his ministers then went before the fire offerings and after the items had been burnt, they returnd to the shrine. Ming Taizu and his ministers then withdrew.

12 Ibid., 117:
初, 斫山石地成坎六十, 漫以堊. 至是, 令軍卒五百負湯實之. 湯蒸氣成雲, 諸僧速幽爽入浴, 焚象衣, 使其更以彩幢、法樂, 引至三解脫門. 門內五十步築方壇, 高四尺. 上升壇東向坐, 侍儀使浦博西向跪. 受詔而出, 集幽爽而戒飭之.

As a result of Ming Taizu personally attending the Mount Jiang Dharma Service, the Water and Land Rite became by characteristic a national sacrifice. In particular, looking at the similarities between a traditional "suburban sacrifice" and the "Mount Jiang Dharma Service", we see the following:

| Suburban Sacrifice (*Jiaosi* 郊祀) | | | Mount Jiang Dharma Service | | |
|---|---|---|---|---|---|
| | Song (*Yuequ* 樂曲) | Dance (*Wu* 舞) | | Song (*Yuequ* 樂曲) | Dance (*Wu* 舞) |
| Welcoming the gods (*Yingshen* 迎神) | Song of *Zhonghe* (*Zhonghe qu* 中和曲) | | Welcoming the Buddha (*Yingfo* 迎佛) | Song of benefiting the world (*Shanshi qu* 善世曲) | |
| Presenting silk (*Dianbo* 奠帛) | Song of *Xiaohe* (*Xiaohe qu* 蕭和曲) | | Burning incense and presenting silk (*Xunxiang dianbi* 熏薌奠幣) | Song of illuminating the belief (*Zhaoxin qu* 昭信曲) | |
| Presenting food (*Jinzu* 進俎) | Song of *Ninghe* (*Ninghe qu* 凝和曲) | | | | |
| First ritual offerings (*Chuxian* 初獻) | Song of *Taihe* (*Taihe qu* 泰和曲) | Dance of Military Achievements (*Wugong wu* 武功舞) | First ritual offerings (*Chuxian* 初獻) | Song of Extending Mercy (*Yanci qu* 延慈曲) | Dance of Pleasing the Buddhas (*Yuefo wu* 悅佛舞) |
| The middle offerings (*Yaxian* 亞獻) | Song of *Yuhe* (*Yuhe qu* 豫和曲) | Dance of Moral Indoctrination (*Wende wu* 文德舞) | The middle offerings (*Yaxian* 亞獻) | Song of Dharma Joy (*Faxi qu* 法喜曲) | Dance of Pleasing the Buddhas(*Yuefo wu* 悅佛舞) |
| The final offerings (*Zhongxian* 終獻) | Song of *Ninghe* (*Ninghe qu* 凝和曲) | Dance of Moral Indoctrination (*Wende wu* 文德舞) | The final offerings (*Zhongxian* 終獻) | Song of *dhyāna* Pleasure (*Chanyue qu* 禪悅曲) | Dance of Pleasing the Buddhas(*Yuefo wu* 悅佛舞) |
| Withdrawing the food (*Chezhuan* 撤饌) | Song of *Yonghe* (*Yonghe qu* 雍和曲) | | Withdrawing the food (*Chedou* 撤豆) | *Song of Universal Response* (*Bianying qu* 遍應曲) | |
| Sending off the gods (*Songshen* 送神) | Song of *Anhe* (*Anhe qu* 安和曲) | | Sending off the Buddha (*Songfo* 送佛) | Song of Marvelous Salvation (*Miaoji qu* 妙濟曲) | |

| Suburban Sacrifice (*Jiaosi* 郊祀) | | Mount Jiang Dharma Service | |
|---|---|---|---|
| Burning of texts and paper money (*Wangliao* 望燎) | Song of *Shihe* (*Shihe qu* 時和曲) | Burning of texts and paper money (*Wangliao* 望燎) | Song of Benevolence Perfected (*Shancheng qu* 善成曲) |

From the above comparison, we can see that the suburban sacrifice in the order of rites are basically similar. There are only two differences between them. First, the Mount Jiang Dharma Service added prayers for the deceased, and therefore it includes rituals for summoning spirits, offering food, preaching the Dharma, and receiving the precepts. Second, the prayers for the Mount Jiang Dharma Service are directed to buddhas and bodhisattvas, which is why first they would make prayers and offerings to them and adorn the shrine hall, and only then make three sacrifices to the ancient kinds of the past. To sum up, the Mount Jiang Dharma Service primarily constituted a Water and Lands Rite that absorbed the structure of the rituals of suburban sacrifices, and moreover restructured the music and dances, thereby realizing the aim of being a national sacrifice.

### 1.2 *Ming Taizu's Religious Views on Spirits and the Demands of "Rites" and "Time" in Sacrifices*

On the one hand, Ming Taizu held the Mount Jiang Dharma Service as important in order to bring an end to the popular disorder that followed the conflict after the collapse of the Yuan dynasty while addressing social disruptions, which placated popular sentiments and brought about stability. Ming Taizu's "Yuzhi Jiang Shan si guangjian Fohui wen" states the following:

> We were born to a farmer family and raised by Buddhists since a tender age. Unexpectedly, we faced great disorder and had no alternative but to join the army, an experience that turned out to be as long as two decades. During those days, when rivalling with the groups of warlords, we were committed to troop training and to save the people from the unrest. Now, disasters and chaos have been cleared away, and the country has been pacified; we are not swinging between Buddhist monks and Daoist priests, nor have we been reckless with our ignorance and offered sacrifices to ghosts and spirits. It has always my view that sacrifice must be undertaken according to the proprieties, and if sacrifices need to be offered, it must be scheduled on proper dates. We still meditate on the

> warriors and civilians having suffered a catastrophe. The dead were either subject to the blade or devoured by flood or flames; or they hung themselves or threw themselves into the river when driven into desperate situations; or they fled into the mountain and forest, injured by snakes or mauled by tigers. Some perished in natural disasters, and some died from missing their families, as well as diseases. In some cases of these diseased people, the whole family died out, and the souls received no sacrifices and have not any shelter; in some cases, their families survive, but they could not take care of them any more; and in other cases, their parents, wives, and children fled and were scattered to different places because of warfare, and how could the unsettled alive manage to make sacrifices? These ghosts and souls, we reckon, without exceptions, are all moaning in the winds and rains or, on fine days, wailing under the Moon and stars. Some may have gone astray in the darkness, having no way to liberate themselves.[13]

The commencement of the Mount Jiang Dharma Service exercised an important function in putting at ease popular will, which is why Ming Taizu adopted contemporary Buddhist services as a means of sending off lone ghosts. This was also particularly connected to his experience of having ordained as a monk.

That the Mount Jiang Dharma Service could become a national sacrifice on the other hand is intimately related to the religious views on spirits on the part of Ming Taizu. Generally speaking, the Son of Heaven (Emperor) would execute sacrifices to the gods and spirits of Heaven and Earth, as well as carry out rites at the altars of state, none of which were primarily carried out as Buddhist rituals. In the Mount Jiang Dharma Service, however, Ming Taizu also ascended the altar and read decrees in a ritualized manner meant to summon spirits. It is clear that he was intent on controlling the present life and afterlife, which confirms his belief in the existence of spirits. When establishing the fundamental policies for governing the nation, Ming Taizu handed down decrees in search of proposals from his ministers, with titles such as "Wen shengxue"

13 *Jinling fancha zhi*, 3.311-312:
朕本農夫, 自幼托身佛門, 忽經大亂, 不得已而從戎於二十年矣. 向與群雄並驅之時, 務在操兵整壄, 救民於徬徨之中. 今禍亂已平, 天下已定, 未嘗朝僧暮道, 妄祀鬼神, 有所祀必以禮, 有所祭必以時. 尙慮軍民, 身經大難. 凡死者或遭兵刃, 或陷水火, 或迫於危急而自縊投河, 或潛入山林而蛇傷虎咬, 或天災而殞滅, 或思父母妻子因疾而亡身, 凡此諸等死者, 或蒲門滅絕, 無祭無依, 或雖有眷屬, 不能顧念, 或有父母妻子因兵流離, 生者未安, 死者誰爲之祭. 朕以己心度之, 此等鬼魂遇天陰時, 莫不呻吟於風雨之間; 遇晴明之時, 莫不悲號於星月之下. 或因生前作惡, 留連冥冥之中, 無由自脫.

問聖學 (Inquiry on Sacred Learning), "Wen xingfa" 問刑罰 (Inquiry on Punishments), "Wen Tianshi" 問天時 (Inquiry on Heaven and Time), "Wen tiandi guishen" 問天地鬼神 (Inquiry on the Spirits and Gods of Heaven and Earth), and "Wen Fo Xian" 問佛仙 (Inquiry on Buddhas and Immortals). In the third of these, he ordered the scholars to answer whether there existed spiritual connections between Heaven and humanity. In "Wen tiandi guishen" and "Chiwen wenxue zhi shi" 敕問文學之士 (Imperial Inquiry on Learned Men), he orders his scholars to answer whether spirits exist, and under what sort of circumstances they reveal themselves, in addition to whether or not they can preside over human fortunes. This shows a brilliant demeanour that reminds one of Emperor Wu (r. 141-87 BCE) of the Han dynasty who sought suggestions from Dong Zhongshu 董仲舒 (179-104 BCE). Ming Taizu later produced the "Songjing lun" 誦經論 (Discussion on Recitation of Scripture), "Shidao lun" 釋道論 (Discussion on the Exposition of the Way), "Sanjiao lun" 三教論 (Discussion on the Three Teachings), "Ganlu lun" 甘露論 (Discussion on Nectar), "Guishen youwu lun" 鬼神有無論 (Discussion on the Existence of Spirits and Gods), "Tiansheng simin lun" 天生斯民論 (Discussion on "Heaven Giving Life to People"), and "Xiujiao lun" 修教論 (Discussion on Cultivation of Teachings), all of which were answers to questions of a spiritual connection between Heaven and humanity, as well as spirits and gods. These ideas became conscious expressions of the Ming dynasty. Ming Taizu in the "Guishen youwu lun" states the following:

> Ghosts and spirits are either highly active or otherwise highly inactive. This is why the ancient sagely kings who established canons for sacrifices believed them to exist like this. Concerning the Way of activity and inactivity, they believed there was something that could be done and then accomplished it. Why is it so? There are those who died a proper death and there are also those who did not, and there are those who died at an opportune moment and those who did not. What are the causes of failing to die a proper death? There are those who perished in the prime of life and those who expired with grievances, and these two kinds of people did not meet proper deaths. Due to their human affairs in the world remaining unfinished, they remain active. As to those who met a proper death, since their human affairs have finished, they are inactive. This is only a brief description. The matters I proposed above, with various details, are all cases where things could be done and were finally done.[14]

14 Ibid., 1.113-114:
其鬼神之事, 未嘗無甚顯而甚寂, 所以古之哲王立祀典者, 以其有之而如是. 其於

There was great governance of the whole nation during the time of Yao and Shun. Few people died, so the world was without wandering ghosts. After the Qin and Han, there were so many dead from wars that many spirits appeared. If people believed that there were no spirits, people would have no fear of Heaven and Earth, and be ashamed to face their ancestors. Ming Taizu therefore emphasized the following: "Now spirits suddenly appear and vanish. Some people observe them. Whether it is fortune or misfortune, it will not be far in future. Could you not believe that they exist in myriad forms, crying out?"[15] At the same time, Ming Taizu sincerely believed in cause and effect (karma), thinking that "it is difficult to escape from settled karma, and the fruits of karmic retribution are obvious"[16]. We can see here how karmic theory functioned as a means to educate the populace.

Ming Taizu therefore very much emphasized the "rites" and "timing" of sacrifices to spirits. His "Yuzhi Jiang Shan si guangjian Fohui wen" states the following:

> What has been passed down from antiquity to the present concerning making sacrifices to ghosts and spirits, as we call tell, isn't it of importance? Dealing with ghosts and spirits demands propriety and timing. One should not trespass his status or violate the propriety or dismiss the importance of proper time. Do not disregard the existence of ghosts and spirits; otherwise, when one becomes a ghost or spirit, the situation will become difficult. Being a spirit means being intelligent and righteous, and changing and transforming unfathomably. When granting weal and woe, they do not discriminate between personal relations. The worldly people, however, are ignorant and greedy, and their mind of desire is vast, so much so that they trespass statuses and violate propriety. They do not know the key to supplicating spirits by piety lies in propriety and right timing.[17]

---

顯寂之道, 必有爲而爲. 夫何故？蓋爲有不得其死者, 有得其死者; 有得其時者, 有不得其時者. 不得其死者何？爲壯而無, 屈而滅, 斯二者乃不得其死也, 蓋因人事而未盡, 故顯. 且得其死者, 以其人事盡而矣, 故寂. 此云略耳. 且前所奏者, 其狀若干, 皆有爲而作.

15 Ibid., 1.115:
今鬼忽顯忽寂, 所在某人見之, 非福即禍, 將不遠矣. 其於千態萬狀, 呻吟悲號, 可不信有之哉.

16 Ibid., 1.119: 定業難逃矣, 果報昭然矣.

17 Ibid., 3.310:
觀自古至今相傳, 祭禮鬼神之事, 豈不重乎？然事鬼神必有禮有時, 毋犯分、毋越禮, 毋非時、毋昧於鬼神. 若昧於鬼神, 則爲鬼神亦難矣. 且聰明正直, 變化不

One was to not violate conventions of portion, rites, timing, and/or disregard the presence of ghosts and spirits. "Rites" refers to the order of rites of the sacrifice. "Timing" refers to the time when the sacrifice is performed. The spirits will only react when the rites and timing of the sacrifice are aligned.

It was through the Mount Jiang Dharma Service that Ming Taizu summoned the Buddhists of the early Ming to Nanjing, which no doubt assembled the power of the Buddhist world in contemporary Jiangnan. This was also a conciliatory policy aimed at the Buddhist world. On the other hand, the eminent monks participated in the Mount Jiang Dharma Service, which was a national sacrifice, carrying out a state act of sacrifice and prayer whereby the primary power of Buddhists was placed under imperial governance. This notably functioned to consolidate and regulate Buddhism during the early Ming. At the same time, the Mount Jiang Dharma Service extended the influence of Buddhism at court among ministers and to wider society. It laid an incredibly important foundation for Buddhist services, such as the Water and Land Rite, to become popular during the Ming-Qing period. Moreover, Ming Taizu promoted the consolidation of Buddhist services through organizing the rituals of the Mount Jiang Dharma Service in response to the requirements concerning "rites" and "time" in relation to sacrificing to the spirits.

### 1.3 *Regulation and Promotion of Buddhist Services by Ming Taizu*

Ming Taizu, named Zhu Yuanzhang, was the founding emperor of the Ming dynasty. Having been a monk, he was keenly interested in Buddhism. From him, government policies toward Buddhism as well as its models originated. From the Yuan dynasty onward, esoteric and exoteric Dharma practices flourished among the common populace. The people who engaged in these activities were mixed. Therein frustrated communities, including the White Lotus Teachings 白蓮教 and White Cloud Sect 白雲宗 frequently carried out nominally Buddhist services to delude people. Zhu Yuanzhang reflected on the shortcomings of the Yuan dynasty's veneration of Tibetan Buddhism. He divided Buddhist temples and monks into three types (meditation or Chan, lecturing, and doctrinal), which addressed the on-the-ground situation of Buddhism during the early Ming. This continued with the Yuan policy of dividing temples according to their assigned functions. The *Yuan shi* 元史 (History of Yuan) states, "The command of all monasteries in the realm will come under the inner and outer Court for the Spread of Governance: namely, Chan,

---

測之謂神. 禍福所施, 必不以親疏而異. 但世人愚而貪, 欲心浩大, 遂至犯分越禮. 不知以敬求神, 在於有禮有時也.

FIGURE 33 1457 stele inscribed with "Eunuch Zheng He 鄭和" in Lingyan Chan Monastery 靈岩禪寺 on Mount Guji 谷積山, Beijing.

doctrine, and *vinaya*. Each will maintain its respective activities."[18] However, Zhu Yuanzhang promoted these monastic divisions through compelled government order. In the fifth lunar month of 1382, he issued the following decree:

> When establishing Buddhist monasteries, all dynasties in history divided them into three kinds, namely Chan monasteries, exposition monasteries, and teaching monasteries. Chan monasteries authorize no words or letters, and only [permit] seeing one's nature as the tenet; exposition monasteries are oriented toward illuminating the purport and doctrines of the scriptures; and teaching monasteries expansively promulgate the rituals taught by the Buddha to benefit and liberate beings, to eliminate all bad karma committed in this life, and cleanse the guilt done by the dead. All are meant to edify the worldly people.[19]

"Chan" refers to Chan Buddhism. Chan Buddhism is based upon the idea that one does not rely upon texts, but rather one sees one's own nature and thereby attains buddhahood. "Lecturing" refers to the Buddhist traditions that explain Buddhist doctrine, such as Tiantai and Huayan. "Doctrinal" refers to the Buddhist traditions that recite mantras, which developed into the esoteric and exoteric Dharma practices of "Yoga" that quelled negative karma and facilitated the passing of the dead. In this manner, monks were appropriately classified as Chan, lecturing or doctrinal.

The division and regulation of monasteries and monks by Ming Taizu also included special distinctions in terms of styles of dress. Fascicle sixty-seven of the *Ming shi* 明史 (History of Ming) states the following:

> In year 14 of Hongwu (1381), it was established that Chan monks will always wear tea-brown garments and jade-colored robes with blue stripes. Lecturing monks will always wear jade-colored garments and light-red robes with green stripes. Doctrinal monks will always wear black garments and light-red robes with black stripes. The monastic officers complied with this. Only monastic overseers will wear green emblems on their robes, and their rings will be adorned with gold.[20]

---

18 *Yuan shi*, 202.4524: 天下寺院之領於內外宣政院, 曰禪、曰教、曰律, 則固各守其業.

19 *Shi jian Jigu lüe xuji*, *T* no. 2038, 49: 2.932a7-11:
佛寺之設, 歷代分爲三等：曰禪、曰講、曰教. 其禪不立文字, 必見性者, 方是本宗; 講者務明諸經旨義; 教者演佛利濟之法, 消一切現造之業, 滌死者宿作之愆, 以訓世人.

20 *Ming shi* 67.1656:
洪武十四年, 定禪僧, 茶褐常服, 青條玉色袈裟; 講僧, 玉色常服, 綠條淺紅袈裟; 教僧, 皂常服, 黑條淺紅袈裟. 僧官如之. 惟僧錄司官, 袈裟綠文及環皆飾以金.

Not only this, Ming Taizu also issued a special order as follows:

> Now appoint the monk Xingguo 行果 (d.u.) to the post of Interpreting the Teachings of the Left (*zuo chanjiao* 左闡教) and the monk Rujin 如錦 (d.u.) to that of Awakened to the Doctrine of the Right (*you jueyi* 右覺義), who head for Nengren si 能仁寺 to set up a "Sanctum of the Buddha" (*yinggong daochang* 應供道場). Monks from all Monasteries Responding to Requests in the capital and provinces, larger or smaller, are all allowed to come to Nengren si and stay together, reading scriptures, and conduct all kinds of Buddhist services. If there are those who do not follow this but privately conduct Buddhist rituals under other names, officers of Nengren si will investigate their guilt. As for those who travel far away, or read scriptures, or live on alms begging, or employed by the commoners, these monks are not covered by this rule.[21]

This made Nengren si a specially designated temple with monastic officers holding special responsibilities. They held a monopoly on all Buddhist activities. Nengren si would enact punitive measures if such activities were carried out in private.

Ming Taizu's regulation of doctrinal temples and monks was comprehensive. A year after designating Nengren si as special, in the fifth lunar month of 1383, he formally issued the following decree:

> For the present time, exoteric and esoteric rituals of the Yoga and various secret mantras should be thoroughly checked and corrected and validated as established practices once for all. They should then be implemented in all monasteries of the country, to be followed for eternity and be resorted to by filial descendants for ancestral remembrance and by folks in local areas for pious invocation. Let the Bureau of Monastic Affairs issue an official document to abbots of all monasteries and inform the monastic officers in various regions. Let them all send monks to the capital and receive the ritual formulary from the Palace Treasury. Let the monks bring it back to learn and practice. After three years, all monks who practice the Yoga come to the capital will be tested in exam; only those who have fully grasped the established ritual procedures are authorized as

---

21 *Shi jian Jigu lüe xuji*, *T* no. 2038, 49:2.932a12-17:
見除僧行果爲左闡教, 如錦爲右覺義, 前去能仁開設應供道場. 凡京城內外大小應付寺院僧, 許入能仁寺會住看經, 作一切佛事. 若不由此, 另起名色, 私作佛事者, 就仰能仁寺官問罪. 若遠方雲遊, 看經抄化, 及百姓自願用者, 不拘是限.

> monks. As for those who do not understand [the ritual procedures], allow them to read the text and, after a full year, to take the exam again. If there are those who are good at memorization and recitation and had no monastic certificates, let them visit the government after the exam and be granted the certificates. If they could not pass the exam, make them commoners (laity).[22]

The emperor's original intention was to promote the regularization of Buddhist services, thereby giving public status to "monks on call" (*fuying seng* 赴應僧) and "Yoga monks" (*yuqie seng* 瑜伽僧). The court first organized the Monk Recorder (*Senglu si* 僧錄司) to produce unified regulations for ritual manuals that were promulgated throughout the monasteries of the realm. Dharma services aimed to promote ethics of filial sacrifices to ancestors and to fulfill the popular need for religious rituals. Abbots of each head monastery had to dispatch monks to the capital to receive the ritual manuals. After three years, all Yoga monks had to come to the capital to participate in an exam. It was through execution of rituals and strict testing that they could become formal "doctrinal monks" and only then be qualified to perform rituals for people. This regulation not only promoted a process of unifying rituals, it moreover provided strict requirements to qualify as a "doctrinal monk".

Dharma rituals were carried out as customary practices of a social nature. They were important symbols in the transmission of Buddhism. Ming Taizu's consolidation and regulation of Yoga monks, on one hand, was to clean up the disorder of post-Yuan Buddhism, and on the other, was reflective of problems that existed in the developmental process of Buddhism during the early Ming.[23] The "Shenming fojiao bangce" 申明佛教榜冊 (Placard Elucidating the Buddha's Teachings) established many regulations and restrictions on monks engaging in rituals.[24]

1. It iterates the need to respect the regulations governing rituals established in Hongwu 16 (1383), stressing that ritual performances, "in the Realm of Light, can communicate to people, and, in the Realm of Dark-

---

22 Ibid., 2.932c24-933a5:
即今,瑜伽顯密法事儀式及諸真言密咒,盡行考較穩當,可爲一定成規,行於天下諸山寺院,永遠遵守,爲孝子順孫慎終追遠之道,人民州里之間祈禳伸請之用.恁僧錄司行文書與諸山住持,並各處僧官知會,俱各差僧赴京,於內府關領法事儀式,回還習學.後三年,凡持瑜伽教僧,赴京試驗之時,若於今定成規儀式通者,方許爲僧.若不省解,讀念且生,須容週歲再試.若善於記誦,無度牒者,試後就當官給與.如不能者,發爲民庶.

23 Zhou, *Zhengzhi wenhua*, 119.

24 *Shi jian Jigu lüe xuji, T* no. 2038, 49: 2.936a4-c13; *Jinling fancha zhi* 2.231-239.

ness, can communicate to spirits."[25] Improper forms could not allow for communication with spirits.

2. With respect to "Yoga monks", there were concrete regulations governing how much income they could receive as compensation. "Each day a single monk could receive 500 *wen* for their services. As for monks who strike the chime, write commentaries, and perform the ritual of invocation, each will receive 1,000 *wen*."[26]

3. With respect to the fees for recitation at services, this was based upon the regulations outlined in the *Daochang zhupin jingzhou bushi zeli* 道場諸品經咒佈施則例 (Conventions for Offerings During Various Recitations at Temples).

   *Huayan jing* 華嚴經 (*Avataṃsaka-sūtra*, i.e., Flower Adornment *Sūtra*): 10,000 *wen*.
   *Bore jing* 般若經 (*Prajñāpāramitā-sūtra*): 10,000 *wen*.
   Buddhist or non-Buddhist mantras: 2,000 *wen*.
   *Niepan jing* 涅槃經 (*Mahāparinirvāṇa-sūtra*): 2,000 *wen*.
   *Liang Wu chan* 梁武懺 (Liang Wu Repentance): 1,000 *wen*.
   *Lian jing* 蓮經 (Lotus *Sūtra*): 1,000 *wen*.
   *Kongque jing* 孔雀經 (*Mahāmāyūrī-vidyārājñī*): 1,000 *wen*.
   *Da baoji jing* 大寶積經 (*Ratnakūṭa-sūtra*): Each part 10,000 *wen*.
   *Shuichan* 水懺 (*Water Repentance*): 500 *wen*.
   *Lengyan zhou* 楞嚴咒 (*Śūraṃgama-dhāraṇī*): One gathering for 500 *wen*.[27]

   The above money was distributed with the reciting monk receiving one third and the others in his assembly receiving an equal share each of the remaining two thirds. Even if a wandering monk happened upon a service, he would also be entitled to a part of the money. However, if the benefactor was pleased with the service, they could make additional offerings, or if the benefactors relatives and friends made offerings of meals or similar offerings, it was not subject to the above restrictions.

4. Priestly tasks such as installing Buddhist images and making offerings of incense and lamps: 1,000 *wen*.

5. There were strict regulations governing the forms of documents issued by monasteries. Nobody was to create things for additional fees, nor were they to waste money.

---

25 Ibid., 2.936b13-14: 明則可以達人, 幽則可以達鬼.

26 Ibid., 2.936b22-23:
每一日、每一僧錢五百文, 主磬、寫疏、召請三執事每僧各一千文.

27 *Jinling fancha zhi* 2.233.

6. At the same time the monastic administrators could not illegally restrict monks in common temples with these regulations: "Give latitude to monks who have expansive karmic association, who have noble spiritual attainment and profound practice, and who have intimate knowledge about the purports of various scriptures. Allow benefactors who have admiration for them to offer meals and gifts, and do not be tied down by the rules."[28] This reveals the liveliness and completeness of the regulations.
7. The tenets and efficacy of the Yoga teachings were repeatedly emphasized. "The esoteric and exoteric teachings of the Yoga must be practiced and observed with moral purity, and the pronunciation of each and every syllable should not be mistaken. When invocation is delivered, beings of the Ghost Destiny in the Darkness are all informed and they arrive instantly. This type of teachings could not be practiced by the defiled and filthy body of the worldlings."[29] There were many among the commoners who emulated the Yoga monks, referred to as "virtuous friends" (*shanyou* 善友). This had to be banned since it was impure with respect to the Buddhadharma and did not work well in relation to the esoteric and exoteric teachings.

In terms its effect on society, Yoga-doctrinal monks primarily served people in society in accordance with what was needed ritually (such as dispelling disasters or funerary services), thereby these monks and believers joined to form a market that was operated by religious supply and demand. Their defects could be easily seen as they appeared. On one hand there existed doctrinal monks who sought large amounts of money and wealth from devotees, and on the other the prices for their services differed, possibly producing unequal distribution of wealth among the doctrinal monks, which then led to conflicts in the community. Ming Taizu therefore made clear regulations governing the economic income that could be received by doctrinal monks reciting scriptures.

## 2 Buddhist Services and Monastic Regulations under the Ming-Qing Periods

Buddhism in the Ming and Qing perfected and revised many regulations atop a foundation of Buddhist laws that were popular during the Song and Yuan

28 *Shi jian Jigu lüe xuji*, *T* no. 2038, 49: 2.936c4-6:
從有緣僧, 有道高行深者, 或經旨精通者, 檀越有所慕, 從其齋禮, 毋以法拘.

29 Ibid., 2.936c7-9:
瑜伽之教, 顯密之法, 非清淨持守, 字無訛謬. 呼召之際, 幽冥鬼趣, 咸使聞知, 即時而至, 非垢穢之軀世俗所持者.

periods, in particular with respect to the liturgies of the two times (*er'shi kesong* 二時課誦), and the revision of the *Shuilu yigui* 水陸儀軌 (Water and Land Ritual Procedures). Modern Chinese monasteries employ the liturgical forms of Buddhism from the Ming and Qing.

### 2.1 *The Popularity and Disorder of Buddhist Services in the Ming and Qing*

After Ming Taizu divided monasteries into three types (Chan, lecturing, and doctrinal), doctrinal temples sprung up in the north and south. An example, the proportion of temples in the regions of Jiangnan: Huzhou county 湖州府 had 37 doctrinal temples, 6 lecturing temples, and 24 Chan temples, and 17 of uncertain affiliation, altogether totaling 84 temples. The combined number of temples and nunneries totaled 251. Gusu county 姑蘇府 had 71 doctrinal temples, 23 lecturing temples, 31 Chan temples, and some of uncertain affiliation, altogether totaling 131 temples, with the combined number of affiliated places totaling 558 temples.[30] From these numbers it is clear that doctrinal temples occupied the largest proportion and moreover were popular in regions of eastern China, in which Buddhism flourished and there existed a rich and populous economy.

The popularity of Buddhist services was connected to the strong demands of the Ming and Qing imperial households and common society. In 1407 under Ming Chengzu, the Empress Xu of Renxiao 仁孝徐皇后 (1362-1407) died of illness. A decree titled "Baoen si xiuguan zhai chi" 報恩寺修觀齋敕 (Decree for Establishing Purification Gathering at Baoen si) was issued, assembling monks of the realm to recite scriptures for a hundred days for her benefit. "Recently, Empress Renxiao passed away, and a ceremony of tribute and a great Assembly of All Beings were held, when monks were widely gathered to chant scriptures. In one hundred days, auspicious omens appeared."[31] Ming Chengzu hoped that through this purification gathering "she might quickly ascend the stage of awakening, benefiting beings and manifesting to aide my imperial household. By order of the Emperor. Hence this decree."[32] Ming Chengzu also organized Buddhist recitations of invocations, gathering together invocations circulating among the people in China as well as those translated from Sanskrit preserved in Tibetan from the Yuan dynasty, producing the *Dacheng jingzhou* 大乘經咒 (Invocations of Mahāyāna Scriptures). The head of the fascicle notes it was

30 Ryūchi, "Zhengce", 15.

31 *Jinling fancha zhi* 31.1080:
比者仁孝皇后崩逝, 舉薦揚之科, 啓無遮之會, 廣集僧伽諷揚經典, 百日之間, 嘉禎翕集.

32 Ibid., 1081: 期早登於覺地, 利生助化翼我皇家, 欽哉！故諭.

imperially organized. The fascicle includes five prefaces that were written by emperors in years 9 and 10 of Yongle. These scriptures and invocations may have been definitive editions espoused by people in the palace.[33]

The "Yongle yuzhi shuichan xu" 永樂御製水懺序 (Preface to the Yongle Imperially Sanctioned Water Repentance), from the first day of the seventh lunar month in year fourteen of Yongle (1416.7.24), states the following:

> *Samādhi* exists only in people's minds and needs not be sought anywhere else. We have written this piece to place it at the beginning of the work. Also, the work is going to be committed to print, as a means to benefit the world. This is drawing on the ocean of *samādhi*s to spread over the worlds as many as the sands of the Ganges and wash out the eons as many as all the atoms in the universe. Those who read this work, I suppose, would become cautious about their conducts.[34]

It is clear from Ming Chengzu's veneration and reliance upon Buddhist services that these services became incredibly important for celebrations and even court religious life. In particular we might note the empress dowager Cisheng 慈聖 (1546-1614). After Shenzong (r. 1572-1620) married, in 1581, she entrusted Hanshan Deqing 憨山德清 (1546-1623) to go to Mount Wutai to carry out a *Qi huangsi wuzhe dahui* 祈皇嗣無遮大會 (Unhindered Ceremony for the Imperial Line), from which it is clear that she devoutly cherished Buddhist services.

From the Ming-Qing period onwards, services that recited scriptures from the Tibetan tradition regularly increased following the proliferation of Tibetan Buddhism at court, but Chinese Buddhist services were also still popular at court.

For instance, the first fascicle of *Jin'ao tuishi biji* 金鰲退食筆記 (Writings of the Golden Sea Turtle and Post-Court Breakfast) states:

> The Chongzhi Hall 崇智殿 (the Advocacy of Wisdom) was renamed to Wanshan Hall 萬善殿 (Hall of Myriads of Goodness) during the Shunzhi era. It enshrined the statues of the various Buddhas of the Three Times. [The court] selected aged and virtuous palace eunuchs, dressed them in robes and tonsured them as monks, who burn incense and conduct services. When coming to the capital under the imperial decree, the two senior monks Muchen 木陳 (1596-1674) and Yulin 玉林 (1614-1675) resided in the Wanshan Hall. At the Middle Primordial Festival every year, an

33 Chen, "Yuqiejiao", 68.

34 "Yuzhi shuichan xu", *T* no. 1910, 45: 1.968a22-25.

> *Ullambana* Ceremony has been held. From the thirteenth to the fifteenth day [of the seventh month], lanterns are floated down in the river, junior eunuchs are asked to hold lotus leaves, inside which kindles are lit. With glowing green, [the lanterns] are set out on both the banks, numbering in the thousands. Lotus lanterns are made with coloured glaze, numbering several thousand, and going up and down with waves. Dragon boats sail in the mainstream, in which Buddhist music is played and meditative chanting is conducted.[35]

During the Shunzhi reign era (1644-1661), the Ullambana Festival was still carried out in the Qing court. Releasing lanterns on the river became a celebration in the imperial garden. Fascicle 161 of the "Qinding Daqing huidian zeli" 欽定大清會典則例 (Imperially Endorsed Precedents of the Collected Statutes of the Great Qing Dynasty) records that "during the three days before the imperial birthday and the three days after it, religious services are held."[36] It is clear that Buddhist services were a religious activity frequently carried out at court.

From the Ming-Qing period onward, repentance ceremonies flourished in common society. For instance, during the Wanli era, a lady surnamed Xue became ill in 1587 and before she faced her end she called a monk to do a repentance rite for her, before she finally died sitting upright, to be reborn in the western Pure Land.[37] Layman Du from the Wanping county of Shuntian, dedicated himself to recitation of the Buddha's name for three years and he knew of his impending end, and practiced repentance. He so earnestly recited the repentance text that he was strained to the limit from tears. He finally took a bit of water and died sitting upright carrying out repentance.[38]

At the same time the literati and commoners assembled communities in order to carry out repentance and recitations of invocations, such as Liu Yushou 劉玉受 (d.u.) from Changzhou 長洲. He recited the *Cundi dhāraṇī* (*Zhunti zhou* 准提咒) daily. When he participated in the civil service examination, he built an altar and recited the *dhāraṇī* for seven days. The result was that during the exam his "thoughts gushed forth like spring-water and it went superbly."[39]

---

35 *Jin'ao tuishi biji*, SKQS, 588: 1.411:
崇智殿 …… 本朝順治年間, 改爲萬善殿, 供三世佛像, 選老成內監披剃爲僧, 焚修香火. 木陳、玉林兩老衲奉召至京師, 曾居萬善殿. 每歲中元, 建盂蘭道場, 自十三日至十五日, 放河燈, 使小內監持荷葉燃燭其中, 青碧熠熠, 羅列兩岸, 以數千計. 又用琉璃作荷花燈數千盞, 隨波上下, 中流駕龍舟, 奏梵樂, 作禪誦.

36 *Qinding da Qing huidian zeli*, SKQS, 625: 161.245: 萬壽聖節前後三日皆啓建道場.

37 *Wangsheng ji*, *T* no. 2072, 51: 2.146a17-b1.

38 Ibid., 2.149b29-c7.

39 *Jushi zhuan*, XZJ no. 1623, 149: 47.977a7: 思如泉湧, 遂得雋.

In 1607, he became a *jinshi* 進士. Yushou, as a result of this, advocated recitation of the *Cundi Dhāraṇī* in his hometown, and his juniors joined him to form a *Cundi* club and built a *vihāra* on the site of Tang Yin's 唐寅 (1470-1524) residence in Suzhou and engaged in good work.[40]

Yu Chunxi 虞淳熙 (1553-1621), the vice director of the bureau of records of the Ministry of Official Personnel, was a native of Qiantang. After succeeding in the provincial examination, "he and his friends in the society recited the *Lianghuang chan*."[41] In 1583, he became a *jinshi*. He lived in the capital for a short time before his father passed away. As a result of this he decided to go into the mountains to cultivate spiritual practices as a way of repaying the kindness of his father. While residing in the mountains, he frequently fed the animals there.[42]

The popularity of Buddhist services was undoubtedly connected to a deep belief in the efficacy of various Buddhist services and rituals, such as funerary rites, and rituals directed at the eliminating disasters. For example, a ferocious tiger appeared in the vicinity of Yunqi si 雲棲寺 and injured people. Yunqi Zhuhong 雲棲袾宏 (1535-1615) "generated compassion and recited a thousand scrolls of scriptures, establishing a Yoga offering to bring relief. After this, the tiger did not injure anyone."[43] Fascicle two of the *Liunan suibi xu bi* 柳南隨筆續筆 (Continuance of Literary Notes by Liunan), written by Wang Yingkui 王應奎 (1683-1759/1760) in the Qing dynasty, records a story about "feeding a monk to get sons". In the late-Ming, one surnamed Wang from the Shantang 山塘 town of the Changshu 常熟 county was aged forty without any sons. He asked for teachings from Master Lianchi (i.e. Yunqi Zhuhong). Later at Yunqi si he built an altar for the Water and Land Rites in hopes of gaining sons.[44] The service of the "Yoga Flaming Mouth" (*yankou* 焰口) to placate the ferocious tiger and the Water and Land Rites reveals the popular religious consciousness.

The need for Buddhist services by the government and the whole of society led to their continual propagation in temples, with monks gaining quite a lot of income. As a result, Buddhist services became the primary activity of temples and monks. For instance, "Shi Zhiyuan deng santiao" 示直院等三條 (Three Dharma talks given to Auxiliaries and others) from the *Yunqi Dashi yigao* 雲棲大師遺稿 (Posthumous Writings of Master Yunqi) states the following:

40 Ibid., 47.977a7-15.

41 Ibid., 42.946a12: 與同社友誦《梁皇懺》.

42 Ibid., 42.946a07-947a06.

43 *Wulin fan zhi*, 2.44: 乃發悲愍, 諷經千卷, 設瑜伽施食津濟之, 自是虎不傷人.

44 *Liunan suibi xubi*, 2.163.

> The Water and Land Services are conducted successively, and scriptural recitation and repentance ritual are staged in succession. Search through the scriptural catalogues, they bustle around as if they were selecting officials; looking for scriptural masters, they are as busy as if they were announcing good news. The monastery treasurers work over night to keep accounting, only to allot money to different errands; transport workers shuttle back and forth, to do nothing but prepare all goods all goods for the services.[45]

It is clear that Buddhist services made temples and monks busy and profit-seeking. At the same time, since such services were easily learnt and practiced, people would make do so long as they could learn the recitations. The *Kaigu lu* 慨古錄 (Record of Lamenting the Past) by Zhanran Yuancheng 湛然圓澄 (1561-1627) states the following: "In recent times, new generations never do seated meditation, nor do they learn contemplative techniques. They only mimic the tone of masters and illicitly gained priesthood."[46] The number of Yoga-doctrinal monks engaged in worldly matters rapidly increased.

Driven by economic interests, the popularity of Buddhist services brought about numerous problems in the Ming-Qing period. For example, laypeople also learned and carried out the services. In the fifth lunar month of Yongle 10 (1412), Ming Taizong made the following decree to the Ministry of Rites:

> Buddhist monks and Daoist priests of the time mostly do not observe the precepts. When hosting religious services and scriptural recitation, they are always haggling over whether the reward is munificent or small. The monks and priests are devoid of the pious mind, and in some cases they even drink alcohol, eat meat, mess about, and debauch themselves, with little scruples. There are another kind of ignorant people, who falsely claim to be men of the Way. They delude all others without exception, and they live in mixture without any distinctions of sexes, offending the morals. During the years of Hongwu era, Buddhist monks and Daoist priests did not commit themselves to their patriarchs' norms, and there were secular men who practiced Yoga rituals and called themselves "Hearth-dwelling Men of the Way". There were strict prohibitions against them which was announced in government postings, and anyone that violates the prohibition would be mercilessly executed.[47]

---

45 *Lianchi dashi quanji*, 4759-4760.

46 *Kaigu lu*, XZJ no. 1273, 114: 1.740b13-14: 近來新學晚輩曾不坐禪, 又不習觀, 但學腔科, 濫登此位.

47 *Da Ming huidian*, XXSKQS, 791:104.66:
天下僧道, 多不守戒律, 間修齋誦經, 動輒較利厚薄, 又無誠心, 甚至飲酒食肉, 遊

Mixing monks and laity and seeking only profit runs completely contrary to the original intention underlying the idea that Buddhist services are a means to benefit others, and therefore this greatly destroyed Buddhism's pure image in society. In the reign era of Qianlong 乾隆 (1735-1795) during the Qing, several times Emperor Qianlong ordered the defrocking of "*yingfuseng* 應付僧 (Monks Responding to Requests) and *huoju daoshi* 火居道士 (Hearth-dwelling Men of the Way)." Qian Yong 錢泳 (1759-1844) in the *Sanjiao tongyuan* 三教同源 (Common Origin of the Three Teachings) points out that "monks use their services in order to cheat people for clothing and food. It is always for profit."[48] It is clear that the inundation of such services led to disaster.

Of course, the Buddhist world in the Ming and Qing continually attempted to restore and regulate Buddhist services in response to this chaos.

### 2.2 *The Production and Perfection of Buddhist Repentance in the Ming and Qing*

Ming Taizu emphasized the "rites" and "timing" of dharma services. He established anew the procedures for the Mount Jiang Dharma Service and moreover integrated all the Buddhist services of the country. This forced the Buddhist world to reform and perfect their existing repentance rituals. On the other hand, the popularity and disorder of Buddhist services also made eminent monks consider which elements of their repentance rituals were incomplete and incorrect. One after another they revised these rituals.

The compilation of repentance rituals of the Ming-and-Qing Buddhist world is the supplement to and perfection of the repentance rituals of the Song and Yuan periods. This includes the following titles:

Ming Dynasty:

- *Zhunti sanmei xingfa* 准提三昧行法 (The ritual practice of *Cundi samādhi*) and *Yaoshi sanmei xingfa* 藥師三昧行法 (The ritual practice of *Bhaiṣajya samādhi*) by Shoudeng 受登 (1607-1675), both one fascicle.
- *Wuzhong shifo xianghao chanyi* 吳中石佛相好懺儀 (The repentance ritual of the marks of the stone Buddha in Wuzhong) by Chuandeng 傳燈 (1554-1628)
- *Zhancha shan'e yebao jing xingfa* 占察善惡業報經行法 (The ritual practice of the *Sūtra on the Divination of the Effect of Good and Evil Actions*) and *Zanli Dizang pusa chanyuan yi* 贊禮地藏菩薩懺願儀 (The repentance ritual of

蕩荒淫, 略無顧忌. 又有無知愚民, 妄稱道人, 一槩蠱惑男女雜處無別, 敗壞風化. 洪武中, 僧道不務祖風, 及俗人行瑜珈法, 稱火居道士者. 俱有嚴禁, 即揭榜申明, 違者殺不赦.

48 *Lüyuan conghua*, 1.177.

FIGURE 34 Stele of the five patriarchs of the Fajie 法界 (i.e. Huayan 華嚴) tradition at the Zhixiang Monastery 至相寺 on Mount Zhongnan 終南山, erected in 2007.

praising the Kṣitigarbha bodhisattva) by Zhixu 智旭 (1599-1655), each one fascicle.
- *Yi Lengyan jiujing shi chan* 依楞嚴究竟事懺 (The repentance ritual according to the profound significance of *śūraṃgama*) by Shichan 釋禪 (1577-1632) in two fascicles.
- *Deyu longhua xiuzheng yi* 得遇龍華修證儀 (The practice ritual of encountering the dragon-flower assembly) by Ruxing 如惺 (fl.1600) in four fascicles.
- Qing dynasty:
- *Zhunti fan xiuxidi chanhui xuanwen* 准提焚修悉地懺悔玄文 (The repentance text of practicing burning incense and *siddhi* of *Cundi*) by Xia Daoren 夏道人 (d.u.) in one fascicle
- *Xiaozai yanshou Yaoshi chanfa* 消災延壽藥師懺法 (The repentance ritual of the calamity-erasing and life-prolonging Bhaiṣajya) and *Cibei Dizang pusa chanfa* 慈悲地藏菩薩懺法 (The repentance ritual of the compassionate Kṣitigarbha bodhisattva), both three fascicles each, by an unknown compiler.
- *Xigui xingyi* 西歸行儀 (Rites for returning to the West) in one fascicle by Gukun 古昆 (?-1892)
- *Sheli chanfa* 舍利懺法 (The repentance ritual of *śarīra*) by Jiseng 繼僧 (d.u.).
- *Gong zhutian keyi* 供諸天科儀 (The ritual practice of making offerings to the heavens), *Li sheli ta yishi* 禮舍利塔儀式 (The ritual practice of worshiping the *śarīra-stūpa*), and *Li Fo yishi* 禮佛儀式 (The ritual practice of worshiping the Buddha) by Hongzan 弘贊 (1612-1686).
- *Jingang jing keyi* 金剛經科儀 (The ritual practice of the Diamond *Sūtra*) by Jianji 建基 (d.u.) in one fascicle.
- *Shui chan fa suiwen lu* 水懺法隨聞錄 (The explanatory notes on the water repentance ritual) by Zhizheng 智證 (d.u.) in three fascicles.
- *Shuichan fa kezhu* 水懺法科註 (Commentary on the water repentance ritual) compiled and annotated by Xizong 西宗 (?-1688) in three fascicles.

### 2.2.1 The *Lengyan Shichan* 楞嚴事懺 (*Śūraṃgama* Repentance) by Shichan 釋禪 (1577-1632)

The monk Shichan of Xitan si 悉檀寺 on Mount Jizu 雞足山 in Yunnan during the Ming dynasty produced the *Yi Lengyan jiujing shi chan* 依楞嚴究竟事懺 (*Śūraṃgama* Repentance of the Profound Significance, abbreviated as *Lengyan shichan* 楞嚴事懺) in two fascicles. Shichan was originally born as Zhang Chujun 張初俊 in Kunming 昆明. At the age of nineteen, he ordained at Mount Xiu 秀山 in Tonghai 通海, serving under Miaokong 妙空 (d.u.) there as a student. He was given the Dharma name Shichan, and the accompanying title

Benwu 本無. Shichan's activities as a youth are uncertain. In the year 1617, he received a request from Mu Zeng 木增 (1587-1646), the native magistrate of Lijiangtu 麗江 to proceed to Xitan si of Mount Jizu in Binchuan 賓川, Dali 大理, where he was invited to be the founding patriarch of the monastery. He also received an appointment as regional manager. He went to the capital to request that a Buddhist canon be installed at Mount Jizu. He received special treatment by Ming Guangzong (r.1620), being made a Monks Registrar and Left Chief of the National Buddhist Bureau, and receiving purple robes. He became a celebrated figure of his generation. He was intelligent by nature and throughout his life read through the Buddhist canon while also reading Confucian texts. Contemporary literati, such as Ping Shike 馮時可 (fl.1571), Chen Jiru 陳繼儒 (1558-1639), and Tao Ting 陶珽 (1576-1635) all interacted with him. He produced Buddhist, Confucian and Daoist works, such as the *Fengxiang ji* 風響集 (Compilation of the Sound of the Wind), *Lengyan chanfa* 楞嚴懺法 (*Śūraṃgama* Repentance), *Chanzong songgu* 禪宗頌古 (Verse Commentary of the Chan School), and *Laozi zhu* 老子注 (Commentary on Laozi).[49] With respect to the transmission of Shichan's study of Chan, it originated with the Tonghai line 通海系 in the Yuan and Ming periods of Yunnan that was initiated by the monk Huiting 慧庭 (d.u.). As a result of his influence, this lineage through him and his disciples Hongbian 弘辨 (fl.1641) and Anren 安仁 (d.u.) saw some resurgence. This had importance significance to the later development of Chan Buddhism in Yunnan.

At the same time, Ming Taizu dispatched monks to Yunnan to build temples and transmit teachings. In 1388, Zhu Yuanzhang ordered the Bureau of Monastic Registration to issue an official note to local Monasterial Offices in various places: "Monks who own official monastic certificates and are 17 years of age or older are sent to Wuman 烏蠻, Qujing 曲靖, and other regions, where they are to build a temple every thirty *li*s 里, take up farming, live on their own, and moralize the local peoples."[50] Chinese Buddhism therefore was introduced into Yunnan on a large scale during the early Ming period. The "mode of teachings" for responding to the demands of worldly society also were transmitted

---

49 *Jizushan zhi*, 6.409. Chen Yuan believes that Shichan also composed *Yinming lun suijie biaoshi* 因明論隨解標釋 (Explanatory Notes on the Buddhist Logic), and the *Laozi zhu* 老子注 was *Laozi xuanlan* 老子玄覽. See Chen, *Fojiao kao*, 248-49. In the *Kunming fojiao shi*, it is written that Shichan also composed the *Chanlin foshi* 禪林佛事 (Affairs in Chan Monasteries). See Kunmingshi zongjiao shiwuju & Kunmingshi fojiao xiehui, *Fojiao shi*, 250.

50 *Shi jian Jigu lüe xuji*, *T* no. 2038, 49: 2.935b9-11:
但有討度牒的僧, 二十已上的, 發去烏蠻、曲靖等處, 每三十裡造一座庵, 自耕自食, 就化他一境的人.

into Yunnan.[51] The popularity of Buddhist services in Yunnan sparked native monks of Yunnan to aspire to produce repentance practices.

Muzeng was named Shengbai 生白. He was the native magistrate of Lijiang. In the later years of the Wanli period, apart from the one at Xitan si on Mount Jizu, he built a canon repository at Huayan si 華嚴寺, the building Yina Xuan 一衲軒 on the peak of Jiuchong ya 九重崖, the Zunshengta Cloister 尊勝塔院 on Mount Wenbi 文筆. All were exquisite and majestic. Chen Yinke 陳寅恪 (1890-1969) states the following: "Zeng is foremost when it comes to the merit of building in the mountains."[52] Muzeng once at Chongsheng si 崇聖寺 in Yeyu 葉榆 got hold of the *Huayan jing haiyin daochang chanyi* 華嚴經海印道場懺儀 (Repentance Ritual in the Ocean Seal Altar of the *Huayan Jing*, XZJ 1452) in forty-two fascicles. He then asked the monks to send it to Suzhou for it to be printed. Later he took the text and placed it in Lengyan si 楞嚴寺 in Jiaxing 嘉興. The inscription at the end of the *Huayan jing haiyin daochang chanyi* reads as follows:

> The Buddhist Mu Zeng 木增 (1587-1646), the Administrative Commissioner of the Sichuan province, a native of Liyang 麗陽 in Yunnan, with the imperially honoured title "Of Loyalty, Righteousness, and Sincerity", his son Mu Yi 木懿 (1608-1692) who is the Participant in Determining Governmental Matters of the Lijiang 麗江 government, his grandson Mu Zheng 木疇 (=Mu Jing 木靖 [1628-1671]) who was to succeed to the title, the students of the Grand School Mu Qiao 木喬 and Mu Can 木參, and graduates of local schools Mu Su 木宿, Mu You 木櫾, Mu Yun 木橒, Mu Sen 木, Mu Ji 木極, and Wu Le 悟樂, all donated salaries and invited monks and sent servants to carry the *Dafangguang fo huayan jing sanmei chanyi* 大方廣佛華嚴經三昧懺儀 (i.e., *Huayan jing haiyin daochang chanyi*), in 42 fascicles and 61 volumes, and travel to the Jigu Ge 汲古閣 Printing House run by the Buddhist layman and vegetarian Mao Fengbao 毛鳳苞 (d.u.) in Hunan 湖南 village in the Changshu county in the Suzhou city in the Nan Zhili province where fine craftsmen were gathered to carve the woodblocks. The project started in the early summer of the *gengchen* year (1640) in the Chongzhen era and completed in the late spring of the year of Xin si (1641), a work taking a year to finish. Now copies of this edition are preserved in the library of the Lengyan si 楞嚴寺 in the Jiaxing city in Zhejiang province. May this scripture be spread to the four groups of Buddhists, and may they, with many *kalpas* of practices,

51 Kunmingshi zongjiao shiwuju & Kunmingshi fojiao xiehui, *Fojiao shi*, 39.
52 Chen, *Fojiao kao*, 341.

> uphold the teachings forever after seeing and hearing them. Our wish is that this Sudden Teaching of One Vehicle will spread over the human sphere and that the various beings of the Three Kinds of Existence will all awake to the ocean of original nature. The monks who carried the copies of the scripture are monk Daoyuan 道源 (1596-1670) and Xuanqi 玄契 (d.u.) from the Xitan si 悉檀寺 in Mount Jizu 雞足, among others.[53]

We can clearly see Mu Zeng's piety for Buddhadharma and the importance he place on repentance. After Shichan produced the *Lengyan shichan*, Muzeng also provided financial assistance to have it published. The inscription at the end of the first fascicle of the text reads as follows:"Mu Zeng, the Buddhist devotee from Liyang, of the Second Bureaucratic Rank, an Earl of the Region, the major donator of the Muni Chapel, financed the printing of this work, to promote its merit: "I wish that my lifespan equals that of legendary Jian Keng and may my family line thrive forever."[54]

After Shichan completed the *Lengyan shichan*, he offered some short comments, explaining the causes for his cultivation of repentance as well as the production of his work:

> The liturgy of repentance is able to deliver the world because it could eliminate sins and beget good. It has a long history. The *Huayan* [*jing haiyin daochang*] *chan*[*yi*] is so voluminous as to cost one a month to read it through, and therefore it could not be widely spread. The *Fahua* [*sanmei*]*chan*[*yi*] and *Jin'guangming chan*[*fa*] have not been seen by people in the south. Circulated there is the 10-fascicle *Jingzhu zi* 淨住子 (Pure Abider) shortened by masters of the Liang such as Fayun 法雲 (467-529) and Sengyou 僧佑 (445-518), also known as *Lianghuang chan* 梁皇懺 (Emperor Liang Repentance). The work was originally in 20 fascicles and composed by Xiao Ziliang 蕭子良 (460-494), Prince Wenxuan

53 *Huayan jing haiyin daochang chanyi*, XZJ no. 1452, 128: 42.718b7-18:
欽褒忠義忠藎四川左布政雲南麗陽佛弟子木增， 同麗江府知府授參政男木懿，應襲孫木靖 (= 靖)，暨諸子孫太學生木喬、木參，生員木宿、木楙、木櫄、木梡、木極、悟樂等，各捐淨俸，延僧命役敬奉《大方廣佛華嚴經三昧懺儀》一部共四十二卷, 六十一冊, 直達南直隸蘇州府嘗（ = 常）熟縣隱湖南村薦素居士毛鳳苞汲古閣中鳩良工雕造. 起於崇禎庚辰孟夏, 終於辛巳暮春, 凡一載功成. 今置此版於浙江嘉興府楞嚴寺藏經閣, 祈流通諸四眾, 歷劫熏修, 見聞此法, 永持不捨. 所願一乘頓教, 遍布人寰; 三有群生, 俱明性海者耳. 賚經僧系雞足山悉檀禪寺比丘道源、玄契等.

54 *Yi Lengyan jiujing shi chan*, XZJ no. 1456, 129: 1.28a6-8:
創建牟尼菴香火大檀越、大方伯、二品服色、麗陽奉佛弟子木增，損資刊，用助此功德, 所願壽躋籛鏗, 雲仍者.

of Jingling 竟陵文宣王, with inspiration from a dream. During the years of Emperor Xiaozong 孝宗 of the Southern Song, the monk Ruone 若訥 (1110-1191), Monastic Registrar of Left Street, took excerpts from the 15-fascicle *Foming jing* 佛名經 (*Sūtra* of Buddhas' Names) and compiled them as the 3- fascicle *Shuichan* 水懺 (Water Repentance, i.e., *Sanmei shuichan* 三昧水懺). These two works of repentance, as one can see, though differing in levels of details, both include all principles and matters, leaving nothing to be complimented. People's minds are fickle, however, and could not keep reverent and solemn for long on occasions of sacrifice which demand piety. The *Lianghuang chan* costs four days to wade through and is considered fatiguing, and families of the middle and lower levels refuse to put it into practice, considering the costs exorbitant. In contrast, there are cases in which the *Shui chan* is practiced three times within one day, and this may owe to the choices for elaboration and simplification not being properly made. I, the monk Shichan, after withdrawing into Mount Muni 牟尼, devoted myself to meditation practice and in the meanwhile realized that my past karma was rather heavy. Thinking to cleanse it, I based [my writing] on the *Lengyan jing* 楞嚴經 (*Śūraṃgama-sūtra*) and composed this 2-fascicle liturgy, which taught over four hundred steps. The liturgy could be performed all day to clean the stains of sin. Devoting myself to polishing my mind-mirror, I had never been ready to show it to others, until I suddenly changed my mind and said to myself, "How could this be derived from my wish only! Therefore, I began to allow any of my followers to make copies. Men could be dismissed, but words should never. If one does not value what he hears over the work close at hand and tests out the liturgy, it could be instrumental for the rebirth in the Pure Land and the attainment of enlightenment. If it was not agreeable, he would just put it aside.[55]

55 Ibid., 2.44a8-b5:
懺法度世, 仗以滅罪生善, 繇來尚矣. 而《華嚴懺》, 卷帙富博, 彌月方竟, 不甚傳布. 《法華懺》、《金光明懺》, 南中人目所未睹. 今之流通者, 梁法雲僧祐諸師, 以齊竟陵文宣王子良夢感所撰《淨住子》二十卷, 節爲十卷, 即《梁皇懺》也. 南宋孝宗之世, 左街僧錄若訥, 摭取《佛名經》十五卷之文, 爲《水懺》三卷. 觀夫兩懺, 詳略雖殊, 理無不該, 事無不盡, 無所容置啄矣. 然人心輕佻, 於祭祀之誠, 肅敬難久. 今《梁懺》竭蹶四日, 以屬倦怠, 中下之家, 以費鉅阻辦. 而《水懺》一日有拜三部者, 似乎系簡未中. 釋禪既獲退居牟尼山, 止觀之際, 覺其根塵之宿業偏重, 思欲湔洗, 乃依《楞嚴經》, 修次懺法二卷, 四百餘拜, 終日可畢持, 以澡雪罪垢. 楷磨靈臺, 不敢輒以示人, 已而幡然曰：此豈一人之私願乎？遂聽徒屬抄寫. 夫有可廢之人, 無可廢之言. 誠能不賤近貴耳, 試熏修之, 未必不爲淨土禪悟之助因也. 苟不當意, 置之也可.

Shichan assessed various types of repentance practices and some of the production processes of some repentance practices. The *Huayan jing haiyin daochang chanyi* in forty-two fascicles was so vast that it required several months to practice all the teachings, which was disadvantageous if it were to be transmitted. Tiantai repentance practices, such as the *Fahua sanmei chanyi* and *Jin'guangming chanfa*, were never circulated in the region of Yunnan. The repentance practice that was widely circulated in Yunnan was the *Lianghuang chan*. Shichan believed monks such as Fayun and Sengyou from the Liang dynasty had abridged the text *Pure Abider* by Xiao Ziliang from twenty fascicles into ten. With respect to the *Sanmei shuichan*, Jingyuan 淨源 (1011-1088) believed that during the period of Emperor Xiaozong of the Southern Song (r. 1162-1189), the Monks Registrar of the Left and Right Streets Ruone had copied the repentance text of the *Foming jing* and turned it into the *Sanmei shuichan* in three fascicles. The creator of this *Sanmei shuichan* was likely Ruone, but at present we cannot find connecting evidence. The *Sanmei shuichan* was already quite popular in the time of Zanning in the Northern Song period.

Shichan very much praised the *Lianghuang chan* and *Sanmei shuichan*. The principle and phenomenal types were perfectly brought together. However, the *Lianghuang chan* in ten fascicles required four days to practice it once, which could easily make a practitioner weary. At the same time, if the benefactor wanted to request monks to practice the *Lianghuang chan*, the cost was high, so it would be difficult to manage if the benefactor was not wealthy. At the same time, someone practicing the *Sanmei shuichan* could manage three times in one day. Shichan believed the *Sanmei shuichan* was too simple. Shichan withdrew to behind Mount Muni, driven by the disorder of the contemporary practice of repentance, where in addition to practice meditative contemplation, he produced the *Lengyan shichan* in two fascicles based upon the *Lengyan jing*. It includes four-hundred prostrations altogether, which was suitable, given that it could be completed in a day. Moreover, he felt that regular practice of this could lead to rebirth in the Pure Land and awakening in meditative contemplation.

Given that Shichan placed much importance upon the *Lianghuang chan* and *Sanmei shuichan*, and at the same time there were no Tiantai repentance practices circulating in Yunnan, so Shichan emulated the structure of the two types of repentance practices in the former and produced the *Lengyan shichan*. Like this, the *Lengyan shichan* is not divided into "gates" (methods), but rather is just worship of some buddhas' names and recitation of a repentance text, which is clearly quite simple. This was a model for the production of repentance practices from the Ming dynasty onward.

At the beginning of the *Lengyan shichan*, Shichan gives some simple requirements for the practice:

> Those who are practicing *Lengyan jiujing chanfa* 楞嚴究竟懺法 (i.e., *Lengyan shichan*) do not need to adopt other Buddhist practices, or to submit memorials of request or explanation, nor does it cost money or valuable items or require various ritual instruments. What they need only to do is to invite renowned monks or good men to read aloud the repentance text while they are contemplating the nature of the sin, visualizing images of buddhas images, and making obeisance in all sincerity; thus they must be able to evoke sympathetic responses. If the water is clear, the moon's reflection will appear, and if a mirror is clean, images will become visible. The matter to control the mind depends on one's self, and therefore whatever none of his wishes will be unfulfilled.[56]

Practicing the *Lengyan shichan* will definitely bring about a spiritual experience so long as one piously recites the repentance text and sincerely prostrates to the names of the buddhas. One does not need to present documents, gold, silver, paper or any other Dharma vessel when carrying out the service. On the altar, one is to set up images of buddhas, bodhisattvas, arhats, and devas, according to one's ability. In front of the Buddha, one could place pure water, pure tea, pure mirrors, fine incense, lamps, fragrant flowers, fruits, and vegetables. One could also lay out one's treasures and textile. One was to not hide the new and fine items by using old items or crude things as offerings instead. Shichan had no demands that one was to set up the altar offerings according to what is required in the *Lengyan jing*. This differs from the *Shoulengyan tanchang xiuzheng yi* 首楞嚴壇場修證儀 (Ritual of Cultivating Realization via the *Śūraṃgama* Altar) of Jingyuan during the Song dynasty.

When practicing the *Lengyan shichan*, one must first recite the Śūraṃgama Dhāraṇī and later carry out strict and pure celebratory praises. The altar is set up in this manner. Next, one starts the practice of repentance. As a result of Shichan being so highly learned and proficient with the teachings of Buddhism, Confucianism, and Daoism, the repentance text of the *Lengyan shichan* might have been derived from scriptures, but it has a high literary quality from having gone through Shichan's hand.

The first fascicle of the *Lengyan shichan* consists of ten sessions of prostrations to the Buddha, altogether totaling 260 prostrations. The second fascicle includes six sessions of prostrations that totals 150 prostrations. It is clear that the structure is relatively meticulous and simple. The names of the Buddhas to

56 Ibid., 1.10a3-7:
凡熏修《楞嚴究竟懺法》，不須別作佛事，不必申奏表牒，不用金銀錢袱，不動鐃、鈸、雲、羅，但當延名僧善士，朗誦懺文，靜觀罪性，觀想佛像，至誠禮拜，必致感應. 夫水清月現，鏡淨像生，克念在我，無有不如願者矣.

which one prostrates during the repentance were, as recorded by Shichan himself, taken from the *Foming jing* and *Qian Fo yinyuan jing* 千佛因緣經 (*Sūtra* of the Causes and Conditions of a Thousand Buddhas, *T* 426), translated by Bodhiruci. Shichan was fond of bringing the Buddha-names that contained numbers from the *Foming jing* into the *Lengyan shichan*, such as the Sixty Merit-Treasures Buddha (Liushi gongdefo 六十功德寶佛), the Sixty-Two Piliuluo Buddha (Liushi'er piliuluofo 六十二毘留羅佛), the Buddha of Mastery-Flag with Eighty-Four Thousand Names (Bawan simian mingzizaifo 八萬四千名自在佛), the Buddha of Three Hundred Great Flags (Sanbai dachuangfo 三百大幢佛), the Five Hundred Pure Voices King Buddha (Wubai jingshengwangfo 五百淨聲王佛), and the Five Hundred Lotus Flowers King Buddha (Wubai botoumowangfo 五百波頭摩王佛).[57] It was likely his intention to leave practitioners with the impression of massive merits, for worshipping one Buddha was equal to worshipping tens or hundreds of Buddhas, or even innumerable Buddhas. At the same time, the buddha names in the *Lengyan shichan* follow another mode: ... *fang* 方 (direction) ... *fo* 佛 (Buddha); ... *shijie* 世界 (realm) ... *fo* 佛 (Buddha). This gives people a quite concrete and definite sensation. This also helps bring about faith in the practitioner of repentance. The *Lengyan shichan* is to a large extent derived from the *Lengyan jing*. It also pulls material from the *Foming jing*, *Puxian xingyuanpin* 普賢行願品 (Samantabhadra Chapter) of the *Huayan jing*, *Guan yaowang yaoshang er'pusa jing* 觀藥王藥上二菩薩經 (*Bhaiṣajyarāja-bhaiṣajyasamudgata-sūtra*), *Sanju jing* 三聚經 (*Sūtra* of Three Heaps), *Pusazang jing* 菩薩藏經 (*Bodhisattva-piṭaka-sūtra*), *Niepan jing* 涅槃經 (*Mahāparinirvāṇa-sūtra*), *Lengqie jing* 楞伽經 (*Laṅkāvatāra-sūtra*), *Jin'gang jing* 金剛經 (Diamond *Sūtra*), and *Jin'guangming jing* 金光明經 (*Sūtra* of Golden Light). The purpose of the repentance text is to explain the importance of repentance, the causes behind beings' creation of karma, the suffering on the six paths that result from karmic retribution, and the making of vows. The repenter realizes, for instance, the impermanence, sufferings, and emptiness of the world, regrets the eight kinds of suffering in the human world, the negative results caused by the six sensory organs, etc.

Shichan in the *Lengyan shichan* stresses merging Buddhist schools during the Ming and the flourishing of the Chan and Pure Land traditions. *Lengyan shichan* points out that one should "generate the seven types of mind and repent to dispel the three types of obstacles."[58] However, Shichan inserts the Tinatai repentance practice of the "ten minds contrary or in line with saṃsāra"

57 *Foshuo Foming jing*, *T* no. 440, 14: 1. 115a1-7; *Yi Lengyan jiujing shi chan*, *XZJ* no. 1456, 129: 1.15b11-13.

58 *Yi Lengyan jiujing shi chan*, *XZJ* no. 1456, 129: 1.13b2: 發七種心, 懺三種障.

(*nishun shixin* 逆順十心) into his *Lengyan shichan*.[59] This was characteristic of his writing. The *Lengyan shichan* also has "repentance to dispel the three obstacles" at its core, but given the intellectual background of the *Lengyan jing*, it had a unique development (see Appendix 4.2).

The *Lengyan shichan* gives a detailed explanation of karmic retribution. All of the second fascicle and part of the first explain this, but the interpretation of obstacles related to afflictions and karma is quite simple. The content of the lower fascicle of the *Lengyan shichan* is primarily derived from fascicle two of the *Lengyan jing*, including ideas such as the ten habituated causes (*xiyin* 習因), the six (*jiaobao* 交報), the seven inclinations (*qu* 趣), the ten types of spirits (*gui* 鬼), the ten animal births (*chusheng* 畜生), the ten types of people (*ren* 人), and the ten (*xianqu* 仙趣). These are all explained in detail in the *sūtra*. In addition, some of the repentance text comes from the *Foming jing*, such as the line, "The *sūtra* says that since time without beginning up until the very present day, … the evil karma produced by the three kinds of behaviours, four kinds of oral activities, and four kinds of mental activities have led me to retributions and the perils and hardship of the six destinies. I sincerely express my penitence."[60]

The *Lengyan jing*'s explanation of the origin of ignorance and afflictions in beings is that all beings since beginningless time have been subject to cyclic existence as a result of not understanding that their permanently abiding real mind-nature is pure and luminous, nor understanding the presence of delusion. Real nature is perfect and luminous, in which there is neither birth nor cessation. It is always originally abiding. All sentient beings transmigrate among different realms due to the two distortions and delusions caused by false discrimination: (1) False views caused by karmas specific to individuals; (2) False views caused by karmas common to all beings. All physical and mental faculties of sentient beings plus their aggregates are pure and originally such in the *tathāgatagarbha*, but due to the three continuities of the world, beings, and karmic fruits, various flawed phenomena move and change following karma, and deluded causes and deluded effects have thusness as their essential. One should discriminate the true from the false and realize that the body and mind are formed by the Five Aggregates and are not truly existent. One should also realize that the world is fundamentally empty, and destroy the attachment to a personal self and the attachment of one's self to a phenomenon. In an ultimate view, the Five Aggregates are the *tathāgatagarbha* and the

59 Ibid., 1.13b5-12.

60 Ibid., 1.21a9-b8: 經云從無始來, 至於今日 …… 身業三種, 口四意三惡業受報, 六趣險難, 誠心懺悔. *Fo shuo foming jing*, *T* no. 441, 14: 14. 239c15-27.

wondrous nature of thusness. True intellect and true elimination will not give rise to delusion again, and, therefore, the Buddha attained reality and thus became devoid of delusions. The true nature of the Four Elements permeates the universe, and enlightenment is nothing but the ceasing of the deluded mind, which is not given by other people. The *Lengyan shichan* states,

> Since the beginningless past, sentient beings form delusive notions; turning affairs upside down, they get themselves into the trouble of transmigration. They are ignorant about that the mind is "briskly alive", free of defilement, and transcends all media, and therefore they vainly infer that it is in the self, or outside the self, or with the sensory organs, or in the middle of the self. Unable to appreciate emptiness, they are shackled by form. They lost the essence and do not realize that they need to return. They have different delusive sights because of their different karma, and they go against enlightenment and enjoy the sensory fields. According to what they realize and what they understand, they set up theories that happen to agree or disagree with each other, which cause confusion and create troubles which are so opaque and end up as an annoyance. Day and night, they keep thinking without stopping for a moment, and good thoughts are always few and evil ones are always the most [frequent]. Even the evil thoughts have not yet been put into action, they somehow build negative karma. Thinking of good, one receives a superior reward; thinking about evil, one submerges [in the sea of sorrow], not to mention those glaring actions: how could one numerate them and point out their retributions![61]

Sentient beings do not understand the real mind of profound luminosity and therefore give rise to delusional views, creating various types of karma: (1) Delusional views of separate karma (*bieye wangjian* 別業妄見), which refers to beings losing the real nature, giving rise to delusional views, and seeing all states of delusion as either suffering or pleasure. If a person does not lose the original reality, then they will not see the state of delusion. (2) Delusional views of common portion (*tongfen wangjian* 同分妄見), which refers to beings losing the real nature, and together seeing all states of delusion, together experiencing suffering and pleasure, and the fruition of karma. Hence, the *Lengyan shichan*

61 Ibid., 1.17b7-13:
從無始來, 用諸妄想, 顛倒行事, 自取流轉. 不知此心活潑潑地, 離塵出指, 妄推在內、在外、在根、在中, 昧空結色, 遺本迷還, "別業妄見", 背覺合塵. 所覺所明, 立同立異, 擾亂生勞, 渾濁成惱. 晝夜思想, 念念不停, 於中善念恆少, 惡念恆多, 事即未行, 幽對冥構, 憶善受勝報, 思惡自沈淪. 何況明爲顯作, 安能條列縷指.

explains the afflictive hindrances and cognitive hindrances with these ideas of delusional views and delusional karma, but it lacks detailed analysis.

In terms of ideas related to repentance, Shichan stressed principle repentance. The last of the first fascicle of the *Lengyan shichan* states the following:

> I wish various World-Honoured Ones witness thus for us. Before knowing the Three Jewels, we have been indulging ourselves with the Three Poisons, and committing and accumulating the Ten Evils. Now, we repent of all karmic hindrances, afflictive hindrances, hindrances from various sentient beings, obstructions to hearing the Dharma, obstructions in transmigration, all of which we have invited. We repent again, and from now on dare not court any more. … Various dharmas, the Buddha preaches, arise from causes and conditions, and since the Three Times are devoid of essence, and there are no karmic hindrances. Where there is no karmic hindrance, the various actions that are being done meet no karmic obstructions. Dharmas are all empty and lack a self; their inherent nature is emptiness and tranquillity, which is the absolute reality and flawless realm. Succeeding in removing all his obstructive dharmas, one finds tranquility.[62]

The *Lengyan jing* explains defilement and purity via the ideas of reality and delusion, hence delusional phenomena, such as karmic obstacles etc, are originally pure. However, if one is able to observe the nature of phenomena as empty, i.e., the original nature being empty, then there are no karmic or phenomenal obstacles.

At the same time, Shichan in the second fascicle of the *Lengyan shichan* at the end concludes with a complete repentance as follows:

> Investigate and penetrate it, and trace it back to back. Repenting through principle, one can break through the barrier of doubts, when karma caused through sensory organs, sensory fields, and senses are all eliminated, the present life and next lives are all purified, the hell is destroyed, the ocean of karma has dried up. … Now one repents before Buddhist believers and various sentient beings. Do good deeds that are difficult to do, and repent the evil actions that are difficult to repent. Take the nectar

62 Ibid., 1.27b8-28a2:
願諸世尊爲我證明, 與我作眼. 我等未識三寶時, 隨順三毒, 疊造十惡, 所有業障、煩惱障、諸眾生障、法障、轉後來世障, 懺悔已, 復懺悔, 更不敢作. …… 佛說諸法, 從因緣有, 三世無體, 無有業障. 無業障處, 現作諸行, 亦無業障. 一切諸法, 空無有我. 本性空寂, 是則實際、無漏際, 能淨一切法障, 而得寂靜.

> (i.e., the Buddha's teaching), the wondrous medicine, and enter the land of immortality. The Ten Obstructions and Twenty-two Kinds of Folly are dissolved in response to the thoughts of repentance, and the Eighty-one Fetters are destroyed immediately. The person and the dharma become empty of self, and the two views of nihilism and eternalism are both banished. With the Two Extreme Views wiped out, the sun of wisdom shines in the mid-sky. The Three Kinds of Contaminations are melted down, and the sharp point of the wisdom is unsheathed. Here and now there is not a single thing, and *śamatha* and *vipaśyanā* are unified. Verbal explanations are uttered spontaneously, and the distinction between right and the wrong is abolished. Questing for the mind in seven locations, the mind becomes limpid; determining the subject of perception in the eight analyzable phenomena, the subject becomes sharp. Being able to transform the perception, one parallels the Buddha; with the insane mind subsiding, one attains the right enlightenment. The views of non-causality, of non-conditionality, and of uncaused existence are all intellectual play; the process of combination, harmonization, separation, and approach all show the Real and Eternal.[63]

Shichan brings principle repentance and Chan concentration together on the basis of sudden awakening as described in the *Lengyan jing*. This is joined with his own realization of Chan practice, while at the same time believing that Repentance by Principle could eliminate transgressive misdeeds that would be difficult to perform through Repentance by Phenomena (*shichan* 事懺). In this manner, one attains true realization identical to that of the Tathāgata through discovering the real mind and the two types of emptiness related to persons and phenomena.

Shichan in the *Lengyan shichan* expresses ideas connected to ethics and morality as well as national protection, related to his deep cultivation of Confucian learning, the grace he received from Ming Guangzong, and the Dharma guardianship provided by Muzeng. Shichan in the *Lengyan shichan* states the following:

---

63 Ibid., 2.43a8-b3:
向上參究, 理懺決透疑關, 根塵識業已銷除, 現生後報俱清淨, 地獄粉碎, 業海枯乾 ...... 今則禮懺眾信, 並及有情等, 行難行之善事, 懺難懺之惡條, 服甘露之妙藥, 入不死之壽邦, 十障、二十二愚, 應念銷落, 刷結八十一使, 即時併除. 人法悉空, 斷常斯遣, 二邊刷蕩, 慧日當天, 三漏陶鎔, 智鋒出匣. 現前無少物, 寂照一如; 當下出言詮, 是非雙泯. 七處徵心, 心已徹; 八還辨見, 見惟精. 轉物即同如來, 歇狂便登正覺. 因緣自然皆戲論, 合和離即示真常.

> His Majesty, the current emperor, enjoys myriads of years, absolute ease, myriads of blessings, myriads of fortunes, the protection from myriads of heavenly beings, and the assistance from myriads of gods. At his leisure amid myriads of duties, he has the myriads return to oneness; joining the myriads into this oneness, he puts myriads of affairs in order and brings the myriads of people ease and happiness. … The Five Planets stay in their proper orbits, and the Five Crops yield a bumper harvest. … The chief ministers and generals, officials of various ministries and bureaus, and censors of the Censorate are all loyal, steadfast, honest, and upright. Local governors in commanderies and cities are all clean, incorruptible, just, and impartial. Those promoted to high offices promote and protect Buddhist teachings. They always keep in mind the Buddhas' instruction on the Vulture Peak and serve forever as the Dharma's impregnable fortress.[64]

Shichan not only announces aspirations for the emperor and nation, he moreover hopes that the great ministers will be loyal and fair. At the same time, he hopes that the emperor and great ministers will protect Buddhism and propagate it together.

Also, *Lengyan shichan* expresses ideas in which Shichan emphasizes that repentance is "cause for the Pure Land and Chan awakening." In his practice of repentance, he emphasized returning back to the Pure Land in the west. The *Lengyan shichan* states, "The founder of the teachers and root teacher Śākyamuni Buddha possessed deep pity and great compassion, elucidating the *gong'an* of the west. The method of cutoff and immediacy, the first bridge to ferry [beings across] in the Dharma Ending Age. We rely on the teachings and faithfully respect [them], offering our revered respects, prostrating and carrying out repentance, while taking sincere refuge."[65] Bringing together recitation of the Buddha's name, prostrations and repentance, he introduced Pure Land thought into repentance practices as the final goal of such practices. This was a trend in the development of repentance practices from the Song dynasty onward.

---

64 Ibid., 2.39b17-40a05:
當今皇帝, 陛下萬壽萬安, 萬福萬祿, 萬天保佑, 萬神護持. 萬機之暇, 萬法歸一, 以一統萬, 萬事得理, 萬民安樂 …… 五星順序, 五穀豐登 …… 輔弼將相, 部寺百僚, 臺憲監司, 忠貞亮直. 郡邑臨民, 清廉公正. 高遷品秩, 弘護教門, 恆憶靈山之付囑, 永爲佛法之金湯.

65 Ibid., 2.41a12-14:
教主本師, 釋迦牟尼佛深慈大悲, 開示西方公案, 橫截直超法門, 爲末世第一救度津梁, 依教信受尊敬, 奉持禮懺, 眾等一心歸命.

### 2.2.2 Ruxing's *Deyu Longhua Xiuzheng Chanyi* 得遇龍華修證懺儀 in the Ming Dynasty

During the Ming dynasty, Ruxing compiled the *Deyu Longhua xiuzheng chanyi* 得遇龍華修證懺儀 (Repentance of Encountering *Nāgakesara* and Cultivating Realization, *XZJ* 1466) in 1606, hereafter abbreviated *Longhua chanyi*. This is the most complete repentance ritual among those directed at the worship of Maitreya.

Ruxing was a Tiantai monk, hence his *Longhua chanyi* was produced based upon conventions of Tiantai repentance practices. He encouraged people to cultivate twelve expedient means on the basis of "Mahāyāna *sūtra*s and the *Fazhu ji* 法住記 (Record of the Perpetuity of the Dharma, *T* 2030)."

First, to develop correct belief; second, to widely search for good friends; third, strictly observe precepts; fourth, to arouse the mind to attain enlightenment for the sake of all sentient beings; fifth, to thoroughly learn the ritual procedure; sixth, to pay obeisance to and invoke the Three Jewels; seventh, to repent the pass sins; eighth, to single-mindedly recite the *Fahua jing*; ninth, to cultivate the field of merit by making offerings to the Three Jewels; tenth, an overview of the Tuṣita; eleventh, the special contemplation on the Dragon-Flower Assembly; twelfth, the mindfulness of the One True Mark.[66]

The "Longhua chanyi bayu" 龍華懺儀跋語 (Postscript of the Longhua Repentance) by Rujian 如鑒 (1580-1666) states, "In the *bingwu* year of Wanli (1606), the Tiantai Ciyun Repentance Master Huanwei [Ru]Xing compiled the *Longhua chanyi* in four fascicles according to *sūtra*s such as the *Guan Mile [pusa] shangsheng [Doushuaitian jing]* 觀彌勒 [菩薩] 上生 [兜率天經] (*Sūtra* on Contemplation of Maitreya Bodhisattva's Birth in Tuṣita Heaven) and divided the text into twelve sections."[67] Hence, were the *Guan Mile pusa shangsheng Doushuaitian jing* and the *Fazhu ji* were the primary scriptures from which the *Longhua chanyi* was produced.

"Di shisan bieguan longhua" 第十三別觀龍華 (The Eleventh Separate Contemplation of Longhua) in the *Longhua chanyi* cites different accounts in scriptures with respect to Maitreya's attainment of buddhahood, such as the *Mile xiasheng jing* 彌勒下生經 (*Sūtra* on the Descent of Maitreya, *T* 453) by

66 *Deyu longhua xiuzheng chanyi*, *XZJ* no. 1466, 129: 1.167a16-b3:
第一開發正信, 第二廣求良友, 第三嚴持戒律, 第四發菩提心, 第五明結壇儀, 第六禮請三寶, 第七懺悔往罪, 第八專誦法華, 第九三寶福田, 第十總觀兜率, 第十一別觀龍華, 第十二念一實相.

67 Ibid., 4.204a7-8:
萬曆丙午歲, 天臺慈雲懺主幻爲惺公, 按《觀彌勒上生》等經, 集《龍華懺儀》四卷, 列十二門.

Zhu Fahu 竺法護 (239-316), *Mile xiasheng chengfo jing* 彌勒下生成佛經 (*Sūtra* of Maitreya's Birth and Attainment of Buddhahood, *T* 454) and *Mile da chengfo jing* 彌勒大成佛經 (*Sūtra* of Maitreya's Great Attainment of Buddhahood, *T* 456) by Kumārajīva, the *Mile laishi jing* 彌勒來時經 (*Sūtra* of Maitreya's Coming, *T* 457) by an unknown translator, and *Mile xiasheng chengfo jing* 彌勒下生成佛經 (*Sūtra* of Maitreya's Birth and Attainment of Buddhahood, *T* 455) by Yijing 義淨 (635-713). Hence, when the *Longhua chanyi* was compiled, it actually cited all scriptures related to Maitreya. The *Fazhu ji*'s full title is *Da aluohan Nantimituoluo suoshuo fazhu ji* 大阿羅漢難提蜜多羅所說法住記 (The Record of the Perpetuity of the Dharma by the Great *Arhat* Nandimitra), which is primarily an account of the names and abodes of the Sixteen *Arhat*s and their retinues, as well as an account of the temporal limit of the True Dharma abiding in the world. The end of the text explains the situation in which Maitreya will be born in the world, encouraging beings to come to cultivate the supreme causes of Maitreya so that in the future they could meet and serve Maitreya.

Among the twelve means of the *Longhua chanyi*, the first type of means is generating true faith, the second is extensively seeking out good friends, the third is strictly upholding precepts, and the fourth is generating *bodhicitta*, which is the foundation for the practice of repentance. Explaining the superiority of faith in Maitreya and the assisting conditions of the repentance ritual connected to him, the practitioner must possess suitable faculties. At the same time, the order of the rites in the *Longhua chanyi* was produced based upon the *Fahua sanmei chanyi*. Elements of the Maitreya cult were added to the *Longhua chanyi*, distinguishing it from the *Fahua sanmei chanyi*.

The *Longhua chanyi* not only follows the order of Tiantai repentance, it is also inclined toward the *Fahua jing*, which is why the eighth rite includes "exclusively reciting the *Fahua* [*jing*]". Ruxing emphasized the three causes for exclusively reciting the *Fahua jing*.

> The first reason, [is that] the Dragon Flower Assembly is as vast as the ocean, and Buddhist practitioners on various paths are all to meet there. What a brilliant choice! Practitioners, however, aspire and approach differently, unsure of their destinations, and therefore, while conducting goodness in a casual manner, they remain driven by various desires. Hence, the mind of vigour and absorption is spoiled. Contain the mind by focusing on one object, like the arrow the arrow on the bowstring aimed at the target. When the efforts could join into a continuity, the essence of the Way will easily manifest itself. The second reason, since the

> *Fahua* [*jing*] says that the *sūtra* itself is the king of all *sūtras*, what other *sūtras* could surpass it? The third reason, this *sūtra* is started by Maitreya posing questions and concluded by Samantabhadra's encouragement.[68]

Ruxing emerged from his Tiantai stance, believing that the *Fahua jing* and Maitreya Bodhisattva possessed a deep connection. Moreover, he believed that the *Fahua jing* was the king of scriptures, which is why he emphasized exclusive recitation of it. Furthermore, when establishing the altar and carrying out the practice, there are two required altars: "The *Longhua* [*chanyi*] is based upon the *Fahua* [*jing*] and requires two altars: one is for Samantabhadra and one is for Maitreya. The altar for Samantabhadra is for cultivation of the *Lotus* Repentance. The Maitreya altar is only for aspiring for rebirth in the inner court [of Tuṣita heaven]."[69] Thus, the *Longhua chanyi* clearly displays tinting of Tiantai and therein possesses a great amount of teachings, which appear to have no direct connection to the *Shangsheng li* 上生禮 (Ascension worship), which purely utilizes practices such as recitation and prostrations.

### 2.3 *The Revisions and Popularity of Morning and Evening Recitations*

Recitations include those scriptures and mantras recited in temples daily or every evening plus the accompanying processions. With respect to the origins of Buddhist recitations, the "*Fashi pin* 法師品 (Chapter of the Dharma Teacher)" in the *Fahua jing* mentions teachers that memorize, read scriptures, and recite. Hence, the custom of recitiation in China was, we might infer, introduced through Buddhist translators from the Western Regions. The earliest account of recitations in China is the appended outline of Ze Rong 笮融 (?-195) in Liu Yao's 劉繇 (156-197) biography in the *Wu shu* 吳書 (Book of Wu). Ze Rong built a Buddhist shrine to accommodate three thousand people, allowing many to enjoy listening to Buddhist recitations.[70] Successive generations of emperors also promoted recitation, such as Xuanzong of the Tang, who ordered Amoghavajra (Bukong 不空, 705-774) to recite the *Renwang jing* 仁王經 (*Sūtra* for Humane Kings, *T* 246).[71] Daizong ordered twenty-seven monks to

---

68 Ibid., 2. 181b5-9:
一者, 龍華如海, 殊途同歸, 一何擇焉？第恐行人志趣不一, 所適靡定, 所以散善日馳, 則精一之心蕩矣. 且令制心一緣, 如射望的, 工成一片, 道體易彰. 二者,《法華》自曰經王, 孰能超勝？三者, 此經首因彌勒示疑, 終則普賢勸發.

69 Ibid., 2. 173b5-7:
既依《法華》爲龍華之本, 須結二壇：一爲普賢道場, 一爲彌勒道場. 普賢道場, 令修法華懺; 彌勒道場, 惟發願求生內院.

70 *Sanguo zhi* 49.1185.

71 *Fozu tongji*, *T* no. 2035, 49: 29.295c14-18.

recite the *Sitātapatroṣṇīṣa-dhāraṇī* (*Foding zhou* 佛頂咒) over a period of time for the benefit of the country.[72] Fascicle fifty-three of the *Fozu tongji* 佛祖統紀 (Complete Chronicle of the Buddha and Patriarchs, *T* 2035) includes a section on the rich merit of recitation, in which it lists nineteen examples of monastics carrying out recitation in special events over the course of more than seven centuries, from the time of Emperor An in the Eastern Jin (Dong Jin Aidi 東晉哀帝; r. 397-419) until Emperor Guangzong of the Song (Song Guangzong 宋光宗 [r. 1189-1194]).[73] It is clear that recitation had a long history and deep prolifersation.

As to the rules governing recitation, ancient India had a system of "three commencements (*sanqi* 三啓)". At the time, the *Fo suoxing zan* 佛所行讚 (Praises of the Buddha's Deeds, *T* 192) by Aśvaghoṣa was widely recited. First are the verses compiled by Aśvaghoṣa praising the Buddha, and then next the recitation of *sūtra*, followed by merit dedication. The whole process is called "three commencements by section (*jieduan sankai* 節段三開)", which is why it is called "three commencements". After reciting *sūtras*, all the people chant "*subhāśita* (*suposhiduo* 蘇婆師多)" or "*svāhā* (*suopodu* 娑婆度)" which means "praising the *sūtra* as subtle and profound".[74] The foundation of recitation in China was also done in the fashion of "three commencements": regardless of the Dharma service being carried, first there are the preliminary praises (with incense or verses recited) followed by the text recitation (scripture or mantra, or a related ritual text), and then finally merit dedication. Only the chanting of "*subhāśita* (*suposhiduo* 蘇婆師多)" or "*svāhā* (*suopodu* 娑婆度)" at the end is rare in recitation rituals in China. However, "good (*shan* 善)" or "how good (*shanzai* 善哉)" is also chanted at the end in some Chinese ritual texts, which is just what *svāhā* means.

The system of recitation in China originated with the monastic regulations established by Daoan during the Eastern Jin. Therein are regulations governing daily procession at six times, and the recitations at meals. China originally had relatively simple recitations in the forms of scriptures and verses. Repentance practices developed after the Jin period, and later more complex practices emerged, such as the "Yoga Flaming Mouth" and Water and Land Rites. During the Tang, when Mazu Daoyi 馬祖道一 (709-788) was building up monasteries, and Baizhang Huaihai 百丈懷海 (720-814) was establishing the Pure Rules of Chan, recitation became gradually regularized, especially later in the Ming, when morning and evening recitations were widely fixed.

72 Ibid., 52.456a13-16.

73 Ibid., 53.468c19-469b4.

74 *Nanhai jigui neifa zhuan*, *T* no. 2125, 54: 4.227a4-19.

FIGURE 35 The Pagoda for Yicun 義存 (822-908) of the Linji 臨濟 sect on Mount Xuefeng 雪峰 in Minhou 閩侯, Fujian.

### 2.3.1 Morning and Evening Recitations in the Pure Rules

The morning recitations in the *conglin* 叢林 system primarily utilize the *Śūraṃgama dhāraṇī*, while the evening recitations include the *Amituo jing* and Eighty-Eight Buddhas (*Bashiba fo* 八十八佛). This is related to the "Śūraṃgama Gathering (*Lengyan hui* 楞嚴會)" and "Summer retreat *Nianfo* (*xiazhong nianfo* 夏中念佛)" from the Song Dynasty.

The *Lengyan jing* in ten fascicles was translated by Pramiti during the reign-era of Zhongzong (r. 683-684; 705-710) during the Tang. In Chinese its full title is *Da Foding Rulai miyin xiuzheng liaoyi zhu pusa wanxing Shoulengyan jing* 大佛頂如來密因修證了義諸菩薩萬行首楞嚴經, also called *Zhong Yindu Nalantuo da daochang jing* 中印度那爛陀大道場經, or abbreviated to *Lengyan jing* 楞嚴經 or *Da Foding jing* 大佛頂經. Thanks to the many differences between its contents and discussions in various other exoteric scriptures and treatises, as well as the contradictory explanations concerning the time and translator behind its translation in Buddhist catologs, this text's authenticity has long been subject to. This *sūtra* explains the principle that "cognitive faculties and their objects are of the same origin; bondage and release are non-dual"[75] as well as the methods for liberating *samādhi* and the stages of the bodhisattva. It is an important scripture that teaches meditation, the complete penetration of the auditory faculty, and the Māra states of the five aggregates. The pure essence of the nature of the true mind that is permanently abiding aligns with the doctrines of the perfected teachings as seen in Tiantai and Huayan. The seven points of mind and eight distinctions concerning what is viewed as explained in the *Lengyan jing* perhaps greatly assisted and inspired Chan contemplation. At the same time, detailed explanation of the way to perfect sudden awakening via meditation also encouraged Chan practitioners.

From the Song dynasty onward, the *Lengyan jing* flourished both within the Chan tradition and other doctrinally-oriented traditions. Monks from each school offered their commentary on the text according to the viewpoints of their respective schools. There were forty-eight commentaries on the text, coming after the number of commentaries of *Huayan jing*, *Fahua jing*, *Jin'gang jing*, and *Xin jing* 心經 (Heart *Sūtra*).[76] At the same time, from the Song and Yuan periods, the summer retreat regulations in Chan monasticism included prayers so that the retreat would go well, and for the establishment of the "*Śūraṃgama* Altar" (*Lengyan tan* 楞嚴壇). From the thirteenth day of the fourth lunar month to the thirteenth of the seventh, the monks would assemble in the main shrine hall to recite the *Śūraṃgama dhāraṇī*.[77] This was the "*Śūraṃgama* Gathering" (*Lengyan hui* 楞嚴會). Zhenxie Qingliao 真歇清了 (1088-1151) of the Southern Song at Mount Putuo recited the *dhāraṇī* and dedicated merit for the sake of an ill monk, which was the beginning of the *Śūraṃgama* Gathering.[78] In the *Śūraṃgama* Gathering, the illustration of the seating arrangement of the assembly is called the "*Śūraṃgama* Illustration" (*Lengyan tu* 楞嚴圖).

Fascicle seven of the *Baizhang qinggui* 百丈清規 (The Pure Rules of Baizhang, *T* 2025) records that the rector selects someone with a good voice to be the "*Śūraṃgama* Head" (*lengyan tou* 楞嚴頭). They recite three times, "Namo Buddhas and Bodhisattvas of the Śūraṃgama Gathering (*Namo Lengyan huishang fo pusa* 南無楞嚴會上佛菩薩)." The assembly recites together. Next, they

75 *Da Foding Rulai miyin xiuzheng liaoyi zhu pusa wanxing Shoulengyan jing*, *T* no. 945, 19: 5.124c6-7: 根塵同源, 縛脫無二.

76 Muranaka, "Ryōgongyō", 71-77. According to Muranaka Yūshō's statistics, there are 76 commentaries on *Avataṃsaka-sūtra*, 67 commentaries on *Lotus Sūtra*, 57 commentaries on *Diamond Sūtra*, 55 commentaries on *Heart Sūtra*, and 48 commentaries on *Śūraṃgama-sūtra*.

77 *Chixiu Baizhang qinggui*, *T* no. 2025, 48: 7.1151c2-d17.

78 *Zenrin shōkisen*, *B* no. 103, 19: 16.509b16-510a4.

recite the *sūtra* heading of "Excellent and Profound *Dhāraṇī Āryācalanātha* (*Miaozhan zongchi budong zun* 妙湛總持不動尊)." They then recite the *Śūraṃgama dhāraṇī*. Afterward, they recite, "*Mahāprajñāpāramitā* (*mohe boreboluomiduo* 摩訶般若波羅蜜多)" three times.[79]

Finally, the "Pu huixiang ji" 普回向偈 (Vast Dedicatory Verses) by the rector Zhenxie Qingliao read, "The monks assembled here [to] recite the secret *dhāraṇī* of the *Śūraṃgama* ... *Mahāprajñāpāramitā*."[80] The order of rites in the *Śūraṃgama* Gathering is basically similar to present-day morning recitations, the only difference being the absence of Dhāraṇī of Great Compassion (*Dabei zhou* 大悲咒) or ten lesser *dhāraṇīs*. It is clear that the *Śūraṃgama* Gathering is the origin of the *Śūraṃgama Dhāraṇī* being recited in the morning.

However, the evening recitations in the Conglin system are basically Pure Land at their core. This was the result of the integration of Chan and Pure Land from the Song and Yuan periods onward. During the Qing, Yirun 儀潤 (fl.1823) records in fascicle eight of the *Baizhang qinggui zhengyi ji* 百丈清規證義記 (Commentary on the Pure Rules of Baizhang, XZJ 1233) "Summer Nianfo". In other words, during the summer retreat, Nianfo or recitation of Amitābha's name was done in place of meditation. After the morning meal, the assembly recites the *Daishizhi yuantong zhang* 大勢至圓通章 (Chapter on Mahāsthāmaprāpta Bodhisattva's Perfect Penetration with Mindfulness of Buddha [in the *Lengyan jing*]) once, Dhāraṇī of Great Compassion, the ten lesser *dhāraṇīs*, and the *Xin jing*, plus the name of the Buddha five-hundred times, the dedicatory chant, the ten aspirations, and then concluding with the three refuges. In the second service in the hall, they recite the *Zaxiang guan zhang* 雜想觀章 (Chapter of Meditation on Complex Concepts) of *Guanjing* 觀經 (Contemplation *Sūtra*) and the Rebirth *Dhāraṇī* (*wangsheng zhou* 往生咒) three times. The name of the Buddha is recited five-hundred times and twelve prostrations are done toward Amitābha Buddha. Each of the three bodhisattvas receive prostration. After the three refuges, the assembly withdraws from the hall. After the midday meal, they recite the *Da chanhui wen* 大懺悔文 (Great Repentance Text), the name of the Buddha five-hundred times, and then after the three refuges they withdraw from the hall. In the evening they recite the *Amituo jing* and conduct the ritual of distributing food to hungry ghosts, which was designed by Master Budong 不動 (d.u.) on Mount Mengshan. In the evening, they recite the "Shangpin shangsheng zhang" 上品上生章 (Chapter on the Highest of the Highest Stage of Birth) of *Guan jing* once, and the Rebirth *Dhāraṇī* three times, and the name of the Buddha one-thousand times, followed by twelve

---

79 *Chixiu Baizhang qinggui*, *T* no. 2025, 48: 7.1151c4-d10.

80 Ibid., 7.1152a1-8: 上來現前比丘眾, 諷誦楞嚴秘密咒 ...... 摩訶般若波羅密.

prostrations to Amitābha Buddha. The three bodhisattvas receive three prostrations each. After the three refuges, everything is concluded.[81] Hence, the evening recitations of the Conglin system during the Ming and Qing hold the *Amituo jing* and *nianfo* as primary. This is primarily the result of *nianfo* practice flourishing within the Conglin system.

#### 2.3.2 The *Zhujing Risong Jiyao* 諸經日誦集要 (Collection of Daily Recitations from Scriptures) by Zhuhong 袾宏 (1535-1615)

On the basis of extant literature, the earliest time in which morning and evening recitations appeared within the Conglin system is the Ming dynasty. For example, the "Conglin liangxu xuzhi" 叢林兩序須知 (Notes for the two rows in monasteries) by Feiying Tongrong 費隱通容 (1593-1661) and edited by his dharma disciple Baichi Xingyuan 百癡行元 (1611-1662) in the section on "things the head monk should know" mentions that "morning and evening recitations should not be missed."[82] The *Yongjue Yuanxian chanshi guanglu* 永覺元賢禪師廣錄 (Records of sayings of Chan Master Yongjue Yuanxian) compiled by the monk Yuanxian 元賢 (1578-1657) and re-edited by Weilin Daopei 爲霖道霈 (1615-1702) states, "After evening recitations, meet with people."[83] The regularization of morning and evening recitations was connected to the importance the Ming government laid upon the Pure Rules.. Prior to the extant version of Baizhang's *Pure Rules*, Zhongzhi 忠智 (d.u.) (abbot of the Chan temple Dazhi Shousheng 大智壽聖 on Mount Baizhang) in Zhengtong 7 (1442) stated the following in a petition: In Hongwu 15 (1382), Ming Taizu decreed that "Monks of the monasteries who do not conform to the Pure Rules shall be bound by law."[84] In Yongle 10 (1412), Ming Taizu further decreed that "Monastics must abide by former regulations. Each shall pursue the demeanour of the patriarchs, be diligent in maintaining the Pure Rules, and be of pure conduct in body and mind."[85] In Yongle 22 (1424), he made the following decree in connection to those monks not abiding by the regulations: "They are to be rectified according to the provisions of the Pure Rules."[86] Under the influence of government policy strictly binding monastic activities, it is clear the *saṃgha* sought to self-govern in connection to the regularization of the Pure Rules, while the regulations and full integration of morning and evening recitations in the *conglin* system were an expression of that regularization.

81 *Baizhang qinggui zhengyi ji*, *XZJ* no. 1233, 111: 8.832b10-833a3.
82 *Conglin liangxu xuzhi*, *XZJ* no. 1340, 112: 1.151b10: 早晚課誦勿失.
83 *Yongjue Yuanxian chanshi guanglu*, *XZJ* no. 1418, 125: 4.448a5-6: 至晚課後, 與諸人相見.
84 *Chixiu Baizhang qinggui*, *T* no. 2025, 48: 1.1109c25-26: 諸山僧人不入清規者, 以法繩之.
85 Ibid., 1.1109c28-29: 僧人務要遵依舊制, 各務祖風, 謹守清規, 嚴潔身心.
86 Ibid., 1.1110a3: 照依清規料治.

In Wanli 28 (1600), Zhuhong compiled the *Zhujing risong jiyao*, which provided a model for daily recitations for the monastics and laypeople of the time. According to the account by Zhuhong in the preface ("Chongke zhujing risong xu" 重刻諸經日誦序), the *Baiba ban jing* 百八般經 (Hundred and Eight Scriptures) that was widely circulated in shops was the book recited by monastics and laypeople in the morning and evenings. Zhuhong believed it to be "a mix of true and false. Those aware will mock it."[87] As a result of this, with the *Baiba ban jing* as a basis, the contents were selected, the table of contents changed, and finally he removed the false scriptures therein. He also looked through the *sūtra*s and *vinaya* plus the works of past authors, selecting the most suitable scriptures and mantras, while inserting some sections into the text. It was then printed and circulated. During a later reprinting, he added further revisions and printed it as a booklet, which was preserved at Yunqi si 雲棲寺.[88] However, we have no way of knowing the definite contents of the *Baiba ban jing*.

Zhuhong revised the *Zhujing risong jiyao* when he was abbot of Yunqi si, completing the work based upon the needs of monks in training. Zhuhong in Longqing 5 (1571) went into residence at Yunqi si and gradually started reviving the temple. At the same time, for the purposes of regularizing the daily practices of the *saṃgha*, he established his unique system of training. Zhuhong started establishing the regulations for his congregation, the "Yunqi gongzhu guiyue" 雲棲共住規約 (Regulations Governing Co-Habitation at Yunqi). He thereby made Yunqi si the largest society of Nianfo practice in the late Ming. In said text, the day is divided into four periods: "At three times, worship and recitation. At one time, carry out meditation."[89] The first five periods of the day constitute the first time, in which the Śūraṃgama Dhāraṇī and *Guanjing* are recited, in addition to recitation of Amitābha's name one-thousand times plus the merit dedication of the *Xiao Jingtu wen* 小淨土文 (Small Pure Land Text). The second time, between dawn and the midday meal, would include the recitations of the "Sishiba yuan wen" 四十八願文 (Text of Forty-Eight Aspirations), recitation of Amitābha's name one-thousand times, and the same merit dedication as before. The afternoon is the third time, in which there are evening recitation of the *Amituo jing*, the "Bashiba chanhui wen" 八十八懺悔文 (Text on Eighty-Eight Repentances), the Mengshan version ritual of distributing food to hungry ghosts, recitation of Amitābha's name one-thousand times, and merit dedication from the "Da Jingtu wen" 大淨土文 (Large Text of the Pure Land). The evening is the fourth time, which includes recitating Amitābha's

87 *Yunqi fahui*, JXZ no. B277, 32: 1.565a3: 真僞交雜, 識者誚焉.

88 Ibid., 1.565a2-10.

89 Ibid., 22.157b13: 三時禮誦, 一時入觀.

name one-thousand times, returning to the sleeping quarters, and meditation and rest. Zhuong offers some evaluation of the training during the fourth time: "A day of pure conduct, is neither complicated nor simple. Those who always uphold this will never be weary."[90] Zhuhong's recitations required one to be quite strict, since those who lacked discipline were fined ten *wen* of cash.

The restrictions of the *Zhujing risong jiyao* existed primarily to provide a norm for daily training of monks at Yunqi si. They were divided into a "general collection" and "specific collections". The former are the morning and evening recitations. The latter are the daily recited mantras and works of eminent monks. The contents are clearly given in Appendix 4.3.

The *Zhujing risong jiyao* shows many similarities to contemporary Conglin recitations in the way it regulates morning and evening recitations. It is clear that this text was enormously influential on the standardization of recitations.

### 2.3.3 The *Zhujing Risong* 諸經日誦 (Daily Recitations from Scriptures) and *Chanmen risong* 禪門日誦 (Chan Gate Daily Recitations)

Zhuhong's revision and implementation of the *Zhujing risong jiyao* was never able to facilitate an immediate integration of daily recitations among all temples in the country. While this text was popular, eminent monks of the Chan school further perfected it. Zhixu 智旭 (1599-1655), one of the four eminent monks of the late Ming, carried on with Zhuhong's personal mission. At the age of seventeen, he read Zhuhong's *Zizhi lu* 自知錄 (Account of What I Know) and *Zhuchuang suibi* 竹窗隨筆 (Writings by the Bamboo Window), and then became a Buddhist monk. After ordaining under Xueling 雪嶺 (d.u.), he resided at Yunqi si and listened to lectures about the *Cheng weishi lun* 成唯識論 (*Vijñaptimātratāsiddhi-śāstra*). It is clear that he was very familiar with the content of the *Yunqi gongzhu guiyue*. Fascicle six of Zhixu's *Lingfeng zong lun* 靈峰宗論 (Treatise on the Tenets of Lingfeng) includes a "Ke chongding zhujing risong zixu" 刻重訂諸經日誦自序 (Preface to the Reprint of the Daily Recitations from Scriptures) as follows:

> Ever since Master Mazu created the Chan monasteries and Master Baizhang established the Pure Rules, they have been carried on, and, in the meantime, many put forth their prejudices and wantonly added articles. *Baizhang qinggui* [was] included in the canon and the 3-fascicle *Zhujing risong* circulated in society, for example, abound with fabricated and strained contents. They do not know the correct way of spiritual cultivation; moreover, as for the single matter of morning and evening

90 Ibid., 22.157b20: 一日淨業, 不繁不簡, 永持無斁.

> recitations, they contradict one another and [have a] lack of etiquette, occupying themselves only [by] singing, praising, drumming, and clashing cymbals. How lamentable it is! Master Yunqi collated and produced a definitive edition and sponsored the engraving [of the *Zhujing risong*]. Many places of ancient Hangzhou tended to espouse the text. The malpractices seen in the Rear Capital (i.e. Nanjing) have not been reformed in the slightest. I recently, joined by fellows living in seclusion, have been working hard to correct the errors and [I am] considering reprinting the work after cutting out the inessential again and keeping only the imperative and the integral. Also, we have picked contents from the *Vinaya* Piṭaka, which are wholesome to the body and mind of beginners and made marginal supplements, and publicized them to those holding the same aspiration. We wish that those who are lofty and brilliant maintain the purity and grace of the meditative contemplation. Thus they could follow the text and enter enlightenment, not admiring the voice and sound of the Yoga any more.[91]

From Zhixu's account, it is clear that the *Zhujing risong* comprised three booklets, which was popular in the *conglin* system during the late Ming, and was completely different from Zhuhong's *Zhujing risong jiyao*. The *Zhujing risong jiyao* was widely popular in Hangzhou, but in Nanjing there was not even the slightest change. Zhixu lamented that the contemporary *conglin* system of recitation only focused on beating the Dharma drum and chanting, and as a result reprinted the *Zhujing risong jiyao* to correct the Buddhist community. Zhixu and the monks at Yunqi si at the time reprinted, edited, and preserved the important parts of the *Zhujing risong jiyao*, and moreover selected some elements from the *vinaya* canon that would be inspirational and helpful for beginners. According to the account in the "Lingfeng Ouyi Dashi zonglun xu shuo" 靈峰蕅益大師宗論序說 (Preface to the Treatise on the Tenets of Master Lingfeng Ouyi), Zhixu had the *Chongding zhujing risong* 重訂諸經日誦 (Reprint of the Daily Recitations from Scriptures) in two fascicles, but the *Ouyi Dashi quanji* 蕅益大師全集 (Complete Works of Grand Master Ouyi) and others do not record this, hence there is no way of clearly knowing the content.

91 *Lingfeng zong lun* 6.509:
自馬祖建叢林, 百丈立清規, 世相沿襲, 遂各出私見, 妄增條章. 如藏中《百丈清規》一書, 及流通《諸經日誦》三冊, 杜撰穿鑿, 不一而足. 寧惟罔知正修行路, 秪早晚課誦一事, 參差失款, 惟事唱贊鼓鈸, 大可嘆矣. 雲棲和尚, 較刻定本, 古杭諸處, 多分遵行; 而留都積弊, 分毫未革. 邇與幽棲學侶, 力正其訛, 重謀付梓, 再刪繁蕪, 獨存切要, 並於律藏, 取警策身心有益初學者, 略補一二, 以公同志. 願高明者, 守禪觀之清雅, 庶可隨文入證, 莫羡瑜伽音響也.

FIGURE 36 The Longzang 龍藏 canon, stored in the scripture hall of Ayuwang Monastery 阿育王寺, Ningbo 寧波.

In the late Ming and early Qing, morning and evening recitations were never integrated. There were various types of *Zhujing risong*. From the middle-period of the Qing dynasty onward, various recitation manuals differed in content (daily recitations, Chan recitations, Chan services, etc), but all included morning and evening recitations of mantras, scriptures, in addition to assorted rituals and praises.

The present *Chanmen risong* used in the Conglin system was mainly established during the Yongzheng era (1722-1735), primary containing the "Tang Taizong Wen Huangdi yuci Xuanzang sanzang shengjiao xu" 唐太宗文皇帝御賜玄奘三藏聖教序 (Tang Emperor Taizong's Preface Bestowed unto the Holy Teachings of *Tripiṭaka* Master Xuanzang), plus morning and evening recitations, and assorted rituals, repentances, praises, incantations and other ceremonies (tonsuring, etc). The *Fuzhou Baiyang Fashun Chanshi shizhong* 撫州白揚法順禪師示眾 (Teachings of Chan Master Baiyang Fashun's of Fuzhou) include texts and scriptures dealing with admonishments and teaching. The most recent is the *Fozu xindeng* 佛祖心燈 (Mind Lamp of the Buddhas and Patriarchs). However, the contents of the morning and evening citations in the

*Chanmen risong*, the morning recited *Śūraṃgama Dhāraṇī*, the ten lesser mantras, the evening reciting of *Amituo jing*, the performance of the Mengshan ritual of feeding hungry ghosts are identical to the present *Fomen bibei kesong ben* 佛門必備課誦本 (Manual of Necessary Buddhist Recitations) of the Conglin system, but the aspirational and dedicatory verses and the praises following the three refuges are different.

To conclude, the morning and evening recitations of the *conglin* system have been continually perfectly and revised. Each monastery has edited their content according to their respective circumstances.

### 2.4 *Reflection and Criticism of Buddhist Services in the Ming, Qing, and Republican Periods*

Following the malpractice in Buddhist services, after the mid-Ming period, there was reflection and criticism within the Buddhist world. In particular, Yunqi Zhuhong attempted to regulate and admonish temples and monks. His strict regulations of monks engaging in services included the following: "Those monopolizing *sūtra* recitation shall be ejected from the monastery."[92] "Those gathering together men and women to engage in worldly feasts shall be ejected from the monastery."[93] "Those studying worldly arts such as composition and music shall be ejected from the monastery."[94]

At the same time, he regulated the activities of monks carrying out services using cash fines. The relevant section in the *Yunqi gongzhu guiyue fuji* 雲棲共住規約附集 (Supplement to the Regulations Governing Co-Habitation at Yunqi) states the following:

- Those who are not present at the moment of Glory and Purity will be fined 26 cashes.
- Those who arrive after 1 *ye* 葉 since the *sūtra* recitation and repentance start will be fined 40 cashes. They must double the recitation of the *sūtra* passages missed.
- Those who make idle chat and exchange banter while others are reciting *sūtra*s or repenting will be fined 120 cashes. If doing them during the break, they will be fined 60 cashes.
- Those who involve in dispute will be fined 60 cashes; those who involve in scuffle and breach etiquette will be fined 120 cashes.

92 *Yunqi fahui*, *JXZ* no. B277, 33: 22.162c22-23: 泛攬經事者出院.

93 Ibid., 22.162c23-24: 聚集男女做世法齋會者出院.

94 Ibid., 22.162c26-27: 習學應赴詞章笙管等雜藝者出院.

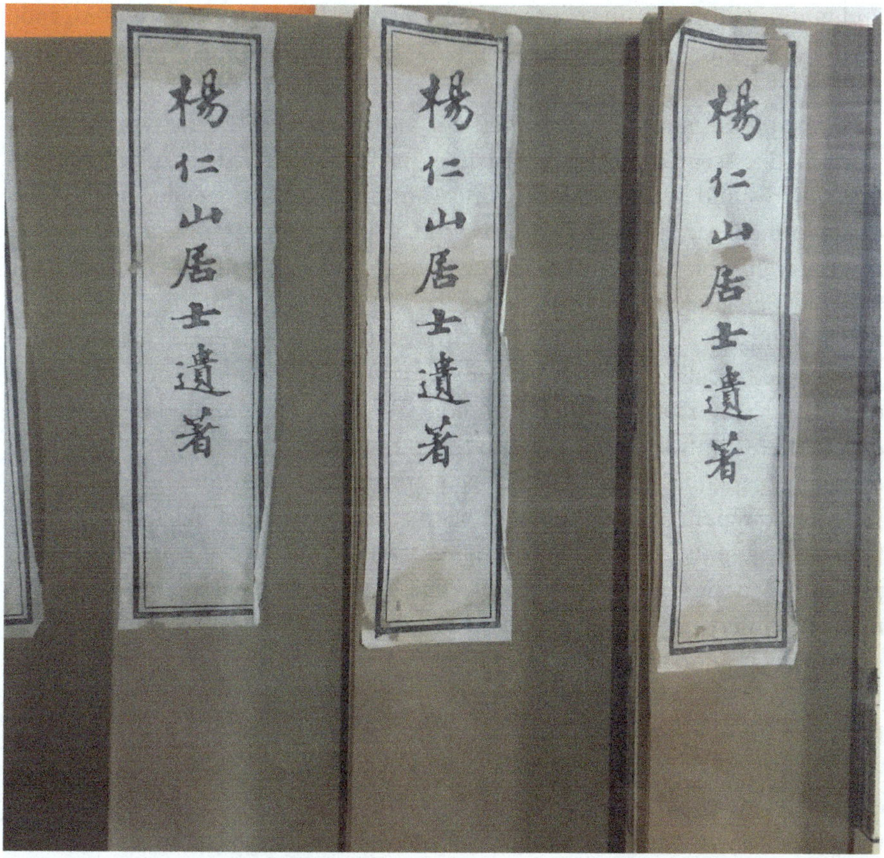


FIGURE 37 The works of the lay Buddhist reformer Yang Renshan 楊仁山 (1837-1911), stored in the Jinling Buddhist publishing house 金陵刻經處.

– Those who do not make the sound in recitation will be punished with doing the recitation once again.[95]

When Zhuhong was at Yunqi si, he rectified the monastic discipline. On one hand, he regulated Buddhist services, and on the other advocated that *nianfo* practice be done in place of *sūtra* recitation and repentance services.

In the early years of the Republic period, Taixu 太虛 (1890-1947) analyzed Buddhism's contemporary situation and divided the tradition into four streams. The first was the pure high stream. This stream did not care for profit

---

95 Ibid., 22. 171b14-21:
嚴淨時不至者, 罰錢二十六. 誦經懺過一葉方至者, 罰錢四十文, 經要多少刻加倍補誦. 雜談戲論當經懺中者, 罰錢一百二十文; 在經懺歇時者, 罰錢六十文. 鬥爭者, 罰錢六十文; 大爭失威儀者, 罰錢一百二十文. 不出聲者, 罰重念過.

and honor. They were pure in their conduct. However, since they had no good instruction, many were lax and in the dark. Few were refined. This stream of people were quite rare. At the time they were the hardest to find. The second was the stream "sitting meditatively for incense-periods". This type of monk just practices seated meditation strictly for five or six years, and, afterwards they could stand beating and scolding, gaining a slight knowledge of the ways of life in the Chan monastery. Then they will be called "senior practitioner," to be promoted from the position Official Duty to Group Head, and further to the abbot, which constitutes the entire goal of their lives. The inferior ones among them would just seek to be fed. The third was the stream of lecturing on *sūtras*. They could be called Dharma Master since they could recite from memory ancient commentaries. The inferiors among them hear and remember only one or two stories, only learning to flaunt their knowledge. The forth was the stream of "remorse aflame". They would learn chanting and instruments, and do recitations and repentance on behalf of people, as well as different rituals, gaining fame and benefits for themselves, thereby selling out the Dharma. They would play music in the streets and seek offerings.[96] Of these four streams, the fourth made up ninety percent of monastics. Taixu said of their misconduct and depravity that "There are still those that I could not stand to mention."[97] From this, it is evident that the malpractices connected with Buddhist services flourished in Chinese society.

Following the introduction of Western Modernism, science, rationalism and democracy became a tide. Scientists used their unique critical consciousness to oppose anything that could not be proven true. They opposed any formal deduction or analytical deduction. They not only attacked religion, but they attacked traditional worldviews. Thus, their criticism resembles Francis Bacon's criticism of idealism and empiricists' attack against religion. Their worship of science can be regarded as a substitute for religion, or might be a "religion of science".[98] Scientists blamed the obstruction of Chinese science on the flourishing of superstitious beliefs and cults. As a result, the later stream of Chinese Buddhism clashed, in particular regarding the practice of various services, which was subject to fierce criticism.

The famous revolutionary of the capital class in the late-Qing, Zhu Zhixin 朱執信 (1885-1920), emerged from the natural sciences and inherited the tradition of ancient Chinese atheistic thought. He adamantly rejected the religious

96 Taixu, *Quanshu*, 29.42. Besides the four streams, Taixu also mentioned one type of people who did not receive ordination or recite *sūtras*. He considered those people, though living in temples, did not count as Buddhists.

97 Taixu, *Quanshu*, 29.43.

98 Kwok, *Weikexue zhuyi*, 25-26.

beliefs (afterlife, the existence of spirits, karma, etc) propagated by the late stream of modern Buddhism, pointing out that monks reciting *sūtras* to "ease the passing of the departed" was also completely impossible.[99] Chen Duxiu 陳獨秀 (1879-1942) also harshly criticized the superstitions of Buddhism, pointing out that "science shall replace religion". He believed that Buddhism "Makes light of reality and tends toward [an] empty perspective, being weary and thoughtless, leading to social degeneracy, and the decline of the Indian people. The ancient religion cannot but be guilty."[100] At almost the same time, Cai Yuanpei 蔡元培 (1868-1940) proposed that "fine education replace religion." At the same time, he hoped to reform Buddhism, and to look after the well-being of the nation: (1) *Nianfo* practice and repentance should be eliminated, and attention should be paid to Buddhist matters. (2) The Japanese charter of Hongan ji 本願寺 should be emulated, in which study halls were widespread. (3) Fitness should be encouraged for military purposes as a way of supporting national defense. (4) The prohibition against eating meat promotes refraining from killing. This is Buddhism's most essential point.[101] Cai Yuanpei's point mixed with his own ideas of fine education, plus Darwinist evolution and his inclinations toward separation from religion. At the same time, he believed that he had to find a substitute for religion. Not only did not intellectual thought bring about a tide of anti-Buddhist ideas, but at the same time it sparked fierce criticism of Buddhism among the masses and the state.

In the process of criticizing the superstitions of Buddhism, the most common criticism was that of Buddhist services, which led to a call to abandon them. However, speaking from the Buddhist world, there was a need to reply to the voice of society, but at the same time there was also a need to consider the reality of Buddhism. As a result, the Buddhist world's reflection and criticism of religious services had to be stronger and deeper. There was a need to change the image of Buddhism as superstitious, which required properly dealing with Buddhism and its relationship to various types of superstition. As a result, monks at the time and laypeople advocated views that "Buddhist is not a superstitious teaching," "Buddhism is a faith of reason," and "Buddhism destroys superstition." There was a large movement in Buddhism at the time to purify Buddhism of superstition and to address wrongs while bringing out virtues. However, the Buddhist world not only offered theoretical explanations and

99 Zhu, *Zhu zhixin ji*, 880.

100 Chen, *Wencun*, 16-17: 薄現實而趣空觀,厭倦偷安,人治退化,印度民族之衰微,古教宗風,不能無罪也.

101 Ma, *Xuanlan*, 179.

purification, they also attempted to save a desperate crisis, reforming and correcting the negative elements of Buddhism.

Taixu was a leader of the modern movement of Buddhist reform, and was always clearly opposed to various types of superstition that damaged the true image of Buddhism. He offered the following thoughts on the original intention underlying Buddhist services and their malpractices:

> As for reciting *sūtra*s and presenting repentance, such Buddhist practices stem from one's mind of piety, honesty, firmness, and keenness. Reciting *sūtra*s and conducting liturgy of repentance on occasions when requested by people to deliver the dead from suffering and to pray for blessings on their behalf, [monastics] should muster up all their heart of sincerity to cultivate merit for the benefactors. Nowadays, [monastics] recite *sūtra*s and conduct repentance liturgy, concerning themselves with only the daily payment of one or two *jiao* 角 of cashes. Monasteries in various regions have thus become workshops that seek opportunities of high profit, losing the fundamental virtue of pious commitment.[102]

The original intention underlying Buddhist services was that one's own sincere execution of dedication and recitation of scripture plus repentance was originally a personal practice, but the merit could be dedicated on behalf of other people or for prayers of good fortune. However, present services became a commercial exchange and temples because factories that sold to the highest bidder. How could Buddhism flourish? Thus, the core of services was in sincere cultivation of virtues, not in money.

Taixu returned such services back to being a form of spiritual cultivation, and moreover removed superstition elements, thereby reforming "Buddhism for the dead" and "Buddhism of spirits", and advocating for "Humanistic Buddhism" (*Rensheng Fojiao* 人生佛教). He states,

> "Buddhist learnings for human life" should put aside and avoid discussing the topics of heavenly beings and ghosts. [One should] fulfill the commitment in this very life of a human and extend it to super and super-super life, cleansing away all sorts of superstition such as the cult of heavenly beings and cult of ghosts. [One should] follow the life philosophy and

102 Taixu, *Quanshu*, 35.95:
即於經懺佛事而論, 本是從自己誠實懇切之心. 念經、拜懺, 有人請薦靈祈福, 乃將一片誠心以回向施主; 如今念經、拜懺者, 只知一天可得一二角錢了事; 各地寺院, 遂成善價而賈之工場！把原來誠心修行之美德喪失.

> base it on popularization and scientization in modern society and then establish a Mahāyāna Buddhism that approaches the unsurpassed, correct, universal, perfect, and gradual enlightenment.[103]

"Humanistic Buddhism" originally meant to do away with all superstitions dealing with gods and spirits. On a foundation of modern humanism, accessibility, and science, he established a type of Mahāyāna Buddhism that met with modern needs.

However, "Humanistic Buddhism" is not just emphasis on addressing said aspects of death and spirits. It goes further and finds a place for all gods and spirits. As Taixu in 1920 stated:

> "Taking refuge in the Buddha" has two meanings: (1) The subject hereby, holding a definite mind of correct conviction, takes refuge in the Buddha's teachings, and therefore, all heavenly deities, ghosts, and spirits are no object of his/her belief, nor a name in which he/she takes refuge. (2) The subject hereby, holding a definite mind of correct conviction, takes refuge in the Buddha's teachings and wishes *deva*s, *nāga*s, ghosts, and spirits, as well as various beings all take refuge in the Buddha.[104]

The stance of Buddhism is to not only correct beliefs in spirits, but to incorporate them. Hence, Taixu's new Buddhist ideal was engaged in the world. It was also a way to aid society through a Buddhist approach, assisting humanity to progress and improve the world. Society, humanity and the world were to be things to address and improve. It was not about the life to come.[105]

Taixu's criticized Buddhist services in order to rectify the malpractices. The problems facing the faith and nation at the time were grave. People found it difficult to live. If Buddhism did not actually engage in service to humanity, how could they be called Mahayanists? However, criticism of Buddhist services never meant that they had to abandon all such practices, since Buddhist religiosity could be expressed through important funerary practices.[106] Taixu's

---

103 Taixu, *Quanshu*, 5.209:
"人生佛學"者, 當暫置"天"、"鬼"等於不論, 且從"人生"求其完成以至於發達爲超人生、超超人生, 洗除一切近於"天教"、"鬼教"等迷信, 依現代的人生論、群眾化、科學化爲基, 於此基礎上建設趨向無上正遍覺之圓漸的大乘佛學.

104 Taixu, *Quanshu*, 1.225:
歸宿佛有二義：一、我今以決定正信之心歸宿佛教故, 則一切天神鬼靈等均非我之所信仰, 即非我所歸宿; 二、我今以決定正信之心歸宿佛教, 則願他人及一切天龍鬼神及諸眾生, 皆歸信佛.

105 Lin, "Jingshi fojiao", 27.

106 Li, "Zongjiaoxing", 53.

stance on services therefore suggested that they be brought back to their original role. At the same time he advocated for "Humanistic Buddhism", which was changing Buddhism's focus while advocating for social engagement and concern for humanity.

Modern Buddhism's self-awareness concerning its services was quite in line with reality. In their reforms, many temples shifted to either not doing them or making them flexible. For instance, the monk Tanxu 倓虛 (1875-1963) opposed profit from services. Zhanshan si 湛山寺 in Qingdao stopped doing services. However, some lay benefactors who had contributed to the construction and maintenance of temples repeatedly required that there be some flexibility. Tanxu had no choice and reconsidered, making an exception to only the lay Buddhists of the above kind. The temple possessed all the offerings of laypeople, but later the temples integrated their finances and gave receipts to monks reciting *sūtras*. The time during which Dharma services were carried out was also to be after the classes at Zhanshan Seminary, with attention given to halting negative social influences.

Yinguang 印光 (1861-1940) came from the Pure Land faith, and fundamentally opposed Buddhist services. He firmly inforced that his temples should not engage in such services. In his "Lingyan si yongzuo shifang zhuanxiu jingtu daochang ji cici jianzhu gongde beiji" 靈岩寺永作十方專修淨土道場及此次建築功德碑記 (Stele Inscription for the Building of the Pure Land Temple Lingyan si), he asserted that the temple would focus on *nianfo* practice and do away with other paid services.[107] They did not receive money for services, but Yinguang used *nianfo* as a substitute for services. His "Nanjing Sanchahe chuangjian Fayun si yuanqi beiji" 南京三汊河創建法雲寺緣起碑記 (Stele Inscription for the Building of Fayun si in Nanjing) states:

> There are believers who admire the trend of spiritual cultivation of the area, and they request opportunities to hold the seven-day meditation retreat, so as to prolong the lifespan of their parents, deliver the souls of their ancestors from suffering, eliminate their own sins, and bring blessings to their descendants. What they do, however, is only to make merit transference three times after the usual practice of reciting the names of buddhas. The practice of feeding the burning mouth is not conducted, lest monks-on-call impair the capacity of the retreat site. On the occasion of the seven-day retreat, only one or two persons are allowed to attend, but only to pay homage, [and they must] return within the same day. It is

107 Yinguang, *Xubian*, 2.148.

> not permitted for family and fiends, as well as young female attendants, to gather and stay at the retreat until it concludes before returning.[108]

Previously, saving souls from suffering and praying for blessings must be fulfilled by pentitent liturgies and rituals of feeding hungry ghosts, or other Buddhist rites. At this point, it was replaced by the seven-day retreat of chanting the Buddha's name and the transference of the generated merits. It was not permitted that too many of the benefactor's family attend the retreat, to ensure the purity of the ritual site. This principle is expressed in his "Ji'nan Jingu si chongxing beiji" 濟南淨居寺重興碑記 (Stele Inscriptions for the Restoration of the Jingju si in Ji'nan) and "Chuangjian Puti Jingshe yuanqi beiji" 創建菩提精舍緣起碑記 (Stele Inscriptions for the Building of the *Bodhi Vihara*).[109]

Yinguang believed that Buddhist services were empty and had no real effect. He wrote to layman Wen Guangxi 溫光熹 (d.u.) the following: "Gratitude to one's parents is deep and one should truly ask for *nianfo* from a monk with the Mind of the Way. One should not ask a monk who does services to recite scripture, repent, or do Water and Land Rites, as this is all just empty."[110] Not only did he reject that renunciates should do such services, he also pointed out that these also included many non-Buddhist elements. In his letter to layman Guo Jiemei (1900-1950) ("Fu Guo Jiemei jushi shuyi" 複郭介梅居士書一) he states the following:

> One should, in the acme of her sincerity and adoration, recite the name of the Amitābha Buddha, in the hope of eliminating the past karma, purifying the mind, and never committing a sin from then on. Realizing that in the *sahā* world her actions are bound for sins, she should set a resolute aspiration to be reborn into the West Pure Land. This is the correct way. Why not repent her sins in the mind instead of trying to eliminate sins only relying on fake *sūtras*? As long as one believes that the Buddha is able to save her from sufferings, why not recite the Mahāyāna *sūtras* preached by the Buddha, such as the *Jin'gang jing*, the *Amituo jing*, the *Xin jing*, the *Dhāraṇī* of Great Compassion, the *Dhāraṇī* of Rebirth into the Pure Land, as well as the *Fahua jing*, and the *Lengyan jing* for the purpose

108 Ibid., 160:
有信士慕此間道風, 祈打念佛七, 以期延椿萱之壽算, 超祖宗之靈魂, 消己躬之罪愆, 培子孫之福祉者, 仍照常念佛, 加三次回向而已. 焰口亦決不放, 以杜住應赴僧, 伏破壞道場之機也. 凡祈打七者, 只可來一二人, 以行禮敬, 即日便回. 若廣集親友, 及小年女眷, 住此待圓滿方歸者, 決不應許.

109 Yinguang, *Zengguang*, 4.15, 31.

110 Yinguang, *Sanbian*, 3.600.

> of eliminating sins and increasing blessings? The liturgy of Feeding Flaming Mouths of the Hungry Ghosts is the essential teaching for saving beings in the wilds; unexpectedly, they do not trust the teaching but take the rituals such as "Breaking the Hell of Blood Pond" and "Breaking the Hell" as requisite Buddhist undertakings. They receive no real benefits, making those who appreciate worldly ways but those who are ignotant of the Buddhadharma, thinking these [worldly ways] are Buddhadharma, and spawning various nonsenses denigrating the Dharma. Nonetheless, they consider themselves right; a pack of blinded beings, they still hold those practices as the principle.[111]

Yinguang emphasizes that repentance based upon *nianfo* could eliminate past transgressive karma. He said this was based upon the *Guanjing*. Shandao in the Tang and Ciyun in the Song both combined *nianfo* and repentance, producing various types of rituals, such as the *Jingtu fashi zan* 淨土法事贊 (Praises of the Pure Land Dharma) and *Wangsheng jingtu chanyuan yi* 往生淨土懺願儀 (Ritual of Repentance and Aspirations for Rebirth in the Pure Land). At the same time, Yinguang emphasized that reciting Mahāyāna scriptures could also eliminate past transgressive karma. False scriptures had been produced and some Buddhist services were based upon these (called destroying the blood lake, destroying hell, etc), and these brought Buddhism many negative consequences.

At the same time, following the revival of modern Buddhism, Chan Buddhism was also shaken up, with many majorly influential Chan monks appears, such as Xuyun 虛雲 (1840-1959), Laiguo 來果 (1881-1953), and Yuanying 圓瑛 (1878-1953). They worked to revive Chan Buddhist centers and revived the Chan Pure Rules. They advocated Chan meditation and retreats. As a result, in addition to rejecting Buddhist services in Chan temples, while putting in order Gaomin si in Yangzhou, Laiguo clearly proposed that all Buddhist activities apart from Chan practice not be permitted, such as ceremonies for the hall, Lotus societies, esoteric practices, *nianfo*, repentance, precepts, repentance, etc.[112]

---

111 Yinguang, *xubian*, 1.74:
當以至誠恭敬念佛, 以期消滅往業, 洗心滌慮, 不作後愆. 以娑婆動多罪愆, 決志往生西方, 方爲正理. 何可不在自心懺罪過, 專靠僞經懺滅罪過乎！既信佛能度苦, 何不念佛所說之大乘經, 如《金剛經》、《彌陀經》、《心經》、《大悲咒》、《往生咒》,及《法華經》、《楞嚴經》等,以期滅罪增福乎！《焰口》, 乃濟孤要法,反不相信,而群以破血湖、破地獄,爲必不可不作之佛事.自己不得真利益, 反令知世理而不知佛法之人, 謂此即是佛法, 因茲生出種種謗法之胡說巴道,尙自以爲是,一班瞎子,反奉爲圭臬.

112 Cheng, "Mingcha", 55-58; Chen & Deng, *Fojiao*, 291-92.

Xuyun's position on Buddhist services was more relaxed than that of Laiguo. In 1920, at the request of Tang Jiyao 唐繼堯 (1883-1927), the Governor of Yunnan at that time, he moved to Huating si in Kunming and restored an old monastery, which he renamed to Yunqi si. In 1930, he set up the *Yunqi si wannian bu* 雲棲寺萬年簿 (Ten-Thousand Year Register of Yunqi si). Therein is the following article:

> Monasteries should address rules governing services. They cannot be organized, since [the community] shall drift downstream. Hereafter this temple shall only consider a request from a benefactor for recitation or repentance on the mountain or in an affiliated temple, and apart from important Dharma protection, no one shall leave the gate, for it would interfere with activities of the path.[113]

Xuyun saw the degeneracy of Buddhist services carried out in monasteries, and as a result of this ruled that such services could only be carried out at Yunqi si or an affiliated temple. They were not to carry out services, since it would interfere with activities of the path. He therefore emphasized that monks could not privately respond to requests for services. This point was identical with Tanxu's.[114]

Xuyun not only regulated such services to be carried out in a specific location, but he also provided rectification and regulations for them. As a result, in 1920 he established the "Shuilu Fahui nianson zhishi guiyue" 水陸法會念誦執事規約 (Rules for the Water and Land Recites and Recitations). He explained the meaning of the services as follows:

> The Chan monasteries of old approached the lofty and isolated themselves from the worldly; except for praying for blessings, they never accepted invitations. This is because the great matter has yet to be settled, one has no time even to trim the nails, and how are they willing to handle worldly things and distract from the mindfulness of the Way? Moreover, one having yet to save themselves, how are they be able to save others? The *sūtra* says, "The teaching of Yoga is the commitment of bodhisattvas, who are already on the Ten Grounds, and it is not suitable for the ordinary beings who have initially developed the aspiration towards

113 Xiuyuan, *Fahui*, 798:
諸方叢林，應付經懺規矩，不能整理，漸趨下流．此後本寺常住，如有檀越請念經、拜懺，只准在山或下院念之，除重要護法外，概不出門，致妨道業．

114 Xiuyuan, *Fahui*, 807.

> enlightenment. Due to that the Chan monasteries suffered a recession and there was a constant concern over the shortage of all requisites, they slightly involved themselves in the Yoga practice of mindfulness and chanting. Entering the altar, one must consider it as the site of enlightenment; facing the images, one must consider himself as facing buddhas. Reciting the texts, remembering the ritual sequences, conducting the mission, and putting it into practice, one must synchronize the mouth and the body and match the speech to the mind. Do not be muddled or drowsy, do not be loose or distracted, do not be slack, and do not be greedy. One must be alert to the law of cause and effect and have a sense of shame, keeping wary and careful. In so doing, one will be able to convert people without expecting so and to benefit people without expecting so. As usually described, people offer me money, and I offer them Dharma; since these two actions of almsgiving are equal and not different in nature, it may be done on certain occasions. If one is reading *sūtra*s as if they were operating bellows while operating bellows or practicing repentance liturgy as if they were pounding rice with a pestle, or if one looks away while facing the divine images or has something else in the mind while reciting *sūtra*s or repentance texts, one inevitably invites invite criticism in the present life and receive retributions in future lives. It turns the Dharma treasure to benefit one's self and others into negative examples that lead one's self and others astray. One must exercise caution![115]

Conglin originally referred to a place of practice which had life and death at its core. Scripture recitation and repentance were originally bodhisattvas' expedient means for the benefit of beings. They were not something ordinary monks could carry out, but it had to be done due to hardships of living in the *conglin* system. As a result of this, when carrying out such services, they ought to be carried out from a position of spiritual practice. The benefactor makes an offering of cash to the monks, and the renunciates provide Buddhadharma. Offerings of wealth and Dharma are equal. If during the service, it is done for

---

115 Xiuyuan, *Fahui*, 831:
古之叢林, 高蹈絕俗, 除祝釐外, 不通應酬. 正爲大事未明, 剪爪不暇, 那肯應酬, 散其道念. 況且未能自度, 何能度人. 經云：瑜伽一法, 乃登地菩薩利生之事, 非初心凡夫所宜. 惟是叢林淡薄, 四事供應, 每虞缺乏, 故不得已, 乃略應念誦也. 然進壇必須生道場想, 對經像如對佛想. 誦其文, 思其義, 行其事, 踐其實, 必使身與口合, 口與心唯. 不昏沈, 不散亂, 不懈怠, 不貪利, 明因果, 知慚愧, 兢兢業業. 若是, 則不期度人而自度人, 不期利益而自利益. 所謂人以財與我, 我以法與人, 等施無異, 猶可權爲. 若鼓籥橐而看經, 舂杵碓而禮懺, 身對尊像而目視他方, 口誦經懺而心存別念. 如是必招現前之毀謗, 受未來之業報. 使自利利他之法寶, 反成自誤誤人之罪案, 可不慎哉.

money, with no focus on the intention, then it is just a formality which will invite criticism, and create future negative karmic consequences in the form of suffering. Thus, people should not fool themselves or others when carrying out services.

Moreover, Xuyun established detailed rules. An excerpt of them is as follows:

1. If seeing one's name on the noticeboard, the *sūtra* reciter needs to take a bath and in the next morning conduct the recitation and repentance liturgy. One must keep the Three Modes of Activities serious and sincere and match the speech to the mind. One is not allowed to profane the recitation and repentance practices with irrelevant chats, let alone acting frivolous and wildly or frolicking. Those who are deliberately chatting or frolicking during the recitation will be punished by making up for the recitation. Or if chatting, frolicking, or clamouring during the rest period after the repentance session, they will be fined with kneeling down for the burning time of an incense stick.
2. During the recitation, one is not allowed to turn one's head back or look at people around them. One must single-mindedly voice the recitation, every word must be clear and distinct, and repetition is not allowed. Those who arrive after the moment of Glory and Purity or even after one page has been recited will be punished with *sūtra* recitation and repentance liturgy; still, they need to make up the lost work of recitation.
3. The announcer should not be hasty and brief; one should recite one after another, conforming with every point of the text. They and drummers and bellmen should make the sounds stately and graceful, which should not be dissonant and short.
4. Those who take care of lamps and incense inside and outside of the site must all keep pious and clean, and beware of the danger of fire. The situations of various altars and halls must be paid extra caution.
5. When distributing food to the hungry ghosts, one should conform with every point of the text and form *mudrās*, intone spells, and visualize in all sincerity, with the Three Mode of Activities corresponding to one another. It is not allowed to carelessly vibrate the tongue and rashly finish the work. The same rule [applies] to plain texts.
6. Everyone conduct one's work according to the timetable, and when the hour comes, the drum and bell are struck. Those who do not show up will be punished.
7. The outer six altar sites all wait for the great altar to launch the penitential liturgy, and these altars launch the liturgy at the same time. Act without fail, and those who violators will be punished.

8. On occasions of *sūtra* recitation, penitential liturgy, and distributing food to hungry ghosts, it is not permitted to collect statues of buddhas, various decorations, and instruments before the conclusion of service.
9. Incense, candles, and fruits, once dropped on the ground, should not be used as offerings. Those have been used as offerings are not to be used again.
10. Vegetables, rice, and other foods must be fully cooked before using as offerings. Do not offer dry or raw food.
11. All members of the Dharma assembly, if violating the rule against brawling, losing the dignity of demeanour, resisting to be disciplined, and defing authority, are to be expelled from monastery.[116]

Xuyun took on the responsibility of establishing regulations for various Buddhist activities, and moreover punished those who disobeyed, all of which was to preserve the solemnness and order of Buddhist services, truly aiming for the liberation of oneself and others.

## 3 Philanthropy and the Life-Release in Ming and Qing Buddhism

The development of Ming and Qing Buddhism, on one hand, inherited the trends of the Song and Yuan, with a focus on philanthropy, engagement in socially beneficial activities, and popular leadership. At the same time, due to the flourishing of Dharma societies and the growth of clan powers, the task of social organization gradually came to societies and clans, which is why there was a decline of Buddhist organization of philanthropy in the Ming and Qing

116 Jinghui, *Quanji*, 4.33:
一、誦經人, 先日見牌上有名, 即沐浴. 次早誦經禮懺, 須三業志誠, 口誦心唯. 不得於念誦禮拜時, 夾雜閒言, 更不得輕狂戲笑. 若誦經故意雜談戲笑者, 於經懺中罰補誦; 或在懺後歇息時, 戲談喧嘩者, 跪香.
二、念誦時, 不得回頭轉腦, 看看人物, 一心稱念, 字字分明, 不得重念. 過嚴淨不至, 誦過一頁方至者, 罰, 經懺仍須補罰.
三、表白人, 不急遽簡略, 宜一一依文, 次第念誦. 其鐘鼓等, 亦宜莊雅, 不宜繁碎.
四、內外香燈行人, 俱要誠潔, 小心火燭, 以及各壇堂中, 尤宜加倍慎重.
五、施食要一一依文, 精誠結印, 誦咒作觀, 三業相應. 不得含糊彈舌, 急促了事, 白文亦然.
六、每日按定鐘點作事, 鐘到鳴鼓一通. 如有不至者, 罰.
七、外六壇場均聽大壇起懺, 各壇亦宜同起, 不得有誤. 如違者, 罰.
八、經懺及施食等, 不得法事未竟, 先收佛像莊嚴器物.
九、香燭供果等, 倘落地者, 不得用; 供過者, 亦不用.
十、上供疏菜飯食等, 必熟得味, 不得用乾物、生物.
十一、法會內外人等, 犯鬥爭者, 因爭失威儀, 不勝調伏, 不服者, 出院.

periods. On the other hand, the Buddhist faith deeply penetrated into society during this period, with a significant influence on people's lives. Zhuhong advocated life-release, establishing ponds for this purpose while building "Life-Release Societies". He established the rules governing this practice, and actively pushed for regularization of it within Buddhism.

### 3.1 *Buddhist Philanthropy in the Ming and Qing*

Following the promotion of the integration of the Three Teachings (Buddhism, Confucianism, and Daoism), society during this period was established with Confucian-type regal kingship at its core, integrating Buddhist notions of compassion and cause and effect together with the ideas promoted in morality books, such as doing good deeds to gather merits and saving and benefiting people. This greatly promoted the development of philanthropic activities. Ming and Qing Buddhism seldom participated in the establishment and operation of public welfare institutes and other public philanthropic systems such as apothecaries. They primarily engaged in popular philanthropy. State-funded Buddhist systems such as Tang dynasty institutes that were "fields of merit for care of the ill" and Song dynasty "field of merit institutes" never appeared in the Ming and Qing. The most important part of Ming and Qing philanthropy was the many organizations that emerged, such as orphanages and hospices. This was intimately connected to the flourishing of Ming period gentlemen's Dharma societies. Under the call and guidance of scholarly societies, these organizations did not require temples or monks to participate. The gentlemen of scholarly societies fulfilled such responsibilities themselves. Literati of the Ming and Qing shook up their world and promoted the spirit of Confucianism through their fellowships. They also realized the ideal of their societies through philanthropic institutions.

However, many Buddhists participated in these institutions, combining their cultivation of virtue with their Buddhist faith, which is also an important point of Buddhist philanthropic activities during the Ming and Qing. For instance, Luo Yunmei 羅允枚 (d.u.) called for *nianfo* and established a Pure Land society, in which " everyone practiced life release, raised orphans, fed the hungry, for which all rejoiced."[117] Peng Jiqing 彭際清 (1740-1796) in 1773 at the age of thirty-four was at Zhendi si 真諦寺. He received the bodhisattva precepts from the elder of Mount Xiang, Shiding 實定 (1712-1778), and then passed away in 1796. He produced a work tilted *Huayan nianfo sanmei lun* 華嚴念佛三昧論 (Huayan and Nianfo *Samādhi*), advocating for the union of Huayan and Pure Land teachings based upon the translation of the chapter of

117 *Jingtu shengxian lu*, *XZJ* no. 1525, 135: 8.360a6: 凡放生、育嬰、賑饑諸善事, 咸樂成之.

"Samantabhadara's Vows" in the *Huayan jing* by Prajñā (Bore 般若, fl. 745-805). He sincerely implemented Pure Land doctrine and also energetically advocated the union of Confucianism, Buddhism, and Daoism. On the other hand, he also supported educating families, and the power of society-clans, "[The court] opened up Halls of Vicinity of help the destitue, installed Fields Nurturing [the Lower Class] Tribe to support the poor, created the Relict Care Fellowship in aid of widows, and establish Life Relieving Fellowship to save lives. Each had its own vow text which stated that the merits were made for rebirth in the Pure Land."[118] He also established the Hall of Vicinity (*Jinqu tang* 近取堂) and The Pengs' Fields Nurturing the Tribe (*Pengshi runzu tian* 彭氏潤族田). The Hall of Vicinity was similar to the Fellowship of Sharing Goodness, consisting of branches such as the Department Providing Coffins (*shiguan ju* 施棺局), the Department Providing Clothings (*shiyi ju* 施衣局), and Fellowship Relieving Lives (*fangsheng hui* 放生會). The Relict Care Fellowship (*xuli hui* 恤嫠會) was established to help women who remained chaste after the death of their husbands. The Pengs' Field Nurturing the Tribe later developed into the Pengs' Charitable Landed Trust (*Pengshi yizhuang* 彭氏義莊), which brought benefits to the local people. It is clear that Ming and Qing Buddhists displayed strong Buddhist notions of faith when engaging in philanthropy.

Temples and monks of Ming and Qing Budhdism engaged in traditional philanthropic activities such as building roads and bridges. For instance, in 1453, the "Chongxiu tongji qiao ji" 重修通濟橋記 (Chronicle of the Rebuilding of Tongji Bridge) from Jinjiang county 晉江縣 in Fujian records that this bridge was rebuilt several times from the Norther Song to Ming periods, which was always under the supervision of monks.[119] Between 1056 and 1064, the monk Benguan 本觀 (1039-1100) rebuilt it and it was named "*jimin* 濟民 (ferry the people)." In 1084, transport magistrate Xie Zhonggui 謝仲規 (fl.1049-1084) rebuilt it and was re-named "*tongji* 通濟 (ferry)." In 1143, the monk Wenhui 文會 (d.u.), the Judicial Commissioner (*tixing* 提刑) Chen, and the Palace Secretary (*shumi* 樞密) [...][120] built a stone bridge with sixteen intervals. It was more than seventy feet tall, and a few feet wide, with both sides having railings, and buddha images set atop the bridge. This construction was completed in 1169. Between 1195 and 1200, the monk Liaoxing 了性 (fl.1186-1200) rebuilt three small stone bridges. In 1413, the stone beams of a bridge collapsed. In 1453, with the efforts of Xie Chen 謝琛 (d.u.), Department Vice Magistrate in the

118 *Jingtu shengxian lu xubian*, XZJ no. 1526, 135: 2.416b8-10:
開近取堂以周窮乏, 置潤族田以贍貧族, 舉恤嫠會以濟孀居, 立放生會以全物命, 各有發願文, 回向淨土.

119 Zheng & Dean, *Beiming*, 70-71.

120 The character is missing in original text.

Quanzhou government, Zhang Qin 張欽 (d.u.) took on the responsibility for rebuilding. The monk Minmo 湣默 (d.u.) oversaw construction work and completed the rebuilding of the bridge. Also, the "Xiu Hai'an changqiao ji" 修海岸長橋記 (Chronicle of the Long Bridge Construction at Hai'an) records that Zhijing 智鏡 (d.u.) of Chengtian si 承天寺 in Quanzhou and Tizhao 體照 (d.u.) of Lingyuan si 靈源寺 both respectively participated in the construction of said Long Bridge throughout the years.[121]

At the same time, the monks also participated in disaster relief and burials of exposed bones. For instance, in the year 1594, Hanshan Deqing 憨山德清 (1546-1623) at the age of forty-eight gave all the temple's rations to the people near the mountain when there was a great famine in Shandong with many people dying. The rations were insufficient, so Deqing travelled to Liaole 遼樂 to buy beans to save the people from disaster. As a result of his diligent efforts, the nearby people escaped disaster and nobody met with death.[122] Later, Deqing, at the age of fifty-two (1598), buried the bones of those many who had died in Huicheng 會城, and also created a funerary shrine for them for seven days and nights.[123]

The Buddhist world in the Ming and Qing periods might have lacked support from the national system, but given the appeal of compassion and ideas of karmic fruition, there was still active engagement in philanthropy.

### 3.2 *The Custom of Life-Releasing in Ming and Qing Buddhism*

Following the economic prosperity of society in Jiangnan, the neighboring regions of Hangzhou and Ningbo flourished in the sale of seafood. The people were fond of eating and increasingly consumed seafood and meat. At the same time, the silk industry of Jiangnan developed, leading to the inevitable destruction of many beings. The Buddhist world of the Ming and Qing actively advocated life-release, especially Yunqi Zhuhong, in response to the lifestyle of Jiangnan society. For instance, the "Yunqi Lianchi Hong Dashi taming" 雲棲蓮池宏大師塔銘 (Pagoda Inscription to Lianchi) by Hanshan Deqing has the following: "He absolutely proscribed killing beings. He esteemed life-release. His penned works have long circulated in the realm, and all within the [borders] of the seas respected him."[124] His influence on the Buddhist world of the Ming and Qing was extremely great.

121 Zheng & Dean, *Beiming*, 70-71.
122 *Hanshan Laoren mengyou ji*, *XZJ* no. 1438, 127: 53.964a15-18.
123 Ibid., 54.966b15-16.
124 Ibid., 27.598a7-8:
極意戒殺生, 崇放生, 著文久行於世, 海內多奉尊之.

"Proscribing killing and protecting life" is an important expression of the Buddhist view on life. Yunqi Zhuhong proposed ideas such as that "animals possess buddha-nature," "animals possess sentience," "animals can be reborn," and "animals can also experience mental anguish and suffering" in an attempt to reform popular perceptions of animals in order to proscribe slaughtering. Zhuhong's notion of buddha-nature was that "all possess this mind and surely can become buddhas", which expresses the idea that animals can recollect the buddha as well as be reborn in the Pure Land. He states the following in his *Amituo jing shuchao* 阿彌陀經疏鈔 (Commentary on the *Amitābha-sūtra*):

> In the term "sons and daughters of good families", "good" has two referents: one is the "good" or positive karmic causes from previous lifetimes, and the other is having been reborn as "good" or superior type of beings. "Sons and daughters" is a generic term for all sentient beings in all of the Six Destinies, both of the clergy and the laity and both of sharp faculties and of dull faculties. ...Hungry ghosts, animals, and beings in the hell, of both sexes, can also be addressed by "sons and daughters". If only chanting the name of the Buddha, one will be reborn to the pure land, and therefore the practice is universally effective for all beings.[125]

Zhuhong interpreted "good sons and daughters" to mean "all beings on the Six Paths who possess karmic connections", i.e., that animals have minds that can "produce meditative stabilization through recollection". Animals also possess the ability to attain buddhahood. This is a position on animal life raised from the angle of spiritual practice and liberation. As animals and people equally possess buddha-nature, to harm animals is improper conduct like the strong bullying the weak. The section on the transgression on killing in the *Zhuchuang erbi* 竹窗二筆 (Two Brushes by the Bamboo Window) states the following: "All beings possess buddha-nature. An ant and human are one and the same. Why speak of differences in volume? It is like the rich deceiving the poor, the strong overcoming the weak; why also speak of differences in volume when humans can kill and eat?"[126] Zhuhong advocated that people should not differentiate

---

125 *Amituo jing shuchao*, XZJ no. 326, 33: 3.440b6-441a4:
善男子女人者, 善有二義：一是宿生善因, 一是今生善類. 男女者, 通指緇素利鈍, 及六道一切有緣眾生也. …… 又鬼畜地獄, 雌雄牝牡, 亦可均名男女. 但念佛者, 俱得往生, 是通一切眾生也.

126 Mingxue, *Quanji*, 3799:
據含靈皆有佛性, 則蟻與人一也, 何厚薄之足云？如其貴欺賤, 強陵弱, 則人可殺而食也, 亦何厚薄之足云.

between any sense of volume of buddha-nature, and that they should treat animals equally.

Next, Zhuhong argued that animals and people are on and the same, encouraging people not to kill them, since they also experience sensation and awareness. The section on the "Calamity of Boiling Water" in *Zhuchuang suibi* 竹窗隨筆 (Writings by the Bamboo Window) states the following:

> I see in the butcher's and wine shop lay turtles, eels, shrimps, crabs, and the like. When to be cooked by boiling in the pot, they are told, "The power of the various beings you could not resist, and you are too humble and low to make voices. If you could resist their power, you should have reacted like tigers and leopards; if you could make voices, the cry of injustice and howl of anguish should have shook the whole universe."[127]

Zhuhong made people aware of the pain of animals through the reality of boiling animals: "One cannot bear the pain." His aim was to proscribe killing animals, and to protect life. In addition, animals also had relatives, and were unwilling to separate from them, just like a parental love in the human world: "All beasts love their offspring."[128]

Zhuhong encouraged people to reflect on their own lifesyles and feeling, imagining that animals also similarly feel things, thereby bringing about a likeminded approach, empathy, and an intolerance for their suffering. In his "Jiesha fangsheng wen" 戒殺放生文 (Text on Life Release and the Proscription of Killing), he asks people to refrain from killing on birthdays, and when someone is born, plus at sacrifices, weddings, feasts, prayers, and on the job. Moreover, Zhuhong invokes stories of cause and effect to figuratively explain the merits of refraining from killing.

At the same time, refraining from killing is not only an expression of the mind of compassion, it is furthermore a method with which to attain rebirth in the Pure Land. As the "Jiesha fangsheng wen" states, "Pure karma and the three merits: not killing [due to] the mind of compassion abides as the first. Now not killing anything, one also releases life. Having released life, one also gives cause for rebirth in the Pure Land via the dharma. This sort of application when coming to fruition results no doubt in ascending the *Lotus* Platform on the Ninth

127 Mingxue, *Quanji*, 3694:
予見屠酤之肆, 生置鱉鱔蝦蟹之屬, 於釜中而以百沸湯烹之, 則諭之曰：彼眾生力弗汝敵, 又微劣不能作聲音. 若力敵, 則當如虎豹; 噉汝若能作聲, 冤號酸楚之聲, 當震動大千世界.

128 Ibid., 3347.

Grade."[129] This proscription against killing was included among methods of spiritual practice, leading to religion liberation from human empathy.

Zhuhong not only advocated the idea of refraining from killing, he moreover actually built the Shangfang life-release pond and the Changshou life-release pond to the south and north of the Hangzhou city respectively in order to benefit devotees everywhere who could practice virtue through life-release. Zhuhong's "Chongxiu Shangfang si zao fangsheng chi ji" 重修上方寺鑿放生池記 (Account of the Life-release Pond Redeveloped at Shangfang si)[130] records that Shangfang si was first built in 921. The temple fell apart in 1453. People then occupied the land, only one-tenth of which remained.. Layman Shen Shanneng 沈善能 (d.u.) originally occupied the land, and in 1544 was promoted in rank. He then rented out the land.

The property rights were left to a daughter. After his daughter married into the Wang family, she respected her father's wishes, and transferred the land rights to Yunqi si. As a result of this the land became monastic land again. After the daughter of the Wang family and her husband passed away, layman Song Huqing 宋化卿 (d.u.) heard of her donation and greatly praised it, giving money to the descendants of the Wang family, and moreover making a contract for the settlement. Zhuhong, after hearing laymen give various explanations, pinched and scraped and finally redeemed the site as the home of the Shangfang si. At the time, the laymen suggested that a temple could be built on the former site. Zhuhong inspected the layout of the land and constructed a waterway and embarkment for the life-release pond. He also reestablished quarters that had been abandoned, allowing three sincere monks to look after the site and carry on with their practice. Not long after Zhuhong had built the life-release pond at Shangfang si, he continued extending the pond at Changshou Hermitage. According to the "Beimen Changshou an fangsheng chi ji" 北門長壽庵放生池記 (Account of the Life-Release Pond at Changshou Hermitage at the North Gate), the Changshou Hermitage was the former site of Xiangluan yuan 翔鸞院 during the Later Tang. After years of ruin, Zhuhong and local gentry collected money to restore the life-release pond.[131]

The construction of the pond was a great task, requiring substantial investment in terms of money, manpower, and material support. At first, Zhuhong transmitted his ideas on life-release and refraining from killing through talks on *sūtras*, encouraging contemporary gentleman to accept his ideas. The

129 Mingxue, *Quanji*, 3379:
淨業三福, 慈心不殺實居其一. 今能不殺, 又放其生; 既能放生, 又以法濟令生淨土. 如是用心, 報滿之時, 九品蓮臺高步無疑矣.

130 Ibid., 3384-3386.

131 Ibid., 3390-3391.

biography of Yu Changru 虞長儒 (1553-1621) in the *Jushi zhuan* 居士傳 (Biographies of Laymen) records the following: "At that time, Master [Zhu]hong resided in Nanping 南屏 and lectured on the *Yuanjue jing* 圓覺經 (*Sūtra* of Perfect Awakening). He raised money, purchased the Wan'gong Pond 萬工池 and established the Life-Release Society (*fangsheng she* 放生社). The chanting of thousands of monks and laypeople resounded in the valley. Many virtuous elites attended the assembly, which was just led by [Yu] Changru."[132] Zhuhong lectured on the *Yuanjue jing*, and thereby gained the cooperation of gentlemen at the time, especially via Yu Changru's promotion, guidance, and leadership. At the time, the "Beimen Changshou an fangsheng chi ji" records that laymen, monks, and gentlemen contributed either financial support, foodstuffs, or participated in the labor.

At the same time, the support of the life-release pond required enormous finances. On one hand, the laymen and devotees contributed cash, and on the other, the monastics of the temple economized and provided funds. The *Yunqi jishi* 雲棲紀事 (Chronicle of Yunqi) states the following: "Yunqi set a place for life-release in the mountain, which abounded with various animals. As there were animals, monks reduced their provisions to feed them. Weeding cost about 200 *shi* 石 of grains. The two life-release ponds in and outside of the city cost over one hundred *jin* 金, which had never been insufficient."[133] It is clear that the building and maintenance of the life-release pond was the result of the integration of the notion, system, and practice of life release..

Under the influence of societies during the Ming dynasty, Zhuhong established "Life-Release Societies". Based upon the conventions of the institute (*Shangfang shanhui yue* 上方善會約), we know of the "Shangfang Benevolent Society (*Shangfang shanhui* 上方善會)" and "West Lake Life-Release Society (*Xihu fangshengshe* 西湖放生社)". The said conventions of the institute established the charter, timeframe, recitations, offerings, lectures, and governance of this society.[134] The charter of the "Shangfang Benevolent Society" was to "recite Mahāyāna precepts scripture and together with this release life while recollecting the Buddha, this being a place for the benevolent people of Shang[-fang]."[135] Therein "Mahāyāna precepts scripture" refers to the *Fanwang*

132 *Jushi zhuan*, *XZJ* no. 1623, 149: 42.946b18-947a3:
時宏公方坐南屏演《圓覺經》, 募錢贖萬工池, 立放生社, 緇白數萬, 伽陀之音震動川谷, 一時清節之士多與其會, 實長孺倡率之.

133 Mingxue, *Quanji*, 5077:
雲棲在山中設放生所, 飛走各類充牣其中; 既有生食, 眾僧復減口以養之; 除菑茭, 約費粟二百石; 城內外放生二池歲費百餘金, 自來無缺乏.

134 Ibid., 4941-4944.

135 Ibid., 4941: 讀誦大乘戒經, 兼之放生念佛, 是諸上善人同會一處.

*jing* 梵網經 (Brahma Net *Sūtra*). It is clear that "Shangfang Benevolent Society" was a gathering of lay practitioners in which the precepts were maintained, *nianfo* was practiced, and life was released into the pond. On New and Full Moons every month, the devotees would gather in Shangfang si. Those willing to participate registered their names. It is clear from the number of people recorded as registered that this Dharma service was held on regular days. After the assembly had some together in an orderly fashion, a monk would lead them and recite the *Fanwang jing* in one fascicle and recite the name of Amitābha Buddha five-hundred or one-thousand times. After the recitation, there would be tea and fruits of three colors offered. After *nianfo*, the fruits would be consumed. The expenses for the tea and food came from the participants who each provided five *fen* of silver, which was then organized by the supervisory monk. After the Dharma service, there would be an exchange of Dharma discussions. Each provided silver for life-release, without any set amounts, while others bought their own animals to release. The organization of the Shangfang Benevolent Society took turns appointing their head. The required membership contribution was a fixed five *fen* of cash. The primary job of the head was to prepare the incense, candles, tea, and hot water, and to record the participating members. In short, Zhuhong hoped to maintain the equality, simplicity, and ease of the life-release society, for it could last long if so.

At the same time, the *Fangsheng yi* 放生儀 (Life-Release Rite) was revised atop the foundation of the life-release rites of Siming Zhili 四明知禮 (960-1028) to ensure ease of execution.The steps primarily included quiet contemplation, sprinkling of water, preaching of Dharma, repentance, and making vows. Zhuhong's greatest reform was adding the *Dhāraṇī* for Rebirth in the Pure Land (*Wangsheng jingtu shenzhou* 往生淨土神咒) and the chapter "Ten Dedications" in the *Huayan jing*. He hoped to express the meaning of life-release through dedication of merit to beings, and rebirth in the Pure Land.

Zhuhong under the influence of societies in the late Ming constructed life-release ponds, brought together societies for life-release, revised rites for life-release, established a society charter for life-release, and built up a system for Buddhist life-release, thereby making a system for life-release that was systematic and regular. Life-release was made appropriate to the values of the time at a spiritual level, and at a formal level it became organized and systematized. Under Zhuhong's influence, life-release flourished in the Buddhist world of the late-Ming and early-Qing. Eminent monks, such as Zhanran Yuancheng and Miyun Yuanwu 密雲圓悟 (1567-1642), as well as Feng Mengzhen 馮夢禎 (1548-1595), Yu Chunxi, and Tao Wangling 陶望齡 (1562-1609), all greatly supported activities related to life-release. Yu Chunxi at Xihu organized a Superior Lotus Society, encouraging members to practice life-release. The *Wulin zhanggu congbian* 武林掌故叢編 (Collection of Wulin Tales) includes a charter for said society that Yu Chunxi compiled (*Shenglian sheyue* 勝蓮社約). Tao Wangling and Zhang Ziyun 張子雲 (d.u.) also established a life-release society in the south of the Hangzhou city in the year 1601.

## 4 The Formation of the Belief in the Four Buddhist Sacred Mountains in Ming and Qing Periods[136]

James Robson writes, "When Buddhism made its way into China from India, it did not bring along a systematically organized set of Buddhist sacred mountains. Buddhist sacred geography in India was primarily keyed to sites associated with the life story of the Buddha or the distribution of his relics, as well as some sites connected with particular bodhisattvas."[137] In China, however, Buddhist sacred sites came into being through the long-term accretion of Buddhist beliefs and traditions. They took shape in a variety of ways, such as travels in pursuit of religious instruction, the building of monasteries, and going on pilgrimages.

Travelling in search of instruction from masters was a traditional means of learning for followers of Buddhism. In this way, some famous mountains and large monasteries gradually established themselves as centres for devotees in quest of learning. The "Five Mountains and Ten Monasteries" (*Wushan shicha* 五山十剎) of the Song dynasty, a general term for Chan monasteries in the Jiangnan region, was based upon that Buddhist system; hence, it was distinctly different from the "Sacred Buddhist Mountains"(*Fojiao mingshan* 佛教名山) which is essentially faith-based.[138] During the Ming and Qing periods, as Chan monasteries declined, clerics and laypeople gradually used traditional famous mountains like Wutai 五臺, Emei 峨眉, Putuo 普陀, and Jiuhua 九華 as major destinations for visits and pilgrimages. Due to this, the social influence of

136 This section is rewritten on the basis of an article previously published as: Kai Sheng, "On the Veneration of the Four Sacred Buddhist Mountains in China," *The Eastern Buddhist* 44.2 (2013): 121-143. The author wishes to thank *The Eastern Buddhist* for permitting this republication.

137 Robson, *Power of Place,* 52.

138 Here the term "sacred Buddhist mountain" is used to refer to *Fojiao mingshan* 佛教名山, but for convenience it makes an exception by using the term "marchmount veneration" to indicate the belief that has been formed centering on these sacred Buddhist mountains. Marchmount, originally, is a translation of the Chinese term *yue* 嶽 and refers to what has become established in China as the Five Marchmounts 五嶽. Edward Schafer was probably the one who came up with the translation, and James Robson has a detailed discussion on it in his *Power of Place*. My borrowing of this term is partly justifiable given that there were Buddhist complexes on some of the *yue*, specifically Mount Song 嵩 and Mount Heng 衡.

FIGURE 38 Jinding 金頂 Peak of Mount E'mei 峨嵋山.

sacred mountains expanded and finally formed the basic framework for the concept of the Four Sacred Buddhist Mountains.

Recent scholarship has been mainly focused on case studies of Putuo Island and Mount Wutai,[139] but has paid little attention to the reasons for the formation of the Four Sacred Mountains concept and to the exact time period during which it took shape. In fact, although each of the Four Sacred Mountains witnessed a flourishing of faith at different times, the joint appellation, the "Four Sacred Mountains," appeared only when Mount Jiuhua rose in status. Historically, regarding the formation of the sacred Buddhist mountains, Chinese Buddhism and Chinese society have had differing opinions that have changed and developed over time. In spite of these varying understandings, famous mountains like Mount Lu and Tiantai have never been included among the ranks of sacred Buddhist mountains. This suggests that the concept of a sacred

139 For studies on Mount Putuo, see Ishino, "Fudarakusen no junreiji", 143-59. For studies on Mount Wutai, see Cui, *Wutai shan Fojiao shi*; Choi, "Koseiryōden", 192-94; idem, "Godaisan", 15-29.

Buddhist mountain must have some special connotation. So far, scholarship has revealed very little about what the veneration of "Buddhist mountains as sacred sites" implies.[140] Clarifying this will thus help us to understand the rationale behind the Sinicization of Buddhist belief and the historical causes for its formation.

### 4.1 *The Time Frame in Which the Four Sacred Buddhist Mountains Concept Appeared*

Historically, the joint appellation "Four Sacred Buddhist Mountains" for Mount Wutai, Emei, Putuo, and Jiuhua evolved over time. Many famous mountain monasteries were built by Buddhist monks and were often centres for Chinese Buddhism. In spite of this, the Sacred Mountain concept has varied with time. For example, in his essay, "Gu Hengyue lü dashi Xiangtang Tangxingsi Yangong bei" 故衡岳律大師湘潭唐興寺儼公碑 (Commemorative Stele Engraving for the Monk Yan[zhi] of the [Southern] Peak *Vinaya* Tradition, [Resident of] the Tangxing Monastery at Xiangtan City), Liu Yuxi 劉禹錫 (772-842) made a survey of the Buddhism of his time:

> Within the Nine Divisions (i.e. China), Buddhism varies according to locality. [People] in central China are preoccupied with [personal] reputation and interest. Since nothing is more effective than marvelous enlightenment in breaking [the illusion of] reputation, those who practice meditative stillness admire Mount Songshan. Northern folk are eager to exert martial force. Nothing is better than the myriad physical manifestations of the Buddha for deterring people from the use of martial force, so those who pursue the way of holiness venerate Mount Qingliang. People of the South are imprudent and frivolous. Nothing counteracts such behavior better than the cultivation of a dignified manner, so people practicing the *Vinaya-piṭaka* admire Mount Hengshan. These three famous mountains constitute the sublime realm.[141]

Liu Yuxi pointed out that among the renowned Chinese Buddhist Mountains of his time, Mount Songshan was the centre for Chan Buddhism, Mount Wutai

140 Sheng, "Sida mingshan", 80-82. Building on this article, this chapter further explores the formation of marchmount veneration.

141 *Quan Tangwen* 610.2730-31:
佛法在九州間, 隨其方而化, 中夏之汨於榮利, 破榮莫若妙覺, 故言禪寂者宗嵩山. 北方之人銳以武力, 懾武者莫若示現; 故言神道者, 宗清涼山. 南方之人剽而輕, 制輕莫若威儀; 故言律藏者, 宗衡山. 是三名山爲莊嚴國.

was the centre for mysterious inspiration, while Hengshan was the centre for those who practiced the precepts and cultivated a dignified manner.

According to the research of Daoyu 道昱, a Taiwanese scholar, Mount Wutai is known as the "Qingliang" 清涼 mountain because it has a year-round accumulation of snow and the weather there is never hot. This characteristic matches the account of Mount Qingliang given in the "Pusa zhuchu pin" 菩薩住處品 (Chapter on the Residing Places of the Bodhisattvas) of the *Huayan jing*, wherein Bodhisattva Mañjuśrī takes up residence on this mountain, thereby generating divine inspiration and mass fervor. As early as the fifth century, the legend that Mañjuśrī Bodhisattva was manifest at Mount Wutai was already in circulation. As for Mount Emei, it was merely a famous mountain for tourism during the Six Dynasties (220-589). It was reported that while out harvesting medicinal herbs, old Mr. Pu 蒲翁 encountered the Bodhisattva Samantabhadra there, but this legend lacks the confirmation of textual evidence.[142] During the mid-Tang era (618-907), Chengguan 澄觀 (738-839) made a pilgrimage, first going to Wutai and then to Emei, hoping to encounter Samantabhadra. When annotating the *Huayan jing*, he praised Mañjuśrī and Samantabhadra as two of the three saints of Huayan, which led to Mount Emei being known as the "Silver Realm" during the Five Dynasties period (907-960). For Mount Putuo, it was during the early Tang dynasty that accounts of the efficacious response of Guanyin 觀音 (i.e. Avalokitêśvara) at Mount Butanluojia 布呾洛迦 (i.e. Potalaka) was introduced into China. With the construction of Guanyin chapel 觀音院 by the Japanese monk Huie (Jp. Egaku) 慧鍔 (fl. 863) for the statue of Guanyin that was unwilling to leave [and be ferried eastward to its former country], the legend that Guanyin had taken up residence on Mount Putuo started. During the Song dynasty (960-1279), people on ships imperiled in the nearby seas prayed to be rescued by the Putuo Guanyin; during the Southern Song (1127-1279), Mount Putuo's reputation was established due to the reappearance of Guanyin's inspiring, efficacious responses at Chaoyin cave 潮音洞 and the Chan Buddhist cultivation of Chan Master Zhenxie Qingliao 真歇清了 (1088-1151) and others. During the Yuan dynasty (1271-1368), stories about Guanyin's instant assistance on Mount Putuo grew more diverse, and the mountain repeatedly received imperially-bestowed titles and money. Due to a combination of Putuo's Chan tradition and Guanyin's efficacious responses, Mount Putuo evolved into a sacred site for Guanyin. The story of Mount Jiuhua began with the cultivation practice of the Sillan master

---

142 *Fozu tongji*, *T* no. 2035, 49: 43.395b18-20:
峨眉志云 : 昔有蒲翁, 因採藥入山, 望峯頂五色雲放白光, 忽一鹿前導至岩上, 見普賢大士真相, 自茲顯迹.

Kim Chijang (Chin. Jin Dizang) 金地藏 (705-803) on that peak. Due to a paucity of capable monks to continue his tradition, as well as to a lack of incidents demonstrating the inspirational, efficacious responses of the Bodhisattva Dizang 地藏 (Skt. Kṣitigarbha), this tradition came to be overshadowed by a group of literati known as the "Jiuhua Poetry Society" (Jiuhua shishe 九華詩社) during the Song and Yuan periods; hence, the mountain was the last one to be listed as a sacred peak.[143]

So, when did the joint appellation, "the Four Great Sacred Peaks" actually appear? That is a difficult question.[144] By the Ming dynasty (1368-1644), the title "Three Great Sacred Peaks" had appeared. In Wanli 萬暦 17 (1589), in his "Butuoshan zhi xu" 補陀山志序 (Preface to the Mount Butuo Gazetteer), Tu Long 屠隆 (1543-1605) wrote:

> Of the three major [Buddhist] sites in China, [Mount] Emei in the west is the seat of Samantabhadra, Wutai in the north is the seat of Mañjuśrī, while Butuo in the East Sea is the seat of Guanshiyin 觀世音. Since the north and west are not far from the Buddhist country (i.e. India), they have enjoyed close, easy contact and have been gradually influenced by the Way of the Dharma. The East Sea is a deeply isolated location. This remote wasteland is far removed from contact with Buddhism; hence, people there have been submerged [in the sea of *saṃsāra*] for a long time and are tainted by the five kinds of impurity. Through the Buddha's deep compassion, Guanshiyin has bestowed cultivation and salvation on Butuo [Island] and [in her manifestation as the rain-bestowing Dragon King] Sagara-nāgarāja, is an efficacious and helpful guide. Deep, steep, and magnificent, both Emei and Wutai are the most gorgeous holy sites in China, while Butuo, in a remote location in the vast sea, is especially extraordinary.[145]

Unambiguously, this preface establishes Mount Putuo as Guanshiyin's sacred seat, Emei as Samantabhadra's, and Wutai as Mañjuśrī's.

---

143 Daoyu, "Mingshan kao", 58-106.

144 In the article referenced above, Daoyu cited the *Baizhang qinggui zhengyi ji* 百丈清規證義記 as evidence and claimed that the "Four Sacred Mountains" appeared only after 1878.

145 *Putuo shanzhi* 6.595-96:
震旦國中, 三大道場, 西峨眉以普賢, 北五臺以文殊, 而東海補陀以觀世音. 西北距佛國不遠, 道法漸摩, 近而且易. 東海僻在深阻, 聲跡荒遐, 衆生久苦沉淪, 薰染五濁, 如來重滑之. 茲觀世音之開化補陀, 津梁婆竭, 良有以也. 峨眉、五臺深峭雄拔, 秀甲神州. 而補陀獨立大瀛海中孤絕處, 尤爲奇特.

In Wanli 33 (1605), Li Changchun 李長春 (?-1607), the Minister of Rites, also mentioned the "three great sacred peaks" in his essay, "Emei Dafosi luocheng song bing xu" 峨眉大佛寺落成頌並序 (Extolling and Introducing the Construction of the Giant Buddha Temple on [Mount] Emei), saying:

> I have heard that there are three Buddhist sites in China: namely, Emei, Wutai, and Putuo. They stand firmly as the three legs of a cauldron within the universe, serving as guides for humans and gods.[146]

But a piece by Chaoyong 超永 (?-1693+) records that after Chan Master Tianyin Yuanxiu 天隱圓修 (1575-1635) left home at the age of twenty-four in Wanli 27 (1599) to become a monk, a fellow monk told him, "I have heard that Bodhisattvas manifest themselves on the 'Four Great Sacred Peaks'; their supernatural power is vast."[147] Judging from this, it can be seen that the designation of either three or four great sacred peaks appeared gradually during the Wanli period (1573-1620).

The biography of Yetai 夜臺 (?-1610) in the *Buxu Gaoseng zhuan* 補續高僧傳 (Supplement to Extended Biographies of Eminent Monks) records Yetai's experiences of divine responses during a pilgrimage to Wutai, Emei, Putuo, and Jiuhua. Not only does it clearly mention that "the master has recently visited 'the Four Great Sacred Peaks,'" but it also ends with the statement: "Yetai visited the 'Four Great Sacred Mountains' and left his footprints everywhere in the imperium."[148] The *Buxu Gaoseng zhuan* was compiled by Minghe 明河 (1588-1640) who, right before his death in Chongzheng 13 (1640), asked his disciple Daokai Zhijong 道開自扃 (1601-1652) to continue the project. It was in Shunzhi 4 (1647) of the Qing dynasty that Daokai did the final editing of the book, and declared that the project was more or less completed, but the commentary attached to Yetai's biography was written by Minghe himself.

In fascicle 17 of the *Yunxi Liangting [Jing]ting chanshi yulu* 雲溪俍亭 [淨] 挺禪師語錄 (The Recorded Sayings of Liangting [Jing]ting of the Yunxi Monastery), there is a petition essay (*shu* 疏) eliciting support for the building of a *stūpa* entitled *Yunxiu jianta shu* 雲岫建塔疏 (Petition to Erect a Temple in the Misty Peaks). Here, the monk Jingting 淨挺 (1615-1684) of the Yunxi si 雲溪寺 relates: "at the top of it are the 'Four Sacred Mountains' dedicated to the worship of the four Bodhisattvas."[149] Jingting was a native of Renhe 仁和,

146 Ibid., 286: 蓋聞震旦國中有道場三, 曰峨眉、曰五臺、曰普陀. 鼎立宇內, 爲人天津梁.

147 *Wudeng chuanshu*, *XZJ* no. 1547, 141: 374b13: 聞四大名山, 菩薩出現, 神通廣大.

148 *Buxu Gaoseng zhuan*, *XZJ*. no. 1501, 134:20.326a6: 走四大名山, 足跡徧海內.

149 *Yunxi Liangting Ting chanshi yulu*, *JXZ* no. B294, 33: 797a: 此其上爲四大名山奉四菩薩.

Huangzhou. His secular name was Xu Ji'en 徐繼恩, his courtesy names were Liangting 俍亭 and Shichen 世臣, and his literary name was Yiting 逸亭. In Shunzhi 18 (1661) when he was forty-seven years old, he received the full precepts from Chan Master Sanyi Mingyu 三宜明盂 (1599-1665) and served as the abbot of Yunxi temple 雲溪精舍. This proposal to erect a pagoda must have been written while he was in charge of this monastery. Here, Yunxi expressly mentions the Four Sacred Mountains.

In the *Jiaxing Canon* 嘉興藏, in Hongjue Daomin's 弘覺道忞 (1594-1674) *Tiantong Hongjue [Dao]min Chanshi beiyou ji* 天童弘覺 [道] 忞禪師北游集 (Collected Essays of the Northern Travel of Chan Master Hongjue [Dao]min of Tiantong [Temple]), it records that "Meditation Master Xingxu 行虛 (d.u.) of Haiyu 海虞 drew [his own] blood to copy the *Fahua jing* for the Four Sacred Mountains."[150] In *Zizhulin Zhuanyu Heng heshang yulu* 紫竹林顓愚衡和尚語錄 (The Recorded Sayings of Monk Zhuanyu [Guan]heng of the Purple Bamboo Forest Temple), Zhuanyu Guanheng 顓愚觀衡 (1579-1646) mentions "visiting the four great sacred peaks and travelling all over the four quarters of the world."[151] In fascicle five of *Pinji [Zhi]xiang Chanshi yulu* 頻吉 [智] 祥禪師語錄 (The Recorded Sayings of Chan Master Pinji [Zhi]xiang), "*Shi Quezhi [Quan] Sui Chanren* 示闕止 [全] 遂禪人" (Showing How the Chan Monk [Quan]sui Followed his Master's Teachings), Pinji Zhixiang 頻吉智祥 (1637-1709) mentions the "four bodhisattvas"—Mañjuśrī, Samantabhadra, Guanshiyin, and Dizang[152]—as corresponding to the "Four Sacred Mountains." In the *Konggu Daocheng chanshi yulu* 空谷道澄禪師語錄 (Recorded Sayings of Chan Master Konggu Daocheng), Konggu Daocheng 空谷道澄 (1616-1683+) wrote of the Four Sacred Mountains in Kangxi 19 (1680).[153]

Given that the woodblock carving for the Jiaxing canon began during the Wanli period and mostly concluded during the Kangxi period (1662-1722), the term "Four Sacred Mountains" must have been very popular during the Kangxi period. For example, in Kangxi 26 (1687), Cao Suzhi 曹素徵 (d.u.), then the Surveillance Commissioner (*ancha shi* 按察使), claimed, "The 'three Es' (i.e. Mount Emei) are higher than the Five Peaks. It is the most beautiful peak in the Nine Divisions (i.e. China), the foremost mountain in China. It is not included among the Five Peaks, but is instead listed as one of the Four Great

150 *Tiantong Hongjue Min chanshi beiyou ji*, JXZ no. B180, 26: 5.303a10-11: 海虞行虛禪人瀝血書雜華大典, 用藏四大名山.

151 *Zizhulin Zhuanyu Heng heshang yulu*, JXZ no. B219, 28: 3.671c15-16: 到四大名山, 走遍四天下.

152 *Pinjixiang chanshi yulu*, JXZ no. B454, 39: 5.622c23-28.

153 *Konggu Daocheng chanshi yulu*, JXZ no. B471, 39: 8.963a11-12.

Sacred Peaks."[154] In Kangxi 37 (1698), in the *Nanhai Putuoshan zhi* 南海普陀山志 (Mount Putuo of the Southern Seas Gazetteer), Qiu Lian 裘璉 (1644-1729) recounts:

> Mañjuśrī, Samantabhadra, Avalokiteśvara, and Kṣitigarbha are all bodhisattvas who have attained the realization of *dharmakāya*. But due to their eagerness to save sentient beings, they are present everywhere. Additionally, they want sentient beings to have proper places in which to render respect. Therefore, Mañjuśrī manifests his response bodies (Skt. *nirmāṇakāya*) at Mount Wutai, Samantabhadra at Mount Emei, and Avalokiteśvara and Kṣitigarbha at Mount Putuo and Jiuhua [respectively]. Some people think that earth, water, fire, and wind correspond with the Four Sacred Mountains. The mundane world believes that each peak is respectively governed by one of the fundamental elements—earth, water, fire and wind (Skt. *mahābhūta*); however, in my opinion, that idea is false and unfounded.[155]

During the Kangxi period, not only did the 'Four Great Sacred Peaks' appellation appear, but the four fundamental elements of earth, water, fire, and wind were also utilized to characterize them. Thus, the concept of the Four Great Sacred Peaks must already have reached widespread popularity before this period.

Therefore, the concept of the Four Great Sacred Peaks probably appeared during the Wanli period and attained a general consensus among Chinese Buddhists and Chinese society by the Kangxi period. This was due to Emperor Wanli (r. 1573-1620), who esteemed the Buddhist presence on Mount Jiuhua, and to the writing and compilation of gazetteers regarding Mount Jiuhua which occurred shortly before the Wanli period. These include:

1. *Jiuhua shanzhi* 九華山志 (Gazetteer of Mount Jiuhua), six fascicles, compiled by Wang Yihuai 王一槐 (d.u.) during the Jiajing period
2. *Jiuhua shanzhi* 九華山志 (Gazetteer of Mount Jiuhua), six fascicles, re-edited by Su Wanmin 蘇萬民 (d.u.) and compiled by Sun Sui 孫檖 (d.u.), finished in Wanli 7 (1579)

---

154 *Emeishan zhi*, 7: 三峨高出五嶽, 秀甲九州, 震旦第一山也. 顧其山不入五嶽, 而列於四大名山之一.

155 *Putuo shanzhi* 6.558:
文殊、普賢、觀音、地藏, 皆久成佛道之法身大士. 以度生心切, 遍界現身, 又欲眾生投誠有地, 故文殊示應跡於五臺, 普賢示應跡於峨眉, 觀音、地藏示應跡於普陀、九華也. 世有以地、水、火、風分配四大名山者, 乃知地、水、火、風爲四大之義, 而以己見妄會之, 不可爲據.

3. *Jiuhua shanzhi* 九華山志 (Gazetteer of Mount Jiuhua), eight fascicles, reedited by Cai Lishen 蔡立身 (d.u.), finished in Wanli 21 (1593)

The listing of Mount Jiuhua among the Four Great Sacred Peaks must have occurred during the Wanli period, during which the overall faith-based framework for the concept of the Four Sacred Mountains took its final shape. The formation of the "four Great Sacred Peaks" was a landmark in the history of Chinese Buddhist belief and the most representative product of the Sinicization of Buddhism. Their veneration of the Four Great Sacred Peaks was an expression of popular faith. These places were where devout people, men and women alike, could go on pilgrimage to express their religious feelings; thus, they are a vivid representation of Buddhist culture.

### 4.2 *The Significance of Veneration of the Four Great Sacred Peaks*

The veneration of these four mountains was the result of a long-term accretion of Buddhist belief centered around them and others like them. Historians studying Buddhist history have explored their geographic and demographic environments, as well as ancient historical sites, and their efforts have shaped a unique genre of "mountain gazetteers," which constitutes a significant component of local Buddhist gazetteers.[156] In compiling a mountain gazetteer, writers must address a core question: Why did this particular mountain become a famous Buddhist peak? Thus, the components of these sacred peak gazetteers furnish us with an important foundation for understanding the significance of this sort of mountain veneration.

The *Gu Qingliang zhuan* 古清涼傳 (Ancient Record of Clear and Cold), compiled by the monk Huixiang 慧祥 (d.u.) of the Lan'gu si 藍谷寺 during the reign of the Tang emperor Gaozong (r. 649-683), is the first gazetteer to be exclusively focused on Mount Wutai. This two-fascicle book, which is structurally patterned after the *Shijia fangzhi* 釋迦方志 (Śākyamuni Local Gazetteer), recounts the evolution of Mount Wutai as a Buddhist sacred peak from five angles: (1) "Becoming a Standard Sacred Site" gives reasons why "Qingliang" mountain became renowned as a standard sacred site for manifestations of Mañjuśrī; (2) "The Territory's Mystical Beauty" covers the peak's geography and its favorable topology; (3) "Famous Ancient and Modern Historical Sites" provides a study of the peak's monasteries and famous sites; (4) "Mystical Rapture Experienced by Pilgrims" is a collection of miracle tales associated with

156 Cao Ganghua summarized the characteristics of Buddhist gazetteers as religious, historical, textual, and regional. He points out, "Buddhist gazetteers are historical accounts that record the development of geographical and human environments of Buddhism. They are compendiums of works and materials of Buddhist historical geography in a given region." See Cao, *Fangzhi yanjiu*, 2.

Mañjuśrī. (5) "Minor Miscellaneous Writings" explains the mountain's flowers, grasses, medical herbs, trees, and so on.[157] The preface to this book states:

> This famous Daoist mountain dedicated to Mañjuśrī, the teacher of seven Buddhas, is where practitioners cultivate their original vitality (*zhenyuan* 真元), while the divine realm of [Mount] Qingliang is where ten thousand bodhisattvas hide their traces. [The fame of the mountain] has spanned from ancient times to the present, and has been well recorded in maps and books. Rare flowers and spiritual grasses are fragrant, and quiet stones and cool springs are sparkling and pure. Auspicious air is emitted from its forests, and propitious clouds lie across its ridges. At night, on dark crags, [Buddha's] lamps and candles always shine brightly. In the morning, in green caves, the sounds of drums and bells constantly reverberate. Old men walk leisurely in valleys, while children play games amidst misty clouds. Buildings and pavilions are splendid, and temple halls are magnificent. Eminent monks come from afar, and the noble visits it personally. [People] lay the foundation for achieving the Way by observing the Buddhist teachings, and make the sincerest vows after witnessing the magnificent marks of the Buddha. From that very day, [they begin] to cultivate special merit, and will realize the wonderful fruits of [enlightenment] in future lifetimes.[158]

According to this preface, geography and environment, large-scale *stūpa*s and monasteries, as well as pilgrimages all made significant contributions to Mount Wutai becoming known as the locus where Mañjuśrī Bodhisattva manifests his transformation body. Zhang Gong 張弓 points out that around the Northern Wei period (386-557), Buddhist circles started viewing Mount Wutai as Mount Qingliang, the sacred site for Mañjuśrī, alluding to the *Huayan jing*'s chapter on the Residing Places of the Bodhisattvas. And it was during the Sui-Tang transition that the culture of Mount Wutai as a sacred Buddhist site took shape. It

157 The titles of these five chapters in Chinese are, "Liming biaohua" 立名標化, "Fengyu lishu" 封域里數, "Gujin shengji" 古今勝跡, "Youli gantong" 遊禮感通, "Zhiliu zashu" 支流雜述.

158 *Gu Qingliang zhuan*, *T*, no. 2098, 51: 1.1092c5-13:
紫府名山, 七佛師棲真之處; 清涼聖境, 萬菩薩晦跡之方. 亙於古今, 備於圖籍. 芬馥之異華靈草, 瑩潔之幽石寒泉, 瑞氣吐於林中, 祥雲橫於嶺上. 蒼岩入夜, 烱烱而燈燭常明; 碧洞侵晨, 殷殷而鼓鐘恒響. 老人蕭散於溪谷, 童子遊戲於煙霞; 燦燦之樓閣莊嚴, 巍巍之殿堂崇麗. 或則高僧遠訪, 或則貴族親臨, 觀化儀結得道之緣, 瞻相好發至誠之願, 修殊因於此日, 證妙果於他生.

FIGURE 39 Pagoda at Zhulin Monastery 竹林寺 on Mount Wutai 五臺, dated to the Ming Dynasty (1368-1644).

took as its basic contents the history of local Buddhism, scenic spots, Buddhist monasteries, divine traces, and miracle tales.[159]

Concerning veneration of sacred Buddhist mountains in medieval China, the value of the *Gu Qingliang zhuan* lies in the fact that it is the first source to associate Mount Wutai with this sort of veneration, and has since established a new model for works focusing on such sacred mountains. Thereafter, the Song-dynasty *Guang Qingliang zhuan* 廣清涼傳 (Expanded Record of Clear and Cold) by Yanyi 延一 (fl. 1060) and the *Xu Qingliang zhuan* 續清涼傳 (Further Record of Clear and Cold) by Zhang Shangyin 張商英 (1043-1121) were both modeled after the *Gu Qingliang zhuan* and enhanced Mount Wutai's significance as a sacred mountain. In particular, the author of the *Guang Qingliang zhuan* divides his information into categories that are supplemented by chronicles of events. The book comprises twenty-three distinct sections dealing with questions like the Bodhisattva's location, information on him, his

159 Zhang, *Wenhua shi*, 2: 716.

merits and virtues, accounts of the bodhisattva's divine efficacy, when the bodhisattva arrived on the mountain, reasons for the name 'Mount Qingliang,' traces of divine actions and divinity, scenic monasteries as well as descriptions of temple structures and dwellings.

The earliest surviving gazetteer of Mount Putuo is the Yuan-dynasty *Butuoluojia shan zhuan* 補陀洛迦山傳 (Gazetteer of Mount Putuo). Its author divided the contents into four chapters (*pin* 品) and three appendices. These are entitled (1) "The Virtues of Guanyin," (2) "The Geography of the Island and Temples," (3) "Guanyin's Auspicious Responses," and (4) "The History of Building Construction," (5) "Appendix," (6) "Encomium for Avalokiteśvara Mahāsattva," and (7) "Poems by Renowned Worthies."[160] During the Wanli period (1573-1619), Zhou Yingbin 周應賓 (d.u.), a disciple of Master Yunqi Zhuhong, feeling that the mountain had received more attention than the temples, revised the mountain gazetteer, calling it the *Chongxiu Putuo shanzhi* 重修普陀山志 (Revised Gazetteer of Mount Putuo). This six-fascicle gazetteer is divided into fourteen sections: (1). "Imperial Writings," (2). "Maps and Paintings," (3). "Landscapes," (4). "Buildings and Temples," (5). "Building Specifications," (6). "Histories of Buildings," (7). "Supernatural Events," (8). "Imperial Gifts," (9). "Envoys," (10). "Buddhist Monks," (11). "Products," (12). "Art and Literature," (13). "Events," and (14). "Poetry."[161] In the *Putuoluojia xinzhi* 普陀洛迦新志 (New Gazetteer of Mount Putuo), completed by Wang Hengyan 王亨彥 (d.u.) in 1931, there are twelve chapters entitled (1) "Guanyin's Miraculous Responses," (2) "Scenic Locales," (3) "Supernatural Events," (4) "Donors," (5) "Buddhist Temples," (6) "Chan Masters," (7) "Building Construction," (8) "Rules and Regulations," (9) "Travellers' Refuges," (10) "Fine Arts," (11) "Supplementary Materials," and (12) "Postscript."[162]

The format of the *Jiuhua shanzhi*, compiled by Desen 德森 (1883-1962) in 1938, is the same as that of the *Putuoluojia xinzhi*. The *Emeishan zhi* 峨嵋山志 (Gazetteer of Mount Emei) compiled by Xu Zhijing 許止淨 (1876-1938) of the Republic of China consists of eight fascicles. Its contents are as follows: (1) "Illustrated Geography", (2) "Divine Activities of Bodhisattvas", (3) "Scenic Spots

160 The Chinese chapter titles are: 1. "Zizai gongde" 自在功德, 2. "Dongyu fengyu" 洞宇封域, 3. "Yinggan xiangrui" 應感祥瑞, 4. "Xingjian yan'ge" 興建沿革, 5. "Fulu" 附錄, 6. "Guanyin dashi zan" 觀音大士讚 and 7. "Mingxian shiyong" 名賢詩詠, respectively.

161 The Chinese titles of these sections are as follows: 1. "Chenhan" 宸翰, 2. "Tukao" 圖考, 3. "Shanshui" 山水, 4. "Dianyu" 殿宇, 5. "Guizhi" 規制, 6. "Jianzhi" 建置, 7. "Lingyi" 靈異, 8. "Banci" 頒賜, 9. "Mingshi" 命使, 10. "Shizi" 釋子, 11. "Wuchan" 物產, 12. "Yiwen" 藝文, 13. "Shilüe" 事略, and 14. "Shilei" 詩類.

162 The Chinese titles of these chapters are: 1. "Benji" 本跡, 2. "Xingsheng" 形勝, 3. "Lingyi" 靈異, 4. "Tanshi" 檀施, 5. "Fansha" 梵剎, 6. "Chande" 禪德, 7. "Yingjian" 營建, 8. "Guizhi" 規制, 9. "Liuyu" 流寓, 10. "Yiwen" 藝文, 11. "Zhiyu" 志餘, and 12. "Ba" 跋.

FIGURE 40 Shengshui Chan Monastery 聖水禪寺 on Mount E'mei 峨嵋山.

[to Be Found] on the Entire Mountain", (4) "Outstanding Features of Buddhist Temples and Nunneries", (5) "Wonderful Responses and Supernatural Events", (6) "Eminent Monks Through the Ages", (7) "Patronage of Emperors and Officials", (8) "Immortals, Hermits, and Travelers' Refuges", (9) "Ancient and Modern Fine Arts", (10) "Animals, Plants, and [Local] Products", and (11) "Supplementary Materials".[163]

Through an examination of the *Qingliang shanzhi, Emei shanzhi, Putuo shanzhi,* and *Jiuhua shanzhi,* the important elements and significance of veneration of sacred Buddhist mountains can be deduced. In my opinion, one can view the evolution of this veneration as a historical process that has resulted from the following six elements: (1) records from classical texts; (2) geography and scenic spots; (3) miracle tales; (4) pagodas, temples, and eminent monks; (5) pilgrimages made by devotees; (6) state support. It is the clearest signification of the Buddhist faith in China. These six facets are also the core contents of the sacred mountain gazetteers, which are analyzed in the following section.

### 4.2.1 Records from Classical Texts

Records contained in classical texts are the source texts for holy faith; they paved the way for the formulation of the "Four Great Sacred Mountains" concept. Although other famous Chinese mountains fulfill these conditions, a lack of textual support prevented them from acquiring the status of holy peaks among Buddhist circles. For example, Mount Tiantai, Mount Lu, and Hengshan 衡山 are all the foci of abundant long-term Buddhist traditions, but compared with the Four Great Sacred Peaks, they lack the textual evidence of sanctity recorded in *sūtras*.

In the Jin translation of the *Huayan jing* completed by Buddhabhadra (Fotuobatuoluo 佛馱跋陀羅 [359-430]), it is recorded that "in the Northeast, there is an abode of the Bodhisattvas called Qingliang Mountain. In the past, many bodhisattvas resided there. Currently, a bodhisattva called Mañjuśrī lives there who has ten thousand fellow bodhisattvas, to whom he often preaches the Buddhist Dharma."[164] In the Tang-dynasty *Wenshushili fabaozang tuoluoni jing* 文殊師利法寶藏陀羅尼經 (Scripture on the *Dhāraṇī* of Mañjuśrī's Precious

163 The Chinese titles of these fascicles are as follows: 1. "Xingye tushuo" 星野图说, 2. "Pusa shengji" 菩薩聖迹, 3. "Quanshan xingsheng" 全山形勝, 4. "Sian shenggai" 寺庵勝概, 5. "Ganying lingyi" 感應靈異, 6. "Lidai gaoseng" 歷代高僧, 7. "Wangchen waihu" 王臣外護, 8. "Xianyin liuyu" 仙隐流寓, 9. "Gujinyiwen" 古今藝文, 10. "Dongzhiwuchan" 動植物產, and 11. "Jiangbianzhiyu" 蔣編志餘.

164 *Da Fangguangfo huayan jing, T.* no. 278, 9: 29.590a3-5:
東北方有菩薩住處, 名清涼山. 過去諸菩薩常於中住, 彼現有菩薩, 名文殊師利, 有一萬菩薩眷屬, 常爲說法.

Treasury of the Dharma) translated by Bodhiruci (Putiliuzhi 菩提流志; 572?-727), it is recorded, "After I enter nirvana, there will be a country called Da zhen'na 大振那, located northeast of Jambūdvipa (Shanbu zhou 贍部洲). In that country, there is a mountain called Wuding 五頂 (literally Five Peaks), in which the child form of Mañjuśrī wanders, lives, and expounds the Buddhist Dharma to sentient beings."[165] Based on these two scriptures, we can see that Mañjuśrī's sacred site is located on Mount Wuding, also known as Qingliang, in the country of Da Zhen'na.

A Jin translation of the *Huayan jing* records: "In the Southwest, there is an abode of bodhisattvas called Mount Shuti Guangming 樹提光明山. Previously, bodhisattvas frequently resided there. Currently, there is a bodhisattva named Xianshou 賢首 who has three thousand fellow bodhisattvas, to whom he often preaches the Buddhist Dharma."[166] The *Huayan jing* translated by Śikṣānanda (Shicha'nantuo 實叉難陀; 652-710) in the Tang dynasty, replaces "Xianshou" with "Xiansheng" 賢勝,[167] but the two editions both consider Mount Guangming to be a sacred site for the bodhisattvas.

The Tang translation of the *Huayan jing* relates, "To the south, there is a mountain called Butanluojia 補怛洛迦, where a bodhisattva called Guanzizai 觀自在 [resides]."[168] The *Da Tang Xiyu ji* 大唐西域記 (Great Tang Record of Travels to Western Regions) records, "To the east of Mount Molaye 秣剌耶 is Mount Butanluojia 布呾洛迦. ... where Bodhisattva Guanzizai wanders."[169] In the chapter entitled "Pumen" 普門品, there is a description of Guanyin Bodhisattva heeding the sounds of sufferers and coming to their rescue. Although there is actually a Mount Butanluojia 布呾洛迦 in India, Guanshiyin is venerated due to her compassionate vitality and her role as a tutelary god/goddess of seafarers.

Mount Jiuhua became known as Kṣitigarbha's seat largely due to the association of this bodhisattva with the Sillan monk Kim Chijang (Chin. Jin Dizang) 金地藏. This combination does not seem to have happened until the Ming, but miraculous stories related to the monk had already appeared on that peak as early as the ninth century.

---

165 *Foshuo Wenshusili fabaozang tuoluoni jing*, *T* no. 1185A, 20: 791c11-14: 我滅度後, 於此贍部洲東北方, 有國名大振那, 其國中有山, 號曰五頂. 文殊師利童子遊行居住, 爲諸眾生於中說法.

166 *Da Fangguangfo huayan jing*, *T*. no. 278, 9: 29.590a8-10: 西南方有菩薩住處, 名樹提光明山, 過去諸菩薩常於中住, 彼現有菩薩名賢首, 有三千菩薩眷屬, 常爲說法.

167 Ibid., 45.241b29-c3.

168 Ibid., 68.366c3-4: 於此南方, 有山名補怛洛迦, 彼有菩薩名觀自在.

169 *Da Tang Xiyu ji*, *T*. no. 2087, 51: 10.932a14-17: 秣剌耶山東有布呾洛迦山 ...... 觀自在菩薩往來游舍.

### 4.2.2 Geography and Scenic Spots

In order to be designated as a sacred mountain, a peak must fulfill two geographic conditions: (1) its topographical features must tally with those described in classical texts; (2) it must be sufficiently spacious to accommodate the building of a large number of monasteries, thereby providing a clean and pure site for spiritual cultivation.

For example, Chengguan personally investigated Mount Wutai for ten years. Noting the severely cold weather on northeast India's Wutai Mountain, as well as its five peaks, he suggested, "Mount Qingliang is actually Mount Wutai in the Yanmen prefecture of Daizhou 代州; there is a Qingliang si 清涼寺 there. It is called Qingliang because solid ice remains there all the year round; it snows there even in the summertime, and the weather is never hot. Its five barren peaks tower loftily and resemble earthen terraces, from whence comes the name *wutai* (literally, five terraces)."[170] No trees grow on its peaks; seen from afar, they look like earthen terraces, which is the source of the name "Wutai." The mountain towers high and is always wrapped in mist and fog. Hidden behind a misty screen, its shape is obscured; it only appears during clear weather when the clouds disperse. Huixiang, the author of the *Gu Qingliang zhuan*, marveled at the similarities in locality and weather between Mount Wutai and Mount Qingliang, which the *Huayan jing* claims as the abode of Mañjuśrī. For such a pure realm, the *Kuodi zhi* 括地志 (Records of Geography of the Whole Land) says, "The mountain's ... divine peaks and holy crevices are not suitable as the dwellings of vulgar, mundane folk. Its residents are all people practising meditation and dwelling on profound thoughts. [Therefore], when the dharma thunder sounds and fragrant smoke converges from the four directions, the heart of the compassion and enlightenment will naturally be spread abroad."[171] It is clear that not only does Mount Wutai possess a mysterious and divine atmosphere, but it is also a good place to cultivate the Way and practise meditation.

Mount Emei, located in southwest China, tallies with the prescribed characteristics of a "luminous mountain" (*guangmingshan* 光明山) because it has "Buddha light" (*foguang* 佛光) in the daytime and "holy lamps" (*shengdeng* 聖燈) at night. When it comes to Mount Putuo, the preface to its gazetteer reads:

---

170 *Da Fangguangfo huayan jing shu*, *T.* no. 1735, 35: 47.859c6-10:
清涼山, 即代州雁門郡五臺山也, 於中現有清涼寺. 以歲積堅冰, 夏仍飛雪, 曾無炎暑, 故曰清涼. 五峰聳出, 頂無林木, 有如壘土之台, 故曰五臺.

171 *Gu Qingliang zhuan*, *T* no. 2098, 51: 1.1093a16-19:
其山.... 靈岳神巇, 非薄俗可棲. 止者, 悉是棲禪之士, 思玄之流. 及夫法雷震音, 芳煙四合, 慈覺之心, 邈然自遠.

> Starting with the Tang dynasty, when foreign monks came to witness [Guanyin's] miraculous transformation, the fame of Butuoluojia began to spread. [The mountain] stands imposingly in the eastern Yue region, gleaming from afar amid great waters (i.e. the East Sea). Stone caves are embedded in cliffs, and forested ridges there are pure and deep. Followers of the Way reside there, and countless Buddhist monasteries have been constructed there. Those who are not curious about exploring remote regions and travelling by boat are seldom able to reach the mountain.[172]

Undoubtedly, the name Putuoluojia 普陀洛迦 originated due to its island landscape and special geographical features. Mount Jiuhua is also strikingly beautiful; it protrudes through clouds with row upon row of peaks and ridges. Its nine peaks rise like lotus blossoms; hence, it is called Mount Jiuhua, or "Nine-Blossom Mountain".

### 4.2.3 Miracle Tales and Pilgrimages of the Faithful

With the introduction of *sūtras* associated with the four bodhisattvas, all kinds of bodhisattva legends were disseminated throughout China. Meanwhile, the various religious experiences obtained on the sacred peaks as reported by monks and adherents were taken as evidence of the bodhisattvas' presence. Such tales unceasingly aroused religious fervor and encouraged others to make pilgrimages. Therefore, legends of miraculous responses were a driving force for the growth of veneration of these sites.

Both Mañjuśrī's transformation body at Mount Wutai and that of Guanyin in the Cave of Tidal Sounds (*Chao*[*fan*]*yin dong* 潮 [梵] 音洞) at Mount Putuo are very charismatic, and have thus attracted countless pious believers to make pilgrimages to these places. During the Tang dynasty, when the Japanese monk Ennin 圓仁 (793-864) made a pilgrimage to Mount Wutai, he described his feelings in this way:

> In May, the nights are extremely cold on Mount Qingliang [i.e. Wutai], and people usually wear padded jackets. Trees on the ridges and in the valleys stand upright and tall—not a single one is crooked. After entering the realm of the Great Sage (i.e. Mañjuśrī), [I] dare not despise even the

---

172 *Butuoluojia shan zhuan*, *T* no. 2101, 51: 1.1135bb1-5:
始自唐朝梵僧來睹神變,而補陀洛迦山之名,遂傳焉.盤礴於東越之境,窅芒乎巨浸之中,石洞嵌岩,林巒清邃,有道者居之,而阿蘭若兆興焉.自非好奇探幽,乘桴泛槎者,罕能至也.

> basest of people. When encountering donkeys or other animals, [I] also suspect them to be transformation bodies of Mañjuśrī. Whatever I see, I always suspect them of being Mañjuśrī's transformation bodies. In the realm of the holy spirits, the scenery naturally inspires awe in the hearts of people.[173]

Ennin's veneration of "the transformation body of Mañjuśrī" is representative of the psychological state of all pilgrims to Mount Wutai.

For example, the *Fozu tongji* says that in Qiande 4 (966), "Jiazhou 嘉州 [officials] frequently reported sightings of Samantabhadra at Baishui si 白水寺."[174] In Taiping xingguo 7 (982), Wang Gun 王袞 (d.u.), a supervisory official from Jiazhou, submitted a memorial, stating: "When [I] recently went to Mount Emei to supervise the building of Baishui Temple, [I] saw that the brick roofs had all become golden, and within this glow appeared the six-yard-tall (*zhang*) golden body of Samantabhadra. At noon on the following day, [I] saw two arhats riding on purple clouds and walking in the sky."[175] These auspicious signs associated with Samantabhadra secured for Mount Emei the direct support of Northern Song (960-1126) emperors. Such measures to profit by and protect the mountain's Buddhist presence undoubtedly played a crucial role in the final establishment of the mountain as a sacred site for the bodhisattva.

In discussing the transformation of Mount Putuo into a sacred site for Guanyin Bodhisattva, Chün-fang Yü states:

> Miracles and pilgrimage sites played an important role in the Chinese cult of Guanyin. Both contributed to the domestication and Sinicization of Guanyin. Miracle tales, local lore, literature, and art were the media through which information about pilgrimage sites was made known. They created certain expectations in the hearts of potential pilgrims, and probably shaped their experiences during the pilgrimage. Both monastic and lay pilgrims were the agents who transmitted local traditions to other parts of the country.[176]

---

173 *Nittō guhō junrei kōki* 2.108:
此清涼山, 五月之夜極寒, 尋常著棉襖子. 嶺上谷裡, 樹木端長, 無一曲戾之木. 入大聖境地之時, 見極賤之人, 亦不敢作輕蔑之心; 若逢驢畜, 亦起疑心, 恐是文殊化現歟. 舉目所見, 皆起文殊所化之想, 聖靈之地, 使人自然對境起崇重之心也.

174 *Fozu tongji, T* no. 2035, 49: 43.395b17-18: 嘉州屢奏白水寺普賢相見.

175 Ibid., 43.398a19-22:
近往峨眉提點白水寺修造, 見瓦屋山皆變金色, 中有丈六金身普賢, 次日中午見羅漢二身乘紫雲行空中.

176 Yü, *Kuan-yin,* 355.

The compilers of mountain gazetteers carefully collected and preserved these traditions, as can be seen in the various *Putuo shanzhi* published through the years. Thus, miracle tales and pilgrimages were important formative factors in the veneration of these sacred Buddhist mountains, and both facilitated the domestication and Sinicization of Guanyin.

### 4.2.4 *Stūpa*s, Temples, and Eminent Monks

In order to be recognized as a famous mountain, a peak must have the effect of scale. Only forests of *stūpa*s, temples, and statues and the presence of generations of eminent monks can spark belief and religious fervor. Buddhism was first disseminated on Mount Wutai in the Northern Wei dynasty. During the Qi dynasty (479-502), it was reported that "there are nearly forty thousand temples in the realm (i.e. China); among these are more than two hundred monasteries [on the Wutai ranges]. Additionally, the land taxes of eight sub-prefectures are given [by the government] to pay for the clothing and medicine of the resident monks. With such privileges, this sacred site, an abode of the immortals endowed with spiritual and monetary gifts, has flourished."[177] At the time, Master Lingbian 靈辯 (477-522) composed the *Huayan lun* 華嚴論 (Commentary on the *Huayan Jing*) of one hundred fascicles, the first Chinese commentary on the *Huayan jing*. From then on, Mount Wutai gradually became the Northern Chinese centre for *Huayan jing* research and study. During the Sui-Tang era, Emperor Taizong (r. 626-649) built temples and ordained monks there, Emperor Gaozong (r. 649-683) exempted mountain-dwellers from paying taxes, and Empress Wu (r. 690-705) constructed pagodas as a religious offering. In Longshuo 2 (662), the empress ordered Huize 會賾 (d.u.), a monk of the Huichang si 會昌寺 in the Western Capital [Luoyang or Xi'an], to write the single-fascicle *Qingliang shan lüezhuan* 清涼山略傳 (A Brief Gazetteer of Mount Qingliang), and also ordered State Preceptor Degan 德感 (659?-704?), who was then serving as Buddhist Supervisor (*sengtong* 僧統), to reside at the Qingliang si 清涼寺 on Mount Wutai. During the Tang Kaiyuan period (713-741), the cult of Mañjuśrī centered on Mount Wutai reached its peak, causing the mountain to become the sacred seat of Mañjuśrī; concurrently, the scale of its temples and monastic compounds also reached an apex of expansion. In the Yuan and Qing dynasties, as a result of the promotion of esoteric Buddhism, there was a dramatic increase in tantric temples. During the Wanli

177 *Gu Qingliang zhuan*, *T* no. 2098, 51: 1.1094a1-4:
宇內塔寺, 將四十千; 此中伽藍, 數過二百. 又割八州之稅, 以供山眾衣藥之資焉. 據此而詳, 則仙居靈貺, 故觸地而繁矣.

period, more than three hundred temples and monasteries stood on Mount Wutai.

In the early fifth century, Huichi 慧持 (337-412) had the first temple on Mount E'mei constructed, the Puxian si 普賢寺. From the Tang dynasty onward, the phenomenon of "Buddha light" appearing on the mountain was widely known. With people explaining this "Buddha light" as "Samantabhadra's auspicious omens," coupled with further support from the Northern Song emperors, Mount Emei gradually became the sacred seat of Samantabhadra. Buddhism reached its peak on the mountain during the Ming dynasty; there were more than 170 monasteries there, housing over three thousand resident monks and countless adherents.

The history of Mount Putuo began in Dazhong 1 (847) when an eminent Indian monk took up residence on the peak. In the Later Liang era's Zhenming 2 (916), when the Japanese monk Hui'e built the cloister Bukenqu Guanyin yuan 不肯去觀音院 (the temple of "Guanyin-who-refused-to-leave"), the cult of Guanyin became increasingly popular and temple construction rapidly increased. By Daoguang 12 (1832), according to the "Chongxiu Nanhai Putuoshan zhi" 重修南海普陀山志序 (Praface to the Newly-revised Southern Seas Mount Putuo Gazetteer) by Wang Dingxun's 王鼎勳 (?-1834+), "There are no fewer than seventy temples in the mountains, with over a thousand resident and guest monks."[178]

In the Zhide era (756-758) of the Tang, a Jiuhua country squire named Zhuge Jie 諸葛節 (d.u.) and others built the Hucheng si 化城寺 for Jin Qiaojue 金喬覺 (i.e., Kim Chijang, 705-803), marking the start of Buddhism on Mount Jiuhua. Gradually, it was said that there were a thousand temples on that mountain, all scattered in clouds and fog. In the Qing-dynasty *Jiuhua shangzhi*, "Huacheng si sengliao ji" 化城寺僧寮记 (Records of the Dormitory of Monks in Huacheng si), Zhou Wenyun 周文贇 (d.u.) claimed that at most, there were a thousand resident monks in each of China's flourishing Buddhist temples. Clearly, with monasteries scattered throughout the land as plentifully as stars in the sky, crowds of eminent monks, splendid Dharma assemblies, and frequent Buddhist ceremonies, these grand scale effects provided an atmosphere that was highly conducive to veneration of these mountains.

### 4.2.5 State Support

A sacred mountain would never be able to expand its influence without imperial support. The coinage, the "Four Great Sacred Mountains," was authorized as a result of imperial and royal patronage. Northern Qi emperors channeled

178 *Putuoshan zhi*, 12.625: 山中僧寮不下七十餘所，緇流及外方掛單約一千餘眾.

the taxes from eight prefectures into funds for the clothing and medicine of Mount Wutai's monks.[179] Amoghavajra vigorously spread the cult of Mañjuśrī with the support of Emperor Daizong (r. 762-779). In Dali 4 (769), the emperor sanctioned Amoghavajra's memorial requesting that Mañjuśrī occupies the seat of honor (*shangzuo* 上座) in all temple refectories, with Samantabhadra and Guanyin acting as attendants. In this way, Mount Wutai became the foremost among all sacred mountains.[180]

Mount Emei obtained various kinds of support from the Northern Song emperors. In Qiande 4 (966), Emperor Taizu (r.960-976) ordered the eunuch Zhang Zhongjin 張重進 (d. u) to travel to Puxian si 普賢寺 to decorate Buddha statues.[181] In the first month of Taiping xingguo 5 (980), Emperor Taizong (r. 976-997) dispatched the eunuch Zhang Renzan 張仁贊 (d.u.) to oversee the casting of a bronze image of Samantabhadra. It was two yards (*zhang*) in height, and was erected in the Puxian si at Baishui 白水 along with a large pavilion to cover it. In this way, five temples were also rebuilt, including Baishui Puxian si 白水普賢寺, Huayan si 華嚴寺, Heishui si 黑水寺, as well as Zhongfeng Qianming si 中峰乾明寺 and Guangxiang si 光相寺.[182] In Yongxi 4 (987), Emperor Taizong ordered eunuchs to deliver precious caps [to bedeck Buddhist images], jade decorations, and monk's cassocks to the Puxian si.[183] In Duangong 2 (989), acting under imperial order, the eunuch Xie Baoyi 謝保意 (d.u.) brought craftsmen and three hundred taels of gold to the mountain to decorate Samantabhadra's statue and renovate the temple compound.[184] In Dazhong xiangfu 4 (1011), Emperor Zhenzong (r. 997-1022) granted three thousand taels of gold to enlarge the mountain's Puxian si and to fund vegetarian feasts for thirty thousand monks. He also ordered the ordination of four monks each year.[185] With this imperial patronage, the Buddhist presence on Mount Emei increased rapidly at the cost of Daoism. Due to imperial support, the mountain became renowned throughout China and abroad as the sacred seat of Samantabhadra. during the Song dynasty During the Ming dynasty, Emperor Taizu (r. 1368-1398) honored Master Baotan 寶曇 (1335-1395) as the state Buddhist preceptor,[186] and the Wanli emperor built a beamless brick hall to protect the statue of Samantbhadra riding on a white elephant. Meanwhile, he

179 *Gu Qingliang zhuan, T* no. 2098, 51: 1.1094a2-3.
180 *Zhenyuan xinding shijiao mulu, T.* no. 2157, 55: 16.887c7-10.
181 *Fozu tongji, T.* no. 2035, 49: 43.395b16-18.
182 Ibid., 43.397c25-29.
183 Ibid., 43.400a9-11.
184 Ibid., 43.400b4-26.
185 Ibid., 43.404b24-26.
186 *Emeishan zhi*, 5.215.

personally wrote a name tablet for the Shengshou Wannian si 聖壽萬年寺 [187]; for the newly-built bronze hall, he bestowed the name tablet "Yongming Huazang si" 永明華藏寺 by imperial decree.[188] Emperor Kangxi (r. 1661-1722) of Qing composed poems, couplets, and name tablets for temples there.[189] Emperor Shunzhi 順治 (1643-1661) bestowed a collection of the Northern Canon that was delicately printed by the bronze block of the Yongle period to Master Mingzheng 明正 (d.u.) of the Xiwa Hall 錫瓦殿.[190] With the direct support of Ming and Qing emperors, there were more and more temples there, and the mountain's roads and environment were improved, making pilgrimages more convenient.

The development of Buddhism on Mount Putuo had much to do with emperors of the Ming and Qing dynasties, who esteemed it highly. Wanli donated several copies of the Buddhist canon to the mountain; Emperor Chongzhen 崇禎 (r. 1628-1644) ordered Tian Hongyu 田弘遇 (?-1643?), a member of the royal family, to pray to Guanyin there and offer imperial incense. In Kangxi 28 (1689), the emperor ordered eunuchs to send a thousand taels of silver for mountain temple construction. Ten years later (1699) when the emperor visited Hangzhou, he ordered eunuchs to burn incense on Mount Putuo and deliver a thousand taels of gold as gifts for the front and the back temples. He also issued an edict claiming that "the mountain is an imperial temple." In Yongzheng 9 (1731), seventy thousand taels of gold were bestowed in order to rebuild the front and the back monasteries.[191] Consequently, the rise of Buddhism at Mount Putuo was closely related to the political attentions of Ming and Qing emperors.

It was also during the Ming and Qing eras that Buddhism on Mount Jiuhua developed. The Wanli emperor donated the Buddhist canon to Huacheng si 化城寺 twice. The Kangxi emperor dispatched eunuchs to burn incense there three times, and granted it the name tablet "*Jiuhua shengjing* 九華聖境 ". In Qianlong 41 (1776), the emperor granted Huacheng si the name tablet "*Fengtuo pujiao* 芬陀普教 ".[192] That Mount Jiuhua was able to take its place among the "Four Great Sacred Mountains" is closely related to the state support furnished by the Ming and Qing dynasties.

---

187 Ibid., 5.282.

188 Ibid., 6.266-67.

189 Ibid., 6.259.

190 Emeishan fojiaozhi bianzuan weiyuanhui, *Fojiao zhi*, 479.

191 *Putuoshan zhi* 4.209-227.

192 Ibid., 5.141.

### 4.3 *The Formation of Sacred Mountain Veneration and the Overcoming of the "Borderland Complex"*

The appellation of the "Four Great Sacred Mountains" likely appeared during the Wanli period; by the Kangxi period, it had already reached a consensus among Chinese Buddhist circles and within Chinese society. However, not only did the Chinese venerate Mount Wutai as a sacred Buddhist site, it was also venerated by eminent Indian monks. From the Song and Yuan dynasties on, the rise of Mounts Emei and Putuo as sacred Buddhist sites was allied with the decline of Indian Buddhism and the "national centrality" of Chinese Buddhism. Chinese Buddhists had a "borderland complex" concerning some of the territories associated with Indian Buddhism.[193] During the Tang-Song transition, the Sinicization of Chinese Buddhism was accomplished in a three-tiered process that entailed Buddhist beliefs, thought, and regulations; the Chinese formulated their own versions of these three components. With the decline of Indian Buddhism, the status of China as the centre for Buddhism became even more evident, lending the "Four Great Sacred Mountains" a more dramatic importance.

Chinese Buddhist veneration of these mountains is not a replica of Indian Buddhist sacred sites. Instead, it is based upon "canonical records" conjoined with "geography and scenic locales," the continuous presence of eminent monks practising cultivation, and travelling students of Buddhism. State support for the construction of *stūpa*s, temples, and for the provision of monastic furnishings and supplies contributed to the formation of large-scale temples and monasteries, which were the material foundation for this phenomenon. Finally, miracle tales stimulated religious fervor, bringing in a continuous flow of pilgrims and thereby forming the psychological foundation for the veneration of these sites.

On the basis of these holy, material, and psychological factors, the four bodhisattvas—Mañjuśrī, Samantabhadra, Guanyin, and Kṣitigarbha—were transported to China. In this way, China overcame its "borderland complex" and erected its own unique Buddhist beliefs, thus demonstrating its zeal to become the world centre for Buddhism. In a broad view, High Tang China was the cultural centre of the entire world, and Chinese people from the Song dynasty onwards continued to harbor this dream. The emergence of the "Four Great Sacred Mountains" satisfied China's aspiration to become the centre of the world.

193 For relevant studies, see Wang, "Tiaozhan", 45-53; Chen, "Biandi qingjie", 22-41.

## 5 Conclusion

In the five hundred years from the Yuan dynasty to the Qing Qianlong period, the most unique characteristic of Buddhism in China was that Tibetan Buddhism continuously held the highest position. Although Tibetan Buddhism was under the control of the rulers and was restricted in spreading its teachings, Han Buddhism did not face such obstruction in propagation. However, Han Buddhism lacked innovative ideas, and on the whole, various rulers since the Ming dynasty adopted policies that suppressed Buddhism. Due to efforts by three eminent monks—Zhuhong, Ouyi and Deqing—to revive Buddhism during the Wanli period in the late Ming, monastery developments thrived. However, during the Qing dynasty, Chan Buddhism was controlled by imperial power and gradually lost autonomy. The only social function of Buddhism during the Ming and Qing periods that was not weakened or changed, but greatly strengthened, was making offerings to the deceased and liberating them. The role of Buddhism in society changed from "treating the mind" to "making offering to the deceased."[194] As such, the form of the "secularization" of the monastic community gradually regressed from the level of daily life and organizational systems, to the faith and lifestyle of liberating the deceased. Buddhism had lost its function of providing the people with a "meaningful world." It was slowly reduced to a kind of tool and technique for liberating departed spirits. In short, Buddhism shifted from "lifestyle Buddhism" to "Buddhism for liberating the deceased." Han Buddhism during the late Qing and Republican periods was once again at a stage of transformation. Upheavals in modern history include the Taiping Rebellion, the Building Schools with Temple Property movement, and battles among warlords, as well as contentions between conservatives and reformers in the monastic community. Also, the proposition of "Buddhism for the Human Realm" was no doubt in order to restore two elements that Han Buddhism should have, that is, "regulation insertion" and "lifestyle integration."

Emperor Ming Taizu emphasized the "ritual" and "timing" of Dharma services. He standardized *sūtra* recitation and repentance services nationwide, which led to Buddhists improving their existing repentance ritual procedures. At the same time, the popularity and disarray of *sūtra* recitation and repentance services prompted eminent monks to reflect upon how repentance ritual procedures were incomplete and not in accord with the Dharma. They revised the repentance ritual procedures. "Mount Jiang Dharma Service" was the Water and Land Great Feast Dharma Service established by Emperor

194 Chen & Deng, *Zhongguo Fojiao*, 161.

Ming Taizu at the beginning of the dynasty. It was established to save the spirits of the innocent and those who had died in battle. Through establishing the "Mount Jiang Dharma Service", Emperor Ming Taizu summoned eminent monks of the early Ming period to Nanjing, which undoubtedly unified the strength of Jiangnan Buddhist circles. As eminent monks participated in the "Mount Jiang Dharma Service" in the form of national offerings and carried out offerings and prayers as a national undertaking, the majority of Buddhist power was under the rule of imperial authority. It played an important function in consolidating and regulating Buddhism in the early Ming period. Through laying down the requirements of "ritual" and "timing" for making offerings to ghosts and gods, and organizing the "Mount Jiang Dharma Service" ritual, Emperor Ming Taizu was the driving force behind the rectification of *sūtra* recitation and repentance services in Ming dynasty.

With the development of *sūtra* recitation and repentance services during the Ming dynasty, there was chaos in the practice of repentance rituals with the phenomena of *yingfu seng* 應赴僧. In order to rectify the situation, the monk Shichan of Xitan si in Yunnan compiled the *Lengyan shichan* in two fascicles. The text was compiled based on the *Lengyan jing*, modelled on the central repentance ritual structure of "repenting the three hindrances" found in the *Sanmei shuichan*, and adopted the names of the Buddhas and repentance text from the *Foming jing*. In the *Lengyan shichan*, Shichan emphasized the function of repentance by principle, and demonstrated the teachings of the excellent illuminating true mind and sudden awakening Chan. It embodied Confucian ethics like patriotism, loyalty and filial piety, as well as holding the position of ultimate rebirth in the Pure Land. Among the three *Śūraṃgama* repentance rituals, the *Lengyan shichan* exhibited characteristics of Chan Buddhism. The popularity of *sūtra* recitation and repentance services in the imperial court and among the people during the Ming and Qing dynasties led to a chaotic and inundated situation. Yunqi Zhuhong revised the monastic morning and evening chanting services, and formulated the *Zhujing risong jiyao* for the promotion of a regulated monastic practice lifestyle. In addition, he discussed the disorder and malpractice of the *sūtra* recitation and repentance services among Ming and Qing Buddhists. He revised repentance ritual texts, rectified monastic discipline and advocated recitation of the Buddha's name to replace *sūtra* recitation and repentance services.

Due to the thriving formation of groups and the growing power of clans, organized activities in society were mainly fulfilled by social groups and clans. Hence, the function of charitable activities organized by Buddhists during the Ming and Qing period was in decline. Also, Zhuhong promoted life release. He set up life release ponds, established "Life-Release Societies" and formulated life release ritual procedures. He actively pushed for the regulation of Buddhist life release.

The development of the "Four Great Sacred Buddhist Mountains" is the most representative product of the Sinicization of Buddhist faith. The faith in sacred mountains has six essential elements: scripture, geography, miracle tales, pagodas and temples, devotees and state support. The "Four Great Sacred Mountains" became widespread in society after the time of Qing Emperor Kangxi. A shift in the location of the sacred mountains meant a shift in the centres of Buddhist faith. China thereby became the "second homeland" of Buddhism.

## Appendix 4.1: The Times, Locations, Eminent Monks Participating in the Mount Jiang Dharma Service (Hasebe, *kyōdanshi*, 18-20)

| Year | Time | Title | Place | Eminent Monks who Preached |
|---|---|---|---|---|
| Hongwu 1 (1368) | 11th day of the 9th month (10.22) | Unhindered Rites (*wuzhe dahui* 無遮大會, Water and Land Rite (*shuilu hui* 水陸會) | Mount Zhong 鍾 Taiping Xingguo si 太平興國寺 (Jiangshan si 蔣山寺) | Tianzhen Weize 天真惟則 (1303-1373); Chushi Fanqi 楚石梵琦 (1296-1370); Biefeng Datong 別峰大同 (1289-1370); Zhu'an Huaiwei 竹庵懷渭 (1318-1376); Nichuan Zhishun 逆川智順 (1327-1373); Xingzhong Zhiren 行中至仁 (1309-1382); Yizhong Zhiji 以中智及 (1311-1378); Rizhang Zu'ni 日章祖儞 (1309-1379); Fuyuan Fubao 復原福報 (d.u.); Xiangyuan Renshu 象原仁淑 (?-1380); Lan'an Tingjun 懶庵廷俊, (1299-1368), etc. |

APPENDIX 4.1 The Times, Locations, Eminent Monks Participating (*cont.*)

| Year | Time | Title | Place | Eminent Monks who Preached |
|---|---|---|---|---|
| Hongwu 2 (1369) | 13th day of 3rd month (4.19) | | Mount Zhong 鍾 | Baiyun Zhidu 白雲智度 (1304-1370); Chushi Fanqi; Wumeng Tan'e 無夢曇噩 (1285-1373); Yizhong Zhiji |
| | 10th month (10.31-11.29) | Universal Salvation Buddha Assembly (*Puji fohui* 普濟佛會) | | Dongming Huiri 東溟慧日 (1291-1379); Bifeng Baojin 碧峰寶金 (1306-1370) |
| Hongwu 3 (1370) | 15th day of 1st month (2.11) | (Water and Land Rite 水陸會) | (Zhongshan 鍾山) | Bifeng Baojin; Chushi Fanqi; Wumeng Tan'e; Quanshi Zongle 全室宗泐 (1318-1390); Jiefeng Shiyu 杰峰世愚 (1302-1371); Yizhong Zhiji; Xingzhong Zhiren; Songhe Zhengshou 松壑正壽 (d.u.) |
| Hongwu 4 (1371) | Spring | | | Tianyuan Qingjun 天渊清濬 (1328-1392); Bai'an Lijin 白庵力金 (1328-1374) |
| | 15th day of 12th month (1372.1.21) | | | Ten Virtuous monks beginning with Jianxin Laifu 見心來復 (1319-1391) and their two thousand disciples |
| Hongwu 5 (1372) | 15th day of 1st month (2.19), ended in autumn | Service of Extensive Offerings (*Guangjian fahui* 廣薦法會) | Zhongshan 鍾山 | Quanshi Zongle; Dongming Huiri; Yuezhi Chongyu 約之崇裕 (1304-1378); Xingyuan Huiming 性原慧明 (1318-1386); Bai'an Lijin; Muyin Wenqian 牧隱文謙 (1316-1372/1373); Tianjing Yuanjing 天鏡元瀞 (1312-1378); |

APPENDIX 4.1 The Times, Locations, Eminent Monks Participating (*cont.*)

| Year | Time | Title | Place | Eminent Monks who Preached |
|---|---|---|---|---|
| | | | | Bifeng Baojin; Mu'an Sicong 木庵司聰 (1312-1381); Xiangyuan Renshu; Taipu Ruqi 太璞如玘 (1320-1385); Qu'an Dayou 蘧庵大佑 (1334-1407); Zhongshan Xingrong 鍾山行容 (d.u.) and two thousand disciples |
| Hongwu 6 (1373) | | | Tianjie si 天界寺 | Yizhong Zhiji and other more than ten virtuous and knowledgable monks |
| Hongwu 11 (1378) | | | Jinshan 金山 | Dai'an Puzhuan 呆庵普莊 (1347-1403); Xingyuan Huiming |
| Hongwu 17 (1384) | | Universal Salvation Feast Gathering (*Pudu zhai* 普度齋) | Zhongshan 鍾山 Linggu si 靈谷寺 | |
| Hongwu 19 (1386) | | Great Feast Gathering (*Da zhaihui* 大齋會) | Linggu si 靈谷寺 | Tianyuan Qingjun |
| Hongwu 20 (1387) | | Universal Salvation Great Feast Gathering (*Pudu dazhai* 普度大齋) | Linggu si 靈谷寺 | Tianyuan Qingjun |
| Yongle 2 (1404) | | Universal Salvation Great Feast Gathering (*Pudu dazhai* 普度大齋) | Zhongshan si 鍾山寺 | Guru Halima 哈立麻上師 (d.u.); Xuexuan Daocheng 雪軒道成 (1353-1433) |
| Yongle 5 (1407) | | Universal Salvation Great Feast Gathering (*Pudu dazhai* 普度大齋) | Linggu si 靈谷寺 | Halima 哈立麻 (Fajixiangxian 法吉祥賢) |

## Appendix 4.2: Three Hindrances (*Sanzhang* 三障)

| Three hindrances (*sanzhang* 三障) | | Content | Reference (*Da foding rulai miyin xiuzheng liaoyi zhu pusa wanxing shou lengyan jing*, *T* no. 945, vol. 19) |
|---|---|---|---|
| Afflictive hindrances (*fannaozhang* 煩惱障) | Afflictions of views and perceptions (*jiansi fannao* 見思煩惱) | the first five consciousnesses (*qian wushi* 前五識) | |
| | | the sixth manovijñāna (*diliu yishi* 第六意識) | |
| | | manas (*monashi* 末那識) | |
| | | ālayavijñāna (*alaiyeshi* 阿賴耶識) | |
| Karmic hindrances (*yezhang* 業障) | | six sense faculties (*liugen* 六根) | |
| | | six data-fields (*liuchen* 六塵) | |
| | ten habitual causes (*shi xiyin* 十習因) | habits of lust and reciprocal interactions (*yinxijiaojie* 淫習交接), habits of greed and intermingled scheming (*tanxijiaoji* 貪習交計), habits of arrogance and resulting friction (*manxijiaoling* 慢習交凌), habits of hatred which give rise to mutual defiance (*chenxijiaochong* 嗔習交衝), habits of deception and misleading involvements which give rise to mutual guile (*zhaxijiaoyou* 詐習交誘), habits of lying and combined fraudulence which give rise to mutual cheating (*kuangxijiaoqi* 誑習交欺), habits of animosity and interconnected enmity which give rise to grievances (*yuanxijiaoxian* 怨習交嫌), habits of views and the admixture of understandings (*jianxijiaoming* 見習交明), habits of injustice and their interconnected support of one another (*wangxijiaojia* 枉習交加), habits of litigation and the mutual disputations which give rise to covering (*songxijiaoyi* 訟習交誼) | 8. 143c04-144a28 |

APPENDIX 4.2: THREE HINDRANCES (*SANZHANG* 三障) (*cont.*)

| Three hindrances (*sanzhang* 三障) | | Content | Reference (*Da foding rulai miyin xiuzheng liaoyi zhu pusa wanxing shou lengyan jing*, *T* no. 945, vol. 19) |
|---|---|---|---|
| | Through a continuous process of restraint, samsara occurs in this world (youyin shoji liu'ai lunhui 由因世界留礙輪迴) | annihilation and dispersion samsara (*xiaosan lunhui* 銷散輪迴), illusory imaginings samsara (*wangxiang lunhui* 罔象輪迴), dullness and slowness samsara (*yudun lunhui* 愚鈍輪迴), parasitic interaction samsara (*xiangdai lunhui* 相待輪迴), mutual enticement samsara (*xiangyin lunhui* 相引輪迴), false unity samsara (*hewang lunhui* 合妄輪迴), enmity and harm samsara (*yuanhai lunhui* 怨害輪迴) | 7. 138c14-139a12 |
| Hindrances of retribution (*guobaozhang* 果報障) | impermanence, suffering, emptiness of human realm (*renchu wuchang kukong* 人處無常苦空) | | |
| | eight kinds of suffering of humans (*renjian baku* 人間八苦) | birth, aging , sickness , death , separation from that which we love (*aibieli* 愛別離), association with that which we hate (*yuanzenghui* 怨憎會), inability to fulfill our desires (*qiubude* 求不得) and the suffering from the instability of the five skandhas (*wuyinchisheng* 五陰熾盛) | |
| | six interacting retributions (liujiaobao 六交報) | retribution of seeing that arises from eyes (yan'gen jianbao 眼根見報), retribution of hearing that arises from ears (er'gen wenbao 耳根聞報), retribution of smelling that arises from nose (bigen xiubao 鼻根嗅報), retribution of tasting that arises from tongue (shegen weibao 舌根味報), retribution of touching that arises from body (shen'gen chubao 身根觸報), and retribution of thinking that arises from mind (yigen sibao 意根思報) | |

APPENDIX 4.2: THREE HINDRANCES (*SANZHANG* 三障) (*cont.*)

| Three hindrances (*sanzhang* 三障) | | Content | Reference (*Da foding rulai miyin xiuzheng liaoyi zhu pusa wanxing shou lengyan jing*, *T* no. 945, vol. 19) |
|---|---|---|---|
| | seven destinies (*qiqu* 七趣) | deva (*tiandao* 天道), man (*rendao* 人道), spiritual being (*xianqu* 仙趣), asura (*axiuluo* 阿修羅), animal (*chushengdao* 畜生道), hungry ghost (*eguidao* 餓鬼道), hell (*diyudao* 地獄道) | |
| | ten kinds of ghosts (*shizhong gui* 十種鬼) | greed for material objects—strange ghost (*guaigui* 怪鬼), greed for lust—drought-ghost (*bagui* 魃鬼), greed to lie—mei ghost (*meigui* 魅鬼), greed for hatred—gu poison ghost (*gudugui* 蠱毒鬼), greed for animosity—pestilence ghost (*ligui* 癘鬼), greed to be arrogant—hungry ghost (*egui* 餓鬼), greed to be unjust to others—paralysis ghost (*yangui* 魘鬼), greed for views—wang-liang ghost (*wanglianggui* 魍魎鬼), greed for deception—servant ghost (*yishigui* 役使鬼), greed to be litigious—messenger ghost (*chuansonggui* 傳送鬼) | |
| | ten kinds of animals (shizhong chusheng 十種畜生) | species of owl (*xiaolei* 梟類), species of weird creature which gives inauspicious prognostications (*jiuzheng* 咎徵), species of fox (*hulei* 狐類), species of venomous creature (*dulei* 毒類), species of tapeworm (*huilei* 蛔類), species of eating animal (*shilei* 食類), species of animal used for clothing or service (*fulei* 服類), species of migratory creature (*yinglei* 應類), species of auspicious creature (*xiuzheng* 休徵), species of domestic animal (*xunlei* 循類) | 8. 145a20-b8 |
| | ten kinds of persons | persons that come from owls (*xiaolun* 梟倫), persons that come from creatures that are inauspicious (*jiuzheng* 咎徵), persons that come from foxes (*hulun* 狐倫), persons that come from creatures of the venomous category (*dulun* 毒倫), persons that come from tapeworms (*huilun* 蛔倫), persons that come from edible types of creatures (*shilun* 食倫), persons that come | 8. 145b9-29 |

APPENDIX 4.2: THREE HINDRANCES (*SANZHANG* 三障) (*cont.*)

| Three hindrances (*sanzhang* 三障) | | Content | Reference (*Da foding rulai miyin xiuzheng liaoyi zhu pusa wanxing shou lengyan jing*, *T* no. 945, vol. 19) |
|---|---|---|---|
| | | from creatures that are used for clothing or service (*fulun* 服倫), persons that come from creatures that migrate (*yinglun* 應倫), persons that come from auspicious creatures (*xiuzheng* 休徵), persons that come from domestic animals (*xunlun* 循倫) | |
| | ten kinds of spiritual beings | earth-traveling immortals (*dixingxian* 地行仙), flying immortals (*feixingxian* 飛行仙), roaming immortals (*youxingxian* 遊行仙), space-traveling immortals (*kongxingxian* 空行仙), heaven-traveling immortals (*tianxingxian* 天行仙), immortals of penetrating conduct (*tongxingxian* 通行仙), immortals with Way-conduct (*daoxingxian* 道行仙), immortals with illumining conduct (*zhaoxingxian* 照行仙), immortals with essential conduct (*jingxingxian* 精行仙), immortals of absolute conduct (*juexingxian* 絕行仙) | |

## Appendix 4.3: Morning and Evening Chanting

| | | |
|---|---|---|
| General Collection (*Zongji* 總集) | Morning chanting (*Zhaoshi kesong* 朝時課誦) | *Da foding shoulengyan zhou* 大佛頂首楞嚴咒 (*Sitātapatroṣṇīṣa dhāraṇī,* The dhāraṇī of Śūraṃgama of the Great Corona of the Buddha), *Qianshou qianyan wu'ai dabeixin tuoluoni* 千手千眼無礙大悲心陀羅尼 (*Nīlakaṇṭha dhāraṇī,* Dhāraṇī of the Bodhisattva With a Thousand Hands and Eyes and Unimpeded Great Compassion), the *Ruyi baolunwang tuoluoni* 如意寶輪王陀羅尼 (Dhāraṇī of the Wheel-King of Wish-Granting Jewels), the *Xiaozai jixiang shenzhou* 消災吉祥神咒 (Eliminating Disasters Auspicious Fortune Dhāraṇī), *Gongde baoshan shenzhou* 功德寶山神咒 (Dhāraṇī of the Mountain of Merit and Treasure), *Fomu zhunti shenzhou* 佛母準提神咒 (Cundīdevī dhāraṇī, Dhāraṇī of the Goddess Cundī), *Sheng Wuliangshou* |

APPENDIX 4.3 Morning and Evening Chanting (*cont.*)

| | | |
|---|---|---|
| | | *jueding guangmingwang tuoluoni* 聖無量壽決定光明王陀羅尼 (Dhāraṇī of the Resolute Light King Amitâyus), *Yaoshi guarding zhenyan* 藥師灌頂真言 (Consecration Mantra of Medicine Buddha), *Guanyin linggan zhenyan* 觀音靈感真言 (Mantra of Avalokitêśvara's Efficacious Responses), *Qifo miezui zhenyan* 七佛滅罪<br>真言 (Mantra of The Seven Buddhas Eliminating Sin), *Wangsheng jingtu shenzhou* 往生淨土神咒 (Dhāraṇī of Rebirth in the Pure Land), *Shantiannü zhou* 善天女咒 (Dhāraṇī of the Divine Goddess), the *Heart Sūtra*, *nianfo yuanqi* 念佛緣起 (*The Origin of the Recollection of the Buddha*), and *Huixiangwen* 回向文 (*Text of Merit Transference*) (see Specific Collections) |
| | **Evening Chanting** (*Mushi kesong* 暮時課誦) | *Fo shuo Amituo jing* 佛說阿彌陀經 (*Amitâbha-sūtra*), *Chanhui wen* 懺悔文 (Penitence Text), *Mengshan shishi yi* 蒙山施食儀 (Ritual of Feeding Hungry Ghosts), *Nianfo huixiang wen* 念佛回向文 (see Specific Collections, Text for Recollecting the Buddha and Transferring Merits), *Sanguiyi* 三歸依 (Taking the Three Refuges), and *Shandao heshang linshui ruguan wen* 善導和尚示臨睡入觀文 (Text of Master Shandao for Entering Contemplation Before Sleep) |
| **Specific Collections** (*Bieji* 別集) | **The *Sūtras*** (*Jinglei* 經類) | *Huayan xingyuanpin zhang* 華嚴行願品章 (Chapter on the Vows of Samantabhadra in the Flower Adornment *Sūtra*), *Lengyan Shizhipusa nianfo zhang* 楞嚴勢至菩薩念 |
| | | 佛章 (Chapter of Bodhisattva Mahāsthāmaprāpta's Teaching on Perfect Mindfulness of the Buddha in the *Śūraṃgama-sūtra*), *Guan Wuliangshoufo jing shangpin shangsheng zhang* 觀無量壽佛經上品上生章 (Chapter on the Highest of the Highest Stage Rebirth in the Pure Land in the *Sūtra* for Visulizing thee Buddha of Immeasurable Life), *Wuliangshou jing sishibayuan* 無量壽經四十八願 (the forty-eight vows from the *Sūtra* of Immeasurable Life), and *Guan Puxianpusa jing Puxian zhang* 觀普賢菩薩經普賢章 (the section about Samantabhadra from the *Sūtra* of Meditating on Samantabhadra Bodhisattva) |

APPENDIX 4.3 Morning and Evening Chanting (*cont.*)

| | | |
|---|---|---|
| | ***Dhāraṇīs*** (*Zhoulei* 咒類) | *Foding zunsheng da tuoluoni* 佛頂尊勝大陀羅尼 (Uṣṇīṣa Vijaya dhāraṇī, *Dhāraṇī* for the Honorable Ones of the Buddha Peak), *Shoujie dayi zhou* 受戒搭衣咒 (*Dhāraṇī* for Taking Monastic Precepts and Putting on the Monastic Robe), *Bore wujinzang zhenyan* 般若無盡藏真言 (*Dhāraṇī* of the Inexhaustible Storehouse of *Prajñā*), *Huayan buque zhou* 華嚴補缺咒 (Huayan Supplementary *Dhāraṇī*), *Huiji jin'gang shenzhou* 穢跡金剛神咒 (*Dhāraṇī* of Ucchuṣma Vajrapāla), *Shi'er yinyuan zhou* 十二因緣咒 (*Dhāraṇī* of the Twelve Links of Dependent Arising) (with various *dhāraṇīs* appended), and *Buque zhenyan* 補缺真言 (the Supplementary Mantra) |
| | **Various Records** (*Zalu* 雜錄) | The Admonition Text for Reading *Sūtras* (*Kanjing jingwen* 看經警文, by the Chan master Baoning Renyong 保寧仁勇, d.u), the Text in Homage to the *Flower Ornament Sūtra* (*Li Huayan wen* 禮華嚴文, by the Chan master Sui 遂 of Mount Dahongshan 大洪山 in Suizhou 隨州, d.u), the Verses of the Vows of the Great Mercy Bodhisattva (*Dacipusa fayuanji* 大慈菩薩發願偈), the Text of Pure Land (*Jingtu wen* 净土文), another Text of Pure Land (*You Jingtu wen* 又净土文, by the penitent Ciyun 慈雲), the new revision of the Vow Text of the West (*Xinding xifang yuanwen* 新定西方願文, by Yunqi Zhonghong), the Text for Worshipping the Buddhas and Making Vows (*Lifo fayuan wen* 禮佛發願文, by the Chan master Ran 然 of Mount Yishan 怡山), the Text in Homage to Avalokitêśvara (*Li Guanyin wen* 禮觀音文), another Text in Homage to Avalokitêśvara (*You li Guanyin wen* 又禮觀音文, by the Chan master Dahui Zonggao 大慧宗杲), The Admonition Text of the Chan master Weishan Dayuan 潙山大圓 (771-853) (*Weishan Dayuan chanshi jingce wen* 潙山大圓禪師警策文), the Liturgy for Buddhist Fasting (*Zhaifo yi* 齋佛儀), the Liturgy for Approach the Two Meals of the Day (*Er'shi linzhai yi* 二時臨齋儀), the Liturgy of Praying for the Emperor (*Zhusheng yi* 祝聖儀), the Liturgy of Making Offerings to Skanda (*Zhu Weituo yi* 祝韋馱儀), the Liturgy of Making Offering to Temple Deities (*ZhuQielan yi* 祝伽藍儀), the Liturgy |

APPENDIX 4.3 Morning and Evening Chanting (*cont.*)

| | |
|---|---|
| | of Making Offering to Patriarchs (*Zhu zushi yi* 祝祖師儀), the Liturgy of Making Offering to Deities Monitoring Monastic Food (*Zhu Jianzhai yi* 祝監齋儀), the Rite for Striking the Bell (*Jizhong yi* 擊鐘儀), the Liturgy for Organizing an Assembly to Recollect the Buddha (*Jiehui nianfo yi* 結會念佛儀), Incense Praise (*Xiang zan* 香贊), and the Praise of Western Pure Land (*Xifang zan* 西方贊) |

CONCLUSION

# The Characteristics of Chinese Buddhist Faith

The three major objects of Buddhist faith include the Buddha, the Dharma and the *Saṃgha*. Chinese Buddhism inherited Buddhist faith from regions of India and Central Asia. Based on this foundation, it fused elements of faith based on Chinese patriarchal system, Confucian ritual systems and Daoist faith, to give creative interpretations and expressions to devotion to the Buddha, Dharma and *Saṃgha*. During the process, it abandoned parts of the original devotional modes from India and Central Asia that were incompatible with Chinese culture. The Chinese also generated their own innovations. Therefore, under the scope of the institutional histories, society and culture, the characteristics of Chinese Buddhist faith were investigated and concluded on as the objects which were emphasized or newly created by Chinese Buddhist faith, and the background and mode in which these expressions occurred. These are the most important findings from the study in Chinese Buddhist faith and lifestyle.

## 1 Spatial Creation for Objects of Chinese Buddhist Faith

The framework within which Chinese Buddhist faith constructs, interprets and expresses itself is still based on the Three Jewels, the Buddha, Dharma and *Saṃgha*, and takes Mahāyāna Buddhist doctrine as its backdrop. However, in terms of selecting and creating objects of faith, characteristics of Han Buddhism like discourse, identity and reproduction of expressions of faith were shown. At different times and places, Chinese Buddhists still created structure and modes of expressions of faith that were in accordance with characteristics of Chinese culture, ethical society and mass psychology. Buddhist faith was closely intertwined with social relations, making it a concern for the daily lives of common people. Hence, when studying Chinese Buddhist faith, we need to approach it from aspects of history, "holism" and locality in order to grasp the practices of Chinese Buddhist faith. The lifestyle of faith should be understood in specific contexts of daily life, and connect threads of society as a whole. This would certainly incline to a view of lifestyle practices that transcends differences in class, region and sect.[1] The Sinicization of Buddhist faith unfolded

1 Ting, *Hanren minzhong*, 56.

 | DOI:10.1163/9789004431775_007

itself through the connecting threads of practices, and was an inevitable process in history and society.

Faith in the Buddha was based on reminiscing about the Buddha. For instance, reverence toward the Buddha's remains, heirlooms, and places associated with him were all examples of this reminiscence. Also, Buddhists showed their reverence and admiration for the Buddha himself. Furthermore, exploration into the path of awakening led to devotion in the Buddha's birth stories and the bodhisattva path. The distance between China and India is vast. The change in space brought about a change relating to the faith in the Buddha. For instance, the Buddha's heirlooms and places associated with him are sacred objects and sacred sites respectively. These are immovable spaces. However, the Buddha's remains, his *śarīra*, are movable sacred objects. They are popular in China, forming a rich *śarīra* devotion. Moreover, the creation of the Four Great Sacred Mountains in Chinese Buddhism demonstrates the relocation of sacred sites. These fully represent spatial creation in Chinese Buddhist faith.

The most important elements in faith in the Buddha were the body and land. That is, the Buddha's body and the Buddha-land. In terms of the Buddha's body, there are the Buddhas of the three times and the Buddhas of the ten directions in Indian Buddhism. The Buddhas of the three times include the seven or 24 Buddhas of the past, Śākyamuni Buddha of the present and Maitreya Buddha of the future. The Buddhas of the ten directions is a special concept referring to the Buddhas of the worlds of the ten directions. Following the popularity of concepts of merit and Buddhas of the ten directions in Han regions, the names of many different Buddhas were developed. According to the objectives in scriptures of the Buddhas' names, through the merits of worshiping and chanting the Buddhas' names one can drive out evil, protect oneself, remove obstacles, eradicate transgressions, strengthen the power of meditative contemplation and recitation, rapidly be reborn into the Pure Land, or ultimately attain Buddhahood. Since the Wei and Jin periods, many scriptures on the Buddhas' names were widespread and popular in the Central Plain. Many Buddhists believed that through chanting, worshiping or repenting with the Buddhas' names, they could obtain various merits described in the scriptures on the Buddhas names, as well as fulfilling the wholesome wish of finding luck and avoiding calamity. By combining the scriptures of the Buddhas' names and repentance rituals, chanting and singing the Buddhas' names, and prostrating and repenting, the foundation for the development of repentance ritual texts was established.[2] The decline of the devotion to the Buddhas of the three times

2 Wang, "Foming jingdian", 35. In the Collected *Sūtras* Section of the *Taishō Tripiṭaka*, there are 24 scriptures of the Buddhas' names in total. Most of them are just lists of the names of the

and the flourishing of devotion to the Buddhas of the ten directions in Han regions reflects the changes in space in Chinese Buddhist faith.

In terms of the Buddha's body, the remains of the Buddha and subsequently the remains of eminent monastics, have always received veneration and offerings by Buddhists. The Buddha's *śarīra* arrived in China during the Northern and Southern dynasties. Promoted by Emperor Wen of Sui, people in society actively participated in making offerings to the *śarīra*, and it became a collective religious activity in society. Devotion to the *śarīra* was an important component in constructing medieval images of politics and society.

In terms of faith in the Buddha-land, the Wondrous Joy Pure Land of Akṣobhya Buddha has never gained popularity. On the other hand, the faith in the Pure Land of Maitreya's Ascension and Amitābha Buddha's Western Pure Land have been widely accepted. In other words, the Pure Land faith of this place and this land was not accepted by the Chinese. This fully indicates the ethical and historical character of Chinese thinking, which rejected the sacralization of this land. The reason why Amitābha Buddha's Pure Land was accepted by the Chinese was not simply because of the simplicity of the recollection of the Buddha method. Rather, it was because the "West" acts as another land in this world, and it extends the Chinese concept of space. Hence, it enabled China to become a complete space.

Besides the Buddha's body and the Buddha-land, Chinese Buddhism accentuated faith in bodhisattvas. This finally led to the formation of faith in the Four Great Sacred Mountains and the Four Great Bodhisattvas. They are: Mount Wutai of Mañjuśrī Bodhisattva, Mount Emei of Samantabhadra Bodhisattva, Mount Putuo of Avalokiteśvara Bodhisattva, and Mount Jiuhua of Kṣitigarbha Bodhisattva. This reflects that Chinese Buddhism, in a historical sense, proactively defined itself as a future Buddha-land. Following the decline of Indian Buddhism, the status of China as the center of world Buddhism became even more prominent. The formation of the Buddhist Four Great Sacred Mountains is the most representative outcome of the Sinicization of Buddhist faith. The devotion to sacred mountains has six major elements, namely: scriptures, geography, sympathetic resonance, pagoda temples, devotees, and state support. The Four Great Sacred Mountains became widely known in society after the time of Emperor Kangxi.[3] The shift in the location of sacred

Buddhas and their merits as the main content. Among them, there are 15 scriptures of "merit of invocation and praise", which mainly expound on the merit of the Buddhas' name. There are nine scriptures of "invocating and worshiping the Buddhas' names", which primarily focus on chanting, singing and prostrating to the Buddhas' names.

3 Sheng, "On the Veneration", 121-143.

mountains meant a shift in space at the center of Buddhist faith. From then on, China had truly become the second home land to Buddhism.

Faith in the Dharma primarily reflected the worship of Mahāyāna Buddhist scriptures, combined with faith in the Buddhas and Bodhisattvas. It is especially so for devotion to Mahāyāna scriptures like the *Fahua jing* and *Huayan jing*, as well as devotion to Maitreya and Avalokiteśvara Bodhisattvas. Devotion to Medicine Buddha was formed through practices like prostrating to Medicine Buddha, recitation of the *Yaoshi jing*, or combining the setup of "life extension practice" shrines, conducting life release and charitable activities. These Medicine Buddha Dharma service practices drove the formulation of Medicine Buddha repentance rituals. Pagoda devotion and upholding the text of the *sūtra* were two core elements in *Fahua jing* devotion. Kumārajīva and his disciples' interpretation of the *Fahua jing* influenced the later iconography of two Buddhas sitting together. On the other hand, due to the spread of the wish that "the true Dharma remains long in the world", and the influence of the concept of the Dharma ending age, transmitting scriptures through transcription to ensure their wide dissemination became a pressing task. Scripture transcription first began by using hard rock as the medium. This ensured that the transcriptions would withstand against destruction in the chaotic world during the Dharma ending age and be able to be disseminated for a long time. Examples include stone carved scriptures from the Northern dynasty and the Fangshan stone scriptures. Among all the transmitted scriptures through transcription, scriptures transcribed with blood were of unique significance. This embodied the combination of scripture worship, bodily sacrifice, merit making and ascetic practice.[4] In addition, scriptures transcribed with blood took blood, the essence of the physical body, as a medium for writing. This transformed the physical body into a sacred space whereby scripture as a material form underwent sacralization to become a sacred medium.

In order to disseminate Buddhism and to ensure its penetration into society, there were two styles of explaining the scriptures. There was a philosophical style of lecture by monastics, and another style like public lectures which were easy to understand. Through illustrative lectures and public lectures, Buddhist faith permeated into common society and finally integrated to become part of the daily life of the people in society. Chinese Buddhism placed great emphasis on the actualization of scriptures. Hence, this prompted a series of specific practice methods that were also in harmony with Chinese ritual culture. Among them, the most representative one was the formation of repentance rites. Repentance rituals centered on scriptures became popular. For example,

4 Murata, "Yuanyuan", 56-63.

Zhiyi's *Fahua sanmei chanyi* was composed during the prevalence of the cult of the *Fahua jing* in the Sixteen Kingdoms, Northern and Southern dynasties. It was modeled on Huisi's *Fahua jing Anle xing yi* and incorporated the method of the *Lotus Samādhi* of the time, to become a complete system of repentance and meditative contemplation.

The faith in the *Saṃgha* primarily referred to the institutional expressions of faith, or in other words, the sacred expressions of the monastic community's lifestyle. For instance, the *arhats*, the Buddha's *śrāvaka* disciples are among these expressions. According to the *Fazhu ji*, sixteen *arhat*s remained in the world and did not enter *parinirvāṇa*, for the sake of acting as merit fields for sentient beings in the Dharma ending age and to protect the Dharma body of Mahāyāna Buddhism. This gave rise to the formation of devotion to *arhats* in Chinese Buddhism. Devotion to patriarchs was an internal faith system within the monastic community of Chinese Buddhism. It assimilated the patriarchal system of Chinese traditional society to develop an ideology of Dharma lineage that was unique to the Chinese. This structure was adopted to establish and regulate faith in patriarchs in Chinese Buddhism.

Therefore, in the discussion of the Three Jewels, Buddha, Dharma and *Saṃgha*, as the objects of faith in Chinese Buddhism, the phenomena of creation of space and relocation of sacred space are evident. Moreover, the faith in the "*Saṃgha*" was influenced by the ancestor worship of lineage-based religion to create a unique devotion to the patriarchs.

## 2 Rituals of Chinese Buddhist Faith, Politics of Imperial Power and Systems of Ritual

Chinese Buddhist religious faith takes the centralized bureaucracy and systems of ritual as its foundation and presupposition, which are the most influential factors in the expression of faith. In terms of politics, Chinese Buddhism has the special feature of being a "state Buddhism", which is fully expressed in its prayers for the state, its political will, and its involvement in power. In ancient China, the idea that "beneath the broad heavens, all land belongs to the monarch" was already a natural truth ordained by heaven and earth. This kind of divinely mandated power extended to all aspects of the state, and on this piece of territory, political will possessed a sense of leadership over religious organizations. Within the Dharma service activities, ritual procedures for practice and cultivation, and constructed images in stone caves of Chinese Buddhism, we see preserved a great amount of votive texts of prayers for the state. Prayers of blessing and repentance rituals on behalf of the state show the special character of Chinese Buddhism as a state Buddhism, acknowledging that religion survives beneath imperial authority. For the emperor, being the authority of centralized power, his religious activities serve as the best point of union between the state and Buddhism. The most important expressions of these were inner altars and *śarīra* worship. During the Sui and Tang periods, in particular the times of Emperor Wen of Sui and Empress Wu Zetian, Buddhism became part of the ideology in the construction of the empire, bringing together different levels of society and acting as a medium for various ethnic groups within the empire. Therefore, inner altars which appeared in the Sui and Tang periods were centers used to call together well known monastics and act as centers for the propagation of Buddhism. This helped make considerable progress in exchange between Buddhism in the north and south, directly influencing the rise of Buddhist traditions in the Sui and Tang periods. The establishment of inner altars fully shows the cooperation between imperial and religious power, and was the point of intersection in the relationship between Buddhism and the state, not only embodying the personal religious faith of the ruler, but also showing the status of monastics in society and politics. During the regnal period of Renshou, Emperor Wen of Sui bestowed *śarīra* on the state and established *śarīra* pagodas, and held dharma services for the installation and receiving of *śarīra* at many locations throughout the land. This fixed the ideology of imperial governing power as well as the emperor's personal will to implement them within the foundational levels of society. Through this method, acceptance for the emperor's governing authority was strengthened in different areas, ethnic groups and all strata of society. The offerings to *śarīra* at Famen si by the Tang emperors also displayed the depth of unification of imperial power and the Buddhist faith. Buddhism aided the emperor in educating the populace, and also helped in gaining the people's acceptance to the emperor's political power.

State Buddhism also appears as power directly involved with Chinese Buddhism. For example, the formation of the tradition of vegetarianism, which was from Liang Wudi's promotion of his own Buddhist policy. Taking Fayun 法雲 (467-529) and others as examples and directed at the malpractice of the traditional Buddhist *saṃgha,* he raised a new spirit of bodhisattvas strictly upholding the precepts out of compassion, starting from the practice of "Proscription of Meat and Alcohol" to rectify Buddhism. Since then, the tradition of vegetarianism has crystalized to become an important way of life for Chinese Buddhists. Through establishing the Jiangshan Dharma Service, Ming Taizu summoned eminent monks of the early Ming period to Nanjing, which undoubtedly unified the strength of Jiangnan Buddhist circles. As eminent monks participated in the Mount Jiang Dharma Service in the form of national offerings and carried out offerings and prayers as a national undertaking, the majority of Buddhist power was under the rule of imperial authority. It played an important role in consolidating and regulating Buddhism in the early Ming period. Through laying down the requirements of ritual and timing for making offerings to ghosts and gods, and organizing the Mount Jiang Dharma Service ritual, Ming Taizu was the driving force behind the rectification of Buddhist *sūtra* recitation and repentance services in Ming dynasty.

Ritual (*li*) is a value goal of ancient Chinese society, which seeks the common social ideal of order in hierarchical rank between different people. The *Saṃgha* community is the main element of the embodiment of the Buddhist religion. "Religious community" is made up of monastics, the monastic community and monasteries. This organized religion was embedded in the Han-cultural-circle regions of China. Its forces and counter-forces exhibited a kind of real "life experience" and historical setting. Therefore, apart from the underlying ideological conflict between Indian and Han cultures, there was a more realistic, practical, and living conflict between institution and way of life. In the very process of ongoing conflicts and contentions between Indian Buddhist ideas about disciplinary regulations and customs in daily life, and that of traditional systems of ritual in Han culture, Chinese Buddhism gradually adopted practices that suited the Chinese ritual culture. An example is the Monastic Regulations formulated by Daoan, which has "Procedures for sending envoys and confession of transgressions and so on at *poṣadha*". In the Northern and Southern dynasties, repentance rites including practices of preaching, *sūtra* recitation and purification gathering, were continuously refined based on the needs and beliefs of the community.

Repentance is an important practice method in Buddhism. Following the transmission and translation of Buddhist repentance scriptures into China, repentance rites were brought into the beliefs and lifestyles of Chinese Buddhists. However, repentance rites possess characteristics of Chinese Buddhism because of the influence of native Chinese culture, especially from Confucian and Daoist thought. Chinese Buddhist repentance rites were developed by eminent monks. On the basis of repentance rites from India and Central Asia, they were formed from the debates among the three teachings during the Wei, Jin, Northern and Southern dynasties, and gradually adopted practices that suited the Chinese "ritual" culture as a form of expression. For example, the doctrines of contemplation of the empty nature of transgression through contemplating the true characteristic, repentance of the six faculties, and the emphasis on seeing the physical body of Samantabhadra Bodhisattva from the *Puxian guanjing* became the basis for developing Tiantai repentance rites.

From the perspective of Buddhism's own ability to transform itself, its own wisdom of skillful means and system of two truths of the ultimate and conventional reveal Buddhism's original functions of openness, fusion and creativity. Inter-subjectivity as an expression of Buddhist faith was formed within the background of politics and systems of ritual. Based on the wisdom of the two truths, this is not in contradiction with Chinese imperial politics and systems of ritual, but further displays the transcendent nature of Buddhist religious faith.

## 3 Rationalism and Communalism as Chinese Buddhist Expressions of Faith

Having passed through the chaos brought to China by the five barbarian tribes and the chronic disorder of the North and South dynasties, in the subsequent unification of the Sui dynasty, various forms of Buddhism from India and other areas of northern and southern China gathered together in Chang'an. This brought about contention between the many traditions of thought and the most splendid period of Sui and Tang Buddhism. Buddhism, which had already Sinicized its religious faith, went through the process of blending into daily life, and then slowly seeped into Chinese systems of thought and regulation. Actualizing an unprecedented development and transformation, it produced the greatest accomplishment of Chinese Buddhism: the various traditions, in particular Sanlun, Tiantai, Huayan, Chan, Pure Land, Esoteric and so forth. These traditions held the exchange and transformation between Indian thought and Confucian and Daoist thought, to reflect the richness and changes of Buddhist thinking. This manifested Buddhism's successes in terms of conceptual thought and novelty of institutional systems, another high peak in the convergence between the heights of Chinese and Indian thought. The establishment of these schools represented the completion of the Sinicization of Buddhist thought. Chinese Buddhist thought was formed by taking the ideas of *Zhouyi*, *Laozi* and *Zhuangzi* as its standards, lecturing and commenting on *sūtras* as its method, the Buddhist philosophical schools of the Northern and Southern dynasties as its foundation, and the Buddhist sects of the Sui and Tang dynasties as its representative characteristic. With respect to lifestyles of faith and the standardization of regulations, the establishment of Buddhist schools in the Sui and Tang even further displays rationalism in the expression of religious faith in Chinese Buddhism. Furthermore, many more intellectuals and literati became Buddhists, and to a certain extent the expression of

Buddhist rational faith replaced folk religion to become common spiritual values of the Sui and Tang society.

As Buddhism became prevalent during the Northern and Southern dynasties, groups gradually formed with the assembly of those connected by the bonds of the same faith. When monastics with the power of virtuous inspiration were carrying out indoctrination, devotional groups centered on them were formed. These collective bodies, organizations or assemblies based on faith were called: *she* 社 (society), *fashe* 法社 (Dharma society), *yi* 邑 (group), *yihui* 邑會 (club), or *yiyi* 邑義 (devotional society), *yiyi* 义邑 (association), *yihui* 義會 (congruence), and so on. Through these organized bodies, Buddhists of the Northern and Southern dynasties constructed Buddha statues, cave temples or conducted services like purification gathering, transcribing *sūtra*, *sūtra* recitation and so on. They also engaged in meritorious activities such as building bridges, roads, digging wells, planting trees, providing burial grounds for the destitute, giving food to the poor and others. Buddhist faith organizations like "groups" and "societies" showed the communal nature in the expression of faith within Chinese Buddhism. Within this, kindness and compassion in Mahāyāna Buddhism became the slogans of communal activities. Sui and Tang Buddhism was an important force in society, actively participating in charity and philanthropic works. Together with the government, it set up compassion field infirmaries, hospitals and so forth, developed disaster relief for the poor, and did civil engineering works. Buddhist temples and monasteries were living spaces for public society, and through providing short-term dwelling accommodation for scholars and literati, further advanced the influence of Chinese Buddhism on the learned classes. Buddhist charitable activities were very well-developed in the Song dynasty. There were charitable institutions like institutes for shelter and care and nursing homes for taking in sick and destitute elderly, orphanages for taking in abandoned infants and children, grain subsidies to assist indigent families in raising their children, as well as public cemeteries providing professional funeral services for the poor and unidentified deceased. Buddhist organizations were actively involved in many public welfare works. They provided funding and labor for affairs such as building bridges, water works, roads and local security patrols. In addition, monastics set up life release ponds in the monasteries. The development of life release customs later became an important tradition in Buddhism's penetration into society after the Song dynasty.

## 4 Pragmatism as Chinese Buddhist Expression of Faith

The thought of Indian Buddhism revolves around and developed from suffering. With the four noble truths at the core, doctrines like suffering, emptiness, impermanence, and no-self evolved. The four noble truths are the understanding of suffering—its arising, the causes for its arising, the cessation of suffering, and the method to the cessation of suffering. That is, the four noble truths of suffering, arising, cessation and the path. An emphasis on suffering and emptiness is a special quality of Indian Buddhism. The hot climate of India brought about the Buddhist theory of "suffering" and concepts of transcendence, such as the fasting precepts, bathing, sitting meditation, and other religious activities. After Buddhism was transmitted to China, it went through clashes and merging of concepts, thoughts and regulations, and its point of focus moved to the present moment, which was applied within human life.

Chinese Buddhist faith expresses pragmatism in practical life. Repentance, recitation of *sūtra*s, meditative contemplation and other practices to cultivate the path were fully put in the service of pragmatic goals for the physical body, power and the state. Chinese Buddhist faith in Buddhas and bodhisattvas shows extremely strong features of relief in the present life. For example, during the Northern and Southern dynasties, the already thriving faith in Medicine Buddha has eradication of calamity, longevity and treatment of illness as its religious aims. Through the acts of faith such as worship, production of statues, repentance, transcription of *sūtra*s and Dharma services, the devotion to Medicine Buddha shows its focus on "happiness in the present life" as its religious character. Furthermore, Chinese Buddhist methods of repentance also display the trait of stressing benefit in the present world. There are prayers and dedications of merit for the state, the emperor and so forth throughout repentance texts. Apart from repentance practices containing state Buddhism content, we cannot overlook the pragmatism of Chinese Buddhist faith.

Under the background of Confucian humanistic thought, as Chinese society focused on benefits in the present life, Chinese people lacked concern for life and death. Buddhism emphasized the nature of mind and concern for life and death, which supplemented the gap in Confucian and Daoist theories, and fulfilled people's spiritual needs. Buddhism's function of offerings to the deceased became the greatest supplement on the level of concern for life and death by the Chinese.

Around the start of the Common Era, following the cultural exchange between the East and West under the climate of commercial trading, Buddhism was transmitted to the great land of China. Through Wei, Jin, Northern and Southern dynasties, up to the Sui unification of China at the end of the 6th century, there were clashes and merges between Buddhism and Confucianism, and Daoism, Buddhism helped to shape and supplement Chinese culture, and Buddhism's unifying and communicative role among the ethnic groups of China, all of which formed a rich and multifaceted historical context. The core factors contributing to the clashes between Buddhism and Confucianism as well as Daoism were concepts and regulations. For instance, between monastic renunciation and filial piety, liberation and assuming responsibilities of benevolence and righteousness. These were fused together on the basis of the spiritual needs of faith and the pragmatic needs of daily life. Through the vocation of values that transcend clan, race and region, and the medium of organizations such as devotional societies, Buddhism successfully transformed the value of faith into a force for the practical merging of resources with the distinct mode of a world religion. This joined together the particular estrangement of "family" society in China and shaped the Chinese world view from the world of faith. Through practical need and the merging of lifestyles, it went beyond the dichotomy of disputes between barbarians and Chinese. Hence, the first Sinicization that was accomplished during the Northern and Southern dynasties was Sinicization of faith. The Chinese accepted Buddhist faith, and expressed their own world of faith through the rituals of Chinese culture. Furthermore, the Chinese also accepted, studied and expressed modes of lifestyle that were directed by Buddhist faith.

Following the scope of the history of society, institutions and culture, Chinese Buddhism accepted the influence of politics of imperial power and systems of ritual. On the level of faith in the Buddha, there were the creation of faith in sacred mountains, *śarīra*, the Buddhas of the ten directions, and so on. On the level of faith in the Dharma, there were the production of methods of repentance, stone carved scriptures, blood transcriptions of scriptures, and other forms of spatial expression. In terms of faith in the *Saṃgha*, there were faith in the *arhat*s and faith in the patriarchs, displaying a definite inclination toward substantialization. In terms of expressions of faith, Chinese Buddhism displays the characters of rationalism, pragmatism and communalism. These fully reflect that Chinese Buddhist faith is a fusion of Indian Buddhism with Chinese thought and lineage-centered religion.

# Bibliography

## Abbreviations Used in Bibliography

B — Chinese manuscripts from Dunhuang collected in Beijing tushu guan 北京圖書館 (currently National Library of China [Zhongguo guojia tushuguan 中國國家圖書館 ]), Beijing, China.

*BB* — *Dazangjing bubian* 大藏經補編 (Lan Jifu comp., 1986; see Bibliography III).

*JXZ* — *Mingban Jiaxing dazang jing* 明版嘉興大藏經 (see Bibliography III).

*SKQS* — *Yingyin Wenyuange siku quanshu* 景印文淵閣四庫全書 (see Bibliography III).

P — Chinese manuscripts from Dunhuang in the Pelliot Collection, Bibliothèque Nationale, Paris.

S — Chinese manuscripts from Dunhuang in the Stein Collection, British Library, London.

*T* — *Taishō shinshū daizōkyō* 大正新脩大蔵経 (Takakusu, et al., comps., 1924-1932; see Bibliography III).

*XXSKQS* — *Xuxiu siku quanshu* 續修四庫全書 (Xuxiu siku quanshu bianweihui, comps, 2002; see Bibliography III).

*XZJ* — (*Wan*) *Xuzang jing* (卍) 續藏經 (see Bibliography III).

## Primary Sources


*Amituo jing shuchao* 阿彌陀經疏鈔, 4 *juan*. By Zhuhong 袾宏 (1535-1615). *XZJ* no. 326, vol. 33.

*Amituo jing shuchao wenbian* 阿彌陀經疏鈔問辯, 1 *juan*. By Zhuhong 袾宏 (1535-1615). *XZJ* no. 328, vol. 33.

*Anle xingdao zhuanjing yuansheng jingtu fashi zan* 安樂行道轉經願生淨土法事讚, the second *juan* in 2 *juan*. By Shandao 善導 (613-681). *T* no. 1979, vol. 47.

*Baizhang qinggui zhengyi ji* 百丈清規證義記, 10 *juan*. By Yirun 儀潤 (fl. 1816-1823) (completed in 1823). *XZJ* no. 1233, vol. 111.

*Baqiongshi jinshi buzheng* 八瓊室金石補正, 130 *juan*. By Lu Zengxiang 陸增祥 (1816-1882) (first published in 1925). References made to the Wenwu chubanshe 文物出版社 edition (Beijing, 1985).

*Bei Qi shu* 北齊書, 50 *juan*. By Li Baiyao 李百藥 (564-648), completed in 636. References made to *Er shi si shi* 二十四史, Zhonghua shuju 中華書局 edition (Beijing, 1995).

*Bei shi* 北史, 100 *juan*. By Li Yanshou 李延壽 (fl.629-659), completed in 659. References made to *Er shi si shi* 二十四史, Zhonghua shuju 中華書局 edition (Beijing, 1995).

*Bianzheng lun* 辯正論, 8 *juan*. By Falin 法琳 (572-640). *T* no. 2110, vol. 52.

"Bi'naiye xu" 鼻奈耶序, by 道安 (314-385) in ca. 382. In *Bi'naiye* 鼻奈耶, 10 *juan*. Translated by Zhu Fonian 竺佛念 (331?-417+) in 382. *T* no. 1464, vol. 24.

*Biqiuni zhuan* 比丘尼傳, 4 *juan*. By Baochang 寶唱 (fl. 505). *T* no. 2063, vol. 50.

"Butuoluojia shan zhuan tici" 補陀洛迦山傳題辭. In *Butuoluojia shan zhuan* 補陀洛迦山傳, 1 *juan*. By Sheng Ximing 盛熙明 (fl. 1344). *T* no. 2101, vol. 51.

*Buxu Gaoseng zhuan* 補續高僧傳, 26 *juan*. By Minghe 明河 (1588-1640). *XZJ* no. 1501, vol. 134.

*Chang'an zhi* 長安志, 20 *juan*. Compiled by Song Minqiu 宋敏求 (1019-1079). *SKQS* vol. 587.

*Chanlin beiyong qinggui* 禪林備用清規, 10 *juan*. By Yixian 弋咸 (?-1311+) in 1311. *XZJ* no. 1239, vol. 112.

*Zenrin shōkisen* 禪林象器箋, 20 *juan*. Compiled by Mujaku Dōchū 無著道忠 (1653-1745) in 1715. *B* no. 103, vol. 19.

*Chanyuan qinggui* 禪苑清規, 10 *juan*. By Zongze 宗賾 (1053-1113) in ca. 1103. *XZJ* no. 1234, vol. 111.

*Chanzong songgu lianzhu tongji* 禪宗頌古聯珠通集, 40 *juan*. Compiled by Faying 法應 (?-1175+) in 1175 and supplemented by Puhui 普會 (?-1318+) in 1318. *XZJ* no. 1283, vol. 115.

*Chaxiangshi congchao* 茶香室叢鈔, 106 *juan*. By Yu Yue 俞樾 (1821-1907). References made to the Zhonghua shuju 中華書局 edition (Beijing, 1995).

*Chisheng guang daochang niansong yi* 熾盛光道場念誦儀, 1 *juan*. By Zunshi 遵式 (964-1032). *T* no. 1951, vol. 46.

"Chisheng guang daochang niansong yi shiyi xu" 熾盛光道場念誦儀拾遺序. By Lingjian 靈鑑 (fl. 1048-1062). In *Chisheng guang daochang niansong yi* 熾盛光道場念誦儀, 1 *juan*. By Zunshi 遵式 (964-1032). *T* no. 1951, vol. 46.

*Chixiu Baizhang qinggui* 敕修百丈清規, 8 *juan*. Compiled by Dehui 德輝 (?-1335+) at the request of the Yuan court. *T* no. 2025, vol. 48.

*Chu sanzang ji ji* 出三藏記集, 15 *juan*. Initially compiled by Sengyou 僧佑 (445-518) in 515. *T* no. 2145, vol. 55.

*Chushi Fanqi chanshi yulu* 楚石梵琦禪師語錄, 20 *juan*. By Zuguang 祖光 (?-1363), et al. *XZJ* no. 1400, vol. 124.

*Cibei daochang chanfa* 慈悲道場懺法, 10 *juan*. Compiled by a number of monks between 502 and 519 during the Liang dynasty 梁. *T* no. 1909, vol. 45.

*Cishou Huaishen chanshi guanglu* 慈受懷深禪師廣錄, 4 *juan*. By Shanqing 善清 (1535-1615), et al., ca. between 1133 and 1135. *XZJ* no. 1433, vol. 126.

*Conglin jiaoding qinggui zongyao* 叢林校定清規總要, 1 *juan*. By Weimian 惟勉 (active under the Xianchun era [1265-1275]) in 1274. *XZJ* no. 1238, vol. 112.

*Conglin liangxu xuzhi* 叢林兩序須知, 1 *juan*. By Tongrong 通容 (1593-1661). *XZJ* no. 1340, vol. 112.

*Da bo niepan jing* 大般涅槃經 (Skt. *Mahāparinirvāṇa-sūtra*), 40 *juan*. Translated by Tanwuchen 曇無讖 (Dharmakṣema, 385-433) in ca. 421. *T* no. 374, vol. 12.

*Da bo nihuan jing* 大般泥洹經 (Skt. *Mahāparinirvāṇa-sūtra*), 6 *juan*. Translated by Faxian 法顯 (337-422) and Fotuobatuoluo 佛馱跋陀羅 (Buddhabhadra, 359-429) between 416 and 418. *T* no. 376, vol. 12.

*Da Fangguangfo huayan jing* 大方廣佛華嚴經 (Skt. *Buddhâvataṃsaka-mahāvaipulya-sūtra*), 60 *juan*. Translated by Fotuobatuoluo 佛馱跋陀羅 (Buddhabhadra, 359-429) between 418 and 420. *T* no. 278, vol. 9.

*Da Fangguangfo huayan jing shu* 大方廣佛華嚴經疏, 60 *juan*. By Chengguan 澄觀 (738-839). *T* no. 1735, vol. 35.

*Da Fangguangfo huayan jing sui shu yanyi chao* 大方廣佛華嚴經隨疏演義鈔, 90 *juan*. By Chengguan 澄觀 (738-839). *T* no. 1736, vol. 36.

*Da foding rulai miyin xiuzheng liaoyi zhu pusa wanxing shou lengyan jing* 大佛頂如來密因修證了義諸菩薩萬行首楞嚴經 (Skt. *Śūraṃgama-sūtra*), 10 *juan*. Translated by Boramidi 般剌蜜帝 (Pāramiti, 656?-706+) in 705. *T* no. 945, vol. 19.

*Da ming du wu ji jing* 大明度無極經 (Skt. *Aṣṭasāhasrikā prajñāpāramitā-sūtra*), 6 *juan*. Translated by Zhi Qian 支謙 (197?-253+) sometime between 223 and 253. *T* no. 225, vol.8.

*Da Ming Gaoseng zhuan* 大明高僧傳, 8 *juan*. By Ruxing 如惺 (fl. 1600-1617) in 1617. *T* no. 2062, vol. 50.

*Da Ming huidian* 大明會典, 228 *juan*. Recompiled by 申時行 (1535-1614) and others, first published in 1587. *XXSKQS* vol. 791.

*Da zhidu lun* 大智度論 (Skt. *Mahāprajñāpāramitā-śāstra*), 100 *juan*. Translated by Jiumoluoshi 鳩摩羅什 (Kumārajīva, 334-413) between 402 and 405. *T* no. 1509, vol. 25.

*Dacheng wusheng fangbian men* 大乘無生方便門, 1 *juan*. Author unknown. *T* no. 2834, vol. 85.

*Daizong chao zeng Sikong Dabianzheng Guangzhi sanzang heshang biaozhi ji* 代宗朝贈司空大辨正廣智三藏和尚表制集, 6 *juan*. By Yuanzhao 圓照 (718-799+). *T* no. 2120, vol. 52.

*Dasheng Wenshushili pusa zanfo fashen li xu* 大聖文殊師利菩薩贊佛法身禮序, 1 *juan*. Translated by Bukong 不空 (Amoghavajra, 705-774) in 765. *T* no. 1195, vol. 20.

*Da Song sengshi lüe* 大宋僧史略, 3 *juan*. By Zanning 贊寧 (919?-1001?) in 977. *T* no. 2126, vol. 54.

*Da Tang Da Ci'ensi sanzang fashi zhuan* 大唐大慈恩寺三藏法師傳, 10 *juan*. By Huili 慧立 (615-665+) and later supplemented by Yancong 彥悰 (595›-699›) in 688. *T* no. 2053, vol. 50.

*Da Tang gu dade zeng Sikong Dabianzheng Guangzhi Bukong sanzang xingzhuang* 大唐故大德贈司空大辨正廣智不空三藏行狀, 1 *juan*. By Zhao Qian 趙遷 (722›-771+). *T* no. 2056, vol. 50.

*Da Tang gu sanzang Xuanzang fashi xingzhuang* 大唐故三藏玄奘法師行狀, 1 *juan*. By Mingxiang 冥祥 (active under the reigning era of Tang Gaozong [649-683]). *T* no. 2052, vol. 50.

*Da Tang neidian lu* 大唐內典錄, 10 *juan*. By Daoxuan 道宣 (596-667) in 664. *T* no. 2149, vol. 55.

*Da Tang Qinglongsi sanchao gongfeng dade xingzhuang* 大唐青龍寺三朝供奉大德行狀, 1 *juan*. By Zhao Qian 趙遷 (722 › -771+). *T* no. 2056, vol. 50.

*Da Tang Xiyu ji* 大唐西域記, 12 *juan*. By Xuanzang 玄奘 (602-664) and Bianji 辯機 (ca. 618-ca. 648) in 646. *T* no. 2087, vol. 51.

*Deyu longhua xiuzheng chanyi* 得遇龍華修證懺儀, 4 *juan*. By Ruxing 如惺 (fl. 1600). *XZJ* no. 1466, vol. 129.

*Dongpo houji* 東坡後集, 20 *juan*. Compiler unknown. References made to *Su Dongpo quanji* 蘇東坡全集, Shijie shuju 世界書局 edition (Taipei, 1964).

*Emeishan zhi* 峨眉山志, 8 *juan*. By Jiang Chao 蔣超 (1624-1673) in 1672 and re-edited by Yinguang 印光 (1861-1940) in 1934. References made to the Jiangsu guangling guji ke yin she 江蘇廣陵古籍刻印社 edition (Yangzhou, 1997).

*Fahua jing anlexing yi* 法華經安樂行義, 1 *juan*. By Huisi 慧思 (515-577). *T* no. 1926, vol. 46.

*Fahua jing shu* 法華經疏, 2 *juan*. By Zhu Daosheng 竺道生 (355-434). *XZJ* no. 1661, vol. 150.

*Fahua sanmei chan yi* 法華三昧懺儀, 1 *juan*. By Zhiyi 智顗 (539-598). *T* no. 1941, vol. 46.

"Fahua sanmei chan yi kanding yuanben xu" 法華三昧懺儀勘定元本序. By Zunshi 遵式 (964-1032). In *Fahua sanmei chan yi* 法華三昧懺儀, 1 *juan*. By Zhiyi 智顗 (539-598). *T* no. 1941, vol. 46.

*Fan wang jing* 梵網經 (Skt. *Brahmajāla-sūtra*), 2 *juan*. Translated by Jiumoluoshi 鳩摩羅什 (Kumārajīva, 334-413) in 406. *T* no. 1484, vol. 24.

"Fangdeng sanmei xingfa xu" 方等三昧行法序. By Zunshi 遵式 (964-1032). *In Fangdeng sanmei xingfa* 方等三昧行法, 1 *juan*. By Zhiyi 智顗 (539-598), recorded by Guanding 灌頂 (561-632). *T* no. 1940, vol. 46.

*Fayuan zhulin* 法苑珠林, 100 *juan*. By Daoshi 道世 (ca. 596-668+) in 668. *T* no. 2122, vol. 53.

*Fo shuo foming jing* 佛說佛名經, 12 *juan*. Translated by Putiliuzhi 菩提流支 (Bodhiruci, ?-535) sometime between 520 and 524. *T* no. 440, vol. 14.

*Fo shuo guan Mile pusa shangsheng doushuaitian jing* 佛說觀彌勒菩薩上生兜率天經, 1 *juan*. Translated by Juqu Jingsheng 沮渠京聲 (?-464) approx. in the early fifth century. *T* no. 452, vol. 14.

*Fo shuo guan Puxian pusa xingfa jing* 佛說觀普賢菩薩行法經, 1 *juan*. Translated by Tanwumiduo 曇無蜜多 (Dharmamitra, 356-442) sometime between 424 and 442. *T* no. 277, vol. 9.

*Fo shuo guan Puxian pusa xingfa jing ji* 佛說觀普賢菩薩行法經記, 2 *juan*. By Enchin 円珍 (Chin. Yuanzhen 圓珍, 814-891). *T* no. 2194, vol. 56.

*Fo shuo shi'er foming shenzhou jiaoliang gongde chuzhang miezui jing* 佛說十二佛名神咒校量功德除障滅罪經, 1 *juan*. Translated by She'najueduo 闍那崛多 (Jñānagupta, 523-600) sometime between 561 and 592. *T* no. 1348, vol. 21.

*Fo shuo Wenshushili fabao zang tuoluoni jing* 佛說文殊師利法寶藏陀羅尼經, 1 *juan*. Translated by Putiliuzhi 菩提流志 (Bodhiruci, a.k.a. Dharmaruci, 572?-727). *T* no. 1185, vol. 20.

*Fo shuo zhu de futian jing* 佛說諸德福田經, 1 *juan*. Translated by Fali 法立 (255?-308+) and Faju 法炬 (259?-309+) in ca. 308. *T* no. 683, vol. 16.

*Fozu gangmu* 佛祖綱目, 42 *juan*. By Zhu Shi'en 朱時恩 (1563-1632+) (published in 1634). *XZJ* no. 1570, vol. 146.

*Fozu lidai tongzai* 佛祖歷代通載, 22 *juan*. By Nianchang 念常 (1282-1344+) in 1344. *T* no. 2036, vol. 49.

*Fozu tongji* 佛祖統紀, 54 *juan*. Compiled by Zhipan 志磐 (?-1269+) between 1258 and 1269. *T* no. 2035, vol. 49.

*Fuzhou fuzhi* 抚州府志, 86 *juan*. By Xu Yingheng 許應鑅 (1820-1891) and compiled by Xie Huang 謝煌 (fl. 1837-1876) (first published in 1876). References made to the Chengwen chubanshe 成文出版社 edition, *Zhongguo fangzhi congshu* 中國方志叢書, vol. 253 (Taibei, 1975).

*Gaoseng Faxian zhuan* 高僧法顯傳, 1 *juan*. By Faxian 法顯 (334-420) sometime between 413 and 420. *T* no. 2085, vol. 51.

*Gaoseng zhuan* 高僧傳, 14 *juan*. Initially completed by Huijiao 慧皎 (497-554) sometime between 519 and 522 (final version probably completed ca. 530). *T* no. 2059, vol. 50.

*Gu Qingliang zhuan* 古清涼傳, 2 *juan*. Compiled by Huixiang 慧祥 (active 660s-706) sometime between 680 and 683. *T* no. 2098, vol. 51.

"Gu Qingliang zhuan xu" 古清涼傳序. By Guangying 廣英 (d. u) in 1181. In *Gu Qingliang zhuan* 古清涼傳, 2 juan. Compiled by Huixiang 慧祥 (active 660s-706) sometime between 680 and 683. *T* no. 2098, vol. 51.

*Guan nian Amituofo xianghai sanmei gongde famen* 觀念阿彌陀佛相海三昧功德法門, 1 *juan*. By Shandao 善導 (613-681). *T* no. 1959, vol. 47.

*Guang Hongming ji* 廣弘明集, 30 *juan*. Compiled by Daoxuan 道宣 (596-667) in 664 and under continuous revision until at least 666. *T* no. 2103, vol. 52.

*Gujin tushu jicheng shijiao buhui kao* 古今圖書集成釋教部彙考, 7 *juan*. *XZJ* no. 1498, vol. 133.

*Guoqing bailu* 國清百錄, 4 *juan*. By Guanding 灌頂 (561-632). *T* no. 1934, vol. 46.

*Hanshan Laoren mengyou ji* 憨山老人夢遊集, 55 *juan*. Recorded by Fushanri 福善 (active under the Wanli era [1573-1620]) and edited by Tongjiong 通炯 (1578-1639?). *XZJ* no. 1438, vol. 127.

*Hongming ji* 弘明集, 14 *juan*. Compiled by Sengyou 僧佑 (445-518) sometime between 502 and 518. *T* no. 2102, vol. 52.

*Hongzhi Huizhoufu zhi* 弘治徽州府志, 12 *juan*. By Peng Ze 彭澤 (fl. 1490-1522) and compiled by Wang Shunmin 汪舜民 (?-1507) in 1502. References made to the Shanghai guji shudian 上海古籍書店 edition, *Tianyige Mingdai fangzhi xuankan* 天一閣明代方志選刊, vol 21 & 22 (Shanghai, 1981).

*Hou Han shu* 後漢書, 120 *juan*. Compiled by Fan Ye 范曄 (398-445) between 432 and 445. References made to *Er shi wu shi* 二十五史, Guji chubanshe 古籍出版社 &Shanghai shudian 上海書店 edition (Shanghai, 1986).

*Huayan jing haiyin daochang chanyi* 華嚴經海印道場懺儀, 24 *juan*. By Yixing 一行 (1535-1615) and Huijue 慧覺 (d. u). *XZJ* no. 1452, vol. 128.

*Huayan jing tanxuan ji* 華嚴經探玄記, 20 *juan*, By Fazang 法藏 (643-712) (largely completed by 690). *T* no. 1464, vol. 24.

*Huixiang wen* 廻 向文, 1 *juan*. Author unknown. *T* no. 2848, vol. 85.

*Ji gujin fodao lunheng* 集古今佛道論衡, 4 *juan*. By Daoxuan 道宣 (596-667) in 661. *T* no. 2104, vol. 52.

*Ji Shenzhou sanbao gantong lu* 集神州三寶感通錄, 3 *juan*. By Daoxuan 道宣 (596-667) in 664. *T* no. 2106, vol. 52.

*Ji zhujing lichan yi* 集諸經禮懺儀, 2 *juan*. By Zhisheng 智昇 (fl. 730-786) in 730. *T* no. 1982, vol. 47.

*Jin guangming chanfa buzhu yi* 金光明懺法補助儀, 1 *juan*. By Zunshi 遵式 (964-1032). *T* no. 1945, vol. 46.

*Jin guangming jing* 金光明經 (Skt. *Suvarṇa-prabhāsôttama-sūtra*), 4 *juan*. Translated by Tanwuchen 曇無讖 (Dharmakṣema, 385-433) sometime between 424 and 430. *T* no. 663, vol. 16.

*Jin guangming jing wenju* 金光明經文句, 6 *juan*. By Zhiyi 智顗 (538-597), transcribed by Guanding 灌頂 (561-632). *T* no. 1785, vol. 39.

*Jin shu* 晉書, 132 *juan*, extant 130 *juan*. Compiled by Fang Xuanling 房玄齡 (579-648) and others between 646 and 648. References made to *Er shi si shi* 二十四史, Zhonghua shuju 中華書局 edition (Beijing, 1995).

*Jin'ao tuishi biji* 金鰲退食筆記, 2 *juan*. By Gao Shiqi 高士奇 (1645-1704). *SKQS* vol. 588.

*Jinyuan ji* 金園集, 3 *juan*. By Zunshi 遵式 (964-1032) and re-edited by Huiguan 慧觀 (active under the Shaoxing era [1131-1163]) in 1151. *XZJ* no. 948, vol. 101.

*Jin'gang sanmei jing* 金剛三昧經 (Skt. *Vajrasamādhi-sūtra*), 1 *juan*. Translator unknown. *T* no. 273, vol. 9.

*Jin'gangding yuqie lüeshu sanshiqi zun xinyao* 金剛頂瑜伽略述三十七尊心要, 1 *juan*. Translated by Bukong 不空 (Amoghavajra, 705-774). *T* no. 871, vol. 18.

*Jingci Huihui chanshi yulu* 淨慈慧暉禪師語錄, 6 *juan*. Compiled by Liaoguang 了廣 (probably active under the Chunxi era [1174-1190]). *XZJ* no. 1409, vol. 124.

*Jingtu shengxian lu* 淨土聖賢錄, 9 *juan*. By Peng Xisu 彭希涑 (1761-1793) in ca. 1783. XZJ no. 1525, vol. 135.

*Jingtu shengxian lu xubian* 淨土聖賢錄續編, 4 *juan*. By Hu Ting 胡珽 (1822-1861). XZJ no. 1526, vol. 135.

*Jingtu wuhui nianfo lüe fashi yi zan* 淨土五會念佛略法事儀讚, 1 *juan*. By Fazhao 法照 (746-838). *T* no. 1983, vol. 47.

*Jinling fancha zhi* 金陵梵剎志, 53 *juan*. By Ge Yinliang 葛寅亮 (1570-1646) (first published in 1607). References made to the Danqing tushu gongsi 丹青圖書公司 edition, *Zhongguo fosi zhi huikan* 中國佛寺志匯刊, series 1, vol. 3 (Taibei, 1985, first edition).

*Jinshi cuibian* 金石萃編, 160 *juan*. By Wang Chang 王昶 (1725-1806) in 1805. References made to the Zhongguo shudian 中國書店 edition (Beijing, 1985).

*Jiuhuashan zhi* 九華山志, 8 *juan*. Recompiled by Yinguang 印光 (1862-1940) in ca. 1938. References made to the Guangling guji keyinshe 廣陵古籍刻印社 edition (Yangzhou, 1997).

*Jizushan zhi* 雞足山志, 6 *juan*. By Qian Bangqi 錢邦芑 (1602-1673) and supplemented by Fan Chengxun 范承勳 (1641-1714) in 1692. References made to the Danqing tushu gongsi 丹青圖書公司 edition, *Zhongguo fosi zhi huikan* 中國佛寺志匯刊, series 3, vol. 1 (Taibei, 1985, first edition).

*Jushi zhuan* 居士傳, 56 *juan*. By Peng Jiqing 彭際清 (1740-1796) between 1770 and 1775. XZJ no. 1623, vol. 149.

*Kaigu lu* 慨古錄, 1 *juan*. By Yuancheng 圓澄 (1561-1627). XZJ no. 1273, vol. 114.

*Kaiqing Siming xuzhi* 開慶四明續志, 12 *juan*. By Wu Qian 吳潛 (1195-1262) and compiled by Mei Yingfa 梅應發 (fl. 1253-1270) and Liu Xi 劉錫 (fl. 1247) in 1259. References made to the Zhonghua shuju 中華書局 edition of the *Song Yuan fangzhi congkan* 宋元方志叢刊, vol. 6 (Beijing, 1990).

*Konggu Daocheng chanshi yulu* 空谷道澄禪師語錄, 20 *juan*. By Daocheng 道澄 (1616-1694) and edited by Deru 德儒 (active under the Kangxi reigning era [1662-1722]). JXZ no. B471, vol. 39.

*Langfeng ji* 閬風集, 12 juan. By Shu Yuexiang 舒嶽祥 (1219-1298). SKQS vol. 1187.

*Lengqie shizi ji* 楞伽師資記, 1 *juan*. By Jingjüe 淨覺 (683-750?) before 716. *T* no. 2837, vol. 85.

*Li chan wen* 禮懺文, 1 *juan*. Author unknown. *T* no. 2856, vol. 85.

*Li ji* 禮記, 20 *juan*. Compiled by Dai Sheng 戴聖 (d. u.) in ca. 80. Annotated by Qian Xuan 錢玄 (1910-1999), et al. References made to the Yuelu shushe 岳麓書社 edition (Changsha, 2001).

*Lianchi dashi quanji* 蓮池大師全集, 3 vols. Compiler unknown. References made to the Putian Guanghuasi fojing liutongchu 莆田廣化寺佛經流通處 edition, 1990.

*Liangxi ji* 梁谿集, 180 *juan*. By Li Gang 李綱 (1082-1140). SKQS vol. 1125-1126.

*Libu zhigao* 禮部志稿, 100 *juan*. Compiled by Lin Yaoyu 林堯俞 (?-1626) and others in ca. 1620. *SKQS* vol. 597-598.

*Lidai sanbao ji* 歷代三寶記, 15 *juan*. Submitted by Fei Zhangfang 費長房 (?-598+) to the court at the very beginning of 598. *T* no. 2034, vol. 49.

*Lingfeng zong lun* 靈峰宗論, 10 *juan*. By Zhixu 智旭 (1599-1655). Compiled by Chengshi 成時 (?-1678) in ca. 1663. References made to the Fujian putian guanghuasi fojing liutongchu 福建莆田廣化寺佛經流通處 edition (Putian, 1992).

*Liunan suibi xubi* 柳南隨筆續筆, 4 *juan*. By Wang Yingkui 王應奎 (1684-1759?). References made to the Zhonghua shuju 中華書局 edition of the *Qingdai biji shiliao congkan* 清代筆記史料叢刊, vol. 34 (Beijing, 1983).

*Lüyuan conghua* 履園叢話, 24 *juan*. By Qian Yong 錢泳 (1759-1844). References made to the Zhonghua shuju 中華書局 edition (Beijing, 1979).

*Mengliang lu* 夢粱錄, 20 *juan*. By Wu Zimu 吳自牧 (1161?-1237). *SKQS* vol. 590.

*Miaofa lianhua jing* 妙法蓮華經 (Skt. *Saddharmapuṇḍarīka-sūtra*), 7 *juan*. Translated by Jiumoluoshi 鳩摩羅什 (Kumārajīva, 334-413) in 406. *T* no. 262, vol. 9.

*Miaofa lianhua jing xuanyi* 妙法蓮華經玄義, 20 *juan*. By Zhiyi 智顗 (539-598) and edited by Guanding 灌頂 (561-632) in 593. *T* no. 1716, vol. 33.

*Mohe sengqi lü* 摩訶僧祇律 (Skt. *Mahāsāṃghika-vinaya*), 40 *juan*. Translated by Fotuobatuoluo 佛陀跋陀羅 (Buddhabhadra, 359-429) and Faxian 法顯 (337-422) in 418. *T* no. 1425, vol. 22.

*Mohe zhiguan* 摩訶止觀, 20 *juan*. By Zhiyi 智顗 (539-598). Compiled by Guanding 灌頂 (561-632) and completed in 594. *T* no. 1911, vol. 46.

*Nan shi* 南史, 80 *juan*. By Li Yanshou 李延壽 (fl.629-659), completed in 659. References made to *Er shi si shi* 二十四史, Zhonghua shuju 中華書局 edition (Beijing, 1995).

*Nanchao fosi zhi* 南朝佛寺志, 2 *juan*. By Sun Wenchuan 孫文川 (19th century) and compiled by Chen Zuolin 陳作霖 (1837-1920). References made to the Mingwen shuju 明文書局 edition (Taipei, 1980).

*Nanhai jigui neifa zhuan* 南海寄歸內法傳, 4 *juan*. By Yijing 義淨 (635-713) in 691. *T* no. 2125, vol. 54.

*Nanyue Si da chanshi lishi yuanwen* 南嶽思大禪師立誓願文, 1 *juan*. By Huisi 慧思 (515-577). *T* no. 1933, vol. 46.

*Nittō guhō junrei kōki* 入唐求法巡礼行記, 4 *juan*. By Ennin 円仁 (Chin. Yuanren 圓仁, 793-864). References made to the Shanghai guji chubanshe 上海古籍出版社 edition (Shanghai, 1986).

*Pinjixiang chanshi yulu* 頻吉祥禪師語錄, 15 *juan*. By Zhixiang 智祥 (1637-1709) and edited by Deneng 德能 (active under the Kangxi reigning era [1662-1722]), et al. *JXZ* no. B454, vol. 39.

*Putuoshan zhi* 普陀山志 (i.e., *Butuoluojia xinzhi* 普陀洛迦新志), 12 *juan*. By Wang Hengyan 王亨彥 (1865-1923+) in 1923. References made to the Jiangsu guangling guji ke yin she 江蘇廣陵古籍刻印社 edition (Yangzhou, 1993).

*Qinding da Qing huidian zeli* 欽定大清會典則例, 180 *juan*. Compiled under the imperial decree of Emperor Qianlong (r. 1736-1795) of Qing in 1764. *SKQS* vol. 620-625.

*Qing Guanshiyin Pusa xiaofu duhai tuoluoni sanmei yi* 請觀世音菩薩消伏毒害陀羅尼三昧儀, 1 *juan*. By Zunshi 遵式 (964-1032). *T* no. 1949, vol. 49.

*Quan Tang shi* 全唐詩, 900 *juan*. Compiled by Peng Dingqiu 彭定求 (1645–1719) and others ca. 1707. Beijing: Zhonghua shuju 中華書局, 1960.

*Quan Tang wen* 全唐文 (i.e., *Qinding Quan Tang wen* 欽定全唐文), 1,000 *juan*. Compiled by Dong Hao 董皓 (1740-1818), et al., in 1814. Shanghai: Shanghai guji chubanshe 上海古籍出版社, 1990.

*Ru busatang shuo jiwen deng* 入布薩堂說偈文等, 1 *juan*. Author unknown. *T* no. 2852, vol. 85.

*Ru lengqie jing* 入楞伽經 (Skt. *Laṅkāvatāra-sūtra*), 10 *juan*. Translated by Putiliuzhi 菩提流支 (Bodhiruci, ?-535) in 513. *T* no. 671, vol. 16.

*Ruzhong xuzhi* 入眾須知, 1 *juan*. By Zongshou 宗壽 (active under the Jiading era [1208-1225]) in 1209. *XZJ* no. 1236, vol. 111.

*Sangguo zhi* 三國志, 65 *juan*. Compiled by Chen Shou 陳壽 (233-297). References made to *Er shi si shi* 二十四史, Zhonghua shuju 中華書局 edition (Beijing, 1995).

*Shanjian lü piposha* 善見律毗婆沙 (corresponds in part of the Pāli text *Samantapāsādikā*), 18 *juan*. Translated by Sengqiebatuoluo 僧伽跋陀羅 (Saṃghabhadra, ?-488+) in 488. *T* no. 1462, vol. 24.

*Shengman shizihou yicheng dafangbian fangguang jing* 勝鬘師子吼一乘大方便方廣經 (Skt. *Śrīmālā-devī-siṃha-nāda-sūtra*), 1 *juan*. Translated by Qiunabatuoluo 求那跋陀羅 (Guṇabhadra, 394-468) in 436. *T* no. 353, vol. 12.

*Shi chan boluomi cidi famen* 釋禪波羅蜜次第法門, 12 *juan*. By Zhiyi 智顗 (539-598). *T* no. 1916, vol. 46.

*Shi jian Jigu lüe xuji* 釋鑑稽古略續集, 2 *juan*. By Huanlun 幻輪 (?-1638+) in 1344. *T* no. 2038, vol. 49.

*Shijia rulai niepan lizan wen* 釋迦如來涅槃禮讚文, 1 *juan*. By Renyue 仁岳 (992-1064). *XZJ* no. 1480, vol. 130.

*Shimen zhengtong* 釋門正統, 8 *juan*. By Zongjian 宗鑑 (active under the Jiaxi era [1237-1241]) in 1237. *XZJ* no. 1490, vol. 130.

*Shishi jigu lüe* 釋氏稽古略, 4 *juan*. By Jue'an 覺岸 (1286-1355+). *T* no. 2037, vol. 49.

*Shishi tonglan* 施食通覽, 1 *juan*. By Zongxiao 宗曉 (1151-1214) in 1204. *XZJ* no. 959, vol. 101.

*Shishi yaolan* 釋氏要覽, 3 *juan*. By Daocheng 道誠 (?-1019+) in 1019. *T* no. 2127, vol. 54.

*Shisong lü* 十誦律 (Skt. *Daśa-bhāṇavāra-vinaya*), 61 *juan*. Translated by Furuoduoluo 弗若多羅 (Puṇyatāra, 305?-404) and Jiumoluoshi 鳩摩羅什 (Kumārajīva, 334-413) between 404 and 405. *T* no. 1435, vol. 23.

*Shittan yōketsu* 悉曇要訣, 4 *juan*. By Myōgaku 明覚 (1056-?). *T* no. 2706, vol. 84.

*Shiwu yuanhui* 事物原會, 40 *juan*. By Wang Ji 汪汲 (active under the Qianlong [1736-1795] and Jiaqing reigning era [1796-1820]). Reprint of the edition published by Guyu shanfang 古愚山房 in 1796. References made to the Guangling guji keyinshe 廣陵古籍刻印社 edition (Nanjing, 1989).

*Shoulengyan tanchang xiuzheng yi* 首楞嚴壇場修證儀, 1 *juan*. By Jingyuan 淨源 (1011-1088). *XZJ* no. 861, vol. 95.

*Shoulengyan yishu zhu jing* 首楞嚴義疏注經, 20 *juan*. By Zirui 子璿 (965-1038). *T* no. 1799, vol. 39.

*Shūgyō yōketsu* 修業要決, 1 *juan*. By Shōkū 證空 (1177-1247). *T* no. 2621, vol. 83.

*Sifen jieben shu* 四分戒本疏, 3 *juan*. By Huishu 慧述 d. u. *T* no. 2787, vol. 85.

*Sifen lü* 四分律 (Skt. *Dharmaguptaka-vinaya* or *Cāturvargīya-vinaya*), 60 *juan*. Translated by Fotuoyeshe 佛陀耶舍 ((Buddhayaśas, fl. 400) and Zhu Fonian 竺佛念 (Skt. Buddhasmṛti?, fl. 400) between 410 and 412. *T* no. 1428, vol. 22.

*Sifen lü shanfan buqüe xingshi chao* 四分律刪繁補闕行事鈔, 12 *juan*. By Daoxuan 道宣 (596-667) between 626 and 630. *T* no. 1804, vol. 40.

*Sifen lü xingshi chao zichi ji* 四分律行事鈔資持記, 16 *juan*. By Yuanzhao 元照 (1048-1116). *T* no. 1805, vol. 40.

*Siming zunzhe jiaoxing lu* 四明尊者教行錄, 7 *juan*. By Zongxiao 宗曉 (1151-1214). *T* no. 1937, vol. 46.

*Sishu zhangju jizhu* 四書章句集註, 19 *juan*. By Zhu Xi 朱熹 (1130-1200) in 1190. References made to the Qilu shushe 齊魯書社 edition (Ji'nan, 1992).

*Siwei lüeyao fa* 思惟略要法, 1 *juan*. Translated by Jiumoluoshi 鳩摩羅什 (Kumārajīva, 334-413) sometime between 401-409. *T* no. 617, vol. 15.

*Song gaoseng zhuan* 宋高僧傳, 30 *juan*. By Zanning 贊寧 (919?-1001?), et al., in 988. *T* no. 2061, vol. 50.

*Song shu* 宋書, 100 *juan*. By Shen yue 沈約 (441-513) sometime between 487-502. References made to *Er shi si shi* 二十四史, Zhonghua shuju 中華書局 edition (Beijing, 1995).

*Sui shu* 隋書, 85 *juan*. Compiled by Wei Zheng 魏徵 (580-643) and others in ca. 629. References made to *Er shi si shi* 二十四史, Zhonghua shuju 中華書局 edition (Beijing, 1995).

*Sui Tiantai Zhizhe dashi biezhuan* 隋天台智者大師別傳, 1 *juan*. By Guanding 灌頂 (561-632) ca. 605. *T* no. 2050, vol. 50.

*Taiping guangji* 太平廣記, 500 *juan*. Compiled by Li Fang 李昉 (925-996) between 977 and 978. *SKQS* vol. 1043-1046.

*Tang Tae Ch'ŏnboksa kosaju pŏn'gyŏng taedŏk Pŏpjang hwasang chŏn* (Chin. *Tang Da Jianfusi gu sizhu fanjing dade Fazang heshang zhuan*) 唐大薦福寺故寺主翻經大德法藏和尚傳, 1 *kwŏn*. By Ch'oe Ch'iwŏn (Chin. Cui Zhiyuan) 崔致遠 (857-900). *T* no. 2054, vol. 50.

*Tang huiyao* 唐會要, 100 *juan*. Compiled by Wang Pu 王溥 (922-982). 2 vols. References made to the Shanghai guji chubanshe 上海古籍出版社 edition (Shanghai, 2006).

*Tang zhiyan* 唐摭言, 15 *juan*. By Wang Dingbao 王定保 (870-954). References made to the Shanghai guji chubanshe 上海古籍出版社 edition (Shanghai, 1978).

*Tanwudebu sifenlü shanbu suiji jiemo* 曇無德部四分律刪補隨機羯磨, 8 *juan*. By Daoxuan 道宣 (596-667) in 648. *T* no. 1808, vol. 40.

*Tiantai si jiao yi* 天台四教儀, 1 *juan*. By Chegwan 諦觀 (Chin. Diguan, ?–970). *T* no. 1931, vol. 46.

*Tiantong Hongjue Min chanshi beiyou ji* 天童弘覺忞禪師北遊集, 6 *juan*. By Daomin 道忞 (1596-1674) and edited by Zhenpu 真樸 (fl.1662-1722). *JXZ* no. B180, vol. 26.

*Tianzhu bieji* 天竺別集, 3 *juan*. By Zunshi 遵式 (964-1032) and re-edited by Huiguan 慧觀 (active under the Shaoxing era [1131-1163]). *XZJ* no. 949, vol. 101.

*Wangsheng ji* 往生集, 4 *juan*. By Zhuhong 袾宏 (1535-1615). *T* no. 2072, vol. 51.

"Wangsheng jingtu chanyuan yi hou xu" 往生淨土懺願儀後序. In *wangsheng jingtu chanyuan yi* 往生淨土懺願儀, 1 *juan*. By Zunshi 遵式 (964-1032) in 1015. *T* no. 1984, vol. 47.

*Wangsheng lizan ji* 往生禮讚偈, 1 *juan*. By Shandao 善導 (613-681). *T* no. 1980, vol. 47.

*Wenyua yinghua* 文苑英華, 1,000 *juan*. Compiled by Li Fang 李昉 (925–996) and others between 982–987. References made to the Zhonghua shuju 中華書局 edition (Beijing, 1966).

*Wŏnjong munryu* 圓宗文類, 2 *juan*. Compiled by Ŭich'ŏn 義天 (Chin. Yitian, 1055-1101). *XZJ* no. 1010, vol. 103.

*Wudeng quanshu* 五燈全書, 120 *juan*. Compiled by Chaoyong 超永 (active under the Kangxi reigning era [1662-1722]) in 1693. *XZJ* no. 1547, vol. 140-142.

*Wulin fan zhi* 武林梵志, 12 *juan*. By Wu Zhijing 吳之鯨 (fl. 1609). References made to the Hangzhou chubanshe 杭州出版社 edition, *Hangzhou fojiao wenxian congkan* 杭州佛教文獻叢刊, vol. 1 (Hangzhou, 2006).

*Wuqian wubai foming shenzhou chuzhang miezui jing* 五千五百佛名神咒除障滅罪經, 8 *juan*. Translated by She'najueduo 闍那崛多 (Jñānagupta, 523-600) sometime between 561 and 592. *T* no. 443, vol. 14.

*Xiangfa jueyi jing* 像法決疑經, 1 *juan*. Translator unknown. *T* no. 2870, vol. 85.

*Xiao pin bore boluomi jing* 小品般若波羅蜜經 (Skt. *Aṣṭa-sāhasrikāprajñā-pāramitā*), 10 *juan*. Translated by Jiumoluoshi 鳩摩羅什 (Kumārajīva, 334-413) in 409. *T* no. 227, vol. 8.

*Xuanzong chao Fanjingsanzang Shanwuwei zeng Hongluqing xingzhuang* 玄宗朝翻經三藏善無畏贈鴻臚卿行狀, 1 *juan*. By Li Hua 李華 (715-767). *T* no. 2055, vol. 50.

*Xu Fozu tongji* 續佛祖統紀, 2 *juan*. Author unknown. *XZJ* no. 1492, vol. 131.

*Xu Gaoseng zhuan* 續高僧傳, 30 *juan*. Initially completed by Daoxuan 道宣 (596- 667) in 645. *T* no. 2060, vol. 50.

*Xuepo ji* 雪坡集, 50 *juan*. By Yao Mian 姚勉 (1216-1262). *SKQS* vol. 1184.

*Xutang heshang yulu* 虛堂和尚語錄, 10 *juan*. Compiled by Miaoyuan 妙源 (1207-1281). *T* no. 2000, vol. 47.

"Yaoshi rulai benyuan gongde jing xu" 藥師如來本願功德經序. By Huiju 慧矩 (active under the Daye era [605-618]) in ca. 617. In *Fo shuo Yaoshi rulai benyuan jing* 佛說藥師如來本願經, 1 *juan*. Translated by Damojiduo 達磨笈多 (Dharmagupta, 529-619), et al., between 616 and 617. *T* no. 449, vol. 14.

*Yaoshi liuliguang rulai benyuan gongde jing* 藥師琉璃光如來本願功德經 (Skt. *Bhagavato-bhaiṣajyaguruvaiḍūryaprabhasya-pūrvapraṇidhānaviśeṣavistāra*), 1 *juan*. Translated by Xuanzang 玄奘 (602-664) in 650. *T* no. 450, vol. 14.

*Yaoshi liuliguang rulai xiaozai chu'nan niansong yigui* 藥師琉璃光如來消災除難念誦儀軌, 1 *juan*. Attributed to Yixing 一行 (683-727). *T* no. 922, vol. 19.

*Yi Lengyan jiujing shi chan* 依楞嚴究竟事懺, 2 *juan*. By Chanxiu 禪修 (1577-1632). *XZJ* no. 1456, vol. 129.

*Ying'an Tanhua chanshi yulu* 應菴曇華禪師語錄, 10 *juan*. Compiled by Shouquan 守詮 (ca. 12th century) and others. *XZJ* no. 1343, vol. 120.

*Yinhua lu* 因話錄, 6 *juan*. By Zhao Lin 趙璘 (fl. 834-853). References made to the *Da Tang xinyu (wai wuzhong)* 大唐新語 (外五種), Shanghai guji chubanshe 上海古籍出版社 edition (Shanghai, 2012).

*Yongjue Yuanxian chanshi guanglu* 永覺元賢禪師廣錄, 30 *juan*. By Daopei 道霈 (1615-1702). *XZJ* no. 1418, vol. 125.

*Youyang za zu* 酉陽雜俎, 30 *juan*. By Duan Chengshi 段成式 (803-863). References made to the Zhonghua shuju 中華書局 edition (Beijing, 1981).

*Yuan shi* 元史, 210 *juan*. Compiled by Song Lian 宋濂 (1310-1381) and others between 1369 and 1370. References made to *Er shi si shi* 二十四史, Zhonghua shuju 中華書局 edition (Beijing, 1995).

*Yuanjue jing daochang lüeben xiuzheng yi* 圓覺經道場略本修證儀, 1 *juan*. By Jingyuan 淨源 (1011-1088). *XZJ* no. 1455, vol. 129.

*Yuanjue jing daochang xiuzheng yi* 圓覺經道場修證儀, 18 *juan*. By Zongmi 宗密 (780-841). *XZJ* no. 1454, vol. 128.

*Yuanjue jing dashu shiyi chao* 圓覺經大疏釋義鈔, 26 *juan*. By Zongmi 宗密 (780-841). *XZJ* no. 211, vol. 14-15.

*Yuansou Xingduan chanshi yulu* 元叟行端禪師語錄, 8 *juan*. Compiled by Falin 法林 (ca. 14th century) and others. *XZJ* no. 1399, vol. 124.

*Yuding yuanjian leihan* 御定淵鑒類函, 450 *juan*. Compiled by Zhang Ying 張英 (1637-1708), Wang Shizhen 王士禎 (?-1711), et al. Endorsed by Emperor Kangxi 康熙 (r. 1661-1722) in 1710. *SKQS* vols. 982-990.

*Yuejiang Zhengyin chanshi yulu* 月江正印禪師語錄, 3 *juan*. Compiled by Jujian 居簡 (d.u) and others. *XZJ* no. 1389, vol. 123.

*Yunqi fahui* 雲棲法彙, 34 *juan*. Compiled by 邹匡明 (fl. 17th century) and others in 1615 and re-edited by Daxian 大賢 (fl. 17th century) and others in 1624. *XZJ* no. B277, vol. 32.

*Yunxi Langting Ting chanshi yulu* 雲溪俍亭挺禪師語錄, 18 *juan*. By Jingting 淨挺 (1615-1684) and edited by Zhicong 智淙 (active under the Kangxi reigning era [1662-1722]), et al. JXZ no. B294, vol. 33.

"Yuzhi shuichan xu" 御製水懺序. By Emperor Yongle 永樂 (1360-1424) in 1416. In *Cibei shuichan fa* 慈悲水懺法, 3 *juan*. By Zhixuan 知玄 (811-883). *T* no. 1910, vol. 45.

*Zheng fahua jing* 正法華經 (Skt. *Saddharmapuṇḍarīka-sūtra*), 10 *juan*. Translated by Zhu Fahu 竺法護 (Dharmarakṣa, 239-316) in 286. *T* no. 263, vol. 9.

*Zhenxie Qingliao chanshi yulu* 真歇清了禪師語錄, 2 *juan*. Compiled by Dechu 德初 (ca. 12th century). XZJ no. 1407, vol. 124.

*Zhenyuan xinding shijiao mulu* 貞元新定釋教目錄, 30 *juan*. By Yuanzhao 圓照 (727-809) between 799 and 800. *T* no. 2157, vol. 55.

*Zhiguan fuxing chuanhong jue* 止觀輔行傳弘決, 40 *juan*. By Zhanran 湛然 (711-782). *T* no. 1912, vol. 46.

*Zhuanjing xingdao yuan wangsheng jingtu fashi zan* 轉經行道願往生淨土法事讚, the first *juan* in 2 *juan*. By Shandao 善導 (613-681). *T* no. 1979, vol. 47.

*Zhufa wuzheng sanmei famen* 諸法無諍三昧法門, 2 *juan*. By Huisi 慧思 (515-577). *T* no. 1923, vol. 46.

*Zhujing yao ji* 諸經要集, 20 *juan*. By Daoshi 道世 (ca. 596-668+). *T* no. 2123, vol. 54.

*Zizhi tongjian* 資治通鑑, 294 *juan*. Compiled by Sima Guang 司馬光 (1019-1086), et al., and presented to the court in 1084. References made to the Zhonghua shuju 中華書局 edition (Beijing, 1956).

*Zizhulin Zhuanyu Heng heshang yulu* 紫竹林顓愚衡和尚語錄, 20 *juan*. By Guanheng 觀衡 (1579-1646) and re-edited by Zhengyin 正印 (active under the Shunzhi [1638-1661] and early Kangxi reigning era [1662-1722]). JXZ no. B219, vol. 28.

*Zong jing lu* 宗鏡錄, 100 *juan*. By Yanshou 延壽 (904-976) (completed in 961). *T* no. 2016, vol. 48.

## Secondary Sources

Andō, Toshio 安藤俊雄 (trans. Su Rongkun 蘇榮焜). *Tiantai xue: Genben sixiang ji qi zhankai* 天台學 —— 根本思想及其展開 (Japanese title: *Tendaigaku: kōponshisō toso no tenkai* 天台学：根本思想とその展開). Taibei: Taibei huiju chubanshe 臺北慧炬出版社, 1998.

Argyle, Michael. *Psychology and Religion: An Introduction*. London: Routledge, 2000.

Averill, Stephen C. ed. *Zhongguo dazhong zongjiao* 中國大眾宗教. Nanjing: Jiangsu renmin chubanshe 江蘇人民出版社, 2006.

Bai Huawen 白化文, et al, coll. and annot. *Ru Tang qiufa xunli xingji jiaozhu* 《入唐求法巡禮行記》校注. Shijiazhuang: Huashan wenyi chubanshe 花山文藝出版社, 1992.

Bai Jinxian 白金銑. *Tangdai Chanzong chanhui sixiang yanjiu* 唐代禪宗懺悔思想研究. Taipei: Wen shi zhe chubanshe 文史哲出版社, 2009.

Beijing Daxue Tushuguan 北京大學圖書館, comps. *Beijing daxue cang dunhuang wenxian* 北京大學藏敦煌文獻. Shanghai: Shanghai guji chubanshe 上海古籍出版社, 1995.

Beijing Tushuguan Jinshizu 北京圖書館金石組, comp. *Beijing tushuguan Zhongguo lidai shike taben huibian* 北京圖書館中國歷代石刻拓本匯編, vol. 6. Zhengzhou: Zhongzhou guji chubanshe 中州古籍出版社, 1989.

Bowie, Fiona (trans. Jin Ze 金澤 & He Qimin 何其敏). *Zongjiao renleixue daolun* 宗教人類學導論 (English title: *The Anthropology of Religion: An Introduction*). Beijing: Zhongguo renmin daxue chubanshe 中國人民大學出版社, 2004.

Brook, Timothy. *Praying for Power: Buddhism and the Formation of Gentry Society in Late-Ming China*. Cambridge, MA: Harvard University Asia Center, Harvard University Press, 1993.

Cao Ganghua 曹剛華. *Mingdai fojiao fangzhi yanjiu* 明代佛教方志研究. Beijing: Zhongguo renmin daxue chubanshe 中國人民大學出版社, 2011.

Chen Bing 陳兵 & Deng Zimei 鄧子美. *Ershi shiji Zhongguo fojiao* 二十世紀中國佛教. Beijing: Minzu chubanshe 民族出版社, 2000.

Chen Duxiu 陳獨秀. *Duxiu wencun* 獨秀文存. Hefei: Anhui renmin chubanshe 安徽人民出版社, 1987.

Chen Jinhua 陳金華. "Dongya fojiao zhong de 'biandi qingjie': Lun shengdi ji zupu de jiangou" 東亞佛教中的 " 邊地情結 ": 論聖地及祖譜的建構. *Foxue yanjiu* 佛學研究 21 (2012): 22-41.

Ch'en, Kenneth. *The Chinese Transformation of Buddhism*. Princeton: Princeton University Press, 1973.

Chen Qingxiang 陳清香. *Luohan tuxiang yanjiu* 羅漢圖像研究. Taibei: Wenjin chubanshe 文津出版社, 1995.

Chen Yuan 陳垣. *Mingji Dianqian fojiao kao* 明季滇黔佛教考. Shijiazhuang: Hebei jiaoyu chubanshe 河北教育出版社, 2000.

Chen Yunü 陳玉女. "Mingdai yuqiejiao seng de zhuanzhihua ji qi jingchan huodong" 明代瑜伽教僧的專職化及其經懺活動. *Xinshiji zongjiao yanjiu* 新世紀宗教研究 3.1 (2004): 38-88.

Chen Zuolin 陳作霖. *Nanchao fosi zhi* 南朝佛寺志. Taibei: Mingwen shuju 明文書局, 1980.

Cheng Shude 程樹德. *Lunyu jishi* 論語集釋. Beijing: Zhonghua shuju 中華書局, 1990.

Cheng Zhang 成章. "Jiangsu Chanzong san da mingcha — Jinshansi Gaominsi Tianningsi" 江蘇禪宗三大名刹 — 金山寺、高旻寺、天寧寺. *Fayin* 法音 5 (1998): 55-58.

Chikusa Masaaki 竺沙雅章. (*Zōteiban*) *chūgoku bukkyō shakaishi no kenkyū* (增訂版) 中国仏教社会史研究. Kyoto: Hōyū shoten 朋友書店, 2002.

Choi, Bok Hee 崔福姫. "Koseiryōden kara Kōseiryōden heno Monju shinkō no hensen — Monju gainen wo chūshin ni"「古清涼伝」から「広清涼伝」への文殊信仰の変遷 — 文殊概念を中心に. *Indogaku bukkyōgaku kenkyū* 印度學佛教學研究 52.1 (2003): 192-94.

Choi, Bok Hee 崔福姫. "Godaisan Monju shinkō ni okeru kegen" 五臺山文殊信仰における化現. *Bukkyō daigaku daigakuin kiyō* 佛教大学大学院紀要 33.3 (2005): 15-29.

Cui Zhengsen 崔正森. *Wutaishan fojiaoshi* 五臺山佛教史. Taiyuan: Shanxi renmin chubanshe 山西人民出版社, 2000.

Dai Xiaoyun 戴曉雲. *Fojiao shuilu hua yanjiu* 佛教水陸畫研究. Beijing: Zhongguo shehui kexue chubanshe 中國社會科學出版社, 2009.

Daoyü 道昱. "Zhongguo fojiao sida mingshan kao" 中國佛教四大名山考. *Pumen xuebao* 普門學報 45 (2008): 57-106.

Dong Zhiqiao 董志翹. *Guanshiyin yingyanji sanzhong yizhu* 觀世音應驗記三種譯注. Nanjing: Jiangsu guji chubanshe 江蘇古籍出版社, 2002.

Du Doucheng 杜斗城. "Xi Qin fojiao shulun" 西秦佛教述論. *Zhonghua foxue xuebao* 中華佛學學報 13 (2000): 212-32.

Durkheim, Émile (trans. Joseph Ward Swain). *The Elementary Forms of the Religious Life*. New York: Dover Publications, 2008.

Fang Guangchang 方廣錩. "Dunhuang yishu de Miaofa lianhua jing ji youguan wenxian" 敦煌遺書的《妙法蓮華經》及有關文獻. *Zhonghua foxue xuebao* 中華佛學學報 10 (1997): 38-55.

Feng Youlan 馮友蘭 (trans. Tu Youguang 涂又光). *Zhongguo zhexue jianshi* 中國哲學簡史 (English title: *A Short History of Chinese Philosophy*). Beijing: Zhongguo renmin daxue chubanshe 中國人民大學出版社, 1996.

Feuchtwang, Stephan. *Popular Religion in China: The Imperial Metaphor*. Richmond: Curzon Press, 2000. Translated into Chinese by Zhao Xudong 趙旭東, *Diguo de yinyu: Zhongguo minjian zongjiao* 帝國的隱喻：中國民間宗教. Nanjing: Jiangsu renmin chubanshe 江蘇人民出版社, 2009.

Fujitani Atsuo 藤谷厚生. "Konkōmyōkyō ni motozuku sangemetsugō no girei ni tsuite" 金光明経にもとづく懺悔滅業の儀礼について. *Indogaku bukkyōgaku kenkyū* 印度学仏教学研究 41.2 (1993): 25-27.

Fukui Fumimasa 福井文雅. "Shubi shinkō—Gireiteki shōchō no ichikōsatsu" 麈尾新考—儀礼的象徴の一考察. *Taishō daigaku kenkyūkiyō: Bukkyōgakubu・Bungakubu* 大正大学研究紀要：仏教学部・文学部 56.3 (1971): 79-101.

Fukui Fumimasa 福井文雅. "'Tokō' no shokunō to kigen—Chūgoku・Indo kōshō no ichisetten"「都講」の職能と起源—中国・インド交渉の一接点. In Kushida Ryōkō hakushi shōju kinenkai 櫛田良洪博士頌寿記念会, ed., *Kōsōden no kenkyū: Kushida hakushi shōju kinen* 高僧伝の研究：櫛田博士頌寿記念. Tokyo: Sankibō Busshorin 山喜房仏書林, 1973, pp. 795-822.

Fukui Fumimasa 福井文雅. "Kōkyō gishiki ni okeru fukugu no gireiteki imi" 講経儀式における服具の儀礼的意味. In Nihon bukkyō gakkai 日本仏教学会, ed., *Bukkyō girei—sono rinen to jissen* 仏教儀礼—その理念と実践. Kyoto: Heirakuji shoten 平楽寺書店, 1978, pp. 101-18.

Fukui Fumimasa 福井文雅. "Kōkyō gishiki no soshiki naiyō" 講経儀式の組織内容. In Fukui Fumimasa 福井文雅 & Makita Tairyō 牧田諦亮, eds., *Tonkō to Chūgoku bukkyō* 敦煌と中国仏教. *Kōza Tonkō* 講座敦煌, vol. 7. Tokyo: Daitō shuppansha 大東出版社, 1984, pp. 359-82.

Fuma Susumu 夫馬進. *Chūgoku zenkai zendō shi kenkyū* 中国善会善堂史研究. Kyoto: Dōhōsha 同朋舍, 1997.

Funayama Tōru 船山徹. "Rikuchōjidai ni okeru bosatsukai no juyōkatei—Ryūsō · Nanseiki wo chūshin ni" 六朝時代における菩薩戒の受容過程—劉宋・南齊期を中心に. *Tōhō gakuhō* 東方學報 (1995), 67: 1-135.

Gao Zhennong 高振農. "Fahuajing zai zhongguo de liuchuan" 《法華經》在中國的流傳. In *Guangshan Jingjusi yu Tiantaizong yanjiu* 光山淨居寺與天台宗研究. Hongkong: Tianma tushu youxiangongsi 天馬圖書有限公司, 2001, pp. 25-40.

Ge Zhaoguang 葛兆光. *Qishiji qian Zhongguo de zhishi sixiang yu xinyang shijie* 七世紀前中國的知識、思想與信仰世界. *Zhongguo sixiangshi* 中國思想史, vol. 1. Shanghai: Fudan daxue chubanshe 復旦大學出版社, 1998.

Gernet, Jacques (trans. J. R. Foster). *A History of Chinese Civilization*. Cambridge: Cambridge University Press, 1982.

Gernet, Jacques (trans. Franciscus Verellen). *Buddhism in Chinese Society: An Economic History from the Fifth to the Tenth Centuries*. New York: Columbia University Press, 1995. Translated into Chinese by Geng Sheng 耿昇, *Zhongguo 5-10 shiji de siyuan jingji* 中國 5-10 世紀的寺院經濟. Shanghai: Shanghai guji chubanshe 上海古籍出版社, 2004.

Hanazuka Hisayoshi 花塚久義. "Nichigonji no kenritsu ni tsuite" 日厳寺の建立について. *Indogaku bukkyōgaku kenkyū* 印度学仏教学研究 30.2 (1982): 166-67.

Handlin-Smith, Joanna. "Benevolent Societies: The Reshaping of Charity During the Late Ming and Early Ch'ing." *The Journal of Asian Studies* 46, no. 2 (1987): 309–37.

Handlin-Smith, Joanna. "Liberating Animals in Ming-Qing China: Buddhist Inspiration and Elite Imagination." *The Journal of Asian Studies* 58, no. 1 (1999): 51-84.

Hao Chunwen 郝春文. *Tang houqi Wudai Song chu Dunhuang sengni de shehui shenghuo* 唐後期五代宋初敦煌僧尼的社會生活. Beijing: Zhongguo shehui kexue chubanshe 中國社會科學出版社, 1998.

Hao Chunwen 郝春文. *Zhonggu shiqi sheyi yanjiu* 中古時期社邑研究. Taibei: Xinwenfeng chuban gongsi 新文豐出版公司, 2006.

Hasebe Yūkei 長谷部幽蹊. *Min Shin bukkyō kyōdanshi kenkyū* 明清仏教教団史研究. Kyoto: Dōhōsha 同朋舎, 1993.

He Shizhe 賀世哲. "Guanyu Shiliuguo Beichao shiqi de Sanshifo yu Sanfo zaoxiang zhu wenti 1" 關於十六國北朝時期的三世佛與三佛造像諸問題（一）. *Dunhuang yanjiu* 敦煌研究 4 (1992): 1-20.

He Shizhe 賀世哲. "Dunhuang bihua zhong de Fahua jingbian" 敦煌壁畫中的法華經變. In Dunhuang yanjiuyuan 敦煌研究院, ed., *Dunhuang yanjiu wenji: Dunhuang shiku jingbian pian* 敦煌研究文集：敦煌石窟經變篇. Lanzhou: Gansu minzu chubanshe 甘肅民族出版社, 2000, pp. 127-217.

Hirakawa Akira 平川彰. *Shoki daijō bukkyō no kenkyū* 2 初期大乗仏教の研究 II. *Hirakawa Akira chosakushū* 平川彰著作集, vol. 4. Tokyo: Shunjūsha 春秋社, 1997.

Hirakawa Akira 平川彰. *Shoki daijō to Hokke shisō* 初期大乗と法華思想. *Hirakawa Akira chosakushū* 平川彰著作集, vol. 6. Tokyo: Shunjūsha 春秋社, 1997.

Hirano Kenshō 平野顕照. "Kōkyōbun no soshiki naiyō" 講経文の組織内容. In Fukui Fumimasa 福井文雅 & Makita Tairyō 牧田諦亮, eds., *Tonkō to Chūgoku bukkyō* 敦煌と中国仏教. *Kōza Tonkō* 講座敦煌, vol. 7. Tokyo: Daitō shuppansha 大東出版社, 1984, pp. 321-58.

Hirokawa Gyōbin 広川堯敏. "Tonkō shuddo Shichikai butsumyōkyō ni tsuite—Sangaigyō to Jōdokyō to no kōshō" 敦煌出土七階仏名経について一三階教と浄土教との交渉. *Shūkyō kenkyū* 宗教研究 55.4 (1982): 71-105.

Hirokawa Gyōbin 広川堯敏. "Raisan" 礼讃. In Fukui Fumimasa 福井文雅 & Makita Tairyō 牧田諦亮, eds., *Tonkō to Chūgoku bukkyō* 敦煌と中国仏教. *Kōza Tonkō* 講座敦煌, vol. 7. Tokyo: Daitō shuppansha 大東出版社, 1984, pp. 425-70.

Hong Jinchun 洪錦淳. *Shuilu fahui yigui* 水陸法會儀軌. Taibei: Wenjin chubanshe 文津出版社, 2006.

Hou Chong 侯沖. *Zhongguo fojiao yishi yanjiu: yi zhaigong yishi wei zhongxin* 中國佛教儀式研究—以齋供儀式爲中心. Shanghai: Shanghai guji chubanshe 上海古籍出版社, 2018.

Hou Xudong 侯旭東. *Wuliu shiji beifang minzhong fojiao xinyang* 五、六世紀北方民眾佛教信仰. Beijing: Zhongguo shehui kexue chubanshe 中國社會科學出版社, 1998.

Hu Shi 胡適. *Lengqiezong kao* 楞伽宗考. In *Hushi wencun* 胡適文存, vol. 4. Hefei: Huangshan shushe 黃山書社, 1996.

Huang Minzhi 黃敏枝. *Songdai fojiao shehui jingjishi lunji* 宋代佛教社會經濟史論集. Taibei: Taiwan xuesheng shuju 臺灣學生書局, 1989.

Huang Yongwu 黃永武, comp. *Dunhuang baozang* 敦煌寶藏. 130 vols. Taibei: Xinwenfeng chuban gongsi 新文豐出版公司, 1984.

Huang Zheng 黃征 & Wu Wei 吳偉, coll. and annot. *Dunhuang yuanwen ji* 敦煌願文集. Changsha: Yuelu shushe 岳麓書社, 1995.

Huang Zheng 黃征 & Zhang Yongquan 張湧泉, coll. and annot. *Dunhuang bianwen jiaozhu* 敦煌變文校注. Beijing: Zhonghua shuju 中華書局, 1997.

Ikeda Rosan 池田魯參. *Kokusei hyarroku no kenkyū* 国清百録の研究. Tokyo: Daizō shuppan 大蔵出版, 1982.

Ishino Kazuharu 石野一晴. "Fudarakusan no junreiro—Sekkōshō Fudasan ni okeru jūshichiseiki zenhan no kōtokuhi wo megutte" 補陀落山の巡礼路—浙江省普陀山における 17 世紀前半の功徳碑をめぐって. *Tō Ajia bunka kōshō kenkyū* 東アジア文化交渉研究 3 (2010): 143-60.

Iwasaki Hideo 岩崎日出男. "Fukū no jidai no naidōjō ni tsuite—tokuni Daisō no jidai no naidōjō ni aterareta kyūchūshoden no kōsatsu wo chūshin toshite" 不空の時代の内道場について—特に代宗の時代の内道場に充てられた宮中諸殿の考察を中心として. *Kōyasan daigaku mikkyō bunka kenkyūjo kiyō* 高野山大学密教文化研究所紀要 13.2 (1999): 65-77.

Jan Yün-hua 冉雲華. "Zhongguo zaoqi chanfa de liuchuan he tedian—Huijiao Daoxuan suozhu 'xichan pian' yanjiu" 中國早期禪法的流傳和特點—慧皎、道宣所著 " 習禪篇 " 研究. *Huagang foxue xuebao* 華岡佛學學報 7 (1984): 63-99.

Jan Yün-hua 冉雲華. *Cong Yindu fojiao dao Zhongguo fojiao* 從印度佛教到中國佛教. Taibei: Dongda tushu gufen youxian gongsi 東大圖書股份有限公司, 1995.

Jia Yingyi 賈應逸. "Jiumoluoshi yijing yu Bei Liang shiqi de Gaochang fojiao" 鳩摩羅什譯經與北涼時期的高昌佛教. *Dunhuang yanjiu* 敦煌研究 1 (1999): 146-58.

Jiang Boqin 姜伯勤. *Dunhuang yishu zongjiao yu liyüe wenming* 敦煌藝術宗教與禮樂文明. Beijing: Zhongguo shehui kexue chubanshe 中國社會科學出版社, 1996.

Jin Zhongshu 金中樞. "Songdai jizhong shehui fuli zhidu—Juyangyuan anjifang louzeyuan" 宋代幾種社會福利制度—居養院、安濟坊、漏澤園. *Xinya xueshu niankan* 新亞學術年刊 10 (1968): 127-69.

Jinghui 浄慧. ed. *Xuyun heshang quanji* 虛雲和尚全集. Zhengzhou: Zhongzhou guji chubanshe 中州古籍出版社, 2009.

Kamata Shigeo 鎌田茂雄. *Chūgoku bukkyō shi* 中国仏教史. Tokyo: Iwanami Shoten 岩波書店, 1979.

Kandatsu Chijun 神達知純. "Riben dui Nanyue Huisi yanjiu zhi xianzhuang" 日本対南岳慧思研究之現状. In Huang Xinchuan 黃心川, et al., eds, *Guangshan Jingjusi yu Tiantaizong yanjiu* 光山浄居寺與天台宗研究. Hongkong: Tianma tushu youxian-gongsi 天馬圖書有限公司, 2001, pp. 289-294.

Kang Le 康樂. *Fojiao yu sushi* 佛教與素食. Taipei: Sanmin shuju 三民書局, 2003.

Kanno Hiroshi 菅野博史. *Chūgoku Hokke shisō no kenkyū* 中国法華思想の研究. Tokyo: Shunjūsha 春秋社, 1994.

Karashima Seishi 辛嶋静志. *Shōhokkekyō shiten* 正法華経詞典. Tokyo: Sōka daigaku kokusai bukkyōgaku kōtō kenkyūjo 創価大学国際仏教学高等研究所, 1998.

Kawaguchi Kōhū 川口高風. "Shibunritsu gyōjishō ni arawareta inyōtenseki no kenkyū—Kyōronbu" 四分律行事鈔にあらわれた引用典籍の研究—経論部. *Sōtōshū kenkyūin kenkyūsei kenkyūkiyō* 曹洞宗研究員研究生研究紀要 6 (1974): 114-32.

Kieschnick, John. "Buddhist Vegetarianism in China", in Roel Sterckx ed., *Of Tripod and Palate: Food, Politics and Religion in Traditional China*, pp. 186-212. New York: Palgrave-Macmillan Press, 2005.

Kimiya Yasuhiko 木宮泰彦 (trans. Chen Jie 陳捷). *Zhong Ri fojiao jiaotong shi* 中日佛教交通史 (Japanese title: *Chūnichi bukkyō kōtsūshi* 中日仏教交通史). In *Shijie foxue mingzhu yicong* 世界佛學名著譯叢, vol. 49. Taibei: Huayu chubanshe 華宇出版社, 1985.

Knoblock, John, and Jeffrey K. Riegel (trans.). *The Annals of Lü Buwei*. Stanford: Stanford University Press, 2005.

Kunmingshi Zongjiao Shiwuju 昆明市宗教事務局 & Kunmingshi Fojiao Xiehui 昆明市佛教協會, comps. *Kunming fojiao shi* 昆明佛教史. Kunming: Yunnan minzu chubanshe 雲南民族出版社, 2001.

Kuo Li-ying. *Confession et contrition dans le bouddhisme chinois du Ve au Xe siècle*. Paris: Ecole française d'Extrême-Orient, 2005.

Kwok, Daniel W. Y. (trans. Lei Yi 雷頤). *Zhongguo xiandai sixiang zhong de weikexue zhuyi (1900-1950)* 中國現代思想中的唯科學主義 (1900-1950) (English title: *Scientism in Chinese Thought: 1900-1950*). Nanjing: Jiangsu renmin chubanshe 江蘇人民出版社, 1995.

Lai Pengju 賴朋舉. "Binglingsi 169 ku Wuliangshou fokan suo sheji zhi yixue yu chanxue" 炳靈寺 169 窟無量壽佛龕所涉之義學與禪學. *Dongfang zongjiao yanjiu* 東方宗教研究 2 (1990): 157-82.

Lai Pengju 賴朋舉. "Guanhe de sanshixue yu hexi de qianfo sixiang" 關河的三世學與河西的千佛思想. *Dongfang zongjiao yanjiu* 東方宗教研究 4 (1994): 233-259.

Lai Pengju 賴朋舉. "Hou Qin Sengzhao de "Fahua sanmei" chanfa yu longdong nanbei Shikusi de Qifo zaoxiang" 後秦僧肇的 " 法華三昧 " 禪法與隴東南北石窟寺的七佛造像. *Foxue yanjiu zhongxin xuebao* 佛學研究中心學報 2 (1997): 211-31.

Lai Yonghai 賴永海. *Zhongguo fojiao wenhua lun* 中國佛教文化論. Beijing: Zhongguo qingnian chubanshe 中國青年出版社, 1999.

Lai Yonghai 賴永海 & Wang Yueqing 王月清. *Zongjiao yu daode quanshan* 宗教與道德勸善. Nanjing: Jiangsu guji chubanshe 江蘇古籍出版社, 2002.

Lan Jifu 藍吉富, comp. *Dazangjing bubian* 大藏經補編. Taibei: Huayu chubanshe 華宇出版社, 1986.

Lee Do-op 李道業. *Kegonkyō shisō kenkyū* 華厳経思想研究. Kyoto: Nagata bunshōdō 永田文昌堂, 2001.

Legge, James. *The Chinese Classics: Translated into English with Preliminary Essays and Explanatory Notes, Vol. 2, The Life and Works of Mencius*. London: N. Trübner, 1875.

Li Faliang 李發良. *Famensi zhi* 法門寺志. Xi'an: Shaanxi renmin chubanshe 陝西人民出版社, 2000.

Li Li'an 李利安. *Guanyin xinyang de yuanyuan yu chuanbo* 觀音信仰的淵源與傳播. Beijing: Zongjiao wenhua chubanshe 宗教文化出版社, 2008.

Li Silong 李四龍. "Renjianxing yu zongjiaoxing" 人間性與宗教性. *Pumen xuebao* 普門學報 1(2002): 51-55.

Li Xiaorong 李小榮. *Dunhuang mijiao wenxian lungao* 敦煌密教文獻論稿. Beijing: Renmin wenxue chubanshe 人民文學出版社, 2003.

Liang Mancang 梁滿倉. *Han Tang jian zhengzhi yu wenhua tansuo* 漢唐間政治與文化探索. Guiyang: Guizhou renmin chubanshe 貴州人民出版社, 2000.

Lin Boqian 林伯謙. "Beichuan fojiao yu Zhongguo sushi wenhua" 北傳佛教與中國素食文化. *Wuzhong wenxuebao* 吳中文學報 4 (1998): 93-138.

Lin Mingchang 林明昌. "Jingshi fojiao—Taixu de xin fojiao yundong" 經世佛教—太虛的新佛教運動. *Pumen xuebao* 普門學報 10(2002): 17-43.

Liu Changdong 劉長東. *Songdai fojiao zhengce lungao* 宋代佛教政策論稿. Chengdu: Bashu shushe 巴蜀書社, 2005.

Liu Shufen 劉淑芬. "Wu zhi liu shiji Huabei xiangcun de fojiao xinyang" 五至六世紀華北鄉村的佛教信仰. *Zhongyang yanjiuyuan lishi yuyan yanjiusuo jikan* 中央研究院歷史語言研究所集刊 63.3 (1993): 497-544.

Liu Shufen 劉淑芬. "Bei Qi Biaoyixiang yicihui shizhu—zhonggu fojiao shehui jiuji de ge'an yanjiu" 北齊標異鄉義慈惠石柱—中古佛教社會救濟的個案研究. *Xin shi xue* 新史學 5.4(1994): 1-50.

Liu Shufen 劉淑芬. "Cibei xishe—Zhonggu shiqi fojiaotu de shehui fuli shiye" 慈悲喜捨—中古佛教徒的社會福利事業. *Taibei xianli wenhua zhongxin jikan* 台北縣立文化中心季刊 40(1994): 17-20.

Liu Shufen 劉淑芬. *Zhonggu de fojiao yu shehui* 中古的佛教與社會. Shanghai: Shanghai guji chubanshe 上海古籍出版社, 2008.

Lü Cheng 呂澂. *Zhongguo fojiao yuanliu lüejiang* 中國佛教源流略講. Beijing: Zhonghua shuju 中華書局, 1979.

Ma Tianxiang 麻天祥. *Fan'guan rensheng de xuanlan zhilu: jinxiandai zhongguo foxue yanjiu* 反觀人生的玄覽之路—近現代中國佛學研究. Guiyang: Guizhou renmin chubanshe 貴州人民出版社, 1994.

Makita Tairyō 牧田諦亮. "Suirokue shōkō" 水陸会小考. *Tōhō shūkyō* 東方宗教 12 (1957): 14–33.

Makita Tairyō 牧田諦亮. *Rikuchō koitsu Kanzeon ōkenki no kenkyū* 六朝古逸観世音応験記の研究. Kyoto: Heirakuji shoten 平楽寺書店, 1970.

Mather, Richard B. "The Bonze's Begging Bowl: Eating Practices in Buddhist Monasteries of Medieval India and China". *Journal of American Oriental Society* 101.4 (1981): 417-22.

Matsumoto Bunzaburō 松本文三郎. "Kannon no gogi to kodai Indo Shina ni okeru sono shinkō ni tsuite" 観音の語義と古代印度、支那におけるその信仰について. In Hayami Tasuku 速水侑, ed., *Kannon shinkō* 観音信仰. Tokyo: Yuzankaku 雄山閣, 1991, pp. 8-16.

Michibata Ryōshū 道端良秀. *Chūgoku Bukkyō to shakai fukushi jigyō* 中国仏教と社会福祉事業. Kyoto: Hōzōkan 法蔵館, 1967.

Michibata Ryōshū 道端良秀. "Hōjō shisō to dan nikushoku" 放生思想と断肉食, in Michibata Ryōshū ed., *Chūgoku Bukkyō shisō shi no kenkyū* 中国仏教思想史の研究. Kyoto : Heirakuji Shoten 平楽寺書店, 1979, 228-230.

Michibata Ryōshū 道端良秀. *Tōdai bukkyōshi no kenkyū* 唐代仏教史の研究. Kyoto: Hōzōkan 法蔵館, 1983.

*Mingban Jiaxing dazang jing* 明版嘉興大藏經. 40 vols. Taibei: Xin wenfeng chuban gongsi 新文豐出版公司, 1987. Reprint of *Zhonghua dazang jing di er ji*.

Mingxue 明學, comps. *Lianchi dashi quanji* 蓮池大師全集. Shanghai: Shanghai guji chubanshe 上海古籍出版社, 2012.

Mizuno Kōgen 水野弘元. "Bodaidaruma no Ninyū shigyō setsu to Kongō zanmai kyō" 菩提達摩の二入四行説と金剛三昧経. *Komazawa daigaku kenkyūkiyō* 駒沢大学研究紀要 13.3 (1955): 33-57.

Mizuno Seiichi 水野清一 & Nagahiro Toshio 長広敏雄. "Unkō kinsekiroku" 雲岡金石録 in *Unkō sekkutsu—Seireki goseiki ni okeru Chūgoku hokubu bukkyō kutsuin no kōkogakuteki chōsahōkoku* 雲岡石窟一西暦五世紀における中國北部佛教窟院の考古學的調査報告, vol. 2. Kyoto: Kyoto daigaku jimbunkagaku kenkyusho unkō kankōkai 京都大學人文科學研究所雲岡刊行會, 1955.

Mochizuki Ryōkō 望月良晃. *Daijō Nehangyō no kenkyū: Kyōdanshiteki kōsatsu* 大乗涅槃経の研究一教団史的考察. Tokyo: Shunjūsha 春秋社, 1988.

Moroto Tatsuo 諸戸立雄. *Chūgoku bukkyō seidoshi no kenkyū* 中国仏教制度史の研究. Tokyo: Hirakawa shuppansha 平河出版社, 1990.

Mou Zongsan 牟宗三. *Foxing yu bore* 佛性與般若. Taibei: Taiwan xuesheng shuju 台灣學生書局, 1992.

Muranaka Yūshō 村中祐生. "Ryōgongyō no kaishaku ni miru Tendai kyōgi" 楞厳経の解釈にみる天台教義. *Tendai gakuhō* 天台学報 26 (1984): 71-77.

Muranaka Yūshō 村中祐生. "Hokuseidai no hōbutsu to bosatsu no shugyōhō no keisei—Chūgoku bukkyō ni okeru Hokekyō no shinkō II" 北斉代の奉仏と菩薩の修行法の形成一中国仏教における法華経の信仰 (二). *Taishō daigaku kenkyūkiyō: bukkyōgakubu būgakubu* 大正大学研究紀要 : 仏教学部・文学部 76. 3 (1991): 19-48.

Murata Mio 村田澪. "Xuejing de yuanyuan jiqi yiyi 血經的淵源及其意義". *Foxue yanjiu* 佛學研究, 21 (2012): 56-63.

Naba Toshisada 那波利貞. *Tōdai shakai bunkashi kenkyū* 唐代社会文化史研究. Tokyo: Sōbunsha 創文社, 1988, 3rd edition.

Nagai Masashi 永井政之. "Chūgoku bukkyō seiritsu no ichisokumen—Sanbutsuki no seiritsu to tenkai" 中国仏教成立の一側面一三仏忌の成立と展開. *Komazawa daigaku bukkyō gakubu ronshū* 駒沢大学仏教学部論集 25.10 (1994): 129-58.

Nagai Masashi 永井政之. *Chūgoku Zenshū kyōdan to minshū* 中国禅宗教団と民衆. Tokyo: Uchiyama shoten 内山書店, 2000.

Nishiguchi Yoshio 西口芳男. "Tonkōshahon shichishu taishō 'kanjinron'" 敦煌写本七種対照「観心論」. *Zengaku kenkyū* 禅学研究 74.3(1996): 123-70.

Nomura Yōshō 野村耀昌. "Chūgoku bunka to Hokke sangyōshi no renkan" 中国文化と法華鑽仰史の連関. In Sakamoto Yukio 坂本幸男, ed., *Hokekyō no shisō to bunka—Hokekyō kenkyū* 法華経の思想と文化—法華経研究. Kyoto: Heirakuji shoten 平楽寺書店, 1965, pp. 97-127.

Okabe Kazuo 岡部和雄. "Zensō no chūshō to gigi kyōten" 禅僧の注抄と疑僞経典. In Shinohara Hisao 篠原壽雄 & Tanaka Ryōshō 田中良昭, eds., *Tonkō butten to zen* 敦煌仏典と禅. *Kōza Tonkō* 講座敦煌, vol. 8. Tokyo: Daitō shuppansha 大東出版社, 1980, pp. 335-76.

Ōmura Seigai 大村西崖. *Chūgoku bijitsushi chōso hen* 中国美術史彫塑篇. Tokyo: Kokusho kankōkai 国書刊行会, 1980.

Ōno Hideto 大野栄人. *Tendai shikan seiritsushi no kenkyū* 天台止観成立史の研究. Kyoto: Hōzōkan 法蔵館, 1994.

Ōtani Kōshō 大谷光照. *Tōdai no bukkyō girei* 唐代の仏教儀礼. Tokyo: Yūkōsha 有光社, 1937.

Pan Guiming 潘桂明. *Zhiyi pingzhuan* 智顗評傳. Nanjing: Nanjing daxue chubanshe 南京大學出版社, 1996.

Pan Guiming 潘桂明. *Zhongguo jushi fojiao shi* 中國居士佛教史. Beijing: Zhongguo shehui kexue chubanshe 中國社會科學出版社, 2000.

Pan Guiming 潘桂明 & Wu Zhongwei 吳忠偉. *Zhongguo Tiantaizong tongshi* 中國天台宗通史. Nanjing: Jiangsu guji chubanshe 江蘇古籍出版社, 2001.

Ran Wanli 冉萬里. *Zhongguo gudai sheli yimai zhidu yanjiu* 中國古代舍利瘞埋制度研究. Beijing: Wenwu chubanshe 文物出版社, 2013.

Robson, James. *Power of Place: The Religious Land scape of the Southern Sacred Peak in Medieval China*. Cambridge: Harvard University Press, 2009.

Ryūchi Kiyoshi 竜池清. "Ming Taizu de fojiao zhengce" 明太祖的佛教政策. In *Zhongguo fojiaoshi lunji: Ming Qing fojiaoshi pian* 中國佛教史論集：明清佛教史篇. *Xiandai fojiao xueshu congkan* 現代佛教學術叢刊, vol. 15. Taibei: Dacheng wenhua chubanshe 大乘文化出版社, 1977, pp. 1-16.

Sakaki Ryōzaburō 榊亮三郎. "Fanzanghanhe siyiduijiao fanyi mingyi daji" 梵藏漢和四譯對校翻譯名義大集. In Shi Ciyi 釋慈怡, et al., eds., *Shijie foxue mingzhu yicong* 世界佛學名著譯叢, vol. 12. Taibei: Huayu chubanshe 華宇出版社, 1984.

Sakamoto Kobaku 坂本広博. "Shishu sanmai—Tokuni hikō hiza sanmai to zuijii, kakui sanmai ni tsuite" 四種三昧—特に非行非坐三昧と随自意、覚意三昧について. In *Tendai kyōgaku no kenkyū—Tada Kōryū sensei shōju kinen ronbunshū* 天台教学の研究—多田厚隆先生頌寿記念論文集. Tokyo: Sankibō Busshorin 山喜房仏書林, 1990.

Sakamoto Yukio 坂本幸男. "Chūgoku bukkyō to Hoke shisō no renkan" 中国仏教と法華思想の連関. In Sakamoto Yukio 坂本幸男, ed., *Hokekyō no shisō to bunka* 法華経の思想と文化. Kyoto: Inoue Shirō 井上四郎, 1965, pp. 489-548.

Sakawa Senkyō 坂輪宣敬. "Chūgoku no sekkutsu ni okeru Hokekyō no zōkeihyōgen ni tsuite" 中国の石窟における法華経の造形表現について. In Nomura Yōshō 野村耀昌, ed., *Hokekyō shinkō no shokeitai—Hokekyō kenkyū* 法華経信仰の諸形態—法華経研究. Kyoto: Heirakuji shoten 平楽寺書店, 1976, pp. 283-302.

Satō Chisui 佐藤智水 (trans. Zhang Shaoyan 張韶岩 & Ma Lei 馬雷). "Hokuchō zōzō mei kō" 北朝造像銘考. In Liu junwen 劉俊文, ed., *Riben zhongqingnian xuezhe lun Zhongguoshi Liuchao Sui Tang juan* 日本中青年學者論中國史六朝隋唐卷. Shanghai: Shanghai guji chubanshe 上海古籍出版社, 1995, first edition, pp. 56-115.

Satō Tatsugen 佐藤達玄 (trans. Shi Jianhan 釋見憨, et al.). *Jielü zai Zhongguo fojiao de fazhan* 戒律在中國佛教的發展 (Japanese title: *Chūgoku bukkyō ni okeru kairitsu no kenkyū* 中国仏教における戒律の研究). Taibei: Xiangguang shuxiang chubanshe 香光書鄉出版社, 1997.

Satō Tetsuei 佐藤哲英. *Tendai daishi no kenkyū—Chigi no chosaku ni kansuru kisoteki kenkyū* 天台大師の研究—智顗の著作に關する基礎的研究. Kyoto: Hyakkaen 百華苑, 1961.

Satō Tetsuei 佐藤哲英. *Zoku Tendai daishi no kenkyū—Tendai Chigi wo meguru shomondai* 続・天台大師の研究—天台智顗をめぐる諸問題. Kyoto: Hyakkaen 百華苑, 1981.

Shaanxisheng Kaogu Yanjiuyuan 陝西省考古研究院. *Famensi kaogu fajue baogao* 法門寺考古發掘報告. Beijing: Wenwu chubanshe 文物出版社, 2007.

Shen Haibo 沈海波. "Beisong chunian Tiantai jiaoji chonggui zhongtu de shishi" 北宋初年天台教籍重歸中土的史實. *Zhonghua foxue yanjiu* 中華佛學研究 4 (2000): 187-205.

Sheng Kai 聖凱. "Lun chanhui yuanyu de hanyi" 論懺悔原語的含義. In *Jüequn・Xueshu lunwen ji* 覺群・學術論文集, vol. 1. Beijing: Shangwu yinshuguan 商務印書館, 2001, pp. 357-66.

Sheng Kai 聖凱. "Zhixuan yu Sanmei shuichan" 知玄與《三昧水懺》. *Fayin* 法音 11(2001): 20-29.

Sheng Kai 聖凱. "Lun Zhongguo fojiao chanfa de linian ji qi xiandai yiyi" 論中國佛教懺法的理念及其現代意義. *Fayin* 法音 3 (2003): 9-18.

Sheng Kai 聖凱. "Lun Tiantai chanfa de sixiang ji qi xingcheng" 論天台懺法的思想及其形成. In *Zhongguo fojiang chanfa yanjiu* 中國佛教懺法研究. Beijing: Zongjiao wenhua chubanshe 宗教文化出版社, 2004, pp. 79-113.

Sheng Kai 聖凱. *Zhongguo fojiao chanfa yanjiu* 中國佛教懺法研究. Beijing: Zongjiao wenhua chubanshe 宗教文化出版社, 2004.

Sheng Kai 聖凱. *Zhongguo hanchuan fojiao liyi* 中國漢傳佛教禮儀. Beijing: Zongjiao wenhua chubanshe 宗教文化出版社, 2004.

Sheng Kai 聖凱. "Ming Qing fojiao 'sida mingshan' xinyang de xingcheng" 明清佛教"四大名山"信仰的形成. *Zongjiaoxue yanjiu* 宗教學研究 3 (2011): 80-82.

Sheng Kai 聖凱. “On the Veneration of the Four Sacred Buddhist Mountains in China”. *The Eastern Buddhist* 44.2(2013): 121-143.

Shi Darui 釋大睿. “Zhongguo fojiao zaoqi chanzui sixiang zhi xingcheng yu fazhan” 中國佛教早期懺罪思想之形成與發展. *Zhonghua foxue yanjiu* 中華佛學研究 2(1998): 313-37.

Shi Darui 釋大睿. *Tiantai chanfa zhi yanjiu* 天台懺法之研究. Taibei: Fagu wenhua 法鼓文化, 2000.

Shi Shengyan 釋聖嚴. “Zhongguo fojiao yi ‘Fahuajing’ wei jichu de xiuxing fangfa” 中國佛教以《法華經》爲基礎的修行方法. *Zhonghua foxue xuebao* 中華佛學學報 7(1994): 1-16.

Shi Weixiang 史葦湘. “Dunhuang Mogaoku zhong de Futian jingbian bihua” 敦煌莫高窟中的福田經變壁畫. In Dunhuang yanjiu yuan 敦煌研究院, ed., *Dunhuang yanjiu wenji: Dunhuang shiku jingbian pian* 敦煌研究文集：敦煌石窟經變篇. Lanzhou: Gansu minzu chubanshe 甘肅民族出版社, 2000, pp. 320-28.

Shiga Takayoshi 滋賀高義. “Minsho no hōe to bukkyō seisaku” 明初の法会と仏教政策. *Ōtani daigaku kenkyū nenpō* 大谷大学研究年報 21.3(1969): 197-237.

Shimoda Masahiro 下田正弘. *Nehangyō no kenkyū—Daijō kyōten no kenkyūhōhō shiron* 涅槃経の研究—大乗経典の研究方法試論. Tokyo: Shunjūsha 春秋社, 2000.

Shioiri Ryōdō 塩入良道. “Senbō no seiritsu to Chigi no tachiba” 懺法の成立と智顗の立場. *Indogaku bukkyōgaku kenkyū* 印度学仏教学研究 7.2(1959): 45-55.

Shioiri Ryōdō 塩入良道. “Chūgoku bukkyō ni okeru sange no juyōkatei” 中国仏教儀礼における懺悔の受容過程. *Indogaku bukkyōgaku kenkyū* 印度学仏教学研究 11.2(1963): 353-58.

Shioiri Ryōdō 塩入良道. “Chūgoku bukkyō ni okeru raisan to butsumyō kyōten” 中国仏教に於ける礼懺と仏名経典. In Yūki kyōju shōju kinen ronbun kankōkai 結城教授頌寿記念論文集刊行会, ed., *Bukkyō shisōshi ronshū: Yūki kyōju shōju kinen* 仏教思想史論集：結城教授頌寿記念. Tokyo: Daizō shuppan 大蔵出版, 1964, pp. 569-90.

Shioiri Ryōdō 塩入良道. “Tendai Chigi zenji ni okeru sange no tenkai” 天台智顗禅師における懺悔の展開. *Taishō daigaku daigakuin kenkyū ronshū* 大正大学大学院研究論集 9.2 (1985): 1-16.

Simmel, Georg (trans. Curt Rosenthal). *Sociology of Religion*. New York: Philosophical Library, 1959.

Spiro, Melford E. “Religion: Problems of Definition and Explanation”. In Michael Banton, ed., *Anthropological Approaches to the Study of Religion*. ASA Monogrphs 3. London: Tavistock, 1973.

Spiro, Melford E. (trans. Xiangguang shuxiang bianyizu 香光書香編譯組). *Fojiao yu shehui: Yige dachuantong bing qi zai Miandian de bianqian* 佛教與社會：一個大傳統並其在緬甸的變遷 (English title: *Buddhism and Society: A Great Tradition and its Burmese Vicissitudes*). Jiayi: Xiangguang shuxiang 香光書香, 2006.

Stevenson, Daniel. "Text, Image, and Transformation in the History of the Shuilu fahui, the Buddhist Rite for Deliverance of Creatures of Water and Land," in Marsh Weidner, ed. *Cultural Intersections in Later Chinese Buddhism*. Honolulu: University of Hawaii Press, 2001, 30–70.

Sun Changwu 孫昌武, coll. and annot. *Guanshiyin yingyanji sanzhong* 觀世音應驗記三種. Beijing: Zhonghua shuju 中華書局, 1994.

Sun Kaidi 孫楷第. "Tangdai sujiang guifan ji qiben zhi ticai" 唐代俗講軌範及其本之體裁. In Zhou Shaoliang 周紹良 & Bai Huawen 白化文, eds., *Dunhuang bianwen lunwen lu* 敦煌變文論文錄. Shanghai: Shanghai guji chubanshe 上海古籍出版社, 1982, pp. 71-127.

Suwa Gijun 諏訪義純. "Chūgoku Bukkyō ni okeru saishoku shugi shisō no keisei ni kansuru kanken—Bukkyō denrai yori Ryōsho ni itaru jiki" 中国仏教における菜食主義思想の形成に関する管見一仏教伝来より梁初にいたる時期. *Nihon Bukkyō gakkai nenpō* 日本仏教学会年報 43 (1977): 73-99.

Suwa Gijun 諏訪義純. *Chūgoku chūsei bukkyōshi kenkyū* 中国中世仏教史研究. Tokyo: Daitō shuppansha 大東出版社, 1985.

Suwa Gijun 諏訪義純. "'Shibunritsu ganchū kaihonsho gyōshūki' ni miru Dōsen no jijo to sanshu no Dōsenden: Dōsenden no saikentō" 「四分律含注戒本疏行宗記」にみる道宣の自叙と三種の道宣伝：道宣伝の再検討. *Aichigakuindaigaku bungakubu kiyō* 愛知学院大学文学部紀要 20 (1990): 369-75.

Suzuki Daisetsu 鈴木大拙. *Zen shisōshi kenkyū daisan* 禪思想史研究第三. Tokyo: Iwanami shoten 岩波書店, 1987.

Taixu 太虛. *Taixu dashi quanshu* 太虛大師全書. Taibei: Shandaosi fojing liutongchu 善導寺佛經流通處, 1980, 3rd edition.

Takakusu Junjirō 高楠順次郎, Watanabe Kaikyoku 渡邊海旭, et al., comps. *Taishō Shinshū Daizōkyō* 大正新修大蔵経. 100 vols. Tokyo: Taishō issaikyō kankōkai 大正一切経刊行会, 1924-1932.

Tan Chanxue 譚蟬雪. *Dunhuang suishi wenhua daolun* 敦煌歲時文化導論. Taibei: Xinwenfeng chuban gongsi 新文豐出版公司, 1998.

Tang Yongtong 湯用彤. *Han Wei Liang Jin Nanbeichao Fojiao shi* 漢魏兩晉南北朝佛教史, 2 vols. Beijing: Zhonghua shuju 中華書局, 1983.

Tay, C. N. (trans. Zheng Zhenhuang 鄭振煌). *Guanyin—Bange Yazhou de xinyang* 觀音一半個亞洲的信仰 (English title: *Kuan-Yin: The Cult of Half Asia*). Taibei: Huayu chubanshe 華宇出版社, 1987.

Teiser, Stephen F. *The Ghost Festival in Medieval China*. Princeton: Princeton University Press,1988. Translated into Chinese by Hou Xudong 侯旭東, *Youling de jieri: Zhongguo gu shiji de xinyang yu shenghuo* 幽靈的節日：中國古世紀的信仰與生活. Hangzhou: Zhejiang renmin chubanshe 浙江人民出版社, 1998.

Teiser, Stephen F. *Scripture of the Ten Kings and the Making of Purgatory in Medieval Chinese Buddhism*. Honolulu: University of Hawaii Press, 1994.

Ting Jen-Chieh 丁仁杰. *Dangdai hanren minzhong zongjiao yanjiu: Lunshu, rentong yu shehui zaishengchan* 當代漢人民眾宗教研究：論述、認同與社會再生產. Taipei: Linking Publishing, 2009.

Tokuno Kyoko. "The Book of Resolving Doubts Concerning the Semblance Dharma". In Donald S. Lopez Jr. ed., *Buddhism in Practice: Abridged Edition*, Princeton: Princeton University Press, 2007.

Tsuchihashi Shūkō 土橋秀高. "Bini to sange" 毘尼と懺悔. *Indogaku bukkyōgaku kenkyū* 印度学仏教学研究 26.1(1979): 83-90.

Turner, Victor. *The Ritual Process: Structure and Anti-Structure*. New York: Routledge, 1969.

Vaidya, P. L., ed. *Aṣṭasāhasrikā Praiñāpāramitā. Buddhist Sanskrit Text*, No. 4. Darbhanga: The Mithila Institute, 1960.

(*Wan*) *Xu zangjing* (卍) 續藏經. 150 vols. Taibei: Xin wenfeng chuban gongsi 新文豐出版公司, 1968-1970. Reprint of Nakano, et al., comps., *Dai Nihon zokuzōkyō*.

Wang Bangwei 王邦維. "Fojiao de 'zhongxinguan' dui Zhongguo wenhua youyuegan de tiaozhan" 佛教的 " 中心觀 " 對中國文化優越感的挑戰. *Guoxue yanjiu* 國學研究 25 (2010): 45-59.

Wang Deyi 王德毅. "Songdai de yanglao yu ciyou" 宋代的養老與慈幼. In *Songdai yanjiu lunji* 宋代研究論集, 2 vol. Taibei: Dingwen shuju 鼎文書局, 1972, pp. 369-88.

Wang Juan 汪娟. "Tangdai Mile xinyang yu fojiao zhu zongpai de guanxi" 唐代彌勒信仰與佛教諸宗派的關係. *Zhonghua foxue xuebao* 中華佛學學報 5 (1992): 193-231.

Wang Juan 汪娟. *Dunhuang lichanwen yanjiu* 敦煌禮懺文研究. Taibei: Fagu wenhua 法鼓文化, 1998.

Wang Juan 汪娟. *Tang Song guyi fojiao chanyi yanjiu* 唐宋古逸佛教懺儀研究. Taibei: Wenjin chubanshe 文津出版社, 2008.

Wang Wencai 王文才. "Sujiang yishi kao" 俗講儀式考. In Gansusheng shehui kexueyuan wenxue yanjiusuo 甘肅省社會科學院文學研究所, ed., *Dunhuangxue lunji* 敦煌學論集. Lanzhou: Gansu renmin chubanshe 甘肅人民出版社, 1985, pp. 100-111.

Wang Yarong 王亞榮. *Chang'an fojiao shi lun* 長安佛教史論. Beijing: Zongjiao wenhua chubanshe 宗教文化出版社, 2005.

Wang Zhongyao 王仲堯. *Nansong fojiao zhidu wenhua yanjiu* 南宋佛教制度文化研究, 2 vol. Beijing: Shangwu yinshuguan 商務印書館, 2012.

Weber, Max (trans. & ed. Hans H. Gerth). *The Religion of China: Confucianism and Taoism*. Glencoe, Ill.: The Free Press, 1951.

Xiang Da 向達. "Tangdai sujiang kao" 唐代俗講考. In Xiang Da 向達, *Tangdai Chang'an yu Xiyu wenming* 唐代長安與西域文明. Shanghai: Sanlian shudian 三聯書店, 1987, pp. 294-336.

Xiao Dengfu 蕭登福. *Daojiao yu fojiao* 道教與佛教. Taibei: Dongda tushu gongsi 東大圖書公司, 1995.

Xie Chongguang 謝重光. *Zhonggu fojiao sengqie zhidu he shehui shenghuo* 中古佛教僧伽制度和社會生活. Beijing: Shangwu yinshuguan 商務印書館, 2009.

Xiuyuan Chansi 修元禪寺, comps. *Xuyun lao heshang fahui nianpu zengdingben* 虛雲老和尚法匯、年譜增訂本. Taibei: Xiuyuan chanyuan 修元禪院, 1997.

Xuxiu Siku Quanshu Bianweihui 續修四庫全書編委會, comps. *Xuxiu siku quanshu* 續修四庫全書. Shanghai: Shanghai guji chubanshe 上海古籍出版社, 2002.

Yamazaki Hiroshi 山崎宏. *Shina chūsei bukkyō no tenkai* 支那中世仏教の展開. Kyoto: Kiyomizu shoten 清水書店, 1932.

Yamazaki Hiroshi 山崎宏. *Zuitō bukkyōshi no kenkyū* 隋唐仏教史の研究. Kyoto: Hōzōkan 法蔵館, 1967.

Yan Shangwen 顏尙文. "Liang Wudi de junquan sixiang yu pusa xingge chutan—Yi 'duan jiurou wen' xingcheng de beijing weili" 梁武帝的君權思想與菩薩性格初探—以《斷酒肉文》形成的背景爲例. *Guoli Taiwan shifan daxue lishi xuebao* 國立台灣師範大學歷史學報 16(1988): 1-36.

Yan Shangwen 顏尙文. "Beichao fojiao shequ gongtongti de Fahua yiyi zuzhi yu huodong—Yi Dongwei 'Lishi heyi zaoxiangbei' weili" 北朝佛教社區共同體的法華邑義組織與活動—以東魏《李氏合邑造像碑》爲例. *Zhonghua foxue xuebao* 中華佛學學報 1 (1996): 167-84.

Yan Shangwen 顏尙文. "Fahua sixiang yu fojiao shequ gongtongti—Yi Dongwei 'Lishi heyi zaoxiangbei' weili" 法華思想與佛教社區共同體—以東魏《李氏合邑造像碑》爲例. *Zhonghua foxue xuebao* 中華佛學學報 10(1997): 233-47.

Yan Shangwen 顏尙文. *Liang Wudi* 梁武帝. Taibei: Dongda tushu gongsi 東大圖書公司, 1999.

Yan Yaozhong 嚴耀中. *Fojiao jielü yu Zhongguo shehui* 佛教戒律與中國社會. Shanghai: Shanghai guji chubanshe 上海古籍出版社, 2007.

Yanagida Seizan 柳田聖山. "Denbōhōki to sono sakusha—Pelliot 3559 gō bunsho wo meguru hokushūzen kenkyūshiryō no satsuki 1" 伝法宝紀とその作者—ペリオ3559 号文書をめぐる北宗禅研究資料の札記 -1. *Zengaku kenkyū* 禅学研究 53 (1963): 45-71.

Yanagida Seizan 柳田聖山. *Shoki zenshū shisho no kenkyū* 初期禅宗史書の研究. Kyoto: Hōzōkan 法蔵館, 1967.

Yanagida Seizan 柳田聖山. *Daruma no goroku: Ninyū shigyō ron* 達摩の語録：二入四行論. *Zen no goroku* 禅の語録, vol. 1. Tokyo: Chikuma shobō 筑摩書房, 1969.

Yang Bojun 楊伯峻, coll. and annot. *Liezi jishi* 列子集釋. Beijing: Zhonghua shuju 中華書局, 1979.

Yang Huinan 楊惠南. "Zhiyi dui Qin yi 'Fahuajing' de panshi" 智顗對秦譯《法華經》的判釋. *Foxue yanjiu zhongxin xuebao* 佛學研究中心學報 2(1997): 1-24.

Yang Mei 楊梅. "Zhongguo gudai de Dingguangfo xinyang—jianlun Tang Song yilai de minjian 'zaofo yundong'" 中國古代的定光佛信仰—兼論唐宋以來的民間 "造佛運動". *Shijie zongjiao yanjiu* 世界宗教研究 4 (2006): 50-63.

Yang Zengwen 楊曾文, coll. and annot. *Dunhuang xinben Liuzu tanjing* 敦煌新本六祖壇經. Shanghai: Shanghai guji chubanshe 上海古籍出版社, 1993.

Yang Zengwen 楊曾文, coll. and annot. *Shenhui heshang chan yulu* 神會和尚禪語錄. Beijing: Zhonghua shuju 中華書局, 1996.

Yao Dianzhong 姚奠中, comp. *Yuan Haowen quanji* 元好問全集. Taiyuan: Shanxi guji chubanshe 山西古籍出版社, 2004.

Yazaki Shōken 矢崎正見. "Hokekyō denyaku to sono keitai" 法華経伝訳とその形態. In Sakamoto Yukio 坂本幸男, ed., *Hokekyō no shisō to bunka—Hokekyō kenkyū* 法華経の思想と文化—法華経研究. Kyoto: Heirakuji shoten 平楽寺書店, 1965, pp. 227-48.

Yin Fu 尹富. *Zhongguo Dizang xinyang yanjiu* 中國地藏信仰研究. Chengdu: Bashu shushe 巴蜀書社, 2009.

Yinguang 印光. *Yinguang fashi wenchao sanbian* 印光法師文鈔三編. Putian: Fujian putian guanghuasi fojing liutongchu 福建莆田廣化寺佛經流通處, 1992.

Yinguang 印光. *Yinguang fashi wenchao xubian* 印光法師文鈔續編. Putian: Fujian putian guanghuasi fojing liutongchu 福建莆田廣化寺佛經流通處, 1992.

Yinguang 印光. *Zengguang Yinguang fashi wenchao* 增廣印光法師文鈔. Putian: Fujian putian guanghuasi fojing liutongchu 福建莆田廣化寺佛經流通處, 1992.

*Yingyin Wenyuange siku quanshu* 景印文淵閣四庫全書. 1,500 vols. Taibei: Taiwan shangwu yinshuguan 台灣商務印書館, 1983-1986.

Yinshun 印順. *Zhongguo Chanzong shi* 中國禪宗史. Nanchang: Jiangxi renmin chubanshe 江西人民出版社, 1990.

Yinshun 印順. *Chuqi dacheng fojiao zhi qiyuan yu kaizhan* 初期大乘佛教之起源與開展. Taibei: Zhengwen chubanshe 正聞出版社, 1992.

Yinshun 印順. *Zhongguo fojiao suotan* 中國佛教瑣談. In *Huayu ji* 華雨集, vol. 4. Taibei: Zhengwen chubanshe 正聞出版社, 1993.

Yokoi Katsunobu 横井克信. "Chūgoku ni okeru uchidōjō no kigen ni tsuite" 中国における内道場の起源について. *Taishō daigaku sōgō bukkyō kenkyūjo nenpō* 大正大学綜合仏教研究所年報 28 (2006): 190-202.

You Xiangzhou 游祥洲. "Lun Zhongguo fojiao chanhui lunli de xingcheng ji qi linian yunhan" 論中國佛教懺悔倫理的形成及其理念蘊涵. In Fu Weixun 傅偉勳, ed., *Cong chuantong dao xiandai—Fojiao lunli yu xiandai shehui* 從傳統到現代—佛教倫理與現代社會. Taibei: Dongda tushu gongsi 東大圖書公司, 1990, pp. 121-36.

Yuan Gang 袁剛. *Sui Yangdi zhuan* 隋煬帝傳. Beijing: Renmin chubanshe 人民出版社, 2001.

Yuan Jin 袁瑾. *Fojiao Daojiao shiye xia de yankou shishi yishi yanjiu* 佛教、道教視野下的焰口施食儀式研究. Beijing: Zongjiao wenhua chubanshe 宗教文化出版社, 2013.

Yūki Yoshifumi 由木義文. "Chigi to Fugen kangyō" 智顗と普賢観経. *Indogaku bukkyōgaku kenkyū* 印度学仏教学研究 23.1(1974): 360-63.

Yü Chün-fang. *Kuan-yin: The Chinese Transformation of Avalokitesvara*. New York: Columbia University Press, 2001.

Zhang Baoxi 張寶璽. "Binglingsi de Xi Qin shiku" 炳靈寺的西秦石窟. In Gansu wenwu gongzuodui 甘肅文物工作隊 & Binglingsi wenwu baoguansuo 炳靈寺文物保管所, eds., *Zhongguo shiku · Yongjing Binglingsi* 中國石窟・永靖炳靈寺. Beijing: Wenwu chubanshe 文物出版社, 1989, pp. 182-92.

Zhang Gong 張弓. "Tangdai de neidaochang yu neidaochang sengtuan" 唐代的內道場與內道場僧團. *Shijie zongjiao yanjiu* 世界宗教研究 3 (1993): 81-89.

Zhang Gong 張弓. *Han Tang fosi wenhua shi* 漢唐佛寺文化史, 2 vols. Beijing: Zhongguo shehui kexue chubanshe 中國社會科學出版社, 1997.

Zhang Gong 張弓, comps. *Dunhuang dianji yu Tang Wudai lishi wenhua* 敦煌典籍與唐五代歷史文化, 2 vols. Beijing: Zhongguo shehui kexue chubanshe 中國社會科學出版社, 2006.

Zhang Zong 張總. *Dizang xinyang yanjiu* 地藏信仰研究. Beijing: Zongjiao wenhua chubanshe 宗教文化出版社, 2003.

Zhao Puchu 趙樸初. *Zhao Puchu wenji* 趙樸初文集. Beijing: Huawen chubanshe 華文出版社, 2007.

Zheng Zhenman 鄭振滿 & Kenneth Dean, comps. *Fujian zongjiao beiming huibian: Quanzhoufu fence* 福建宗教碑銘匯編・泉州府分冊. Fuzhou: Fujian renmin chubanshe 福建人民出版社, 2003.

Zhou Qi 周齊. *Mingdai fojiao yu zhengzhi wenhua* 明代佛教與政治文化. Beijing: Renmin chubanshe 人民出版社, 2005.

Zhou Shujia 周叔迦. *Zhou Shujia foxue lunzhu ji* 周叔迦佛學論著集. Beijing: Zhonghua shuju 中華書局, 1991.

Zhu Zhixin 朱執信. *Zhu Zhixin ji* 朱執信集, 2 vols. Beijing: Zhonghua shuju 中華書局, 1984.

Zürcher, Erik. *The Buddhist Conquest of China: The Spread and Adaptation of Buddhism in Early Medieval China*. Leiden: E. J. Brill, 1959.

# Index

Printed in the United States
By Bookmasters